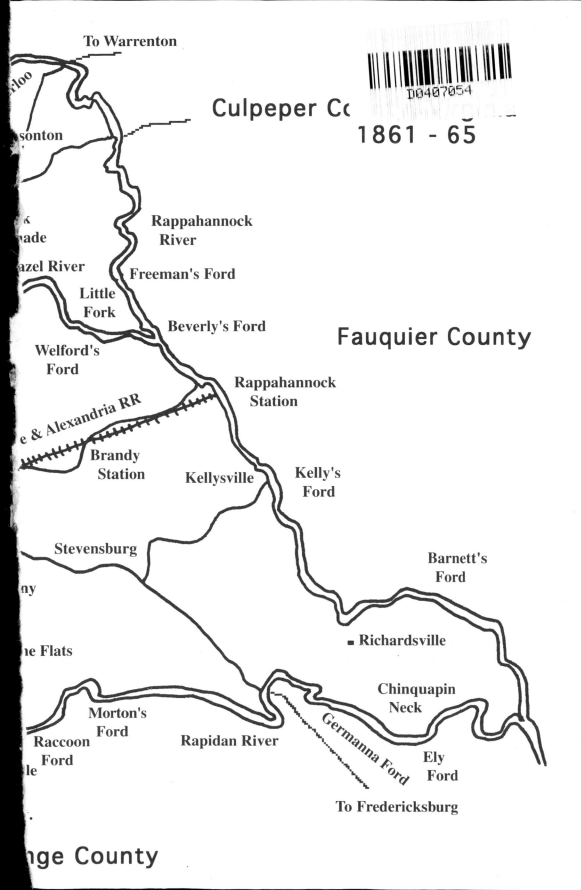

To Warrenton

Culpeper C〈...〉

1861 - 65

Rappahannock
River

Freeman's Ford

Little
Fork

Beverly's Ford

Welford's
Ford

Rappahannock
Station

Fauquier County

e & Alexandria RR

Brandy
Station

Kellysville

Kelly's
Ford

Stevensburg

Barnett's
Ford

Richardsville

Chinquapin
Neck

Morton's
Ford

Raccoon
Ford

Rapidan River

Germanna Ford

Ely
Ford

To Fredericksburg

ge County

Seasons of War

THE ORDEAL OF A CONFEDERATE COMMUNITY, 1861–1865

DANIEL E. SUTHERLAND

THE FREE PRESS

New York   London   Toronto   Sydney   Tokyo   Singapore

For Anne

The Free Press
A Division of Simon & Schuster Inc.
1230 Avenue of the Americas
New York, N.Y. 10020

Printed in the United States of America

printing number

1 2 3 4 5 6 7 8 9 10

Text design by Carla Bolte

Library of Congress Cataloging-in-Publication Data

Sutherland, Daniel E.
    Seasons of war: the ordeal of a Confederate community, 1861–1865/
Daniel E. Sutherland
      p. cm.
    Includes bibliographical references (p.) and index.
    ISBN 0-02-874043-2
    1. Culpeper County (Va.)—History.   2. Virginia—History—Civil
War, 1861-1865. I. Title.
F232.C9S88 1995
975.5'392—dc20   95–18357
                                                        CIP

CONTENTS

Preface   *v*

PART I: SPRING

Chapter

1   A Place and a People   3

2   A Promise of Glory and Greatness   29

3   Glorious, Terrible War   61

PART II: SUMMER

4   Invasion   87

5   Occupation   117

6   Liberation   153

7   Lost in Admiration   181

PART III: AUTUMN

8   To Be a Confederate Soldier   205

9   Perplexed, but Not in Despair   231

10   Return of the Yankees   263

11   Equinox   289

PART IV: WINTER

Chapter

12   A Yankee Village   317

13   An Unsettled State   349

14   To Every Thing a Season   371

Notes   387

Bibliography   449

Acknowledgments   472

Index   475

LIST OF MAPS

Culpeper County, Virginia, 1861–65   Endpapers

Cedar Mountain and Approaches, August 1862   135

Confederate Virginia, 1861–65   201

Brandy Station and Approaches, June 1863   247

PREFACE

orty-eight months of war, that is what the years 1861-65 meant to the people of Culpeper County, Virginia. Forty-eight months of military training, invasion, occupation, liberation, battle, hardship, triumph, and sorrow, forty-eight months and their ever-changing seasons of war. This is the story of the people of Culpeper, and the story of the soldiers, Blue and Gray, who fought, lived, and sometimes died there. Robert E. Lee and Ulysses S. Grant, Thomas J. "Stonewall" Jackson and George G. Meade, James E. B. "Jeb" Stuart and George Armstrong Custer, Richard S. Ewell and John Pope—they all knew Culpeper. Culpeper was one of the most important strategic spots in the war. Nestled below the Rappahannock River and north of the Rapidan, it became a natural point of invasion for the Union army and a place from which some of the most important campaigns of the war were launched, including First and Second Manassas, Gettysburg, and the Wilderness. Few Confederate communities hosted more soldiers or witnessed more combat than Culpeper.

But this is more than the wartime experience of a single community. The story of the Civil War has been told and retold more often than any other in American history. We have the northern view and the southern view, the views of generals and privates, the views of politicians and civilians. We have military histories, political histories, economic histories, diplomatic histories, and social histories. Yet, with all this, we remain haunted by poet Walt Whitman's dismal prediction that the "real war" will never "get in the books." Whitman was thinking of the gritty and grisly side of war found in the army camps and hospitals, the side of war that soldiers seldom mention to nonsoldiers. But more than that, besides the drunkenness and swearing, beyond the blood and excrement, we are ultimately confronted by the monstrous size, scope, and duration of the war. The mind boggles at the task of making sense of it, of comprehending it.

One way to do this is to stay put, that is, to tell the story from a single place, a single vantage point. Most narratives of the war keep the reader in perpetual motion, moving from battlefield to battlefield, or from Richmond to Washington, or from Virginia to Texas. But that is not how the majority of the people engulfed by the war—southern civilians—experienced it. Most people, even the soldiers to a large extent, were spectators of the war, much like us. So, as spectators, we need a perch on which to sit and watch the action unfold. Culpeper is a good place to do that without losing any of the drama or humor of the war. So it is from Culpeper that we shall watch two nations do battle, admire the efforts of soldiers and civilians to cope with war, and try to understand the rise and decline of the Confederacy. Like Whitman, who, incidentally, plays a part in Culpeper's story, we shall watch anew the "Battles, the horrors of fratricidal war, the fever of doubtful news, the fitful events."

As for that all–important vantage point, it is largely "southern." This is not to say the story neglects those Yankees whose lives were shaped by events in Culpeper. It is only to acknowledge that a majority of its vast array of characters are southern civilians and soldiers. In organization, too, the story is southern. The "seasons" of war, besides drawing on the wisdom of Ecclesiastes, refer largely to the changing fortunes of the Confederacy. Thus the four seasons of this book: "Spring" is 1861, when the Confederacy was born and southern hopes were buoyant; "Summer" is 1862, when the Confederacy reached its full strength and maturity; "Autumn" is 1863, the year in which defeats at Gettysburg and Vicksburg muted Confederate enthusiasm;

"Winter" is 1864–65, which saw the death of the Confederacy. What emerges then is a portrait of a people initially keen to wage war but increasingly plagued by self-doubt, weariness, and fear. The people of Culpeper gradually turned away from rebellion, not so much because they lost faith in their cause but because they became intimidated by the destructive power and demoralizing forces of war.

Finally, the story is told largely in the present tense. This is not an attempt to copy the technique used by Albert Castel in a recent book about the Atlanta campaign. *Seasons of War* was launched long before publication of Castel's fine work. In important ways, too, Castel and I use the present tense differently. Larger portions of Culpeper's story are told in the past tense, and there are no historiographical digressions like those used by Castel. I have chosen this technique for two reasons. First and most importantly, it is meant to provide a sense of immediacy, to place readers in the vortex of the war. Second, it is meant to recreate the confusion and chaos of war. The narrative unfolds only as rapidly as the story will allow. No knowledge of events is permitted beyond those being described. Readers must not even assume that they know how the war will end.

PART I

Spring

CHAPTER ONE

A PLACE AND A PEOPLE

*T*he colors strike you first—greens, and browns, and blues, all of them bright, all of them vivid. Especially the greens. God, it is green, every conceivable shade of green. New grass, perpetual pines and cedars, and the freshly-minted leaves of hazel, beech, and fruit trees spread unchecked toward the horizon. And the greening has only begun. Before many weeks have passed, clover, corn, wheat, oats, and tobacco will enrich the spectrum. Until then, moist, glistening patches of tan and black, in furrows of newly-turned earth, protect embryonic seeds and adolescent plants. The land's contours lend the colors subtle shadings, for this is no flat, dreary plain. Colors melt and flow, one into the other, as pounding ocean tides fifty leagues to the east shove and squeeze the earth's surface into the hills and hollows of Virginia's central Piedmont. There is no predicting this terrain. In one direction, broad sweeps of unblemished land roll for miles while elsewhere thick woodlands obscure the view. A mountain here, a series of hills there, leave you gasping at the variety of nature's adornments. Near the horizon, rich blue skies and the sun's brilliant rays force you to squint against the onrush of spring.

Green and silver ribbons of moving colors slice through the land. They separate the hills, create the valleys, and confine the earth. The

3

ribbons have names: Rappahannock, Rapidan, Robinson, Thornton, and Hazel. And they have scores of children in the creeks, runs, and rivulets that honeycomb the scene. These ribbons mean much to the people who live here. They feed the colors, they nourish the greens and browns that proclaim the wealth of the land. They add to the earth's allure, clinging erotically to its contours. The colors complement the earth's configuration, as fashionable attire accents the body of a beautiful woman.

The land is quiet, too. You are not aware of the quiet at first; it does not seize you like the colors. Only when the stillness is broken does it speak. A child's gleeful shout echoes against a hill. A train whistle shrieks through a valley. More often a gradually swelling breeze whispers through the pines and cedars. That is as noisy as it gets, at least until late afternoon. Then spring skies frequently darken, and the muffled rumble of thunder rolls over you, eastward from the Blue Ridge.

This place is called Culpeper, ancient, proud, happy Culpeper. Its boundaries once confined nearly a thousand square miles, a gift from Charles Stuart II to John Lord Culpeper. Only Indians—mostly Seneca—and white trappers roamed the land then. Lord Culpeper's domain grew and shrank and changed hands more than once before white settlement began. The entire story, filled with rapacious noblemen, ambitious politicians, and a mistress or two, is still murky. In the end, the lands fell to Margaret Lady Culpeper and her daughter Catherine, who became, in turn, Lady Fairfax. Family bequests and the encroachments of civilization played havoc with the land. Bits and pieces were whittled away, subdivided, and severed. Fewer than 400 square miles remain, a modest landholding, of no great account in the world's affairs, unless, of course, this is your world.[1]

Now it is April 1861. The people of Culpeper shed the sloth and slough of winter. Farmers have been in their fields for several weeks; merchants and shopkeepers prepare for the spring trade; and families roll up carpets, air out mattresses, and attack the residue of winter decay. The weather encourages them. The days are slowly warming, and the danger of a deep frost has passed. Nights can still be chilly, the early mornings brisk, but no one minds. Winter has fled. The skies are brighter, the colors livelier, the air fresher. The air smells of water, the water of rivers, of dews, of rains. It is a time of hope and expectations; it is a season of birth and renewal.

Sheriffs James Harris and Jacob Eggborn recorded 12,000 inhabitants in last year's census. Only 44 of Virginia's 148 counties have more people. Over half of the 12,000 are slaves; only 23 counties have more. That seems like a lot of people, but plenty of elbow room remains in Culpeper. In fact, Culpeper, like many long-settled Virginia communities, has been losing residents until recently. Some blame the decline on exhausted soil, wasted by decades of heavy tobacco planting. Others blame it on the restlessness of the people and their hankering for adventure or a new life. Traces of restlessness remain. Young men continue to drift westward or to nearby cities in search of fortune and fame. Still, the worst of the exodus seems to have passed, and Culpeper, if not growing, is no longer in decline.[2]

The white families are mostly farmers, and most own their land. This is a prosperous community, where the average farm is 260 acres, but it is quite unlike the Deep South. Culpeper produces no cotton or sugar, only a small amount of rice, and modest crops of tobacco. The biggest money crop is wheat. The most important crop, used to feed free people, slaves, and livestock alike, is corn. Sheep are the most numerous livestock, followed by hogs, cattle, and horses. Add to this large quantities of butter, hay, oats, potatoes, peas, beans, flax, honey, and wool and you have a farming community more akin to Pennsylvania or New York than to Georgia or Alabama. Reforms that began in the 1790s and accelerated in the 1820s have placed Culpeper farmers among the southern leaders of progressive, diversified agriculture. By replenishing the soil with fertilizers (mostly lime and guano), rotating crops, and planting legumes such as clover and peas, they have increased the production of all crops since 1850, especially tobacco. The value of the county's farms has exploded from less than $3 million to over $5 million, thirteenth highest in the state.[3]

With the annual planting routine under way, farmers, slaves, and hired hands labor with fairly primitive tools—hoes, shovels, and rakes mostly. It is not that Culpeper is ignorant of the latest farm machines. After all, Cyrus McCormick grew up and introduced his wonderful reaper just a few miles away, in Rockbridge County. Since moving to

Chicago, McCormick has added mechanical threshers, rakes, and mowers to his inventory. But Culpeper farmers find McCormick's machines, as well as those of people like Obed Hussey, more useful for harvesting (mostly wheat) than for planting. Their most important planting tool remains the horse-drawn iron moldboard plow. The quality and number of these plows and other horse-drawn implements may lag behind machines used on northeastern and midwestern farms, but Culpeper, and Virginia generally, remains the South's most progressive farming region. On the other hand, few farmers regard the machines as suitable replacements for slave labor. Of the 22 men who own at least a thousand dollars' worth of machinery in Culpeper, only two own no slaves.[4]

Of course, most farmers get along fine without machines or slaves. For every member of the Culpeper gentry, three to four small farmers and herders remain, in their defiantly individualistic fashion, unconcerned with cultivating large expanses of wheat and corn. Pursuing the leisurely life of their mostly Celtic ancestors, they seem content to live on a few acres, much of it unimproved woodland, and tend an acre or two of corn and tobacco while their livestock, mostly hogs and cattle, fend for themselves. They live in cabins rather than trim farmhouses. The men hunt and fish rather than till fields, and they seem happier arguing about politics and the weather at local taverns and mills than frequenting church, although they attend revival meetings now and then. They like to drink and fight, and because these pastimes get them into trouble in town, they steer clear of settlements with more than a half dozen buildings. Their numbers have declined in past decades, for the largest segment of the Culpeper exodus has been a great plain-folk migration to the West and Southwest. Yet many remain, and they are unchanging in their ways.[5]

The biggest exception to the generally British settlement is a healthy German community. Small groups of Germans first arrived in the early eighteenth century. Within a generation, they established communities at Germanna on the Rapidan River, Criglersville on the Robinson River, and in the Little Fork region between the Hazel and Rappahannock rivers. These hard-working, prosperous farmers scorned their lazy non-German (mostly Scotch-Irish) neighbors. "I would not mind if there were a thousand times as many inhabitants here, who, if possible, should all be Germans," confided one of their number in 1766. "While others indulge in idleness, do nothing but ride about and plant scarcely so much as to provide for their households, the Germans are reputed for their diligence and industry which probably prompted the saying hereabouts that a German can thrive on a rock." The German did not get his wish, but the Yagers, Spicers, Leggs, Inskeeps, Criglers, Aylors, Utterbacks, Huffmans, and Waylands of the county have lived fairly amicably alongside the Taylors, Weavers, Stringfellows, Smiths, Hudsons, Browns, Armstrongs, Hills, McDonalds, and O'Bannons. Of the county's current 51 foreign-born residents, 36 are Irish and 7 are German.[6]

The hills and piney woods northwest of Culpeper Court House, the county seat, offer the biggest haven for plain folk. There, around the little settlement of Griffinsburg, the countryside abounds in "flint rock, chinquapins, and brandy." A village evolved at Griffinsburg, or the "Box" as it is known, because a store and post office happened to be in the same general area. Local farmers and herders find it a convenient place to rendezvous. It is a place where, as one alarmed citizen insists, "they vote and fight audaciously, for they are a pugnacious sort."[7]

Slightly more tame are the denizens of the Little Fork region around Jeffersonton. Jeffersonton is a booming metropolis compared to Griffinsburg, yet it remains a placid place. The town, with a population of about 160 souls, still serves as the home of the Jefferson Academy, which assured the parents of young scholars upon opening in 1836 that the town was "free from the haunts of vice and dissipation." That is probably still true. Remember all the Germans who settled there. Certainly the residents of the Little Fork, famed for their camp meetings and watermelons, "differ from the dweller in the 'pines' [around Griffinsburg] in not being much addicted to fighting." Still, these people are seldom rushed for time. Adhering to the Celtic rather than the Protestant work ethic, they habitually "meet at the store of 'old Mac [in Jeffersonton],' whittle sticks and tell monstrous yarns about fox hunting."[8]

Other crossroads villages and settlements—18 all together—have sprouted up around the county. Many, like Griffinsburg, exist only because of a mill, tavern, or river ford in the area. The few exceptions are places like Rixeyville, which thrives because the Rixey family, extensive landowners along the Hazel River north of Culpeper Court House, willed it into being. Mitchell's Station, near the Rapidan, is a product of the Orange & Alexandria Railroad. The story goes that Billy Mitchell, whose land blocked the railroad's right-of-way, opposed construction of the line and stood ready, shotgun in hand, to prevent its passage across his land. John Wharton, a wealthy neighbor, intervened to suggest that any station built along that portion of the train's route bear Mitchell's name, and that the engineer of each passing locomotive blow his whistle in tribute. Uncle Billy, as Mitchell is known, beamed and relented.[9]

The village of Brandy first drew notice because a deep well made it a natural watering place for wagoners and herders passing through the region east of Culpeper Court House. Then a crossroads tavern, dubbed the "Brandy House" after a visit by thirsty soldiers during the War of 1812, gave the place a name. When the Orange & Alexandria Railroad began to stretch westward from Fauquier County, the place seemed a good spot for a station. Soon Brandy Station became a village with a post office, although it is still not a very impressive settlement. One county resident describes it as "a doulful looking place" with "two stores, a tavern, blacksmith shop and no streets."[10]

There is only one town of consequence: Culpeper Court House. Located pretty much in the center of the county, it has just over a thousand residents. The town's official name is Fairfax, but when it became the home of the county court, people started calling it Culpeper Court House, the Court House, or simply Culpeper. Call it what you will, it is the fulcrum of county political and economic life. Besides hosting the county court, Culpeper boasts the largest merchants, the biggest market, and the principal railroad depot. Its growth has helped to save the county. Yet for all its growth, Culpeper remains a friendly place, free of the rural versus town estrangement that plagues some parts of Virginia.[11]

The merchants, artisans, professionals, and manufacturers who reside in these villages and towns lend the sort of diversity every farming community needs. Culpeper boasts nearly 60 merchants and shopkeepers, and over 30 clerks and bookkeepers. It supports 88 carpenters, 20 shoemakers, 19 wheelwrights, 18 blacksmiths, 13 weavers, 9 coach or wagon makers, 8 coopers, 8 saddlers, 8 tailors, 7 bricklayers, 5 masons, 5 cabinetmakers, 4 millwrights, 4 plasterers, and a sprinkling of gunsmiths, silversmiths, and harnessmakers, about twenty different crafts in all. In the professional community there are 46 teachers (but no public schools), 30 physicians, 12 lawyers, 8 ministers (but twenty-four churches), 3 dentists, and 2 druggists. A mutual dependence has developed between these people and their farmer clients as Culpeper's markets have opened up to Virginia and beyond.[12]

Perhaps the closest ties run to the mercantile community. Merchants work 14-hour days to oblige their customers, especially in spring. Saturday, the traditional market day in southern towns, is the single busiest day of the week, but court days, muster days, and election days are equally frantic. Not all who stop purchase something. Many visit the stores only to socialize, swap stories, warm up in cold weather, or cool off in hot weather. Still, the merchants must be ready for them, and so spring, a traditional time to restock stores, is a busy season. Goods arrive more promptly now that a railroad passes through the county, a convenience that has even led some shopkeepers to abandon the traditional pattern of placing orders only in the spring and fall. But spring sales remain important, and some merchants, leaving nothing to chance, have made personal visits to eastern cities to ensure the quality and prompt delivery of goods. James Rudasill and John T. Stark, seeking to get a leg up on their competitors, advertise: "*Groceries! Groceries!* We have just returned from Richmond, and having bought a good supply of the goods, we think we can do as well by all who want to encourage Southern trade, as any house in town, either for the cash or credit, (cash very much preferred)."[13]

Culpeper's industries also depend on agriculture. The county has 27 mills, two of them steam powered. Most millers survive on the corn and wheat crops, although several also grind gypsum (for plaster), cut lumber, and card wool. Fierce competition means that only seven millers earn more than $500 a year. The seven biggest mills employ free labor, a combination of 98 laborers (71 men and 27 women) with a payroll approaching $19,000. Garnett Hudson operates a small iron foundry, and some mining—gold mining of all things—survives in the county's southeastern corner, around Richardsville. However, the heyday of Virginia gold mining, which peaked in the 1840s, has long since passed.[14]

Much of Culpeper's prosperity can be attributed to the Orange & Alexandria Railroad, which has only recently supplanted the old transportation network of roads, rivers, and canals. A turnpike boom hit the county, as it did much of Virginia, shortly after the War of 1812. The state incorporated scores of private companies to construct roads, but it bore, in the process, as much as three-fifths of the costs. The best roads, constructed of stone, require a toll of from 1 to 20 cents, the amount depending on the number of animals pulling and the size of the vehicle they pull. Four such thoroughfares pass through Culpeper, all of them originating at Sperryville, in Rappahannock County, and confined to the northern half of Culpeper. Most of Culpeper's roads are plain dirt, which turns to mud during much of the year. There have been efforts to maintain planks along the most heavily traveled routes, but lack of revenue makes this difficult.[15]

Canals attracted advocates in the 1840s and 1850s as alternatives to Culpeper's principal rivers. The rivers have never been very dependable highways. Their waters run deep enough for heavily laden craft only after heavy rainfalls. The most promising canal, still used in 1861, is the Rappahannock Canal. It runs 55 miles from Waterloo to Fredericksburg, which has traditionally been the county's best market and supplier. Wheat, flour, timber, and assorted merchandise travel downriver to Fredericksburg, while guano, lime, plaster, bricks, fish, whiskey, seed, and salt are returned to Culpeper, all on substantial flatboats. Yet business on the Rappahannock Canal has been seriously curtailed by the railroad. In the process, Alexandria and Lynchburg have largely replaced Fredericksburg as markets and suppliers.[16]

Railroad construction began at Alexandria in 1849, and the tracks reached Culpeper ten years ago, in 1851. The completed line stretches 148 miles from Alexandria southward through Manassas and Culpeper and on to Gordonsville, Charlottesville, and Lynchburg. Culpeper raised nearly $30,000 for the project, and more than half of the nearly $21,000 paid to secure rights-of-way went to Culpeper landowners.

The county now has five stations along the route, including Rappahannock, Brandy, Mitchell's, and Rapidan, and the Court House. Culpeper's own John S. Barbour, Jr., has served as president of the line since 1851.[17]

Although the O&A does offer passenger service, it is primarily a freight line. The same is true of most of Virginia's 17 railroads, of which the O&A is the fourth longest. These lines were meant to usher in a new age of prosperity for Virginia by making the state economically independent of the North and strengthening commercial ties with other southern states. The results for Culpeper have certainly been as intended. The O&A offers the lowest rates in the state to ship grain, flour, guano, coal, iron, plaster, and manure. The railroad has also brought more goods to Culpeper shops—far more, and in greater variety, than the county has ever known. Garland Sisson now sells "all popular Magazines and Literary Papers" at his bookstore. Alexandria, Baltimore, and Richmond merchants advertise in Culpeper, and local merchants offer such luxuries as "Sweet Havana Oranges," English port, and "cassimere."[18]

Only a few people have suffered from this prosperity. As the railroad has opened Culpeper to competition with manufactured goods from the East, some local craftsmen, including gunsmiths, tailors, cobblers, and furniture makers, find it hard to compete. They have been forced either to move to less commercialized regions or to become more shopkeeper than craftsman. In a similar fashion, the amount of "home manufacturing"—barrels, ironware, clothing—has fallen sharply with the arrival of the O&A. No wonder that while the population at the Court House continues to grow, the rural population has declined slightly. Of course, Culpeper is not alone in its dilemma. Other Virginia counties given readier access to markets via railroad have suffered similar fates, as have communities across the nation.[19]

Contributing to the general prosperity are Culpeper's 6,653 slaves. Nearly seven hundred people own or hire slaves in Culpeper. Eighty-four people have 20 or more slaves, which is the usual measure of a "planter," but the average holding is nine to ten. The county has three slave markets, the oldest and most active one operating at the Court House, but most sales, as seems to be true for much of the South, result from private negotiations. Prices have been running high lately, which has forced many people to hire rather than purchase black labor. In fact, 10 percent of the slave population is hired out, and only 68 percent of slaveholders own all of the slaves they hold.[20]

Owned or hired, it is all the same to Culpeper's slaves, who are less enthusiastic than white folks about the arrival of spring. The late autumn and winter months, generally known as "slack time," provided cool weather and demanded little arduous work. Shucking corn, storing fodder, stripping tobacco, killing hogs, some plowing, fixing fences, mending harnesses, and repairing equipment and outbuildings occupy most of these months. But spring quickens the tempo. Slaves not assigned to field work face the formidable task of spring cleaning. Everyone else, including skilled craftsmen, may be asked to help with planting, and those slaves who are normally allowed to hire out their free time will find fewer opportunities (and possess less energy) to do so. Alexander Jackson, the property of William Day, earns money as a saddle and harness maker during slack time. By now, however, Jackson has likely joined Day's seven field hands to work his master's nearly 400 acres.[21]

Elsewhere, Culpeper slaves work at varied tasks. John P. Kelly's sprawling farm, which includes lands on both the Culpeper and Fauquier sides of the Rappahannock, not only produces thousands of bushels of corn, wheat, and oats, but also supports a thriving industrial plant, known locally as Kellysville. The twice-widowed Kelly leaves domestic tasks in the capable hands of his white housekeeper, Frances Thornhill, while he and son Granville oversee the operation of a three-story flour mill, a cloth factory, a sawmill, and wheelwright, cooperage, and shoe shops. The flour mill is the biggest industry. It employs a hundred men, free and slave, who work six and a half days a week and can produce 100 barrels of flour a day. Slaves, who supply most of the other labor, card and spin flax and wool in their cabins, and weave yarn on looms in the cloth factory. The shoe shop is operated primarily by and for slaves, who use hides that have been tanned in Fredericksburg. Two slave women, Mary Latham and Sarah Hurley, tend 50 head of milch cows, as well as draw and strain the milk, skim the cream, and churn the butter. Kellysville also boasts two icehouses, a bean house, a smokehouse, and a sausage grinder. The grinder receives its heaviest use each October and January when a slave named White slaughters the hogs he has tended through the year.[22]

The presence of so many slaves has caused tension in Culpeper, where white residents have been debating the merits of their "peculiar institution" since the 1820s. Having carefully discussed and weighed the dangers of slave rebellion, the moral obligations of slaveholders, and the consequences of emancipation, most residents have concluded that slavery is necessary. A few slave owners have emancipated their servants, but most such instances occurred before the 1830s, before the Nat Turner rebellion and the rise of abolitionism in the North. As the South has become more defensive about slavery and less tolerant of any talk about emancipation, ranks have closed in Culpeper. Slaves who have been freed and who wish to remain in the county find the court less willing to approve their petitions. The most recent legal gesture in support of emancipation occurred this very month, when Ann Hall, who lives at the Court House, provided for the eventual manumission of six servants in her will. However, Hall appreciates the legal and popular resistance to her action, and so has also arranged for the slaves to be sold with the rest of her property should state laws at the time of her death make emancipation impossible.[23]

Those few slave owners who, like Miss Hall, wish to make amends to their servants generally accept colonization or transportation out of Virginia as the most suitable solution. Colonization claims an old and honorable southern lineage, dating back to the turn of the century. Inspired by the writings of colonizing advocate Thomas Jefferson, one Culpeper farmer, J. Pembroke Thom, instigated an almost legendary colonization scheme in 1839. Thom, long uncomfortable with slavery, resolved to free his 18 slaves and provide for their settlement in Pennsylvania. He even sent his eldest son to inspect and purchase suitable lands for the transfer. Thom's scheme hit only one snag: his slaves refused to go. Their reasons are unclear, but, in any case, Thom listened not. He conscripted several slaves to initiate the plan and sent them packing. The plantation, recalls a younger son, became "a house of mourning," and all efforts to dissuade Thom in his good work failed. He soon found, however, his exiled slaves just as resolute. Nearly all fled the colony and returned to Culpeper within the year.[24]

Philip Slaughter, a Baptist minister in Culpeper, campaigned to revive interest in colonization in the 1850s. When the Virginia legislature voted to fund colonization to Africa, Slaughter helped to promote African settlement by establishing and editing the *Virginia Colonizationist*. The plan never attracted much attention, and Reverend Slaughter has proved notably unsuccessful in exciting his Culpeper neighbors. Perhaps they doubt his sincerity, for Slaughter still owns nine slaves.[25]

Popular opinion in Culpeper is more in tune with another Baptist preacher, Thornton Stringfellow. Stringfellow, who manages 32 slaves and 1,000 acres, has been constructing an elaborate Biblical defense of slavery since the early 1840s. In both Sunday sermons and published essays, he maintains that slavery is sanctioned by both Old and New Testament and protected by the U.S. Constitution, the "only National Constitution which ever emanated from God." He argues that Africans are suited to slavery by virtue of their race and intellectual inferiority, and that they have benefited physically, morally, and spiritually from bondage. Slavery, he insists, is "full of mercy," and he assures skeptics that the South's slaves are better cared for than "any other equal number of laborers on earth."[26]

Stringfellow's approving neighbors have been particularly anxious about defending slavery during the past five years, as rumors of possible slave rebellions have grown. The rumors became so widespread in December 1856 that the county court doubled the number of slave patrols to eight and requested additional arms from Richmond. Created in the 1820s, slave patrols had been responsible for breaking up unlawful assemblies of slaves and arresting slaves found abroad without permission. Since the mid-1850s, they have watched for far more sinister activities. "People are very much alarmed—the ladies particularly," one patroller reported during the 1856 crisis. "Alarming and exciting rumors are in circulation that during the Christmas week all the whites are to be massacred. In Rappk, in Orange, in Fauquier, and in this County negroes have been arrested who are supposed to be engaged in these plots—weapons of various kinds have been found and in some places ammunition." Nothing came of the "insurrection," part of a tremor felt throughout the South, but several Culpeper slaves "*emigrated*" during the weeks of tension.[27]

True, Culpeper slaves get into mischief from time to time. They love, for instance, to match wits against the slave "patterolls." A favorite trick, when caught out at night and chased by patrollers, is to stretch grapevines across a darkened road or path. While the patrollers pick themselves up out of the dust, the fugitives make good their escape. Malinda Perry, the property of Polly Brown, loves to attend illicit parties in the neighborhood of Eggbornsville, in the northeastern part of the county. She regularly wears on these occasions petticoats that have been starched in hominy water. The effect is to produce a loud "pop" whenever she moves. The "pop" is her means of escaping the patrols, for she instructs her children to listen for her return home. When they hear the popping, they are to throw open the cabin door and let her in ahead of the patrol.[28]

But all things considered, Culpeper slaves do not pose a serious threat to law and order. Theft, an occasional assault, or a charge of arson now and then measures the extent of slave crime. Of course, one explanation for this quietude could be the severity of the penalties for those who misbehave. For slaves found guilty of serious crimes, justice is swift and untempered by mercy. In August 1858, John Heflin, a middle-aged overseer, accused Henry, a slave of Lewis Ellis, of assault, a black offense tantamount to murder in white eyes. The court proceeded fairly with its investigation and concluded that the charges should be "quashed for defect." Henry was discharged. However, when Henry appeared before the court in October for "maliciously" assaulting Heflin, the justices found him guilty and ordered him sold and transported "beyond the limits of the United States." Sale and transportation are the most common punishments for troublesome slaves.[29]

The most serious black threat to white tranquility came in 1859, and the event did not even occur in Culpeper. Harper's Ferry is less than 50 miles north of Culpeper. So when John Brown seized the United States arsenal there in October 1859, the county reacted. The county court increased the size of its slave patrols, and the patrols grew more aggressive. "A number of peddlers and suspicious characters have been arrested here of late," reported a newspaper dispatch from Culpeper, "and it is the intention of our citizens to put all strangers who cannot give a satisfactory account of themselves in confinement." Besides beefing up home defenses, the county rushed 25 armed men by train to Charles Town.[30]

Sixty additional volunteers resurrected the Culpeper Minute Men, a militia force founded during the American Revolution, and prepared to join their neighbors. They elected Waller Tazewell Patton, a graduate of and former professor at the Virginia Military Institute, as captain. First sergeant George Williams, with no military experience, expressed fiendish delight at this opportunity to drill "all the lawyers, doctors and merchants" of the county. Yet the men soon believed themselves ready for duty. "Our first parade will be in two weeks," Williams informed his fiancee in late November, "& we expect to agitate the town to its low-est depths. The brass band will precede the company." Alas, the excite-ment passed before the Minute Men left home. Members of the earlier "war party" returned soaked and chilled by heavy rain, and "without a scalp or other trophy." One sunshine patriot sighed, "I don't think I shall go out campaigning again in a hurry."[31]

Still, it would be wrong to underestimate the county's resolve on the slavery issue. Largely to defend against such threats to the public peace as that posed by John Brown, the Minute Men continue to muster regularly. The county remains enthusiastic because the com-pany has restored a colorful page to community life. "We had a great day here on Saturday," reported one Minute Man following a spring drill. "Our company of volunteers was out in full uniform and pre-sented a very handsome appearance. A large crowd attracted by the novelty of the thing witnessed the parade and our ladies especially were well pleased." And truly, even without the need for defense, what could be more rewarding than to please the ladies? A couple of months later, the entire town—led by the ladies—showed its apprecia-tion by sponsoring a ball for its intrepid heroes.[32]

People also agree on the necessity of maintaining a pacific black pop-ulation. Whites who endanger their neighbors by emboldening slaves are unceremoniously hauled into court. The most frequent threats to white solidarity come from selling spirits or liquor to slaves and permitting their unlawful assembly. Then, too, some slave owners, laws unto themselves, persuade their own slaves of the dangers of insubordination, let alone rebellion. Their method is to impose harsher penalties for relatively minor transgressions than the courts impose for civil crimes. "Corpulent, smoothshaven, gray haired" John Kelly, master of Kellysville, is a notorious example. Kelly is a formidable character who reserves a room in his grist mill for "unruly slaves." The room has no windows and only a peephole in the door. Prisoners remain handcuffed and chained to a heavy weight. Kelly releases them each morning to perform their day's labors, but they spend all remaining hours in the cramped, dark, stuffy cell. If in a particularly vile mood, Kelly lets off steam by whipping lazy or insubordinate slaves with a birch. Nor does he hesitate to separate families when selling his slaves, a threat which in itself can be an effective means of discipline. In any case, his slaves fear him.[33]

Only 429 free blacks live in Culpeper. That is about 25 percent fewer than in 1830, although the number ranks high (fortieth) among all the counties in the state. White distrust and jealousy have driven away many blacks. In years past, petitions seeking the removal of all free blacks from the county have occasionally circulated. Petitioners either protested the competition posed by free blacks for jobs or, taking the opposite tack, accused free blacks of being idlers and a threat to the peace. In 1831, some citizens sought to ban all blacks—free and slave—from learning a trade or becoming an apprentice. They blamed cheap black labor for driving away white artisans and mechanics. Indeed, right up to this year of 1861, employers have preferred free Negro labor, particularly for temporary or irregular work. They believe that blacks generally work for lower wages than whites and that they are more obedient and respectful. Free blacks, like disreputable whites, find themselves in court if they threaten to stir up the slaves in any way. The children of indigent blacks are sometimes bound out as servants or apprentices by the court, although it is also true that some black parents request such action. More to the point, adults are bound out if they fail to pay their taxes. Free blacks also receive more severe penalties than whites for minor crimes. Just ask John Miles, who spent five years in jail for stealing a piece of meat.[34]

The least affluent members of the free black community reside, like many white "crackers," in wooded areas remote from towns and villages. Poor whites who hire out to prosperous farmers, a sprinkling of half-breed Indians, and an occasional runaway slave share these dark regions with them. The largest such region is a triangular stretch of low ground south of the Court House and along the Rapidan River. Some farmers favor the rich soil of this region, but it remains a dreary spot. One county resident describes it as "a large tract of dead level country covered from one end to the other with mud and water." Known variously as the Flats and the Free State, its population of poor whites and free blacks mingle and cohabit scandalously. The offspring of their interracial liaisons are called "Free State Negroes." Respectable folk naturally regard the Flats as an unsavory place. At the very least, it is rowdy. "This is a powerful place for drinking and fighting," testifies one county resident. "They drink & fight and fight & drink. . . . They look upon both as pleasant & refreshing."[35]

But most free blacks are reputable people who work hard and pay their taxes, facts admitted by many whites. Some blacks own farms and businesses. Others command valuable skills. True, fewer occupations are open to them than to whites, less than a quarter as many to be exact. Three-fourths of them work as unskilled laborers, as farmhands, or in service occupations. The nature of their jobs, especially those of servants and apprentices, also means that they frequently live in their employers' homes. That is certainly the case for some two dozen children who have been put out to work as domestic servants or apprentices by either the court or their parents. Farmhands fare better, but only marginally so. Warner Bundy is typical. He, his wife, and six children, ages 3 to 19, live in a house provided by Robertson Coons. Coons also pays Bundy $150 a year and allows him to raise his own stock. Generous terms, and they provide the family a modicum of independence. But Bundy sees very little of his wages in cash, for he and Coons have a credit arrangement whereby Coons provides whatever supplies the Bundys may need and deducts the cost from

Warren's wages. Bundy still owes $77 from 1860, and thus far in 1861 he already owes $30 for bacon, salt, and brandy.[36]

At the Court House, where most nonfarming Negroes live, nine black families own personal property, and three own land. One must admire the pluck of these people. Lucy Collman, a 47-year-old washer-woman, lives on her own property and has raised two sons who work as house servants in town. Nancy Asher, a 32-year-old washerwoman, has accumulated $100 in personal property while single-handedly rais-ing an infant daughter. Ann Asher, also a laundress but 9 years Nancy's junior, supports three children, the oldest being 9; and Eliza-beth Madden supports five children, ages 1 to 10, through long hours at the washtub. Other people have an easier time. Ira Field, a 60-year-old barber, and his wife Judy enjoy a comfortable life. Their six chil-dren are now grown and all are employed, including 17-year-old Ruben, who is learning his father's trade. George Hicks, a 20-year-old bricklayer, supports his mother and two younger siblings. Frank and Eliza Smith, both 30, work at the Piedmont Hotel, he as a cook, she as a laundress. They have two children. Arthur and Betty Redmon, both 35, work as carpenter and washerwoman to support their four children and Arthur's 60-year-old mother. Their daughter Martha, 15 years old, works as a cook.[37]

A few black farmers, who constitute a "select group" throughout the South, own their land. Their holdings are generally small, but they can be quite productive. Randall Tate, a 28-year-old farmer with a wife and son, owns a twenty-two-acre farm worth a hundred dollars. He plants, with the help of two relatives, seven acres in corn and wheat. Richard West, 22 years old, recently bought twelve and a half acres from Thomas Fitzhugh, for whom he still works occasionally. West cul-tivates about half the land, mostly in corn. Fitzhugh brags of his pro-tegé, "It was all woodland. He cleared some of it & put up a dwelling house, kitchen, stable, & meat house."[38]

Willis Madden stands out as Culpeper's most prosperous and pro-ductive black citizen. Born free in 1799 to the mulatto daughter of an indentured Irish servant and a slave (family tradition says one of George Washington's footmen), Madden was bound out in accordance with Virginia law until he turned 21. In 1835, Martin and Martha

Slaughter, his former masters, sold him eighty-seven acres of land on the peninsula formed by the convergence of the Rappahannock and Rapidan rivers. The region is known as the Chinquapin Neck because chinquapins, a type of beech tree, grow there in abundance. Indians inhabited the region in colonial times. Now Willis Madden lives there with his son Jack, the only one of eight children still at home. Madden's wife Kitty died a few years ago. She had been something of an aristocrat, born free and the daughter of William Clarke, a Revolutionary soldier. She had been five years younger than Willis, five inches shorter (5 feet, 2 inches tall), and lighter in color. Both were mulattoes, but Willis is regarded as a "dark mulatto."[39]

Together Madden and Jack work nearly three hundred acres worth close to $1,200. In 1860 the land yielded 600 bushels of corn, 260 of oats, 75 of wheat, 30 of rye, 6 of peas and beans, 4 of potatoes, plus 4 tons of hay. Madden's livestock includes five horses, two milch cows, three cattle, and eight hogs, the whole worth over $260. Madden's productivity and wealth cannot challenge those of Virginia's richest free black, a Halifax County farmer named William Epps, whose property is valued at nearly $80,000. But Madden is his nearest challenger in Culpeper.[40]

Madden is also a successful businessman. His property fronts a busy road between the Court House and Fredericksburg, and he takes full advantage of the traffic by operating a general store, tavern, blacksmith shop, and drover's rest. The tavern, actually part of his house, is "deservedly popular" with travelers, for it is the only place between the Court House and Fredericksburg that offers accommodations for man and beast. The drover's rest is equally appreciated, albeit by a rougher class of drover and teamster. These men are not permitted in the tavern, but they may take their drinks on the porch. Madden has entered the entrepreneurial world to the extent of occasionally hiring slaves to work on his farm.[41]

Madden gets along with everyone, black and white. Neighbors call him "Uncle Willis" and acknowledge him as "a highly respectable man." Madden's whiskey supplier in Fredericksburg never worries about receiving payment. On one occasion, he was nearly apologetic about sending Madden a bill. "I would have sent it before," the supplier explained, "but I thought you might think I was dunning you.

You know I told you I was not going to ask you for any money. But you know whenever you send it, it is very acceptable."[42]

As Madden's position suggests, Culpeper is a pleasant place for most people. Granted, blacks are expected to keep their place, and even someone as hard-working as Madden would not last long were he to threaten the authority of his white neighbors. Yet few whites have reason to complain about their world. A spirit of community binds these people together, a spirit evolving over many years that has benefited enormously from two bulwarks of southern society: neighborhood and kinship. Culpeper is fractured into many towns and regions—the Court House, Brandy, the Flats, Little Fork, and others. The people living in each of these enclaves depend on their neighbors. The strength and intimacy of their neighborhoods determines the vitality and friendliness of county life. The intimacy of each neighborhood gives people a sense of well-being. They know their neighbors. They know the property lines, the creeks, the hills, the woods; they can anticipate what will happen, and they believe they control their own destinies. Equally important are ties of kinship and clan. Although families are sometimes fractious and raucous, the bond of blood is more often a mediating influence. Many large families, present among both low and mighty, both black and white, inhabit the county. Kinship bonds individual neighborhoods; it can even strengthen ties between neighborhoods several miles apart. Taken together, neighborhood and kinship give people a sense of place and belonging. Culpeper is home, and these people feel secure within its borders.[43]

This is not to deny the existence of animosity, jealousy, and pettiness in Culpeper. Some poor people grumble about the rich; some affluent folks scorn the lowly. Lutherans abhor Baptists, Germans distrust Celts, and whites, even the least respectable, lord it over blacks. Yet these divisions do not usually run deep. The people of Culpeper share a universal desire. Each person likes to think that someone, somewhere, ranks below them on the social scale. So long as they believe this is so, that their own place is secure, they are content. Thus divisions of race, religion, education, and wealth have never endangered the equilibrium of the community.

For instance, the county's middle classes hold the humbler residents of the Flats in mild contempt, and they can be condescending in the extreme. "There are some queer people in this section," one of the gentry reports of a recent trip through the Flatlands. "The women particularly are remarkable specimens. They eschew hoops and invariably wear long eared caps made of muslin without trimmings." The men, he says, are similarly "unpolished, rude and offensive in the familiarity of their manners. And they insist if a person goes to their houses, that he shall eat to bursting almost their coarse & unpalatable food," a fare which he insists is composed largely of bacon, poke salad, and "hard corn cake."[44]

And talk about ignorant. Lord, think the gentry, these people are simple. The traveler spent the night with one cracker family. At supper, his hostess asked if he preferred "long or short sweetening" in his tea. Puzzled by the expression but assuming that "long" meant several teaspoons of sugar, he asked for a generous measure. "At that," he reports, still shuddering at the memory, "she dipped the forefinger of her right hand into the molasses bottle and then plugged it into my cup of tea." Another person at table asked for short sweetening, whereupon the hostess bit a lump of sugar in two and gave him half. What most amazed the visitor was the high regard with which this particular family was held in the region. "These people are looked up to in their neighborhood as the arbiters of questions of etiquette and their demeanor settles the gentility of the people."[45]

But take note. While this gentleman might scoff at the family's ways and manners, he never questions its right to live as it chooses, and he does not see these people as a threat to the community. After his hostess had withdrawn her finger from his tea, he proceeded to drink it. He admitted that her method of sweetening the tea made him "nauseous," but he would never deliberately insult her. The family, while not "quality folks," had, in fact, treated him generously and courteously. It neither asked nor expected payment for the meal and lodging. Ignorant and crude they may be, but he judges them "an honest set for all that."[46]

Court days betray the most typical fissures in community life. On the one hand, these are holidays, occasions for hard-working country folk to relax. They provide opportunities to shop, to sell produce and livestock, to gamble, to drink, and to talk with neighbors about everything from politics to "the gloomy prospects of the wheat crop." On the other hand, courts are necessary because even neighbors occasionally irritate, insult, or bamboozle one another. The county court's principal job is administrative, to supervise county officials, collect and expend revenues, issue licenses, and generally ensure that local government runs smoothly. Its legal role is limited to cases involving slaves, misdemeanors by whites and free blacks, the settlement of estates, and the appointment of wards. The circuit court, which meets just twice yearly, hears criminal cases and quarrels concerning trespass, fraud, boundaries, broken bonds, and unpaid debts. There are lots of unpaid debts, debts due on estates, services rendered, loans extended, and purchases made. Some of these debts are years, even decades, in arrears.[47]

Hard feelings result from some litigations, for even where small amounts of money are involved and payment is relatively quick, debtors are embarrassed by the public disclosure of their crimes. Yet quarrels over debts betray no serious class resentment in Culpeper. Most court cases involve people of means—frequently merchants and landowners—seeking to remedy a financial arrangement gone wrong. Not a few cases pit relatives or former business partners against each other.

There are, of course, cases where honor of a different sort is at stake, and one such recent court battle has produced snickers and no little tongue clucking. Ellen Smith, ward of a prosperous farmer and slave owner, accused Harris Freeman, a local merchant, of fathering her bastard child. This has been embarrassing for Freeman, not just because he is married with six children, but because he is a county constable. The case has also resurrected memories of another Freeman court skirmish. About 18 months ago, before he was elected constable, a grand jury issued a presentment against Freeman for selling ardent spirits to slaves and for permitting their unlawful assembly. Still, the court, after hearing preliminary evidence, has dismissed Miss Smith's charge.[48]

Then again, the legal system is not big enough to contain the feuds and grievances of some people. John Kelly and two of his neighbors, George and Garland Wheatley, have been at odds for decades. The Wheatley brothers, who live about a mile up the Rappahannock River from Kellysville, can muster less than half of Kelly's wealth in property and slaves, but they have held their own in a feud that started a quarter-century ago. It seems that Kelly built a toll bridge across his part of the river between Culpeper and Fauquier County. The Wheatleys hollered foul, for they had recently constructed at "considerable cost" a bridge across their own span of the river, at Wheatleyville. The Wheatleys retaliated by diverting the flow of water from their grist mills to Kelly's disadvantage. The two sides went to court. Kelly won, but neither side was pacified. Even now, Kelly will unleash a pair of ferocious dogs against Wheatley livestock found wandering on his land. Until recent years, the hot-blooded Kelly stood ready to exchange blows with the Wheatleys, even though the brothers, at least a dozen years younger than Kelly, usually won those bouts. Now his 70-year-old body is less able to join combat, even though his spirit is willing. By the way, both bridges—the sources of this feud—fell into disrepair long ago.[49]

Kelly also holds a grudge against a downriver neighbor, 60-year-old Henry Kemper. Kelly calls Kemper "the Devil," but the cause of their feud is puzzling. Kemper, a denizen of the Flats, owns no property to speak of. Perhaps he poaches on Kelly's land, or sells whiskey to his slaves. In any case, Kelly once ordered his blacks to grab Kemper and fling him into the river. Kelly's face brightened with joy as he watched his nemesis being swept along in a torrent of foam. However, Kelly's glee quickly turned to rage when he spotted Kemper's head bobbing above the water and heard the ornery cracker singing a merry tune as he floated on the river's current. And Kemper soon took revenge. While squirrel hunting one day, he spotted Kelly riding through the woods wearing a tall white beaver hat. Unable to resist such a tempting target, Kemper thoughtfully ventilated Kelly's cover.[50]

Some feuds continue outside the courts. Last spring, John S. Pendleton, one of the county's most honored citizens as a former Whig congressman and foreign diplomat, owed Fayette M. Latham, a prominent attorney and community leader, a modest sum of money. Pendleton paid the debt, or thought he had. Unfortunately, his check bounced, and Latham reacted as though Pendleton had perpetrated a major fraud. He said unkind things about Pendleton and impugned his character. When some women introduced the quarrel into the local gossip mill, the episode became exaggerated beyond reason. Latham soon regretted the rumpus, but Pendleton refused to let the incident pass without a public apology. George Williams, Pendleton's nephew, considered challenging Latham, 20 years Pendleton's junior, to a duel or fistfight as a means of satisfying family honor, but finally decided against martial measures. Latham, he reasoned, was too "small, weak and timid and a man could gain neither satisfaction not credit out of him." In any case, Williams feared that prolonging the dispute would destroy "the harmony of the two families"[51]

Pendleton has also waged war in the only local arena that unfailingly divides the community: politics. Old Jack has not sought elected office since the 1840s, but that has not prevented him from becoming embroiled in local contests. Last year, Pendleton's nephew, Williams, ran for commonwealth attorney in the county. As the only Whig running against four Democrats, Williams felt confident of splitting the opposition vote. He campaigned hard and won a core of dedicated supporters, but many people thought the 26-year-old lawyer too young for the job. Then, too, most Democrats finally rallied around a single candidate, and their cooperative efforts, bolstered by the Baptist vote against Episcopalian Williams, decided the contest by a "large majority." Williams, a level-headed fellow, graciously accepted the defeat and reasoned that he had, after all, made many friends during the campaign, and that the election had been a good experience.[52]

But things did not rest there. Uncle Jack could not restrain himself during the campaign. His political juices had begun to flow, and, given his generally low opinion of the local legal establishment, he felt compelled to enter the fray. He spoke passionately on behalf of Williams, too passionately, and with too many barbed attacks on Democratic rivals. One of his targets, John C. Green, who eventually won the election, took exception. Following his victory, Green prepared a handbill that attacked Pendleton's "character and reputation." Friends on both sides feared the worst. Pendleton is a proud, stubborn man; Green is known for his temper. Williams feared that public circulation of the handbill would produce "disastrous & deplorable consequences" and "a most serious disturbance in the family as well as the community." Cooler heads prevailed, but resentments and bruised feelings linger.[53]

Next to court days, election days mark the most exciting and entertaining occasions in county life. Nearly every man thinks himself qualified for public office. Consequently, candidates are as numerous "as locusts." And there do seem to be a lot of offices to fill. Not counting national and state elections, Culpeper residents must choose a circuit court judge, 24 justices of the peace (to sit on the county court), five constables, two commissioners of revenue, a county sheriff, clerks for both county and circuit courts, a commonwealth attorney for both county and circuit courts, an overseer of the poor, a jailer, and a county surveyor. Voters congregate at one of eight polling places, and five of them are taverns. The polls stay open from sunrise to sunset for three days (one day for federal elections), and all votes are recorded publicly. No wonder that election days make wonderful excuses to drink, argue, and scuffle. Even if fisticuffs are avoided, passions often lead to verbal assaults and hard feelings. Luckily, passions usually subside with the announcement of election results. Life goes on, and a neighborly spirit is restored—generally, that is.[54]

No single political party has ever dominated this free thinking community, and none is likely to do so. Ever since the resurrection of a two-party political system in the United States during the 1820s and 1830s, the good people of Culpeper have voted in their own best interests, national trends and issues be damned. The county supported Andrew Jackson for president in 1828 and 1832, but in the latter year, they sent a Whig to Congress and remained solidly in the Whig camp until 1852. That year, they went narrowly (by 14 votes) for Democrat Franklin Pierce over Winfield Scott, but they sent another Whig to Congress. Not until 1854 did they wholly enter the Democratic fold.[55]

Elections of the past few months show that political consensus remains an elusive commodity. The tumultuous presidential contest of last November produced no votes for Abraham Lincoln, the Republican, and precious few (19 to be exact) for Stephen Douglas and the Northern Democrats. John Bell, the perceived compromise candidate of the Constitutional Union party, won the most support, but by the slimmest of margins. He garnered 526 votes to 525 cast for John C. Breckinridge and the Southern Democrats. Lincoln's triumph in the North induced the secession of the Deep South, but Virginia and Culpeper have resisted that suicidal plunge. When the state finally organized a secession convention last February, Culpeper sent an outspoken unionist, James Barbour, to represent the county. Most people assume that unionist sentiment will prevail in the face of this madness.[56]

Generally, then, Culpeper is a quiet place, despite the potential for trouble between the races and the conflicting economic interests of its citizens. George Williams, one of the most perceptive observers of his community's condition, traveled on business to New York City a couple of years ago. He returned convinced that Culpeper was the place for him. New York was a "great humbug," he decided, nothing but a jumble of omnibuses, carriages, and drays, everyone in a hurry, "people jabbering and sputtering in all the languages of the Earth." Now, understand this: Williams is a level-headed chap, not the sort to think Culpeper's rituals any less foolish than those of Gotham. But for him, as for most of his neighbors, Culpeper's foibles and delusions, being familiar, are easier to accept, more legitimate. Yes, most white people—one might even say most free people—in Culpeper approve of their community and its customs. This is a contented, peaceful place that looks forward to a prosperous, happy future.[57]

CHAPTER TWO

A PROMISE OF
GLORY AND GREATNESS

A few hear the news with alarm. This is not what they want; this is not right. Damn South Carolina! Damn Abraham Lincoln! But most of Culpeper rejoices, or at least feels relieved. How appropriate that Virginia should join the Southern Confederacy in this season of birth. How telling that only now, amid the thunderous blast of guns in Charleston harbor, does the Confederacy seem likely to survive. Its arrival has been painful to behold, the babe wrenched from the womb of Mother Union amid the shrill staccato of political accusations and denunciations. The fledgling nation launched in February at Montgomery, Alabama, has remained a weak, undernourished waif that might well have perished without the aftershocks of Fort Sumter. Lincoln has made the Confederacy. On Monday, April 15, the president as much as declared war on the seceded South. Governor John Letcher refused to send the troops requested of Virginia, and on Wednesday, the Virginia convention approved an ordinance of secession. Arkansas, North Carolina, and Tennessee will likely enlist, perhaps to be followed by Kentucky, Maryland, and Missouri. But even without these last three, the Confederacy's white population will be more than doubled, war made a certainty. It is a time to rend.[1]

A pretty pass things have come to, and here is how it happened. Until the Sumter incident, Culpeper's path, as well as Virginia's, had been most uncertain. Culpeper divided sharply in last fall's presidential election, but Lincoln's victory rapidly shifted opinions. Slaveholder and nonslaveholder alike blanched at the thought of a Black Republican leading the national government. "National," indeed. With nearly all of his votes—and only 40 percent at that—coming from northern states. Inspired by the defiant secession of South Carolina on the day before Christmas, Culpeper held a mass meeting at the Court House on December 26. No Virginia county reacted more swiftly. Everyone had been shocked by the Carolinians' bold stroke, an action occasionally threatened and frequently discussed since the 1830s but now realized. Henry Shackleford, a prominent attorney, organized the meeting so that the community might "consult together upon the present condition of the country, and the best means to protect the rights and honor of the South."[2]

The meeting fairly crackled with excitement as several respected gentlemen, most of whom had supported John Bell in the election, urged their neighbors to lead Virginia out of the Union. Alexander G. Taliaferro and Tazewell Patton set the tone with eloquent, vibrant calls to arms. Neither one mentioned slavery, but both men, like Shackleford and all the other speakers, are connected to landed, slaveholding families. Shackleford himself owns eight blacks, and his father, also Henry, keeps sixteen on his 1,400-acre estate. Taliaferro is worth nearly $90,000, and 45 slaves work his 1,300 acres. Patton, 26-year-old captain of the Minute Men and a law partner of George Williams, is already recognized as a future leader in the county. His father, P. F. Patton, owns a 700-acre farm and 21 slaves.[3]

But it required the oratorical gifts of 63-year-old Jeremiah Morton to set the assembly's blood racing. Morton lives south of the Rapidan in Orange County, but as an ex-Whig congressman representing Culpeper, he consented to address his former constituents. "Let all secede," proposed Morton, "and then hear any propositions the North . . . [might] make for a reconstruction." A Republican administration, with its professed belief in "a higher law than the Constitution," he warned, could not be trusted. "Many a manly cheek was suffused with tears," reported one of the enraptured throng, "while with fervid eloquence he related some of the incidents of hardship and suffering borne by our fathers, in the great struggle for American liberty." Few listeners missed Morton's point: It was time for a War of Southern Independence.[4]

Shackleford then added a few stirring words before proposing five resolutions. Their essence declared that southern security could no longer be guaranteed within the Union, and that all 15 slaveholding states should unite in secession before Lincoln's inauguration on March 4. Lincoln would not dare challenge such a coalition. Meanwhile, Culpeper should pledge to raise $1,000 to purchase arms and equipment for the county's defense. No one dissented, and a committee of 12 citizens was appointed to raise the funds. "Thank God," gushed one man with some irony, "we are no longer a divided people."[5]

Word of the meeting stunned observers in Richmond, who believed that Culpeper had set in motion the "Ball of Revolution." Yet on January 5, Shackleford and other agitators went a step further by organizing the Southern Rights Association of Culpeper. Lewis L. Wood, a 40-year-old farmer with a wife, two daughters, and three slaves, spoke for this radical element when he swore that "if Virginia did not secede, he was going to South Carolina if he had to wade through blood up to his armpits."[6]

Still, many people resisted the war fever. The day before the Southern Rights Association was organized, Culpeper joined in a national vigil of "fasting, humiliation and prayer" called by President James Buchanan. Businesses closed, and a sober citizenry implored God "to avert the dangers that overhang our beloved country like a pall." Even when Virginia's General Assembly approved the convening of a secession convention on February 11, hopeful voices denied the inevitability of secession and war. Southern rights, of course, must be guaranteed, insisted Alfred J. Stofer, editor of the Culpeper *Observer*, and "if war must come," surely every Virginian should "fly to her Banner resolved to conquer or die under the stainless color of her honorable cause." Young men were already rushing to form new cavalry and artillery units, and the Culpeper Minute Men drilled with purpose. Yet, Stofer speculated, perhaps peace and security might yet be guaranteed by measures short of war. Certainly Virginia must choose wisely its delegates to the convention. "It is vastly easier to get into trouble than to get out of it," warned the editor, "and in the selection of Delegates we hope that politicians will be left at home, and intelligent, honest farmers be sent to the Convention that '*wisdom, justice, and moderation*' will characterize their proceedings.'"[7]

Further signs of fading resolve worried fire-eaters. Enlistments in military units faltered. Even the Minute Men numbered only 45, about half of the desired strength. Collecting money for military equipage proved difficult. Worst of all, unionists such as James Barbour began to exploit the vacillation. Barbour, a Democrat, represents Culpeper in the Virginia House of Delegates and chairs that body's Committee of Finance. He authored Virginia's official rejection of petitions from South Carolina and Mississippi to join the secession movement. He also penned the General Assembly's proposal for a national peace conference in Washington, D.C., on February 4. On January 21, he urged "an immense meeting" at the Court House to consider the perils of secession. A supporter called the speech "powerful and eloquent" and swore that were it repeated throughout the state, the cause of disunion would be lost.[8]

In late January, Barbour led a delegation of Culpeper citizens to Washington, where they discussed a compromise with Stephen Douglas, William Seward, and other northern political leaders. Barbour, whom Seward regards as "the master spirit of the Union party" in Virginia, praised the results. The men returned home confident that they had preserved slavery in the South. Despite torrential rain, a large crowd greeted them at the Court House depot, and it cheered jubilantly when Barbour announced that "a plan for the adjustment of our national difficulties" had been reached. He could not reveal the details, but negotiations had been concluded, he assured them, "upon a basis perfectly satisfactory to every Virginian." The whole county rejoiced at this "glorious news," and a few days later, Barbour won election as Culpeper's delegate to the Virginia convention by a 167-vote majority.[9]

The shift in attitude seemed remarkable. Just weeks earlier, secessionists had broken up unionist meetings with noisy disturbances and quiet threats. William Douglas Wallach, who divides his time between Culpeper and Washington, where he edits the *Evening Star* newspaper, had been "hissed down" in a speech at the Court House. Then suddenly, the voice of reason prevailed. People now heeded unionist calls to consider Lincoln's promised compromise. "We raised money," Richard Wallach, brother of Douglas, says in explaining the unionist plan, "and got up meetings and took every means to fortify the union men in Virginia and to prevent the passage of the ordinance [of secession]." Merchants and businessmen, calculating the value of their financial ties to the North, seemed especially anxious to avoid disunion. Older people, too, holding stronger loyalties to the Union than they had realized, shuddered at secession.[10]

It became a season to keep silent for disunionists. Having confidently swaggered and applauded the approach of secession, they now found themselves outnumbered and forced to hold their tongues, "under penalty of being denounced as traitors and threatened with a halter." George Gray, a lawyer and owner of five slaves, admitted to being "sadly depressed about old Virginia." He concluded that the only hope for secession seemed to lie "in Revolution or else in conflict of the Government with the Seceded states."[11]

Sensing the tide turn, unionists warned Lincoln and his men not to falter. Jack Pendleton complained to Seward that if Lincoln had given "more decisive encouragement," Virginia's convention might have been packed with unionists. As things stood, nothing could be assured. Barbour agreed. Unionism had flourished of late, he told Seward, because Virginians believed Lincoln would preserve southern honor by providing constitutional guarantees for slavery. If the new president disappointed those expectations, he would drive unionists back into the secessionist camp. "They are men in earnest," warned Barbour, "devoted to the Union and would mourn over its loss as a private grief. But they are resolute to shiver the bond if their effort to get guarantees fails."[12]

Tragically, Lincoln and Seward ignored Pendleton and Barbour. Culpeper and all Virginia waited in vain for the new administration to announce a compromise. Lincoln promised lamely in his inaugural address not to interfere with slavery, but he said nothing about the constitutional guarantees implied earlier by Seward. Stofer printed the full text of the address in the *Observer*, but Lincoln's words clearly disappointed him. An accompanying editorial expressed a sense of betrayal. "Slavery as it exists in Virginia, regulated by law and tempered by the genius of christianity, has been a great blessing to the Negro," Stofer insisted. Most of Culpeper was convinced of that fact; Lincoln and the Congress had better acknowledge it.[13]

Less than a fortnight after reading Lincoln's address, a crowd rumored to be the largest ever assembled in Culpeper responded with a stunning reversal of sentiment. Secessionist to the core, it rejected the constitutional amendments recently proposed by the Peace Convention. Sad to say, one of those proposals, forbidding Congress to regulate, abolish, or control slavery in the states or territories, gave precisely the guarantees most people sought. But Congress had also rejected the convention's plan on March 2, and when Lincoln remained silent on the issue, the proposals only served to mock the unionists' once-bright hopes and ridicule their naive trust. They could salvage their honor only by publicly denouncing the plan. The meeting, with near unanimous voice, then angrily endorsed secession and instructed Barbour to speak and vote accordingly in Richmond.[14]

Barbour, who also felt betrayed, raised as forceful a voice in favor of secession as he had formerly used to oppose it. Still feeble from a bout of illness that had incapacitated him for several days, Barbour returned to the Richmond convention and denounced Seward. Virginia should be deceived no longer by Lincoln's double-dealing secretary of state, he warned the assembly. Seward's promises were as chaff on the wind, and Virginians could never expect the new government to protect their property, liberty, or rights. Barbour declared that the "remarkable revolution" launched so many weeks before in Culpeper had grown and swept across the state. All Virginians, slaveholders and nonslaveholders alike, now recognized secession as the only safeguard for southern freedom and prosperity. Nor should Virginians fear the consequences of secession, Barbour continued, for the United States government had become so "decrepit," both morally and financially, that it would not dare oppose a united South. The Confederate States of America had shown itself to be a viable and vital nation.

Barbour's voice cracked and faded as he pounded away at the amazed convention. These men knew how dear he held the Union, and that knowledge heightened the impact of his emotional appeal. Visibly weakening, Barbour could barely stand, yet he was loath to yield the floor. One more point had to be made. He still prayed fervently for reunion, but such restoration could be accomplished only if the North respected the South as an equal. Goaded on by the lingering sting of Seward's betrayal, Barbour proclaimed in a final burst, "This great controversy has reached its crisis. You recognize the necessity of regular negotiation and full and final settlement. If ever this Union is to be restored, it is to be after a new bargain between the sections, and under a new compact full of conditions for your security."[15]

Then came Fort Sumter, and it could not have been better timed for Virginia disunionists. The convention approved secession by a vote of 88 to 55. Most of the opposition came from the northwestern part of the state, a region dominated by nonslaveholders and people with close economic ties to the North. But former unionists, if not converted to secession, acknowledge that their cause is lost. In Culpeper, people who have spoken consistently against secession since December remain disgusted and appalled by the act, but they now accept it. Indeed, so stong is the secessionist tide that most remaining opponents dare not speak. William Heflin, an uneducated sawyer, believes it is no longer "prudent" to support the Union. Hiram Amiss, a shoemaker and an independent cuss, fears no one's wrath, but he understands Heflin's caution. "Things . . . [are] so hot," he concedes, "union men wouldn't dare to say they . . . [are] such even privately." They do not know "who to trust" in the present oppressive atmosphere.[16]

Some Culpeper women grieve over secession, but having no vote, they are ignored in the public debate. Mary L. Payne, owner of the Virginia House, one of three hotels at the Court House, is "violently opposed" to recent events. She calls secession "the work of the politicians" and blames this disaster on "fire-eaters" who wish "to rule or to ruin" the South. Both Susan Hall and her husband, a tenant farmer, avoid politics and oppose secession, and they are "afraid to say anything about it, or to express . . . [their] sentiments any way." Sarah Shaw holds an even more precarious position. She and her husband Simeon rent their farm near Kellysville from Jack Stone, an avid secessionist. The couple must be careful not to offend Stone, for Sarah is convinced that they would "be taken up and turned out of doors with . . . [their] children" should they do so. Sarah frets constantly that her husband, who speaks privately of the impending war as "a negro war" and tries to persuade people that they "should not fight against the Union to uphold slavery," will go too far.[17]

Yet these are a self-acknowledged few. Most in Culpeper do not curse secession and war as terrible, destructive forces. People of all social ranks, be they farmers or lawyers, slaveholders or hired hands, see themselves first as members of a community that has been put upon by a despotic Federal government. They rejoice in the glorious crusade that they are now to wage for independence; they glory in the name *Rebel.* It is a time to embrace—to embrace their new nation and its cause, to embrace one another. A fervor and excitement not seen in this land since the Revolution has engulfed the people. They talk excitedly on streetcorners and in shops. Ploughs sit idle; pitchforks lean against fence rails. No one can work, no one can think of anything but this daring act of secession and the war it has brought about. And not just war, but a war of liberation, a war that few people in the world's history have ever dared wage. "Our town is nothing but excitement," gushes one man. Every new rumor of war preparations in the North or of the expected Yankee invasion only incites them further, stoking the flames of liberty and "firing up the Southern heart."[18]

Merchants sell stationery and envelopes decorated with Confederate flags and patriotic slogans. Ordinary citizens donate money to purchase uniforms and military accoutrements. Students at the Piedmont Academy have hoisted the Stars and Bars above their school. Alfred Stofer has added a section on "War Terms" to the Culpeper *Observer* to acquaint citizens with military expressions such as barbette gun, casemate, embrasure, and mortar. He also publishes patriotic poems that at once express and reinforce the public mood. Miss Virginia C'Session writes in "Lines on the Threatened Invasion of Dixie":

Our bosoms we'll bare for the glorious strife,
And our oath is recorded on high,
To prevail in the cause that is dearer than life,
Or crush'd in its ruins, to die!

It is wretched poetry, but no one cares. It is the emotion and the sentiment that counts. People everywhere speak of glory, honor, and the Cause, always the Cause.[19]

The people most affected by April's dramatic turn of events are Culpeper's young men, and, like their counterparts across the South, most of them appear eager to take on the Yanks. The destiny of the South rests in the hands of farmers and clerks, carpenters and lawyers, in hundreds of communities from Virginia to Texas. Amateur soldiers they may be, but they answer the call for troops by the hundreds of thousands. Culpeper's Minute Men, with new recruits coming in daily, drill with fresh incentive and focused will. How romantic this all seems to them. How they relish the gazes and smiles cast on them by Culpeper's fair maids. The spirited, bellicose nature of their drills suggests easy confidence. Their green hunting shirts and bucktails lend a "savage and warlike appearance" to their ranks, so that their motto, "Liberty or Death!" seems no idle boast. One potential recruit, devoid, perhaps, of a proper seriousness of purpose, jokes that he will enlist only if the motto is changed to "Liberty or be Crippled!" Tazewell Patton still serves as their captain, but he is almost certain to gain higher rank. In a war waged by amateurs, men with professional military training must rise quickly.[20]

Meanwhile, additional units organize. The Culpeper Riflemen, led by Stockton Heth, muster at Brandy Station. Their recruits come from all walks of life, so that the heirs of several large estates serve alongside the "fighting Irish" of the village and farmers and carpenters from the surrounding country. The Hazelwood Volunteers flock to Stevensburg, where John Taylor, a wealthy farmer with over 80 slaves, has been elected captain. Other men chose the Letcher Artillery, Rough and Ready Rifles, or one of several companies being raised in neighboring counties.[21]

The most dashing Culpeper company is the Little Fork Rangers, the only cavalry unit being organized in the county. The Rangers formed in the summer of 1860 at Oak Shade, a community in the Little Fork peninsula. They, too, are a democratic crew, mostly farmers but with a generous sprinkling of clerks, craftsmen, and professional men. Each recruit supplies his own horse and weapons, which means they are adequately mounted but pitifully armed. All of the men have sabers, but many carry no firearms. Not that this is an unusual circumstance. In mid-April, nearly a third of Virginia's 4,900 cavalry volunteers have no weapons whatsoever, and another 1,100 men carry only sabers. Amateurs, indeed, and ill-prepared amateurs at that. Still, the Rangers remain brash. Among their most frequently heard boasts: "Rangers eat Yankees for breakfast," or, "One Ranger can whip twenty bluecoats." "We can whip them with cornstalks," declares a slightly more original Ranger. It is said that men are born boys and stay that way. That is why they become soldiers.[22]

The Rangers have drilled every Saturday in good weather since forming. They drilled on foot in the beginning, for as a child must walk before it can run, so cavalrymen must march before they can ride. The Rangers are fortunate to have a pair of professional soldiers to instruct them. Langdon C. Major, a 39-year-old farmer with over 700 acres and 18 slaves, attended West Point, and William H. Cole, a 40-year-old carpenter, served as a sergeant in the U.S. Army. And, of course, the Rangers receive all sorts of gratuitous advice from neighbors and relatives who attend the drills to applaud and encourage their heroes. Boys around Jeffersonton have even formed their own little company to muster alongside the Rangers and imitate them.[23]

The Rangers, like many volunteers, originally donned magnificent uniforms of their own design—blue caps, white trousers, and red jackets with yellow stripes across the front. Perched on their horses, they would have made fine targets for Yankee marksmen. Now that Virginia has joined the Confederacy, they will wear gray uniforms. A campaign on their behalf has raised enough money to purchase gray cloth at the Swartz Woolen Mills, at Waterloo, four miles north of Jeffersonton. A tailor in Fauquier County will cut the cloth, and women living in and around Jeffersonton will meet at the home of Sarah Ann Kirby, wife of a wheelwright, to sew the cut cloth into uniforms.[24]

The reality of war has come with a rush. With northern troops boldly advancing toward Harper's Ferry—gateway to northern Virginia—patriots have assembled swiftly at that strategic town. Culpeper's Minute Men, maintaining the tradition of their namesakes, respond at once. At daybreak this morning, April 18, Captain Patton marched them to the Court House depot. The train, which already carried companies from Augusta, Madison, and Orange counties, arrived at dawn. Unhappily, in the process of boarding, Culpeper has suffered its first casualty of the war. Someone dropped a pistol. It discharged and sent a ball ripping through the forearm of John A. Inskeep, a civilian who had come to see the boys off. Though not seriously hurt, he has had a "narrow escape." Some men have been caught off guard by the rapid mobilization. Alfred Stofer asks all *Observer* subscribers to "pay up" whatever they owe him. He must join the company, he explains, but he wants first to make sure that his wife Ann and their three children (all less than six years old) will be cared for in his absence.[25]

One woman describes the Harper's Ferry rendezvous as "the gathering of the clans." The Celtic spirit of the South has been aroused, and ill-armed and poorly-equipped as many Virginia warriors may be, they declare themselves willing, if necessary, "to try the issue with stones!" George Williams has arrived with the Minute Men, and he is his usual droll self. He fails to see the need for all this rushing about. Personally, he could have used a good night's sleep, denied him in the all-night vigil at the depot and the crowded railroad cars, before getting into a war. And to what end? "There is no danger of a fight here now," he complains to wife Gertrude, "tho' we will be ordered to stay two or three weeks." April 20: More troops have arrived, making a total of nearly 2,500 volunteers. The militia companies have been sworn into Confederate service, formed into regiments, and had their romantic names replaced with letters of the alphabet. The Minute Men are now Company B, 13th Virginia Infantry; the Culpeper Riflemen are designated Company E. Rumors say they are headed for Baltimore or Portsmouth. If they do head east, Captain Patton promises Williams, his law partner and friend, a pass home to kiss Gertrude good-bye.[26]

One week later. Still no action, and the men have grown less than enamored of army life. This is nothing like the light-hearted Saturday afternoon drills back home. The marching and standing at arms seem to serve little purpose. Village maidens no longer wave and laugh. The food is wretched, camp chores mere drudgery, and the long, dull hours between drills nearly as tiring as the drilling itself. Men no longer return home to sleep next to their wives in their own beds. Indeed, they enjoy precious little sleep at all. More than once the 13th Virginia has been roused at 2 A.M. by a drum roll, marched two miles out of camp, ordered to stand in ranks until dawn, and then marched back to camp, all the result of false reports of an enemy advance. If sleep is the first casualty of war, than patience and enthusiasm must place a close second. These men are ready to fight. Bring on the Yanks, they say, and let us be done with it. George Williams, who has been elected sergeant-major of the regiment, declares that the volunteers are spirited enough. Indeed, they are "splendid specimens for soldiers." What they lack, he declares, is leadership. "Never was a finer set [of men] gathered together," Williams insists; "and never was a greater set of blockheads commanding them."[27]

Private John Wesley Bell, a lawyer in civilian life, tries to keep the boys in good humor with quips and comic asides. When the regiment found itself caught in a ferocious hailstorm, Bell fell to his knees and prayed aloud for divine intervention. People were amazed when, just as he ceased his supplication, the storm, did in fact, subside. "Boys," chuckled Bell while wearing an air of nonchalance, "wasn't that the damndest hailstorm you ever saw?" This morning, as part of a work detail that has been ordered to dig drainage ditches in camp, Bell grumbles good-naturedly, "This is a nice business for a lawyer in good standing, a gentleman, and a member of St. Stephen's Church vestry, to be put to ditching the first Sunday in camp!"[28]

Meanwhile, the pace has quickened back home. "The military spirit of Culpeper is fairly aroused," reports the *Observer*, "and almost every train bears away sons to join their comrades in arms at Harper's Ferry. . . . The ladies, God bless them, are busy night and day making up clothes for the absent ones, and for those who are preparing to leave." Culpeper's strategic location on the Orange & Alexandria

Railroad makes it a natural place, much like Harper's Ferry, to stock supplies, rendezvous men, and train recruits. Troop and supply trains flow steadily northward out of Culpeper to Alexandria, Harper's Ferry, and Manassas, but many men are being assigned to garrison and defend Culpeper. A "Home Guard," composed of men too old or too cautious for active campaigning, has also been organized. It stands ready "at a moment's warning to protect the homes and firesides of those who have gone to the wars."[29]

Nothing attracts attention like a general, and at 10 A.M. this morning, April 28, Culpeper got one. Philip St. George Cocke, commanding the Potomac Department, has arrived on the morning train from Alexandria to establish his headquarters at the Court House. Cocke, who hails from Powhatan County, is a West Pointer, but he does not look like a soldier. Past his prime at age 52, he is slight of frame and arrayed in plantation dress. And, in truth, his military experience has been slight. He served less than two years in the army after graduation from the academy in 1832. He has devoted himself for the past quarter-century to his plantations in Mississippi and Virginia, and he is widely known in North and South for his writings on progressive farming methods. Even now, in the midst of war, he maintains a regular correspondence with his overseers concerning crops and slaves. Some people consider him "an excitable person" with "an exaggerated opinion of himself and his position." His mission in Culpeper is to hold the "Potomac border" between Harper's Ferry and Fredericksburg.[30]

Cocke is appalled by the meager staff allotted him and the thinness of his resources. Only his assistant adjutant, Lieutenant Colonel S. Jones, is an experienced officer. Cocke has asked General Robert E. Lee, commanding Virginia forces, for an assistant quartermaster, a surgeon, an ordnance officer, and a military engineer "of talent." He also wants weapons. He has been told that 2,000 rifles will soon arrive from Harper's Ferry, but he also needs powder and two or three batteries of artillery (six-pounders), with ammunition.[31]

Meanwhile, Cocke has been directed to enlist and train enough recruits from Culpeper and surrounding counties to fill ten infantry regiments, two of cavalry, and eight companies of artillery.

May 5. Cocke has issued a proclamation summoning all "brave men" in his district to defend Virginia against northern aggression. "The North has not openly, and according to the usage of civilized nations, declared war on us," he points out. "We make no war on them; but should Virginia soil . . . be polluted by the tread of a single man in arms from north of the Potomac, it will cause open war." Understanding human nature, Cocke also draws slyly on the help of local ladies. "Women of Virginia!" he appeals. "Cast from your arms all cowards, and breathe the pure and holy, the high and glowing, inspirations of your nature into the hearts and souls of lover, husband, brother, father, friend!"[32]

Cocke has worked hard, made progress, but General Lee and Governor Letcher, sitting snug in Richmond, want everything to have been done yesterday. On May 6, Lee asked Cocke to rush troops to defend against an expected attack at Harper's Ferry. On May 7, he asked for a report on the troops: their strength, their organization, and how soon they can be deployed in the field. Poor Cocke tries to comply. He dispatches the Powhatan troop of cavalry, half an artillery battery from the Court House, and a cavalry troop from Amissville to Manassas Junction, but he tells Lee that these "are absolutely all of the forces at all available." He knows the Powhatan men are ready, for he raised and outfitted them himself following the John Brown raid. Recruits are slowly being mustered, but they must be trained and equipped. He must have more rifles or muskets. He still needs a full staff. Colonel Jones has been dispatched to Manassas to requisition supplies while a junior officer, Lieutenant Giles B. Cooke, seeks additional supplies, especially weapons, in nearby counties.[33]

General Lee understands the problems, but Cocke must press on. "It is very important," reminds Lee, "that the volunteer troops be organized and instructed as rapidly as possible. I know you are doing all in your power towards that object." Most important, stresses the commander, instill discipline in the men. Order them to assemble in Culpeper from the towns where they have mustered. Once congregated, "their instruction may be uninterrupted and rigid discipline established." Lee apologizes for not being able to furnish sufficient tents for the men at this time, but perhaps recruits could be quartered in vacant buildings at the Court House, or perhaps they could construct plank huts. However it is done, Lee begs Cocke "to prepare the men for hard effective service."[34]

Cocke has seen it through. He was miffed for several days when informed that the Virginia Convention has reduced him in rank to colonel, but General Lee handled his bruised feelings skillfully. By May 14, Cocke has assembled 918 men in Culpeper, and the Powhatan cavalry is due back from Manassas. His immediate concern is to construct a camp large enough to contain his command. Like troops elsewhere in the district, these men have been scattered, as Lee realized they must be, in vacant buildings, yards, and warehouses. Cocke has even asked the pastors and rectors of local churches to volunteer their buildings as barracks. Most congregations, like that of the Culpeper Baptist Church, have deemed such arrangements "improper." Even so, the Baptists, not wishing to appear unpatriotic, have agreed that the basement rooms of their church might be used when "other suitable places are exhausted." Cocke has solved a large part of the problem by obtaining permission to establish a camp on the lands of Cumberland George, northwest of the Court House. "The Engineers will tomorrow map the land and lay out the Camp," he informs Colonel James L. Kemper, with whom he has discussed the problem, "which for the lack of Canvas we shall have to construct of plank huts." The camp is to be christened in honor of the Revolutionary patriot Patrick Henry.[35]

Cocke's son John, who has joined his father's staff as an ordnance lieutenant, remains optimistic. "We are beginning to get our military arrangements somewhat organized," John informs an aunt, "and getting the regiments formed, and every thing beginning to wear a military appearance." John thinks his father is too tense, and that he makes it hard for others around him to relax. Yet the colonel cannot help but worry. He expects in a few weeks to meet his quotas for recruits, but he still lacks sufficient supplies and arms. He worries about the fate of his men should they be thrown into battle no better trained or equipped than they are at present.[36]

While Cocke frets and complains, builds and organizes, Culpeper residents grow somber. The presence of a vast encampment, filled with so many confident soldiers, is reassuring in some ways, but to witness the construction of a mighty war machine can be unnerving. Might not so many soldiers draw attention to Culpeper? Might not the county become an especial target of Federal armies? A Lynchburg newspaper has even predicted that "the first battle or encounter will be at Culpeper Court House." People feel *"very blue"* about the situation and are "very much frightened" by the thought of invasion. Even the northern public is aware of Culpeper's unenviable position. "From newspaper accounts the scene of the first battle will not be far from your residence," a northerner informs his transplanted brother who has practiced law in Culpeper for many years; "& I judge now that large bodies of soldiers are being marshalled and encamped near you." Then, hitting the nail squarely on the head, the northerner expresses concern that his rebel brother may soon find his "property & effects . . . liable to the dreadful ravages incident to a cruel . . . war."[37]

One already hears talk of flight, of people seeking safe havens further south. A soldier at Manassas has written home to urge unprotected families in Culpeper to pack their household goods, collect their livestock, and leave. Refugees from more northern communities, like Alexandria, pass regularly through the countryside. One refugee has arrived with a harrowing tale. A native Virginian, the man moved to Pennsylvania as a youth. He remained loyal to the South, and he spoke out against Lincoln's policies after the November election. His neighbors tolerated his nonsense until Fort Sumter. Then old friends ceased to associate with him. Unionists tested his loyalty by assigning him to solicit funds for the war and ordering him to raise a Federal flag. The pressure became too much, so he came south to Culpeper, where he has relatives, after placing his wife and child under the protection of his brother-in-law in Maryland. He is destitute, for his business and all of his property are in Pennsylvania, and he now presents a living example of how rebels may expect to be treated by Yankees.[38]

Even if not fearful of invasion, families with soldiers already at the front feel anxious for their safety. They fret particularly over the proximity of Manassas to the Union armies and of the movement of troops all through that region. Do not worry about us, Mildred Halsey instructs her husband Joseph, a lawyer in peacetime but now a member of the 6th Virginia Cavalry. "I feel quite uneasy about *your scalp*," she insists, "don't be too brave." Millie Payne has learned that her beau, John, pines for her so much at Manassas that he suffers from severe headaches and is "not at all well." She responds with a letter so filled with expressions of undying love and devotion that he feels magically cured. People find it hard to get reliable reports about what is happening just 20 miles to the north. They visit the railroad depots daily to learn if the telegraph has brought any "authentic news" of conditions and events.[39]

Fathers miss their children, and wives miss their husbands, but silence and separation work most cruelly on young lovers like Daniel A. Grimsley and Bettie Browning. Daniel, a 21-year-old teacher from Rappahannock County and son of a Baptist preacher, has been courting his cousin Bettie for several months. She is attending school at the Court House, although her father William, a prosperous farmer in the north of Culpeper, may soon bring her home. Daniel joined the Rappahannock Cavalry one week after the surrender of Fort Sumter. "What a spectacle!" he marveled in April. "A nation once so powerful and united" now disrupted and dismembered by "fanaticism." His militia company was among the first to arrive at Harper's Ferry, where he became a corporal in Company B, 6th Virginia Cavalry.[40]

Having exchanged his "quiet home for the uproar of the battlefield," Daniel has asked Bettie to write to him while he serves their country, and to send a photograph of herself. "I think . . . it would inspire me with courage in the days of battle," he gushed romantically, for she must know that the "flame of love" burning so brightly in his heart can "never be extinguished." Bettie, however, was suspicious. She at first refused to send her precious likeness, for she had heard that Daniel has been "a relentless flirt" among the young ladies at Fairfax Court House, where he is now encamped. Not so! responded Daniel. How could she believe such scurrilous rumors! How could she think that he would ever "trifle with the heart's most tender feelings." No, he is innocent, and she must not allow "some very busy-body" to destroy their happiness. Bettie hesitated but has relented. She will send the photograph. After all, she is just sixteen.[41]

Yet most in Culpeper remain confident during these heady spring days in which no blood has yet been shed. At the very least they see the bright side of this upheaval in public and private affairs. "Culpeper, the banner spot of the Old Dominion, has won, as she has deserved, the sobriquet of 'Revolutionary County,'" declares an observer at Mitchell's Station. "The fires of Southern Liberty are burning brightly upon her red hills, whilst her valleys and flat grounds send up the shout of resistance to the death." Even the refugee from Pennsylvania, a Mr. Beckham, unnerved and despondent as he is after parting from his wife and child, finds the atmosphere invigorating. "I am able and willing to do everything that may be required of an honest energetic man," he tells Colonel Cocke, "and respectfully ask you to aid me to some position where I can do something to support my family and at the same time to . . . serve my native state."[42]

Jane Conway, caught up in the excitement of life at the Court House, fully approves the enlistment of her nephew Charley in a volunteer company. "I am glad he has joined," she reasons, "it is better to be a soldier than to be idle. I hope that he may be able to resist all the temptations & evils of Camp life & be brave & faithful." She will keep an eye on Charley as long as his company remains at the Court House, and see that he is properly outfitted. Dozens of school-age boys, like Charley, want to prove their manhood and impress the girls by enlisting. Major Charles E. Lightfoot, who directs the Culpeper Military Institute, attempts to conduct classes as usual, but spirits run high among his 70 cadets. The school must soon dissolve. Other adolescents too young for the army form a company dubbed the Culpeper Yellow Jackets. Sixteen-year-old John J. Wharton has been elected captain; a 12-year-old lieutenant and a 13-year-old sergeant assist him. Schoolgirls plead to be released from their studies. They want to sew uniforms and watch the men drill. Besides, they reason, how can they possibly study amid such excitement?[43]

Isolated families and single women are most likely to imagine the worst, but even these folk seem resolved to do their part. Lucretia Clore is a spunky 40-year-old widow whose husband left her tolerably well off with a 59-acre farm, a horse, three cows, three cattle, and seven hogs. Now, however, in "these war like times when one scarcely knows a friend from a foe," she finds herself living alone with her eight-year-old son. Lucretia knows all about the "indignities" southern women will likely suffer at the hands of "Lincoln's hirelings" and "ruffians," but she is determined to stand her ground. She has only one desire, and she asks it of Governor Letcher: Could he send her a Colt revolver for protection? "I have practised shooting," she assures him, "and I would not be afraid to defend myself but it is impossible to get a weapon here." If the governor will oblige her, she promises to teach her son Curran how to shoot, too.[44]

If war presents danger, it also offers money, and the army's presence brings profits to many people. Culpeper merchants are positively giddy about the county's situation. Not only do the troops at Camp Henry protect them and their property, they also purchase food and camp equipment locally. Cocke began contracting for Camp Henry's needs on May 15, and John Stark was first in line. Stark sold the government six dollars' worth of iron (for crowbars), four spades, and a bucket. Now county merchants may count on being tapped for goods several times a month, and sometimes in large quantities. A dozen different merchants provide the army with brooms, candles, axes, hatchets, blankets, shovels, nails, rope, saws, frying pans, kettles, coffeepots, washbasins, tinware, salt, coffee, and on and on. Even *Observer* editor Stofer, before joining the Minute Men, has found a way to turn a dollar by printing and binding blank receipts and invoices for Cocke.[45]

Some people have the wherewithal to sell goods directly to Richmond. John Foushee has supplied over a hundred dollars' worth of sugar, coffee, and candles during the first weeks of the war. J. G. and Henry Miller, who operate a woolens mill on the Hazel River, enjoy even bigger contracts. They provide thousands of dollars' worth of wool and flannel cloth and clothing, most of it, presumably, to be used for uniforms. The contracts are a boon not only for the Millers, but for their nearly forty factory hands. These are all white people, both male and female, and include many children, six of them younger than 14.[46]

The people of Culpeper have quickly found that nearly everything they have has some value. Most of the county's crops have just been planted, but grain, mostly corn and oats, and hay stored from last year are needed for food and forage. Anyone with some uncleared land can sell lumber and cordwood to the army. People sell their labor and rent wagons and teams for hauling goods and men to the army. Craftsmen, especially carpenters, construct barracks and storage buildings. People rent out vacant buildings and warehouses. In just three weeks, the government has spent $665.09 for forage, $1,272.22 for lumber, $70.01 for transportation, $100.00 for rent, $352.95 for labor, $245.00 for horses, and $59.77 for cordwood.[47]

The economy prospers in other ways, too. At the Court House, George Wells, who manufactures guns, rifles, and pistols on Main Street, expects an increase in sales. Thomas Parr and Gabriel Farish offer liberal commissions for information leading to the purchase of quality slaves, and other people advertise their interest in buying slave property. Real estate is also booming. Several houses are for sale, as is property near the Court House. George and John Strother offer a farm just outside of town, and the farm of recently deceased Robert Welford is for sale near Brandy.[48]

The county court has tried to reinvest some of the new wealth. On May 24, the court officially declared that the northern states have provoked the present national crisis. The war is not of our choosing, maintains the court, but now that it is upon us, the people of Culpeper owe it to the memory of their ancestors and to the security of posterity "to resist to the uttermost" northern aggression. For its part, the court will seek to raise $10,000 by issuing bonds valued at $50 and up at 6 percent annual interest. It will use the money to uniform and equip volunteer companies and to help support the families of volunteers who may need assistance while their men serve the state. As a reward for those "public spirited citizens" who have already helped to equip and provision county volunteers, the court will credit previous donations to the purchase of the new bonds if the purchaser invests double the original contribution.[49]

At Camp Henry, Colonel Cocke works furiously to put troops in the field. By mid-May he has been relieved of some responsibility. Five counties formerly under his command have been given to Colonel George H. Terrett, and both he and Terrett now answer to a new department commander, General Milledge L. Bonham. Cocke has about a thousand men at the Court House with perhaps another five thousand scattered throughout his district. But men constantly flow in and out of Culpeper, being sent northward as soon as they are equipped and given a modicum of training. The lack of preparation bothers Cocke. He wants more time to ready these men, and he needs more experienced noncommissioned and commissioned officers to do that. "For want of an adequate number of good drill masters," he laments, "the progress of improvement in the drill is not as rapid as is desirable." His officers are largely amateurs who know little about tactics or military procedures. Thank God, he breathes, the "physical & moral character" of the rank and file remain "very good."[50]

Among his most enthusiastic new units is the Little Fork Rangers. The Rangers formally entered Confederate service at Oak Shade on May 25. Captain Robert E. Utterback led 54 stouthearted recruits to the Court House on May 27, the last of the Culpeper companies to arrive. They lodge in the old Freeman house, south of the Court House. Being a cavalry unit, they have immediately drawn picket duty along the Rappahannock River, where they guard the old wooden covered railroad bridge at Rappahannock Station, opposite the village of Remington. Six men at a time spend a 24-hour watch at the bridge. It is dull duty but a respite from the even duller drill, inspections, and discipline of Camp Henry. They eat well, too, for in addition to the rations they bring from camp, local folk contribute delicacies. Kindest is Richard H. Cunningham, who sends baskets loaded with ham and cornbread. Cunningham, whose $75,000 estate and 60 slaves lie exposed along the river, appreciates their presence.[51]

But Cocke frets about the Rangers, for they, like many of his men, continue to be poorly armed. Guns and ammunition have arrived at the depot, but in small numbers, and many of the guns are of inferior quality. Cocke has 3,000 flintlock muskets that must be converted to percussion cap before being distributed. Five infantry companies have no cartridge boxes, bayonet scabbards, canteens, or haversacks. One artillery company has no guns. Cocke seeks to ease his conscience by rationalizing the lack of arms. When a cavalry troop ordered to Manassas protests that it has only sabers and but few sidearms, Cocke replies that it cannot be helped; the state has no pistols to provide. Cavalry already in the presence of the enemy are no better armed, he says, and some infantry companies suffer even worse conditions. Besides, concludes Cocke, sabers are "the *only proper* arm for cavalry," and the troop should be able to achieve its mission equipped in that fashion.[52]

Cocke also faces a growing element of discontent and restlessness in camp. The rigors of army life and the restraints of discipline cause grumbling. Some enlisted men resent the officers. One man calls Cocke's staff a pack of "young snobs" from the Virginia Military Institute who believe the war has been "gotten up that they might dazzle the world by their talents." Seven men—five of them from neighboring Madison County—are absent without leave on May 21. At least one Culpeper man, Andrew J. Garner, a 39-year-old carpenter with a wife and seven children, has been placed in confinement for "unsoldierly conduct." New recruits cause the most trouble; as men gain experience, they generally adapt to military necessities. Cocke's Powhatan cavalry, in the opinion of one of its lieutenants, have "performed every duty with cheerfulness and have won applause . . . [as] the most orderly set of men & soldiers they ever saw." Just the same, the county court has made the jail available to the army.[53]

A few men, having had a taste of army life, seek less taxing or hazardous ways to serve the cause. People with political influence use it. Dr. John Ashby closed his "large and valuable medical practice" in Culpeper to enlist as a lieutenant in the Hazelwood Volunteers. Now, a month later, he has asked Henry Shackleford to recommend him for a post as army surgeon. James G. Field, a private in the Minute Men, gave up a lucrative law practice to enlist. He now seeks an assignment as quartermaster. Having spent three years in the U.S. Army pay department, he is familiar with military paperwork, and that experience, argues Field, will serve the new nation well. He also admits that a quartermaster's pay will compensate for lost legal fees and enable him to support his wife and two children. Even so, Field insists that he does not seek to shirk his duty or avoid danger. If a battle begins, he pledges, he will immediately rejoin his comrades in the ranks.[54]

Commissions as officers provide another escape from less appealing duties. Graduates of VMI appear everywhere, and each one naturally thinks himself suited to command the amateurs. Besides, there is glory in command. Dr. Edwin Barbour, a brother of the O&A's president, is even willing to exchange his appointment as an army surgeon for a lieutenancy. Unlike Dr. Ashby, he wants to be in the thick of the action. George Williams finds himself in a more awkward position. Already sergeant-major of the 13th Virginia, he has asked his influential Uncle Jack Pendleton to find him an assignment as aide-de-camp to some senior officer. Pendleton, writing to Governor Letcher, stresses that his nephew is bright and talented, and he assures the governor that, come what may, George will serve in the army, in the ranks if need be. Still, he believes George deserves a post more appropriate to his social position.[55]

As the euphoria of secession and the romance of enlistment give way to the dullness of military life and the possibility of battle, a measure of soul-searching also begins. Giles Cooke, a 23-year-old lieutenant on Cocke's staff, has been struck by the "awful reality" of his situation. He finds himself in a great war, and while he has experienced no hardships and has seen no blood spilled, he senses that hardships will come, and that much blood will be spilled. Thou shalt not kill. Is it damnation he fears? Or is it the thought of being killed? In either case, how far does God extend his mercy?[56]

One Sunday night, as the doubts and fears continued to press upon him, Cooke frantically sought a church in which to worship. Finding none open, he returned to the rented house where Cocke's staff resides and found a quiet place to pray. He asked God "sincerely and fervently" to take pity on him, "a poor sinner," and to give him some sign of His divine will. Since then, Cooke has buried his fears in ceaseless activity—organizing drills, assigning guard and labor details, and generally "arranging the encampment into something like method and system." He speaks not of his inner turmoil, but he prays daily "to the Christ of mercy," and he frequently takes long solitary walks away from camp.[57]

Whatever private doubts and fears men suffer, everyone wants to look like a soldier. War is a glorious pursuit, its combatants stainless warriors. So new boots, pants without holes, and the proper accoutrements must be obtained. Even chaplains may surrender to the vanity of display. John Bocock, chaplain of the 7th Virginia Infantry, is "mortified" by the appearance of his horse and saddle. The nag is not so great an obstacle as the saddle, which has been a tender issue ever since his regiment moved to the front. "When I asked him about it," his sympathetic wife Sarah explains to her brother, who happens to be Colonel Kemper, "he said the *thought of it* humbled him and begged that no more might be said about it." Sarah understands that his honor somehow is at stake, so she continues to scour Culpeper for a respectable saddle.[58]

Sickness has become another unanticipated enemy. In mid-May a mild epidemic of measles hit Camp Henry. That has been followed by outbreaks of typhoid, diarrhea, dysentery, and any number of afflictions that hobble the poor soldier. At first, uninfected men did their best to attend the infected. Now the camp has a hospital to segregate the ill from the healthy and speed treatment. The hospital is not a single building but a collection of military tents, public buildings, and private homes. The camp surgeon, Daniel S. Green, manages this network and directs the treatment of patients, but his professional staff is small. He depends heavily on the women of Culpeper, who have volunteered their homes and services. "It is the office of women to watch by the bedside of the sick & suffering," contends Inez Pendleton, wife of Jack, "and it is our wish to be allowed as all that we are able to do in our country's great struggle for liberty, to fulfil this part of our mission."[59]

As the burden of the hospital increases, the women meet each new challenge. They bring food to the patients, cut and sew necessary linen, write letters for feeble sufferers. They have their hands full. Three hundred patients have quickly overwhelmed the available facilities, and yet the women persevere in their "gorgeous and blessed work." One army chaplain, posted to Camp Henry with a portion of the 18th Virginia Infantry, is so impressed that he writes a public letter to surrounding counties urging them to follow the example of Culpeper's heroines. It is unfair, he points out, to expect one county "to be burthened with the whole care of the sick of a great army." Other communities must contribute, if not their services then their wealth and resources, to Culpeper's hospital. Remember, he reminds people, your menfolk may find themselves sick or, in time, wounded on a cot at Culpeper.[60]

Meanwhile, Colonel Charles W. Wager prepares for the day when most of Cocke's men will be dispatched to the front by raising a militia regiment to serve in Culpeper. It is a thankless task, for militia service has acquired an unenviable reputation. The high-spirited young men who flock to the volunteer companies of the provisional army are not inclined to be militiamen. Many people predict the militia will never see action, that it will sit in Culpeper protecting chicken coops and cornfields. Indeed, that is the intention of Virginia's military leaders, who assume that the war will be fought by the volunteers. Only in "the emergency of actual invasion" will the "bold hearts and strong arms" of the militia be called upon "to make each house a citadel, and every rock and tree positions of defense." Meanwhile, the militiamen will re-main at home, where they may pursue their civilian occupations and so contribute doubly to the war effort. Incidentally, each militiaman must supply his own arms, without expense to the government.[61]

Despite all these problems—lack of weapons, sickness, restlessness, and amateurishness—the men are ready to fight. "The tented fields and battalions drilling would prove to the Yankees that we were going into this contest in real earnest and to talk about subjugating Southern people animated with such feelings as they are is an absurdity," insists an enthusiastic officer at Camp Henry. "They *may* whip us but they will *never* subjugate us to the yoke of a Black Republican President."[62]

Culpeper's civilians are ready, too. On May 23, they joined the major-ity of Virginians in approving the state's ordinance of secession. There is no turning back now; all are bound together by solemn faith and high purpose. Only two of 1,053 voters dared dissent, and most every-one knows who they are. John Brown, a plain-speaking farmer from near Jeffersonton, opposed secession right up to referendum day, and he opposes it still. Hiram Amiss considered the repercussions of voting against the ordinance but did so anyway. "I told the folks when they were voting the State out they were voting their children's blood away," he maintains defiantly. Disturbing talk, bordering on treason-ous. Not at all what true southerners should be saying at this joyous moment.[63]

Generally, however, people recognize that the hour for dissent has passed; it is a time to keep silent. People with misgivings about secession know their votes could not have changed things. They know, too, there may be danger in opposition. James B. Kirk, who moved to Culpeper from Maryland in 1858, remains a quiet dissenter. Kirk owns a 700-acre farm and eight slaves (he rents seven more) worth $19,000. He has opposed secession since December, yet he did not bother to vote on the referendum. "I knew it would not amount to anything and it would involve me in difficulties," he says. "The people all around me were secesh with the exception of one family, and I knew if I voted against the ratification of the ordinance, they would be down on me." A point worth considering, for a man rarely helps himself by rejecting the verdict of his neighbors. Archibald Shaw, brother of Simeon and, like him, a tenant farmer, spoke out but wishes he had not. "I was prevented from voting against it [the referendum] by threats of arrest & of being tarred & feathered," he maintains.[64]

Culpeper's black population observes but says little. Only a few free blacks seem to know that slavery has anything to do with the impending conflict. These few whisper privately that they support the Union and wish to see enslaved blacks freed. Whether or not they understand the root of the trouble, free blacks voice no opinion. If whites who oppose secession fear to speak, it would be suicidal for a black man publicly to approve of the northern cause. White neighbors, preferring to keep the blacks in ignorance, avoid discussing events with them. Warner Bundy, the farmhand who works for Robertson Coons, complains that he does "not hear a great deal about the War from the rebels." He cannot read, so newspapers are useless to him. Whites have been especially suspicious of free blacks ever since Daniel Brooke was caught helping two slaves belonging to William H. Perry escape toward northern lines. The county court has sentenced Brooke to five years in prison.[65]

Yet, perhaps surprisingly, many free blacks regret the threat of war. Culpeper is their community, and they sense that war will destroy them, their families, and their property as surely as it will destroy their white neighbors. They handle the situation about as well as can be expected. Ira Field, the Court House barber, has lived in close association with whites for many years. He wishes them no ill. When customers ask his opinion of events, he responds diplomatically. "Well master," he drawls, "I don't know. This war has started amongst the sons & daughters, the fathers & the mothers and a family affair is the worst thing that ever could be settled." Willis Madden, being highly regarded by Culpeper whites, knows that he need only stay clear of the Court House to avoid trouble. He sits tight and stays mum on the eastern edge of the Flats.[66]

But not all blacks are safe, and woe betide those idlers who lack the reputations of Field and Madden. In early June, all unemployed free blacks are sent into lower Virginia. "Those who remain," reports an observer, "are more industrious than ever, and ask not for a single hour of virtuous liberty, but now 'hoe de corn and blow de horn,' with as ready a grace as those who have enjoyed a whole lifetime of bondage."[67]

The slaves are inscrutable. They give no appearance of rebelling, or even that they are aware of the political and social upheaval around them. Yet they are neither deaf nor blind, which causes slaveholders to worry. Should they move their property further south? Should they insist on a speedy organization of Colonel Wager's militia? Should they request that regular troops be assigned to protect Culpeper? When word comes that all remaining able-bodied men might soon be drafted into military service, letters of concern find their way to Richmond.

Catherine Crittenden is among the first to protest. Crittenden, a 62-year-old widow, owns over 700 acres, worth nearly $11,000, at the foot of Cedar Mountain. It is an extensive farming operation, with $1,355 worth of livestock, $1,100 worth of machinery, and 19 slaves worth thousands of dollars. Last year she produced thousands of bushels of wheat, corn, oats, and potatoes, 10 tons of hay, and 3,700 pounds of tobacco. The overseer of her farm and slaves, George Bowman, must be exempted from any general muster, she has informed Governor Letcher. She and her 22-year-old daughter Anne have no protection now that her son, Lieutenant Charles T. Crittenden, a merchant who serves as second in command in the Minute Men, is at Harper's Ferry. "Not only for myself do I make this appeal," Mrs. Crittenden insists to the governor, "but for my neighbors, Mr. Bowman being the only overseer & nearly every man has volunteered." The result, as the governor might imagine, is "a thinly settled neighborhood, the farms being large, averaging 20 negroes to a farm, and not a man to keep order. . . . Truly the condition of our neighborhood will be a lamentable one if we are left to the mercy of the negroes."[68]

Word has arrived that many Culpeper men at Harper's Ferry have marched westward to Winchester with the 13th Virginia Infantry. The rigors of army life have already eliminated some local men from the regiment's muster rolls. Richard Apperson, John Wesley Bell, James Farish, and William Thompson receive medical discharges in May. Bell and Farish have defective vision, Thompson suffers from consumption, and Apperson has broken his foot. Apperson, at least, promises to reenlist. For a while, people feared that Culpeper's good name had been tarnished by desertion. James P. Ross, a shoemaker from Jeffersonton, disappeared from the regiment's camp on May 17. However, he reappeared a week later to enlist in the Little Fork Rangers. The action is illegal, but everyone, especially his wife, is so glad that he has not shamed himself that he has been allowed to switch regiments. Ross had seen enough of infantry life.[69]

The remaining men of the regiment are excited to learn that Ambrose Powell Hill, born and raised in Culpeper, has been made their colonel. Powell's brother Edward and his family still live at the Court House in a beautiful mansion on East Street. Hill drills the men hard, six to eight hours a day, but he also instills confidence in them. The new colonel's hazel eyes and red beard are distinctive, and his finely-toned five-foot-ten-inch, 160-pound frame give the 35-year-old West Point graduate the look of a warrior. He has a sense of humor, and, while always military in bearing, he disdains uniform dress. Particularly prominent in his outfit are a red or checkered shirt beneath his uniform coat and a black felt hat atop his head. "I like him very much," acknowledges one of his men; "he knows how to act both the gentleman & soldier. On parade he is very strict—off duty he is a perfect gentleman and as kind as can be."[70]

The people of Winchester and the upper Shenandoah Valley are as excited about Hill's men as the soldiers are about Hill. When the first shadowy columns entered Winchester in the hours before dawn, wary residents peeped from their windows. They saw men of Culpeper, former Minute Men, in the vanguard, bearing one of the first Confederate flags to appear in this part of the Valley. Heartened, a few people stepped cautiously outside. Within moments, an admiring crowd filled the streets. "Above them," reports one woman of the gray column, "the flag chosen by the Confederacy slowly furled and unfurled its stars and bars as the wind rose and fell, and as I beheld it my heart beat high, for it seemed a promise of glory and greatness, and of triumph over those who would deprive us of our right to do as we pleased with our own." [71]

In Culpeper, Colonel Cocke rushes to move most of his remaining troops to Manassas. He is anxious but optimistic. He has been as-signed command of a brigade, so he hopes soon to reclaim his rank as general. Mostly militia will be left to defend Culpeper. A few volunteer companies, including the Little Fork Rangers, will remain for the pre-sent, but everyone knows that they, too, must soon move forward. Cocke wrote his last will and testament at the end of May. Reverend Philip Slaughter will accompany the men as chaplain of the 19th Vir-ginia Infantry.[72]

July 4. This afternoon everyone senses that the tension and suspense of the past few months must soon burst. Fighting has already broken out in western Virginia, and Federal troops have entered the Shenan-doah Valley. Northern newspapers clamor for a drive on Richmond, and rumors say that General Irvin McDowell is preparing to move against Manassas. Yesterday, the Little Fork Rangers received orders for Manassas. Captain Utterback dismissed the men so that they might spend one more night with their families. They reassembled this morn-ing at Jeffersonton to make final preparations. Men shoed their horses. Some of them have had Uncle Wash Fitzhugh, the town blacksmith, fashion dirks for them. These knives and their sabers are the only weapons many will carry, for they still lack sufficient firearms. The men stood in ranks to receive a hand-stitched company flag from Miss Emma Latham, a comely 20-year old. Captain Utterback asked, "Boys, will you follow this banner into the face of the enemy, defending it with the last drop of your blood?" They responded with gusto, "Yes, yes!" The entire population of the Little Fork bore witness to their reply and applauded the stirring ceremony. Utterback ordered his men to mount, and prancing steeds now snort and wheel into columns. The Rangers, most of them too young to have regrets, canter jauntily away. As the home folks shed proud tears and wave their heroes out of sight, a band plays "The Bonnie Blue Flag"[73]:

> *We are a band of brothers,*
> *And native to the soil*
> *Fighting for our Liberty,*
> *with treasure, blood, and toil;*
>
> *And when our rights were threaten'd,*
> *the cry rose near and far,*
> *Hurrah for the Bonnie Blue Flag,*
> *that bears a Single Star!*

July 11. All are welcome at Manassas. Daniel Grimsley, promoted last month to sergeant, is delighted to learn the Little Fork Rangers have arrived. "I was very glad indeed to see them," he reported to Bettie a few days ago. "Our camps are very close together and to-day we are enjoying a social chat with them." Today, the Rough and Ready Rifles received the rest of their equipment (haversacks and canteens) and are proclaimed fit for duty. The Rifles represent a combination of Culpeper and Fauquier county volunteers who have been officially designated Company I of the 11th Virginia Infantry. Captain James H. Jameson, a 41-year-old Culpeper farmer and owner of 11 slaves, commands them. The men bid adieu to their loved ones and friends and rendezvous with the rest of their regiment at Manassas. Captain Jameson leaves behind his wife and four children.[74]

So, only the militia and the sick remain in Culpeper. Upwards of seven hundred men are receiving medical care at the Court House, and their numbers grow daily. Many sick troops, mostly victims of measles, have been sent from Manassas to "the commodious hospitals and . . . efficient medical and surgical staff" at Culpeper. Most patients recover, but not all. The hospital lost its first sufferer, Martin Holcomb, in late June. Holcomb, a 22-year-old farmer, had enlisted in the 17th Mississippi Infantry only a month before. His remains now fill the first grave in a plot of land south of town that the hospital will use as a cemetery. Despite the loss of Holcomb and five other brave lads in June, Bettie Browning is proud of the hospital's record. So is Daniel Grimsley, when Bettie tells him of his neighbors' devotion. "It must be consoling to the weary soldier when stricken with disease to know that he has the sympathy of friends and that kind hands will provide for his wants," Grimsley muses. Giles Cooke, of Cocke's staff, is among the ill in Culpeper. He suffers from a "violent fever" that has everyone puzzled, but he seems likely to recover. Cooke returned to the Court House from Manassas under the care of Reverend Slaughter. Dr. Green attended him and has written for the lad's mother and sister to join him from Petersburg. Meanwhile, Slaughter serves as Cooke's "constant companion and nurse" until they arrive.[75]

July 13. Seeking every bit of available manpower, Governor Letcher has ordered the remainder of Colonel Wager's 5th Militia regiment to Manassas. This worries many residents. Influential John Barbour protests to Letcher that the militia represents the last 200 eligible and able-bodied men in the county. Like everyone else, he also points out that the militia are "poor men with families whose departure from home produces distress." Why not, suggests Barbour, summon instead the last volunteer company being recruited and "already practically organized"? What it lacks in size (only 80 men) it will compensate for in zeal and ability. "Can you not accept it as a commutation for the dregs of the militia?" he asks hopefully.[76]

Other people are only concerned with keeping certain militiamen at home. Martha J. Cole, of Brandy, asks Letcher to release her husband, Francis, from active service. She suffers ill health and has two infants with no one to wait on her but an eight-year-old slave girl. Who will harvest her corn, oats, and rye with all the men gone? She must sell her crops in order to pay the merchants, who no longer extend credit. She has two brothers and a brother-in-law, but they, too, are in the army. "I love our Southern Confederacy and will do all I can for the Souldiers," she maintains, but cannot her husband come home for a while? "All of my Neighbors sympathize with me," swears Mrs. Cole. "They think if any man could stay at home Mr. Cole ought to be the one."[77]

But no one can be spared. McDowell draws closer. If anyone doubts his own ability or the state's resolve to repel the invader, he speaks not. Yet surely some people quiver; surely some soldiers, knowing they may soon die, regret this whole affair. Surely the women at home, once the brave flutter of company banners and the melancholy wave of a loved one's hand dips below the last hill, calculate the possible cost of war. Perhaps Joseph Halsey recalls the last letter he received from his New Jersey brother. No northerner, Halsey's brother assured him, felt any "personal hostility" toward the southern people. Northern hatred focused on the South's leaders, who "for their personal aggrandisement plunged the Country into its present state of apparent ruin." Yet, he warned sadly, it would be the common people who would suffer. And make no mistake, he stressed, the South would suffer: "You may think your people well appointed and able to withstand all the forces the North can move against you. It may be so, but you will not leave your battlefields with unbroken ranks. The hordes you speak of and vandals will devastate your fair land and mar your happiness."[78]

July 18. It must soon begin.

CHAPTER THREE

GLORIOUS, TERRIBLE WAR

So this is war. It is not entirely what people expected. Oh, it was wonderful, exhilarating, to see Lincoln's blackguards tumble in confusion back across Bull Run. It was uproarious to watch the jumble of carriages and horses as self-important Yankee civilians fled in terror toward Washington City. Those arrogant gentlemen and their ladies had sashayed out from Washington to enjoy a picnic on the hills above Manassas while they watched the rebels get drubbed. Well, by God, Virginia boys had put on a show for them, and had taught Lincoln's minions a thing or two about fighting. True, the Virginians had some help from equally courageous sons of the Carolinas, Mississippi, and Louisiana, but as one witness testifies of the Virginians, "They just *kivered* tharselves with glory!"[1]

Quite a few Culpeper boys received their baptism of fire in the battle. Companies C and E of Colonel Kemper's 7th Virginia Infantry, mostly lads from around Hazelwood, enjoyed a taste of glory at Blackburn's Ford on July 18. They got off to a rocky start when, in the confusion of their first battle, they started to fire into the ranks of General James Longstreet's Fourth Brigade. Luckily they inflicted no damage and, eventually, did noble work in shoring up the Confederate line. The 11th Virginia also skirmished at Blackburn's Ford, but only the

7th regiment participated in the main fight of July 21, the one southern newspapers are calling the battle of Manassas.[2]

The Little Fork Rangers also came under fire for the first time at Blackburn's Ford. Not all the Rangers behaved bravely in the fell clutch of battle, but as a unit they acquitted themselves well. On the evening of July 20, the Rangers joined General Pierre G. T. Beauregard as an escort. Their subsequent responsibilities as couriers and guides for the general kept them out of combat on the 21st, but they remained exposed to sporadic rifle and cannon fire throughout the day. They even suffered two casualties, of sorts. A spent cannonball toppled and stunned Burr Utz, a young farmer, but he has since recovered. More tragically, John Hawkins' fine mount, worth $125, died from a blast of grapeshot. In the late afternoon, as the Federals fled the field, a portion of the Rangers, commanded by Captain Utterback, enjoyed a signal honor. President Jefferson Davis had arrived at General Beauregard's headquarters and requested a tour of the battle site. The Rangers escorted him.[3]

Two Culpeper soldiers are among the 45 men of the 7th Virginia wounded at Blackburn's Ford and Manassas. O fortunate warriors! To be sent home displaying bandaged emblems of courage and sacrifice! Henry Clay Burrows is the very first to have his name huzzahed at home. A handsome youth, fair complected with hazel eyes and dark hair, and unusually tall at six feet in his seventeenth year, Henry first enlisted in the Letcher Artillery. He had been in the 7th less than a month before falling at Blackburn's Ford. Henry worked as an apprentice silversmith under T. D. Johnson before the war. He even lived with the Johnson family, and he now returns there to convalesce. Twenty-year-old Gabriel Colvin received his wound on July 21. He, too, lived and worked at the Court House, where he clerked for the merchant D. J. Norris and lived, as did fellow clerk Edward Flint, in Norris's home.[4]

Some Culpeper men envy Burrows and Colvin for their wounds and are angry because they missed the battles. The 13th Virginia Infantry had tried desperately to join Beauregard's army from Winchester. As the rest of their command rushed eastward by railroad under General

Joseph E. Johnston, the 13th served as a rear guard. They finally arrived at Manassas, but too late to "see the elephant."[5]

Still, the Manassas fight has produced a sobering effect. Proud boasts of martial valor have been muffled by lingering memories of the day's terrors. Participants had never experienced such violent noise or choking dust. Few will forget how the broiling July heat caused men parched by thirst to break ranks and sprawl along the road to lap water from mud puddles like so many dogs. Each will remember how the others looked—grim expressions, faces and hands caked with dirt, sweat, and blood. They had laughed and rejoiced as they equipped themselves with weapons, canteens, and blankets discarded by fleeing Yankees; but now, as they tend their wounded and bury their dead, men pause to survey the battlefield. Their hearts sink; their chests feel heavy, as though they had swallowed much of the lead that recently hissed past them.[6]

"The battle-field presents a sight heart-sickening in the extreme," admits Daniel Grimsley to Bettie Browning. "I have seen men wounded in every conceivable way. You cannot conceive of such havoc and destruction of property." Surely the Yanks, who may be thickheaded but cannot be idiots, will realize the folly of their war, the impossibility of subduing the South. The price of hundreds of dead and wounded comrades must quickly sober them. "I think that this fight has settled the independence of the southern states," Grimsley breathes with a sigh. "I do not pretend to say that there will be no more fighting, but I think that the most severe is over."[7]

Grimsley is right about Bettie not appreciating what has happened. Neither she nor any other civilian could possibly imagine the scene. Yet the home folks have learned enough to have mixed emotions about both the fight and the war. They heard muffled echoes of cannon fire during the fight. They fretted and prayed, agonized and prayed, and prayed some more through those long hours when they knew not how their army had fared. News of a great victory, particularly one earned at so little cost to their own husbands, brothers, sons, and sweethearts, produced relief; but they are taken aback by early descriptions of the carnage and ruination wrought by Mars. Some rous-

ing words from Jefferson Davis as he paused in the county on his return to Richmond has excited them, but now the sick and wounded
begin to arrive. Culpeper is accustomed to treating sufferers of
measles, typhoid, and diarrhea, but the sight of torn and bloodied bodies stuns people. Wounded men also verify in vivid language the
ghastly realities of combat. A private in the 4th Alabama Infantry reports that his regiment was "completely cut to pieces," his company
alone losing 75 of its 105 men.[8]

Culpeper responds magnificently to the challenge. "Great praise is
due to Culpeper County for its hospitality to the sick and wounded,"
reports a visiting clergyman on this second day after the battle.
"Scarcely a family in all the country round but has from two to a dozen
convalescents, feasting them and making them comfortable by every
contrivance they can make." Thomas and Eliza Flint are among the
first to open their doors. Many neighboring women go to the large
house to assist Mrs. Flint and her five servants, as does Robert Lewis, a
local physician. Mrs. James Field sends one of her house servants,
Mary Stuart, who has a particular gift for treating the sick and
wounded. Most of the county's churches have been converted into
sick wards, as have some public buildings, such as the Poor Institute
and the old Smith mansion, the latter used in more recent years as a
seminary. Houses around Brandy and the Court House are especially
busy. All four churches at the Court House—the Baptist, Episcopal,
Presbyterian, and Methodist—shelter wounded men.[9]

There are better systems, grumbles Dr. Green at Camp Henry.
Green, a naval officer, already feels landlocked in Culpeper, and now
he must keep track of patients scattered on farms and in villages all
over the county. By the end of July, he admits that he can account for
only half of the sick men under his care. He is more certain of the
number of wounded, for they remain under his immediate supervision
at the Court House, but a steady stream of unwounded men continues
to seek medical care. Not that Green is ungrateful for civilian help. He
would probably agree, if grudgingly, with the chaplain of one Virginia
regiment who laments that "of all the sorrowful incidents of war, the
military hospital, even under the best regulations, is the most mournful;
it is far more dreaded by the soldier than the battlefield." No, these

sick men receive excellent care in Culpeper's private homes, but this informal system of medical assistance is certainly no way to run . . . well, a ship.[10]

August. Green has created more space for his patients by constructing several temporary hospital wards. Each is 250 feet long and 35 feet wide, neatly whitewashed outside and "pure and sweet" inside. Even the floors are "as clean as the top of a dining table." Pine bunks, set at intervals of two feet, line both sides of the wards. A small table, upon which rests a cup of water, medicines, personal effects, such as pipes and books, and, not infrequently, a bouquet of flowers, stands at the head of each bunk. A hospital kitchen, housing an immense cooking range and an equally impressive oven, has also been constructed. Less appealingly, the barracks that had been used to hold new recruits have been converted into wards. These buildings are less spacious and less clean than the new ones, and they are poorly ventilated. Dr. Green shakes his head, but any port in a storm.[11]

Green lost 59 of 775 patients in July, 31 of them from battlefield wounds, mostly gunshot wounds to the head, chest, and abdomen. Forty-two cases were so severe that he sent them to hospitals in Richmond. Ironically, the first wounded man to die was a Yankee. Thomas Needham, a private in Company H, 1st Massachusetts Infantry, died of a gunshot wound to the chest on July 21. The marbleworker from Suffolk County had enlisted at Boston last May. On July 18, at Blackburn's Ford, he got in the way of a Confederate ball. He is buried in the hospital cemetery near Martin Holcomb, the boy from Mississippi. It is sad to think how Needham's family will react to the news. He was the oldest of several children, and his widowed mother Sarah, aged 50, has depended on Thomas to support her and the family.[12]

Green needs more help. At the end of July, he had a staff of only six surgeons. Since then, he has recruited another 14 doctors, although he also lost two of his original six. Nine of the new doctors are listed as privates on his muster roll, for Green has recruited them from whatever volunteer regiments and militia companies have happened to pass through Culpeper.[13]

Around the county, many other volunteers, unknown to Green, go far beyond what might be expected of them in their devotion to the sick. Philip Slaughter has been caring for Lieutenant Giles Cooke ever since returning with him from Manassas. The most frightening phase of Cooke's illness, a delirium that affected him between July 18 and 24, has passed, and his mother and sister are daily expected to arrive. John Bocock, he of the humble saddle, is another dedicated chaplain. When the wounded of his regiment, the 7th Virginia Infantry, were evacuated to Culpeper, Bocock accompanied them. "I came up here with the wounded on Monday night [July 22]," he explained to Colonel Kemper, his commanding officer and brother-in-law, "thinking that I could render much more service here than at Camp. I wish you would order me to stay here awhile. . . . I feel as if I ought to be with the wounded, but cannot get free access to the Hospital at the [Manassas] Junction as I can here." The wife and daughters of George S. M. Payne have been caring for a Mississippi soldier, T. C. Catchings, confined to bed with typhoid for over a month. The Paynes even wrote to inform Catchings' parents of his condition and welcome the troubled parents into their home. Now recovered, Catchings departs with a light in his eyes and a vow never to forget the Paynes' kindness. He is especially thankful for the attention shown to him by winsome eighteen-year-old Millie Payne.[14]

Mrs. William Herr still is not ready for war. She was very much in the family way when Virginia seceded. Mr. Herr, a tailor, barely had time to greet their third child, christened Mabel, before he departed for Manassas with Culpeper's militia. Left alone at their isolated home near Raccoon Ford, on the Rapidan River, Mrs. Herr has struggled. "I spend a lonesome time here I tell you without Mr. Herr," she confides to an aunt. "The ford is bad enough when all the people are in it, now it seems as if it was deserted." Besides battling loneliness, anxiety for her husband, and fear for her own safety, Bunny, as she is known, is not physically robust. She recovered slowly from birthing and suffered for weeks afterward with a "rising breast." Then Mabel refused to take her teat, weakened, and suffered from "disordered bowels." Dr. Charles Hume and Dr. Stringfellow, a neighbor who took time from the military hospital, both attended the child. Hume prescribed slippery-elm tea and gum arabic dissolved in sugar water for Mabel. For a time, the infant revived, but a sudden reversal released her tiny soul to Heaven on August 16. Bunny grieves, but she consoles herself by thinking that Mabel "will never more be racked with pain, and that safe in her Saviour's arms, she is forever at rest." Ann Stringfellow, the doctor's wife, has been helping Bunny, but the grieving mother knows she must rely on her own strength to survive this saddest, most unjust of human experiences. Besides, grief is a species of idleness. Three days after Mabel's passing, Bunny sits down to make shirts for the sick soldiers.[15]

People seem less eager to help sick or wounded Federal prisoners. This sounds like a harsh assessment, and yet it is so. Few residents provide the same care and comfort to Yankees that they extend to Confederates, and people who appear overly indulgent come under suspicion. Matilda Hudson, a widow since 1842, pities all sufferers, whatever the color of their uniform. She and one of her slaves, Hannah Gibbs, have come to the Court House depot to lend a hand with the wounded. She finds a Federal soldier lying ignored on the station platform. Immediately procuring some bread, milk, and wine, she proceeds to show the lad "a good deal of kindness." No one interferes with her, but no one helps Mrs. Hudson, a woman known for her unionist sentiments. Still, the county has a conscience, and has set aside a ward in the poor house for Federal wounded.[16]

Culpeper's doctors and amateur nurses would be overwhelmed had not supplies and volunteers from nearby counties arrived, and some large towns, like Lynchburg, have accepted the overflow of patients. Margaret Brandon Jordan has come all the way from Huntsville, Alabama, to help. Mrs. Jordan first came, like Mrs. Cooke and the Catchings, to attend her wounded son. She has remained, however, to attend the sons of other mothers. Her son Jesse marvels at his mother's energy and courage. "I never had any idea she could stand & witness the grins of the dying and crying of the wounded," Jesse tells a sister back in Alabama, "but she stands it like a soldier & she says it is a wonder she is not gray for . . . she never witnessed such a sight in her life." Her help and that of others who have pitched in comes not a moment too soon. July, with its 59 deaths, may have been a rugged time to labor in hospital wards, but nearly twice as many men have died in the debilitating August heat.[17]

Monimia Cary and her daughter Constance have come down from Fairfax County to help. Monimia is an inspiration to all around her as she works among the sick and wounded at the Methodist church on West Street. Eighteen-year-old Constance spends most her time flirting with soldiers, but she is proud of how her mother rises from an army cot at dawn to play the ministering angel until dusk. Mrs. Cary dresses wounds, writes letters to the families of her patients, holds a boy's hand during an operation, comforts a dying man in his final moments, and whispers words of faith, hope, and cheer to everyone. "They call to me all over the church like a set of boys after their mother," she confides to Constance, "and tell me they should give up and die if I left them." What a terrible burden; what selfless devotion; but it is not difficult to understand Monimia's generosity. She labors so diligently and provides such loving care because her own son, Clarence, is a navy midshipman. He has already succumbed once to fever, and he may, before this cruel war is over, find himself lying on a cot in a distant place, his life dependent on a volunteer like his mother.[18]

> *Into the ward of the clean, white-washed halls,*
> *Where the dead slept and the dying lay,*
> *Wounded by bayonets, sabres and balls,*
> *Somebody's darling was borne one day.*
>
> *Somebody's darling, so young and so brave,*
> *Wearing still on his sweet, yet pale face*
> *Soon to be hid in the dust of the grave,*
> *The lingering light of his boyhood's grace.*
>
> *Somebody's darling, somebody's pride,*
> *Who'll tell his mother where her boy died?*[19]

Constance helps boost morale after a fashion. She has been joined recently by two cousins from Baltimore, Hetty and Jenny Cary. Federal authorities advised Hetty and Jenny to leave Maryland because of their Confederate sentiments. They complied, and after smuggling a cache of drugs and uniforms to Richmond, the young women went to visit friends in Orange County, across the Rapidan from Culpeper. All three cousins are beauties, and they have caused quite a stir as they roar around the countryside visiting Confederate camps and towns. At Manassas, they sang a rendition of "Maryland," a stirring poem written in April by James R. Randall, for troops of the Maryland Line. Hetty has set the poem to music by adapting Randall's words to "Lauriger Horatius," a college song introduced to her a few years ago by Burton N. Harrison, then an undergraduate at Yale and presently private secretary to Jefferson Davis. The Confederate version has become an overnight sensation. The vivacious trio has also been asked to sew three samples of a new Confederate battle flag. Each young lady will send her completed banner to a general of her choice. Hetty has selected Joseph E. Johnston. Jennie chose G.T. Beauregard. Constance will bestow her favor on Earl Van Dorn, a dashing cavalryman from Mississippi.[20]

Now it is mid-September. With most of her patients recovered, Monimia has joined Constance, stationary at the moment, for a much-needed rest at Bel Pre estate, where they are staying with the Wise family. But like her daughter, Monimia is a restless spirit. She is already looking for another camp or hospital that will accept her services. She cannot go just anywhere, for not all doctors welcome women. "I have found my stay here very pleasant," she confesses, "the country is so beautiful; but of course so many causes of anxiety as I have weigh a good deal on my spirits." Her family's home in Fairfax, she has learned, is being occupied by Federal soldiers. And there is always Clarence. She wants to work in Richmond, where she will be closer to him, but Dr. Green has asked her to stay near Culpeper for a while, at least.[21]

Monimia stayed a few more weeks, and Dr. Green was glad to have her. By November, 2,659 men have entered the hospital; 53 have died. Most of the patients suffer from diarrhea and fevers. Nearly half of the deaths result from wounds, but an appalling number of men still succumb to diarrhea (9 cases) and typhoid (13 cases). And this is only the toll at the general hospital, where precise records are kept. Throughout the county, 119 deaths have occurred during the past two months.[22]

Some people serve less willingly than Mrs. Cary. A few months ago, on July 15, the county court, on authority of an ordinance passed by the state convention, ordered the sheriff and commissioner of revenue to compile a list of free black men aged 18 to 50 who could work for the government. Many of those blacks have since been assigned duties as hospital stewards and teamsters. White men who have not joined the army have been assigned similar tasks, as well as temporary militia duty. Some whites resent being dragooned into service. George T. Jennings, suspected by many people of holding unionist sympathies, refused to answer his summons to the militia. The sheriff arrested him, but after a week's detention, Jennings was released because of poor health. Churchill M. Gordon has not been so lucky. He, too, refused to join the army, though his reasons remain unclear. Some say he opposes slavery, but four blacks are as much a part of his property as his sawmill and 200-acre farm. Perhaps he was influenced by his Pennsylvania-born wife, who has a brother in the Union army. In any case, after being called to help nurse wounded men, Churchill contracted typhoid fever at the hospital and died on October 12. He is Culpeper's first civilian death in the war.[23]

Equally unsettling episodes vibrate through the county. Letters received from the front remain generally positive, but they also contain hints of discontent and sometimes relay tragic tidings. Daniel Grimsley usually exudes confidence. "I am really fond of a military life," he insists to Bettie, "and am satisfied no matter if we have to endure hardships, there is something of romance & novelty about it that suits my disposition." But even the sheltered and largely innocent Bettie can see that not all goes well. Daniel mentions more than once the carnage of Manassas, as though, like a recurring nightmare, the memory of that ghastly field lingers. "It beggars all description," he told Bettie nearly two weeks after the battle, "and the mind sick in contemplation turns from it in disgust." He also chafes under the restrictions on his life and the deep mystery surrounding the army's intended movements, but he is especially miffed at his inability to obtain a pass to see Bettie. Alas, he broods, the army reserves such tickets to freedom for "important business," under which heading lovemaking does not appear. He is glad to learn how many sick and wounded men are being cared for in Culpeper, but he has already adopted the commonly held opinion about army medical care. "I have been in the hospitals here frequently," he tells Bettie, "and I tell you that should I be so unfortunate as to be sent into a hospital I should go in with the conviction that I never should come out alive."[24]

Joseph W. Embrey's family learns of the dark side of military life in tragic fashion. Joseph, a 22-year-old farmer, joined the Culpeper Riflemen in May. He enjoyed his early days of campaigning, although he occasionally lamented the scarcity of letters from home. "Give my love to all inquiring friends if I have any in Culpeper," he told one of his five sisters sarcastically shortly before Manassas. "I do not think I have any it do not seem so at any rate. . . . I do not think you all have any paper in Culpeper or you all would writ sometimes." Like the rest of the 13th Virginia, Embrey missed the action at Manassas, but even when he did do some fighting a few weeks later, he carefully avoided telling his family any of the details. Instead, he noted when and where he fought, including the regiment's casualties, in a diary. He told his family how well the army was fed, if not from official rations than from foraging and the generosity of Virginia civilians. "We get a plenty to eat now," he assured the folks at home. "We get a plenty of milk and pies and some vegetables now and than. We milk all the cows we can find."[25]

Embrey complained more openly about the army when he felt victimized by the military pecking order. While encamped near Fairfax Court House, his company received a visit from some Culpeper boys of the 7th Virginia camped nearby. The visitors ribbed their hosts about missing the action at Manassas, and the ribbing soon became boasting. Most of the 7th was to receive furloughs home from Colonel Kemper, supposedly as rewards for their role in the battle. Embrey's company, indeed his whole regiment, bristled at this news. Many men of the 13th had sought furloughs, but few secured them. Colonel Hill, commanding the regiment, approved Embrey's request, but General Arnold Elzey, brigade commander, rejected it. Embrey could not conceal his contempt for Elzey, who is a Marylander in any case, not a Virginian. "I would shoot him as soon as I would a yankee," exploded Joseph. Others in his regiment became equally bitter over their treatment; camp talk bordered on mutiny.[26]

Now Embrey's family learns that Joseph died on September 20. Details are sketchy. Perhaps he died of wounds suffered in fighting at

Hall's Hill, on September 16. All the Embreys know is that their family is among the first in Culpeper to pay the ultimate price for independence. They receive the brief diary Joseph kept in the month before his death and learn of events and personal reflections he left out of his letters. They discover that his regiment eventually shook off its anger and depression over the furlough incident. Joseph even seemed to forgive General Elzey, a comforting thought to the family. They are similarly heartened to read that he attended church at least once during August, when the preacher had reminded him that the eyes of the Lord are upon us in both good and evil. But they also learn that Joseph had been "low spirited" on occasion. They learn of the skirmishes and casualties the regiment endured, of quarrels, drunkenness, and fistfights in camp. Taken together, the news provides the Embreys with a different view of war than the one they held in April.[27]

Local unionists contribute to the uneasiness of people like the Embreys. Some of these traitors, for so they are viewed by loyal Confederates, continue to criticize secession and the new southern nation. Reverend Slaughter is losing patience with them. Slaughter is a kindly man who wishes no one harm, but he cannot understand, let alone tolerate, unionist treachery. He privately calls one of his neighbors, James B. Kirk, a "traitor" and suggests that he be arrested. Other people demand tougher action against Kirk, even though he is an undemonstrative chap who speaks openly only to other known unionists. But Kirk refuses to admit Confederate sick or wounded into his house, or even to provide food to passing soldiers. His actions have attracted attention, and another unionist in the neighborhood, William Purks, fears for Kirk's safety. "I have heard secesh people threaten to go there [to his house] and strip him of everything," frets Purks. Rough characters call Kirk "a damned union man," even "a damned Yankee." Some people curse him as an "abolitionist," although that probably goes too far since Kirk owns eight slaves and hires another seven.[28]

William A. Soutter, a tenant farmer, draws more ire than other Culpeper unionists. Soutter has steadfastly refused to join the army, and gleefully insists in public that the South will never defeat the North. The sheriff nearly arrested him in April, but people largely ignored his ravings during the hectic days of May and June. When summoned to the Court House for militia duty, he agreed to serve only as a hospital steward for Union prisoners. The authorities accepted this compromise, little knowing the dangerous game Soutter would soon play. Soutter learned after a few weeks in his ward that two Federals intended to escape once their wounds had healed. Using the utmost tact, he gained their trust and proposed a plan that would spirit them safely across the Rappahannock. On the night of the escape, he conducted them through the woefully lax hospital guard, provided them with three days' rations and a bottle of "spirits," and pointed them toward Warrenton. No one has ever been able to prove Soutter's complicity in the escape, but everyone suspects him. He continues to refuse service in the army, his half-brother will not speak to him, and one neighbor threatens to shoot him. Soutter himself boasts that the community generally will have "nothing to do with me."[29]

Such unabashed defiance angers people. How can men like Soutter so blindly ignore their own best interests, the best interests of Culpeper, and the best interests of Virginia? Loyal Confederates ignore such perverse behavior as best they can, but so long as people like Soutter speak their minds and engage in subversive activities, the threat of wider treachery remains a clear and present danger. Even in the flush of early military success, portents of moral decay and social disintegration, quite apart from unionist activities, abound. The hospital has witnessed a startling rise in cases of venereal disease. In July, doctors treated only two such cases; in September, the number swelled to 28. Reports circulate of increased banditry and violence in neighboring counties, where both civilians and soldiers have been assaulted on public highways, and people have been beaten and robbed in their homes.[30]

Most frightening of all, some Culpeper slaves have grown restless and defiant. A shiver ran through the county when, on September 14, one of William Colbert's twenty slaves murdered his 51-year-old daughter, Eveline. The crime occurred in Colbert's barn, about 200 yards from his house near Waterloo, on the upper Rappahannock. Sixteen-year-old Clary Ann, the murderess, claims that she acted in self-defense when Miss Colbert threatened to whip her. She admits striking

Miss Colbert on the head with a piece of fence rail, but she also insists that she did not mean to kill her mistress. Unfortunately, she cannot explain why she then proceeded to choke Miss Colbert to death. Clary Ann was found guilty in county court on October 21, and sentenced to be hanged on December 6. However, the execution has been delayed until May because Clary Ann is "quick with child." Meanwhile, the Colbert family fears that similar outrages might follow. One of William Colbert's married daughters has asked Governor Letcher to release her nephew from military duty so that he might return to Culpeper and protect his grandfather from "a large lot of rude Negroes."[31]

The curtailment of church activities, and even the temporary closing of some churches, has doubtless heightened the sense of disarray. Small congregations have suspended worship services because their buildings are filled with wounded and sick soldiers. The pitifully small attendance at churches able to maintain regular worship services reminds everyone of how much the community has shrunk. The loss of so many men to the army and the flight of some families has drained a degree of robustness out of both civil and secular life. Bettie Browning complains that the number of worshipers is "quite small" at Gourdvine Baptist, with scarcely any young men attending. Male attendance at Mt. Pony Baptist has dwindled to four members. Most churches failed to send either delegates or letters to the meetings of their regional associations this year.[32]

Churches like Gourdvine, Mt. Pony, Crooked Run Baptist, New Salem Baptist, and Culpeper Baptist have suspended monthly business meetings even when gamely carrying on with their sabbath routine. Few people see this as a great loss in and of itself. People are always looking for reasons to postpone or miss the business meetings. Any excuse will do—inclement weather, a sick cow—let alone a war. As the secretary of Pleasant Grove Baptist notes wryly in his minute book, "Church members, on meeting days, are generally very much afraid of rain." Still, to curtail such a vital arm of any church voluntarily and completely seems ominous in these uncertain times. Not that people fear for the continued physical operation of their churches. They accept the inconvenience and confusion that will result without regular business meetings, but they sense that the disruption has robbed them of some bit of spiritual solace and may, indeed, displease the Lord.[33]

Yet amid turmoil and shapeless fears, the mood remains confident. As part of Beauregard's army falls back from Manassas, and Confederate soldiers once more flood the county, a feeling of security returns. The soldiers are happy to be here, too. They have proven their determination to the Yanks and their courage to themselves. They think they deserve a respite from Yankee rifle balls. Men arriving in Culpeper for the first time admire the place. One lad is much impressed by this "beautiful country of hills and dales, and pure running brooks, fine farm houses and barns, rich lands with a promising crop of wheat and clover." He is equally dazzled by the view beyond, where, to the west, he spies the Blue Ridge, looking like "a bank of dark clouds, or smoke, low down on the horizon, . . . intensely blue." Even the much maligned local militia seems to be a more formidable defense force since the remainder of their promised equipment—mostly canteens and blankets—has arrived from Richmond.[34]

Returning troops also mean a resumption of profits for Culpeper merchants, farmers, and artisans. Camp Henry, the general hospital, and detachments of troops bivouacked in fields and woods throughout the county require supplies. But Colonel A. S. Taylor, who now commands the troops at Camp Henry, opposes one source of private profit. It has become apparent to him that far too many men have fallen prey to local dealers in spirits and liquors. The county is honeycombed with taverns and grog shops, and many retail merchants sell liquor. Two Court House hotels, the Piedmont and Mary Payne's Virginia House, have barrooms, and Colonel Taylor has become so enraged by the activities of these dispensers of Devil's brew that he has closed them. Taylor is no prude or teetotaler, but he insists that the hotel bars have shown no patriotic restraint in their trade with soldiers. First, they have been making enormous profits, upwards of $50 a day, which means they are either charging inflated prices or conducting an incredible volume of business. Second, all of these drinking establishments have created serious discipline problems by luring thirsty men away from their units. Worse yet, convalescents from the hospital frequently suffer a relapse from the effects of the whiskey. Soldiers have also been known to sell their blankets, shoes, or other equipment in return for a drink. He may not be able to regulate every tavern and merchant in Culpeper, admits Taylor, but he can make an example of the hotel bars and hope to show the "impropriety of selling liquor ad libitum *and* without the slightest discrimination to whoever may ask for it." For her part, Mary Payne has protested this outrageous attack on civil liberties to Governor Letcher.[35]

As for more honorable trade, profits blossom anew as the year draws to its close. August expenditures by the army increased by over 400 percent, to above $6,000. Construction of storage buildings and hospital facilities continued, and the construction, in turn, has fueled demand for lumber, nails, hardware, and labor. Twenty-one residents supplied lumber valued at over $1,200, and the army paid civilian carpenters almost $900 to turn the raw materials into sheds and hospital wards. Forage, including corn, oats, and hay, valued at over $1,300, came from 16 different farms. The army even had to purchase 26 additional horses, and their average purchase price of over $100 per horse provided acceptable profits for many families. The army purchased large amounts of cordwood from local farmers. The hospital purchased buckets, dusting brushes, matches, brooms, tincture bottles, wash pans, tin cups, knives, forks, rope, and a barrel of whiskey.[36]

Demand continued at a less frantic pace through September, and has tailed off in the last few months of the year. The biggest continuing expenditures, as usual, come from the hospital, even though most of the hundreds of patients that arrived after Manassas have either been released or buried. In October, over half of all expenditures paid for additional surgeons and carpenters, the former to heal, the latter to shield. In November, most monies went to the surgeons and to civilians renting out buildings and land to the army. December expenditures, up slightly, have paid for the same services as well as for additional cordwood and lumber. Poignantly, William F. Colvin, a Court House carpenter, received $47.71 on December 3 for digging graves. A few months earlier, another carpenter, D. T. Jones, earned $626.79 for making coffins.[37]

This is not to say that all citizens profit from the war. Even as they enjoy lucrative financial arrangements with the army, many merchants have stopped giving credit to civilians, and this at a time when prices have started to rise. Merchants have also been active in the courts collecting past debts. People complain about "enormously high" prices at the Court House, and even G. F. Carter, who operates a store at Rapidan Station, charges more for many goods. A gallon of molasses, which went for 40 cents in August, cost $1.00 in October. Fifty pounds of sugar cost $2.00 more in late December ($9.50) than in mid-November. A pound of tobacco sold for between 25 and 65 cents in October and November; in mid-December it went for 75 cents.[38]

Inevitably, too, some citizens have sustained the army without volunteering to do so. It is hard to regulate thousands of soldiers scattered over a vast countryside. Camp Henry still holds the majority of the men, but several independent regimental camps now supplement it. The outlying camps tend to rely more on foraging and voluntary civilian contributions to fill their needs. Soldiers are incorrigible foragers in any case, and however good-natured they may be, they do not always ask permission or offer payment for the food or firewood they "requisition." An old custom in many parts of the South holds that travelers are welcome to a top fence rail should they require fire for warmth or cooking. But the custom was never intended to accommodate several thousand visitors within a few months' time. A few soldiers, assuming that a tree here and there will never be missed from such dense forests, even cut standing timber. The men have not yet made confiscation "a business," admits one resident, but growing numbers of farmers are "grumbling" about the losses. Soldiers respond that if they do not use the rails and timber, the next army to pass through the region will. They leave an unsettling question as to whether the new army will be clad in blue or gray.[39]

But it is the return of many gray-clad Culpeper boys on furloughs and sick leave that has captured people's attention for the moment. By December, quite a few Little Fork Rangers, known officially since September as Company D, 4th Virginia Cavalry, have crawled home sick. Bettie Browning estimates that nearly half have returned. "They had such an easy time when they first went into service," she reasons, "exposure now goes hard with them." Quite a few Rangers have succumbed to pneumonia, and their camp, like so many others, has battled an epidemic of measles. Some invalids, like Lieutenant William A. Hill, return to the company after resting a few weeks. Other men show less resilience. Dennis Kelly, a private in the company, accepted a disability discharge in October. Robert Sheads, a 21-year-old farmer, died in September while on sick leave. He had returned home to recover from measles. Tragically, he tried to rebound too quickly, went out, over-exerted himself, and contracted pneumonia. His brother George continues to serve in the Rangers.[40]

Richard Y. Field, a 28-year-old lawyer, enlisted in the Minute Men rather than the Rangers, but some of his company are also home sick. Field returned to the Court House in August, and people say he still "looks dreadfully." The lawyer claims to have had enough soldiering for a while and will not return to the army until next year. Captain James H. Jameson, 11th Virginia Infantry, is the most recent and celebrated returnee. He suffered a thigh wound while leading his men into action at Dranesville, Virginia, on December 20. Everyone admires his courage and regrets his misfortune. Jameson thinks the wound a stroke of great luck, for it allows him to spend Christmas with his wife Mary and their four children.[41]

Pray that Jameson does not repeat the error of Sheads, for the death rate rolls up at an alarming rate among both native sons and those entrusted to Culpeper's care. Fifty more men died at the General Hospital in November; 38 have passed over in December. That makes a total of 372 deaths since July 1. Only 43 men have died directly from wounds. The largest numbers have fallen victim to typhoid (138), pneumonia (42), and typhoid pneumonia (41). Another dozen have died from a combination of these three killers with some other affliction, such as wounds, measles, or diphtheria. Three of the recent hospital dead are Culpeper lads, all in their twenties. One of them, 25-year-old Argelon F. Gaines, died of typhoid in August. Before joining the Minute Men, Gaines had worked on the farm of his father-in-law, William H. Freeman. Now Mary Freeman Gaines is a widow at 24, and two-year-old Mildred has no father.[42]

This is not to say that healthy men do not return home for a spell. Pollard Wood and James P. Ross, both shoemakers in their mid-thirties, drew a break from the rigors of camp life with the 4th Cavalry. They spent September and October at home in Jeffersonton on detached service making boots for their company. Wood, incidentally, has also been elected first sergeant of the company. The Culpeper Riflemen have returned en masse. The men had offered their services to the Confederate government for only six months. That time has now expired, and they were officially released from service on November 8. Many of the men speak of reenlisting in other units, but for the moment, they intend to savor their freedom and spend the winter months at home. Somewhere in northern Virginia, the Culpeper Minute Men, obliged to serve until January 17, are muttering about the luck of the Riflemen. Local gossip says that the Minute Men will try "right hard to get off" as soon as their time expires. Meanwhile, those lucky enough to find a way home parade in their uniforms, display wounds and war trophies, spin "*lengthy* yarns," and generally bask in their roles as heroes.[43]

And the ladies are delighted. Whether a man is sick, well, transferred, or retired, it matters not to them. Suspecting that the war may go on a while longer, and anxious to have someone to write to, pray for, and pine over when the boys return to the front, many single women set their sights on catching husbands before the next campaign. Many fellows, too, are eager to capture the tender looks, soft caresses, and sweet kisses of some fair maid before returning to possible death and damnation. And the local fellows find themselves at a distinct advantage. Many former rivals are still with the army, and the Culpeper women generally prefer to be courted by men they know rather than by the hundreds of "outlander" suitors in their neighborhoods. Bettie Browning is rather disgusted with the behavior of her cousin Will on this score. Seeing the broad field before him, Will is no longer content with his old girlfriend, Asa. Home on sick leave, he has been paying particular attention to a darling little thing named Allie. "I rather expect he likes Allie best of the two," judges Bettie (who is partial to Asa), "though it is not known how long it will last, as he is so fickle, like most of the gentlemen."[44]

The skein is not so tangled for some people, and Culpeper's church bells have hardly stopped ringing since the boys came home. Fifteen pairs of wedding vows have been exchanged since July, seven of them during December. And a gray coat does not always win the day, for plenty of eligible bachelors remained behind when more spirited rivals rushed off to war. The civilians have now enjoyed several uncontested months in which to press their suits, and a few have come away the victors. The most notable nonmilitary wedding has been that of John Stark and Kate Nelson. Their union forms a financial alliance between two of Culpeper's most important mercantile families. John is unlikely to join the army, his talents being necessary to direct the family business.[45]

The danger to the soldier of a visit home is that he will not want to return to the rigors of army life, at least not to the rigors he has known. Seeing newlywed couples, smelling perfumed hair, attending the funerals of lifelong friends, all of these can convince even patriots to seek easier, safer berths on a ship-of-war. Requests and recommendations for military commissions flow from Culpeper to Governor Letcher's office. Many of the requests are quite legitimate and understandable, although one wonders why they are only being made now, many months after the war commenced. Colonel Kemper, still commanding the 7th Virginia, is similarly swamped with requests for transfers and special favors. Perry J. Eggborn, one of the county's largest farmers with 23 slaves and 600 acres, is concerned about his son William's health. William, just 17, fought bravely at Manassas, but then turned deathly sick with dysentery. This only son means the world to Eggborn, already a widower, so he asks that the lad be allowed to convalesce at home. Besides, Eggborn persuades Kemper, "It would be some satisfaction to him to come up as he has never been allowed to leave his post from the day the co[mpany] was organized. . . . Every other member of the co has been allowed to go home at some time or other." William has also been reassigned from the infantry to service as a courier for Joe Johnston.[46]

People at the top solicit Kemper, too. Tazewell Patton, promoted to major and transferred from the Minute Men to the 7th Virginia, is finding it hard to cope with winter weather in camp. He has already returned to Culpeper from his regiment's "cold and dreary" camp at Centreville. Taze is only 26, but his liver ails him, and he suffers from "a general prostration and disorganization of the functions." More to the point, he is "extremely sensitive to cold, and suffer[s] amazingly even in a good house during winter." He wonders, then, if Kemper might not place him in command of the troops at Culpeper until next year's campaigns. The post is vacant, Colonel Taylor having been relieved of duty (supposedly over the infamous bar closings), and Tazewell swears that he desires it only as a temporary assignment. Besides, he adds mysteriously, "I have other reasons, not necessary to be mentioned, having no connection with the army or military matters, which make me desirous of coming to Culpeper." Patton is one of Culpeper's most eligible bachelors. Could his "other reasons" have anything to do with the perfumed hair?[47]

But in truth, as many men seek adventurous and dangerous assignments during this lull in the war as request sinecures. Abner Beckham was attending the Virginia Military Institute when the war began. Since then, he and many other cadets have been serving as drillmasters for new recruits in Richmond. Now Beckham longs for action. He asked his influential father James A. Beckham to plead his case with Colonel Kemper. The senior Beckham, who owns 56 slaves and a 2,000-acre estate, tells Kemper quite plainly, "I have a great distaste—& in fact—a horror for letters of recommendation . . . as I think a man ought to earn a reputation before he asks for letters." But he knows the heart of his eldest son, "a very modest youth," and has heard him declare that he would "rather be killed than to remain here in the woods doing nothing" while his country is being "over-run by Yankees." Abner has been offered a post as orderly sergeant in a new local company that one of the Barbours seeks to raise, but that effort seems to have collapsed. Besides, Abner's training at VMI entitles him to a commission. Kemper has obliged by assigning young Beckham to his own staff as a captain.[48]

The Confederacy cannot expect any better men than these volunteers from Culpeper, but the county does not harbor many more men able to serve. Oh, here and there a few adolescents hope the war will last long enough for them to come of age (unlikely); but discounting hard-core unionists, nearly everyone fit for duty or not needed at home is already in the ranks. Barbour failed to raise his company because, as one resident has observed, "No one seems to be disposed to volunteer." John L. Brooke understands the situation and has a solution. Most of the remaining able-bodied men, he believes, are "men of small means" who cannot easily leave their farms and shops without causing economic distress for their families. Yet these men are, by and large, patriots who wish to serve their country, if only they did not have to leave home for an entire year, the usual term of enlistment. Brooke suggests that Governor Letcher authorize the formation of a new militia company, rather than one of regular volunteers, to serve as both "an offensive as well as defensive force." Such a company would provide added security for the county, allow these men to remain productive contributors to the economy, and allow even short-term volunteers to "render most efficient service" for three or four months at a time.[49]

Meanwhile, Culpeper citizen's try to pursue normal lives. Unfortunately, despite the game effort, life in Culpeper is not—cannot be—normal. The graveyard filled with the remains of brave lads from Georgia, Louisiana, South Carolina, and, yes, Virginia, forbids normality. Thousands of soldiers, the dictates of martial law, the possibility of being invaded by a wicked foe, these and many extraordinary circumstances have altered life beyond recognition. The luster of a glorious war has been somewhat tarnished, too. News comes of a Federal thrust into Missouri, an impending invasion of the peninsula southeast of Richmond, the fall of Fort Hatteras, North Carolina, the capture of Paducah, Kentucky, Robert E. Lee's defeat at Cheat Mountain, the seizure of diplomatic commissioners James Mason and John Slidell, and an outrageous attempt by John C. Frémont, the original Black Republican presidential candidate, to liberate slaves in Missouri. On the other hand, southerners can savor the Union debacle at Ball's Bluff, the removal of Frémont from command, the release of Mason and Slidell, and, of course, Manassas, glorious Manassas. Surely the Yanks will soon be discouraged and quit. The war has not ended in the six months that most expected, and tragically, more men have died than anyone could have anticipated; but the next few months will probably decide the issue.

Yet these northerners are a curious race and a stubborn lot. They seem not to realize the impossibility of their goal. As the year closes, Joseph Halsey's family must be amused, and perhaps a bit frustrated, as it reads the latest letter from the New Jersey Halseys. "We are all well & prospering as well as the condition of the country will permit," asserts Samuel. "We judge from the present condition of affairs that the war will be ended in about six months." (Yes, that is also the assessment here, think the Virginia Halseys, but they read on.) "You are doubtless ruined in fortune, and perhaps in health," assumes the terribly misin-formed Samuel. "But I write you now as I did before the war broke out that a difference of political opinions shall make no difference in the brotherly affection which has always existed between us." Samuel, gen-erous to a fault, offers to help them with their financial collapse after the war. Can he be serious in his appraisal of the situation? Has the Yankee government hidden its reverses so thoroughly from even intelli-gent citizens like Samuel? This is puzzling, but the Halseys have scarce time to ponder. Culpeper will celebrate Christmas soon and the New Year. Then another planting season will begin. Confederate armies will march forth once more, and this time, they will win the nation's inde-pendence by summer. What a glorious summer it will be.[50]

PART II

Summer

CHAPTER FOUR

INVASION

*T*he sharp glint of a January sun belies the frosty weather. Sitting inside, without the contrariness of wind and temperatures, one can be fooled by the magnified light that slashes through the window. Impatient for the summer of victory to commence, one can easily ignore still-brown hills and barren trees. A new year breeds new hopes, regardless of the season.

January 6, 1862. Today Governor Letcher issued a proclamation designed to stir the passions of Virginians. The murderous and barbaric actions of the United States government during nine months of war have more than justified Virginia's decision to secede, avers its chief executive. Abraham Lincoln's government, by its "unnatural" and "wicked" behavior, has "violated" and "annulled" the old compact between the states. More than that, Lincoln's personal conduct has served to remind southerners of another tyrannical and oppressive monarch who sought to enslave a free people some four score years ago. In another summer, in another century, that free and irrepressible people had risen up, joined together, cast off self-doubt, shoved aside its sunshine patriots, defied the penalty for failure, and declared its independence. That, "our first revolution," proclaims Letcher, can only

87

serve to inspire Virginians and all southerners in the unfinished task ahead. "We must be content with nothing less than the unqualified recognition of the independence of the Southern Confederacy and its nationality," he continues; "and to this end we must meet the issue . . . with spirit, energy, and determination."[1]

Sleepy Culpeper hears the call but responds slowly. Surely it is not yet time to rejoin the battle. Whole men on leave and shattered men still convalescing are all loath to forsake the warmth and safety of home. William Crigler, a teacher in peacetime, has arrived from the winter camp of the 4th Virginia Cavalry to round up the boys of Company D who have overstayed their furloughs. Crigler is a little disgruntled himself. He has had enough of Colonel Beverly Robertson, the regiment's commander. The balding, unsmiling, mustachioed West Pointer works the men too hard, says Crigler; he is unsympathetic. Crigler still believes in the cause, but he will not reenlist if Robertson stays in command. He knows that some of the other boys dread another campaign, too. John Hawkins, in his forties, still has not recovered from the last one. Hawkins imagines he will die any day now. Crigler understands; he will leave him in Culpeper.[2]

Civilians, too, are distracted and disturbed. Much sickness (typhoid in some quarters) lingers in the community. Charles W. Rixey voices concern about the effects a prolonged war may have on the education of Culpeper's youth. He has hired a tutor for his own children and invites other families in his neighborhood to help form a school. He is even willing to take three of four "small boys" as boarders in his home (for $150 per ten months) to encourage enrollment. More urgently, people worry about the ineptness of the Confederate troops in Kentucky, where the only real scrimmages of the year have been fought. People worry about the morale of the armies. Beauregard, some say, must "so fill the troops with enthusiasm and daring as to make them invincible." Other people wonder why England hesitates to pledge itself to southern independence. Surely the cotton embargo is hurting English manufacturing. Perhaps Governor Letcher's speech will circulate in Britain, impress John Bull with the historic connection between America's two revolutions, and entice British might onto the side of right.[3]

At the very least, England might defy the flimsy Federal naval blockade. Virginians are beginning to mutter about high prices and shortages of goods. Shortages have even caused suffering in some quarters. The Confederacy needs more imports. Prices in Culpeper are not outrageous, but some items, including salt, lamp oil, and shoelaces, are scarce. A bag of salt, holding less than two bushels, sells for $23. Gertrude Williams finds it impossible to acquire red flannel, hairpins, bath soap, or knitting cotton at any price. She asks George, who, following the breakup of his company, has gone to Richmond in search of a government post, to purchase them in the capital.[4]

By February, mercantile activity at the Court House has slowed to a trickle. Less than a year ago, the *Observer* carried pages of advertisements for both local and distant merchants. Now the ads are nearly all local, and they are confined to a single column. Some signs of vitality remain. C. B. Hoop, opposite the Virginia House on Main Street, promotes a new inventory of boots, shoes, gloves, toilet articles, knives, whips, umbrellas, and an array of clothing direct from Richmond. L. W. McVeigh and H. C. Slaymaker have opened a new dry-goods store, although it is located in the rather cramped quarters formerly occupied by the Garland & Sisson bookstore. Still, Joseph B. Gorrell's attitude is more telling. Gorrell has been the town druggist for many years. People know him, and their patronage has made life comfortable for Gorrell, his wife Mary, and their two children. But that was peacetime. Now, money is tight; goods are scarce. Gorrell must pay cash for his inventory, so he asks even longtime customers to settle their accounts.[5]

February 17. Governor Letcher worries. He has detected a dangerous lethargy among Virginians, and so has launched a legislative campaign to pull people out of their doldrums. On February 8, the General Assembly ordered, at Letcher's urging, all white males between 18 and 45 years of age to enroll for county militia service. Two days later, it gave Letcher the power to use militiamen to fill levies for volunteers. That was not good enough for the governor. Recent military defeats in Kentucky, at Fort Donelson, and on Roanoke Island have shown that the war is far from being won. If this is to be the summer of victory, Virginians and all southerners must rededicate themselves to the cause. More men are needed, yet the legislators have only grudgingly complied with his demands for more troops, and they have insisted on liberal occupational and health exemptions from active service. On February 11, Letcher asked that home guards be organized to protect Virginia's towns and cities. To make it easier for businessmen and craftsmen to drill and serve in these units, he recommended that all businesses in Virginia close at 2 P.M.[6]

Now, on the 17th, Letcher asks the solons to increase the number of volunteers in the field. The demand for more troops, he assures them, is "instant and pressing, and it should be met promptly by people of all classes." "We are too apathetic," he warns, "too insensible to the wants and necessities of the times. . . . I desire to impress upon the minds of our people that no time is to be lost. Now is the day and now is the hour." His message is clear: The war will be lost without a larger army. More to the point, *Virginia* will be endangered without a larger defense force. The Confederacy is immense, reminds the governor, far too large for the national government to protect every hamlet and ensure the safety of every citizen. It is rather for the states "to look after their local interests."[7]

Alfred Stofer, home from the wars, agrees. A paper shortage has forced Stofer to reduce the size of the *Observer*, but he voices his opinions as forcibly as ever. "A great crisis is upon us," he echoes, "and we cannot disguise the fact, nor hide it from our eyes, that we are in imminent peril. Numerous and well appointed armies and navies, flushed with recent triumphs, are bearing down upon us." Young men must enlist now, either as volunteers or in the militia, if the South is to be saved. Catastrophic western defeats must be avenged. The South must demonstrate its spirit and vitality by bouncing back from such setbacks. Repeated military failures and depleted ranks will not inspire foreign powers like France and England to assist the Confederacy. "Volunteer! volunteer!! volunteer!!!" pleads Stofer. "Let all who can volunteer."[8]

Patriotic watchdogs have picked up the scent, although they actually have two, sometimes quite different, complaints. On the one hand, they speak critically—baying as it were—of neighbors who shirk their duty. In this, as Letcher and Stofer have said, there is cause for concern. Yet some people believe the problem goes far deeper than a desire to avoid military service. They see a society in decay.

The decay is not always obvious; it cannot be understood simply by looking at infractions of laws or abuses of power. The county court has heard only one criminal case since the start of the war, and that a fairly minor one of a man stealing a pair of mules. Some people still have not paid their taxes from last year, but the missing sum amounts to only a few hundred dollars. No, the decline is best seen in little things, in the way people behave, the way they speak. Rowdiness, vulgarity, knavery, and dishonesty abound. Ladies awaiting trains at the Court House depot have been compelled lately to stand in bitter cold and rain on the station platform. Why? Because, complains one outraged citizen, "the reception room . . . is filled with old baggage, dirty soldiers, or low, vulgar citizens . . . who are uttering blasphemous oaths or blackguard expressions."[9]

The watchdogs have many supporters on the latter score, but no little amount of debate is brewing in Culpeper over the issue of military service. Who *should* serve? What is a legitimate reason to avoid service? Few citizens would support John A. Stone, who has requested exemption from militia duty because he is the postmaster at Brandy. Although Stone's request is based on the letter of the law, which exempts local officials from conscription, men with far graver responsibilities have joined the army. But what about someone like 45-year-old David Faulkner? Mrs. George Pannill, like Catherine Crittenden last year, has urgently requested that Faulkner, her overseer, be excused from the army. Her husband is serving in the volunteers, and Faulkner has already served three months himself. Should he be recalled, complains Mrs. Pannill, "I will be left on the farm with a great many negros & not a white man or boy within three mls." Mrs. M. E. Walker wants her brother, D. W. Gibson, excused for a similar reason. "Without him we will come to want," she tells the governor, and, indeed, her case is persuasive. Mrs. Walker is a widow with four children and eight slaves, of whom only two—both women—are adults.[10]

Other citizens believe that once a man has served a term of enlistment he should be allowed to retire gracefully. Charles Crittenden very nearly fell into trouble over this issue. Crittenden replaced the popular Tazewell Patton as captain of the Minute Men when Patton was promoted to major. He is a capable officer, even though he lacks military training. When his company disbanded in January, Crittenden tried to organize a new one. Rumors spread instantly that he had done everything in his power, including writing letters to influential politi-cians and army commanders, to prevent the old company from being disbanded. The motives of the rumormongers are unclear, although they evidently seek to sully Crittenden's good name. Perhaps they covet his post as captain should a new company be raised. Perhaps they think he tried to keep the men in service for selfish reasons, to maintain his own berth as captain.

It is true that Crittenden bristled to see the men mustered out of service, but he is only guilty of being a patriot. He believes his men had just begun to work together, and that it was "an injustice" to disband the company before it could prove itself in battle. He absolutely denies charges of political maneuvering, whatever his motive. "I endeavored to pursuade them [his men] while in camp," Crittenden insists, "that in my opinion, they were not acting with a due sense of propriety to leave the field just at this particular time." He is determined to return a company to the regiment, even going so far as to request permission to draft militiamen should an insufficient number volunteer. The prospective conscripts, doubtless irritated by Crittenden's meddling, may also have spread rumors injurious to his character. But the trouble seems to have passed. A large portion of the original company has reenlisted for the duration of the war, and Crittenden has been re-elected captain.[11]

Other companies have also been reformed or newly organized. Company E, the old Culpeper Riflemen, mustered out of service last November, has reformed. Robert Utterback, captain of Company D, 4th Virginia Cavalry, has been recruiting in Culpeper for the better part of two months. Former lieutenant John Strother is reforming Company C of the 7th Virginia Infantry. Strother, one of three broth-ers to join the army, attended VMI, but chose law for a profession. In advertising for recruits in the *Observer*, he reminds young men about the state's $50 enlistment bounty.[12]

So the county, despite some doomsayers, is rising up—how did Shelley put it? Like lions after slumber? Men who lack legitimate rea-sons for staying at home are returning to the front. Something of last spring's excitement has returned. Bettie Browning has been invited to several balls and parties in the neighborhood, where people are having "quite a merry time." A sense of gaiety pervades all, she tells Daniel, who impatiently chafes for action in winter camp at Centreville, a dozen miles beyond Manassas. The certainty of victory has restored Culpeper's spirits; fear of failure's consequences has strengthened resolve. "Nothing is spoken of but the *war* and soldiers reenlisting," insists a starry-eyed Bettie.[13]

Letcher, of course, remains unsatisfied. He is embarrassed by a national report that shows Virginia, as of March 1, providing fewer volunteers for the duration of the war than any state except Florida, Missouri, and Maryland. The Old Dominion has provided more 12-month volunteers and more total volunteers than any other state, but most of those men have been mustered out, and the rebuilding process, with long-term enlistments, lags far behind other states. So the governor, pursuing one of his favorite themes, has asked the legislature to limit the possibilities for exemptions and substitutes. "In a time like this," Letcher elaborates, "there is a duty to be performed by all classes—the men of wealth not only, but also the poorer classes. Each has a personal duty to perform in driving back the invader from our soil." Wealth and power, in particular, should not be allowed to purchase exemption. And not least, Virginia's volunteers should be Virginians, not substitutes or lackeys from other states. Let each man fight for his own land, and let no state win its freedom by depending on the courage and fidelity of others.[14]

Most of Culpeper nods agreement, and now, one week before the Ides of March, the rhetoric from Richmond assumes real meaning. Joe Johnston has ordered Confederate troops at Fairfax Court House, Manassas, and Centreville to rendezvous at Culpeper. Johnston believes that General George B. McClellan is about to lead a monster army out of Washington toward Richmond. He is uncertain of McClellan's route, but he fears it may be toward Manassas. He anticipated such a move last December, when he ordered a reserve depot of food placed at the Court House. In February, determined to concentrate his forces south of the Rappahannock River, Johnston ordered his quartermaster and subsistence departments to evacuate their stores from Manassas to Gordonsville, about 15 miles south of Culpeper. Now Culpeper's reserve depot will be transferred to Gordonsville while the county becomes the center of a new defensive line.[15]

General Gustavus W. Smith's division arrived first, and today, March 12, the divisions of James Longstreet, Richard S. Ewell, and Jubal Early have finished crossing the Rappahannock. The withdrawal has not been flawless. The weather, for one thing, has been terrible. Heavy rains have soaked the men, who have been forced to march overland and to sleep each night without benefit of shelter. "I am fairly launched on a sea of mud," sighed General Smith, as his men slogged toward Warrenton. "The road is said to be very bad; some good judges say it is impracticable." Johnston feared this would happen. The withdrawal is President Davis's idea. Premature, warned Johnston. He wanted to wait until later in the spring "on account of the difficulties and hardships of marching" so early in the year.[16]

Nonetheless, his men have survived the ordeal, and the miserable conditions have been offset by the generosity of civilians along the route who cheer the troops and offer them cakes, hard-boiled eggs, and other delicacies. Men from flatter parts of the South marvel, as usual, at the steep hills and distant mountains, "wrapt in their bluish robes" and presenting "a most enchanting picture." "*Our* boys altogether stood the march remarkably well," brags a Georgian, the journey done; "none better, tho' the heavy knapsacks gave them jesse. I suffered no inconvenience from it except weary pedestals." One young lieutenant marvels at the endurance of the average soldier: "How patiently he trudged along those muddy roads, carrying musket and knapsack, cold and wet and hungry day after day—without murmuring, without ever a thought of giving the thing up."[17]

The removal of supplies and equipment has been a far greater disaster, and Johnston holds the Orange & Alexandria Railroad responsible. In truth, Johnston must share at least part of the blame. He asked John Barbour to operate the railroad to its "utmost capacity," but the overeagerness of both men has resulted in 61 miles of track (between Manassas and Gordonsville) being clogged by 332 engines and cars. A normal 6-hour journey now requires 36 hours. Johnston, furious over the delays, rails against the "wretched mismanagement" of the O&A. The delays have forced him to abandon or destroy 750 tons of food and forage in the depots at Manassas, Centreville, and Thoroughfare Gap, as well as untold amounts of clothing, accoutrements, ammunition, and artillery. Barbour resents the accusation that his company is at fault, and he is furious that Johnston has ordered the destruction of all railroad bridges between Manassas and Catlett's Station. Johnston claims that the destruction is necessary to slow Federal pursuit, but his premature action has only compounded the congestion below Culpeper and resulted in an unnecessary sacrifice of stores.[18]

The muddle of the withdrawal aside, many men are embarrassed by this apparent retreat, and a bit worried. Some write to reassure home folks that all is well. "Let it be understood," Colonel William N. Pendleton, Johnston's artillery chief, tells his wife, "that this is by no means a retreat, but a change of position for purposes of great value to our cause. People may rest assured the state is not going to be given up." Still, he advises Mrs. Pendleton that the Federals may attempt a strike up the Shenandoah Valley toward their home at Lexington. She should be ready to move the family to Hanover. Captain Robert Scott, 8th Virginia Infantry, admits that the retrograde movement represents "a dark hour," even though he remains hopeful of "the *final* result." He does not fear for his wife's safety, but the start of another campaign reminds him of how much he misses her. "This uncertain absence is almost overpowering," he confesses to his darling Fanny. "When will it end?" Even Johnston is sensitive to appearances. He has forbidden journalists to enter his lines.[19]

To his credit, Johnston has acted swiftly to deploy his troops and prepare for any Federal advance. He now thinks that McClellan will not try to move directly against him. More likely, the Young Napoleon will continue toward Richmond but send additional forces to strike up the Valley or against Fredericksburg. Johnston must be ready to move in either direction. Meanwhile, he is most concerned about staying on good terms with Culpeper's civilians. To ensure harmony, he has appointed Major Cornelius Boyle provost marshal, to be headquartered at the Court House. Boyle's chief task will be to keep stragglers—always a potential source of trouble—out of town. Outside the boundaries of the Court House, divisional commanders will be held responsible for men who "disturb private property or burn the fences in the neighborhood of their encampments."[20]

The army is behaving itself, mostly. No serious conflicts have arisen between civilians and soldiers. A few disturbances ripple through the camps, but they generally involve the rambunctiousness and pranks inherent in army life. One colonel had his horse stolen by "marauding soldiers," but he found it the following day. Captain Scott, a lawyer in peacetime and a devout man at all times, is one of the few officers who seems dissatisfied. "The spirits of our men impresses me," the captain admits, "never saw people apparently in better. They make fun of & cheer every thing they pass." Yet they are too often rude and insubordinate, and the "oaths and vulgarity that constantly issue from their mouths" cause him to "shudder" and feel "sick at heart." He complains that even one of his lieutenants shirks his duties and spends evenings away from camp, probably searching for women in the neighborhood. Not a good example for the men. "There is no place so demoralizing, so full of temptations," concludes Captain Scott, "as the army."[21]

Whatever their behavior, the men sense the building drama. They know something big will happen soon. The entire army, like Scott's company, is in high spirits, even though the men—enlisted men at least—continue to sleep without shelters in cold, rainy weather. "We now fairly enter upon the routine work of the campaign," Colonel Pendleton reports, "and many expect to be going continually until some great battle, or other decisive event." Some division commanders, like Gustavus Smith, drill and exercise their charges to keep them fit and out of mischief. The men grumble unconvincingly. They know what is at stake. Last week Daniel Grimsley's father delivered a sermon to a mixed congregation of civilians and soldiers from the text, "Be ye ready also." "To me it was quite impressive and at the same time consoling," reflects one soldier. "Oh! that our enemies would soften their hearts and be content to let us alone and terminate this unholy and unnatural strife," he laments to his wife. "They can never conquer men determined to be free and to throw off the yoke of an oppressive despotism. I think our enemies will find us determined *even to desperation.*"[22]

March 18. Just as quickly as it arrived, most of the army departs as Johnston orders three divisions south of the Rapidan. He has decided that McClellan will advance toward Richmond along the coast, and he wants to be nearer the capital. He leaves behind Ewell's infantry division and James E. B. "Jeb" Stuart's cavalry brigade, which includes the Little Fork Rangers, to shield his rear and guard the upper Rappahannock. He is confident that he has enough troops to divide his army in this fashion. The day before Johnston left Manassas, Governor Letcher mobilized the state militia, estimated at 40,000 men. The day after Johnston arrived in Culpeper, Letcher authorized all Confederate generals in Virginia to muster such militia within the boundaries of their commands as they deemed necessary for successful operations. Now, as Johnston plunges across the Rapidan, Letcher receives the gratifying news that Virginians are responding to his earlier call for recruits. "So many have volunteered," reports his adjutant general, "that there is a fair prospect of the deficiency being filled up without a draft, or by a comparatively small one."[23]

Even though they have been expecting it, the men grouse about the move. Soldiers hate to move. You just get settled and comfortable when some general decides it is better to camp on the other side of the river or a few miles in another direction. It is bad enough in good weather, but cold rain continues to fall in Culpeper. "I tell you it is trouble to move such a large army," a Georgian complains. The roads consist of "stiff mud," even above the Flats. "You could see men Giv out and lie down on the coald, wet ground," he reflects. "The Generals Had Gards put behind the army to take up every [man] that fell out of ranks. . . . I saw sevral horses lying in the middle of the road completely giv out. Thir was more blankets throan away on the march than horse teem could pull, and cloaths of the very best kind."[24]

Culpeper reacts variously to the flurry of military activity. Most people regard the militia mobilization as little more than conscription, and they are not at all pleased. The scramble for deferments has resumed as men seek release on account of hardship or physical disabilities. A few search for substitutes. Letcher is not pleased by the reaction, which is much the same throughout the state. In response, he has tightened procedures for obtaining exemptions, particularly for physical disabilities. He wants universal military service. The governor's attitude depresses George Williams. Still safe in his war department berth, Williams believes he has fulfilled his military duty by serving a year with the Minute Men, and he is making a valuable contribution now to the Confederacy. Yet he also knows that in the public mind only those men serving in the field merit real praise. It is they, he predicts, who after the war will "stand a much better chance of attracting the support of the people in his calling or profession than those who have dodged the draft or who have sheltered themselves in the comfortable & safe quarters of Govt Depts." Worse yet, he confesses to Gertrude, "I feel my own little wife almost ashamed of myself for sitting here idle when every man is needed for the defence of the country."[25]

More importantly, the army's presence means danger. It is all very well to have a training camp or a reserve depot in the county, to be a bustling terminal for departure to the front. It is quite another thing to *be* the front. "People in this region & where we have passed a good deal scared," reports one officer from Culpeper. "Not a few breaking up & going southward." Those people not taking personal flight consider moving their livestock and slaves to safer havens.[26]

From Richmond, George Williams worries about Gertrude and the baby. "There is darling good cause for fearing that most of our county will be over run," he admits. Yet he does not want Gertrude to fret. She should pack and be ready to join him in Richmond at a moment's notice, but until then she should stay calm and rely on the protection of Uncle Jack. The Yanks, of course, would like nothing better than to toss old Pendleton in jail, but he has a "firm friend" in Douglas Wallach's wife, Margaret, and she will shield him, his property, and his family should the Federals drive out Ewell and Stuart. Still, it would hardly do to wait quietly for disaster to strike. Williams says he may try to raise a company of infantry or artillery that would be posted at

Culpeper as "a sort of police or Rangers to watch & bring information of the enemy."[27]

But now March has nearly passed, and the initial panic has subsided. People appraise the situation and are reassured. After all, Ewell and Stuart remain in place, Major Boyle is still at the Court House with his provost guard, and Johnston is just across the river in Orange. Slave owners who had considered evacuating their property now think better of it. Few people want to live as refugees. They recall that the presence of soldiers means profits. Culpeper merchants, being low on stock, do not realize last year's bonanza, but the army still purchases enormous quantities of cordwood and forage. In March alone, it will likely pay over $1,500 for the former and $2,300 for the latter.[28]

Young ladies of the county delight in being surrounded by so many men, and they feel a patriotic responsibility to entertain them. With Major Boyle and the regimental commanders keeping a sharp eye on the enlisted men, it is the unmarried junior officers who benefit most from their proximity to civilization. They find it fairly easy to obtain passes to visit neighborhoods around the camps. "Heretofore the sight of a woman was so rare that everyone would run to the window to look," jokes a randy young man when contrasting duty in Culpeper and Orange to the camp life of a few weeks ago, "& all were pronounced pretty or beautiful." Alas, he sighs with a mock air of boredom, there are now so many women to choose from that all the men have become "more fastidious." On the other hand, it is also maddening when on duty to see so many lovely creatures passing in the distance and not be able to "get up flirtations."[29]

Ah, but come evening. One group of officers posted at Rapidan Station find a warm welcome at Annadale, the home of Alexander G. Taliaferro. Colonel Taliaferro is away from home, but his wife and three "pretty & charming daughters" remain. The daughters—21 year-old May, 18-year-old Sarah, and 17-year-old Margaret—have been joined recently by a few "refugee friends," so that Annadale does indeed offer a rare oasis of beauty and gentleness. Young officers, determined that such an agreeable bevy "should not be left to waste their sweetness on the desert air," pay frequent visits. The ladies are always cordial and agreeable. The combined company jokes, sings, and dances until well past midnight. Other men invited to dine with the Taliaferros marvel at the elegance of their surroundings in this island of "civilization."[30]

March 28. The gaiety has been rudely shaken. Federal troops tried for the first time to cross the Rappahannock into Culpeper this morning. The people have always appreciated the possibility of such an attack, but they are still shocked that it has happened. The high banks and breadth of the Rappahannock have made the river seem as formidable as a medieval moat. Of course, a couple of bridges span the river and several fords leave the county vulnerable, but Stuart's cavalry has been able to cover these gaps, at least until now.

Here is what has happened. A Federal reconnaissance of four infantry brigades and one cavalry brigade advanced from Alexandria along the O&A, threatening a far smaller force of Ewell's infantry north of the river. Stuart's cavalry slowed the column's advance, led by General Oliver O. Howard, by harassing the Federal flanks as dismounted skirmishers. All who could joined the action. A newly-promoted lieutenant on Stuart's staff, John S. Mosby, dashed forward with a Sharp's carbine to help his old company pour a deadly fire into the bluecoats. Slowly, the skirmishers gave way. When about three miles from the Rappahannock, they spotted the remainder of Ewell's infantry—about three hundred men—frantically boarding a southbound train. Trains and cavalry headed at top speed for the protection of Ewell's artillery and entrenched infantry on the Culpeper side of the river. Their job of shielding the infantry accomplished, the cavalry cut for the fords and soon splashed across to safety while the train hurtled across the bridge at Rappahannock Station. No sooner had the last car of the train cleared the span than two terrific explosions shattered the air, rising even above the boom of artillery, which had commenced a covering fire. Ewell had been ready. His engineers had blown one of the three stone pillars supporting the bridge. As the wooden trestles began to burn, Howard halted the pursuit but aligned his force along the bluffs.[31]

The volume of fire increased. Ewell posted a battery on either side of the bridge. Most of his 5,000 infantry anchored the left flank while a smaller number plus Stuart's cavalry—now dismounted and fighting under Ewell—secured the ground below the bridge. Another crash erupted above the din of battle as another portion of the burning bridge collapsed into the river. The firing, almost entirely an artillery duel, continued for perhaps an hour. Near dusk, Ewell ordered most of his infantry to withdraw toward Brandy. There were no casualties to speak of. The Federals captured three of Ewell's men, and a bursting Federal shell knocked the chaplain of the 21st Virginia Infantry off his horse. He remains dazed and unable to speak. The Federals pulled back, too, beyond effective cannon range, to bivouac for the night.[32]

March 29. Sporadic firing echoed along the river all day, most notably near Rappahannock Station, where the Federals opened up on a Confederate detail sent to retrieve some hay from the depot. Not wishing to challenge Ewell any further, and having confiscated forage and about 230 head of cattle from farms along the Fauquier County side of the river, Howard decided to withdraw. About sixty of the cattle belong to a unionist named William Bowen who has sworn allegiance to the United States. Howard sent his apologies to Bowen, but he kept the cattle, too. Stuart has already confiscated or destroyed most of the forage and supplies as far north as Warrenton. As the Federals withdrew, Stuart's men recrossed the river to pursue and harass them. The 4th Virginia Cavalry has joined the pursuit, but the 1st Virginia has won most of the glory by capturing two dozen Yankees and wounding several more. Stuart returned before dark with some fifty captives. It has rained nearly all day, a cold rain. The dazed chaplain has recovered. After doctors bathed him last night, he regained his ability to walk and move, although he could not speak until this afternoon.[33]

A fortnight has passed quietly. Ewell's stalwart defenders have turned back the first serious threat to Culpeper's freedom. Still, the attempted invasion has unnerved a few more families, mostly those living along the river. Richard H. Cunningham is the most prominent new refugee. With 60 slaves and nearly 600 head of livestock (mostly sheep and cattle), Cunningham cannot afford to sit vulnerable to an attack across the Rappahannock. He leaves his "splendid estate," including his furniture and a dozen bottles of Madeira wine, in the care of John Wiltshire, a small farmer who lives nearby and operates Cunningham's mill. Wiltshire has orders to torch the house and all within should the Yanks arrive. Ewell has made the house his headquarters. All seems well. With the bridge gone and Stuart's pickets more vigilant than ever at the fords, peace should reign. Oh, a few Federal patrols have crept back to march, countermarch, and rattle their sabers across the river; but they keep their distance. Some Confederate soldiers actually express chagrin at the quietude; they are anxious for a another crack at Billy Yank. Lieutenant Mosby is "perfectly confident of being able to whip the Yankees" wherever he encounters them. "Our men are in the finest spirits & eager for a fight," he insists. His only concern is in finding a good *cavalry* horse. He has two horses, but neither one, he claims, is suitable for combat.[34]

But peace does not always bring comfort. The first weeks of April have produced more rain, even some sleet and snow. Most officers and a few enterprising enlisted men find shelter in private homes and outbuildings, but the vast majority of Ewell's division did not receive tents until April 6. Before then, the men had constructed rude huts from whatever materials came to hand. Many soldiers simply slept on straw spread beneath two or three dislodged fence rails placed against a still standing top rail. Morning usually found them thoroughly "chilled with wet and cold." Unfortunately the construction of such shelters required them to ignore General Johnston's prohibition against disturbing Culpeper's fences, and straw is not issued by the army either.[35]

Food is scarce, too. With much of the army's supplies having been shipped to Gordonsville, rations are generally limited to hardtack and bacon. Luckily, a generous citizenry helps many men. The community contributes even such precious commodities as coffee, sugar, and salt to the troops. Some families, like the Taliaferros, invite small numbers of men to join them at table. One lucky fellow on a particularly nasty day, stumbled upon a house where the family invited him in to dry himself and share a hot meal. On his return journey to camp, he passed a house where he was beckoned to rest and warm himself. He spent a lively evening singing and joking in the company of "two very pretty ladylike girls." One of the new songs they taught him was Jennie

Cary's increasingly popular rendition of "Maryland." The family invited him to spend the night, but he pressed on to camp.[36]

But there is something these cold, tired men welcome even more than a hot meal, a dry bed, or a frolic in a real parlor: letters from home. In this, they are unlike soldiers in most previous wars. Not that soldiers have not always longed for home, and welcomed any sign that they are remembered, but in past centuries soldiers have come mostly from illiterate families. They knew few people who could write to them, and they could seldom read. This Confederate army, and the Federal army too, is quite different. Most of the men can read; many of their loved ones can write, and nothing so inspires them or lightens their hardships as a sweet, familiar voice rising from a written—and often scented—page.

"How exultantly I seated myself on my bunk," rejoices one soldier in telling his family of his reaction to their missives, "and strewing my letters around, devoured them one by one, over and over again." This same lad, writing home on his 20th birthday, expressed the thoughts of many a poor soldier when he quoted from a book of poetry loaned to him by a Culpeper family:

> *The voices of home! I hear them still!*
> *They have been with me through the dreamy night—*
> *The blessed household voices, wont to fill*
> *My heart's clear depths with unalloyed delight!*

Another soldier writes to tell his mother of a merry evening in the company of some of Culpeper's fairest maids. "It made me wish for an evening at home with all the pretty girls there, singing, dancing, & happy once more."[37]

Dick Ewell writes home, too, but he has something other than pretty girls on his mind. Ewell is unhappy with his army and its position. His men consider Ewell "a stern, fierce old soldier" and "a rigid disciplinarian." At age 45, the West Pointer has a jawbone, upper lip, and chin that sport far more hair than does his bald dome. He is a master of profanity—none better. And he does not suffer fools. No response angers him more than, "I don't know, sir." His staff lives in "fear and trembling" of being unable to supply the information he desires.

The general's irritability is doubtless exacerbated by his poor health. He suffers from indigestion which, in turn, provokes recurring bowel problems and ulcers. Still, his men feel some affection for "Old Bald Head," if that can be regarded as an expression of endearment.[38]

From his headquarters at Richard Cunningham's abandoned estate, Ewell watches the Rappahannock and fumes. His men, he complains, "are more afraid on picket than the Yankees, as they are always shooting at whatever they see, friend or foe, cows or pigs." More than that, Ewell, a man of action, aches to strike at a despicable foe. The Federals sit within his grasp, and Stuart's cavalry reports that they are "very much scattered and demoralized." He also hears that the "stupid, ignorant Dutch," or German-born troops, that oppose him are behaving in a low, thieving way, "ill-treating the people [in Fauquier], robbing and stealing and wantonly killing all the stock." Just what one would expect of ignorant immigrants, Ewell grunts. "These people are committing more wanton injury than they did in the Mexican War," fumes the Mexican War veteran, "and are as cowardly as villainous." How he would love to cross the river and knock hell out of them![39]

But Joe Johnston and Robert E. Lee, the latter directing all Virginia troop movements from Richmond, urge patience. Ewell's men must remain fresh, says Lee, for they will move to aid Thomas J. "Stonewall" Jackson in the Valley. Until then, Ewell must limit his action to artillery duels across the river. On one occasion, frustrated beyond endurance, Ewell lined up the 10th Virginia Infantry along the river bluffs. As Federal shells dropped among them, General Arnold Elzey, the 10th brigade commander, raced up to Ewell and demanded to know why his men were being exposed. Ewell turned to him and replied matter-of-factly, "Ostentation." "Ostentation, hell!" shouted an infuriated Elzey, who then marched his men back to camp. Ewell has been especially cautious since April 10, for on that day Johnston sent Longstreet's division from Orange to Richmond. Ewell's division is pretty much alone.[40]

The dwindling force in Orange affects civilian morale in Culpeper. More folks speak of following Cunningham and other refugees. Ewell mutters in disgust as he shares a bottle of Cunningham's wine with General Isaac R. Trimble. He is gratified by a recent rush of volunteers that has swelled his ranks from 6,500 to 8,000, but he thinks few of these men hail from Culpeper. He is particularly down on the county's "so-called 'Chivalry.' " "Here they seem to be pretty generally played out," he contends. "Very few re-enlisting—none to all intents and purposes." Ewell is overreacting, for hundreds of Culpeper men are in the ranks, including the Minute Men and Brandy Rifles of his own 13th Virginia. But Ewell is devoted to the Confederate cause, and he knows that timidity and apathy will scuttle it quicker than anything. "If our people will it," he assures his sister, "our cause will in all probability prosper."[41]

Uncertainty may be blamed for a large degree of the worry. No one, civilian or soldier, knows much about what is happening outside of Culpeper. Rumors abound, and many of them are dismal. So is much of the verifiable news. On the day Johnston left Manassas (still spoken of as a "retreat" by some), the Federal ironclad warship *Monitor* ran the *Virginia*, pride of the Confederacy's ironclad fleet, out of Newport News. Since then, New Madrid, Missouri; New Bern, North Carolina; and Fort Pulaski, Georgia have been captured. General Albert Sidney Johnston, the South's best general say some people, has died at Shiloh, and General Beauregard, who replaced him, has been shoved out of Tennessee. One report says the Confederates have retaken Nashville, but that seems doubtful. "You can hear almost any thing you want from different points," decides one frustrated citizen. And, perhaps naturally, people tend to credit the most pessimistic reports. It matters not that Culpeper and most of northern Virginia are still safely in Confederate hands, or that the inhabitants enjoy "much comfort, even luxury, in the manner of living." By mid-April, much of the joy and gaiety is muted.[42]

And now Culpeper's army is disappearing. Jackson needs Ewell to counter a swelling Federal presence in the Valley. Old Bald Head leaves reluctantly. He still wants a crack at the damned Dutch, and he nearly got one. Johnston gave him qualified approval for an attack, today, April 17, provided he clearly outnumbered the enemy and could guarantee low Confederate casualties. But the still-falling rain has made it hazardous to ford the Rappahannock, and this afternoon, word came from Jackson. Ewell must go at once. He has contented himself with a final, brief artillery duel. He will strike his tents tomorrow, Good Friday.[43]

Over the past several days, Ewell's men have moved silently across the Rapidan toward Orange Court House. It is a miserable march. They slog through mud while cold, driving rain blisters their faces. At Orange they board a train that carries them to Gordonsville, but because they ride in open cars, the rain continues to pelt them. They sleep in the rain, their clothes and blankets soaked through. They receive no rations for two days. "Ground wet, wood soggy, air cold, men starved," summarizes one veteran; "one of the severest experiences we have ever had." Meanwhile, Stuart has been ordered to join Johnston on the Peninsula. He leaves just three companies to picket the Rappahannock.[44]

And Culpeper has lost more than Ewell and Stuart. With them has gone nearly all of the military apparatus that protected Culpeper and made it prosper. Camp Henry has been disbanded; so, too, the general hospital, physically as well as practically. Ewell ordered any hospital buildings constructed over the past year to be torn down and burned. Culpeper's inhabitants cooperate in dismantling the structures, but they cannot bear to see so much lumber wasted. They salvage the wood and use it for fence rails and firewood. Meanwhile, the surgeons and volunteer nurses have also departed. "We will be somewhat lonesome until the Yankees arrive," speculates Deputy Sheriff Charles Short, only half in jest. Few people laugh, for a Yankee invasion seems almost inevitable. Jefferson Davis's universal conscription act, signed on April 16, adds to this fear. The act requires that all white men between 18 and 35 serve three years in the Confederate army. Exemption is possible, but fewer men will now escape service; fewer men will be left to protect hearth and home. This realization is bad enough, but the act also seems like a measure of desperation to some people; it suggests that the war is going badly.[45]

People fear the Yankees will take advantage of Culpeper's vulnerability. "You can form no idea how lonely it is here," Martha Coons informs a married sister who has departed the county. With her father dead and three older brothers in the army, Martha resides with a stepmother, two younger brothers, and an overseer on the family estate,

Northcliff. "I understand the Yankees are treating the people generally very bad [in adjoining counties]," she continues, "but we hear so many rumors that it is impossible to get the truth. . . . We are in a very help-less condition." Yankee cavalry patrols, like buzzards gliding above a wounded animal, already probe the Rappahannock. Many people re-gard travel over even relatively short distances an unnecessary hazard. The pastor of one Baptist church has suspended regular worship ser-vices "in consequence of the presence of the publick enemy and the excitement incident thereto."[46]

Reactions at the Court House are mixed. Sheriff Short is summoned to break up a fight on Main Street a few days after Ewell leaves. The combatants are civilians, so the provost marshal, left behind to keep a check on the sometimes rowdy cavalrymen, looks on. But Short and the provost marshal share concern about what to do with Clary Ann, the slave who murdered Eveline Colbert last summer. She presently resides in the county jail, sentenced to hang on May 4; but what if the Yanks arrive before then and free her? Better not take a chance. She is sent to Richmond. Such actions suggest tension and anxiety, but most people seem to be coming to grips with the situation. They are increas-ingly inclined to work, shop, go to school, and move about in their daily activities much as they always have, at least in town. "The most of the folks are becoming more composed & determined to meet the Yankees with a bold front," judges Short, "and bear their misfortune as best they can."[47]

The shifting mood accompanies clearer weather. Rain and a little snow continued into the last week of April, but now, in early May, the world has brightened. The sun, so long missing, reappears. Crops in the fields reach heavenward. "The spring has arrived very suddenly," reports a startled witness who just a week ago had felt more like a duck than a man. "Vegetation has sprung as it were from death to vigorous life without the usual intermediate stages." Fruit trees and dogwoods begin to bloom. River banks and fields sprout a first growth of weeds and wild flowers. Ferns spring from rocky crevices. And one reminder of the heavy rains looks like a Godsend, for the rivers remain high, es-pecially the Rappahannock, Culpeper's moat. Yet one cannot help wondering—What will happen when it recedes?[48]

Monday, May 5. The answer was not long in coming. The defilement has been brief, only 18 hours, but a battalion of the 1st Maine Cavalry, commanded by Major D. Porter Stowell, crossed into Culpeper at Beverly's Ford, opposite the Cunningham farm and less than two miles above Rappahannock Station. It was not yet 1 A.M. when their horses stumbled up the Culpeper bank. The column cautiously approached the Cunningham house, where it halted to dry out and rest. Major Stowell located Wiltshire and ordered him to unlock the door. While horses grazed and most of the men bedded down outside or in adjacent outbuildings, the officers and a few lucky troopers lounged "promiscuously" on Cunningham's comfortable beds, sofas, and easy chairs. Three hours later, the men swung back into their saddles and, with Wiltshire drafted as guide, advanced toward Brandy Station.[49]

Wiltshire, of course, had drawn an assignment he could not refuse. Some in Culpeper suspect him of being a unionist, yet he guided the Federals not along the roads but across intervening hills, thus exposing them to view and providing time for interior residents to spread the alarm. Stowell questioned several citizens, both black and white, along his route. One of the whites, 15-year-old Beverly Beckham, son of James A. Beckham and brother of two Confederate officers, presented himself as a Union sympathizer and assured Stowell that Rebel troops at the Court House were in flight. But other informants warned that the 2nd Virginia Cavalry had formed a skirmish line near the Court House and that two infantry regiments had been summoned from Orange. Stowell proceeded cautiously. Uncertain of the size and strength of the Confederate force, he sent ahead several squadrons at 10-minute intervals to probe the unknown while he advanced his main force to within a half-mile of the Court House. Finally, impatient and increasingly nervous, he galloped ahead with his staff to assess the situation. He found the town devoid of Confederate soldiers, although his men had seized a few rifles and eight civilian prisoners. After occupying the Court House for 45 minutes, Stowell ordered a withdrawal and moved his command briskly toward the Rappahannock. By the time he reached the river, at about 6 P.M., it had risen seven inches from the previous night. He pushed his weary men and horses across immediately. The crossing has taken nearly two hours, and a pair of men and their mounts have nearly drowned; but Stowell seems deter-mined to reach Warrenton by morning.[50]

Several days have now passed since the raid, but a numbness remains. No one is hurt, no property has been damaged, not even at Cunning-ham's place, but the prisoners! Their "capture" is nothing less than kidnapping, a cowardly way for soldiers to behave—taking hostages to shield their retreat. Rumors fly as to the identity of the captives. Thomas Lewis, proprietor of the Piedmont Hotel, is certainly one of them. David Stallard, a 42-year-old depot agent and the father of five children (the eldest being nine) is another. Henry Shackleford, the at-torney, and Ned Freeman, a merchant, have evidently been taken, too. My God! these are harmless civilians, people known to everyone in the county. If such folks may be snatched from their homes by a ran-dom patrol, what might happen if the Yanks should strike in force, say with a brigade, or even a division? "It must be a gloomy time indeed in Culpeper," speculates Lemuel Corbin, a Court House merchant who has refugeed to safer climes, "no regular mail, and business of every kind so frustrated & paralized. I sincerely hope the war will soon cease that our independence will be acknowledged and that we can return to our *once happy home.*"[51]

Events during the remainder of May have toyed with people's emo-tions. They feel hope one day, despair the next, relief at one hour, ter-ror a short time later. The release of the hostages a few days after the raid has caused celebration. Tom Lewis was the last to return home. He had been detained longer because he was armed when captured and resisted arrest. With all the men returned, people begin to take heart. "I think Culpeper as safe as any other portion of Virginia," in-sists Sheriff Short; but then sheriffs are supposed to talk that way—be confident, positive, buck up the populace. Other people scoff. Short may be right, they acknowledge, but that is not saying much, for no place in Virginia now seems safe. Certainly refugees from Culpeper have not been inspired to return. Sarah Parr, who fled to Amherst Court House with her husband and four children, believes, "This is a *horrible war,* & I have no idea now that it will end for five years." She misses her Culpeper neighbors "dreadfully," but she cannot think of returning under present conditions. John Turner, an elderly gentleman who refugeed to the Court House from Rappahannock County, was overcome with emotion when a portion of Culpeper's remaining cavalry guard left for the Valley in late May. As the detachment passed through town, this usually "passive, undemonstrative" man stood silently watching "with the tears rolling down his furrowed cheeks."[52]

The level of concern is measured to a large degree on where people reside. Do they live isolated from the rivers and main roads, or do they regularly witness increasingly bolder Yankee patrols? Have they had contact with the Federals, or is the Yankee threat still just a rumor to them? Mary A. B. Payne, who has had Federals at her front door, bemoans life's "trials and troubles." "Although they have not been so bad what they could be worse," she declares, "I am expecting far worse every day as we are almost surrounded by the Yankeys." Bettie Browning, on the other hand, remains cheerful. Her beloved Daniel, promoted to captain last month, was safe at last report, and she has not yet "had the pleasure of seeing a Yankee." She feels free to travel through her neighborhood, even though she knows the Yanks are nearby. They have been swarming all over neighboring Rappahannock County, where some of her friends report being "very much frightened." But except for the Stowell raid, they have steered clear of Culpeper, so Bettie remains more curious than concerned.[53]

Early June. Martha Coons has rebounded somewhat, and her stepmother, Susan, believes they are out of harm's way at Northcliff, which is located far north of the Court House and midway between Rixeyville and the Rappahannock. The Coons enjoy a harvest of watermelons, strawberries, and cherries. Their flocks of ducks and turkeys multiply. They will harvest their wheat—a "tolerably good" crop—in a few weeks, and the corn—"backward" but plentiful—soon afterward. Martha's main complaint is loneliness. She writes to Lemuel Corbin's wife, Mary, and urges her to return to Culpeper if only for a visit: "I sometimes think if this state of affairs continues a year longer, and I am separated as I am from those I hold dear to my heart that I will lose my mind. Every body says I am looking so badly; and some think I am *going in a decline.*"[54]

Late June. Susan believes the worst has passed, and that they face little danger of being "molested" by the Yankees. Perhaps she is so confident because her stepson has visited recently on leave from the army, but she also believes Northcliff has been "blessed." She thanks God that she resisted an earlier impulse to flee Culpeper like the Corbins. "Here we have all the comforts of life," she insists, "go where we please, come when we please, and I must say, I have felt happiness, and had less to trouble me at home." She tells Sarah Parr that she "would'nt for anything exchange places with any of the refugees." Some timid folk still hesitate to leave their homes, but generally people now venture out to harvest wheat, plant gardens, and visit neighbors.[55]

Yet doubts hover in some quarters. In faraway Richmond, George Williams hears only of the travail and fears the worst. The excited state of Richmond, in the face of McClellan's long-anticipated advance up the Peninsula, colors and possibly exaggerates his reaction. "This is a vast store house of excitement and rumor," he informs Gertrude, "and the sullen boom of the cannon . . . has set the women nearly crazy." He is on edge; he worries about his wife's safety. Keep a sharp eye on the servants, he warns her. These are dangerous times, and who knows what thoughts, whether of flight or violence, fill their minds. "Treat them kindly," he emphasizes, "but never have much to say to them. The nearer they approach to intimacy the further they go from respect."[56]

His frustration and fear are born partly of fatigue. Williams has a hundred cares, none of them easily resolvable. He worries about his ability to care for a wife and child on his meager government salary. He can barely pay for his board and room, located above "one of the noisiest bar rooms" in Richmond. Prices are soaring. Potatoes currently sell for $8 a bushel, butter is at $1.25 a pound, "small & poor" chickens go for $1.25 each. Salt and sugar are enormously high, and coffee impossible to secure. He is seeking a second job, one where he can work a few hours each day after leaving the War Department at 4 P.M. An extra $300 to $400 a year would help "mightily." Concern sometimes overwhelms Williams. When Gertrude asks if she should plant flowers at Redwood and enclose the yard with a fence, he is stupefied. What is the use of doing that, he asks this silly woman, when either army could descend at any moment, commandeer the house, picket horses in the yard, and ruin the entire estate? My God! does she not understand what is happening? Can she not perceive the precariousness of her world? [57]

Mostly, though, Williams is irked by supposed Confederates who, after a few setbacks, appear to be changing their colors. He heaps varying degrees of scorn on neighbors who abet the Union cause. He is angered by reports that unionists, meeting secretly in Culpeper, will induce wavering and frightened neighbors to take an oath to the United States when Federal troops arrive in force. "Those people do us more harm, our cause greater injury, than twice as many open enemies," Williams maintains. "We must punish these people or I fear we will not succeed in the struggle." He considers merchants who will seemingly do anything to turn a profit a particularly noxious breed. Thomas S. Alcocke, a merchant with a son in the 13th Virginia, is an outrageous case. Alcocke will no longer accept Confederate money in payment of goods or debts. Worse than that, he has recently taken to entertaining Wallach's daughters in his home. Alcocke would never have done that three months ago, and he can only be doing so now to curry favor with a prominent unionist family. "I have never had much faith in him," mutters Williams, "though he has the talent for humbugging others and they confide greatly in him."[58]

"Now is the time when every man must do what he can to serve his country," continues the lawyer, warming to his subject. "If unable to do so in the field with a musket, [he] must elsewhere with a pen or something." Williams remains sensitive on this subject of Confederate service. Unable to bear the physical hardships of campaigning himself, he feels obliged to act in some capacity, lest people whisper that he is not doing all he might to further the cause. He would quit his Richmond post altogether and return home, provided he could "strike on anything" that would exempt him from conscription. Unfortunately, such a move would expose him to the same appearance of shirking his duty that he levels at others. "I must do something for the cause or be disgraced," he tells Gertrude. "[H]ere I am of some service and my conscience acquits me." Having subdued the Devil within, he is impatient with weaker men who make no pretense of sacrifice.[59]

Many people in Culpeper share Williams's concerns, and lengthening casualty lists have not relieved their anxiety. While Culpeper hangs on the edge of violence, Culpeper men and boys have been fighting and dying elsewhere in Virginia. Some die in battle; others suffer from wounds or succumb to sickness or disease. As word leaks home of these sorrows, Culpeper feels pain. George Williams tries to confirm for his neighbors the names of those men who have fallen in recent fighting around Richmond. Culpeper's contingent in the 13th Virginia lost 16 men in late June and early July, the county's heaviest losses to date. Charles Crittenden has been "shot dangerously through both legs." Maybe that will silence his critics of the spring. Abner Alcocke, 18-year-old son of the Court House merchant, has been wounded in the right arm; surgeons talk of amputation. James T. Beckham, 19-year-old brother of Beverly and Abner, did not enlist until last March, but he did not waste any time attracting a Yankee bullet at Gaines Mill. Bettie Browning breathes easier when she learns that Daniel Grimsley escaped serious injury when his horse was shot from under him at Front Royal.[60]

When the summer breeze is sighing
Mournfully along,
Or when autumn leaves are falling,
Sadly breathes the song.

Oft in dreams I see thee lying
On the battle plain,
Lonely, wounded, even dying,
Calling, but in vain.

Weeping, sad and lonely,
Hopes and fears, how vain.
When this cruel war is over,
Praying that we meet again.[61]

Early July. The United States is apparently planning a massive new offensive in north-central Virginia. Abraham Lincoln, frustrated by the inability of his eastern generals to make any headway against Richmond, and threatened by the rising volume of political adversaries, has vowed to get tough. Less than a fortnight before Lee shoved McClellan back down the Peninsula, the president summoned General John Pope to Washington. Pope will command a new army, the Army of Virginia, and he will lead it into Culpeper. Pope is to secure a foothold south of the Rappahannock, seize control of the O&A, sever communications between the Shenandoah Valley and Richmond, and strike southeastward toward the Rebel capital.

Pope plans his invasion carefully. He consults with Douglas Wallach and David Strother, the latter a topographer familiar with the region, about the people and the terrain of Culpeper and adjacent counties. He grows impatient with Wallach, who cannot seem to describe the simplest crossroads or mountain gap without providing lengthy genealogies of families in the area. Pope is all business, and as he looks at maps and gathers information, he envisions an advance of 80,000 men as far south as Charlottesville. From there he could menace Lynchburg and Richmond, besides controlling the canals and railroads along the James River. Pope has a reputation as a braggart, but Strother decides, "Pope is a much cleverer man than I at first took him for."[62]

With Yankee patrols already thick around Warrenton, General Irvin McDowell, commanding one of Pope's three corps, ordered a Rhode Island cavalry regiment to cross the Rappahannock into Culpeper on July 3. The invasion has begun. Federal patrols are more frequent, and they penetrate deeper into Culpeper and adjacent counties, as far south as Gordonsville. Strong pickets have been established along the Rappahannock, as far east as Fredericksburg, as far west as Front Royal. Culpeper sits squarely at the center of this advance; it is the key to Federal success. "You must throw forward your cavalry to Culpeper Court House," Pope ordered a second corps commander, General Nathaniel P. Banks, on July 5, "and carefully watch the whole country toward Richmond and Gordonsville. This watch must be very vigilant and constant, and in sufficient force not to be driven back by small parties of the enemy." On July 7, Pope, who continues to direct the invasion via telegraph from Washington, ordered General John B. Hatch, commanding the cavalry of McDowell's corps, to establish his headquarters at the Court House and to post pickets at least twenty miles toward Richmond. Today, July 12, Hatch arrived in Culpeper with his cavalry and a battery of artillery and some infantry. He has scattered a company of Louisiana cavalry, killing one, wounding five, and capturing eleven. They were the last Confederate soldiers in Culpeper. The county belongs to the Union.[63]

CHAPTER FIVE

OCCUPATION

*I*t will be a hot summer. Breezes that ripple through trees and stir crops mislead. Cool, shimmering reflections on rivers are mere mirages. It remains hot, hot and sticky. By late June, the air is warm and heavy. Rain, sometimes hard rain, freshens most afternoons, but the heavens produce more mud than relief.[1]

John Pope does not mind. Delighted by his army's success thus far, he busily plans the next phase of his invasion. He has ordered a general advance across the Rappahannock and, today, July 14, he has issued a proclamation to his men. "Let us understand each other," Pope tells the Army of Virginia. "I have come to you from the West, where we have always seen the backs of our enemies; from an army whose business it has been to seek the adversary and to beat him when he was found; whose policy has been attack and not defense." The general continues this brash announcement by insisting that he is not concerned with "taking strong positions," or establishing "bases of supplies," and certainly not with securing "lines of retreat." Eastern soldiers, says he, have been demoralized by defeat; they must believe they can and will advance, can and will defeat the rebels, can and will march through the streets of Richmond. "Success and glory are in the advance," he concludes. "Let us act on this understanding, and it is safe to predict that your banners shall be inscribed with many a glorious deed and that your names will be dear to your countrymen forever."[2]

No one has ever accused Pope of modesty, or perhaps even of good sense. A Kentuckian and related by marriage to Mary Todd Lincoln, Pope has spent his adult life in the army. He graduated from West Point in 1842, fought in the Mexican War (gallantly, of course), and has performed competently thus far in the war between North and South. He helped to suppress guerrillas in Missouri, and he captured Island No. 10 in the Mississippi River above Memphis. He has, in truth, never shown his back to the enemy, and, to be fair, Federal troops in the western armies have enjoyed far more success and made far larger gains against the enemy than have Lincoln's eastern troops. Many of Pope's new soldiers resent his remarks, but Pope understands the need to send this army off on the right foot. His address is a hard-edged means of instilling spirit and boosting morale. At least this "tall, corpulent, and athletic" man with "keen dark eyes and beard and hair black as midnight" looks the part of a bold, courageous captain.[3]

Pope's exploits have impressed Abraham Lincoln. The president likes his aggressiveness. Being related to Mary Todd has also helped Pope catch the President's attention, but then Lincoln has his own connections to the Popes. Back in Illinois, Lincoln practiced law before Judge Nathaniel Pope, the general's father, and Pope's father-in-law is a Republican congressman from Ohio. John Pope himself served as part of the President's escort from Springfield to Washington for the inauguration. No wonder Lincoln has embraced this Lochinvar as his new eastern champion. Lincoln knows Pope and believes he can work with him. If Pope blusters, is quick-tempered, vain, petulant, "impatient of contradiction," and "rude in manner," he remains, nonetheless, "gifted with a vivid imagination," and he is "shrewd, active, and skilled in the rules of warfare." At least Lincoln hopes so.[4]

Culpeper has reacted as best it can. Some citizens take to the woods to plague detachments of Federal troops as guerrillas. Staccato exchanges of pistol and rifle fire vibrate across the county for the first time in the war. Amateur saboteurs attempt, with only minor success, to derail supply trains and cut telegraph wires. "The horrid Yankees have arrived," reports one young lady. "There is skirmishing every day about the Rapidan River." The county makes so bold because they have heard rumors that Stonewall Jackson is rushing to the rescue. With McClellan contained south of Richmond, Lee has ordered Jackson, Ewell, and Powell Hill with three divisions to Gordonsville on July 13. Jackson's assignment is to halt Pope's advance at that point and re-open railroad communication to Richmond, but no one doubts that Stonewall will press on to liberate Culpeper.[5]

That includes the Union troops. It is as Pope had feared. Whatever confidence his address may have momentarily inspired is being corroded by the sniping and the dreaded name of Jackson. As more men have been ambushed, captured, and wounded in skirmishes, some of Pope's officers bungle assignments. They speak of retreat. Pope has ordered his commanders to be more active; "Not only watch, but harass the enemy," he tells them. When he learns that a mere 325 cavalry occupy the Court House, he orders General Hatch to reconcentrate his forces there. "It is the most central point for operations against the enemy," he reminds the general, "and should be strongly held. . . . Do not fail to push and press the enemy from this point, and ascertain his force, position, and plans." But Pope's troops have been unnerved. They show signs of panic. They burn bridges to halt the Confederate advance, not appreciating that they thus halt their own advance. They exaggerate the number of Confederates, and they have no notion of Jackson's position. They lack good maps of the region, and heavy rains swelling the Rapidan and Rappahannock threaten to divide the army.[6]

Pope, who has faced similar circumstances in Missouri, knows what to do. Between July 18 and today, July 25, he has issued four general orders, approved by Lincoln, that threaten to nudge the eastern war in a devastating new direction. Pope has authorized his men to confiscate from local citizens whatever food, forage, animals, and other supplies they might require; to exile beyond Federal lines all male citizens who refuse to swear allegiance to the United States; to execute all persons who fire upon Federal troops; to destroy the property of all such persons; to force local residents to repair any railroads, wagon roads, or telegraphs destroyed in their neighborhoods; and to deny guards for the homes of citizens who seek protection. Parts of these orders are not unprecedented in warfare, and Pope and other western generals found some of them necessary to control guerrilla-infested Missouri. But those orders, issued by local authority, had not borne the stamp of the Lincoln government or countenanced executions and the burning of homes.[7]

Even though Lincoln has encouraged Pope in this direction, largely in response to public clamoring for a tougher, more effective military policy, the general feels obliged to justify some of his tougher measures. The toughest is General Order No. 11, which provides for the execution of all rebels suspected of being spies and permits the confiscation of their property. "I find it impossible to make any movement, however insignificant the force, without having it immediately communicated to the enemy," he complained to Lincoln. Correspondence with Rebel forces by "so-called peaceful citizens" must cease, he said, and the penalties of exile or execution are the only means sufficient to the threat. "A thousand open enemies," insisted the general, "cannot inflict the injury upon our arms which can be done by one concealed enemy in our midst." Pope may also be seeking revenge, for word is circulating through Washington, where Pope still maintains his headquarters, of gruesome "rebel barbarities" upon the remains of the Federal dead at Manassas and the mistreatment of wounded men and prisoners.[8]

Pope is still not satisfied. His army's failure to confiscate sufficient supplies to support itself annoys him. He has ordered division commanders to seize mules and horses not absolutely essential to the maintenance of local inhabitants, "especially in Culpeper County." They should also seize "all stores and supplies in the same vicinity." After again discussing the topography of central Virginia with Strother and Wallach, he has ordered more spies into the region and has hired more blacks to wander into Confederate lines and inform him of Rebel positions.[9]

Now, in early August, the orders have had the desired effect. Hardnosed unionists cheer Pope's initiatives and hope they portend a more "vigorous war policy" by the Lincoln administration. It is time, they insist, to "cease throwing grass at an enemy who throws stones." The soldiers respond, too. The orders not only convince them that they can now deal effectively with the Rebel population, they also change the

Willis Madden, Culpeper's best known and most prosperous free black resident. His land and property were wrecked by the war. (Courtesy T. O. Madden, Jr.)

Ambrose Powell Hill, born and raised in Culpeper, helped to defend his home county more than once during the war. (Courtesy Massachusetts Commandery, Military Order of the Loyal Legion and the U.S. Army Military History Institute)

This panoramic view of Culpeper Court House is representative of the town's position during the war. It was occupied by the army of either North or South almost continually from the beginning to the end of the war. The season of this photograph is autumn 1863. (Courtesy Library of Congress)

The road to Culpeper Court House (probably looking west) as Timothy O'Sullivan arrives to photograph John Pope's occupation. (Courtesy Massachusetts Commandery, Military Order of the Loyal Legion and the U.S. Army Military History Institute)

John Pope commanded the first Union army to occupy Culpeper. In the process, he instituted a new policy of "total war." (Courtesy National Archives)

Civilians rarely appeared on the streets of Culpeper Court House during John Pope's occupation of the town in August 1862. The building on the left with the weather vane is the courthouse. (Courtesy Library of Congress)

The Orange & Alexandria Railroad, seen here with one of its trains leaving the Court House, made Culpeper a prized target for both Federal and Confederate military strategists. (Courtesy Library of Congress)

Federal soldiers from Irvin McDowell's corps settle in during John Pope's occupation of Culpeper Court House. (Courtesy Massachusetts Commandery, Military Order of the Loyal Legion and the U.S. Army Military History Institute)

This view of the battle of Cedar Mountain by northern artist Edwin Forbes shows the alignment of Federal batteries as Pope's army prepares to advance. (*Leslie's Illustrated Newspaper*)

Another view of the battle of Cedar Mountain by Forbes depicts the initial success of General Samuel W. Crawford's men as they drive Stonewall Jackson's men back into the woods that border the cornfield. (*Leslie's Illustrated Newspaper*)

Farmhouses like this one near Cedar Mountain became makeshift hospitals after the fight. (Courtesy Massachusetts Commandery, Military Order of the Loyal Legion and the U.S. Army Military History Institute)

Home of the Reverend Philip Slaughter on the east end of Cedar (or Slaughter) Mountain. (Courtesy Massachusetts Commandery, Military Order of the Loyal Legion and the U.S. Army Military History Institute)

The arrival of wounded men at the courthouse following an unspecified battle. Such a scene was enacted on several occasions during the war. (C. W. Bardeen, *A Little Fifer's War Diary*, 1910)

Officers of the 10th Maine Infantry pose on the Cedar Mountain battlefield following Stonewall Jackson's withdrawal from Culpeper. (Courtesy Library of Congress)

Black refugees take advantage of John Pope's occupation to leave Culpeper. The Rappahannock railroad bridge stands in the background. (Courtesy Library of Congress)

These women in front of a cabin on Cedar Mountain present a scene that might have been witnessed almost daily during the war, as home folk awaited the return of their soldier heroes and carried on with life as best they could. (Courtesy Library of Congress)

men's opinion of Pope. They have been making sport of his bombastic July 14 address and a widely-quoted remark that he liked to maintain his "headquarters in the saddle." The latter is a rather empty boast for a man who has yet to stir from behind his desk in Washington, and it has inspired the nearly inevitable rejoinder that Pope's saddle, if ever he occupies it, would be better suited to his "hindquarters." But the orders end much of the jesting. All are "exultant" over a policy that has apparently "infused new vigor" and "additional strength and courage" into the army. "There has never been such universal good feeling in any army with which I have been as is manifest here now to see the government take strong measures," one enthusiastic soldier informs his wife. "No victory we have gained has been worth as much to the army in the field and the nation's prospects as this order."[10]

Confederates are outraged. Lee regards Pope's orders and his treatment of noncombatants as uncivilized and immoral. He fears that Pope's policy will force the Confederate government to retaliate with similar measures, that the Federals will then counter with even more drastic measures, and that the entire war will degenerate into barbarity. Indeed, even without retaliatory Confederate measures, one general in Pope's own army has exceeded his commander's orders. General Adolph von Steinwehr, commanding a division in General Franz Sigel's corps, has arrested five citizens of Luray, Virginia, and threatens to execute one man for every one of his men killed by guerrillas if the murderers are not surrendered by their neighbors. This is too much for Lee. He orders Jackson not just to defeat the "miscreant Pope" but to "destroy" him. A Richmond newspaper, describing Pope as "a compound of vulgar self-conceit, impudence and brutality," demands that he be captured and executed.[11]

Jefferson Davis tells Lee to lodge a protest with General Henry W. Halleck, Lincoln's general-in-chief, against the "savage war" unleashed by Pope. If the barbarity continues, warns Davis, "We shall reluctantly be forced to the last resort of accepting war on the terms chosen by our foes, until the outraged voice of a common humanity forces a respect for the recognized rules of war." Effective immediately, Davis adds, any of Pope's officers that fall captive (enlisted men are specifically spared) will be denied their rights as prisoners of war. If any southern civilians are murdered or executed under Pope's orders, an equivalent number of Pope's officers will be hanged. It is the escalation Lee feared.[12]

Meanwhile, confiscation, indiscriminate destruction, and intimidation have become the orders of the day in Culpeper. Federal officers are supposed to supervise confiscation and issue vouchers specifying the type, amount, and value of goods taken; but many soldiers, sensing a license in Pope's orders that probably was not intended, seize whatever takes their fancy. A private in the 21st Massachusetts Infantry admits that he and his mates have "immediately proceeded to take advantage" of Pope's confiscation order by stealing a beehive and capturing a sheep. A northern journalist admits, "A large number of our soldiers have an idea that Gen Pope's orders give them permission to help themselves to anything they can find, and consequently they have been roaming through the country killing chickens, sheep, etc., extensively." Pope's orders have "produced a decided revolution in the feelings and practices of the soldiery," admits another northerner. "Men who at home would have shuddered at the suggestion of touching another's property," he observes in only mild reproach, "now appropriate whatever comes in their reach." Too many officers turn their men loose. The colonel of the 1st Rhode Island Cavalry claims to enforce Pope's "severe" orders "modestly, quietly and lawfully." Yet his charge to the regiment, "given with a twinkle of the eye," is, "Don't you let me see you when you take anything."[13]

Other officers are horrified by the spectacle, but can do little to control it. "Straggling soldiers have been known to rob the farm houses and even small cottages, the homes of the poor, of every ounce of food or forage found in them," swears a commissary lieutenant. People safe in their homes, far removed from the swath of war, cannot imagine, he swears, the brutality and suffering in this portion of Virginia. "Families have been left without the means of preparing a meal of victuals." What is more, he adds bitterly, "The villains urge as authority, 'General Pope's order.'" A northern journalist insists that some marauders have been "punished severely by their officers," and that brigandry has nearly ceased. He exaggerates, although some officers make headway. Pope's provost marshal at the Court House, Captain Fitzgerald of the 28th New York, keeps a tight rein, and residents recognize him as a "gentleman." Lieutenant Colonel Joseph Kargé, 1st New Jersey Cavalry, has warned that any officer or enlisted man of his regiment caught "committing depredations or appropriating things of citizens without authority" will be court-martialed. The 1st New Jersey, which had in the past "once or twice attempted wanton destruction and unlicensed pillage," has become a model regiment.[14]

A pity more regiments fail to show restraint, yet confiscation is far from being the worst plague to strike Culpeper. "In every direction there appeared a frightful scene of devastation," reports a sympathetic member of the 1st New Jersey as he surveys the work of fellow soldiers. "Furniture, valuable in itself and utterly useless to them, was mutilated and defaced; beds were defiled and cut to pieces; pictures and mirrors were slashed with sabres or perforated by bullets; windows were broken, doors torn from their hinges, houses and barns burned down." At Berry Hill plantation, soldiers steal all of Lucy Thom's clothes, and she watches helplessly as they carry her melodeon to the slave quarters, destroy all her corn, and take away her horses. After ransacking Reverend Slaughter's house, soldiers proceed to wreck his church by order of their officers. Soldiers burn the house and outbuildings of Confederate army captain John Taylor after rounding up his slaves, confiscating his livestock, and laying waste to "his entire farm."[15]

"The Yanks are now in Culpeper," reports Dick Ewell as word of the wreckage reaches Jackson's army, "and I learn, are systematically destroying all the growing crops and everything the people have to live on. Sometimes they ride into the fields and swing their sabers to cut the growing corn. They seem bent on starving out the women and children left by the war." What is not destroyed is frequently left to die. Culpeper farmers are afraid to harvest their fields, so crops and grass burn and wither in the unrelenting sun. Ewell is furious, and frustrated by not being able to strike the loathed enemy. He protected Culpeper well during his stay. If he had been allowed to hit Howard when he had the chance, all this might have been prevented. Desperate remedies occur to him. "It is astonishing to me," he tells a niece, "that our people do not pass laws to form regiments of blacks. The Yankees are fighting low foreigners against our best people, whereas were we to fight our Negroes they would be a fair offset."[16]

But the Yankees intend to break the spirit of these Rebels by whatever means come to hand. Families, even poor families, have food "wantonly snatched from their mouths and wasted by brutal men." In a raid on Kellysville, the Federals freed John Kelly's slaves, confiscated his livestock and produce, and so frightened the old man that he is now in "a pitiable condition," a shadow of his earlier, rambunctious self. Federal cavalrymen terrorized two sisters who live near Kelly. The rowdies galloped up to the house and demanded to know the whereabouts of the married sister's husband. She swore that he was not here and wept in fear of what outrages might follow the conveyance of this news. The Federals dismounted and cursed the woman as they approached the house with "pistols in hand, sabers clanking, spurs rattling." If they caught the miserable son-of-a-bitch, growled one man, they would hang him in his own front yard. "No," his partner interrupted gleefully, "we will scalp his damn old bald head just here at the door." Laughing, they proceeded to sack the house, breaking every lock, rummaging through every drawer, and carrying away what they pleased. The sisters thanked God that the men rode off without having treated their persons in similar fashion.[17]

Unprotected women invite the worst behavior, for "insult and outrage ever walk hand-in-hand with plunder." "Instances are reported," laments one observer, "of deeds of violence perpetrated upon respectable ladies . . . which are without a parallel, save in the annals of the infamous Yankee race." People are too discreet to mention the victims' names or to dwell on the "repulsive details" of the attacks, but all feel sickened by the acts. "The Yankee rule in the county is severe beyond precedent in the war," reports one resident. "The most abominable outrages are being reported on the females, white and black." A British journalist confirms that the war in Culpeper is being waged "in a way that cast mankind two centuries back toward barbarism."[18]

The occupation has fallen nearly as hard on Culpeper residents not present to suffer Yankee abuse. George Williams is horrified to think of Gertrude exposed to Yankee insults. He advises her to behave toward any soldiers that may occupy Redwood just as she handles the servants. Be "dignified & firm," he cautions. "On no occasion allow them to be free & easy in your presence—if they become so leave them at once." Furthermore, "show them no sort of politeness not absolutely required by the necessities of your situation." If possible, he says, leave the house entirely; go to stay with relatives. He bitterly regrets having left her in Culpeper. As soon as Pope leaves, Williams vows, he will return and make arrangements for Gertrude to stay elsewhere. They will most certainly leave Culpeper after the war. They might go west, maybe to Arkansas. "I really do not believe I should ever be happy in Culpeper again," he laments.

Is this what war means, Williams wonders? No one envisioned such perils a year ago. Happy hopes for a quiet career, a burgeoning family, a peaceful home, all that gone in a moment. It is as though the land has been defiled. Williams cannot consider resuming the old ways amid familiar scenes and people. The more he ponders, the angrier he gets. "It comes so hard with me to leave the place in which my childhood was spent, where my best friends live," he decides. Damn these contemptible Yankees! "What should be done with these wretches, who forget the teachings of civilization and the amenities of civilized warfare?" he asks plaintively. "Where is their boasted religion, their morality, their charity? They seem to have become as savages." The war may well drag on another ten years with such enemies. But take heart, he whispers to his wife. Jackson is on the way, "& when he moves they will probably leave faster than they came."[19]

Culpeper's black residents, slave and free, receive mixed treatment. Pope's invasion has given Culpeper slaves their first good opportunity to escape bondage. Large numbers of slaves who had been placed in the county jail by their masters preparatory to being sent to Richmond for safekeeping have been released by the Federals. Elsewhere, slaves who have not already been spirited away to safe havens delight to see so many blue uniforms. They "gaze with wonder and joy upon the banner of the free," and the Federals, who regard their actions as a form of revenge against Virginia slave owners, take especial pleasure in urging slaves to leave their masters. They regard their actions as a form of revenge against Virginian slaveholders, and they encourage liberated slaves to eat of the same fruit. A coachman in the Somerville family, tempted by the soldiers' invitation, enters his master's bedroom, dons one of Mr. Somerville's best suits, and pilfers a watch and chain. Thus attired, he returns to the parlor, walking stick in hand, and announces in a confident voice (Somerville calls it insolent) that his master "might for the future drive his own coach." Particularly bold female slaves smack the faces of their mistresses as they exit, "and it is not an uncommon thing for them to dress in their mistresses' clothes [and] put on their jewelry and ornaments," reports one observer. Another favorite departing gesture is to "play the Piano for the 'Northern gemmen'" before setting out on the road to freedom.[20]

But not all blacks receive kind treatment from the "gemmen." Union soldiers commit acts of the "most beastly and infamous character" against slave women, and the confiscation order applies to everyone, regardless of color. Willis Madden watches Union soldiers march away from his farm with two horses, a cart, 40 fowls, 40 bushels of corn, 200 pounds of bacon, and 8,000 pounds of wheat, the whole worth nearly $300. At the Court House, Ira Field surrenders a horse worth $200. Even Alexander Jackson, William Day's slave who hires out his time as a saddle-maker, loses his saddle bench, $10 worth of tools, and $10 worth of leather to Pope's army. No one is immune to Pope's concept of total war. All civilians, regardless of sex or race, fear Pope.[21]

Pope's men have not executed or banished anyone, as they are licensed to do, but they have arrested a good many civilians. "Every man of prominence who has come in their [the Federals'] way has been arrested and sent off to Washington," reports one resident, "their personal goods stolen or destroyed, their stock butchered, and their lands laid waste." They incarcerated Miss Ella Slaughter, "a young and lovely lady and one of the most accomplished in Culpeper," because she drew a pistol against a soldier who had entered her house and "grossly and brutaly insulted" her. Soldiers dragged the Reverend John Cole from St. Stephens Episcopal Church and sent him to Washington because he dared lead his congregation in a prayer "for the welfare of the Southern Confederacy and the success of its arms."[22]

The intimidation and arrests have had an effect. The Court House population, at the very center of this summer storm, is thoroughly cowed. "It looked like Sunday when I rode through the principal street," reports a journalist accompanying the army. "The shutters were closed in the shop windows, the dwellings seemed tenantless, no citizens were abroad." He finds William Payne, proprietor of the Virginia House, on the northwest corner of Main and Cameron, in such a state of shock and distress as to be "somewhat out of his head." "A town so sombre as Culpeper I have never known," he reports. Shortages of food and high prices for what remains are reported everywhere. "Absolute starvation" reigns in some quarters, and "pinched, pining faces" betray a ravaged population. Even the dogs are "skinny and savage for want of sustenance." A few people respond by filing meekly into the provost marshal's office. They ask to take the "exorable oath" in order to save self and property. A larger, only slightly bolder, number still refuse to swear allegiance to the United States, but they do promise not to interfere with Federal troops in the county.[23]

The invasion has also tested neighborly feeling by releasing a current of repressed Union sentiment. Culpeper unionists have remained discreetly quiet since the war began. Given their experiences during the secession crisis, even acknowledged unionists have thought better of speaking against the Confederacy. But with Pope's juggernaut apparently ready to liberate them, these previously cautious people have turned to mischief. Archibald Shaw, who has escaped Confederate conscription because of partial deafness, suffers no disability that prevents him from feeding Union soldiers and providing them with information "as to roads, fords, & the position of the enemy." Matilda Hudson gives the army the run of her farm and provides nearly a thousand dollars' worth of food, fodder, and livestock, including eight cattle and fatted calves. "They did the butchering," she explains of her arrangement with the soldiers, "and when they moved away gave me a number of hides and the tallow from 9 beeves."[24]

Even free blacks feel bold enough to supply U.S. troops with food and "information of the rebel movements." Ryburn Bundy does so. George Mars feeds Federal pickets and provides estimates of the strength of Confederate units in the region. A lack of accurate maps has severely hampered Union movements, so Mars also explains the best routes from one place to another and describes the quality of various roads. John N. Colvin and Joe McIntosh go so far as to guide Federal patrols through the county. Many free blacks help the U.S. forces because they have been mistreated by the Confederacy. They resent being pressed into service as hospital stewards and teamsters, and they complain that Confederate forces have confiscated their crops. "The Rebel soldiers often cursed me for a damned Yankee," insists Mars, revealing an even more emotional reason for his loyalties, "& said I was saving my property for the Yankees & threatened to knock me in the head." These unionists are apparently unconcerned that the Virginia legislature has made it a criminal offense to provide intelligence, provisions, or any form of assistance to Federal troops.[25]

Still, Culpeper's Rebels are far from subdued. People have shown their defiance in different ways, but the general air of hostility toward the Federals is marked. "Secession is more rabid and bitter here than in any other place we have been in Virginia," swears a trooper in the 1st Pennsylvania Cavalry. "The men generally retain a sullen silence while the women wear a contemptuous and disdainful Sneer." Mr. Payne may be emotionally paralyzed, but the same cannot be said of his four tempestuous daughters. They scorn the Federal officers who have taken over their parents' hotel—just plain cut them dead. When dining, they make a show of sitting apart from the soldiers and speaking disparagingly of "Yankees." When promenading through town, dressed in their finest crinolines, the sisters never acknowledge the existence of any Federal they may pass, and they relish any opportunity to scorn with a "pert flourish" symbols of Federal authority, particularly the national flag. Other citizens at the Court House have protested against Federal bands playing patriotic northern airs. More aggressively, physical harassment of Union troops continues. "A man was shot a few minutes [ago] down to the creek bathing by some bushwhacker," a Federal informs his wife. Even as he writes, an officer has been dispatched to arrest several suspects.[26]

One Yankee cavalryman encountered a barefoot, dirty, ragged, and hungry family of "poor white trash" typical of large parts of the Flats. He had nothing but contempt for these herders. The mother of the family seemed "reconciled to the kindred sordidness of her life," while both she and her husband apparently lived "in the labors of the day, caring for little outside their farm and homestead, letting the war pass on with no interest beyond that of the safety of their little [live]stock." When even the animals were snatched from them by Union troops, they showed no emotion. Their faces were masked by an apathy resembling "indifference." But was it? These people are not far different from "loyal" citizens like Beckham that Major Stowell encountered in May. Not a few people use apathy, even an apparent willingness to cooperate, as a ploy. They protect themselves in this way. They pose no apparent threat, and so are left largely undisturbed. Yet it is just such people who, under cover of darkness or the terrain, can become deadly bushwhackers and saboteurs. The army, as one of the perceptive invaders appreciates, is "surrounded by secessionists, and watched by spies calling themselves 'Union men.'"[27]

At Federal headquarters, Pope has been expecting Jackson for weeks, and his Army of Virginia is vigilant to the point of tenseness. Officers have become increasingly worried about the poor condition of the Virginia roads. Full of holes and soft as dough, they will severely hamper movement of troops and supplies should the Rebels attack at an unexpected moment. So Pope has continued to probe outward from the Court House, stretching his picket lines toward Madison Court House and Gordonsville. He wants to keep as much distance as he can between the center of his forces and the advancing Confederates, wherever they may be. His engineers tell him that repairs to the railroad bridge at Rappahannock Station, unusable since March, will be completed by August 8. Pope breathes easier. With that lifeline completed, he will be able to concentrate his whole army south of the river. He left Washington to join his army on July 29. Having taken time to inspect several of his divisions en route, he finally arrived at Culpeper today, August 7.[28]

His men are better prepared than Pope had expected. They continue in "high spirits," confident of their ability to whip "whatever forces may . . . be collecting," even Jackson. Desertion had been a problem in July, but even Pope's relatively mild penalties, being branded and drummed out of the service, have given pause to those men who might have been tempted to take "French leave." Of course, the license assumed by the men in the way of confiscation has also won their loyalty, and not a few souls are genuinely committed to the preservation of the Union. The 9th New York Infantry publishes a camp newspaper "devoted to the dissemination of Union principles in this benighted region."[29]

When not on picket or patrol, the men have had a fairly easy time, too. True, the heat causes some problems. Cases of sunstroke are on the rise, and a few men have died beneath this blazing sun. But most men enjoy camp life, their domain marked by the thousands of white canvas tents that stretch from the Court House to the Rappahannock. "Lay in camp near Raccoon Ford nothing particular doing," a New Hampshire man records in his diary. Young men, randy and restless but moral enough not to have joined in the "outrages," enjoy ogling the "good looking women & girls" near the camps. Everyone eats well. So they pass the time doing laundry, playing cards, reading, sleeping, and, of course, writing letters. Some excitement has occurred in one of the camps where a pair of young women have been discovered disguised as soldiers. The "she-soldiers," their hair cropped to look like "two fine looking boys," have followed their lovers on the campaign dressed in baggy uniform shirts, blouses, and pants. The provost marshal has sent them home to Maryland. In spite of such distractions, all the men realize that this peace will not last long. We have "earnest work" ahead, one man tells his wife. He, like his messmates, is anxious for a crack at the Rebs. He wants to be in a great battle. He also wants "to get out safe."[30]

August 8, late afternoon. Pope has spent the day lounging at General Mc-Dowell's headquarters, established a mile from the Court House at the Wallach house. All of his agents and scouts had told him that Jackson was not yet a threat. Then, a few hours ago, the 1st New Jersey Cavalry, one of several detachments picketing the Robinson and Rapidan rivers, dashed "pell-mell" into camp. They report that a large Rebel force, including "immense adjuncts of cannon and artillery," has crossed the Rapidan at Barnett's Ford. Pope confers hurriedly with his staff, which reminds him that, while he probably outnumbers Jackson by 10,000 men, his three corps remain dangerously separated. Only McDowell's corps is actually in Culpeper. Sigel is at Sperryville, some 20 miles to the northeast. Banks, who had been equally distant near Little Washington, has spent the day advancing toward the Hazel River.[31]

Pope is suddenly in trouble, but his situation could be worse, much worse. Jackson had intended that Ewell's division spearhead a massive strike into Culpeper this very day, but the plan has been bungled. Jackson decided on August 7 to move against Pope, after his own spies and scouts had informed him of the widely dispersed disposition of Pope's army. His chief scout, Benjamin Franklin Stringfellow, grew up on the Orange County side of the Rapidan and knows every mile of the occupied territory. Jackson knew his men were primed and ready to wallop Pope. They know all about the ravaging of Culpeper, and just today heard "some heartrending accounts of the savage and barbarous treatment" one farmer received from "Lincoln's bandits." "They plundered him of all he had, his corn, wheat, and pork, killed his hogs, drove off his beef cattle and even his milch cows," says the report. "They even threatened to shoot this gentleman for having a loaded musket in his house." Jackson's men mutter that "the man with the movable headquarters had better commence moving."[32]

But as nightfall approaches, the advance has sputtered. Temperatures hovered around 90 degrees at midday. Veterans, who have learned a trick or two about campaigning, stuffed leaves in their hats to help ward off the sun. Still, men fainted, collapsed, and fell by the wayside as gray woolen columns ambled forward under full packs. Jackson's passion for secrecy has kept him from divulging his plans to even his division commanders. Men and officers have moved forward with no sense of purpose, no urgency. Then, too, the marching orders were confused and contradictory. A tense, brisk exchange of words between Powell Hill and Jackson resulted. Consequently, of the three divisions that should have crossed the Rapidan by midmorning, ready to attack this afternoon, only Ewell's is in position. His men crossed into Madison County at Liberty Mills last night and moved forward to Barnett's Ford, where they encountered McDowell's cavalry, commanded by General George D. Bayard. Hill's men, scheduled to cross at dawn, remain mired in Orange County. Most of General Charles S. Winder's men, the third division, eventually wade across the Rapidan, but

progress no further than a mile into Madison. The fords and approaches on both sides of the river remain clogged with men, wagons,
and animals. No wonder soldiers curse.[33]

Jackson, impatient for a view of the enemy and the ground he
holds, has reached Culpeper. He and his staff now bivouac at the
home of James Garnett, near Crooked Run Church. Jackson has lain
down to sleep on Garnett's porch; his officers choose the long, soft
grass in the yard. Before stretching out, they learned from Garnett further details concerning "the atrocity of Pope's army and the suffering
of the people." Stonewall intends to avenge them tomorrow. Until
then, the army must sleep. It has been drained by the heat, confusion,
and frustration of the day. These men must fight tomorrow; they will
need their strength. Perhaps, as Jackson himself nods off, he recalls
words written to his wife a fortnight earlier: "Christians should never
complain. The apostle Paul said, 'I glory in tribulations.'"[34]

The inhabitants of this southwest corner of Culpeper are uncertain
what to think of the sudden Confederate appearance. For weeks the
river banks and surrounding hills have vibrated with the shouts and
shooting of skirmishers. People have been terrified that a pitched battle might break out in their yards at any time. As gray columns now
wind past their houses, they rejoice yet fear the possible costs of liberation. Wagon trains have rumbled over the rough roads all night, with
the poor infantry, half asleep, trudging behind. But as word spreads
through the neighborhood that these gray warriors belong to
Stonewall, people rush outdoors; they stand along the road to cheer
the troops and bless them for ending Pope's "reign of terror."[35]

Saturday morning, August 9. Pope awoke refreshed and optimistic.
Banks's corps joined him toward nightfall, and although the blunder-
ing Sigel does not seem to appreciate the urgency of the situation, his
men should arrive soon. Bayard's cavalry has withdrawn a prudent distance from the Rebel vanguard, and has been reinforced by General
Samuel M. Crawford's infantry brigade. Most importantly, McDowell's
and Banks's men are in motion, their long snakelike columns winding
southwest along the Culpeper Road. So Pope sits in front of his headquarters tent, smokes a cigar, and chats with his staff. A dozen miles

away, Ewell's men march up the other end of the Culpeper Road, and Winder's division is moving to catch up. It will follow Ewell onto the battlefield, wherever that may be. Hill's men have finally crossed the Rapidan.[36]

Neither army looks particularly impressive to those uninitiated in military matters. The precision, orderliness, and discipline of the drill field are nowhere evident. Columns stagger along a few yards, halt, move again, halt, sit down to rest, resume the march, halt, inch forward again. The temperature will reach 80 degrees long before noon. Men stop at creeks, ponds, any natural depression that has accumulated water. They crave water, if only to moisten their lips. Columns passing within 50 yards of a tree line drift away from the prescribed marching route to savor the shade. If the trees bear fruit, men swing their rifles above them to dislodge it. Snatches of song drift above some regiments. "John Brown's body lies a-moldering in the grave; his soul goes marching on." A melancholy thought on such a day, when so many men will soon share John Brown's condition.[37]

Many men are anxious. This will be their first battle, maybe their last. They think of home, of Mollie, of Mother, of childhood dreams of soldiering. Some wonder if there is a God; they try to remember the Lord's Prayer, the 23rd Psalm, the last sermon they heard. "Father, save me from this hour; but for this cause came I unto this hour," the chaplain of one cavalry regiment told his men. Bracing stuff, but, hell, cavalrymen never get killed. Consciences begin to gnaw. Men duck out of line to bury decks of playing cards, chewing tobacco, and other signs of depravity. Jesus! What if they are killed and someone sends their belongings home to Mother or Lizzie? Some men scribble their names and regiments on strips of paper and pin them to their coats. Others are fascinated by the prospect of battle. What is it like, this experience of "seeing the elephant"? Will they measure up to this supreme test of manhood? Will they flee at the first shot? How does it feel to be wounded? Do not think about it. It does not matter. They are here, and they must fight for their country.[38]

Think of something else, anything else. Men throw taunts and jests at rival regiments and at friends. Someone spots a reporter, scribbling in his notebook. "Give the 55th a good puff!" the men shout in pass-

ing. "Give me a good obituary!" "Bully boy reporter!" Most of the ban-
ter is senseless, but talking, or singing, or shouting is better than puk-
ing. Better than wetting your pants. The Federals have brought their
music. Brave drummer boys, none above 14, rap out "The Girl I Left
Behind Me." Brigade bands blare out a more stately "Hail Columbia!"
An Irish regiment prefers "The Wearin' of the Green"; the Scots,
"Bonnie Dundee." Horse-drawn ambulances follow troops and wait
patiently, morbidly in the rear as columns become lines and men prepare to meet death. Artillery batteries rush ahead, unlimber, and position their guns. Infantrymen pause behind the guns. No need to hurry.
They will bear the brunt of battle soon enough; they know who the
ambulances await.[39]

The pounding and jangle of a cavalry regiment is heard approaching
from the rear. God, they are noisy! Most of the cavalry is already
fanned out several hundred yards ahead, probing and hunting for the
enemy. The newcomers veer toward the flank, scabbards glistening in
the sun, horses' hooves shaking the ground. They will form a reserve.
A regiment already in position carries lances. Lancers, for Christ's
sake! Lances against rifles? The poor sons-of-bitches. Hell, maybe
some cavalrymen will die. There it is again: Death. Don't think of it.
Mind your place in line. Did I bring my cartridges? Yes, there they are,
but I thought I had more. Christ, it is hot![40]

The advancing forces seem destined to collide on a plateau beneath
the western slope of Cedar Mountain, nearly eight miles from the
Court House. The heart of the plateau itself slopes up toward the town
and forms a ridge in front of the approaching Federals. Heavy forests
shroud the rear of the Federal ridge and spread over most of the land
northwest of Culpeper Road. The only open spot to the northwest is a
wheat field, already harvested; cornfields, unharvested, cover the
plateau. The only natural cover on the plateau is a clump of cedar trees
near the base of the mountain, but the plain is also broken by several
knolls, and its generally undulating nature can mask the movement of
troops from some vantage points. Three farms, belonging to William
Major, Catherine Crittenden, and Robert Hudson, sit on the plain.[41]

Both armies have spent the morning positioning themselves. Pope,
just as he directed his invasion from Washington, now directs his bat-

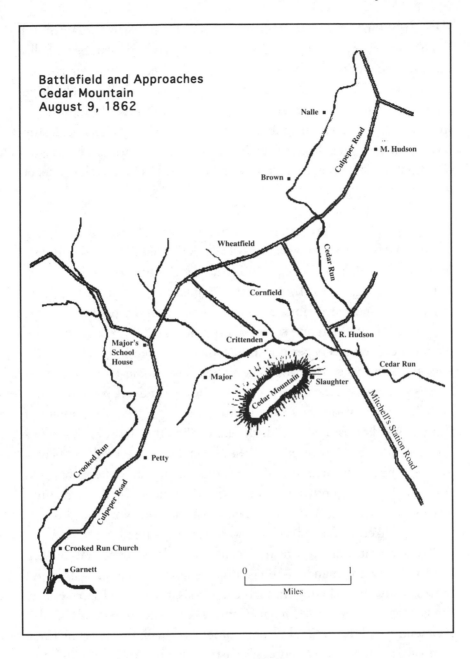

**Battlefield and Approaches
Cedar Mountain
August 9, 1862**

Nalle ■

■ M. Hudson

Brown ■

Culpeper Road

Wheatfield

Cedar Run

Cornfield

Crittenden ■

R. Hudson ■

Major's
School
House ■

■ Major

Cedar Mountain

Slaughter ■

Cedar Run

Crooked Run

Mitchell's Station Road

■ Petty

Culpeper Road

■ Crooked Run Church

■ Garnett

0   1

Miles

tle from the porch of the Wallach house. He still seems relaxed and largely unconcerned. His cavalry, directed by Bayard, watches Ewell's advancing column. Old Bald Head has established his headquarters at the home of Cornelia Petty, a thirtyish widow with three children, about two miles north of the Garnett house. Ewell is playing on the front porch with some neighborhood children when Jackson rides up late in the morning. The two men get down to business and agree on an initial battle plan before stretching out for a brief nap. They expect a long day.[42]

1 P.M. Ewell's men, having received their orders, file past their dozing leader. Two brigades, led by generals Isaac R. Trimble and Henry Forno, and Ewell's artillery swing east and head for the base of Cedar Mountain. Early's brigade, led by the 13th Virginia, moves toward the plain. Early has assigned the 13th as skirmishers. He must realize that the Culpeper Minute Men and scores of other local lads compose this regiment. They have a very personal interest in the impending contest and a personal score to settle with Pope. They have come to liberate *their* homes and families; it will be *"our fight,"* they say. Indeed, some men will be fighting almost on their own farms. Charles Crittenden, captain of Company B, knows these woods through which they pass. His mother's house stands just a few hundred yards ahead. He has worked and played in these fields, roamed the side of this mountain. Fifteen-year-old William D. Colvin, a private in Crittenden's company, did the same until just five months ago, when he joined the regiment. Now this, his first battle, will likely be fought on land owned by his father, John.[43]

"General Early, are you ready?" calls out Colonel James A. Walker, the 13th's new commander. "Yes; go on," replies the general. Walker and the 13th advance. Moving through the woods, the colonel spots enemy cavalry two hundred yards to his front. The mounted Federals see his regiment, too, but the Yankee detachment is small, only two or three companies. The infantrymen easily disrupt its charge and continue to advance. Federal vedettes appear on the right, but they, too, fall back before a well-aimed volley of fire. Reaching the edge of the woods, the regiment spots still more Union cavalry. It opens fire, but these horsemen, though exposed in the open fields, remain out of range. The rest of the brigade soon joins the 13th. Early has lost a few men along the way, not to enemy bullets but to the overpowering heat. The sun has been unrelenting. Many men, especially the "stout" ones, have fallen out of ranks "utterly exhausted, some fainting, some victims of sun stroke, and many from sheer want of strength and will to go further."[44]

It is 3 P.M., and Walker's men now fall back to a position on the brigade's left. Artillery arrives. A fence—a Crittenden fence—barring the advance is torn down. The brigade moves forward, across the road that leads to the Crittenden house, on the right, and to the crest of a small hill. Ahead stretches the plain. Beyond it, a thousand yards distant, sits the enemy ridge. Federal guns have already commenced firing. "We are in for it now," the men whisper among themselves. Early places two batteries in the clump of cedar trees a few yards ahead on his right. The artillery duel begins. The infantry falls back a few steps to lie down behind the crest. They are relatively safe here from Yankee guns, but that accursed sun continues to beat down.[45]

4 P.M. Ewell has arrived to take personal command of his divison, and he flings orders in all directions. He positions General Winder's artillery to the right of the Culpeper Road. He places additional batteries near Reverend Slaughter's house on Cedar Mountain, where a small plateau affords a spectacular view of the Yankee lines. Not far away stands the house of a 24-year-old saddler named John Pope. An 18-year-old captain, Joseph W. Latimer, commands one of the mountain batteries. He is Ewell's best artillerist, and Old Baldy fondly refers to him as his "Little Napoleon." Jackson admires Latimer, too, and calls him the "Napoleon of the Valley." The din of artillery fire echoes and reechoes across the fields.[46]

General Winder has joined his artillerymen, despite the fact that his surgeon advised him not to take the field today. He is a sick man who has been traveling in an ambulance for much of the past week. But Winder is a warhorse and an artillerist by trade, so he could not resist dismounting, stripping off his jacket, and helping to direct the fire of Captain William T. Poague's battery of the Rockbridge Artillery.

4:30 P.M. Winder was about to shout instructions to one of the gunners, Ned Moore, when a Federal shell screeched between the general's body and his upraised left arm. Winder is "fearfully mangled"; his whole left side has been ripped apart, his chest shattered. He has fallen straight backward and lies "quivering on the ground." Lieutenant McHenry Howard, a staff officer, rushes to him and asks, "General, do you know me?" Winder shifts his eyes toward Howard and breathes, "Oh yes," but this man is doomed. He knows it; he begins to speak about his wife and children at home in Maryland. A chaplain arrives and asks the general to lift up his heart to God. "I do," Winder replies mechanically and faintly, "I do lift it up to Him." An ambulance arrives to carry Winder back to a grove near the Major schoolhouse. Meanwhile, Winder's artillery chief, Major Richard S. Andrews, has nearly been disemboweled by an exploding shell. It has been a rough day for artillerists.[47]

Catherine Crittenden stares wide-eyed through a window of her home, Cloverdale, midway between Early's infantry and Cedar Mountain. She does not know that her son lies huddled along their farm road just a few hundred yards away. Her own position is nearly as precarious, with two Confederate batteries blazing away less than a hundred yards from her door. As Federal cavalry swept through her yard this morning, she appealed to the chaplain of the 1st Rhode Island Cavalry, Frederic Denison, to escort her, four daughters, and their servants either to Confederate lines or behind Union lines. Denison declined, pleading lack of time and men. Riding on, he left the widow in "great mental perturbation and nervous excitement." About 2 P.M., as Early's men commenced their march toward her house and sporadic artillery fire commenced, Denison returned to find her "in agony." Artillery and rifle fire from both ends of the field jarred windows and mirrors. Denison stayed long enough to calm her, but he soon had to retreat. She repaid his consideration with a canteen of milk and four biscuits.[48]

5 P.M. Her fields flooded with gray uniforms, Mrs. Crittenden takes heart. Confederate officers stop at the house and urge her either to leave or to take refuge in the cellar. One man thinks he spots her and the other Crittenden women clambering up the side of Cedar Mountain to escape the fray, but she and her daughters, most notably spunky

Annie, have decided to stay and prepare food and bandages for the many Confederate boys who are sure to be wounded on this day. When artillery shells come crashing into the yard, one even slicing through her roof, Mrs. Crittenden reluctantly leads most of the other females below ground. Only 22-year-old Annie remains at her post, where she is already nursing the first casualties of the day.[49]

Other civilians on or near the battlefield respond variously. The most rational course is flight, and many people, both black and white, have already headed for the homes of friends and relatives outside the range of the guns. Abraham Curtis, nearly seventy years old and fearful that his frame cottage will not survive the whistling shells, has found shelter in the substantial brick home of neighbor James Inskeep. Alas, even Inskeep's house stands on the fringes of battle, and while waiting out the bombardment in his neighbor's basement, Curtis is struck stone dead by a shell that crashes through the floor above him. Not far away, a free black woman and her children huddle in their own cabin until the intensifying barrage forces them to flee one mile across open fields to a neighbor's home. A "passel" of neighborhood women and children find shelter in the modest home of J. B. and Sarah Brown. The house is well behind Federal lines, nearly a mile northwest of Culpeper Road. One of the children, an 18-month-old boy, sleeps soundly.[50]

Only a few stubborn or adventurous folk, like the Crittendens, refuse to leave their homesteads. Robert Hudson, whose farm sits in the middle of the Union lines, is not going to leave his house unattended with so many bluecoats around. Miraculously, a heavy concentration of Confederate fire, aimed at a Federal battery less than 20 yards from his door, has not yet struck his house. Equally oblivious to danger, a crowd of slaves belonging to Samuel A. Daniel, of nearby Forest Grove, has climbed onto the roof of a shed to get a better view of the white man's battle. They are probably safe enough. Neighboring families closer to the battle have been arriving all morning to find shelter at Forest Grove. Thirteen-year-old William Nalle, whose father owns a grand brick house behind Federal lines, skipped toward the battlefield with several black and white playmates earlier in the day. When, almost without warning, the boys found themselves trapped between the advancing armies, they wasted little time in retreating to the Nalle house.[51]

Back at the Court House, five miles behind Federal lines, townsfolk are learning that random patrols, martial law, and confiscation pale beside the boom of artillery and the threat of total destruction. The suddenness with which it has all happened, the shock of having their morning peace shattered by the clamor of assembling forces, has unnerved them. As blue columns shuffle through the streets, clouds of "pale, anxious faces" appear in windows. Men, women, and children huddle on porticoes and "gaze with expressions of awe, ridicule, anger, and wonderment" as the martial scene unfolds before them. At the Virginia Hotel, the Payne girls were playing a spirited rendition of "The Bonnie Blue Flag" on their parlor piano when the thunder began to roll. By 3 P.M., as cannon peals shook Court House homes, the young ladies had ceased their merriment. Their parents are emotionally numb.[52]

Catherine Crittenden may yet regret her decision to stay at home, for Nathaniel Banks has ordered his infantry to advance. The men have been in position since 2:30 P.M., withstanding the Confederate artillery barrage much as Early's men are doing. Now, General Alpheus S. Williams's Federal division, led by General Crawford's brigade, moves up the northwest side of Culpeper Road. General Christopher Auger's division advances in like fashion on the mountain side of the road, opposite Early's brigade. Banks tells his staff that Pope has ordered an attack, and, indeed, Pope intends to do just that, even though he is outnumbered two to one and Jackson holds a strong defensive position. Cedar Mountain, with infantry and artillery at its base and the batteries near the Slaughter house able to "sweep the field," effectively protects Jackson's right. His left is "completely ensconced in woods." The only way to strike him is with a frontal assault across open fields.[53]

Pope has been sitting calmly all day at his headquarters near the Court House smoking and examining dispatches from the field. He thinks that Banks has understood the plan: wait for Sigel's men to arrive before attacking. A large portion of Sigel's corps has by now marched into the Court House, but the men need to rest and eat before continuing to the front. If Sigel had arrived last night, as instructed, Banks would outnumber Jackson and be ready to attack, but the damned Dutchman is about as dependable as a canteen with a hole in it. Now suddenly, as Pope sits chatting with McDowell, the artillery exchange five miles away grows sharper. The heightened intensity is unmistakable. Something has gone wrong. Shaken from his lethargy, Pope orders McDowell to assemble a reserve regiment and tells his own staff to mount up.[54]

The 13th Virginia sees it coming. Blue skirmishers appear first, flowing over the ridge and rolling onto the cornfield. Behind them comes a "beautiful line" of infantry. God, there are so many of them! They overlap Early's right flank and the guns in the cedars. If they push through at that point, they can overrun the entire Confederate line. Early summons reinforcements, which arrive in the form of General Edward L. Thomas's brigade, detached from Hill's newly-arrived division. But the pressure is terrific, and it quickly extends across the field. On the left, the Federal advance threatens two batteries under Captain William J. Pegram and Lieutenant William B. Hardy, which have incautiously moved ahead of Winder's infantry and now find themselves a mere 150 yards from Federal skirmishers. Actually, the infantry belongs to General William B. Taliaferro now. Taliaferro has succeeded the fallen Winder, but he is unsure of the intended battle plan. His infantry is still not firmly planted, and as Crawford's infantry advances obliquely against his left, Taliaferro's line buckles.[55]

Virginians under Taliaferro blame the collapse on two Alabama regiments, consisting mostly of green conscripts, who run "like turkeys" before the Federal hunters. "Raw men can't stand that kind of music," a veteran spits decidedly. The fighting is desperate, hand-to-hand along some parts of the line, but that is not the worst of it. The retreating regiments cause such confusion as they crash into the ranks forming behind them that the entire army is endangered. Captain Walter Lenoir, 37th North Carolina Infantry, is furious, not just at the cowardice of the retreating troops but at the "indescribable confusion" they have created. Lenoir, positioned in the wheat field north of the road, works frantically to keep order among his men. Luckily, he and the other officers of the regiment succeed, but Lenoir's effort is particularly remarkable. This is his first battle, and he has been seriously weakened by the "flux." That condition, combined with the suffocating heat that has caused many of his men to faint, has tempted him to fall out of line himself. But his first lieutenant has already succumbed to similar conditions, and Lenoir cannot bear the "mortification" of seeing his men face the enemy without him. Then, too, the excitement of combat and the challenge of holding his company together have driven awareness of the heat, physical weakness, even fear of death completely from his mind. Lenoir, a lawyer in peacetime, feels less frightened entering battle than he does facing a jury. He focuses his attention entirely on his men, on "keeping them in order, and directing and encouraging them." Somewhere in his actions lies a definition of courage.[56]

6 P.M. General Early had moved his brigade forward to protect artillery batteries on the right, but the relentless pressure of the Federal advance is forcing his men back. Only the 13th and a portion of the 31st Virginia Infantry, to the right of Walker's men, hold their ground. Walker pushes both regiments forward some 30 yards, the colonel of the 31st having fallen, to protect a lone artillery piece that continues to rake the Federal line. Taliaferro, witnessing their gallant act, attempts to inspire his fleeing men by calling to them, "Look at the old Thirteenth, rally on her!" The stand seems nothing less than miraculous, yet how often such actions occur in battle. Small units, clearly outnumbered, hold firm while their comrades either limp away in orderly retreat or reform for a counterattack. The Virginians hope for the latter, or they are goners. Federal lead flies everywhere, piercing clothing and plunking into bodies. *Plunk*; *plunk*: the sickening sound of bullets lodging in human flesh. Yet Walker's infantry and their adopted field piece respond with a "well-directed fire" that has blunted the Federal advance. They have saved the Confederate right flank from total collapse and a possible rout.[57]

But the pressure is growing. *Plunk*; *plunk*. More men fall. The Federals threaten to encircle Walker's gallant band, and he will not sacrifice such men needlessly. It is 6:30 P.M. The artillerymen, their ammunition exhausted, are falling back in good order. Walker tells both regiments to fall back to the right—toward the Crittenden house and the covering fire of the 12th Georgia Infantry and Thomas's brigade, which have stood fast throughout the debacle in the center and on the left. Some of Walker's officers are "horrified" by the order to retreat. They fear the men will panic and be slaughtered from behind. But withdraw they do, and in tolerably good order considering the "terrible fire" that continues to pound them. Two hundred yards, and Walker halts to form a new line.[58]

On Walker's left, Stonewall Jackson gallops up to turn Taliaferro's faltering men in a counterattack. This is his old division, including the near-legendary Stonewall Brigade. He knows they have more pluck than this. He tries to draw his sword, something he has never done in battle, but finds the blasted thing rusted tight in its scabbard. Unperturbed, Stonewall releases the scabbard from his belt and waves the whole affair high above his head. He lurches forward on Sorrel and cries out above the roar of battle, "Rally, brave men, and press forward!" Retreating men hesitate. They look toward him. Is it really Old Jack? The men have never seen him display such energy. He is normally "an indifferent and slouchy looking man." The battlefield has transformed him. The "light of battle" radiates from his blue eyes. "Your general will lead you," he shouts again. "Jackson will lead you. Follow me!" More men pause; a few turn back toward the enemy. Seeing their reaction, Jackson drops his reins and grabs a Confederate battle flag from the hands of its startled bearer. Waving both scabbard and flag above his head, Jackson further exhorts the troops.[59]

It is a gesture far surpassing his famous stand at Manassas. Faltering men turn suddenly resolute. Exhausted men seem revived. Scared and panic-stricken men grow ashamed. Lines reform; a counterattack begins. These men will follow Old Jack "into the jaws of death itself." Powell Hill, already stripped down to his famous red battle shirt and drenched in perspiration, sees what to do next. Unwilling to be outdone by Jackson, Hill waves his unsheathed sword overhead and pushes his relatively fresh troops into action on Stonewall's left. Captain Lenoir and his North Carolinians surge forward.[60]

The reversal of fortunes is startling. Moments ago, the Federals had the battle well in hand. Banks, unwise and unauthorized as his attack may have been, had victory within his grasp. It now appears to be slipping away. Volley after volley of Confederate fire shatters Federal lines and dreams. Federal fire is surprisingly inaccurate. Both sides advance on equal terms across open fields, yet it is the Union lines that now falter. It is not a rout; no Federal units flee in panic, as had the Rebels moments earlier. Even the wounded—and there are many—wear "stout countenances" and retain their weapons as they hobble to the rear. Yes, the Federals have fought bravely, but their lines are disintegrating. They stop firing and turn back. The thought flashes through Captain Lenoir's mind that God has intervened on behalf of a "righteous cause."[61]

Federal commanders are stunned. General Williams, the Michigan lawyer, judge, newspaper editor, and politician commanding the division on Banks's right flank, had been laughing and joking with his brigade and regimental commanders over a dinner of coffee and ham. After eating, the officers had lain beneath shady trees with no more concern or apprehension than they would have displayed on the lawn of a watering place. The order to attack had sent hearts pumping, and the initial successes were exhilarating. Then came the counterattack by Jackson and Hill. Many of the men with whom Williams shared dinner are now dead, dying, or seriously wounded. Crawford's brigade, especially the 5th Connecticut, 46th Pennsylvania, and 28th New York, has suffered most severely. Nine hundred of their combined 1,679 men are dead or wounded. Many of the wounded look ghastly. A musket ball has passed through the intestines of Private Philip Hill. He lies on the field with blood and fecal matter oozing from his side. Other men are lucky. Musket balls strike privates Michael Walsh and T. J. Duncan in the head. They tumble to the ground, stunned, but they have only received contusions, although the right side of Duncan's face is paralyzed. Crawford calls the slaughter "fearful."[62]

The 3rd Wisconsin and 2nd Massachusetts of General George H. Gordon's brigade have also been hit hard. The captain of Company E, 3rd Wisconsin, marvels as much as Captain Lenoir at the Federal reversal. One minute, his Badgers were pushing forward enthusiastically against little opposition; within moments, they were reeling backward.

The captain takes satisfaction in the orderly nature of the withdrawal. Men pause, reload, and fire as they fall back; they carry wounded comrades to the rear. Yet they are being pummeled by the Carolinians and cannot withstand the "terrible fire from the bushes and woods." As the 2nd Massachusetts advances haltingly over "an immense number of bodies" that already litter the ground, they face a long line of ghostlike Rebel battalions nearly concealed by smoke. The New Englanders' assault seems to shatter the Rebel lines, but as the regiment draws nearer, it becomes trapped in a wicked crossfire. Men are being riddled by a "shower of bullets, as if it were so much rain." The regimental flag has been shot "through and through, the staff shattered and broken." So are the spirits of the men.[63]

Irritability and recrimination punctuate the retreat. When full-bearded, dark-visaged General John W. Geary, commanding a brigade in Auger's division, is wounded in the left ankle and elbow, the pain and loss of blood force him to retire from the field. As his men carry him to safety, he shouts out to General McDowell that reserves must be sent to fill widening gaps in Union lines. McDowell, in a black mood, tells Geary to mind his own business. The exchange is sparked partly by hard feelings between "Regular" army men like McDowell and "Volunteers" like Geary, a lawyer, engineer, and politician. But the incident also betrays a rapid loss of Federal composure. Everyone has an explanation for the collapse of the Federal right. Some men blame it on confused generals who did not commit the correct brigades at the proper times. Others blame it on a lack of reserves to exploit initial gains. Still others, including General Williams, blame it on the loss of so many officers in the attack. Left leaderless, many confused men have simply wandered off the field.[64]

Black humor punctuates the reversal. General Williams cannot help but laugh at "the skedaddle" of Pope, Banks, and their staff officers as the blue tide suddenly cascades back toward them. Pope sees nothing funny in the disaster. By the time he arrived on the field, all had already been lost, and he might well curse that damned Bobbin Boy and upstart politician Banks for playing the part of Napoleon. Pope would have missed the humor in the remark of a retreating Massachusetts soldier who, as he heads for safety, calls out to an advancing column of belated reinforcements, "Give 'em hell boys, we got 'em started."[65]

The 13th Virginia knows nothing of events on the left. It can barely determine what is happening on its own small part of the battlefield, where, incidentally, the Federal attack shows no sign of weakening. It is so for the common soldier in all battles. His attention is fixed on the narrow plot of ground in his immediate front, the direction from which death will likely come. Sometimes the field is so obscured by smoke and dust that he can see no more than a few yards ahead. Add to this the thunderous boom of cannon, the terrible swoosh and bursting of artillery shells, the constant rattle and popping of small arms, the pounding of horses' hooves, the cries of wounded men, the shouts of officers, and the natural tendency to cower behind available cover whenever the opportunity affords itself, and the average soldier sees and understands little of the historic event in which he participates.

As men load and fire their weapons, often shooting blindly at undistinguishable, smoke-shrouded forms, they talk incessantly. It is much like the march to the field, or like any group of laboring men engaged in a common effort. They could be farmhands, miners, lumbermen, sailors, or ditchers bantering and chatting to pass the time. They question neighbors about the number of cartridges remaining. They call for someone to pass a canteen, even if they know not a drop of water remains in the regiment. They curse their thirst. Men pause to slam inverted rifles against convenient rocks or trees. Black powder has fouled the barrel and must be expelled. They curse their weapons. Water, if they had any, could be poured down the barrel to loosen the crud. That would also cool an overheated barrel. But they have no water, so they curse again. Men have been known under these conditions to haul out their peckers and piss in the barrel. Meanwhile, everyone gives advice to the officers. Doesn't the captain think they should move up, or fall back, or take advantage of the cover provided by that patch of woods to the right? "Looky here, Butler, mind how you shoot," a man calls back to a fellow in a rear rank; "that ball didn't miss my head two inches." Butler replies, "Just keep cool, will you; I've got better sense than to shoot anybody."[66]

Not even the generals are entirely sure of what is happening. Jubal Early finds it impossible to keep up with, let alone control, rapidly changing circumstances along the front of his brigade. He gallops down the line so that the men see him and perhaps think he is master of the situation, but he is not. In battle, units become mixed, men become separated. They have no idea where they are, who is fighting beside them, or from which direction the enemy may next appear.[67]

Oh, the survivors will tell the folks back home all about the fight. The generals will write their reports and, later, their memoirs. All will describe in intricate detail the movements of the army and the reasons for victory or defeat. They will give eyewitness accounts of heroic deeds, though some of them, if occurring at all, took place simultaneously and hundreds of yards apart. Even the "bummers" and "coffee boilers"—shirkers who have an uncanny knack for avoiding battle—will tell riveting tales of life and death struggles and hairbreadth escapes. Soldiers are such liars.[68]

The 13th Virginia, breathing hard after the retreat and braced for another assault, sees the resurgence of Winder's division on its left; but, as it now joins the counterattack, the regiment is inspired less by Winder's men and more by what it spies 200 yards ahead. Bluecoats are forming on the spot they themselves had recently, and so gallantly, defended. Walker's men are determined to recapture the worthless patch of trampled cornstalks. Barely waiting for the colonel's order, they surge ahead and drive back the offending Federals. It is not a pretty charge. It is wild and spontaneous, rather ragged if truth be told. Gaps appear in the advancing line, some caused by fallen wounded, others by men who decide to lie down or turn back. More Federal troops advance to meet the attack, but a heated fight, lasting some ten minutes, convinces the Yanks to withdraw. The 13th leaps ahead once more, this time with a whoop, "driving everything" before it and "strewing the corn field" with Yankee dead.[69]

Banks is desperate. He has decided to try one more attack, a cavalry charge against the Confederate left. Standing in the middle of the field and on a slight rise, Colonel Walker sees the threat. He has been cool under pressure all day, and he has directed his sometimes weary men with an enthusiasm that has aroused and inspired them. Once more, he prepares to rally the regiment. Waving his hat in one hand and his sword in the other, Walker cries out, "Thirteenth, left wheel!" The men respond instantly, as they do again when Walker sends them at the double toward the Culpeper Road. When but ten yards from the rail fence that flanks the road, the regiment halts and delivers a murderous volley into the horribly vulnerable 1st Pennsylvania Cavalry. The Pennsylvanians, thundering down the road in columns of four, look magnificent as they charge Winder's division, but courage and discipline are no match for an ambush. Only at the last minute have they seen the Virginians on their flank, too late to escape the slaughter. Lead riders and horses collapse in a heap. Following ranks pile into one another. Horses wheel and plunge. Orderly retreat is impossible, and all the while men and mounts remain under a heavy crossfire. The Virginians laugh and shout as they reload and fire, reload and fire. A dozen, two dozen, eight dozen Yankees fall. The Pennsylvanians gradually extract themselves, but they leave behind more than half of their 164 men. It is 7 P.M., and the battle seems to be over.[70]

8 P.M. The womb of night cradles the battlefield. Jackson orders Powell Hill's relatively fresh brigades to give chase as Banks's men pour back toward the Court House. Jackson's blood is up now. He envisions pushing Pope across the Rappahannock before morning. He sends for local men from the 13th Virginia to lead his army on a night march through Culpeper, but he is overly optimistic. Sigel's men, after finally leaving the Court House, have collided with Hill's men two miles beyond the battlefield. Both sides are startled. Skirmishers rush forward to exchange fire; gunners wheel artillery into place and blaze away. Willie Pegram, the bespectacled but surprisingly tough artillerist, calls this largely blind duel the "hottest" exchange of the day. To the exhausted infantry, many of whom are now plopping down to rest, the artillery exchange is a grand fireworks display to cap a triumphant day.[71]

Jackson decides it is "imprudent" to press the attack. Operations sputter to a close. Everyone is satisfied with the day's results, everyone, that is, except Jubal Early. Early is still confused. He has lost track of the daring and rapid movements of the 13th Virginia. Thinking that the regiment fled the field earlier in the day, Old Jubal is red hot and cursing thunderbolts. He is a good curser, and the only man ever known to have sworn in the presence of Robert E. Lee. Lee calls him his "bad old man." Now Early spots Colonel Walker in the twilight, gallops up to him, and demands to know, "Where in the hell is the Thirteenth?" Walker is dumbfounded, but he quickly senses the implications of Early's anger. "Gen. Early, damn it," he replies, himself a little hot by now, "if you want to find the Thirteenth, go closer to the enemy. It is a mile in front, holding on for you to come up. The Thirteenth don't stay with the wagon-train!"[72]

Jackson orders his men to bivouac for the night. Many men, in sore need of a spot of repose, drop where they stand. Others crave water. They submerge their faces in one of the two branches of Cedar Run, which run across the eastern edge of the plain and along the base of the mountain. They either do not notice or do not care that the creek runs red with blood. Dead men and horses litter the banks and lie in the water itself. Other men sip from water accumulated in wagon traces and shell-holes (a brief downpour of rain struck part of the field during the battle). They ignore the foulness of the muddy water. They are similarly oblivious to their clothes, crusted with mud and blood, soaked with sweat, alive with lice and vermin. Having long since learned to live with these conditions, they are "past caring" about appearance, comfort, or cleanliness.[73]

Surgeons are fully engaged by this time. They have plied their trade since early afternoon, either in hastily prepared field hospitals or in buildings near the battlefield. Most buildings in the vicinity have been converted into hospitals, including the Crittenden, Inskeep, Daniel, Nalle, and Major homes. The wounded continue to come in, some under their own power, more often leaning on a friend or carried in a blanket. But while some men shake off fatigue to tend their comrades, others seek to rob the wounded. Scavengers blend in with the humanitarians to prowl the field in search of spoils. Mostly they rifle the pockets and steal the clothes of dead Yankees, but well-equipped Confederates are not ignored in this "shameless and disgusting" ritual of war. War is not cruel, only uncaring.[74]

Jackson rides among the troops before seeking shelter for the night. Shelter is not easily found. Every house is filled with wounded, every shed already occupied by exhausted soldiers. Finally, as it has so many of his men, the sweet fragrance and beckoning softness of the grass seduces him. He slips from his saddles and lies face down on the green carpet. Someone offers food. "No," says Jackson, "I want rest, nothing but rest." To sleep when one chooses is a sweet pleasure. Everywhere, gray men try to sleep. Most will succeed, but some will spend fretful nights. Nightmare visions of the day's horrors flash through their minds. Remnants of the carnage lie all around them, and they can hear the "constant and pitiful murmur of the wounded and the groans of the dying." We will help you, whole men tell themselves, we will help you in the morning. But now I must sleep, I must sleep. We will help you in the morning.[75]

Most Federal units will make it back to the Court House before morning, although many men, clearly as worn as the Confederates, prefer grassy plots along the road. Pope and his staff, who narrowly escaped capture in the twilight, bivouac near Colvin's tavern. Federal surgeons work through the night on the most severely wounded. Less serious cases limp back to town or bounce along in the train of ambulances. Wagons and limping men jam the road. Their progress, like the march to the field, is syncopated and jerky. Columns pause every few yards so that more men, either crippled or exhausted beyond endurance, can climb aboard wagons and ambulances. Vehicles creak under increasing loads. The men talk steadily for the first few miles. They call out to friends along the route to ask the fate of other friends. They beseech the drivers and stewards for water. They talk about the battle and dispute its details, even argue about who won. Men tell tall tales of their courage or that of others. Other men laugh at their stories. Some men, moody and melancholy after what they know is a defeat, exchange accusations and mutter bitterly to themselves. Rumors circulate. Sigel has launched a counterattack, say some. The Rebels are in flight. Stonewall Jackson is wounded, captured, dead. "Oh! Get out!" comes a disbelieving response. "That's all blow. Don't try [to] stuff me! We're lathered; that's the long and shawt of it." Those within hearing nod grimly. "Boys, I guess we're beat."[76]

As the column progresses, it grows from the sudden addition of shirkers, skulkers, and coffee boilers who have been hiding in the woods and tall grass behind the lines. Some of the cowards dropped out of column during the advance; others fell back stealthily once at the front. They inquire about the battle. Learning of the defeat, they feel almost vindicated in their cowardice. They were too smart to be "hood-winked and slaughtered." "I was sick, anyway," insists one wretch to explain his sudden reappearance, "and felt like droppin' on the road." Another maintains, "I didn't trust my colonel; he ain't no soldier." A third admits, "I'm tired of the war, anyhow, and my time's up soon; so I shan't have my head blown off." The chatter gradually diminishes, partly because the men grow too weary to speak, partly because there are fewer men. They continue to drop by the roadside to sleep.[77]

CHAPTER SIX

LIBERATION

$\int$unday, August 10, has dawned fair but still hot. The field begins to stir, and everyone can see just how terrible were yesterday's proceedings. The sound of musketry crackles in the distance, but there will be no hard fighting today, you can sense that. Men often itch for a battle, for a chance to smite the foe; but a few hours of fighting quickly satiates them. Jackson is content to keep an eye on Pope. General Jeb Stuart arrived in Culpeper this morning. Jackson sends the cavalryman on a reconnaissance to fix the Federal position. Otherwise, both armies seem relieved to spend the day tending their wounded, burying their dead, and salvaging equipment. Thousands of dead and wounded litter the field. More than a few men awake to discover their nocturnal neighbor is a corpse. Many of the prostrate bodies are "mutilated and grotesquely contorted." People stare and appreciate the horror of it all, but few can summon words to describe either the scene or their own emotions. The scattered murmurs and groans of the previous night have swelled to a disagreeable fugue of agonized calls for help, for water, especially water.[1]

Veterans, men who have seen the elephant, say a battlefield crowded with sweaty, bloody, struggling men and canopied by the roar of battle is the most lonely place in the world. But it is equally lonesome and disheartening the day after a fight. Confederates silently carry or lead their wounded from the field. Some men are "so weak, or so shattered in nerve" that they cannot speak. No time now for the wounded Yankees; Confederates first. But the "agonized shrieks and groans" of the worst-suffering Federals soon require that they be dragged into the shade and given water. Confederate chaplains and stewards, men of God and Hippocrates, circulate through the fields and woods—some two square miles of terrain—in search of more dead and wounded. Those they find, they comfort, but some men are so badly injured and so far from the hospitals that they will surely die. Here and there lie large clusters of men, ghastly heaps of dead men, men who fought and died defending not their homes or sacred principles but each other. One chaplain grows angry as he absorbs the enormity of the scene and calculates the slaughter. He blames it entirely on the "fanaticism, tyranny and injustice" of the North.[2]

Soldiers and civilians come to gape. All are stunned; civilians are stupefied. They have read descriptions of battles in newspapers and in letters sent home by local heroes; they have heard blood-chilling accounts of combat from northern and southern soldiers stationed in Culpeper. Yet none of that has prepared them for what they now see. Unharvested wheat and corn fields have been leveled, their surfaces littered with the carcasses of men and beasts, destroyed or disabled cannons and wagons, splintered gun carriages and limbers, and an indescribable array of clothing, shoes, haversacks, canteens, cups, cartridge boxes, bayonets, knives, blankets, and rifles. Fences girding fields have been torn asunder, either knocked down by advancing troops or shredded into "kindling-wood" by cannon and rifle fire. Forests bear the same scars, "pierced and perforated" by lead. Symbolic of the disruption of ordinary life for Culpeper's civilians, a plow left standing on the battlefield has been sliced in half by a cannon ball.[3]

The early stages of rigor mortis lend dead men and animals a grotesque and horrifying appearance. Bodies are "torn and mangled in a dreadful manner." Men disemboweled, men decapitated, limbless men, faceless men; most people live entire lives without seeing a fellow human being so desecrated. "Looking down one of the rows of corn, I saw the first corpse," reports one witness, "the hands flung stiffly back, the feet set stubbornly, the chin pointing upward, the features losing their sharpness, the skin blackening, the eyes great and white."[4]

Yet much of the field has already been sanitized by late morning. Men have acted quickly to bury the dead, partly from humane impulse, partly because of the horrible smell that already floats on hot August breezes. A scorching sun has accelerated decomposition, and the stench of rotting flesh will doubtless infect the air for many days. The mercury has rocketed to near ninety degrees. For the sake of speed, most of the dead are tossed into long trenches or natural ravines, a dozen or more to a grave. This is the usual method of interment. Only a few "favourite officers" are allowed separate graves. Dead horses and mules, being too large to bury, are sometimes burned. The graves are shallow, covered by perhaps a dozen inches of soil. Either in haste or disgust, the burial teams leave an occasional face, hand, shoulder, or foot protruding from the ground. It is a scene "too awful for description." Dante would have been hard put to get it right.[5]

A slave boy, William Yager, one of those who watched the battle from atop the outbuildings at Forest Grove, wanders onto the field. He discovers a prostrate Yankee too badly wounded to cry out for help. There he lies, "the sun broilin' down in his face, his arms jus' agoin' it." He cannot speak, for he has been wounded in the throat. The boy has just bent down to help the stricken man drink from a canteen when, suddenly, the soldier leaps up, looks around, and, without uttering a word, walks away. Yager, nearly scared to death, races from the field.[6]

Looting continues. Some men seek trophies, evidence that they have survived the Great Death. Other, more practical folk search for food. Most Confederates are famished, not having eaten for more than a day, and Yankee haversacks and still standing corn look appealing. Clothing is also treasured. One officer, having lost his hat, spots a likely replacement lying beside a dead man. He picks it up and is about to crown himself when he sees the inside smeared with the brains of its previous owner. He drops the prize. Even generals roam the field. A. P. Hill spots a magnificent gray stallion wandering free. He claims the horse and names it Champ.[7]

The mood is generally somber and businesslike but not entirely so. A story is already making the rounds about two wounded men who dragged themselves into a barn for shelter during the night. As daylight brightens their abode, each man sees that the other wears a different colored uniform. "Johnny, where are you shot?" asks the man in blue.

"Lost my leg—where are you?" comes the reply.

"Ah, you're in a devil of a fix for dancing. I've only lost my arm."

"I'm sorry for you Yank. You'll never be able to put your arms around your sweetheart again." The Rebel pauses thoughtfully. "What did you come down here for anyway, fighting us?"

"For the old flag," the Federal answers proudly.

"Well, take your darned old flag and go home with it," shoots back Johnny. "We don't want it."[8]

At Stonewall's headquarters, a prisoner arrives to be questioned. As he waits to see the general, the man stands beside Sorrel and stealthily plucks hairs from the animal's tail. Jackson himself notices the odd behavior and asks mildly what the Yank is doing. The man, a sergeant, immediately whips off his cap and stands to attention (whether from habit or out of respect is hard to say) and answers brightly, "Ah, General, each one of these hairs is worth a dollar in New York." Speaking of horses, Dick Ewell is in a lather. Despite the heroics of the 13th Virginia, he remains unhappy with the performance of his division. When a young lieutenant botches a relatively minor assignment on this morning, he becomes a convenient target for Ewell's frustration. "I supposed, General," begins the lad in seeking to explain his sin; he gets no further. "You supposed; you supposed," interrupts the irascible Ewell. "What right had you to suppose anything about it, sir; do as I *tell you*, sir; do as I *tell you*."[9]

The Crittenden house, Cloverdale, has bustled with activity since yesterday afternoon. It is a mess. Walls have been shredded by rifle and cannon, and at least one artillery shell has ripped through the roof. The yard is thoroughly chewed up. One freshly turned patch of earth near the front door marks the grave of a Rebel lieutenant. Mrs. Crittenden is in similar shape, that is, chewed up. She is still recovering from the "awful noise" of battle, and looks, indeed, "half dead." So do most of the men who now share her parlor. Hunter McGuire, Stonewall's surgeon, has converted the room to a surgery. He tried to persuade the Crittenden women that they would find a house filled with wounded and dying men "very disagreeable," but they insisted, even "begged," that the doctor establish a hospital here. The results are as he predicted. His labors have not improved the appearance of the house. It is a "ghastly spectacle," its floors slick with blood, as he and his assistant surgeons do their best to save men's lives.[10]

The scene is duplicated horribly all through the countryside. Other houses on the Crittenden estate, as well as on other farms, like Reverend Slaughter's, serve as hospitals. Slave cabins, tenant houses, overseer's homes, corncribs, taverns, churches, anything with a roof will suffice on this day. Sarah Daniel, who sheltered neighbors in her cellar during the battle, now takes in the wounded at Forest Grove. The activity perhaps helps Sarah to forget that her husband was killed during the Seven Days. Or, if not to forget, at least to ease the ache. She is alone now with her three children, ages four through fourteen.[11]

A half mile and more away, Federal surgeons continue their frantic efforts in other parlors, in other houses. Some men are beyond help. Lieutenant James P. Taylor, 1st Rhode Island Cavalry, attracted no enemy bullets, sabers, or shrapnel during the battle, but the relentless summer sun disabled him. This was not an uncommon occurrence yesterday. Extreme heat and lack of water caused "immense suffering" in most regiments. Taylor stopped at the house of William Flint last night; he died there this morning. Similarly, a number of wounded men died from the effects of lying all night in wet grass, exposed to surprisingly cool temperatures. Many men who had been wounded in the chest or abdomen, the worst possible part of the anatomy to be hit, also died during the night. Lucy Colvin fled her house on the advice of Federal officers when the fighting started. She has returned to find her three featherbeds soaked with the blood of the wounded. Every sheet, blanket, quilt, and counterpane has been used to comfort the wounded or has been ripped into bandages. Furniture has been piled in the yard. The floors of the house are covered with blood and littered with amputated limbs.[12]

Federal surgeons have been invited by Thomas B. Nalle to occupy his fine brick house, Val Verde. It is a magnificent two-story structure built 30 years ago in the Federal style, complete with portico and four Ionic columns. The grounds are already filled with wounded, dead, and dying men. Surgeons have dragged a kitchen table outside to form a makeshift surgery beneath some locust trees. A growing pile of sev-ered arms, legs, hands, and feet measures the furious pace of their work. Stewards hold down the wounded as surgeons wield saws and knives. Some men put up desperate fights as their bodies twist and writhe, their backs arched against the pain. And there are so many. Not a few men die on blood-soaked blankets and mattresses before they can receive attention. "Blood, carnage, and death among the sweet shrubbery and roses," is one blunt assessment of the scene. No one tries to describe the cries and moans of the shattered men.

Another team of doctors working in the parlor soon transforms that room into a butcher's shop. The carpets have been rolled up and furni-ture shoved aside, but blood splatters everywhere. The operating table stands beside the piano, and surgical instruments stand on a side table and the mantelpiece, spots "lately dedicated to elegant books and flowers." Captain Nalle's wife and daughters, unionists all, work as feverishly as do the Crittenden women in tearing sheets and garments into bandages and ministering to the wounded. The lasting impression these scenes make upon the youngest Nalle children, ages four to twelve, may be imagined.[13]

Residents at the Court House, which remains in Federal hands, have the carnage delivered to their doorsteps. Ambulances, wagons, litters, whatever means can be procured, transfer men from the field of death. Trains stand ready at the depot to carry the worst wounded men to Alexandria or Washington, although many will not survive even at those facilities. "Culpeper is one vast hospital," asserts an ob-server. Or, more somberly, "The shady little town" has become "a Gol-gotha." Red hospital flags hang like ensigns from half the houses in town. The 18 rooms of the Virginia House have been stripped of all furnishings save their beds and mattresses. As he surveys the rows of bloody bodies stretched across his floors, Mr. Payne cries out with tears in his eyes to an equally horrified journalist, "My good Lord, sir! Who is responsible for this?" Payne does not expect an answer. He only ex-presses the agony of "a human heart pitying its brotherhood." Local doctors arrive to assist army surgeons, and local women, both union-

ists and Rebels, volunteer to help. One unionist marvels at the way
staunch Confederates take wounded Federals into their homes,
"notwithstanding the fact that they had been for the previous two
weeks most sadly abused" by the same soldiers.[14]

Dr. Alonzo Garcelon, from Maine, praises "the kindness of the people of Culpeper" for furnishing all they can for the "relief of our sick
and wounded." All four Court House churches are full, as are the
Piedmont Hotel and the depot's small Dixie Hotel. The Masonic Hall
has opened its doors, and a tobacco warehouse near the depot shelters
wounded. It all seems so efficient and orderly, but of course it is not.
Dr. Thomas A. McParlin, Pope's medical director, complains angrily
that medical supplies, including dressings, stimulants, and anesthetics,
are still at the front, in the supply wagons that accompanied yesterday's troops movements. No one has thought to return them with the
wounded men.[15]

Things are equally chaotic inside the hospitals. Wounded men with
any stamina call back and forth across the rooms to each other, and
they question all who enter. They want to talk about the battle. They
lie on floors and blankets stained by their own blood, and the close air
reeks of sweat, human excrement, and pus. Clouds of flies buzz around
their heads and wounds, driving already delirious men nearly mad.
Some men, despite the environment, and immobilized and weak as
they are, remain in good spirits. They eat "voraciously" any food that
is distributed to them, and nearly all beg for water. Stewards do what
they can to bring relief. Some of them carry buckets of ice water up
and down the isles. Others fan the men with cedar boughs. This provides some relief from the suffocating heat and helps to dissipate the
foul air, but flies continue to swarm.[16]

A journalist enters the Virginia House. He has been busy all morning interviewing Confederate prisoners and Federal officers. He found
the Rebels particularly interesting. About 50 of them are being held in
the loft of the courthouse. Ragged and dirty, they seem to be "weary of
the war and glad to be in custody." Some of them sit in the courthouse
cupola where they can dangle their legs over the side and enjoy a priv-
ileged view of the busy street below. They seem eager to talk to Yankee

reporters and have their names printed in New York newspapers. A few men are too garrulous. They tell not only their names but those of their brigades and commanders. Now, at the hotel, the reporter records the names of as many wounded and dead as he can identify for his newspaper. He jots down the name of one wounded man, but finds his neighbor apparently asleep. "I don't think he is alive," offers the first man; "he hasn't moved since midnight." The journalist pulls back the blanket to view the subject's face and, sure enough, he finds a corpse. "I hope they'll take it out," the first man continues dispassionately. "I don't want to sleep beside it another night." No one knows the dead man's name.[17]

The known dead will soon be mourned by loved ones far away, but grief has already struck Culpeper. Two county men died yesterday, and another was seriously wounded. The dead men are Samuel Lukett and Rufus Humphreys, both lieutenants, both 22 years old, both in Company E, 13th Virginia. How poignant that they should be cut down in a cornfield below "Slaughter" Mountain. Both men lived in the northern half of the county, where Luckett worked as a wheelwright and Humphreys helped his father manage twelve slaves and a 550-acre farm. James G. Field is the lucky man, relatively so. A nephew of Judge Field and part of an extensive family in Culpeper, the 36-year-old lawyer gave up a prosperous practice to join the army. His education— and perhaps his family name—landed him on Powell Hill's staff, but his lofty status could not shield him from a terrible leg wound. Doctors say it must be amputated, but he is expected to survive.[18]

A torrential rain pummeled Culpeper in mid-afternoon. It was a welcome relief from the heat, but of course, when the rain stopped, the heat resumed and became "insufferable." One Confederate officer thinks the rain adds to the "horrors" of the battlefield, which still remains littered with bodies at sunset. Taken together, he concludes, it has been "a miserable day."[19]

August 11. The day broke clear and warm on a scene as unappealing as yesterday's. Many dead remain unburied, and by now they are "blackening and putrefying under the sweltering sun." The "stench of decaying flesh" is everywhere, and the fierce heat has "well nigh obliterated" any semblance of human form for many corpses. Those bodies still recognizably human have not improved with age. "The eyes had bulged through their apertures in the flesh," reports one shocked observer, "distended to the size of eggs, and the hair lay long, tangled and matted with blood, over a forehead blue and yellow by exposure and hastening corruption." Elsewhere, one sees piles of dead, "heaped upon each other, and withering under a fiery sun." Only a few corpses—mostly officers—have been salvaged from the wreckage. The Federals have transported these corpses to the Court House, to be packed in charcoal and sent to Washington, where they will be placed in "metallic coffins" and shipped home.[20]

This morning, Pope asked Jackson for a truce until 2 P.M. to collect his wounded and bury his dead. Jackson agreed, but there were too many men to be attended. At 2 P.M., with the temperature well past ninety degrees, the truce was extended for another three hours. The Federals bury their dead as the Rebels have done, in long trenches or shallow ravines with a thin covering of earth. Also like the Rebs, a few Yanks receive special treatment. One man digs a single grave for the body beside him. "Pardner o' mine," he explains matter-of-factly to a curious passerby; "him and I fit side by side, and we agreed, if it could be done, to bury each other. There ain't no sich man as that lost out o' the army, private or officer." The armies pursue their grisly work side by side on this day. Both groups are cordial, even though the Federals notice that many of their men have been stripped and robbed. The adversaries mingle and talk, but no one mentions the battle. No one suggests that the surroundings and circumstances are strange or morbid. Is this studied intent? Are the men indifferent, or are they desperate to erase the memory, to finish their work and escape the assault of sights and smells on their senses?[21]

The openness elicits some surprising remarks. Many Yankees, officers and privates alike, confess that they are "quite sick of the war." Some enlisted men speak confidentially of deserting. Some do desert, to be paroled by Jackson and sent home. A Confederate chaplain tries to convert a Federal captain, one of "Lincoln's bandits," to the Confederate cause. They talk for an hour on the blood-soaked plain. The captain insists that he is fighting to maintain the U.S. Constitution.

The chaplain says Lincoln is a charlatan and a liar who has done far more than the Confederacy to subvert the Constitution. The contest ends in a draw. Yesterday, Ewell's men had stacked a considerable number (one estimate is 1,000) of captured rifles on the field. Today, some of Sigel's men try to steal them back. Ewell spots the theft, personally interrupts it, and summons one of Sigel's staff officers to have all purloined rifles returned. The Federal is all cooperation. As the weapons are loaded onto Confederate wagons—it requires six to haul them away—one Yankee laments, "It is hard to see our nice rifles going that way." "Yes," replies his friend, "but they are theirs, they won them fairly."[22]

The scene is brightened by a gathering of old friends. Generals Stuart and Early supervise the truce on behalf of Jackson; Generals Benjamin S. Roberts and George L. Hartsuff represent Pope. The four generals, accompanied by several other officers, gather along Cedar Run to chat. Stuart, as is his habit, quickly seizes center stage. The broad-shouldered, barrel-chested cavalier with the ruddy complexion, sparkling eyes, full beard, and large, joyous mustache, radiates energy. Perched casually on a log, Stuart begins to boast, also his habit, of his military prowess. He recalls, in particular, his ride around George McClellan's army on the Peninsula. "That performance gave me a Major-Generalcy," he proclaims joyfully. When Hartsuff, "fair and burly, with a boyish face," joins the circle, Stuart leaps up to greet his West Point classmate: "Hartsuff, God bless you, how-de-do?" The Federal is more subdued, but he joins Stuart in a brief turn around the battlefield while they talk about old times.

When they return to the group, still gathered about the log, a Yankee surgeon produces a bottle of whiskey from which all the generals take a swig. "Here's hoping you may fall into our hands," toasts Stuart; "we'll treat you well at Richmond!" Hartsuff replies, "The same to you!" and all the men laugh. Of course, Stuart, while joining in the gaiety, did not actually drink his ration. He is a teetotaller who consumes nothing stronger than lemonade, except, perhaps, for a little Christmas eggnog in the Virginia tradition. When Generals Crawford and Bayard, also former classmates of Stuart, join the festivities, the whole affair begins to look like a "roadside gossip" among farmers. General Early, looking something like "a homely farmer," says little. He does not even dismount. He is older than these other men; the war is less of an adventure for him. He did not want to fight the North and does not believe most northerners want to fight the South. He blames this "damned hell-fire war" on New England Puritans, the abolitionists. Perhaps Early is contemplating the insanity of the scene before him. Here are all these laughing young blades, drinking and enjoying themselves in the middle of a field strewn with decaying and stinking corpses.[23]

It is frightening to see how casually men accept the terrible sights and smells. "The fact that many men get so accustomed to the thing, that they can step about among the heaps of dead bodies, many of them their friends and acquaintances without any particular emotion, is the worst of all," considers a Federal officer. "It is only at odd times that we realize what a fearful thing it is to see 100 or 200 men, whom we have lived in the midst of, for more than a year, killed in a few moments." Yet as the shock of battle and the numbness of its aftermath recede, they write home to report on the great battle and to assure loved ones that they have survived. It is not an easy task. Words prove inadequate to convey what they have seen and experienced. "It would be vain for me to attempt to give a description of how it [the battle] looked and sounded," a Confederate admits to his cousin. He can say only "it was awful in the extreme." As for the day after the battle, "I saw some sights on the field . . . which was enough to sicken any one of this war."[24]

Other men are more articulate, but they remain shaken. They strain to come to grips with the enormity of their experience. One Rebel reports six killed and eight wounded in his company. "It was a bloody, desperate fight," he assures his friends. His regiment, the 21st Virginia Infantry, was "literally butchered." "I long to go to some quiet place," he reflects, "to rest body & mind. . . . The smoke of battle seems still around me, & my ears yet ringing with musketry & cannon. . . . I am sick of seeing dead men, and men's limbs torn from their bodies." A lieutenant in his regiment agrees. "Our whole brigade is cut entirely to pieces," he laments, "and to day has no existence as a brigade." The Federals had flanked them in the wheat field, gotten in their rear, and cut them up pretty severely. "My clothing was pierced by balls three times," he tells his brother. Miraculously, he escaped with only a painful bruise in the small of his back. The bruise, he believes, was caused by a rifle ball striking a ring in his sword belt, thus sparing his life.[25]

Captain Lenoir also recalls a narrow escape. He has returned to the field and retraced the route of his company's harrowing advance. Spotting a scarred hickory tree standing where his men first came under fire, he pries from it a bullet that had narrowly missed his head during the battle. A vivid scene flashes to mind. The battle again roars, and he recalls that before it whizzed past him and struck the tree, this same bullet passed through the head of Private William Weaver, an actual weaver in peacetime. Again, he sees Weaver collapse at his feet. "He seemed to look at me in the face with an expression that I cannot forget," cries Lenoir, "a gentle smile on his lips and a look from the eyes that seemed to ask me for aid. The blood gushing from his forehead and from the back of his head gave me too plain evidence that the look was unconscious."[26]

But perspective is everything, and some Confederates have found the clash and fury of battle exhilarating. A Virginian calls the fight "the most sublime sight I have ever seen or imagined." "It was worth all the dangers we passed and more," he insists. Just imagine, he asks his mother, "Two mighty armies rush together. Three hundred cannon pour forth their smoke and fire and thunder." The "clash and roar of muskets" and the "thunder of the cannon" is terrible, but not "*frightening*." He felt "awe" more than any other emotion. Of course, he is saddened by the loss of four men, one of them dead, from his company. A shell had exploded in their midst, he reports, and "scattered the brains and blood of poor Ralph Smith all over a dozen of us." Sad, but unavoidable. Men die in war.[27]

Generals write, too. The easily distracted Jackson must be reminded to do so. He has even forgotten to send a dispatch informing the government of his victory. He finally sat down this morning to scrawl a hasty missive. He credited God with the victory. This act has inspired him to write also to his beloved wife Anna. "God again crowned our arms with victory," he tells her in a stiff communiqué that could well pass for an official report. Many good men have fallen, General

Winder most notably. Still, "If God be for us, who can be against us?" he asks. "That He will still be with us and give us victory until our independence shall be established . . . is my earnest and oft-repeated prayer." Dick Ewell does not pray much and does not think God has a damned thing to do with winning battles. If the South hopes to win the war, it will have to fight a hell of a lot better than it did on Saturday. The Confederacy needs more men of ability in the field, Ewell tells a niece. Hell, it needs more men, period. Too many of the "chivalry" have preferred to stay close to home, or to retire there when the rain falls too hard or the bullets fly too thick. "Such horrors as war brings about are not to be stopped when people want to go home," the grizzled veteran informs her. "It opens a series of events no one can see to the end."[28]

Somber as he may sound, at least Ewell has enjoyed a victory; that is more than the Federals have to lighten the tone of their letters. Some try to see the bright side. "I am sorry I can't twist the facts into a glorious victory," apologizes one lieutenant, but the battle does, in some ways, stand as a "glorious defeat." "A hotter fire then that endured by our men," he explains, "I do not believe ever was poured in on soldiers, certainly not in this war." General Banks is unruffled by defeat. "My command fought magnificently," he insists to his wife. "Their loss was terrible. It is conceded to be the most bloody & the best fought battle of the war. . . . Everybody says we have done well, and our men are pleased." Still, while the men fought gamely, Banks believes Federal strategy is terribly flawed. "It has been so from the first," he confides to his wife, "and I do not see any certain prospect of change." If Banks sounds testy on this point, it may be because he writes from bed, where he is recuperating from bruises and aches caused when his horse tumbled on top of him during the retreat. Meanwhile, General Williams commands the corps. Banks may also fear permanent loss of his command, for Pope is currently "moving heaven and earth" to blame him for the defeat.[29]

Other men join Banks in wondering about the battle plan. General Hatch, relegated to brigade commander under McDowell, blames the defeat on the "stupidity" of commanders like General Crawford who,

Hatch decides, needlessly sacrificed their men. "It was the same old story," he grumbles to his father, "an insufficient body of men sent to do the work of twice their numbers." It is a shame, he contends, for "the resources of the South are about played out." A Pennsylvania cavalryman wonders about strategy, too. Why were reinforcements not sent to follow the initial breakthrough? he asks his diary. Why did Pope not resume the battle on Sunday? "For my part," he sighs, "I shall not pretend to pass an opinion on the opporations of our Genls, as I do not understand them." Other Yankees are less restrained. General Marsena S. Patrick, who despises Pope in any case, calls it "a bloody battle, fought without object & in its results disastrous to us." Yet, he fumes, "the lying reporters and interested parties call it 'Our Victory'." A Hoosier cavalryman, completely unnerved by the defeat, claims the Confederates had an unfair advantage. "Lincoln ought to have a *praying* General pitted against Jackson," he decides, "or else quit fighting him." Jackson, to his mind, possesses an unbeatable combination of traits, being at once "a sly rogue" and a "profound Christian."[30]

Even as Stuart and his cronies laugh and toast one another in the cornfield, Jackson prepares to withdraw across the Rapidan. Stuart's earlier reconnaissance has informed him of Sigel's arrival, and more reinforcements are doubtless en route. He has stung Pope; the Yankees are neutralized. Jackson will move back to Orange County and await Lee's arrival. Then, together, they will advance to liberate Culpeper and destroy the miscreant. Lee deserves to take a hand in that. So back trudges the army. His men are used to it. "Man that is born of a woman, and enlisteth in Jackson's army, is of few days and short rations," groans one soldier in a parody of Job that would have shocked the puritanical Jackson.[31]

August 12. Pope learned of the retrograde movement early this morning. Gloating, he reports to Halleck that Jackson is fleeing for his life "under cover of the night." Pope claims a great victory and announces preparations for a full pursuit. Halleck knows better. "Beware of a snare," he cautions Pope by telegraph. "Feigned retreats are secesh tactics." Halleck orders reinforcements to Culpeper and suggests that "under existing circumstances" Pope should send his locomotives and rolling stock south of the Rappahannock and place a strong guard at the bridge. "Do not," the general-in-chief commands, "advance your force across the Rapidan." It is just as well. As Pope's men cautiously shadow Jackson's army, some Federal units collide, become confused, and start shooting at each other. Pope heeds the omen and his orders. He knows he needs more men, and he is likewise desperate for supplies. Despite the abundance all around him, he lacks forage for his cavalry horses. He cannot provide adequate care for his wounded, and many men who must be evacuated await transportation.[32]

Clara Barton helps. By convincing Federal authorities that a woman's hand is needed in the delicate task of nursing, the New England relief worker has received permission to accompany army ambulances to the front. Nurses abound behind the lines, she argues, but many sick and wounded men who could benefit from their attention never make it off the battlefield. Learning of the suffering in Culpeper, she has raced via railroad with two assistants, a man and a woman, and piles of medical supplies. This will be her first test. She arrived at the Court House yesterday, August 13, at 5 P.M., not a moment too soon. Pope's doctors have nearly exhausted their supplies of dressings, salves, clean clothes, and stimulants. Barton went immediately to the field hospitals, where she assumed her services and supplies would be most needed. Dr. James Dunn, a Pennsylvania surgeon, welcomed this "homely angel"—Clara is not a beauty—and marvels at her emotional and physical stamina. To attend limbless men, half delirious and wallowing in blood and filth, requires "sinews of steel and nerves of iron." This little Massachusetts woman possesses both.[33]

August 14. Barton began work at the Court House today. Men still lay thick on the floors and porches of the town, both at designated hospitals and in private homes. She visits them all. Many men have, by this time, succumbed to maladies that go beyond their battlefield wounds. They have suffered from the sun, from dehydration, exposure, shock, and demoralization. Barton had no idea the suffering, chaos, anguish, and desperation were so extensive. She can touch only a portion of the horrors facing her. She even visits a ward of wounded Confederates, who have received but cursory attention from the overworked surgeons. The Rebels eye this Yankee matron suspiciously, but her kindness and attention soon bring tears of gratitude to their tired eyes.[34]

But Pope's chief problem is the railroad, or rather his own misuse of it. If Joe Johnston failed to take full strategic advantage of the Orange & Alexandria during his withdrawal from Manassas, then Pope has made a complete mess of things. He tried at first to operate the railroad himself. The result has been gross inefficiency. Trains stand idle for days before being loaded or unloaded. Trains that do arrive have not nearly enough cars. Untended roadbeds present hazards, and mechanical failures disrupt any semblance of a schedule. Even Pope now admits that something is awry, and so has asked Halleck to place Colonel Herman Haupt in charge of all railroads in the department. Without Haupt, predicts Pope, his army will likely receive neither stores nor mail below Warrenton. Pope grimaces at the pungent taste of crow. He had dismissed Haupt from this very job when he took command of the army, preferring to have his own quartermaster direct transportation.

Haupt, a 45-year-old West Pointer who earned a solid reputation in the 1850s as a civil engineer and superintendent of the Pennsylvania Railroad, is just what Pope needs. Haupt operates by three simple rules: all trains must run on schedule, all cars must be unloaded immediately upon arrival, and he alone decides which trains run where and when. Haupt arrived yesterday, August 16, in Culpeper and slept last night on the floor of Pope's new headquarters at the Nalle house. He awakens to the sickening smell of dead horses. Pope shows him the nearby battlefield. In contrast to the wreckage he views here, his job promises to be duck soup; but he underestimates the extent of the muddle. Back at the Court House, he finds the O&A paralyzed, "at a standstill; . . . scarcely a wheel in motion." The bearded, defiant Haupt analyzes the situation and tells Pope that too many officers who know nothing about railroads have been working at cross-purposes. He must have absolute control over the railroad. Pope grants it.[35]

While Haupt revives the railroad, Pope tries to revitalize his men. Most are dispirited, but as Pope continues to insist that Jackson has conceded defeat in retreat, the men seem to brighten. Some officers return to the battlefield with a photographer to have likenesses taken at the scene of their triumph. Wounded men grow more cheerful as the memory of battle and the pain in their bodies recede. They actually seem to be "proud of their wounds and more attached than ever to the good cause." They are buoyed, too, by the appearance and sentiments of Confederate prisoners. The Rebels, demoralized by their circumstances, speak in defeated and forlorn tones. Their "semi-barbarous" appearance, with ragged clothes, matted beards and hair, and dirty faces, contrasts unfavorably with Union attire and hygiene. Pope has capped his efforts to rebuild morale by reviewing each of his divisions in the expansive fields around the Court House. Nothing like a review to restore pride! The men clean their weapons, polish their shoes, and don the neatest uniforms they can muster. Regimental bands play. The men march with straight backs and confident strides. Their ranks are thinner, but some hint of gallantry and resolve has returned to their faces.[36]

Unfortunately, many troops have also reverted to their old habits of living off the civilian population, still justified, as they see it, by Pope's orders. If the new wave of brigandage has been less extensive than the first orgy, that is only because less remains to be stolen or vandalized. Certainly Culpeper's larders have been largely exhausted. "Vegetables, fruit, corn and every thing that could be used," records one embarrassed soldier, "are swept as clean as if a swarm of Pharo's locusts had been here." Up on Cedar Mountain, the Slaughter house and the minister's chapel are a mess. Federal soldiers have "completely gutted" the house. Books from Slaughter's magnificent library litter the yard. Most of them have been torn apart so that their liberated pages fly further and further from home on the wings of the slightest breeze. Some Federals say Rebels did it, but the family and the army's provost marshal know differently. At this very moment, Yankees are digging up the yard in search of buried valuables. Excavating a suspicious mound of freshly-turned earth, they find the remains of a horse killed during the battle. The discovery actually excites them. They believe a treasure has been adroitly hidden beneath the rotting carcass.[37]

It is easy to rob and bully these people, particularly the poorer folk, for the Federals despise them as rebels and barbarians. "They are about the poorest specimens of humanity I have met with," concludes one officer as he rides through the Flats, "having more of the vices of civilization, and less of that native manliness [than] we find even among the wild Bedouins." He pities these "poor white trash" in some ways, for he believes them to be the "worst victims of slavery, stigmatized by the haughty slaveholders." Yet, ultimately, he holds them in "contempt." He can hardly blame his troops for slipping out of ranks "for marauding purposes" as the regiment marches through the countryside. To his credit, he overcomes his repugnance of the people on several occasions to drive off squads of men "prowling about the farm-houses after gastro-nomic plunder," but his very attitude inspires such banditry.[38]

Some civilians rate their chances of being pillaged according to the nationality of the soldiers in their neighborhoods. The Irish are not too bad, declares Cumberland George, but he and many others fear Sigel's Germans. The Dutch, as they are called, show little restraint as they ransack houses and gratuitously destroy property, believe these Vir-ginians. Their officers seem not the least inclined to halt the maraud-ing, and the enlisted men enjoy destruction for destruction's sake. Reverend George says the Germans are "about as cleanly and intellec-tual as the overgrown sows of '*der Vaterland*'." Still, George continues, worst of all may be "the Puritans and psalm-singers of pious New Eng-land." The Germans can be excused their excesses and vulgarity as ig-norant foreigners. New Englanders can claim no such immunity. They are just vengeful, spiteful malcontents who have been jealous of south-ern prosperity and gentility for generations.[39]

Jack Pendleton has ridden into town to ask General Banks for relief from the confiscation that has already wasted Redwood. He must ei-ther have food for himself and his family, which includes Gertrude Williams, or be allowed to leave the county. Banks says he can do nothing for him, but Pendleton elects to stay in Culpeper. Others, however, now feel compelled to leave. They tolerated Pope in July be-cause they believed Jackson would soon rescue them. They also felt obliged to stay and protect their property. Indeed, they saw their homes as a refuge. Now Jackson has come and gone. Pope remains, but they have little left to protect, and that little might well be snatched from them tomorrow. The uncertain life of a refugee seems no less desperate than these conditions, so people begin to wind south and west, to Charlottesville, Lynchburg, Danville, and Staunton. Refugees with anything worth saving take it with them.

They load wagons with furniture and valuables and drive their remaining livestock before them.[40]

Not even Rebel graves are safe. A number of Federals have been inspecting the Confederate cemetery near the Court House. The fence enclosing 311 graves, all neatly laid out with head boards identifying men by name and regiment, has long since disappeared, probably gone for firewood. Some soldiers still find it a poignant spot, as from time to time they discover the resting place of a Federal soldier. One man, a New Yorker, found the grave of a former acquaintance. After informing the man's family of their soldier's fate in a hasty letter, he muses about the loneliness of death in war. "I suppose that the old man little thought when he left Cambridge [Massachusetts] that he would die a prisoner," speculates the New Yorker, "not a friend near not even his own family know with any certainty where he was or whether he was living or dead, but so the world goes." The sight of the Federal graves, or perhaps the serenity of the Confederate graves, angers some men. An officer, fearing possible vandalism, warns them "to respect the place."[41]

The decaying battlefield seems to infect everyone near it. Arriving Federal reinforcements who visit the plateau react variously. Men untested in combat express disappointment. These ordinary fields, with the bodies and most of the equipage now removed, fail to meet their expectations. They walk about, picking up small souvenirs of battle, as though collecting artifacts for a museum; but they cannot imagine the fury of August 9, and they certainly fail to appreciate the sacrifices and sorrows that have hallowed this ground. They spilt no blood here; the bodies of their friends do not fertilize the rich earth. Having paid nothing to view the scene, they cannot hold it dear. They see ordinary fields.[42]

Other men, perhaps the majority, are angered by the fields and nauseated by lingering sights and smells. Even men who have lived for several days amid these sights can be strongly affected. When, on August 17, Pope moves his headquarters from the Nalle house across the road to the "queer old-fashioned cuddy of a house" inhabited by Robert Hudson, his staff is reminded yet again of things it would like to forget. Hudson's house, like Catherine Crittenden's home a few hundred yards away, has served as a hospital. Bloodstained rags, clothes, and bedding litter the yard. Grass and earth remain soaked with blood. Three fresh graves decorate the yard, as do thirty animal carcasses in "various stages of decomposition." This is worse even than the Nalle house. Every breeze, rather than bringing relief from the heat, wafts the odor of rotting flesh. General McDowell orders the carcasses burned, but this only produces "roasted carrion instead of raw," complains one man, which he certifies "on honor, is no improvement."[43]

Perhaps the anger and disgust still inspired in these men helps to explain the new wave of destruction; perhaps it is only cold, calculated revenge for the battlefield loss. Whatever the cause, Pope has been forced to do something about it. Both he and Abraham Lincoln have felt the backlash against their policy of total war. Many of Pope's own officers have protested the policy. Rumors circulate that Jackson is holding some of Pope's captured officers as hostages against further destruction or civilian harassment in Culpeper. On August 12, Pope learned about Jefferson Davis's General Order No. 54. He and his staff scoff at it, but Lincoln cannot ignore it, particularly not when Culpeper unionists complain.[44]

Upon returning to Washington from a visit to Culpeper, and on the advice of William Seward, Douglas Wallach wrote an urgent letter to General Halleck. Rein in Pope, his missive pleads. Pope's policies may be breaking the spirit of Rebel resistance (though he errs in this judgment), but they are also demoralizing loyal people in Virginia. All of Pope's supply problems would disappear, swears Wallach, if he would treat the citizenry with civility. His army could have a hundred thousand bushels of wheat (half of it already threshed), thousands of acres of timothy (for hay), and enough beef cattle to supply it with fresh meat for three months in return for government receipts or vouchers. Yet Pope, maintains Wallach, has no plans to cut the timothy or thresh the wheat. He has no mechanics to repair reaping and threshing machines, no wagon teams and drovers to collect the produce and cattle.

Not only has Pope failed to take these steps, he has caused the civilian population to fear and distrust him. "You can hardly conceive of the waste of the resources of that region," Wallach insists. His own wife, who welcomed McDowell, Pope, and other officers into the Wallach home, has counted sixteen cattle and three horses stolen. "Marauders" have butchered a hundred sheep in the field and used but half of them. Soldiers have stolen bushels of corn, wheat, and timothy, and silverware has been "snatched from her breakfast table by the handful." She has received neither payment nor vouchers for any of this. If such treatment is accorded prominent unionists, submits Wallach, what can be the lot of obscure neighbors, loyal though they may be? "Colonels permit their men to straggle . . . after plunder, and the camp followers are under no restraint whatever. My friend Pope's order to live on the country is being plead as licensing all these improper things." Good Union people who earlier offered provisions to the government now hold back. They hesitate to take the oath, which Pope insists is necessary to receive a voucher, because they fear their fate should the army evacuate the county. Should that occur, they would then stand to lose their property and be imprisoned at Richmond. Still, argues Wallach, a measure of optimism could be restored by softening the dreaded general orders. Then, should the Federal armies continue to advance and occupy Culpeper permanently, three-fourths of the remaining population would "gladly take the oath."[45]

Wallach's advice reinforces a decision already made by Lincoln and Halleck. On August 14, the same day Wallach delivered his letter, Pope issued General Order No. 19 condemning men who had "grossly abused" General Order No. 5. The original order had been "entirely misinterpreted," Pope announced. He had never intended that soldiers should enter houses, molest citizens, or disturb private property. "Such acts of pillage and outrage are disgraceful to the army," he declares, "and have neither been contemplated nor authorized by any orders whatsoever." Two days later, Pope reprimanded the provost marshal in one of Sigel's German brigades for allowing soldiers to plunder and pillage the countryside. Yet Pope's apologies have been tardy and half-hearted. He can hardly blame his men for exceeding the letter of his orders when they so clearly acted within the spirit. Some newspapers report that the original orders have only been "slightly moderated" in any case. But Wallach is happy. Pope's orders had brought "disgrace" on the nation, he asserted in the *Evening Star*. General Order No. 19 has corrected serious "irregularities." Already, he tells readers in today's paper, August 18, the new order has "greatly checked the evil it aims to suppress, which had worked infinite mischief to the good cause."[46]

It hardly matters now, for Pope has decided to abandon Culpeper. Shortly after Pope and Jackson collided at Cedar Mountain, Robert E. Lee became convinced that McClellan would evacuate the Peninsula to reinforce Pope. If McClellan and Ambrose Burnside, already funneling troops to Pope from Fredericksburg, should combine south of the Rappahannock, Lee knew he would have the Devil's own time pushing them back across. He has decided to link forces with Jackson and strike at Pope before this potential force can assemble, and before Pope pushes his so-called Army of Virginia any deeper into the state. Lee moved to Gordonsville on August 13; today, August 18, he is in Orange County and ready to cross the Rapidan into Culpeper. Pope has learned from pickets, spies, and captured documents (taken from a luckless member of Jeb Stuart's staff) that the game is afoot. He has ordered his army to fall back and cross the Rappahannock in three columns at Barnett's Ford, Rappahannock Station, and Sulphur Springs Ford. He hopes to be safely across by noon tomorrow. He will fortify the northern bank of the river and dare Lee to attack him.[47]

August 19. The evacuation has proceeded clumsily along Culpeper's by now notoriously poor roads. Pope has 45,000 men, and they all seem to be getting in each other's way, despite the wisdom of a three-column withdrawal. Artillery and wagons clog streets at the Court House. Pope gallops among his men trying to infuse them with some "Western energy," but wagons break down en route to the river; bottlenecks form at the fords. Pope has ordered supply wagons to precede troops in the evacuation, so progress is slow, uneven, and, to the disgust of one general, "without system." Columns move a mile or so, halt, resume the march, and halt again. Halts may last a few minutes or an hour; the men never know. There is no time to relax. Everyone remains in "a state of expectant preparation." Early mornings and evenings are cooler than a week ago, but the days remain hot. The same blistering sun that pummeled both armies during the battle now beats down on the retreating Federals. Knapsacks and accoutrements weigh more heavily with each step. Dust clogs the throat; thirst is slacked at every spring and rivulet within range of wilting men.[48]

The army, moving lethargically, betrays the "characteristic and gloomy calm" of demoralized spirits. Once again it has penetrated enemy territory only to turn tail and run. Numerous rumors explain this latest retreat, but the most frequently repeated one happens to be true: Lee has arrived. This is demoralizing enough, but other stories say he has crossed the Rapidan, that he has already "thrashed" a portion of the army, that he leads an army of a hundred and fifty thousand men. Many Federal officers serve as poor models during these dark hours. They are "a pretty cynical and misanthropic set," claims a Massachusetts soldier of his regiment's leaders. "They all say they are sick of the war, and they are down on every General here, except perhaps Sigel." Where they are going, what their mission may be does not concern them: "No one knows, or seems to care much."[49]

Some men must trudge from as far away as Cedar Mountain. Darius Starr, 2nd United States Sharpshooters, is among them. It has been a disagreeable day for Starr. Marching across the Cedar Mountain plateau, he has seen friends stumble on the undiscovered remains of poor bastards who had crawled into the underbrush to die. Dead horses still litter the field, and where large numbers of horses have fallen together, the stench is intolerable. Starr wants to describe the incredible scene for his mother, but he has no writing paper. Luckily, he is able to snatch a piece of paper blowing across the field. It is the flyleaf of a Greek lexicon belonging to Reverend Slaughter. "At a little school house," he reveals, "there are several graves and when we arrived here, there were quite a number of limbs which had been cut off and thrown upon the ground, but the boys buried them when they found them."[50]

Some civilians are leaving, too. Several unionists, fearing a return of the Rebels, accompany Pope. Most of them are headed for Alexandria. Large numbers of fleeing slaves also slow the army's progress. So long as Pope occupied the county, they were content to remain with it. The army even hired blacks to work as laborers; officers hired them as servants. They are now desperate to accompany the fleeing army. They travel on foot, on horse and mule, in rickety carts and wagons. They carry few possessions, and most of those, including clothes, they have taken from former masters. Their joy at crossing the Rappahannock is hard to imagine. It is as though they have entered the promised land. One mother, having coaxed the family's ox-cart across the ford while carrying the youngest children, feels enraptured as she sets foot on the northern bank. She clasps her hands together, looks heavenward, and calls out, "Bress de Lord—we'se on dis side ob Jo'don!" Not all slaves take flight. "Uncle Ned" Hawkins, owned by a family that lives on the banks of the Rappahannock, watches the procession. He has had plenty of opportunities to slip away, but has pledged to protect his mistress and her property from the Yankees. Uncle Ned is a rarity.[51]

The exodus is slowed further, or at least punctuated, by a final round of confiscation and marauding. Stray or unattended chickens disappear into haversacks. Sheep, calves, and hogs are butchered on the spot. Men break ranks to roam the countryside a mile from their column. "Only the strictest watch on the part of the company officers can prevent this straggling," insists one captain. The men often convince citizens to sell edibles, even to cook a meal for them, by offering greenbacks in payment; but thieves prowl largely unchecked. Even if caught, they have no end of explanations, "and sometimes the excuse is so droll," confesses the captain, "that one is compelled to laugh in spite of himself." Spotting a private with half a sheep tossed over his shoulder, the captain demands an explanation. The private swears that he killed the sheep "in self-defense" when, incited by his blue uniform, it attacked him.[52]

Less humorous are departing threats of violence. Albert Gallatin Simms, a venerable and idiosyncratic Latin teacher who has operated a school for boys since before the war, receives a visit from a gang bent on ransacking his house and satisfying their lust for his two daughters. While Simms stalls the men, his daughters escape through a rear window and conceal themselves in a cornfield. Enraged by the deception, the toughs beat old Simms, plunder his house, and drive off the stock. The girls, terrified by what little they can see and hear from the fields, have decided to remain concealed there through the night.[53]

Of course, Pope's quartermaster stuffs the last train to leave the Court House with as much food, forage, and equipment as he can manage. Barely enough room remains for Pope's wounded, who must also be evacuated by rail. In fact, the most seriously wounded men, those who would never survive the journey, must be left behind.

Confederate prisoners have already been sent north. "As the rear of our column passed through, the village looked gloomy indeed," reports one fellow who has left the Court House. "All the turmoil and bustle of the last two weeks was hushed and hardly a face appeared at the windows."[54]

August 19. Lee is frustrated. Pope's spies and the captured dispatches have given him the jump on Lee, and now Lee has had trouble getting his men across the Rapidan. Confederate troops and supply trains have arrived late at the river crossings. Even his cavalry has been delayed. This morning, anxious and restless, Lee has ridden with his escort to the top of Clark's Mountain, where Jackson had earlier established a signal tower. The spot provides a magnificent view of Culpeper and the movement of Pope's columns. The sight of thousands of wagons and tens of thousands of men escaping vexes Lee. Even at such a distance, he can identify an army in disarray. Stragglers lag behind their regiments, wagons stall, and teamsters curse. "Chaotic confusion . . . emanates from the motley mass." Jackson passes the time by executing three men found guilty of desertion. His men stand in formation to witness the firing squads in action. Jackson wants them to take this lesson to heart. "Horrible sight," admits one soldier, "but rendered necessary for sake of country."[55]

August 20. Today Lee's army, fifty thousand strong, has finally rumbled forward. The cavalry has bounded ahead to nip at the heels of Pope's rear guard, and a series of sharp skirmishes have lent excitement to the chase. A portion of Fitzhugh Lee's brigade has galloped past Willis Madden's tavern to drive frantic Federal pickets across Kelly's Ford. Meanwhile, Beverly Robertson's brigade collided with Federal cavalry between Stevensburg and Brandy. Robertson threw his regiments, including the Little Fork Rangers, against the retreating Bayard. The infantry, consisting of seven divisions and two unattached brigades, is divided into two wings. James Longstreet, commanding the right wing, crossed at Raccoon Ford; Jackson led the left wing across Somerville Ford. The men exuded confidence. They joked and laughed "like a lot of school boys" as they waded across the Rapidan.[56]

Culpeper is delighted, too. Citizens pour out to greet Lee's advancing columns. "God preserve you, my boys!" shouts a grateful gentleman as each regiment passes his gate. Women dispense water to parched throats along the roadside. "Doc" Gorrell does them one better at the Court House. The druggist hauls out a large tub of lemonade to distribute along Main Street. "Just think of it!" exclaims one of his beneficiaries. "Ice cold lemonade, with plenty of lemon in it to make it sour, and plenty of sugar to make it sweet, and ice to make it cold, to a tired, weary, dirty, dusty Confederate soldier, on a hot day in August." But Gorrell cannot match the ladies in other ways. Young women rush forward waving handkerchiefs and flirting with these gallant knights and men-at-arms. Some of them positively swoon at the sight of the most handsome and famous warriors, like Jeb Stuart. Older women content themselves with kissing passing battle flags and shedding tears of joy. Men, women, and children, "many thanking God on their knees for their deliverance from the enemy," surge around their liberators. Old men and boys, all who are able to carry a gun, fall in behind the advancing columns that they might "join in the fight with the detested Yankee."[57]

Soldiers and accompanying reporters see why the people rejoice. They have heard reports of the destruction wreaked by Pope's army, and Jackson's men witnessed some of the results during the Cedar Mountain campaign. But Jackson's men had marched through only a small corner of the county. As Lee's force traverses nearly half the community, including the Court House and villages like Stevensburg and Brandy, they form a fuller picture of Federal occupation. "The people all have the same tales to tell," reports a member of the Richmond Howitzers. "They [the Yankees] took everything they could lay their hands on & not content with that would break up costly furniture, tear down banisters, kick the panels out of doors, etc." A newspaper correspondent is shocked by the "melancholy picture of desolation and devastation." The "unbridled license" of Pope's soldiers, he learns, has left the county "almost a desert." "Unoffending citizens have been impoverished in a day," he reports, "their fencing destroyed, their sheep and hogs and cattle butchered, their grain entirely consumed, their horses all stolen. . . . Many a family has been left in a condition verging upon absolute want and starvation." One officer has seen nothing like it in over a year of war. The "scene of confusion" he witnesses at one farm, with "pieces of broken chairs & furniture scattered in all directions, broken panes of glass, feathers," leaves him stunned. Outside, the fences have nearly disappeared, and not so much as a potato remains in the garden.[58]

In truth, Lee's boys do not help much. While they are not deliberately destructive, the sheer number of Confederates rolling over the countryside produces additional damage. Whatever fields have not been trampled, whatever crops have not been confiscated, whatever fences have not been dismantled, fall victim to swarming Rebels. It cannot be helped. Wagon trains cannot keep pace with the men, so after exhausting the rations carried with them, the soldiers naturally turn to farmhouses and fields along their route of march. Lee's provost marshal tries to limit theft, and Confederates usually pay for what they take. Jackson's quartermaster is even instructed to exchange salt—which the civilians need desperately—for bacon when cash payments are not possible. Still, some people despair. One elderly resident, surveying his trampled fields and the streaks where his fences once stood, remarks ruefully, "I hain't took no side in this yer rebellion, but I'll be dog-gorned if both sides hain't took me."[59]

One other disturbing episode has darkened the day. A Yankee spy, posing as a courier, tried to sow confusion and disrupt the progress of the army by carrying false dispatches to Longstreet. Unfortunately for the spy, named Charles Mason, a genuine Confederate courier carrying dispatches from Longstreet had been found shot dead. Mason aroused suspicion and was searched. Longstreet's message, a Confederate cipher alphabet, and a memorandum book recording Lee's movements since he left Gordonsville were found on Mason. His revolver had an empty chamber. This was evidence enough "to hang a dozen spies," and a drumhead court-martial, convened by Longstreet's assistant adjutant, Major Gilbert M. Sorrel, sentenced Mason to just that fate. The hasty judicial proceeding was held on the farm of Charles Doggett, outside Stevensburg, and it is there that Mason ended his life swinging from one of Doggett's trees. Passing soldiers are too hardened by battle to be much impressed by the gently swinging body, but Culpeper civilians, who soon heard of the episode, now scrutinize suspicious-looking characters passing through their neighborhoods.[60]

CHAPTER SEVEN

LOST IN ADMIRATION

August 21. The rest of Lee's army arrived in Culpeper by nightfall last night. Despite their cheerfulness, his men sighed gratefully for the night. The march had been long, hot, and dusty. The sun blistered their skin, their wool uniforms chafed, and ill-fitting shoes pinched and rubbed at every step. Men who had rarely worn shoes in civilian life preferred to walk barefoot, their footwear tied together and dangling from their rifle barrels. "O, my country, how I bleed for thee!" sang one wag as the columns snaked through the countryside. The rest of his regiment picked up the lament, though "never in a seditious or complaining way," stresses a Virginian, "for a truer or more loyal set of men never marched beneath a banner."[1]

But a bivouac meant water, food, sleep. Their arms stacked, the men prepared a supper of green corn. Their corn eaten, tired men threw themselves on the ground. They felt the weariness and fatigue ebb from their bodies, absorbed by the sweet grass and benevolent earth. They slept without tents, though each man rolled himself in a blanket. The night turned chilly and damp, and nights on campaign are always brief. The men treasure every hour of sleep as one in which they may be "lost to the world and its cares, dreaming of home." Their campfires, twinkling in the cool, fresh air, offered a picturesque sight.

As Lee gazed into the night from his bivouac near Brandy, he felt satisfied. Pope, safely at bay across the river, posed no threat.[2]

This morning, after breakfasting on rye coffee, bread, and honey, Lee ordered Jackson's wing, which had halted at Stevensburg, to join Longstreet along the Rappahannock. Stuart's men were already probing, challenging, trying to find some way to get at Pope. Some cavalry regiments actually crossed the river in anticipation of an immediate attack, but Lee has recalled them. He is anxious. He must find some "practicable fords" for his infantry and pressure Pope if he is to shift the war north, away from Richmond and the James River. Yet outwardly Lee remains unflappable. An admiring private in the 21st Virginia Infantry puzzles over Lee's apparent timidity in not plunging after Pope, but Marse Robert retains the man's confidence. "I have seen him several times today," he excitedly informs his parents, "& as he looks easy and cheerful I dare say he knows what he is about & will let the Yankees know when the proper time arrives."[3]

As artillery on both sides of the river warms up, Lee anchors his right flank between Kelly's Ford and Rappahannock Station with Longstreet's wing, then cautiously pushes his remaining forces up the river as far as Jeffersonton. He has stretched his line dangerously thin, but Pope feels obliged to do likewise. Both men place strong pickets at all the fords. Meanwhile, the artillery keeps pounding. A Federal officer finds the standoff "exciting." "General Lee is said to be in command in front of us with the whole power of the Southern Army," he confides to his diary. "Thus we are enveloped in a dark storm of war for a season." The situation is tense, fraught with danger, he realizes, but it is "better than ignoble idleness." "And if final success crowns our arms," he reasons, "the glory will be all the greater."[4]

An artillery duel favors the Federals. The river bank is higher on their side, so they have a clearer view of their targets and can coax more distance from their guns. The effect is often deadly for the Confederates, and certainly unnerving, although both sides seem to be aiming high. A "continuous and terrific" booming is heard for miles along the river. Hundreds of shells come swooshing and screaming into Rebel ranks. Even if failing to hit anyone, they rock the ground upon impact and batter the woods where Confederate infantrymen seek shelter. Broken tree limbs lurch perilously through the air; splinters and bark leap in all directions. Shell fragments strike rocks, trees, and human flesh with eerie "shrilly pings." One Confederate lad weeps over the prone body of his dead brother, struck down by the hail of shells. "Dad drat those Yankees!" he curses; "if I had known that they were going to throw such things as that at a fellow, I would have stayed in Texas."[5]

The gunners remain detached, if not exactly cool. The heat of the guns and of combat accentuate the sultriness of these summer days, but all things considered, theirs is a sanitary way to kill. They systematically elevate or depress their guns, consider the distance to their targets, and clip their fuses. A Federal cannoneer spies a Confederate brigade moving across an open plain between two sheltering belts of timber. The Rebels are halfway to safety when the shells begin to drop. The line disintegrates as men fall, retreat, and rush forward. When the guns pause, gray-clad figures dart from safety to retrieve their wounded. The Yankees, perhaps a mile away, watch dispassionately. They hear no groans or cries. They see no blood, no dismembered bodies, no splattered brains, no entrails spilling onto the ground. It is not half so impressive "as many a scene on the mimic stage." One gunner's only emotion is an "anxious curiosity for the next act of the battle-drama."[6]

The duel acquires a more personal character at other places along the line, with battery against battery, gunner against gunner. The toll is heavy. The famed Washington Artillery, of New Orleans, has lost nine men killed and nineteen wounded on this day. Not a high count in comparison to an infantry assault. In fact, the unit is able to fashion genuine coffins for its dead from the pews in St. James Episcopal Church, north of Brandy. But the loss totals more than enough men to operate a third of a three-gun battery.[7]

Jackson remains his usual stoic self through it all. He is a queer duck, no doubt about it. He sits astride his horse on a hill overlooking the river. As the cannonading continues, he and his staff prowl the crest of the hill, studying the terrain, fixing the enemy's position, looking for an opening. A solid shot whistles toward the small group and strikes the horse of Jackson's color sergeant. The sergeant, lucky to be alive, goes sprawling. So does his standard, the same one Jackson used to rally the army at Cedar Mountain. The dead horse collapses head first against Sorrel, but Jackson takes no notice. He does not even glance at the sergeant. When Sorrel, who seems to have a better conception of the danger than does Stonewall, skitters away from the falling horse and rider, Jackson reins him in mechanically, without shifting his eyes from the enemy positions.

The sergeant, seeing that his days as a color bearer are over, cuts loose his saddle, tosses it into a passing wagon, picks up the musket of an infantryman who has been felled by the same ball, and marches away with the dead man's regiment. When a staff officer tries to bring Jackson's attention to the sergeant's gallant gesture, Stonewall merely mumbles, "Very commendable, very commendable." It is his favorite expression, used to acknowledge any and all occurrences, particularly when lost in his own thoughts and oblivious to events so recognized.

Jackson now decides to push his men across the Hazel River. The shelling has intensified, and Federal infantry is approaching the Rappahannock, perhaps preparing to cross. Jackson dismounts and sits down on a convenient stump to write a dispatch informing Lee of the changed situation. Shells falling all around him throw up bushels of dirt. Another infantryman is hit, this one tumbling nearly at Jackson's feet. Stonewall continues to write. When yet another shell lands, covering Jackson, the stump, the dead boy, and Jackson's dispatch with dust and dirt, Tom Fool looks up in "an abstracted manner," stands, walks around the stump, sits down again, and goes on writing.[8]

One staff officer is frankly baffled by Jackson. Stonewall is often rude, always secretive, and notoriously unkempt. He is, in nearly every detail, the complete opposite of his mentor and idol, Lee. "He is ever monosyllabic," reports the officer to his family, "and receives and delivers a message as if the bearer was a conduct pipe from one ear to another. There is a magnetism in Jackson, but it is not personal. All admire his genius and great deeds; no one could love the man for himself. He seems to be cut off from his fellow man and to commune with his own spirit only." And yet, the officer admits, Stonewall's men idolize him nearly as much as they do Lee. He is mystified.[9]

August 22. Pope made the first move this morning by advancing portions of two brigades, the same force Stonewall saw massing across Freeman's Ford. Wading ashore north of the Hazel River, into the Little Fork, the Federals thought they had struck a bit of luck, for they had wound up in the rear of Jackson's column as it moved upriver. They pursued and were about to strike at Jackson's unprotected supply wagons when General Isaac Trimble's division intervened. Trimble saw the invaders come ashore and caught them in a cornfield about a mile from the ford. Though outnumbered three to one, Trimble is a "Tartar," and his men leapt savagely upon the Federals. After two hours of fierce fighting, the bluecoats retreated. Trimble, loath to let his prize escape him, has directed a relentless pursuit right to the river. His men pour a murderous fire into the Federals even as they stagger and reel up the opposite bank. Blue-clad bodies choke the ford. It is raining.[10]

Nearly fourteen miles to the east, Jeb Stuart's cavalry has struck Pope's rear. He and fifteen hundred men dashed across Waterloo Bridge and the ford at Hart's Mill earlier today. Their objective was Catlett's Station, on the O&A, where Stuart planned to destroy the bridge across Cedar Creek and sever Pope's communications. When his mounted warriors and horse artillery reached Warrenton, they found the town devoid of Federals, but filled with townspeople who cheered them wildly as they cantered through the streets. Then it began to rain, the same rain that dampened Pope's failed reconnaissance across the Rappahannock. The weather turned out to be appropriate, for up ahead of his prancing column, Catlett's Station was a sitting duck. The cavalrymen thundered through token resistance to capture over three hundred men, a Yankee payroll of over $500,000 in greenbacks and $20,000 in gold, huge amounts of personal equipage and baggage, tons of supplies, and untold horses, mules, and wagons. There is so much that Stuart must destroy most of the supplies and baggage.

By now, the rain falls in torrents. Stuart has ordered a return to

Culpeper. He is satisfied with the raid. It is his finest hour since the ride around McClellan's army. He is especially pleased with one bit of boodle: Pope's personal baggage, including his uniforms and dispatch book. The dispatch book includes not only Pope's correspondence with Halleck but also the numbers and deployment of his army. The very thought of Pope's reaction to this loss brings a twinkle to Stuart's eyes and curls his oversized mustache upward in delight. He heads back to Culpeper, the dispatch book, prisoners, and money chests in tow.[11]

Tonight, Stuart's men have recrossed the rapidly rising Rappahannock in the nick of time, but Jubal Early is not so lucky. His brigade, including the 13th Virginia, crossed the river on a reconnaissance in force before the rains betrayed their full potential. He is trapped, and if Pope discovers him before the river recedes, his brigade faces "inevitable destruction."[12]

If Early's men survive, however, they may well thank the rain; it has stymied everyone. The dust that tormented men for so many days has turned to mud, which gives the soldiers something new to complain about. When they walk, they sink half a leg deep in brown-and-red ooze. They cannot sit, so some men strip off their clothes and dance in the rain. They look like bedlamites on the loose, but they enjoy their first bath in days. The Confederates still have no tents, although a few find shelter in ambulances, under wagons, and in abandoned cabins and sheds. It is the "terriblest" weather one Texan can remember. His only consolation is that the Yankees are as miserable as he. As the Texan stands in a steady downpour at his picket post along the river, he can "hear their feet pop in the mud" as they labor to walk. "But," he reasons in a resigned tone, "it is a poor soldier who can't do impossible things when they have to be done."[13]

August 23. The rain continues for a second day. It prohibits fighting, but there have been some curious casualties on the day. When Trimble's division found itself cut off from its supply train south of the rain-swollen Hazel River, their quartermaster purchased a hundred acres of corn, on the hoof as it were. By noon, hardly "a nubbin" remained on yesterday's battlefield. Last night, men were so hungry that they husked the ears and ate them raw. Today they prepared the corn "in every style known to the culinary art of soldier life." One man is rumored to have devoured thirteen ears. Alas, the crop was green roasting corn. By nightfall, many men are sick, some even vomiting, and nearly everyone is "spouting his bitterest anathemas upon corn, cornfields, corn in any and every style, but especially half-done green corn." Well might the men remember yesterday's battle, if not today's agony, as the "roasting ear fight."[14]

The rains have impeded Pope as much as they have Lee. Whatever his reputation as a braggart, Pope is an aggressive soldier. He is unhappy sitting and waiting for Lee to smite him. He must either fall back or attack. He prefers to attack the Rebel left wing, under Longstreet. Perhaps he has had enough of Jackson; more likely he wants to keep his forces concentrated along the O&A. He began planning an attack yesterday, August 22, to be launched tomorrow, the 24th, but the swollen river has probably washed away all hope of a successful crossing. Then again, the rain may have saved Pope. An assault, even under the best of conditions, would have been risky. His "soldierly conception" might have changed the whole campaign, even the war, but the annals of military mediocrity are filled with failed designs. And what about the disruption of the flanking movement begun by Early? If rain had not aborted that operation, the Army of Virginia might already be reeling off toward Manassas. Pope is luckier than he knows.[15]

Stuart's raid has changed things, too. Haupt had warned Pope about the possibility of such a venture on the very morning of Stuart's crossing. Pope replied that Lee could never outflank him. Upon learning the facts, he realizes that the lost dispatch book is a serious blow. Pope was already in trouble with Halleck for allowing his staff to slip news of the government's plans to the press. No sooner would Pope receive a telegram than it would appear in northern newspapers. Halleck does not seem to have considered that the lax security is at his end of the wire. Instead, he has banned all newspaper reporters from Pope's army and ordered Pope to "clean out" his headquarters. Now Pope, in losing his dispatch book, has done more damage than a brigade of reporters.[16]

August 25. Early's men finally waded back to safety yesterday afternoon after two days of vigilant uncertainty. Despite some skirmishing and a brief exchange of artillery fire on the enemy's turf, they have not suffered a single casualty. The skies cleared enough today for Lee to attempt another crossing. Now Jackson has his infantry lumbering back across the river at Hinson's Mill, four miles above Waterloo. Stuart's cavalry has preceded him, and Longstreet is creating a diversion between Warrenton Springs and Waterloo to hold Pope in place. Jackson hopes to force Pope to withdraw by gaining his rear and cutting the railroad between Warrenton and Manassas and Alexandria. This will allow Lee to cross the river unopposed and crush the "cretin" between the two wings of his army.[17]

August 27. Pope has been diddled, while expending most of his energy over the past few days arguing with Haupt. Intent on carrying the attack to Lee, Pope wanted more men and supplies brought forward from Alexandria. But he does not understand the complexities of railroad transportation, and he would not listen to Haupt's advice. Haupt had been warned by the War Department, "Be patient as possible with the generals. Some of them will trouble you more than they will the enemy." Belatedly, Pope learns that Jackson has circled his right flank, destroyed Federal supplies at Bristoe, propelled his corps through Thoroughfare Gap toward Manassas, attacked Manassas Junction, and cut the telegraph lines at the latter point. Pope has turned to pursue Jackson in hopes of cornering and destroying him before Lee and Longstreet can slip across the Rappahannock. Lee is following Pope.[18]

Suddenly, with both armies gone, Culpeper civilians are left alone to survey the damage and reflect on events of the past six weeks. The silence, after so many days of clamorous activity, is haunting. It is as though a tornado, with its roaring, swirling winds, had touched down and left everything in utter confusion. Now, as the tornado speeds away over the hills, the last swirls of dust and chaff settle to earth. Stillness prevails. As people contemplate their scars, they see hope in the fact that they have, after all, survived. Few people have actually perished; houses can be repaired, and crops can be replanted. Some families were far enough removed from the center of the storm to have been only partially stung by confiscation. Other people tell how they have outwitted the Yanks by cleverly concealing valuables and caches of food. A few preserved property by spunk. Mary Mason may be the only person to have saved the contents of her smokehouse. Learning of an approaching raiding party, she threw all of her hams and bacon into the vegetable garden. When the Yankees galloped into the yard, she pointed at the meat and shouted, "There it is; take it!" The soldiers, suspicious that she had poisoned the meat, left it untouched, although they retaliated by severing the heads of her geese with their sabers.[19]

Life regains some semblance of order, at least it seems so. It has been so long since Culpeper was without an army or two tramping through fields and villages that people are uncertain what normal life is like. They begin to think the world may never be as orderly or predictable as it was before the war. Two hundred or so of Stuart's cavalry still picket the river fords and patrol the countryside. Many sick and wounded men also remain. But the people can at least walk about without being hit by stray musket-balls or tossed into jail.

By the end of September, most sick and wounded soldiers have left Culpeper. All the Yankees are gone. Of those left behind by Pope or captured by Lee, a few have died. Most of the deaths resulted from amputations, although one private in the 82nd Ohio Infantry succumbed to constipation. The survivors have recovered enough strength to be transferred to prisons in Richmond. Unfortunately, over two hundred incapacitated Confederates remain. Most of them suffer from the usual ailments: typhoid, diarrhea, dysentery, rubeola, pneumonia, bronchitis, "camp itch," and venereal diseases. Dr. James L. White is the chief surgeon. He had 13 doctors assisting him at the start of September, including two civilians, Thomas Herndon and William M. Thompson; but six of them have since been transferred to hospitals at Lynchburg and Winchester.[20]

Four subjects dominate public debate: salt, conscription, traitors, and the future. Salt has been a concern since spring. It is a necessity of life, required to cure meat, digest food, and maintain health. Yet the war has seriously diminished salt supplies and raised prices enormously. The problem plagues all southerners, but it is especially frustrating for Virginians, who have some of the South's most productive salt mines in the southwestern part of their state. The county court has contracted for 5,000 bushels, but only a quarter of that amount has arrived. It is not nearly enough, and no one knows when the remaining bushels will be delivered.[21]

Last April's conscription act has inspired equally passionate concerns. Pope's incursion spared Culpeper men from being inducted through the summer, but with the county once more under Confederate control, Culpeper will be expected to fill its quota. The law has caused bickering in some Confederate communities, where its exemption of overseers on plantations with more than twenty slaves is criticized for allowing slaveholders to avoid military service. Most of Culpeper does not see it that way, but people do think the county has supplied enough men to the army. The roll of Culpeper dead and disabled is far longer than anyone anticipated a year ago. Now, 250 more men, many of them terrified at the thought of going to war, have departed for Camp Lee, in Richmond, where they will be mustered, equipped, and trained as soldiers. Many of them are in poor condition, suffering from defective eyesight, lameness, asthma, rheumatism, and "almost every conceivable disease" Not a few inductees have employed lawyers to plead their cases.[22]

Whether the draftees would prefer residing under Federal occupation to being hauled off for the army is uncertain, but another set of civilians is distinctly unhappy with the return of Confederate rule. Those people who, betting on a permanent Federal occupation, have taken the iron-clad oath, or who have aided the Federals in some way, now fear for their lives. A few have already been arrested. Jacque Wood, a widowed shoemaker in his early thirties who seems to have been "very intimate" with the Yanks, is on his way under guard to Richmond. A group of partisan rangers arrested Willis Browning and threatened him with prison. They paroled him instead, but have taken his horses in exchange. William H. Browning, a prominent farmer and slaveholder, has not yet been arrested, but everyone knows he took the Federal oath. He may have done so in a moment of weakness or panic in order to save his property and spare his family, but he is a marked man. When he recently sent an agent to Richmond to collect money due him for renting slaves to the army, the government refused to pay him.[23]

As for the future, well, no one is at all certain about that. Culpeper rejoiced when it learned that Lee has smashed Pope in another battle at Manassas. Pope, it seems, is not a Hannibal or Caesar. Heck, he is not even a McClellan. Pope is simply Pope. Too bad that General Ewell lost a leg in the battle; Culpeper has come to think of Old Bald Head as one of its own. Then rumors spread that Lee planned to move immediately across the Potomac onto Union soil. That seemed almost too good to be true, but it was certainly welcome news. "The time has come for the Yankees to smell southern gunpowder & face southern steel by their own homes," asserts George Williams, "and I hope they may have to smell & feel until they are heartily sick of the war." The joy has been tempered somewhat by news of a fight at Sharpsburg, in Maryland. The Army of Northern Virginia has apparently faced down a force twice its size, and Powell Hill is reportedly the hero of the day; but Marse Robert has since fallen back into Virginia. Was it a victory or not? No one can say.[24]

It is now October, and news has arrived that General Earl Van Dorn, Connie Cary's dashing cavalryman, has been beaten at Corinth, Mississippi. Equally disheartening is news of General Braxton Bragg's defeat at Perryville, Kentucky. Then there is Lincoln's proclamation of emancipation issued on September 22. What effect will that produce on the county's remaining slaves should they hear of it? Rumors have spread of a conspiracy among free blacks and slaves near Amissville, who have apparently already learned of the proclamation. Some slave-owners, leaving nothing to chance, are sending their human property to safer regions of the state, "running the negroes," it is called. [25]

People try to view such setbacks philosophically. "So it goes," reasons a Virginia artillerymen in Culpeper, "first one side is successful, and then the other. We have had our day, the enemy now are beginning to have theirs, yet ours will come around again in due time." Maybe so, reason others, but will the Confederacy's turn come in time to end the war, or will Culpeper again be invaded and threatened with spoliation? The old debate over emigration revives. With the Yankees being held at bay, people are not as inclined to leave as they had been in August. Yet those who fled earlier do not seem eager to return, not yet anyway. Houses stand vacant across the countryside. The county court has instructed justices of the peace to "ascertain the damages sustained" in their districts at the hands of the armies, both those of the Confederate States and of the "so called United States."[26]

Some of these fears and uncertainties seem less formidable as Confederate troops begin to filter back into Culpeper in late October. Lee believes it is time to establish winter quarters, and he regards Culpeper as a good spot to settle down. Strategically, this makes sense. The weather has cooled considerably, and the Federals seem unlikely to attempt another offensive before spring. Lee wants to concentrate large forces in Richmond and in the Shenandoah Valley, but he also thinks it imperative to garrison "a sufficient force" south of the Rappahannock to discourage northern aggression. "We must select points where there is sufficient wood for hutting and fuel for the troops," he reasons, "and within convenient distance from the railroad by which they can be provided." Recalling the natural resources, railroad depot, and friendly population in Culpeper, Lee has ordered Longstreet's corps and the army's artillery reserve to return here. Jackson will occupy the Valley.[27]

Lee's soldiers have mixed feelings about stopping at Culpeper. They welcome a respite in the fighting and an opportunity to stay put. They need rest. They have spent the past few months marching from the Peninsula to Culpeper, from Culpeper to Manassas, from Manassas to Sharpsburg, from Sharpsburg to Winchester, and now, finally, back to Culpeper. And, of course, they did a fair measure of fighting during their travels. With all that freshly in mind, a lazy season in Culpeper comes as a relief. "We are just lying about camp doing nothing except drill a little and stand guard," reports one relieved fellow. "Our camp is entirely off from the main body of the army which suits me very much." As they loll around, word arrives of northern election results. Democrats have scored impressive congressional gains, especially in New York, New Jersey, and Illinois. Old Abe may be on the way out. Some men envision George McClellan, relieved of his command by Lincoln after Sharpsburg, rallying the Copperheads and breaking the Lincoln administration inside twelve months. A pleasant, warm thought on a crisp autumn night.[28]

Despite the devastation of the countryside, Culpeper also offers an opportunity for regular rations. Some soldiers express skepticism about the ability of Culpeper to feed an army. "The country is exhausted," complains General Wade Hampton when he arrives at Brandy Station with his cavalry brigade, "and I do not see how we are to live." The railroad, as Lee knows, will help on that score. So does the generosity of "the kind and hospitable people" of Culpeper. A few men complain about the high prices charged by some civilians, but other appreciate how hard Pope has hit the community. Lee has tried to ensure that neither soldiers nor civilians will be cheated. He sent all his quarter-master and commissary officers ahead of the army to acquaint themselves with local prices in Culpeper. Those officers have established a schedule of fixed prices to be paid by the army that allows a fair profit for civilian suppliers. No one anticipates fancy food, mostly bacon and shortening bread, but there should be more of it than on campaign.[29]

The fact is, Virginia is a difficult place to starve in, and Culpeper has plenty of food or anything else the army may require, if one knows where to find it. The estimates are lower than those made by Wallach in August, but still substantial. Culpeper, after all, is a big place. The further away one lives from the Court House, which had been the center of Federal occupation and raids, the better the chance of having escaped foragers and marauders. Also, many farmers, even those near the Court House, have harvested their crops and moved them, along with much livestock, out of harm's way. Marauders may have bullied people and destroyed property under Pope's orders, but they also overlooked much food.[30]

When not looking for food, soldiers who have not yet seen the Cedar Mountain battlefield pay a visit. The place has become quite a tourist attraction. Some regiments even camp and drill on the field, which is at once a curiosity and a place of horror. A Texas regiment has great sport competing to see which man can pick up the most bullets without moving from a fixed spot. Other men marvel at the bullet-riddled trees, which look as though they have been devoured by swarms of termites. More unsettling are the many disturbed graves. Rooting animals, mostly hogs, have uncovered and feasted on numerous bodies. "It really makes me feel bad to see a Yankee dead body in such a fix," concedes a North Carolinian, "much less those of our own men." Equally unpleasant, the newly exposed carcasses invest the field with a sickening odor.[31]

Companies C and E of the 7th Virginia Infantry are particularly pleased to be in Culpeper, to be back home. Even the men not from Culpeper generally hail from the neighboring counties of Orange, Madison, and Rappahannock. Their camp southeast of the Court House is soon overrun with friends and neighbors bearing gifts of clothes and food. The regiment's ranks have thinned considerably during the past eighteen months. Men have been killed, disabled, captured, transferred, and discharged. A few, to the embarrassment of everyone, have deserted. But the survivors are all veterans who appreciate the fortuitousness of their winter encampment.[32]

Still, some soldiers remain unhappy, not necessarily with Culpeper or its people, but with conditions here and with their personal circumstances. Most men are not as lucky as the 7th Virginia. They remain far from their homes, which lie as distant as Alabama, Mississippi, and Texas, and they have not seen those homes for over a year. Christmas will soon arrive. Yet Lee, for the sake of both discipline and defense, has forbidden furloughs. The fact that some generals, like Roger A. Pryor and Jeb Stuart, have been joined in camp by their wives probably causes grumbling, too, although no one complains publicly. Indeed, the men sympathize with Stuart's case. Flora Stuart has come to console her heartbroken general over the sudden death of their five-year-old daughter. Yet news of the little girl's death only reminds men of the vulnerability of their own families.[33]

"You all have no idea how bad the soldiers want to visit home," a Virginian informs his wife. "It is all the talk you can hear it around every fire but talk is about all no chance for Ferloughs now." One man misses his sister's fried chicken. A North Carolinian is happy with army life generally, but he does feel "out of the world" at times, cut off from any news "except Camp rumours." Most of all he misses a good drink, a good stiff one like he could get at home. "Please," he begs his aunt in faraway Hillsboro, North Carolina, "send me a bottle of good whiskey or peach brandy—nothing of the kind can be had up here for love nor money—and I frequently need it."[34]

Lee's no-furlough policy seems unreasonable to some, but the order has been issued as part of a broader and, from Lee's perspective, entirely necessary plan to improve discipline in the army. Lee is a stickler for discipline, and he sees too many men engaging in conduct "wholly inconsistent with the character of a Southern soldier and subversive of good order and discipline in the army." He has directed his officers to keep their men busy with useful drills and instruction and to discourage "intemperate habits." He has also forbidden gambling, profiteering, and unauthorized absences. He is especially saddened to think that a "habit so pernicious and demoralizing" as gambling "would be found among men engaged in a cause, of all others, demanding the highest virtue and purest morality in its supporters." Every effort must be made to "suppress this vice."[35]

Physical discomfort causes men to pine for home. "The weather is quite cold," complains one officer to his wife, "and the men suffer much for want of clothes and shoes." November can, indeed, be very cold in Culpeper, and it rains or snows frequently. Some men have built cozy huts, or "doghouses," for shelter. Other men must be content with tents, or even a blanket by the fire. The latter crowd groans and suffers the most. "Sleeping out on the ground," reports one unlucky soul. "Very cold . . . impossible to get any thing to eat. . . . It is enough to kill any set of men in the world." Clever men, when forced to sleep in the open, often lie on a pair of fence rails above the damp ground.[36]

Much suffering may also be attributed to a shortage of shoes. Some men have gone barefoot since marching here from Winchester. "I am Barefooted my self," a member of the 14th Virginia Infantry informs his mother, "and no way to Git any Shooes so you may know we see a hard time of it." Please send a pair of boots, he tells her; he is "well off for clothing except Shooes and Socks." Lee, ever mindful of his army's condition, has requested more shoes. Some fifty thousand pairs arrive in mid-November, but Lee complains to Secretary of War George W. Randolph that the army still has 2,000 barefoot men and another 3,000 "whose shoes are in such a condition that they will not last longer than another march." Taking further action, Lee has also placed nearly 250 men on detached service as shoemakers.[37]

So the men keep busy, try to stay warm, and fill their bellies as best they can. Many soldiers pass the time by writing letters. Even generals do that. Lee has a snug headquarters, located about a mile from the Court House and set in the middle of a "thick pine wood, so dense that you cannot see the tents till within twelve yards of them." An English journalist describes it as "a picturesque kind of Robin Hood bower." Still, like his men, Lee misses the warmth of his family and the opportunity to confide in them. Sitting at his camp desk, he writes of his hopes and fears. He tells Mary Custis that he prays the enemy will remain "quiescent" and keep to his "own country." He asks her to tell daughter Mildred not to risk visiting him, as she desires; the enemy is too near. And, oh yes, would Mary please send him two pair of drawers? He tells Mildred that he is happy to learn she is pleased with her new school. "Endeavor to improve yourself," advises papa. "God grant that we may one day be all again united in this world." He asks son Custis to contact their banker concerning the sale of some railroad stock.[38]

The nongenerals have no idea what lies ahead, only that they grow weary of a soldier's life. Many are agitated by pessimistic news from home. They talk about leaving service, or of obtaining easier assignments and playing safer roles in the fight for independence. They seek discharges or transfers because of physical infirmities, or because they believe they would be more useful to the country as overseers or factory hands. Some men take action. A soldier from Franklin County, Virginia, requests a discharge so that he might care for his widowed mother. He claims to have already served 90 days beyond his enlistment. A Georgian wishes to leave service because he cannot support his widowed mother and three sisters on the $11.00 monthly pay of a private. A major in the Jeff Davis Legion seeks reassignment to an Alabama regiment so that he will not have to winter in Virginia. Over a year of campaigning and sleeping on wet ground has caused him great suffering from rheumatism. He sends his request to President Davis himself, along with an impressive list of endorsements from Wade Hampton, Jeb Stuart, and Lee. Two members of the 13th Virginia Cavalry seek transfers to an artillery battery stationed near Petersburg for similar reasons.[39]

Despite the grumbling, consensus holds that this respite from battle is improving the condition and morale of the army. The number of men in hospital continued to decline in October, to fewer than 90 on November 1. The number has risen again, it is true, during November, largely because the winter weather has produced new cases of pneumonia, rheumatism, and like ailments; but a permanent camp means better care for these men. Sarah Pryor, the general's wife, is impressed by the army's generally high spirits. Visiting journalists acknowledge the "ragged, slovenly, sleeveless" appearance of many men, some of them "without a superfluous ounce of flesh upon their bones, with wild matted hair, in mendicant's rags." Yet they also sense an uncommon degree of confidence in this army. "I am lost in admiration of its splendid patriotism, at its wonderful endurance," reports an Englishman, "at its utter disregard of hardships which, probably, no modern army has been called upon to bear up against."[40]

Culpeper's civilians do what they can. The Richard Rixey family is one of many to nurse soldiers and entertain visitors. This winter, their house has been filled with civilians who want to be near the army, or who are looking for an opportunity to "run the blockade." The destination of the latter folk is usually Baltimore, where they may buy medicine or some other precious commodity and smuggle it back into the South. The Rixeys do their best to entertain everyone, and their parlor is ablaze with lights and gaiety on most evenings.[41]

Of course, Culpeper again benefits from the army's presence. All that food, lumber, and forage also puts cash in empty civilian pockets. An army is a healing tonic to a local economy. Corn, oats, hay, and livestock are most in demand. One farmer earns over $1,000 selling corn and hay to a North Carolina regiment. Thomas Hill earns $500 for his flour and corn, and John H. Rixey gets $1,000 for wheat, corn, and cordwood. Many other articles, some in relatively small quantities, can also be marketed profitably. Mary Foushee earns $30 by selling 102 pounds of soap to the hospital. Similarly, she earns $5.40 for fifteen gallons of milk, $6 for a dozen chickens, $2.50 for five dozen eggs, and $6 for twenty pounds of lard. Lemuel Corbin sells the army ten beef cattle for $457.50. Merchants do not fare as well as they did last year, mainly because their supplies of goods have been drastically reduced.[42]

The army pays wages, too. While not requiring the number of car-penters and teamsters it needed during the first year of the war, when Camp Henry and the hospital were constructed, it does employ some people. Philip Slaughter received $100 for a month's service attending sick and wounded soldiers. Two free blacks have hired on at the hospi-tal as laundresses. This is somewhat demeaning for one of the women, 23-year-old Adeline Veighney. She usually works as a cook, a much more respectable and better-paying position, but times are hard.[43]

The restoration of peace stimulates trade among civilians, too. A flourish of real-estate deals accompanies the departure of still more refugees. Most folks doubt the wisdom of the sellers, especially if they accept Confederate scrip in payment. Hearing of two such transac-tions, George Williams declares, "I cannot help thinking it bad policy to sell real estate now, and dont believe one dollar of this money of ours will ever be redeemed." Trade in livestock is also brisk, with thou-sands of dollars changing hands. Lemuel Corbin, who sold ten beeves to the army, has been buying livestock at a ferocious pace since Octo-ber, when many people started to bring their cattle, hogs, and sheep back into Culpeper from neighboring counties. With the Yankees gone, farmers can again safely transport crops and livestock by rail-road, at least to points southward.[44]

But just as life starts to look secure, just as people begin to breathe easy, the Federals have resumed operations along the Rappahannock. During the first three weeks of November, they seized Warrenton and probed the river fords. Raiders in Fauquier County "robbed inhabi-tants [of] everything within their reach, and burned the stacks of wheat in the field." They have been firing on Lee's pickets at the river crossings, and Federal reconnaissance forces prowl beyond the river as far as Amissville. Jeb Stuart's cavalry has been "incessantly scouting, reconnoitering, making dashes, taking prisoners. . . . perpetually skir-mishing with the enemy." In early November, his delighted men cap-tured a Federal wagon filled with Havana cigars and bowie knives, but a few days later, while venturing north of the Rappahannock, they were driven back in a "disgraceful stampede." In skirmishing shortly thereafter, a Yankee bullet neatly clipped half of Stuart's beloved mus-tache. The Federals do not appear ready to hibernate this winter. Lee has ordered all surplus supplies and equipment removed to Madison Court House. John Mosby reported after a week's "scout" that the enemy has abandoned Warrenton and seems to be moving southeast, toward Fredericksburg. On November 17, Lee ordered a division of Longstreet's corps to march to Fredericksburg.[45]

The army is ready. As cavalry skirmishes increase in number and ferocity, as news of raids in Fauquier reaches camp, the men's blood rises. They are mostly veterans. They know the business of war, and they are ready to practice their trade. "I have been fighting Yankees until I am not afraid of them at all," a member of the 10th Virginia Cavalry assures his worried wife. "I love to fight them." The men are buoyed by the remarks and demeanor of Federal prisoners. When Stuart drove the Yanks out of Jeffersonton, he captured several unlucky men, among them a colonel and his adjutant. Both of the officers, "agreeable gentlemen" from Massachusetts, believe the war can never be decided on the battlefield. Private soldiers, as they trudge through crowds of jeering Confederates, try to disguise their humiliation by looking "stonily" ahead, or by laughing with "counterfeited glee." But most wince and flush at their predicament, all of which adds to Rebel morale. On November 19, Mosby's hunch was confirmed when Federals burned the reconstructed railroad bridge at Rappahannock Station and a Federal corps arrived opposite Fredericksburg. Lee packed up the remainder of his army, less one brigade of cavalry, to join Longstreet. Jackson has moved from the Valley toward Madison Court House.[46]

Its private guard gone, Culpeper again worries, even about problems unrelated to security. The salt issue remains unsettled. Governor Letcher has intervened by obtaining 150,000 bushels of salt for distribution to counties in need. Culpeper is due to receive 1,633 bushels, but must pay a staggering $3 per bushel. A recent levy on the county for 200 slaves, needed to strength fortifications around Richmond, also worries people. Slave owners would be paid $16 per month for the labor of each slave, but the county simply cannot afford to give up that many workers, particularly not in the category specifically required by the state: able-bodied men between 18 and 45 years old. "A great many of that class ran away to the Yankees," Fayette Mauzy, acting as clerk of court, complains to Governor Letcher, "and all the rest, except such as are *absolutely indispensable* to the people of the county, have been carried away by their owners to other more southern counties for security." Mauzy fails to mention the large number of slaves, most of them recaptured from the mob that marched off with Pope, locked up in the county jail. Many Culpeper slaves are exempt from the new law in any case, for slaves working on farms devoted exclusively to the production of grain may not be impressed.[47]

And what if Lee is wrong? What if the Federal move toward Fredericksburg is a feint and Union troops swoop down on Culpeper and the O&A once again? Jane McVeigh, an aged and partially crippled widow, begs President Davis to consider this possibility and to send home her son, currently serving in the 55th Virginia Infantry, to protect her. "My home and property [have been] distroyed and dispoiled by the inhuman enemy," she tells Davis. She now finds herself "left entirely without resources of any kind and no one in the world to look to for support for myself and daughter but my son (or the cole charities of the public) with the rigours of winter stairing me in the face."[48]

George Williams, still seeking a government post that will place him closer to home, offers confused advice to Gertrude. In mid-November, he urged her to seek safety with nearby relatives or to board at the Court House. It would be "folly" to stay at Redwood, he asserted, "when opposing armies are trampling every thing under foot." Two weeks later, Redwood seemed safe after all. "I would not be precipitate in leaving home," he decided. "It is the best place you can find & two days is ample time if you have your things constantly packed & in readiness to move." Where to go is the question. By mid-December he advises her to wait for him. He has finally decided to take a position in the quartermaster department with the rank and pay of captain. He will join her in a few days on a month's furlough.[49]

Joseph Halsey thinks Culpeper is safe, though his reasoning is peculiar. The lawyer has resigned his commission and returned to Culpeper and Orange County to attend his law practice and supervise spring planting. Having surveyed the situation, he concludes that the contending armies have stripped the country so completely of supplies "that there will be no inducement for any army to stay long in this sec-

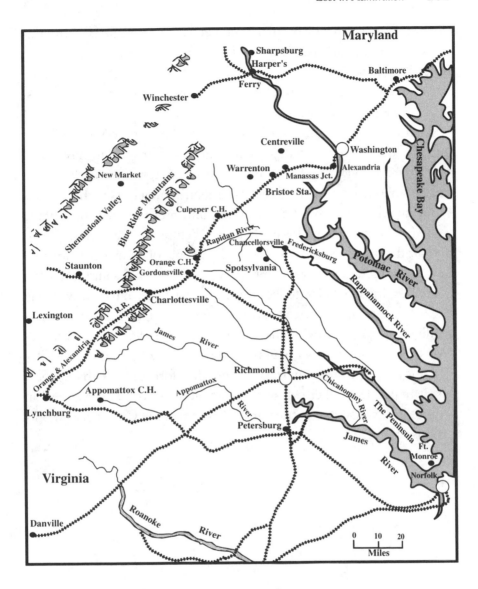

Maryland

Sharpsburg

Harper's
Ferry

Baltimore

Winchester

Centreville

Washington

New Market

Warrenton

Alexandria

Shenandoah Valley

Blue Ridge Mountains

Manassas Jct.

Bristoe Sta.

Culpeper C.H.

Rapidan River

Chancellorsville

Fredericksburg

Staunton

Orange C.H.

Spotsylvania

Gordonsville

Potomac River

Charlottesville

Rappahannock River

Lexington

R.R.

James   River

Orange & Alexandria

Appomattox C.H.

Appomattox

Richmond

Chickahominy River

Lynchburg

River

The Peninsula

Petersburg

James

Ft.
Monroe

Virginia

River

Norfolk

Danville

Roanoke   River

Chesapeake Bay

0   10   20

Miles

tion, and I have little fear of the Yankees ever again attempting this route to Richmond." Farmers should be able to plant spring crops in peace, continues his line of reasoning, for "few places are more secure than this now, and probably a living until the war is over can be as easily made here as elsewhere."[50]

That had been a universal sentiment at the start of the past year, but the season has not fulfilled expectations. This was to have been the summer of victory; it has been, instead, a year of terror. Even the brightest moments resembled but an Indian summer. Now the earth is brown and barren. The war continues, and prospects for the coming year, if not hopeless, are lower than ever before. Yet even now, just as despair threatens to consume them, the people of Culpeper learn that Lee has fashioned a magnificent triumph at Fredericksburg, the most overwhelming Confederate victory of the war. They have not yet read Lee's congratulatory message to his army, but it applies to them as readily as to the troops. "The war is not yet ended," acknowledges Uncle Bob. "The enemy is still numerous and strong, and the country demands of the army a renewal of its heroic efforts in her behalf. Nobly has it responded to her call in the past, and she will never appeal in vain to its courage and patriotism." If the people of Culpeper can only promise as much.[51]

PART III

Autumn

CHAPTER EIGHT

TO BE A CONFEDERATE SOLDIER

The war year of 1862 glides imperceptibly into 1863. The weather remains cold. It snows frequently, and the snow lingers. Even the warmest days remain chilly. It is a dismal scene, the dreariest time anyone can recall. The Fredericksburg victory has already lost its glitter. The Yanks have been hurt, but the war goes on. Blue armies continue to mass along the Rappahannock from the Chesapeake to the Blue Ridge. Culpeper, as always, sits squarely in the middle. Wade Hampton's cavalry protects the country, but he commands only a few hundred men. Is it enough? Could he really stop a determined Federal invasion? Why does Lee sit at Fredericksburg? Surely he sees that Culpeper is the vulnerable, crucial center of the Rappahannock line. The mood of the people here, soldiers and civilians alike, is autumnal.[1]

Yes, Wade Hampton is in Culpeper, and by God he resents it. Winters were never like this in Carolina, grumbles the cavalryman, but it is not just the weather that rankles. Hampton resents being cut off from the world and the army. He resents being unable to feed his men and horses as they deserve to be fed. "There is no news here," Hampton complains to his sister Mary, "except that the river is so high, the Yankees cannot get to me." Newspapers from South Carolina come but irregularly, and even the Richmond papers arrive only once or twice a week. Stuart has assigned Hampton's brigade miserable duty guarding these fords, constantly skirmishing in brutal weather. Even at that, insists the general, "I do not object to the work, but I do object to seeing my command broken down by positive starvation. We cannot get forage, and in the course of a few weeks my Brigade will be totally unfit for service."[2]

Most irritating to Hampton is the damned superior attitude of Stuart, who always gives the easiest assignments to Virginians. Hampton's brigade, consisting of Carolinians and Georgians, gets the dung end of the stick. While Hampton's men, "doing all the hard work," freeze and starve in Culpeper, Virginia cavalrymen "are quietly doing nothing," he fumes. Stuart's "partiality towards these Brigades is as marked, as it is disgusting and it constantly makes me indignant," admits Hampton. After quarreling over this issue since New Year's with the Virginia cavalier, Hampton has appealed to General Lee. Even so, no one is more loyal to the cause or more eager to get at the Yanks than is Hampton. And he sympathizes with Lee's predicament. Marse Robert, he knows, would like to follow up the Fredericksburg triumph with another pounding of the bluecoats. "I suspect he is more disappointed at the failure on the part of the Yankees to cross the river, than they are," ruminates the Carolinian, "for if we could get them well over once, I think we could break up their Army forever."[3]

Hampton reads Lee correctly, and the people of Culpeper need not fear that Lee has forgotten them. Lee understands Culpeper's strategic importance, and he is consumed with how best to get at the Federals. He has already ordered every available quartermaster wagon, some fifty of them, sent to Culpeper and to neighboring Greene and Madison counties. Lee remembers the cache of wheat he discovered in Culpeper last November. He now orders it collected and sent by rail to Richmond, where it can be made into bread for his hungry troops. He could thus feed his army and, at the same time, deprive the Yanks of the grain should they manage to punch through Hampton's cavalry. And Lee has another idea, one suggested to him by Major Henry Hill of Culpeper, now serving in Lee's commissary department. Culpeper, Madison, and Greene retain a large quantity of salt meat, either saved from Pope's occupation or recently cured. Thousands of pounds of bacon could be procured from Culpeper alone. Why not, the general urges Secretary of War James A. Seddon, purchase meat for the army with sugar? Sugar has become a greatly prized commodity throughout the South. The people would value it more than payments in Confederate currency, and by offering a pound of sugar for two pounds of bacon, the army could be well fed.[4]

Lee has also acted to blunt a growing Federal concentration opposite Culpeper. He is especially concerned about the infantry and artillery near the junction of the Rappahannock and the Rapidan. It is "probable," guessed Lee on January 20, that this force would soon attempt a crossing at either Kelly's Ford or Rappahannock Station. Federal infantry has been withdrawing from his front at Fredericksburg and marching upriver, and northern newspapers provided by his spies have convinced him that the Yanks are in motion. There can be no immediate action. The river is too high for either army to cross in significant numbers, and then there is this foul weather. The cold and snow are bad enough, but intermittent warm spells cause even more serious problems for military operations. "We are in a liquid state at present," he told Mary Custis on February 8. "Up to our knees in mud & what is worse on short rations for men & beasts. This keeps me miserable." Still, he must be ready, so he has sent Stuart's cavalry and more artillery to Culpeper. This pleases Wade Hampton. When the first of Stuart's Virginia brigades reached Culpeper today, February 11, under Fitzhugh Lee, Hampton's brigade returned to South Carolina on recruiting duty.[5]

Major John Pelham, chief of Stuart's horse artillery, is among the new arrivals in Culpeper. The tall, slender, strikingly handsome young Alabamian is a favorite of Stuart. Pelham replaced Lieutenant Robert F. Beckham as commander of the Culpeper Battery in September 1861. In the winter of 1861-62, he drilled this and the remnants of several batteries relentlessly at Stuart's Camp Qui Vive, midway between Fairfax Court House and Centreville. Since then, the gallant lad has earned an enviable reputation as an artillery commander while fighting on the Peninsula, against Pope along the Rappahannock, at Second Manassas, during the Maryland campaign, and at Fredericksburg. He has arrived in Culpeper with Major Heros von Borcke, a giant Prussian who enjoyed himself pursuing Pope's cavalry last August, and Lieutenant Thomas R. Price.[6]

The trio had a harrowing if ultimately amusing introduction to the county. As they crossed the Rapidan at Germanna Ford, a blizzard struck. They urged their mounts through the foot deep snow until finding themselves in a thick woods. The day had grown dark, and their horses were nearly exhausted when they suddenly, almost miraculously, saw a light ahead. It was Willis Madden's tavern. The old man opened the door suspiciously when they knocked. One look at the half-frozen, bedraggled spectres and he slammed the door in their faces. Pelham refused to tolerate such treatment from a "stupid old nigger," particularly in light of his company's genuinely perilous situation; but being a gentleman at heart, he decided on a ruse rather than intimidation to enlist Madden's cooperation.

Pelham knocked repeatedly until Madden again opened the door. Look here, intoned the artillerist in his sweetest Alabama drawl, this gentleman (pointing to the bearded von Borcke) is General Robert E. Lee. I am his staff officer, and our companion (indicating Price) is the French ambassador. The "general" had stopped purposely to visit Madden, announced Pelham, and was growing "quite mad" at this rebuff, which kept his entourage shivering in the night. Madden still looked doubtful, so Pelham turned the screws just a bit. If Madden did not let them in immediately, the general would be forced to shell the house with his artillery. Within minutes, the soldiers were seated around a welcoming hearth, their horses sheltered and fed, as Madden scurried to assemble a savory repast for his distinguished guests. The next morning, following a restful sleep, the men paid Madden liberally for his hospitality and admitted their hoax. However, Madden refused to believe them and bid adieu cheerfully to "General Lee" when his uninvited guests departed.[7]

At the Court House, the three men have taken rooms at the Virginia House. They attended a minstrel show last evening, February 18, "got up" by Fitzhugh Lee's men, and Pelham could not resist volunteering an impromptu skit about yesterday's incident at Madden's. During the evening, the Alabamian, who is a notorious flirt, spied a vivacious blue-eyed brunette named Bessie Shackleford in the audience. Bessie is one of a bevy of unmarried Shackleford charmers, all in their twenties and daughters of Henry Shackleford, whose townhouse is directly across the street from the hotel. Today, Pelham enlisted von Borcke to help construct a plank runway from one side of Main Street to the other. Pelham is not particularly interested in civic improvements, but this is the only means of bridging the muddy gorge that separates him from the Shackleford home. He secured an invitation last night to visit Bessie but, however great his infatuation, he would not think of tracking mud into her lovely home. Thus the bridge, and with the Prussian in tow, he has crossed the moat of desire to spend an enchanting day of charades, singing, and small talk with the Shackleford ladies. What confidences, vows, and intimacies they have exchanged no one can say.[8]

But this is wartime, and not even the grandest entertainments are very elaborate affairs. "Confederate parties," they are called. The term implies music, merriment, and dancing but little else. Refreshments are generally confined to punch or tea and sweet biscuits. No one expects fancy dress. Most of the principal generals have attended parties given in their honor. Jack Pendleton and Gertrude Williams have entertained Stuart at Redwood. Those who are excluded from even these modest functions must content themselves with a congenial exchange of waves or polite salutations with their protectors. People are especially keen on catching a glimpse of some of the county's more illustrious visitors. St. Stephen's Episcopal Church is sure to be filled on mornings when Jeb Stuart attends services. It is said that even "timid old ladies" linger outside God's house to watch Stuart mount his prancing steed and gallop away.[9]

Any display of gallantry is reassuring to Culpeper, where the New Year has thus far produced mixed blessings at best. January 1 had been quietly dreaded by the county's slaveholders, for that was the day Lincoln's arrogant proclamation of emancipation was to take effect. As people now go about their daily chores—preparing for a new planting season, securing what goods may be obtained from local shops—the possible consequences of the decree hovers like a gray cloud over Confederate spirits. People wonder what the blacks may know of this pronouncement. Do blue-clad troops across the Rappahannock intend to liberate Culpeper slaves? The blacks had been content during Pope's occupation to slip quietly away with the departing army. Could they be encouraged this time to perpetrate dastardly deeds and heinous crimes? There is no telling what the hateful Yankees might do or say to incite them.[10]

Whether as a show of scorn for the Yankee policy or as a sign of fear that slave property is now endangered, some Culpeper slaveholders have recently engaged in a trading spree. Lemuel Corbin has sold a "sound and healthy" girl named Fanny to Robert Yancey for $1,450. Corbin, in turn, is considering a purchase from John J. Gordon of eight blacks worth $4,500. There is only one man in this bunch; the remainder, save one child, are women.[11]

More joyfully, another spurt of marriages, like that following Pope's departure, has excited the county. Eight couples have exchanged vows thus far, and no fewer than twelve pairs hope to wed before May. As was the case last year, surprisingly few of the grooms currently serve or have ever served in the army. Only in the first year of the war did separated sweethearts seem anxious to secure claims on each other. Several weddings involve older widowers or men above the age of conscription. An exception happens to be the most anticipated wedding of the season, scheduled for late May, when Annie Crittenden will marry the handsome Major James Richard Smoot. Everyone regards Annie as a heroine after her spunky performance in the Cedar Mountain fight. Smoot, who hails from Alexandria, is a lucky fellow. But the reality that death accompanies war has set in for many young people. More than one Culpeper woman now weeps in widows weed's.[12]

At our fireside, sad and lonely,
Often will the bosom swell
At remembrance of the story
How our noble Willie fell;

How he strove to bear our banner
Thro' the thickest of the fight,
And uphold our country's honor
In the strength of manhood's might.

We shall meet, but we shall miss him,
There will be one vacant chair.
We shall linger to caress him,
While we breathe our evening prayer.[13]

News from the North has recently buoyed spirits. The populace there has grown restless over Lincoln's inability to win the war. Democrats won gains in last year's elections, and a copperhead congressman from Ohio, Clement Vallandingham, is rallying antiwar sentiment throughout the section. Richmond newspapers, copies of which have found their way to Culpeper, provide excerpts from a recent Vallandingham speech in New Jersey. Jeremiah Morton, who spoke passionately on behalf of secession two years ago, lauds Vallandingham's harangues as "magnificent." He and other people have begun to think that the war will not last "much longer."[14]

County churches are trying to revive themselves financially and spiritually. What with last year's military occupation and the constant threat of danger since then, most churches had abandoned their business meetings and even canceled some worship services. Crooked Run Baptist Church has suspended its meetings because so many members had been "harassed and driven from their homes by the public enemy." Elsewhere, churches have suffered physical damage, either through malicious destruction or by deterioration attendant to their use as barracks and hospitals. Some preachers are worn out, too. Seventy-year-old James Garnett, Jr., has stepped down as pastor of Gourdvine Baptist in favor of Barnett Grimsley, Daniel's father, a powerful and eloquent speaker. The war has taken its toll on Garnett, who has seen the Federals drive off his 30 slaves and inflict some damage on his house, Spring Hill.[15]

Some congregations are now trying to revive worship services and business meetings. There is much business to conduct. Many churches have mortgages to pay. Money for repairs is essential. And, as at Gourdvine, departed ministers must be replaced. Most ministers welcome the business meetings as added occasions to address the faithful. "God is our refuge and strength, a very present help in trouble," reminds the Psalm as preached at the Baptist church in Criglersville. "Therefore will we not fear, though the earth be removed, and though the mountains be carried into the midst of the sea." And surely the Good Book is speaking of the swollen Rappahannock when it promises, "*There is* a river, the streams whereof shall make glad the city of God, the holy *place* of the tabernacle, of the most High." And of Culpeper, as the promised holy place, "God *is* in the midst of her; she shall not be moved: God shall help her, *and that* right early."[16]

A pressing issue for many churches is the black exodus. Of course, the exodus is a financial blow to church members, but as their personal financial fortunes are diminished, so too are those of the churches. The congregations also feel betrayed by their departed black brethren. Separated from whites though they may be during worship services, with no voice in church affairs, their names on church rolls mere appendages of their masters' names, blacks have still been baptized and counted children of God. The churches continue to believe that slaves brought into fellowship are more loyal than those entirely excluded from the white community. At Crooked Run Baptist Church, no fewer than four families plan to have their servants baptized.[17]

But severe steps are sometimes necessary. The Criglersville church decided last December to expunge from fellowship the names of all slaves who had "absconded from their owners, & gone off with the abolitionists." The issue was again raised at the February meeting. A slave named Diley has been ordered to attend the next church meeting to answer a charge "of being instrumental in the conveyance of a portion of her masters younger servants to the abolitionists." Members have also been reminded of their responsibility as expressed by Paul (Galatians 5:4): "Christ is become of no effect unto you, whosoever of you are justified by the law; ye are fallen from grace." Wisely, the pastor ignored another verse in the same chapter: "Stand fast therefore in the liberty wherewith Christ hath made us free, and be not entangled again with the yoke of bondage."[18]

Churches and congregations at the Court House have suffered most. Portions of gray-bricked St. Stephen's Episcopal on East Street, the oldest church building in town, have served almost constantly as barracks, hospital, or refuge since the first months of the war. Similarly, the rectory has sheltered many terrified citizens in its cellar. Portly

John Cole, the rector, immigrated to Culpeper from Delaware in the 1830s. He liked Culpeper and probably would have stayed here in any case, but his marriage to Fannie Thompson in 1855 settled the matter of residence. Cole is not a dynamic speaker. George Williams thinks he should have retired years ago, that he has "sounded his dull discourse in the ears of the people for so many years [that] . . . a new man is required to awaken them." But Cole has done much to keep the community together during the last two years. He will not leave Culpeper or his congregation, whatever personal danger he may face. To demonstrate his loyalty to the government, he has even invested $500 in Confederate bonds.[19]

The remaining Confederate soldiers, clustered in camps around Brandy Station and Stevensburg, are as uncertain about the future as their hosts, and not nearly so enamored of Culpeper. Richard Watkins, a 37-year-old member of the 3rd Virginia Cavalry from Prince Edward County, has been chilled by snow, soaked by rain, immobilized by mud, and choked by smoking campfires. "Quite a gay time," he grumbles good-naturedly to his wife. He asks her to imagine him "sitting down on a little pile of wet straw surrounded by damp blankets & wet saddles" with a pair of saddlebags as a writing desk. The men finally have tents to shelter them from the rain, he assures her, but dampness pervades everything, and the tents do not retain heat. The only warmth comes from the smoking campfires, though he and two mates plan to remedy that problem. They have torn down an abandoned brick oven on Pope's old campground, and acquired a wagon to haul the bricks to their tent. As soon as they find a brick-mason, they will construct "a real high falutin head quarters chimney."[20]

And Watkins knows he should not complain, at least not until the next campaign. He dreamed one night not long ago that he had applied for a furlough—a luxury he has not enjoyed in a year—only to have it disapproved by General Lee. Marse Robert had attached a note to the disapproved request saying that *he* had not enjoyed a furlough "since *the war commenced.*" The dream sobered Watkins. After all, he reasons, he is well clothed, with a stout pair of boots, an overcoat, thick warm pants, plenty of shirts and socks, even a "warm night cap." Duty is light, "nothing but a little picket duty, a squadron at a time."

He acknowledges the usual miseries and mishaps of camp life. Some men cannot take the cold and damp, and they suffer for it, but a reasonably healthy and cautious man can survive. No, thinks Watkins, army life is not bad. "Who wouldn't be a Confederate soldier & contend for his rights & his home & his country," he decides in his puckish way. "I grow so patriotic that I can hardly restrain my pen after my paper is exhausted. Hurrah for Jeff Davis & southern rights." Now if only the rivers will ride high through the spring. Or the snow. Perhaps a blizzard will immobilize both sides for a few more weeks at least.[21]

February 23. Watkins' daydreams, like his nightmares, have been shattered by yet another Lee, Fitzhugh this time. It has started to snow again, heavy snow, at least a foot deep. Watkins has heeded it not. He has spent the day resting snug and cozy in his tent, which, besides its now completed fireplace, has recently had a foot of dry wheatstraw applied to the floor. He and his tentmates, smug over their good fortune, have been planning a hunting expedition for tomorrow to lay in a supply of rabbits and possums. So what if this evening Watkins is detailed to picket duty? He has heard that pickets in his area enjoy the comfort of a vacant house and are "well protected from the weather." Enter Fitz Lee, restless, ambitious Fitz Lee. He has ordered his brigade, including the 3rd Virginia, to commence a three-day "scout" across the Rappahannock tomorrow. Oh, do the boys grouse about that order. "Fitz Lee must be drunk," declares one soldier. "Hell, all generals are crazy," retorts another man. "Our horses will all perish," predicts a third trooper, "and the men too for where can we sleep?"[22]

Actually, it was Stuart who ordered the reconnaissance. He predicted that Lee's men would face "extraordinary obstacles and difficulties" on their mission, but the army must learn the Federal strength, and so across Kelly's Ford plunged 400 gray cavalrymen. Less than 48 hours later, they have returned in glory. Lee caught the Yanks by surprise near Hartwood Church, drove in their pickets, routed the encampment, and pursued the foe to within five miles of V Corps at Falmouth. He bagged 150 prisoners, along with their horses, arms, and equipment. The brigade returns in a torrent of rain, the horses "almost swimming" across the Rappahannock; but Lee has lost only 14 men.

The 3rd Virginia suffered no casualties. Watkins personally captured an iron gray horse, complete with "a beautiful Yankee saddle (right new) with a splendid Yankee bridle (right new), with two large very heavy dark grey blankets (new)." Life is surely sweet. Who would not be a Confederate soldier?[23]

By the time Fitz returns, Constance Cary is stopping once more at Bel Pre. Most of the Wise family has refugeed to Augusta County with their slaves and livestock. Two daughters, Annie and Fannie, and a family servant, "Uncle" Jeff Fowler, remain to welcome Constance. She hopes to run the blockade to Baltimore, but her journey has been stalled by "the united forces of such a snow, mud, and rain, as the oldest inhabitant himself recks not of." Constance is unhappy. She has a head cold to start with, but even worse is the forced inactivity and resulting boredom. Constance hates boredom. Her hostess is most hospitable, and there is admittedly something inviting about a "glorious, crackling, spluttering noisy" fire in an oversized fireplace in such foul weather. Yet her naturally high spirits droop when she thinks of the contrast between "fluttering, busy, sociable" Richmond and this "country fireside, an odd volume of Mrs. Southworth, and a long evening lit by a solitary tallow dip!"[24]

Now comes Fitz. Connie is a bit smitten with this cavalryman, what with her earlier heartthrob, Earl Van Dorn, seemingly destined to remain out West. Van Dorn is a cavalryman, too. Connie loves "rowdy cavalry-men, all boots and spurs, who dash about in a halo of mud." Their very look, scent, and bearing is erotic. In any event, "General Fitz," as she calls him, with his "soldierly dash" and "jollity," has rescued her from boredom. He and his staff visit Bel Pre nearly every evening for conversation and song, and as the weather slowly warms, he begins to escort her on rides through the countryside and on visits to his camp, where she participates in shooting matches. (He presents her with a miniature Smith and Wesson revolver.) When it comes time for Miss Cary's departure on March 8, Lee provides her with his prize mare, Refugitta, to ride on the journey and a comfortable ambulance for her aunt, with whom she is traveling. He assigns several of his staff to escort the ladies as far as Warrenton, by way of Jeffersonton.[25]

Other people have been running the blockade to Baltimore through

Culpeper all winter. Medicine, clothing, visits to friends, the object of the journeys varies, but this region of north central Virginia seems more open to civilian passage than does the countryside around Richmond. Rixeyville, north of the Court House, is an especially popular spot to rendezvous. Most parties travel by wagon, and Richard and Margaret Rixey always seem able to recruit some tough old teamster who knows the roads and can conduct the pilgrims to safety.[26]

For those left behind, there is not much to choose between the roaring March lion and the tigress that was February. Brutal weather continues as more Confederate soldiers, including the Little Fork Rangers, converge on Culpeper. The Federals are curious about Culpeper's swelling population, and so send patrols across unguarded river fords to survey the rebel buildup. Residents along the Rappahannock grow worried. Civilians near Jeffersonton, which impressed Constance Cary only as a "poor deserted hamlet," complain that they never know what a day will bring. One morning, gray riders stop to feed their horses; that afternoon, bluecoats pass through.[27]

Most Confederate soldiers in Culpeper enjoy the relatively light duty but curse the weather. Having built fireplaces for their tents, like Richard Watkins, they are snug enough inside, but the frosty air still stings when they step outside, even on clear, sunny days. There is "nothing to break the winds between us and the mountains," complains a lieutenant from Powhatan County, "so the cold bleake winds from the summit of the snow clad peaks come sweeping down upon us in all its fury and seems to blow through a person and nearly chills the blood in ones veins." Some men grumble about the lack of food, which remains principally biscuits and beef. "I have got sixty dollars left of my money," a man in the 15th Virginia Cavalry informs his sister in Rockingham County," yet I tell you that I have been spending money like the devil spending for things to eat and washing my clothes." Forage for cavalry horses is equally scarce, and most of the units here are cavalry. "The horses are a starving," continues the man from the 15th. "They only git a little hay evry other day." And it is not just the animals that are threatened. "They say that all that dont furnish horses has to gow in to infantry," he reports with alarm to his sister, "and I dont want to gow in infantry."[28]

Jeb Stuart and John Pelham are back in Culpeper. Stuart has returned to serve as a witness at a court-martial, and he insisted that Pelham accompany him. He is obsessed with the ridiculously handsome boy. Were it not for their mutual reputations with the ladies, the pairing might inspire gossip. Stuart has spent much of his time visiting and going to parties. He seems to know everyone, especially the ladies; and everyone knows him, especially the ladies. This evening, March 16, after dining at the Virginia House, Pelham insisted that he, Stuart, and Colonel von Borcke, who has joined them, accept an invitation to visit the Shackleford home. Pelham has just returned from a visit to a sweetheart in Orange County, but the randy major, "as grand a flirt as ever lived," led the older men across his old plank bridge (Main Street remains a morass) to resume his courtship of Bessie. The Shackleford parlor, a haven as on evenings past, reverberated with music and song. Bessie played the piano and the assembled company harmonized on patriotic airs like "Dixie," "Bonnie Blue Flag," and "Yellow Rose of Texas." Bessie could not take her eyes off Pelham. She is fascinated by this "splendid boy" with the flawless manners, sparkling blue eyes, and golden-brown hair. After treating their worn voices to coffee and crackers, the visitors have departed, Pelham riding out to Redwood where he will spend the night.[29]

March 17. Yesterday had been uneventful for Private Lawson Morrissett of the 4th Virginia Cavalry, but at about the same time the Shackleford house began to ring with music, a portion of his company, Company B, received orders to cook three days' rations and mount up. "Yankees coming," was the word. Sure enough, at dawn this morning, General William W. Averell, seeking revenge for Fitzhugh Lee's February raid, has thrown 2,100 cavalry and a battery of artillery against Confederate pickets at Kelly's Ford. Averell feels confident striking at this point. He knows the land beyond the ford, having fought there last summer. He believes he knows, too, how Fitz Lee, a former West Point classmate, will respond. Averell will anticipate Lee's moves, counter them, and whip him.[30]

But as Averell's men approach the chilly water, all manner of obstacles thwart them. Lee's pioneers have felled trees at the crossing to form abatis on both banks. More deadly, 15 sharpshooters from the 2nd Virginia Cavalry open fire from rifle pits on the Confederate shore. They pour death into the uncertain attackers, even though James Breckinridge, their captain, knows that "15 men in little holes in the ground" cannot hold back the Yanks for long. Detachment after detachment of Federal pioneers move forward to hack through the abatis. Three times Averell's men exploit their progress only to be turned back. Finally, at about 7:30 A.M., and on the fourth attempt, Captain Simeon A. Brown and three other men from the 1st Rhode Island Cavalry clamber triumphantly up the west bank. The remainder of his regiment quickly follows, and Breckinridge's men are out of ammunition. Only three Rebels, including Breckinridge, escape capture.[31]

10 A.M. Averell has his entire force in Culpeper, despite having to cross the swiftly moving current of the Rappahannock. The wheels of his caissons and guns were submerged during the crossing, and the powder in the limbers had to be removed and carried across in nosebags by the cavalry. Yet Averell has lost only ten men, three of them dead, with 15 horses wounded or killed.[32]

Noon. Fitzhugh Lee, contrary to Averell's expectations, has anticipated his classmate's movements. Warning came yesterday morning from army headquarters below the Rapidan that something was afoot. Lee's own scouts brought him definite intelligence yesterday evening that Averell was at Morrisville, six miles from Kelly's Ford. Thus the orders to Private Morrissett to mount up. His regiment has since been joined by the 1st, 2nd, 3rd, and 5h Virginia Cavalry. By now, as Averell moves northwest up the Kellysville road, Lee, accompanied by Stuart, is in position to greet him.[33]

"General, I think there are only a few platoons in the woods yonder," Fitz observed to Jeb as they surveyed Averell's advance. "Hadn't we better take the bulge on them at once?" Stuart agreed, so Lee sent forward a portion of the 3rd Virginia on foot as sharpshooters. They opened up on Averell's men, mostly New Yorkers and Pennsylvanians, about a half mile from the ford. The Federals have taken cover behind a handy stone wall that runs from the road to G. T. Wheatley's ford. The still mounted portion of the 3rd Virginia now charges, but Federal fire, the stone wall, and a ditch traversing their path forces the horse soldiers to wheel left. The Yankees enjoy a strong position. Besides the wall, their left is anchored in heavily wooded terrain.

The 3rd Virginia has escaped heavy casualties, but among the fallen is John Pelham. The impulsive Alabamian had abandoned his unfinished breakfast at Redwood when he learned that Stuart and Lee had headed toward a possible battle. As Lee's skirmishers commenced action, Pelham rode to the rear to check on the progress of his artillery. He returned to the front in time to see the gallant rush of the 3rd Virginia. Caught up in the excitement, Pelham drew his saber and joined them, "the shout of battle on his lips." Within moments he lay very still, struck in the back of the head by a shell fragment. The wound is barely visible. A small rivulet of blood runs down from the hairline; but the boyish smile has vanished, the gay laughter has been silenced, the roving blue eyes are closed.

Meanwhile, five regiments of Confederate cavalry, severely outnumbered, continue a series of sporadic charges. Some of the assaults are met head on by Averell's men. Much of the fighting is close, saber to saber, horses thrashing and lunging against one another. On Averell's left, Colonel Alfred Duffié's brigade throws back the horsemen of the 2nd and 4th Virginia. A Federal charge against the Confederate left meets a similar fate, but the Rebels are falling back steadily toward the farm of James Newby, nearly two miles from Kelly's Ford, before a determined Union advance. Lee positions an artillery battery on a hill to his right rear. Four guns pound Averell's center as gray riders fan out to strike the Yankee flanks. The Rebels also set fire to a stubble field in hopes that the smoke, rolling back before a stiff wind, will scatter the Yanks; but Averell's men have beaten out the flames with their overcoats.[34]

A short time ago, as the smoke snaked upward and gradually dissipated in the March wind, a cavalryman who saw Pelham downed rushed to retrieve the body. Determined that the heroic lad's remains would not fall into enemy hands, he swung it over his own horse's neck and made for the Court House. Halfway there, he was stopped by Captain Harry Gilmor, who insisted on examining the body. Pelham lived! Gilmor frantically requisitioned an ambulance and had the lad taken to a place he knew would welcome him—the Shackleford house. Since then, three surgeons have probed and examined Pelham while Bessie tenderly bathes his brow. They have found the shell fragment, no larger than the tip of one of Bessie's dainty fingers; but it is buried two inches deep in Pelham's skull and has severed many nerves.[35]

By this time, Lee has stymied Averell's advance. The Yankee general decided to withdraw at about 5:30 P.M. He still outnumbered Lee better than two to one, and he had six guns to Lee's four; but his horses were exhausted, and he lacked infantry to press the attack. His artillery had caused little damage, it was running out of ammunition, and much of what ammunition remained was defective. Some of his shells were too large for the pieces, and his fuses, some spending themselves in two seconds rather than five, were unreliable. Averell also fancied that Lee would momentarily receive reinforcements. By 7:30 P.M., twelve hours after forcing a crossing, the Federals have recrossed the Rappahannock. Six men are dead, 50 wounded, and 22 captured. Averell has failed to "rout or destroy" the Rebels, as his orders instructed, but he claims to be pleased. His cavalry fought the vaunted Confederate horsemen to a standstill and, with precise maneuvers and obvious courage, pushed them back in their own territory. He is in such high spirits that he leaves a package for Fitzhugh Lee at the river ford. Lee had left a note for his old classmate following the Rebel raid near Hartwood Church. It read, "If you won't go home, return my visit and bring me a sack of coffee." Averell has replied, "Dear Fitz: Here's you coffee. Here's your visit. How do you like it?"[36]

Lee is also pleased with the performance of his 800 men against 2,100 Federals, but he has defended Culpeper at a high cost. He mourns 11 killed, 88 wounded, and 34 captured. Only one Culpeper lad, 21-year-old Dallas Coons of the 4th Virginia Cavalry, is known to have been seriously wounded. The persistent charges of his men—wild, unbridled Celtic charges on this Saint Patrick's Day—have also resulted in the death of 71 horses, with another 87 wounded and 12 captured. And, of course, one loss looms above all others: Major John Pelham. Stuart rushed, grief-stricken, to the Shackleford house to verify rumors of a fatal wound. About 1:00 A.M., a dozen hours after being felled, Pelham opened his eyes briefly, drew a deep breath, and was gone. This morning, Stuart has assigned von Borcke to accompany the body to Richmond, where it will lie in state. From there, Pelham will be returned to his native Alabama. Stuart will order his horse artillery and division staff to wear a badge of mourning for 30 days. He will also request that Culpeper's own Robert Beckham, now a major, who had favorably impressed Stuart at First Manassas, succeed Pelham as chief of horse artillery.[37]

Jeb Stuart tells Flora that his men "whipped" Averell's division and inflicted a "terrible loss" on it. He is honest enough, however, to admit his own losses. Pelham, of course, but also Colonel Tom Rosser and Major John Puller, both of the 5th Virginia Cavalry, received severe wounds. As one soldier reported to his sister, "General Stuard ses that it was the hardest Caveldry fite that he ever saw." The death and suffering has even led the seemingly unflappable Stuart to a brief moment of introspection. He weighs, possibly for the first time, his own chances of surviving the war, and tells Flora that it is "extremely improbable" that he will outlive her. He does not suggest violent death in battle as his likely end; that would be too cruel. But she will know what he means. He asks her to promise that whatever happens she will never desert the South, and that she will raise their children "on southern soil."[38]

After this brief disruption, life for soldiers and civilians has resumed a measure of routine, if not outright tedium. Fields must be plowed, though so much recent rain—with apparently more to come—makes this slow work. Virginia mud can latch on to plows, men, and mules like a vise. In the cavalry camps, life is "very dull." "Every thing quiet," reports one man. In late March, President Davis proclaimed a national day of fasting and prayer. General Lee suspended all duties not essential for "safety and subsistence," and regimental chaplains took advantage of an extra day (the observance fell on a Friday) to hold religious services. Now, in early April, speculation about the army's next move flies through the camps. It is hard to know. One day the men receive orders to strike their tents, cook three days' rations, and be ready to march at dawn. A few hours later, with all preparations having been made, the orders are revoked. Snow still falls occasionally. March came in like a lion, remarks one man, and is going out like one. Ra-

tions for man and beast remain minimal. Picket duty along the Rappahannock and Hazel rivers is the only real work to be done. "We are in
no hurry to leave here," insists a member of the 3rd Virginia Cavalry
who likes this kind of Sunday Soldiering, "as we will have to give up
most of our tents and all baggage not absolutely necessary."[39]

Men maintain their spirits with the usual camp diversions. A
trooper in the 3rd Virginia Cavalry owns a violin, so his regiment enjoys "music and dancing almost every night." "I wish you could see
them dancing by moonlight," one man tells his family. "The hardships
and self-denials through which they are passing are all forgotten. Some
are acting the part of ladies and others of gentlemen and on goes the
dance till a late hour." Robert Lee's winter decrees against gambling
are still in force, with variations. Colonel William C. Wickham has
told his regiment, the 4th Virginia Cavalry, that he has no objection to
them "playing cards or other forms of amusement within the bounds of
innocence," although he cannot permit "actual gambling."[40]

Fraternization with the Yanks causes consternation among Confederate officers. Their men are supposed to hate the bluecoats, or at least
distrust them. Yet blue and gray pickets along the Rappahannock have
been launching little sailboats, made of planks and rags, from one side
to the other. The cargo of these trim craft is rumored to be coffee and
sugar, with each side swapping its bounty to obtain that which is
scarce. This sort of exchange has thrived since the first day of the war.
Wise officers generally turn a blind eye to the traffic, but the military
situation here is tense. The men must be impressed with the need to
maintain discipline. So today, when some company officers discover
their pickets exchanging newspapers—a possible source of information
about the army's movements—they send a provost guard to arrest the
unsuspecting sentries. Across the river, one can see a Union boat-
builder being led to the rear in similar fashion.[41]

The lack of activity is causing other problems, even creating friction
between soldiers and civilians. With the arrival of spring, cavalrymen
who have watched their horses starve all winter turn them loose in local
pastures. Citizens complain, and General Lee has ordered the practice
to cease. All company commanders, he says, shall be responsible for the

security of farms near their camps. If necessary, he tells them, they must "establish guards who will arrest all persons" violating the orders.[42]

But the biggest danger of this peaceful interlude is that it gives men time to think about the hardships of army life, of how much they miss snuggling up to their wives on chilly nights, of how lucky they are to have survived the war up to now, and how that luck could change in the next skirmish or battle. John Pelham never imagined dying in battle. "I am happy that I can write to you but I hope it wont be long until I will have the pleasure of seeing you and then we can talk over things," one man tells the young lady waiting for him at home. "O how I wish this war was ended and I could return home safe and . . . enjoy the sweet comforts of life." Sure poison, but who can blame a man for feeding his fancy?[43]

Young officers feel the same way. Lieutenant Richard Watkins resolves several times a day to resign his commission and serve the Confederacy in a capacity that will keep him closer to Prince Edward County. He survived the charge of his regiment against the stone wall on Wheatley's farm, but that brush with death has caused him to think more than ever about his family and his own farm. Watching Culpeper farmers plow their fields and commence planting makes Watkins anxious about his place. Has the tobacco been cured, he asks his wife? How are the winter oats? Has the corn been planted? How is she? How are the children? "[I] dread the thought of our Brigade moving lest it may go still further from you," he sighs to wife Mary. "Oh I wish you could write to me every day and tell me exactly how you look, & how you feel, and what you are doing & thinking & saying." Again, sure poison.[44]

Luckily for the army, the men gradually shake off their melancholy and reconcile themselves to the fact that they have a job to do. The task is easier for country lads who have never led a gentle life in any case. "We sleep very well on a hay bed," confesses one farm boy. "We have a stove in our tent. We have right good eating a plenty of bacon and bread and sausage. . . . I had rather be in the Army than home attending to the farm." In this second week of April, the veterans sense impending action. The remainder of the cavalry arrived from Fredericksburg between April 9 and 11. Stuart and his staff headed straight for the Virginia House and, shortly thereafter, the Shackleford house. One of Stuart's staff found Bessie to be a "gay young lady," evidently fully recovered from Pelham's death. By April 13, taking their mission a bit more seriously, everyone has settled into the cavalry camp, a quarter mile southwest of town and known since March 17 as Camp Pelham.[45]

Culpeper's civilians wonder how much longer they can cope with war. It has been two years since Robert Anderson surrendered Fort Sumter, two years that Virginians have been fighting for their independence. Yet Union cavalry and artillery still launch regular attacks against principal fords on the Rappahannock and Hazel rivers. More rain and rising rivers have stymied most Federal efforts, but when the rivers recede, the county could be invaded and reoccupied once again. The most intense pressure has been felt at Rappahannock Station and Kelly's Ford. Colonel Judson Kilpatrick's cavalry, with some men fording the river, others scampering across the bridge, momentarily broke through the crisp rifle fire of sharpshooting Confederate pickets at Rappahannock Station. But they were few in number, and the arrival of Rebel reinforcements sent them reeling back. The fighting there has settled into a series of long-range artillery duels. Hearing that the Yanks are headed toward her home near Kelly's Ford, Fannie Jennings prays that Stuart's men will keep them above the Rappahannock. "We ought to be faithful Christians," she tells a friend to boost her own courage, "to discharge our duty to Him in behalf of this Country as well as for ourselves." But even if they escape another invasion, frets Fannie, the war has taken a dismal turn. Friends have been conscripted. It is impossible to find a Baptist preacher near her home (although a Methodist may be preaching in Brandy by summer). Prices are outrageous, "larseny," says Fannie, with flour selling at $35 to $40 a barrel, butter at $2 to $3, and sugar at nearly $2.[46]

Fears and doubts run highest in the northernmost reaches of the county, where people, distant from the Confederate camps clustered east of the Court House, remain most vulnerable to Yankee patrols. Sally Armstrong, an 18-year-old living on her father's farm, Rose Hill, near Waterloo, finds that her mood fluctuates daily. One moment she sings merrily, flirts with furloughed soldiers, or makes jelly for a neighboring lad who is convalescing from a wound he received on a raid with John Mosby. By the following evening, she is "very much frightened" to learn that Yankees are in Warrenton and marching toward Culpeper. A few days later, the war seems less threatening than an April storm that dumps eight inches of snow on the countryside. The untypically April weather has left her with a "wretched cold," but the occasional appearance of Confederate patrols provides enough reassurance for her to work in the family garden, attend prayer meetings, visit friends and relatives in Jeffersonton, and wander into the mountains to pick wildflowers.

Then comes another round of rumors, interspersed with actual sightings of bluecoats. While visiting Jeffersonton, Sally learns that a Yankee patrol has been spotted on the bluffs across the river from her family's house. Consternation and excitement prevail. Will the Yankees dare to cross? Will she be safer hurrying home or staying where she is? "People begin to dread these Yankees as they would a famine," she asserts. Sally decided to sit tight in Jeffersonton on that occasion, but today, April 21, acting on reports that the Yankees have fled, she starts back home. Upon reaching her uncle's house at Waterloo, she discovers that Federals still prowl the neighborhood. "In the evening about 30 went by," she tells her diary. "Uncle Joe [Settle] got the horse in the cellar when they were in sight. Two men came by in the evening and demanded a ham. Aunt Judie gave them a shoulder."[47]

Robert Lee, still with his infantry at Fredericksburg, shares Sally's concern. What worries him even more than Union patrols are the Yankee prisoners taken in the Rappahannock fights who carried eight days' rations. The Federals clearly have big plans. Lee also notes that the forces in the recent abortive attacks against Culpeper have been cavalry and artillery, not infantry. This means that the real Federal target lies elsewhere than Culpeper. Fredericksburg? Lee is uncertain. He does not know the new Federal commander, General Joseph Hooker, very well. It is hard to anticipate his moves. Lee must locate the bulk of Hooker's army, his infantry. "My only anxiety arises from the present immobility of the army," Lee admits to President Davis, "owing to the condition of our horses and the scarcity of forage and provisions." Lee wants more cavalry, for he knows that the Federal horsemen far outnumber his own, and that their mounts are fresher and better fed. The Army of the Potomac has reorganized its entire cavalry corps and placed it under the command of General George Stoneman. Stonewall Jackson knows Stoneman. They were classmates at West Point. Stoneman is not a particularly clever man, but with an entire corps at his disposal, he need not be clever. He need not even be lucky. He could be dangerous when the Rappahannock recedes.[48]

Monday, April 28. After two days of increased patrols along the river the impatient Federals have struck. "No Yankees today," Sally Armstrong reported in her diary last night, "how can we be thankful enough to our heavenly Father, who keeps these savages from destroying us!" Yet even as Miss Armstrong relaxed, Stoneman acted. Avoiding a direct assault against the fords, Federal infantry—the infantry that Lee has been seeking and that has now joined the Federal cavalry opposite Culpeper—has crossed the Rappahannock in boats and on a rapidly constructed pontoon bridge below Kelly's Ford. By this morning, two corps (XI and XII) were in Culpeper. With this diversion, Stoneman's cavalry has navigated the ford with ease. Stuart is aware of their arrival by 9 P.M., but, uncertain of the Federals' next move, he orders units to advance only as far as Brandy Station.[49]

April 29. A dense fog blanketed the land this morning, so it was early afternoon before Stuart discovered the vanguard of Hooker's army slashing across the top of Chinquapin Neck, headed toward Germanna Ford. Hooker seems bound to cross the Rapidan and drive eastward against Lee's flank at Fredericksburg. Stuart tried to slow the advance by piercing the marching columns near Madden's tavern. Alas, he struck too late and too weakly to have much effect. The Federal cavalry alone numbers some 10,000 men. Lee, informed of the situation, has decided to abandon Culpeper. He has ordered Stuart to join the main army at Fredericksburg. He tells Fitzhugh Lee to lead his remaining regiments (the 9th and 13th Virginia) across the Rapidan to protect the railroad near Gordonsville.[50]

Despite Federal haste to cross the Rapidan, about 4,000 blue cavalry have lingered long enough to cause some anxious moments. Stoneman divided his cavalry in crossing the Rappahannock. One column, led by General John Buford and accompanied by Stoneman, made for the Rapidan and has crossed it with dispatch. The second column, a division led by General Averell, has proceeded by way of Brandy Station toward the Court House. His men were cantering toward Brandy when they encountered Confederate skirmishers, who have by now been joined by the main force. The Yanks have formed a line of battle in anticipation of a full attack, but it is too late for that. The air has turned bitterly cold; a fine sleet falls incessantly. Neither side wants to fight. Averell has fallen back to the edge of a wood where his men, without shelter and clutching the bridles of their unsaddled horses, sleep as best they can. Many men have not eaten in 24 hours.[51]

Morning, April 30. The rain has stopped, but it will be a cloudy day. Sally Armstrong feels safe again. Yesterday she could hear cannonading echo upriver from Freeman's Ford, but today she will go fishing with her cousin Emma Latham. Averell's men are on a fishing expedition of their own. In the saddle by dawn, they continued toward the Court House. The Confederate troops who blocked their path last night have melted away. Averell pays his respects to Culpeper's best-known unionist John Minor Botts as the column swings past his Auburn estate. All his men see of the Rebel cavalry are the remains of dead horses, which lay "thick and unburied" along their route. "The country looks old, war-torn and wasted," observes one officer, "but not so bad as the other side of the river." Most of the houses they pass are deserted, or at least seem to be. They see few white folks.[52]

They reached the Court House late this morning, and have captured a Confederate rear guard. There are still few white civilians to be seen, but numerous black people and dogs greet Averell's men as they ride along Main Street. One New Englander thinks the town "quite a Yankee looking place," with its steeples, whitewashed buildings, and regular streets. Averell has ordered the telegraph lines cut, as he has all along the line of march. His men confiscate a mail sack, 60 barrels of flour, and large amounts of pork and bacon. The hungry bluecoats are allowed to take as much of the confiscated food as they can carry, but then, in a striking show of generosity, Averell distributes the remainder to those whom he considers "the poor people of the place." Averell presses on southwest toward Cedar Mountain.[53]

Afternoon. The 3rd Indiana Cavalry, which suffered heavily in an attack at Beverly's Ford a fortnight ago, forms part of Averell's command. These men have delighted in their gallop through Culpeper, but like most of the other horsemen, they declare it "the hardest ride" they have known. Passing over the Cedar Mountain field, they note some unpleasant sights. "All parts of the human skelton strewed over the field," reports one man, "which hogs have rooted from the [ground]." Men in other units, including the 1st Rhode Island Cavalry, recall comrades who died here; their bones may be the ones gnawed by the hogs. "Such it is to die for one's country!" snorts an officer. He notices that the horses will not eat the grass here.[54]

Evening. As the column moves past the battlefield, still pursuing the retreating Confederates toward Rapidan Station, a heavy rains falls. Some squadrons begin to straggle. As the first riders now approach the river, at about 7:30 P.M., the column stretches back several miles. The horses are exhausted; the men are "tired and hungry." A brief reconnaissance has revealed stiff Confederate resistance ahead. Rebel infantry and artillery are dug in along the south bank of the Rapidan. Light skirmishing has ensued, but Averell has no intention of forcing his way across tonight. His men, once again without shelter from the rain, seek comfort in the muddy, swampy Flats, "the worst camping ground I ever saw," proclaims one soldier. Unable to locate even a patch of dry ground, the men content themselves with finding the "least wet" spots.[55]

May 2. Hooker is angry. He had expected Averell to cross the Rapidan on April 30, three days ago. Averell could have crossed easily yesterday against token resistance. Perhaps he was being cautious; perhaps he wanted to rest his command. Whatever his thinking, Averell's men spent a second night in the Flats. This morning, Averell has pursued the Rebels indirectly by swinging east and marching past Germanna

Ford to Ely's Ford, where he arrived at 10:30 A.M. Now, in early afternoon, the last invader, as well as the last defender, drifts away. The tide of war rolls away from Culpeper toward the sound of pounding guns at Chancellorsville.[56]

CHAPTER NINE

PERPLEXED, BUT NOT IN DESPAIR

The cannonading to the east has not ceased during the early days of May. Though muffled by distance, the sound is ominous. All know that some great issue is being decided. One day, two days, three days, the guns continue. Is it possible? Can a single battle last so long? Who has won? Surely Lee. But would he not return to Culpeper were it so? The people have come to look upon Lee's army as their private guard, a local militia. Surely, if unable to hurry back from his expedition, he would send word to explain the delay. Instead, only the sound of guns drifts westward from . . . where? It sounds like Fredericksburg. Yes, surely Fredericksburg. That would be a real plum for the Yanks, south of the Rappahannock, a position they have been unable to secure by way of defiant little Culpeper. And having been whipped so thoroughly there last December, the Yanks doubtless would like to capture Fredericksburg as a means of salvaging their honor.[1]

Sally Armstrong grows anxious. She wonders when the guns will stop, and why, indeed, they seem to be moving closer. "We have driven the enemy back," she reports to her diary on May 6, but in which direction? Back across the Rappahannock? Toward Richmond? Or toward Culpeper? Did the Yankees slip away from Lee, and now, though doubtless defeated, find themselves positioned between Lee and Culpeper?

How will the wounded beast turn? How will it unleash its fury? "There are a good many of us here," reports Sally, "some desponding, but most of us in confident hope we shall whip our enemies, if God will continue with us."[2]

Fannie Jennings is just as scared and confused as Sally. She has heard "a thousand rumors" about the fate of the army. "It is very dull & lonesome," she tells a soldier friend on May 6, "get no papers & hear nothing that is reliable. I have the Blues as bad as anyone can have them." Fannie may work in her garden tomorrow in order to relieve the tension and pass the time. "It is very discouraging to do anything," she complains. "It is really appalling in this part of the County for a person to live here. The two armies sweep everything away from a body." Fannie has come to believe that the war and its attendant troubles have been pressed upon the community "for the sin of the people & the termination will be through the power of the Lord in the deepest humility of prayers of Christians."[3]

May 7. News of glorious victories at Chancellorsville and Fredericksburg has arrived, but so has the shocking report that Stonewall Jackson, indestructible, saintly Stonewall, has lost an arm in the fighting. But the news comes in driblets and satisfies no one. What are the casualties? Were any Culpeper boys in the fight? What price victory? "Surely these are stirring times," writes Sally; yet she senses, even though her own father is too old to fight and her brother Jonathan too young, how anxious must be the vigil of people with men in the army.[4]

May 9. Still no reliable word. "I feel uneasy," confesses Sally. "It is more difficult to hear from this fight than any we have had."

Sunday, May 10. Sally goes to church, but few others attend; there is no sermon. May 13: This is the saddest day of the war. Stonewall, that "good Christian" soldier, died yesterday. All Culpeper mourns.

Sunday, May 17. Still no sermon for Sally to hear, but people have shown more confidence during the past week by moving around the countryside and visiting friends. Sally does attend a prayer meeting, but it is such a beautiful day outside, her thoughts wander. She pays scant attention to the lesson. She is ashamed.[5]

Culpeper can afford to daydream a little, to breathe easier, for Jeb Stuart is on his way. Lee ordered him back to Culpeper on May 11 with instructions to guard the upper Rappahannock and monitor Federal movements in the area. He is, however, to undertake no large-scale expeditions. Lee is uncertain of Union intentions. Stuart should devote his energies to the "reorganization and recuperation" of his cavalry.[6]

May 22. Wade Hampton is already back in Culpeper, and he does not like it one damned bit. The Carolinian still detests the preferential treatment shown Virginia cavalry by Stuart. He hopes his wife will be able to visit him soon, but he makes plans for her to stay across the Rapidan in Orange County, where he has found "the nicest Boarding House in the Confederacy." Hampton informed his wife on May 19, "Stuart will be here today I suppose, after his trip to Richmond where he went to have himself made Lt. Genl. I do not think he will succeed in this, but there is no saying how far newspaper puffs will go in this State." In fact, unknown to Hampton, Lee had sent Stuart to inquire about reinforcements and equipment in Richmond before joining his three cavalry brigades at Culpeper. You will never convince Hampton of that. His resentment of Stuart runs deep. If a new cavalry division is formed in the army, as rumor has it will, Hampton intends to get it— and a promotion—for himself.[7]

Stuart arrived two days ago, May 20, and today he held a grand review of his cavalry and horse artillery—some four thousand men— near the Court House. Many civilians attended, and they were tremendously impressed by Stuart's splendidly mounted and outfitted veterans. General Lee, however, still at Fredericksburg, worries. Two weeks ago, he beseeched President Davis to supply him with more cavalry. The Federal mounted force has grown dramatically in proportion to the Confederacy's horse soldiers, and Yankee commanders have clearly determined to make use of their superior numbers. Ever since the Saint Patrick's Day fight at Kelly's Ford, they have been sending reconnaissance after reconnaissance below the Rappahannock to threaten Lee's communications and supply lines. "Every expedition will augment their boldness and increase their means of doing us harm," Lee warned Davis, "as they will become better acquainted with the country and more familiar with its roads." He must, Lee told the president, have reinforcements from South Carolina, Georgia, Florida, and anywhere else cavalry can be spared. It is these men who have been reporting and continue to report to Culpeper, and who Hampton hopes will form the heart of his new division.[8]

Meanwhile, Stuart is his old frolicking self, and, as usual, he has selected a particular young lady to tease. Stuart is headquartered at the Samuel Bradford farm, Afton, near Brandy. Major Daniel Grey has lodged his wife Myrta with the Bradfords, and the general cannot resist flirting with the pert young (just nineteen) lady at meals. He teases her about her absent husband, who must attend to duties in camp and rarely sees his wife, and he speculates aloud about how much she must miss him. It is all innocent enough, and to prove his sympathy for the young lovers, Stuart one day ordered Grey away from camp to spend a few hours with Myrta. As Grey galloped up unannounced into the Bradford yard, Stuart leapt from the porch and shouted to a startled Myrta, "I'll get the first kiss!" Quickly realizing the situation, and not one to be outdone, Myrta launched her own very unladylike dash across the yard, passed the laughing Stuart, and fell "breathless and panting" into her husband's arms.[9]

This evening, Stuart has called in his near-legendary banjo-playing companion Sam Sweeney to entertain his staff, the Greys, and the Bradfords. Everyone sings "Old Joe Hooker, Won't You Come Out of the Wilderness?" "Sweet Evelina," and "Oh Johnny Hooker, Help the Nigger!" Myrta thinks Sweeney a solemn, overly dignified man, so much in contrast to his merry playing, but she marvels at his artistry. He has his audience shouting and laughing one minute and in tears the next. Stuart himself leads the company in "The Dew Is on the Blossom" and "The Bugles Sang Truce," and he has Sweeney play "Sweet Nellie Is by My Side" two times while he sits besides Myrta and teases Dan about how much he enjoys her company.[10]

The general has nearly as much sport with Mrs. Bradford, his hostess. "Aunt Sally," as she is known, is a formidable character. She has kept her husband, a quiet, peaceable man in his early forties, out of the army so he can look after their considerable property and two dozen slaves. Yet she twits him mercilessly about staying at home whenever soldiers are within hearing distance. "The place for a *man*," she ungraciously reminds all and sundry, "is on the field. Just give me the chance to fight! Just give me the chance to fight, and see where I'll be!" Stuart cannot resist whispering to his companions whenever Mrs. Bradford works herself into a lather, "I don't think she needs a chance to fight, do you?" Or, "Aunt Sally's getting herself in battle array," or "The batteries have limbered up," or "Aunt Sally's scaled the breastworks."[11]

Elsewhere, Culpeper's civilians try to proceed with life as usual, clinging to any remnant of their old world. The most reassuring symbol of continued civil authority is the county court, their bastion of order and direction before the war. Court routine was seriously disrupted last year, and with so much of life now dictated by military necessity and martial law, its jurisdiction has been circumscribed. Yet thus far in 1863, thanks to the presence of Lee's army, the court has at least managed to hold regular monthly sessions. In the total absence of the circuit court, which has not convened in a year, this is comforting.[12]

Early June. Lee has decided to relocate most of his remaining army at Culpeper. He has been slow in reaching this decision, in part because he wants more definite intelligence of the enemy's disposition, but also because he has been forced to reorganize his army. Jackson's death has left Lee with a serious problem. Who will replace Stonewall? Who *can* replace Stonewall? Deciding that no one man can do the job, Lee has divided his army into three corps. James Longstreet, steady, reliable Old Pete, will retain command of a reduced First Corps. Jackson's old command has been reinforced, split in half, and placed under the commands of Dick Ewell and Powell Hill.[13]

Both of the new appointments find favor with the men. Ewell returns to the army after recuperating from the loss of a leg during the Second Manassas campaign. He is a tough old bird, and his men admire his courage and loyalty in rejoining the army. "All are pleased with him," reports a staff officer. "His health is pretty good now, and he seems quite pleased to get back into the field. He manages his wooden leg very well, and walks only with a stick, and mounts his horse quite easily from the ground." Gentle and gentlemanly Powell Hill will be returning home in triumph. A corps commander, by God! and now, like

Ewell, promoted to lieutenant general, as well as being praised by Lee as "the best soldier of his grade with me."[14]

Troops that have been stationed in Orange County since after Chancellorsville now cross the Rapidan. Gray and butternut columns snake through the countryside. Elements of both Longstreet and Ewell's corps depart Fredericksburg. Only Hill remains behind, momentarily at least, to keep the Yanks guessing. Hoping to swell his numbers as much as possible, Lee requests that all convalescents ready for duty be sent directly to Culpeper. The men know something is up. After all, it is June, "the month of battles."[15]

Most troops arrive in good spirits, even though they are alternately drowned by heavy spring rains and baked by a surprisingly warm spring sun. Regiments wade across the waist-deep Rapidan, still swollen by the rains, and "as red as Albemarle soil," at Raccoon and Somerville fords. The countryside is so lush, the scene so idyllic, that it is hard to think of the grim business that lies ahead. "The banks on either side were lined with willows," reports one man of his crossing at Somerville Ford, "which dipped their branches in the stream and made a beautiful feature in the landscape. Just above the ford there was a waterfall and an old mill in the last stages of decay. . . . Just upon the summit of a little knoll opposite the ford two tall chimneys mark the spot where stood a large old-fashioned country house." Not a few men take off shoes and socks so that the cool water can soothe their weary feet. The water and fresh air put them in "fine spirits."[16]

Rumors have spread quickly about the army's destination. Some say they are headed for the Valley. More authoritative voices speculate about another Maryland campaign. A few even speak of an attack against Washington, D.C. More honest, or perhaps simply cautious, men admit total confusion. "All of our movements are inexplicable to me," claims a Texan. "We never know anything." Most men do not care. They are glad to be going *somewhere*, anywhere. They are eager to fight. The sooner they fight, the sooner the war will end, and the sooner they can go home.[17]

Lee followed his army on June 6, but even now he has no certain plan. If only he could guess what the Yanks are about. They are in motion, but to what end? Lee has been reading northern newspapers, especially the New York papers, for the past month. These and his scouts warn of a large Federal buildup along the Rappahannock, with "every ford defended and closely picketed." Should they launch a sudden offensive, Lee fears he could not resist them. He has been losing men to desertion—mostly conscripts and substitutes—ever since Chancellorsville. He also fears the ability of his cavalry to block a major river crossing. Actually, it is not so much his men as their mounts that worry him. Good cavalry horses are few in number and in a weakened condition.[18]

June 8. Many generals would dig in and wait, but Robert Lee is not any general. It is the day after his arrival in Culpeper. Lee sits down at his camp desk to write. A plan has slowly been forming in his mind. The details are still obscure, but he is certain of one thing, and of that he must inform the secretary of war. There can be no victory without risk, no glory without sacrifice. "Hon. James A. Seddon," he begins. No clerk, no aide, however trustworthy, can write this letter. "As far as I can judge, there is nothing to be gained by this army remaining quietly on the defense, which it must do unless it can be re-enforced." The last phrase sounds harsh, but better to state the facts. He continues cautiously: "I am aware that there is difficulty and hazard in taking the aggressive with so large an army in its front, entrenched behind a river, where it cannot be advantageously attacked. Unless it can be drawn out in a position to be assailed, it will take its own time to prepare and strengthen itself to renew its advances upon Richmond." This melancholy scenario, he knows, may be enacted in any case, but every effort must be made to "prevent such a catastrophe." "All our military preparations and organizations should now be pressed forward with the greatest vigor," Lee concludes, "and every exertion made to obtain some material advantage in this campaign." There; he has stated his case. He will prepare.[19]

The army has been receiving new equipment, not just ammunition and personal accoutrements but also *large* items, like wagons, ambulances, tools, and harness, lots of mules and horses, too. More food and forage must be brought in than on previous visits to Culpeper. The grass is not as tall as in past years. Hogs that should have been slaughtered and cured by now have long since been stolen or driven off. Yet, somehow, the men get enough to eat and do not complain too much. Much trading goes on with local farmers and within the army—sugar for butter, tobacco for milk, that sort of thing. "We had some bread toasted and some black-eyed peas boiled and some ham fried," reports one man, "and though we ate with our pen-knives, we enjoyed it very much." Not elegant fare, but these men have come to appreciate simple food.[20]

The losers are Culpeper's farmers. They who have been so generous—and who have profited so handsomely—during the past two years by supplying the army's needs have little to offer. The Majors, Cunninghams, Hills, Shacklefords, Crittendens, and Rixeys, to name only the most prominent benefactors, have either been driven from their lands or have no surplus crops to sell. More money is made this spring by hiring slaves to the army at $20 per month than by selling produce or renting lands. Only Alfred Stofer has retained a reliable source of income from the army by printing general orders, provost-marshal passports, and other military forms in the office of the *Observer*.[21]

In camp, Lee's men only know that, whatever this flurry of preparation might mean, life, for the moment, is easy. Pickets on both sides assume relaxed postures. "The Yankee pickets and ours talk across the river to each other," reports one Rebel from the vicinity of Rappahannock Station, "and some times they meet on the railroad and trade with each other." Yanks and Rebels alike know something is brewing, but so long as no one actually orders them to *attack*, all are willing to live and let live. Soldiers are as mischievous as ever. Company and regimental officers have strict orders to prevent the men from dismantling Culpeper's fences for firewood, a well nigh impossible task. On the other hand, many men are too lazy and comfortable to bother stealing anything. They lounge around camp smoking, writing letters, and reading the latest—a few days old—newspapers. More energetic types wash their socks or visit nearby homes. The only sign of concern about what lies ahead is the increased numbers of men who attend worship services. This often happens before a campaign. One chaplain reports 57 "penitents," six "converts," and nearly two dozen new church members in a two-day period.[22]

Jeb Stuart, already a devout and God-fearing man, primps and preens his horsemen for the campaign. He has held two grand cavalry reviews and as many balls since May 22. The first review was impressive enough, but the second one, on June 5, surpassed it. Days before the event, Stuart ordered his officers and men to don their best uniforms, groom their horses, black their boots, and polish their equipage. On June 4, in response to Stuart's invitation to the gentry of Culpeper and surrounding counties, well-dressed gentlemen and dazzling ladies began to arrive at the Court House from as far away as Charlottesville. The most prominent guest was George Wythe Randolph, former Confederate secretary of war. He arrived from Gordonsville by special train, the locomotive bedecked with Stuart's personal battle flag. With accommodations secured for guests at hotels and private residences, carriages, army wagons, and ambulances carried people from the railroad depot to their quarters. The response delighted Stuart, and he had already planned a ball at the court house building for that evening. The decorations were modest, only what could be secured in wartime; but von Borcke, who directed the social arrangements, secured enough candles to light the ballroom, and with Stuart's own band providing the music, waltzes, reels, and quadrilles energized the merriment until midnight. John Pelham would have loved it.[23]

By 8 A.M., June 5 already promised to be a warm day. The review site, a broad, flat plain, covered largely by fast-growing young cornstalks, lay about midway between Brandy Station and the Court House on the northern side of the O&A Railroad. Most of the site encompasses the Auburn estate of John Minor Botts. Many of the hundreds of people who would attend the review had already arrived by wagon, carriage, and railroad, and no sooner had they staked out positions on the high ground surrounding the plain and on flatcars parked for their convenience on the tracks than Stuart's entourage appeared. Young women threw flowers and cheered wildly. Inspired by the reception, Stuart and his staff give spur to horse and dashed onto the reviewing field. Stuart, dressed in a "short grey jacket, wide-brimmed whitish hat with long black plume," waved and bowed low from the saddle. Some young ladies, overcome by such an assemblage of manly form and virtue, swooned and fainted.

By late morning, nearly 10,000 men, arrayed in twenty cavalry regiments and five batteries of horse artillery, had formed up. Stuart galloped down the line to inspect each regiment in turn. As he passed, brigade officers fell in behind their commander and followed him as he ascended a knoll overlooking the field. As bugles sounded commands, flags and guidons snapped in the breeze, and three bands blared martial tunes, the pageantry reached its zenith. All now passed in front of Stuart and their officers, led in procession by the horse artillery, commanded by Culpeper's own Major Beckham. Once past Stuart, the artillery wheeled to assume a position along the ridge behind the field. They unlimbered their guns and fired salute after salute as each regiment passed. The horsemen moved at a walk until within a hundred yards of Stuart. Then they quickened their pace, first to a trot, then to full gallop. The earth vibrated and trembled beneath thousand of pounding hooves.

With the formal review completed, the long column divided into teams to engage in mock battle, a "sham battle" one lady spectator called it. Regiments took turns galloping full tilt at each other to engage the "enemy" in combat. The show went on until late afternoon. Men applauded, women squealed with delight. The heat, the noise, the dust, the pounding guns, it was as close as most spectators would come to an actual fight. How little they understood the grim results such displays wrought on other days on other fields.[24]

Yet even now, three days hence, not everyone is pleased with the show. Many enlisted men, while acknowledging the grandeur of the review, would have preferred spending the day in camp. A "useless expenditure of powder and horseflesh," remarks a laconic artilleryman. "The sight was certainly full of grandeur and military beauty," a Georgia infantryman informs his mother, "but rendered somewhat unpleasant by the great quantity of dust." Even cavalrymen grumble about the "useless waste of energy, especially that of the horses." One exasperated trooper complains that he was "worried out" by Stuart's "military foppery and display." Not all civilians are impressed, either. One woman informs President Davis in outraged tones of what has been happening in the county since Stuart's arrival. The recent ball and review, she writes, are typical of the "perfectly ridiculous" behavior of Stuart and his "fops," who spend their time entertaining female companions. Are they not supposed to be fighting a war? What other major general would dare stage "repeated reviews for the benefit of his lady friends, he riding up and down the line thronged with ladies, he decorated with flowers, apparently a monkey show on hand and he the monkey."[25]

John Minor Botts had particular reason to complain, for he gained little satisfaction watching thousands of Rebel horses trample his "Northern" corn. He proceeded to Stuart's camp immediately after the circus to lodge his protest and demand recompense. Stuart listened to the harangue, tried to calm the outraged visitor, but ultimately only laughed and dismissed him. "Mr. Botts ripped and rarred and snorted," reports an army servant, "but Genrul Stuart warn't put out none at all." The "genrul" would allow nothing to spoil the day. He had never been so proud of his men or so full of himself. Not even the ride around McClellan's army could top the day's pageantry.[26]

Indeed, Stuart was so pleased that he called for another ball that same evening. This one, an impromptu affair, was held outdoors near his Brandy camp. Huge, crackling bonfires lighted the grassy dance floor and extracted the chill from the night air. Stuart's officers were fagged out, but they would not dream of disappointing the assembled guests, particularly not the young ladies who had cheered them that day. So they spent yet another evening of quadrilles and waltzes, this time beneath the stars and with soft breezes gently mingling the fragrance of pine trees and perfumed hair.

Still June 8. As Lee finishes his letter to Seddon, he rises to prepare for another Stuart review. Lee does not want to attend; he has a campaign to launch. But he missed the great review, and he knows how much Stuart, like a son wishing to impress his father, wanted him there. Lee is too fond of this laughing man-child. He has asked Stuart to stage another review at the same Auburn site so that he might inspect the cavalry, but he wants few civilian guests and no artillery salutes or sham battles. Lee still plans to march north tomorrow. Stuart agrees; he will agree to anything just to have Lee see his magnificent horsemen. He will dazzle the old man.

Late afternoon, and the show proceeded without a hitch, although Lee seems better pleased with the review than are many of his staff. We "had a ride of it," complains General William Pendleton, "some six miles at full run for our horses, down the line and up again, and then had to sit on our horses in the dust half the day for the squadrons to march in display backward and forward near us." Lee is gratified by the display, but he does not allow it to distract him from deeper concerns. He has committed himself to an offensive which could be costly. As he returns to his tent and ponders all possible obstacles to success, Lee remembers an old and still uncorrected complaint. Pulling off his gauntlets, he reaches for pen and paper and writes a second letter to Seddon. He must remind him that the saddles and carbines manufactured in Richmond for his cavalry are defective. The former ruin the horses' backs, and the latter are "so defective as to be demoralizing to the men." Nothing can be done for the present campaign, but he must ask the secretary of war to correct the problems.[27]

Meanwhile, a few miles to the east, Federal cavalry patrols prowl the Rappahannock. A fortnight past, Sally Armstrong rejoiced that the neighborhood had been quiet. She was spending most of her time tending chickens, and hoping that, unlike last year, her family and not the Yankees would enjoy eating them. But the Yanks have become progressively bolder. Even as Stuart's men pranced and cavorted on the fields of Brandy, Sally saw several blue patrols in the neighborhood. When she and her Aunt Judie on another visit to Jeffersonton spotted Yankee cavalry approaching the village, they raced for their carriage and "went home as fast as the horse could travel."[28]

June 9, 4:30 A.M. Few of Stuart's men have stirred from their blankets. The campfires of five brigades, spread over nearly ten miles from Oak Shade to Stevensburg, flicker and glow. A quick cup of coffee on this cool morning, load the wagons, saddle the horses, and they will be under way soon enough. Stuart's headquarters, transferred to Fleetwood Hill near Brandy Station, has already been reduced to a pair of tent-flies. Let the men sleep a while longer. They are worn out from reviews, dances, and picket duty.[29]

> *Many are the hearts that are weary tonight,*
> *Wishing for the war to cease,*
> *Many are the hearts looking for the right*
> *To see the dawn of peace.*

Tenting tonight, tenting tonight,
Tenting on the old Camp ground.[30]

Four miles east of the sleeping camps, the groggy but mounted Union cavalry of General Alfred Pleasonton crashes across the Rappahannock at Beverly's Ford. Six miles to the southeast, a second wing of Pleasonton's command directed by General John Buford approaches Kelly's Ford. Pleasonton received orders from Joe Hooker two days ago to "disperse and destroy the Rebel forces assembled in the vicinity of Culpeper." Averell had operated under similar orders in March, but Pleasonton, a determined if not entirely competent chap, has sworn to succeed where Averell failed. And where Stoneman failed, for Pleasonton has replaced him, as Stoneman had replaced Averell, as cavalry commander of the Army of the Potomac. The 8th New York Cavalry, led by Colonel Benjamin F. "Grimes" Davis, one of Buford's brigade commanders, and part of a reserve brigade show the way. Pleasonton has made his headquarters with this column, while General David M. Gregg directs the movement toward Kelly's Ford. Pleasonton is being cautious. As is his tendency, he has greatly exaggerated the size of Stuart's force. He believes the Confederates have 30,000 men, when, in fact, his own 11,000 men slightly outnumber them.[31]

"Damn! Where did they come from!" think Confederate pickets at Beverly's Ford. They had not a hint of a Federal force across the river, certainly not a force this big. Not a noise, not the flicker of a fire. They cannot see them now in the pre-dawn gloom and fog that clings to the river bank. Silence and then shouts, the crack and whiz of carbine fire, the pounding of massed horses. Captain Bruce Gibson, Company A, 6th Virginia Cavalry, is the unlucky commander of the pickets. There is nothing he can do. He hurries a courier to inform Major C. E. Flournoy, commanding the 6th Virginia, of the assault, then orders his men to fire their carbines as rapidly as possible into shifting shadows. Gibson attempts a counterattack; but within minutes, his command has been shoved back through the picket camp. Men scramble from under blankets to join the fight, but they can resist only briefly before retreating halfway to Brandy Station and their regimental camp.[32]

Major Flournoy has reacted quickly. After informing brigade commander General William E. "Grumble" Jones, bivouacked at nearby St. James's Church, of the attack, he has ordered his regiment into the saddle. The camp is bedlam. Men race through the dark in search of boots, weapons, saddles, and horses. Flournoy cannot wait. He signals what men he can assemble, no more than a hundred and fifty, to follow him at a gallop up the Beverly's Ford road. He intends to rescue Gibson and give the rest of the army time to mobilize. He is also thinking about the artillery. Four batteries, 16 guns in all, have been positioned on the hills about a mile from the river. Their loss would be disastrous.[33]

His column collides with the Federals midway between the river and his camp. Both sides are startled; it is not yet light. The 8th New York by this time has been joined by the 8th Illinois Cavalry; the Confederates bend. Two Rebel lieutenants, C. B. Brown and J. T. Mann, both of Company I, are among the first to fall. The firing escalates. Soldiers shout and horses shriek. Bullets whine and hiss through the air; the occasional sickening "plunk" identifies those that find their mark. Men tumble from their saddles; horses slump to the ground.[34]

But Flournoy has done his job. If not halting the Federal advance, he has slowed it and forced the Yanks to regroup. As his men pour small-arms fire into the blue ranks, gray artillerists, aroused from sleep by the "whizzing of musket balls" through their camp, increase the storm by wheeling one of their guns into the road and unleashing round after round of canister. The baggage trains and remaining 15 guns, directed by Major Beckham, escape to brigade headquarters. Then, just as Flournoy's weakening line threatens to break, a portion of the 7th Virginia Cavalry adds its weight to the counterattack on the 6th's left flank. Some men of the 7th have leaped into action so quickly that they arrive only half dressed or riding bareback.

These half-clad men have come not a moment too soon, for yet another Federal regiment, the 3rd Indiana, has joined the fray. The additional pressure might have proved fatal, but the 7th's added bulk has permitted an orderly retreat. The Federals, themselves in some confusion, cannot press the attack. One Confederate, Lieutenant R. O. Allen of the 6th Virginia, has lingered in the woods along the road on his badly wounded horse. About to rejoin his regiment, he spots a Federal officer in the road about 75 yards ahead of his regiment. The Yankee is waving his sword and gesturing toward his men, evidently trying to coax them to move forward and press the Rebel retreat. Allen, with but a single shot left in his revolver, canters toward the blue rider. The Yankee wheels and sees Allen when the two are but a saber's length apart. He lunges at the Confederate with his sword, but Allen leans away, aims his revolver, and empties the final chamber into Colonel Davis. The Alabama-born, Mississippi-raised professional soldier who would not turn against the United States is dead.[35]

Stuart has reacted to the attack belatedly but effectively. He had been awakened by the *pop-pop-pop* of carbines soon after Davis crossed the river. From atop Fleetwood, he peered eastward into the darkness and wondered how serious the ruckus might be. When Grumble Jones's courier arrived with a few sketchy details, Stuart sent his baggage wagons to the Court House. He then sent word for Wade Hampton to move up from his camp near Stevensburg and for William H. F. "Rooney" Lee to come south from his camp near Welford's Ford, on the Hazel River. Now, as the sun peeps cautiously over the horizon, the lingering fog becomes an irritating haze. Stuart's vision is limited. He cannot see Beckham's artillery rocking back up the Beverley's Ford road toward St. James's, nor Beckham's haste to position his guns below Fleetwood, on high ground to the front and east of St. James's Church. From there, Beckham will be able to cover the road and the broad plain on either side of it. Stuart cannot see Grumble Jones positioning his infantry to support the guns, nor the simultaneous arrival of the 6th and 7th Virginia. The suddenness of the attack, and now the rapid transition from night to dawn, must make the whole episode seem slightly unreal to Stuart. According to Lee's plans, he and his cavalry should already be moving northward, toward the Valley. Now, in the midst of this peaceful summer interlude, and in defiance of the army's plans, he must prepare once more, it seems, to do battle.[36]

Were this not depressing enough, Stuart now receives word of intruders at Kelly's Ford. Crossing the river far behind schedule, at 9:00 P.M., Gregg's two cavalry divisions plus five infantry regiments and three artillery batteries can hear the battle raging upriver. Gregg sends the infantry north parallel to the river to engage whatever Rebels might be moving against him. He then leads his cavalry west toward Brandy Station to rendezvous with Pleasonton, expecting that their combined force will then swoop down on Stuart's cavalry, encamped, it is supposed, at the Court House.[37]

Clearly, Gregg and Pleasonton have it all wrong, which accounts for John Buford's surprise at the size of the Rebel force he has encountered. These men are not supposed to be here. The miscalculation does not help Stuart. He knows only that he is caught in a pincers movement that threatens both his cavalry and Lee's infantry. Having made what he believes to be adequate arrangements to thwart the column from Beverly's Ford, he now directs General Beverly Robertson's brigade, which had been encamped adjacent to Hampton between Brandy and Stevensburg, to turn back this second force from the southeast. He then orders Fitzhugh Lee's brigade, commanded by Colonel Thomas Munford in place of the ailing Lee, to move south across the Hazel River.[38]

Stuart now descends to inspect the situation at St. James's, but he has already missed several hours of desperate fighting. As the Federals, in pursuit of Jones's brigade, emerged from a fringe of heavy woods, they saw a rapidly forming gray line some eight hundred yards away across an open and fairly level plateau. A barrage from Beckham's guns greeted them, followed by an assault by the 11th and 12th Virginia Cavalry and 35th Virginia Battalion. The Federals, lurching forward, were too stunned by the suddenness of the attack, the cannonade, and the size of the Confederate force to stand their ground. Sabers briefly "gleamed and flashed in the morning sun" before the bluecoats retreated back into the woods. Jones's men have fallen back to their original line.[39]

Buford arrived on the scene shortly after the failed attack, at about 8 A.M. More obstinate than wise, he could think only of his mission, which was to rendezvous with Gregg at Brandy. No matter that 16 guns and a growing line of dismounted sharpshooters and mounted cavalry stood between him and his objective. No matter that skirmishers and sharpshooters from Hampton's brigade pressed and harassed his left flank. He must reach Brandy, so to clear the way, Buford or-

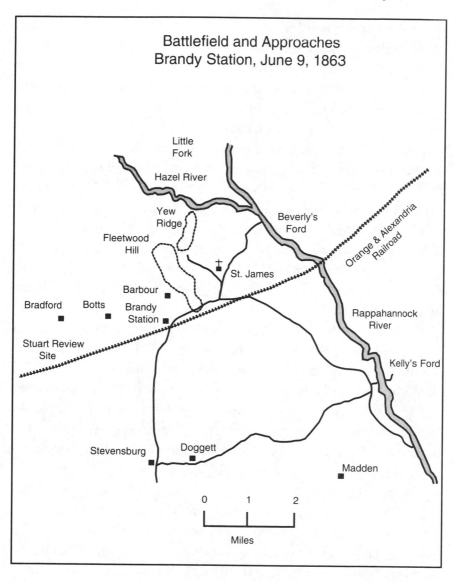

Battlefield and Approaches
Brandy Station, June 9, 1863

Little
Fork

Hazel River

Yew
Ridge

Fleetwood
Hill

Beverly's
Ford

Orange & Alexandria
Railroad

St. James

Barbour

Bradford   Botts   Brandy
                             Station

Rappahannock
River

Stuart Review
Site

Kelly's Ford

Stevensburg   Doggett

Madden

0   1   2

Miles

dered the 6th Pennsylvania Cavalry, reinforced on the left by the 6th U.S. Cavalry, to charge across the same open plateau and dislodge the Rebels. Never one to question his superiors, Major Robert Morris, a descendant of the Revolutionary War patriot, led his Pennsylvanians out of the woods. Victory requires sacrifice. They walked their horses a few yards, then trotted, and, on the bugle's command, charged straight toward Beckham's amazed gunners—amazed, but not paralyzed. "Shells burst over us, under us and alongside, "reports a survivor of the mad dash, "and bullets were singing through the air like a hornet's nest." A few horsemen actually reached the Rebel batteries, but gray riders swiftly engulfed them. Desperate fighting broke out across the field, but the Federals were again outnumbered. Major Morris lost his horse and is now a prisoner. Those of his men able to extricate themselves have returned to the woods in tolerable order, but in a determined "*race for life.*"[40]

Yes, Buford is obstinate, but not stupid. Leaving four cavalry and two infantry regiments in position, he has shifted the rest of his force around the plateau in search of a safer route to the Court House. He thinks he has found one, but Rooney Lee blocks his way. When Rooney Lee received Stuart's orders to move south from the Hazel, he established a defensive position on Yew Ridge, a steep slope that abuts the northern end of Fleetwood Hill and runs north toward the Hazel. Placing two artillery pieces high on the ridge, Lee dismounted his four regiments and aligned them behind a sturdy stone wall at the base of Yew Ridge. Buford's cavalry, which began probing Lee's left flank shortly after 8:30 A.M., slowly dislodged Confederates from two portions of the wall, but the rest of the command continues to thwart him. Buford ordered charge after charge against the wall, but a sheet of Confederate carbine fire, interspaced with counterattacks by the 2nd North Carolina and 10th Virginia Cavalry, have kept the Yankees at bay.[41]

By now Buford is visibly "annoyed." He has summoned Captain George W. Stevenson, a Wisconsin infantry officer. "Do you see those people down there?" he asks Captain Stevenson, gesturing toward the wall. "They've got to be driven out." Stevenson gulps. Lee's men outnumber his own two to one, but he thinks he can sneak some marksmen through a wheatfield on Lee's left and create a diversion with enfilading fire. The rest of the infantry, men of the 3rd Wisconsin and 2nd Massachusetts, might then carry the wall. "Mind," says Buford after hearing Stevenson's tentative but affirmative response, "I don't order you; but if you think you can do it, go in."

It is 10:30 A.M., and go in Stevenson did. He soon had ten sharp-shooters peppering Lee's flank "with terrible accuracy." When the remainder of the infantry rushed forward, the Confederates were too confused to stand their ground. Rooney Lee now realizes that Jones's men are withdrawing, thus exposing his right flank. Lee has no idea of what is happening; he has received no instructions from Stuart. But to remain where he is would be foolish. He orders his men to pull back and take positions on the northwestern end of Fleetwood Hill.[42]

Stuart, after watching light skirmishing in front of St. James's for nearly two hours, faces a crisis. A short time ago, a courier dispatched by Daniel Grimsley, now a captain on Jones's staff, galloped up and leaped from his saddle. Begging the general's pardon, but General Jones wished to report that a sizeable force of Federals had crossed the Rappahannock south of Beverly's Ford and was moving toward Brandy. Hell, Stuart knew that. He had already sent Robertson's brigade to handle the problem. "Tell General Jones," Stuart replied testily, "to attend to the Yankees in his front, and I'll watch the flanks." Stuart does not care for "Grumble," never has. The curt reply would remind him of his subordinate rank. When the courier reported back to "Grumble," the general was livid. "So he thinks they ain't coming, does he? Well let him alone; he'll damn soon see for himself."[43]

Stuart had, indeed, relied on Robertson to handle the affair below Beverly's Ford, but his reliance has been misplaced. Amazingly, Robertson, another officer in whom Stuart places little confidence, has allowed Gregg's cavalry to slip through the countryside almost unopposed. He has reasoned that to block the cavalry would allow Gregg's infantry to march unchecked to Rappahannock Station and thus seize control of the railroad. Stuart learns of the disaster in a frantic message from Major Henry B. McClellan, his adjutant (and a cousin of the erstwhile commander of the Army of the Potomac) at the camp atop Fleetwood. Gregg's men are approaching Brandy! blurts out the messenger. Stuart is incredulous. McClellan is his most trusted staff officer. Surely the courier has garbled the message. "Ride back there," Stuart snaps at a nearby artillery captain while gesturing toward the southern end of Fleetwood, "and see what this foolishness is about." No sooner has the captain sped away than a second McClellan courier gallops up. "General," he cries without even dismounting, "the Yankees are at Brandy!"[44]

It is true. After crossing the Rappahannock and pushing his cavalry across Mountain Run, Gregg divided his force. He sent Colonel Alfred Duffié's Second Division further west, past the Doggett farm to Stevensburg. From there, Duffié was to swing north and attack the Court House while Gregg and the Third Division joined forces with Buford, as planned, at Brandy. To accomplish his part, Gregg pushed the Third north along the Fredericksburg Plank Road that runs past Berry Hill straight to Brandy Station. He has arrived, and Stuart, demonstrating his first real burst of energy today, has responded by ordering the regiments around St. James's to ascend Fleetwood and secure the high ground before Gregg can do so. Stuart himself mounts and rides for the crest; he will direct the coming contest first hand. The race is on.

Stuart's men have arrived first, but barely. Colonel Sir Percy Wyndham, son of a British cavalry officer and possessing the most magnificent mustache in the Army of the Potomac, had already scattered a South Carolina regiment posted at the railroad depot before leading his Second Brigade up the southwest slope of Fleetwood. As his horsemen lunged toward the grassy plateau, their "flags and guidons flying," even Confederate observers admitted that it was an "awe-inspiring sight." Simultaneously, the 12th Virginia Cavalry, slightly disorganized and winded after a mile-and-a-half gallop from St. James's, labored up the other side and hesitated only slightly before racing down to slam into the head of Wyndham's column, still fifty yards from the prize. The 1st New Jersey Cavalry, no strangers to the fields of Culpeper, bore the brunt of this blow. The Virginians, smaller in numbers and lacking stamina, soon disengaged and fell back, but Wyndham's men have been stung, and they, too, now reel and tumble back as the 35th Virginia Battalion follows up the 12th's attack. These Confederates will not surrender Fleetwood.[45]

4 A.M. The remainder of the day has been a fog of dust, smoke, death, and glory. As "the discordant and fearful music of battle floated on the thickened air," the fortunes of these two great armies have hourly ebbed and flowed. First one, then the other gained control of Fleetwood. No sooner had the Virginians fallen back than Georgians and South Carolinians appeared on Fleetwood; no sooner had Wyndham retreated with a bullet in his leg than Judson Kilpatrick charged up the hill at the head of regiments from New York and Maine. Seven thousand men rode into the melée at some time during the afternoon. When Stuart arrived to observe from the fringe, he ordered, "Give them the saber, boys," a rather needless command since his men were already giving them the saber, the knife, the pistol, and whatever other weapon they could lay hands on. Cavalry did most of the fighting. Not dismounted cavalry, mind you, as has been the case for most of the war, but mounted warriors, as in the days of Arthur and Lancelot. Thousands of sabers glistened in the sun of a very warm day as blue and gray riders crowded and thrashed in "promiscuous confusion."[46]

Participants will not soon forget this day. "My saber took him just in the neck," reports a New Jersey cavalryman, "and the blood gushed out in a black-looking stream." Horsemen swerved and dodged, leaning first to one side then to the other of their sturdy mounts to avoid saber thrusts and bullets. As men fell, their "excited, riderless steeds" continued to race up and down the field like "scalded cats." Smoke and dust, the rattle of small arms and the crash of artillery, assaulted and stifled all senses in the "tumultuous and bloody scene." Only gradually, after some three hours of combat, did the pace slacken. The Federals, with both men and horses "utterly exhausted," lost their initial advantage and mounted fewer counterattacks. Not a dozen horses in the 1st New Jersey Cavalry retained enough stamina to launch or withstand another charge; not a man in the regiment "could shout above a whisper." Alongside the gore lurked occasional humor, or what passes for humor under these conditions. It is so in most battles. Early in the fight, a Federal bugler was in such haste to retreat down the hill that he plowed his terrified mount through the wall of a dilapidated icehouse. The horse plunged to its death down the shaft within. The rider tumbled down the hole too, but he miraculously escaped serious injury, to be hauled out on the end of a rope by his laughing comrades. Through it all, and almost unnoticed on the northern end of Fleetwood, Rooney Lee's men held their position, too. Rooney has taken a bullet in his thigh.[47]

Beckham's artillery probably has saved the day. When Stuart pulled men out from around St. James's, Beckham had to redistribute his guns. He dispatched four of them to the southern end of Fleetwood, where gunners found themselves in a vortex of saber-wielding Federal cavalry. Lieutenants C. E. Ford and William Hoxton leveled two blue-coats at point-blank range with pistol shots. Private Sudley knocked another sprawling to the ground with a mighty swing of his sponge staff. The Federals actually captured a pair of guns, commanded by Lieutenant John W. Carter, but could not hold them for long. In the midst of all this, Federal gunners, content with a position at the foot of the hill, unleashed a barrage of grape and shot on their gray counter-parts. "Screaming fragments" tore through the air and human flesh.[48]

Now, some fourteen hours after the Federal crossing began, Plea-sonton is ready to retreat. Fighting continues around the northern end of Fleetwood, but the Federals are clearly "blown." They wish only to rest on their own side of the Rappahannock. To their credit, they with-draw at a deliberate pace and in good order. Stuart's men pursue and harass them, but it is a half-hearted effort, for they, too, are exhausted and famished. They are content to hold the field and watch the Yan-kees gallop across Rappahannock bridge or churn across Beverly's Ford. As the sun sets and the Confederate pursuit slows, a Federal offi-cer atop the river bluffs swears he has never seen "a prettier sight." The river flows below him; the same mist that shielded the Federal ap-proach has reappeared to disguise their return. Best of all, "no living object" stands between his men and the safety of the northern bank. Another day of war concludes.[49]

Robert E. Lee arrived at Brandy shortly after Pleasonton ordered a retreat. He has spent most of the day at his camp near the Court House largely unconcerned about the fighting six miles to the east. He awoke this morning fully prepared to push across the Rappahannock, but when Dick Ewell said his infantry needed another day to prepare, Lee acquiesced. Later in the morning, Lee received his first report from Stuart. The situation did not appear ominous; Lee believed Stuart faced only a reconnaissance force. He could send infantry if necessary, Lee assured Stuart, but he preferred that the enemy remain ignorant of his large force at the Court House. Lee had then settled down to wait, thoroughly confident that Stuart would handle the situation.[50]

Lee used part of the early afternoon to write to Mary, the first opportunity he had found to compose a private letter in several days. He thanked her for the new pillowcase she had sent and described yesterday's review. "It was a splendid sight," he admitted. "The men & horses looked well. They had recuperated since last fall. Stuart was in all his glory. Your sons and nephews well & flourishing." The general then turned to deeper thoughts. "The country here looks very green & pretty notwithstanding the ravages of war," he told Mary. "What a beautiful world God in His loving kindness to His creatures has given us. What a shame that men endowed with reason & a knowledge of right should mar His gifts. May he soon change the hearts of men, shew them their sins & enable them to repent & be forgiven!"[51]

By late afternoon, and having heard no abatement of the clamor east of the Court House, Lee ordered Ewell to prepare his corps to march. The commander then mounted Traveller and led his staff up the road toward Brandy. By the time he halted at the Barbour place, however, Lee could catch only glimpses of the Fleetwood fight from the cupola of the house. The dust and the tumolt were dying. He knew, as did Pleasonton, that the daring attack had failed.[52]

The evening has been spent tending the dead and wounded and marching Federal prisoners to the rear. Losses are heavy for a cavalry engagement. Stuart has as many as 75 dead, nearly 300 wounded, and 132 missing. His adjutant, Major McClellan, estimates Federal losses at slightly over 450 killed and wounded, and Stuart's men have captured nearly 500 Yankees. The heaviest casualties for both sides came in the fighting around St. James's Church, on Yew Ridge, and on the northern slope (Rooney Lee's end) of Fleetwood. The 6th Pennsylvania alone, in its "dash of conspicuous gallantry," lost 146 officers and men. Stuart assures Pleasonton, when the Federal officer asks leave to bury his dead and care for his wounded, that his men will attend to both needs.[53]

Survivors soon fill hastily constructed field hospitals and nearby homes. Mary Wise welcomes the wounded at Bel Pre, even though she must rest many of them in her yard. She, her daughters, and her servants assist the physicians as best they can on this warm June night. Mrs. Charles Wager has her home, The Glebe, opened less voluntarily. At the height of the fighting, when it appeared that the battle might engulf her farm a mile west of Fleetwood, she and her children fled to the house of relatives near the Court House. When she ventured back home this evening, Mrs. Wager stumbled in the dark over two men lying in her yard; two other men had sought shelter on the porch. Even Glenmore, four miles from the field, receives dying men.[54]

Rumors have circulated throughout the neighborhood about the course of the fighting and the names of the fallen. Myrta Grey waited in dread anticipation at Afton for news of her major, and her confidence was not bolstered by the number of wounded soldiers who soon filled the Bradfords' house, porch, yard, and outhouses. Even when she learned that Dan was uninjured, Myrta remained shaken by this sudden turn of events and her proximity to the war. Not that she fears for her own safety; but the sight and sound of all these half-men, men without limbs and with gaping holes in their bodies, and the realization that but for God's blessing her own husband could be lying among them, changes her perspective on the war. Myrta even feels sorry for a young (aren't they all young?) Federal soldier who has been brought to the house. He was found lying in a road, his lower jaw nearly shot away. She considers that somewhere, no doubt, a woman, perhaps a sweetheart, at least a mother, who dearly loves this boy, knows nothing of his suffering. Myrta is sickened. This war, she decides, is "an utterly unjustifiable thing."[55]

Blessedly, no Culpeper lads have fallen, but William A. Hill, kin to the Culpeper Hills, has arrived from Madison County on grim business. Two nephews, James and George Williams, had stayed with his family not long ago when their regiment passed through Madison on its way to Culpeper. Hearing of the Brandy Station fight, Hill has arrived to inquire about their welfare. He had been particularly taken with the younger George, "a youth of good deportment in every way." Hill is devastated to learn that of several relatives and friends who participated in the battle, only George has been killed. George, it seems, was marching a captured Yankee to the rear when the "cowardly prisoner" turned on him with a pistol and shot him between the eyes. It was a pocket pistol, a woman's weapon. Hill has come just in time to help lift the youth's lifeless form from an ambulance. The body, already starting to decompose after lying for five hours in the relentless sun, is too far gone to be sent home. George will be buried tomorrow beside three other men from his regiment in Culpeper soil.[56]

Everyone is tired and hungry. Stuart initially ordered his headquarters replanted on Fleetwood, a gesture meant to show that he had, in fact, held his ground. But this will be impossible. The plateau is littered with dead men and horses, with bluebottle flies "swarming so thick over the blood stains on the ground" that no decent plots remain to pitch tents upon. It is late, and some men have already begun to cook supper and prepare a bivouac.[57]

> *We've been fighting today on the old Camp ground,*
> *Many are lying near;*
> *Some are dead, and some are dying,*
> *Many are in tears.*
>
> *Dying tonight, dying tonight,*
> *Dying on the old Camp ground.*[58]

What does it all mean, this unexpected blood bath at St. James's and Fleetwood? The participants know only that they have been in one helluva fight, and several days later they are still talking about it. Bill Wilson, a survivor of the overwhelmed 12th Virginia, continues to list the names of dead and missing comrades in his diary. In all, his regiment has lost forty dead and wounded. "They were good soldiers & unselfish patriots & we miss them much," he records unabashedly. Elsewhere he writes, "It was the hardest cavalry fight of the war. The enemy gained our rear beautifully but our brigade cleaned them out nicely." Even when Wilson manages to suppress the memory of his dead comrades and visions of the fight, physical reminders still haunt him. "The stench of dead horses around Stuart's head-quarters, where our regiment engaged Windham's Brigade," he writes on June 14, "makes travelling very disagreeable in the immediate vicinity."[59]

Robert E. Lee is far more taken with—and shaken by—the Fleetwood fight, or the battle of Brandy Station, as it is now being called. Of course, his son, Rooney, was badly wounded there. He has been sent to recuperate near Richmond, but the general continues to worry about him, and particularly about the danger of infection, which would almost certainly result in amputation. More than that, though, the general worries about his many other boys, the tens of thousands of boys he leads and who trust him to win this war. On the day after the battle, Lee wrote an anxious letter to Jefferson Davis. As is his habit, Lee was already thinking beyond what had passed, and he had come to two conclusions. First, the bold Federal cavalry strike had made it abundantly clear that the Yanks could now claim superior "numbers, resources, and all the means and appliances for carrying on the war." Even more sobering was the thought that the South could not expect to escape the "military consequences of a vigorous use" of those advantages. "We should not, therefore," Lee continued, "conceal from ourselves that our resources in men are constantly diminishing, and that the disproportion in this respect between us and our enemies . . . is steadily augmenting." Lee's second point followed naturally: The need to strike on northern soil was more urgent than ever before. The North's fervor for war must be subdued; northerners must be divided and their resolve to continue fighting weakened.[60]

The need to strike quickly and formidably against the North has gained added impetus from public speculation that Stuart was actually beaten at Fleetwood. "The cavalry fight at Brandy Station can hardly be called a *victory*," Captain Charles Minor Blackford told his family three days after the battle. "Stuart was certainly surprised and but for the supreme gallantry of his subordinate officers and the men in his command it would have been a day of disaster and disgrace." Blackford's views diverged diametrically from those of his older brother, who served as Stuart's chief engineer, but even Stuart's friends have betrayed some concern. Dorsey Pender, a West Point classmate of Stuart, has told his wife, "I suppose it is all right that Stuart should get all the blame, for when anything handsome is done he gets all the credit." Pender, trying to cast the best possible light on the situation, emphasizes that "in the end" Stuart "retrieved the surprise by whipping them." And no one is having more sport with the episode than the army's infantrymen. "Genl Stuart was beautifully surprised & whipped the other day," chuckles one man. "He drove them back, but not until he had received a considerable chastising. It is amusing to hear the cavalry fellows trying to bluff out of it."[61]

The Richmond press has got hold of the story now and made it all the rage. "The more the circumstances of the late affair at Brandy Station are considered," suggests the Richmond *Examiner*, "the less pleasant do they appear." Lee's "puffed up cavalry" had been surprised in battles more than once this year, insists the paper, and had shown clear signs of "negligence and bad management." "If the war was a tournament," it maintains in slightly concealed reference to the recent grand reviews, "invented and supported for the pleasure of a few vain and weak-headed officers, these disasters might be dismissed with compassion. But the country pays dearly for the blunders which encourage the enemy to overrun and devastate the land." Stuart's men had been "carelessly strewn over the country" prior to the battle, with only the Rappahannock between them and the enemy. The cavalry must be reorganized, insists the *Examiner*, with "stricter discipline" imposed. Wade Hampton might have written that article.[62]

Stuart seethes with indignation. Having read the *Examiner* story (and there are many like stories in other papers), he assures his wife Flora, "The papers are in great error, as usual about the whole transaction. It was no surprise, the enemys movement was known, and he was defeated." The *Examiner*, in particular, "*lies*" about the battle, Stuart declares, and he will "take no notice of such base falsehood." True to his word, Stuart has admitted no fault in his official report of the battle. He has created the impression of a man in full command of the situation, a man who deployed his units with precision and directed them flawlessly, a man who betrayed no sign of doubt, indecision, or surprise. Yet the jokes and rumors continue. So today, June 15, Stuart has issued a general order praising his men and the "prowess of their arms."[63]

Northerners are pleased with the battle, and quite boastful. Certainly Pleasonton is boasting, but then he always does, boasts and lies. His victory, if such it may be called, was not so complete as he claims. Still, most Federals merely lament that the Rebels had not been thumped *more* soundly. This battle, coming on the heels of the Saint Patrick Day's fight and Stoneman's raid, has shown the Federal cavalry to be the equal of the southern. Few people would have thought that possible a year ago. Even Stuart's trusted aide, Major McClellan, admits that the battle will doubtless give Federal cavalrymen "confidence in themselves and in their commanders." Yet probably the South's heaviest loss, the one becoming more difficult to offset, is in horses. They have lost hundreds.[64]

The possibility that Stuart might have thrashed Pleasonton more convincingly does not concern Lee. He only knows the Fleetwood fight has set him back several days. He is uncertain how much the Federals have learned of his strength and his plans. Probably too much; the Richmond papers have seen to that. Their attacks on Stuart and stories about the Fleetwood fight have betrayed the presence of his three corps. He knows, too, that men cannot control time; time has us. He must move quickly. He has not half as many cavalry as he needs, but it is time for "bold measures." Federal patrols continue to poke brazenly across the Rappahannock. Stuart's men chase them back with relative ease, but it is galling to see how little respect they show for these massed forces. Lee sent part of Ewell's corps north toward Front Royal on June 10, the day after the fight. The rest of Ewell's men headed for Winchester, which they captured on June 14. Some of them groaned upon departing Culpeper. Why could they not remain behind like Longstreet's men, or like Hill's men, still sitting snugly in Fredericksburg? "I have the soarest feet I most ever had," lamented a man in the 21st Virginia Infantry, "they have blisters on them as big as Dollars." The rest of Lee's army—excepting the cavalry kept busy on picket—still sits and waits.[65]

The waiting naturally produces a new round of speculation about the army's destination. Most men assume they will move north, probably into Maryland. This suits them just fine. "Since our army is so much larger and better disciplined than ever before I am quite willing to advance upon Yankeedom," declares a member of the 18th Virginia Infantry. "When Lee moves this time I think the Yankees will catch fitts." A Georgian feels the same way. Even before the Fleetwood fight, he had been hoping to invade "yankeedom" and "finally make this a war of piledging, plundering, and destroying private citizens property" on the other side of the Mason-Dixon line. "I feel like retaliating in the strictest sense," he declares unapologetically to his mother. "I don't think we would do wrong to take horses; burn houses; and commit every deprivation possible upon the men of the North. I can't vindicate the principle of injuring or insulting the female sex, though they be never so disloyal to our confederacy and its institutions. . . . But mother, I would not hesitate to take, or burn up any thing belonging to their government or that belonged to a citizen who was loyal to the U.S."[66]

The men seem to be in fine spirits. The Little Fork Rangers, who fought against Duffié's column near Stevensburg, enjoy camping near Oak Shade. How they must revel in this brief reprieve from the war, as neighborhood "lady friends" visit and admire them. Men more distant from home scribble reassurances to family and friends before the campaign begins. Who knows when or if they will have another opportunity? Most soldiers swear that they are well fed, well rested, and just itching for a fight. Some of them send advice, particularly if they think their families may be in danger. "As soon as you can remove every thing of value . . . to some place of greater safety," a Virginia infantryman advises his wife in King William County. "The Yankees will not hesitate to steal & plunder everything on the place if they have an opportunity. . . . They are great at stealing & breaking up pianos and furniture generally." He apologizes for not being at home to protect her, but, perhaps trying to be strong for both of them, he reasons that it is time that she learn "to think & act" for herself. "Ladies must do so [in] these times," he concludes. Another man advises his wife to let the children write their own letters to him; she should not copy or compose them. He prefers to see their own handiwork, even "their scribbling with all their mistakes."[67]

More men than in the past spend time at church or at camp meetings, no doubt looking to hedge their bets in the coming battles. Court House churches have been open the past two days, Saturday and Sunday. General Lee attended the Episcopal church yesterday morning. He saw the Reverend Cole there and was sorry to learn that his wife Frances had died recently. This leaves Cole with three small children, the youngest only three years old. General Pendleton, an ordained minister, delivered, at Mr. Cole's invitation, an inspiring sermon on "the greatness & goodness of God." It impressed Lee. One of his staff, Captain Blackford, was bemused. He calls it a "very good sermon," but confesses that Pendleton's "curiously mixed" apparel distracted him. "The gown covered up his uniform entirely except for the wreath and stars of a general on his collars which peeped out to mildly protest against too much 'peace on earth,'" the captain explains, "and the boots and spurs clanked around the chancel with but little sympathy with the doctrine of 'good will towards men.'"[68]

June 15. This morning, Lee sent Longstreet's corps, accompanied by Stuart's cavalry, after Ewell. The men cooked four days' rations, a sure sign that "a big move is on hand." The men remain uncertain about their destination. Those who venture a guess suppose it to be Maryland, but most do not care. They are "jubilant" just to be moving and break camp "with no regrets."[69]

A portion of John Bell Hood's division is packing up near the Cedar Mountain battleground. Some men could not resist touring the field before leaving. "There were a great many unburied skeletons, presenting a very ghastly appearance," reports a man in the 4th Texas Infantry. He counted 49 skulls in one ditch and numerous bodies dug from their shallow graves and "torn to pieces and scattered about . . . by hogs and other animals." Here and there, a "hand or foot might be seen protruding from the earth." A member of the 5th Texas, who passed over the field last year, thinks it looks much as it did then. As he writes a letter to his uncle describing the scene, a pair of leg bones retrieved from the field sit beside him. "One of the boys pulled [them] out of a pair of blue Yankee breaches yesterday," he explains.[70]

Lee has also ordered Hill's corps to join him from Fredericksburg. Joe Hooker has reacted to Ewell's appearance at Winchester by pulling back from along the Rappahannock. For two more days, gray troops march through Culpeper toward the Blue Ridge and the trail northward. When Hill arrives at the Court House, he is shocked by the appearance of his home town. He doubtless agrees with a Richmond newspaper reporter who, perhaps exaggerating conditions a bit, describes it as "mutilated by barbaric invasion" and "devastated by pestilence and famine."[71]

The weather is beastly hot, the march a hard one, especially for Hill's troops. Hundreds of men faint by the roadside, just as they did last year en route to the Cedar Mountain fight. Exhaustion sets in; men die. "I never saw the like sence I have bin in the armey," declares a North Carolinian. He expects, as do they all, a "big fite" at the end of their march, probably in the Valley, or at Manassas. Wherever it may be, they are ready. "We whip the Yankees ever time we catch up with them and get half a chance at them," he assures his wife. "I will not se you this summer unless I get badly wounded. . . . We are troubled on every side, yet not distressed. We are perplexed but not in despare. Percicuted but not fore saken. Cast down but not destroyed."[72]

As always happens when the army departs, some civilians are certain that *this* time the Yankees will exploit the county's vulnerability. They start packing. Myrta Grey has decided to leave, although for her, it is not just a question of the army's departure; she has also had enough of Aunt Sally. A few days after the fight at Brandy Station, Aunt Sally returned home from a visit to Washington. (How she secured a pass is anyone's guess.) Two wounded Confederates, of all the men who had been cared for at her house, remained in one of her bedrooms. Aunt Sally flew into a rage. Her beautiful yard torn apart and "trampled down"! Her front steps covered with mud! Wounded men in her beds and on her best sheets! "Just like Mr. Bradford!" she fumed. "If I had been here it wouldn't have happened. The idea! Turning the house into a hospital. I won't have it! Nobody knows who they are. . . . Dirty, common soldiers! I never heard of such a thing!" The poor fellows were in a field hospital soon after supper. "I was as afraid of Aunt Sally as of a rattlesnake," admits Mrs. Grey, "but I think I could have shaken her!"[73]

With the wounded, the army, and her husband all gone off to war, Myrta wonders what to do. She spots Captain John Esten Cooke, one of Stuart's staff and, incidentally, a cousin of Flora Jackson, writing at a desk in the Bradford parlor. He is hurrying to finish some reports and correspondence before rejoining the army. Lively Myrta thinks Cooke a "glum old thing," a "very dull, disagreeable man," but she asks his advice. When might the army return? Should she wait for it at Culpeper? Where is the safest place to stay? "Can't say, madam," is Cooke's unenlightening response to all queries. "I felt like shaking him and asking: 'What *can* you say?'" Finally, she hits on the right question: Should she, perhaps, go to Richmond? Cooke considers. Yes, he decides; yes, she should go to Richmond. She will.[74]

Dorsey Pender, leading one of Hill's divisions, is one of the last officers to leave Culpeper. He pauses on June 17 at Stevensburg to dash off a letter to his wife. He is tired, but in better spirits than when he left Fredericksburg. The campaign is off to a brilliant start with Ewell's victory at Winchester. Lee now has the "inside track," for as the army heads north, Hooker must pursue. "I do not think we shall have much severe fighting this summer," he assures his wife. "We will get North for a few months but we shall have to come back by September or Oct. for their force will be increasing while ours will be decreasing." He does not know for certain, but unlike most of the officers and men, who still believe the army is headed for Maryland, Pender thinks Lee intends to invade Pennsylvania.[75]

CHAPTER TEN

RETURN OF THE YANKEES

*D*orsey Pender was right: Lee's destination *had* been Pennsylvania; and alas that it was. By July 24, many days after Culpeper received word of the army's defeat at Gettysburg, the first of Lee's shabby collection of heroes, baked by the sun and worn as never before, have limped across the Hazel River back into Culpeper. Lee has returned because the Federals have threatened the Orange & Alexandria Railroad in a move toward Rappahannock Station. His larger fear is that the Yankees will try to insert themselves between his army and Richmond. For the first time in the war, a Confederate army enters Culpeper as the vanquished.

Not that any of these men admits to being beaten, though the honest ones do own up to being dog-tired and hungry. The march has been "severe" on man and beast. Few opportunities to cook rations, the sun beating down, and several river crossings have not made for an easy time. The men subsisted on bread, berries, and green apples; the horses ate only grass. Not until arriving in Culpeper do the men enjoy a cooked meal, or the horses receive loose corn. Conditions stand in stark contrast to the march into Pennsylvania, where the men had found "chickens, sheep and apple butter in abundance." The fare, insists a Georgian, far surpassed the Pennsylvania women, whom he regarded as the "ugliest set of mortals" he had ever seen—"long-faced, barefooted, big-nose[d] and everything else that it takes to constitute an ugly woman." The same man, utterly spent, challenges his sister: "Ask some of your Western soldiers if they know anything about hard times. If they do not and want to know anything about it, just tell them to come up and join the Army of Northern Virginia and we will give them a few lessons."[1]

Culpeper had prayed for the army's return, but it is always sad to see who has *not* returned. Most noticeable is the absence of Colonel W. Tazewell Patton. The former captain of the Culpeper Minute Men had been severely wounded last year in the second dance at Manassas. Now reports say he was shot in the jaw and died three days ago in a Yankee hospital. Other men from his regiment, the 7th Virginia Infantry, are also listed as casualties: Thornton Brown, captured; Henry Clay Burrows, captured; John D. Canaday, killed; William H. Hill, killed; Andrew J. Kilby, wounded; Joseph O. Matthews, wounded and captured; Alexander Oden, wounded and captured; Robert B. Somerville, killed. The 7th was the worst-hit Culpeper regiment, but the 11th, 13th, and 14th Virginia Infantry sustained losses, too. William Daniel Ross, a Culpeper lad serving in the 14th, died on the third day of the fighting. A few weeks earlier, he had written to his sister, "I would give every thing I ever expect to possess in the world if I could end the war by doing so. There is no pleasure in it but pain and uneasiness from morning till night."[2]

The army's arrival has also created yet another period of ambivalence. The citizens always feel safer with the army here, at least safer than when it is away. Yet they have long since realized that the army also serves as a magnet for trouble. Where Lee is, so will be Pope, or Hooker, or—who is it now? Meade, someone says, George Gordon Meade. Some farmers, having given up hope of the army's return, had begun to drive their livestock into the woods to keep it out of Union hands. Up to the very morning of Lee's arrival, Yankees roamed Culpeper looking for horses, although, rejoices Sally Armstrong, "they did not get any." "These are exciting times," the impressionable girl records in her diary. "We are in dread of the Yankees taking every

mouthful we have, thus we are left to the cruel mercy of our enemies."
But now advance Confederate units have run off the Yankee patrols.
With God's and Lee's protection, all may yet be well.[3]

The army tries to protect civilian property from illegal foraging.
Even unionists, like John Minor Botts, receive protection. Apparently
bearing no grudge against private soldiers for the folly of their political
leaders or the affront delivered in June by Jeb Stuart, Botts allows
Confederates to fill their canteens with milk from his "choice herd" of
cows. Of course, he charges 25 cents a quart, but he allows the Rebels
to pay with Confederate money, a currency which even many Confederates will not accept. "All of us had a good word to say for Mr. Botts
and his family," remarks one soldier.[4]

Some citizens, however, find reason to complain. One of the com-
plainers, strange to say, is Jack Pendleton. Culpeper boasts few truer
Confederates. Pendleton has given all he can materially to the cause,
and he has entertained scores of officers at Redwood. But the war has
failed to dampen his fiery temper, and a recent event has ignited it
once again. The army was trying not to inconvenience citizens when it
decided to feed its horses by cutting grass from local pasturelands,
rather than allowing the animals to graze. Not a wise order, not the
sort a farmer would issue. "Grass long enough to cut can be made into
hay for the winter," marvels an officer who sees the folly of the order.
"Short grass cannot."[5]

Pendleton knows the difference, so when he saw soldiers, scythes in
hand, approaching the beautiful long meadow that runs up to his house,
he bounded out the door with a double-barreled shotgun. He did not
pull the trigger, but he did deliver a "volley of oaths that would have
done credit to a Gatling gun," and promised to shoot any man who cut
so much as a blade of his grass. The scythe-wielders retreated to camp
for reinforcements, and returned with an armed guard and an officer.
The latter, a mannerly, pleasant-spoken fellow named Joe Haskell, explained the situation to Pendleton—the need for the grass, the need to
follow orders—and finally persuaded the old gentleman to let the men
cut enough grass to feed his horses until Pendleton could appeal to Lee.
Having stated his case to the commander, Pendleton returned with a

note ordering Haskell to withdraw. Apparently, Lee had never intended to procure fodder for his horses by cutting grass, but had left the means of accomplishing such a relatively minor action to subordinates. By doing so, his intentions had "got out of the best shape."[6]

Sunday, July 26. This sabbath day provides a natural, almost providential, occasion to thank God for delivering Lee's men safely to Culpeper. Last night's rainstorm may be interpreted variously as an ill omen or as God's effort to refresh these tired soldiers. Morning broke bright and beautiful, and camps all across Culpeper have held prayer meetings through the day, to be continued, no doubt, into the evening. Hungry men pray for food; the sick and lame pray for restored health and vigor; everyone hopes the fighting is over for the year. "The Lord is good to us in letting us rest and hear his blessed word once and a while," asserts a member of the 14th Georgia Infantry. Lieutenant James M. Simpson, unable to attend church, finds a shady spot away from camp where he can worship privately and commune with memories of his dear wife and children in Alabama. Surely God will soon end the war and their unnatural physical separation, he tells his wife. "I believe," Simpson writes, as he draws on the deepest kind of faith, "that he *has* smiled on our cause, and will never forsake us, tho we lose our whole army."[7]

An odd image: The war over, families reunited, but the army destroyed? The vision reflects the ambivalence that runs through both the military and civilian populations. In the week since the army's arrival, soldiers and civilians alike have contemplated the meaning of the past few weeks. One man complains and worries about the mood of the people. "Our sky is dark," he admits, but "the worst feature is that our people seem to be letting down. We have had only our first reverses, yet many people have gone into a fainting fit. The press seems to take infinite delight in publishing everything to increase the depression and chill the enthusiasm of the army."[8]

But most men, while depressed or worried to some degree, put the best face on the Confederacy's condition and the fate of their cause. "The truth about Gettysburg," decides one soldier, "is that we were *repulsed* at the *final* position of the enemy, & that the *want* of *success* was a terrible *calamity*: but we were *not defeated*." He cannot deny that the "repulse" and the loss of Vicksburg, by now confirmed, has produced "dark days," "agonizing days," but southerners must continue to abide in "an absolute, *unconditional* faith" in both their God and their country, and in the belief that "*in spite* of circumstances & prospects," the Confederacy will prevail.[9]

Jeb Stuart seems unaffected by doubts or defeat. He did not serve Lee well in the Gettysburg campaign. He lost contact with the army for several days when the commander needed information from his cavalry chief about the enemy's position and strength. He had been on a raid, rounding up 900 Federal prisoners and 250 supply wagons, Stuart explains. Some people call it an attempt to atone for Brandy Station by duplicating his ride around McClellan's army or his Catlett's Station raid. More likely, he was just being Stuart. He lives for glory and adulation. He gallops into Culpeper expecting a warm welcome. "Here I am on my old stamping ground," he tells Flora, and, except for the weakened condition of his horses, "in fine fighting trim."[10]

Robert E. Lee has told Mary Custis that he has accomplished his goal in crossing the Rappahannock, but he seems to know the defeat is a serious one. Lee refuses to recognize newspaper criticism, for he believes the army "has accomplished all that could have been reasonably expected. It ought not to have been expected to have performed impossibilities or to have fulfilled the anticipation of the thoughtless & unreasonable." Echoing the words and reflecting the pride of so many of his soldiers, Lee tells Jefferson Davis that his army *did* achieve "a general success," even if it could not claim "a victory." "But with the knowledge I then had, & in the circumstances I was placed, I do not know what better course I could have pursued." If the government or the public believe otherwise and seek someone to blame, he tells Davis, let it be him, not his army. "I am alone to blame," he says, "in perhaps expecting too much of its prowess & valour."[11]

The army has recuperated both physically and spiritually this past week. Supplies have arrived so that men may be fed and reclothed. There is still a shortage of shoes, but Lee's quartermaster is filling the need as best he can. Most men consider a full meal an unexpected luxury, so accustomed have they become to short rations. One man informs his sweetheart that he is thinner than he has been in years, but he feels fit; "[I] look like a soldier really," he tells her. Regular afternoon rains that have pummeled the army since July 26 can be depressing, but the weather has also restricted the hard work and drill. Roll call three times daily and a little guard or picket duty is the only work required of most men. The lull also builds hope that the fighting may be "pretty well over for the season." The men resume old friendships with Culpeper's population. A kinship has grown up between some soldiers and civilians. Families greet men they have come to know as though they were sons or brothers. They gladly wash their clothes and feed them hot meals.[12]

Less pleasantly, the week has permitted numerous courts-martial to be convened, for many men have been charged with breaches of military regulations—not the least of them being desertion and cowardice—since the march north began. The weight of war is beginning to tell on many men. They never bargained on such a long ordeal, and the patriotism that once buoyed them is eroding. "I am heartily tired of the service," complains a more desperate Virginian, "[and] am extremely anxious to be in civil life again." This man, and many like him, only grumble, then return to duty. On the evening of July 29, however, about three hundred unhappy North Carolinians deserted the army. Most of the Tarheels are conscripted artisans and craftsmen who think they should be exempt from the draft, and grumbling may be heard among other non-Virginians who resent being sent to fight far from home. Troops from Alabama, Mississippi, and Tennessee claim they "will fight no more."[13]

The early days of August have seen activity along the Rappahannock. The movement of Federal troops toward Fredericksburg made it appear as though their entire army might shift in that direction, but then John Buford launched yet another attack across the Rappahannock on August 1. Confederate infantry and artillery moved up from the Court House to block the advance on Brandy Station, and after a hard day of fighting, turned back the threat. Lee lost 15 dead; Federal casualties are assumed to be higher.[14]

The unexpected attack has confirmed Lee's inclination to move. If he could hold the Rappahannock fords, all might be well; but the swift

Federal penetration has betrayed how weak his line is without high water in Culpeper's moat. Besides, Lee does not want to be caught in Culpeper. Having carefully examined the terrain on more than one occasion, he has concluded that the county has no field "offering advantages of battle." He has thus ordered a retreat. He does so regretfully, for Culpeper possesses sufficient grass for his horses and enough flour for his men.[15]

August 4. The weather was stifling all day as Lee's army, like some mythical giant shifting in repose, rolled across the Rapidan to concentrate around Orange Court House. Men fainted along the road, and the Federals made things even hotter by establishing a picket force south of the Rappahannock. Light skirmishing has broken out along the Rapidan, and at dusk this evening a thunderstorm adds to the clamor and buffets Lee's men on both sides of the river. Tonight's bivouac has been a "cheerless affair." Only Stuart's cavalry remains in Culpeper. Lee is loath to leave the county to the enemy uncontested. If Stuart can hold it without sacrificing his men, "it will be well." If Lee feels any apprehension about his position, he betrays no sign. One artillerist, watching the general ride unattended through the camps, thinks he looks "as unconcerned as an old farmer going to his daily toil." The move should be completed by tomorrow.[16]

Culpeper civilians are apprehensive again. It seems unlikely that Stuart's cavalry can halt a determined Federal advance, and so some people once more drive their stock and slaves below the Rapidan, "out of the way of the Yankees." Stuart has not even enough men to protect them from the Federal raiders who seem to cross the Rappahannock at will. Sally Armstrong's family is still plagued by blue devils. "Nothing but Yankees from morning till night," she protested on July 29, "no signs of their leaving yet." Things have not improved since then. She hears of how horribly the Federals have been treating people in Fauquier County, and so lives "in dread of having the infantry come over and pillage." "Great anxiety we are in," laments Sally. "We must try to be patient, for we have so far fared better than our neighbors who have had almost every mouthful taken from them."[17]

Yet, even with the Yankees claiming a tenuous hold south of the

Rappahannock, neither side seems anxious to challenge the other. A few skirmishes have been fought, and John Mosby has kept the Yankees off balance by launching raids in Meade's rear; but these bellicose interludes remain exceptions. A Federal officer above the river, impatient for action, mumbles about the "perfect amnesty" that exists between the two sides. Some opposing pickets even water their horses in the same creeks.[18]

This unsoldierly attitude toward picketing and fraternization can go too far. A New Yorker has been given 30 days' hard labor and will forfeit five months' pay for manning his post in a sitting position, his back toward the Rebel lines, his musket lying on the ground 20 feet away. His defiant response to the court-martial board that sentenced him was, "I never had orders to walk my beat. I had orders to keep a good lookout." A Federal captain has been suspended from rank for 15 days after he waded into the river at Kelly's Ford to chat with a Rebel and give him a Washington newspaper. The captain swears he thought the man to whom he spoke was a civilian. "These citizens and soldiers are clothed so much alike that it is hard to distinguish between them," he told the court-martial board with some justification.[19]

Federal and Confederate pickets on the upper regions of the Rappahannock, in the neighborhood of Sally Armstrong's house, rely on the Hazel River to keep their counterparts at bay. Both sides seem relieved. One Federal captain, commanding about 150 men, finds the Rebels south of the river "just active enough to keep up one's excitement. Confederates at the fords, he marvels, sometimes no more than ten yards away, are "very sociable." He frets, even in such a pacific atmosphere, about the need for "continual vigilance and perpetual preparation." This is, after all, the enemy. "Still," he concedes, "it is very pleasant . . . away from orders, details, and fatigue duty, . . . the enemy before you and all quiet along the line." Rebel pickets on the Hazel are content to live and let live. "They [the Federals] were looking quietly around, and behaving themselves," reports one man, "so we did not molest them."[20]

Some residents welcome the Yankees. Lieutenant Colonel Rufus B. Dawes, who holds the Rappahannock bridge with a Wisconsin and a Michigan regiment, observes that people, especially the women, are "grateful" for the protection he affords them. "They have been plundered and robbed by both armies," he reasons, "until starvation stares them in the face." More to the point, his sturdy force has emboldened Culpeper slaves to dash toward Union lines all along the river, from Kelly's Ford to Waterloo. On one evening alone, about forty "children of Ham," as Dawes calls them, moved within his picket lines from the neighborhood around the bridge. Many of the boys and men will be hired by Federal officers as body servants, although some officers refuse under any circumstances to hire "wretched 'niggers.'" Most have been mere field hands as slaves, complains one man, and therefore are ignorant of the duties of a personal servant. "To this ignorance," he elaborates, "must be added the natural laziness, lying, and dirt of the negro, which surpasses anything an ordinary white man is capable of." Not everyone agrees with this assessment, and a number of Union soldiers—apparently a growing number—have come to associate the northern cause with black emancipation. These men view the blacks as heroic figures. A member of the 20th New York Militia admires the "thousands" of contraband blacks laboring in Meade's camps as cooks, teamsters, and servants. "I wish you could see with what earnestness they strive to improve their condition," he informs his mother. "They are faithful and honest in their work and they improve their leisure in learning to read." He believes the blacks "as a class" exhibit more "native sense" than the majority of white southerners.[21]

Sally Armstrong's family has lost about a dozen slaves; only one, Alcinda, who seems puzzled that the others should leave, remains faithful. "We are not distressed at their going," Sally proclaims stubbornly, "though I feel very sorry for father & mother. They in their old age will be deprived of help." When some Yankee officers stop by the Armstrong house to see how the family is taking the loss, Sally will not give them the satisfaction of even discussing the matter.[22]

Old John Kelly has had his fill of deserters, Negroes, and Yankees. General Alpheus Williams, a veteran of the Cedar Mountain fight, occupied Kellysville with six regiments on August 1 and 2 while Buford's men held Stuart's attention at Brandy Station. Kellysville was pretty much a shambles when Williams arrived. The flour mill and woolens factory, both "much dilapidated," stood idle. Only a few slaves remained, most of them either aged or very young. The rest had been sent away for safekeeping a week earlier by Kelly. Kelly and his son, whom Williams judged "very seedy" and "a great scamp," met the Federal general in their yard to complain about how the U.S. government had misused them. Williams displayed his sympathy by gathering Kelly's remaining cattle and horses and emptying his icehouse—the latter being the greater prize, thought Williams, in this oppressively warm weather.

General Williams turned over the younger Kelly to the provost marshal when the army fell back across the river. He also took a slave named James. Williams assumed the fellow would welcome the chance at freedom, but James's wife and their five children are among the slaves Kelly sent away for safekeeping early in the war. James wanted only to return to Culpeper, where he hopes his family will eventually be reunited. He claims that his own master, a Mr. James, is "tolerable," and that life among strangers—the Federals—would always be uncertain. Williams allowed him to return to Culpeper while ruminating, "There is a wonderful amount of strong sense in many of these uneducated Negroes."[23]

But as the days drag by and Meade makes no move, Federals on both sides of the river grumble about their commander's inaction. Many men are "anxious to go ahead and finish up the war," but they sense that Meade is not yet comfortable as the army's commander. Word has it that he nearly gave up the fight at Gettysburg after the second day, and now he seems overly deliberate and cautious. He is a "modest and naturally diffident man, who is not yet warm in his seat or thoroughly master in his own house," judges one officer. In any case, men complain. "This lying in an advanced position where one may be attacked at any moment, while at the same time the chances are twenty to one that you will not be attacked at all, is about the most tiresome position one can be in," asserts one officer. But boredom is nothing compared to a discovery made by Colonel Dawes while south of the river. After over a fortnight in the rifle pits, in danger of imminent attack, he has learned that some of his men have "not a single cartridge in their boxes." Dawes concludes, "The negligence and carelessness of some officers is marvelous."[24]

Men curse the weather and the insects, too. The heat is "intense" everywhere, but it is even less bearable on the Fauquier County side of the Rappahannock, where the region between the riverbank and Warrenton has been stripped of timber. A combination of blazing sun and "barren & desolated fields," judges one soldier, make men feel as though they are "living in an oven." At the other extreme, a Pennsylvanian on picket north of the river complains about the "Virginia dews." "On guard you get as wet in a couple of hours here as you would get at home in an ordinary rain," he explains to his brother. The mornings and evenings are relatively cool, but during the hottest part of the day, "the less clothing worn the better. Most of the men run around all day with nearly a Georgia costume, a Hat, drawers and shirt." As for the insects, "I have read of the Musquetoes of the Arkansas swamps and have heard something of those that infest regions of the Nile," vows an Indiana soldier, "but I never came in contact with such gigantic cannibals, such Mammoth blood suckers, such unprincipaled glutons as the Musquetoes of the Rappahannock."[25]

Facing the Union threat, Stuart is content to hold Brandy Station and mind Lee's cautious orders, but inaction makes Stuart irritable. His men find the atmosphere less relaxed in camp than on picket duty, where they hold "frequent interviews" with Yankee vignettes, even though their commander has issued an order forbidding fraternization. "It is impossible to get out of camp," complains one Confederate cavalryman, "discipline is on every tongue. . . . We live on hard bread (stale crackers) & fat bacon, or poor beef." Besides that, Stuart drills them morning and afternoon when they are not on picket. His cavalrymen resent working so hard while the infantry, they imagine, reclines "safe & at ease twenty-five miles . . . to the rear enjoying all the vegetables of the season & an abundance of meat & bread & corn."[26]

The physical reminders of battles past scattered all around the camp at Brandy merely add to the gloom. Trying to sleep one recent night, a Virginia cavalryman tossed and turned uncomfortably, unable to settle down. Finally, he got on his knees to inspect the ground beneath his blanket. He discovered that he had been "laying on Yankee bones," though how he could tell they were Yankee bones is uncertain. He moved his position a few feet away but the next morning found himself resting next to a corpse. A friend, less concerned than he by the remains of death, picked up a portion of a leg-bone and made a ring from it. Even Jeb Stuart feels a little blue. Perhaps the restrictions placed on him by Lee make him restive. He clearly misses Flora on these progressively cooler nights, and he with only one blanket. Stuart is also anxious about his chances for the new lieutenant-general position soon to be filled.[27]

Recent military setbacks and their isolated position have inspired a religious revival in Lee's army. As their numbers dwindle, and they see fewer and fewer of their old comrades around them, men who have fought for two years without a scratch reckon their chances for sur-vival. Consequently, emphasizes one man, this is "no fictitious enthusi-asm" that has struck the army. "It is a serious solemn awakening of hope among men who for years have been walking face to face with all the darkness and honor of a sudden and hopeless death." Should he "bee killed or dye," a South Carolinian informs his family, he wants to be buried next to his brother at home. "Some how I have a horror of being thrown out in a neglected place or bee trampled on as I have seen a number of graves here," he explains from near Stevensburg. Of course, he hopes to survive the war in one piece, but he realizes that "life is uncertain at any time, particularly in the army where a man is exposed to so many dangers."[28]

The army has observed several days of "prayer and fasting" during August. At Stevensburg, a Captain Brown serves as chaplain to a South Carolina regiment. A "pleasant and affible gentleman," Brown has held services twice on Sundays and sometimes on weeknights for the past few weeks. At Brandy, the other large area of encampment for Stuart's men, a revival meeting was held on August 21. "We had the Brigade to our camp to hear it," reports a member of the 10th Virginia Cavalry. "You never saw such a congregation," he informs his wife, "[men] sitting on the ground listening at the word of god." At the ar-tillery park near the Court House, George Neese, a member of Chew's Battery, preached a sermon recently from the text of John 13:17: "If ye know these things, happy are ye if ye do them."[29]

Meanwhile, Culpeper's civilians hunker down. The pickets may be laughing and joking, men in camp may be in a meditative mood, but that cannot last for long. The war is not over; there *must* be a battle, and soon. Captain Charles Francis Adams, Jr., commanding the Union picket force on the Hazel River, feels sorry for neighboring civilians. He knows that these people hate him and his men, but he understands the reason. He has witnessed daily "acts of pillage and outrage on the poor and defenceless" that make his "hair stand on end," and cause him to "loathe all war." Soldiers, usually under cover of darkness, break into homes, rifle closets and drawers, take what they like, and abuse and threaten their victims. Some regimental commanders enforce strict or-ders against such acts, but other units seem to operate without re-straint. Few courts martial result from this marauding. Some citizens are too terrified to sleep. It is as bad as in the days of Pope. "Poor Vir-ginia!" laments Captain Adams. "Her fighting men have been slaugh-tered; her old men have been ruined; her women and children are starving and outraged; her servants have run away or been stolen; her fields have been desolated; her towns have been depopulated."[30]

Adams, like Dawes further down the river, finds himself trying to help and protect defenseless Rebels. When an old woman, approach-ing the three-quarter-century mark, begs him to prevent his men from stealing her sheep (four are all that remain to her), he cusses at his men and swears vengeance on anyone who repeats the offense. The woman has responded by sending Adams a gift of milk and butter, an expression of gratitude that she has privately vowed to repeat each evening that Adams's men stand picket. Adams has reciprocated by giving her a sack of sugar. Were it within his power, decides Adams, he would provide a safeguard for every Rebel who asked for one, "even the most offensively outspoken" traitors. "The horrors of war are not all to be found in the battle-field," he laments, "and every army pil-lages and outrages to a terrible extent."[31]

Sally Armstrong's family has benefited from the kindness of Yankees like Dawes and Adams, but this only confuses Sally. August 1863 has been one of the most trying times of her young life, yet she knows it could have been far worse. Her father received a guard for their farm on August 3, and they have not been bothered since. "Really," decides Sally, "we have abundant cause to thank God for his merciful protec-tion, surrounded by our enemies, yet so little disturbed. Our guard must be the best Yankees in the north. They are always on the lookout." Yet Sally has not seen a Confederate uniform in over a month, and she worries how long the Federal occupation will last. She has been slipping into bed before dark in order to sleep as much as possible and so shorten the days. "What shall I write for these times?" she asks her diary. "Yankees doing all conceivable wickedness." About the middle of August, the Federals who had been encamped near her home fell back beyond the Rappahannock. With her family no longer living within Yankee lines, she feels free to visit in the neighborhood once again. Yet the pickets, her "tormentors," continue to patrol. She feels much like Stuart's men, who seek solace in religion: "If God did not rule we would die in despair. He only can help us."[32]

The rest of Culpeper plows bravely ahead. After all, Stuart's men are in place; Lee is just across the river. Even the circuit court plans to resume its sessions in September. At least one important case is pending. Back in June, a dozen men were indicted by a grand jury for illegally making whiskey and other spirituous liquors. Otherwise, each day without a battle builds hope that Meade will be content to winter in Fauquier. Something of the social scene associated with past Confederate occupations begins to surface, albeit without the sparkle or verve of last year. People with anything left to sell can still make money from the army. Alfred Stofer has given up trying to publish his newspaper, but he continues to print forms and orders for Lee. Langdon C. Major has sold 58 sheep for $1,740. William Major has sold nearly 1,200 pounds of hay for some $320. Thomas Hill has sold hay, corn, fodder, and cattle and pastured horses. Philip Slaughter has sold hay, corn, and oats, and rented out his blacksmith shop and tools. And so it goes for many other families. Even John Botts is willing to support the Confederacy if the price is right. He has earned thousands of dollars (albeit in Confederate money) since the end of July for grazing horses and selling cordwood, wheat, and hay.[33]

Yet an unsettled, almost melancholy mood hovers over soldiers and civilians alike. More Culpeper families have moved south and west, mostly into the Shenandoah Valley. The ghostly hand of Cedar Mountain, the battle just a year past, clings in memory to those who survived the bloody ordeal. Jubal Early has sent a work detail from south of the Rapidan to tend Confederate graves on the field. Hogs have again been rooting and uncovering corpses. The dead, Early knows, are past caring; all seasons are alike to them now. Yet . . . well, damn it, these were soldiers.[34]

And Stuart remains unsettled. He still jokes with Flora in their correspondence—wishing so he could give her "such an old fashioned *squeeze*" that she would squeal "*don't!*"—but he is not at all himself. His plan for a raid against General David M. Gregg's cavalry encampment on September 4 along the Hazel River went awry when the Yanks arrested the citizen who was to serve as Stuart's guide across an unguarded ford. His perceived failure during the Gettysburg campaign still haunts him. He tells everyone that he has been "much blamed by those that knew nothing about it." Another blow landed on September 9 when he learned that Lee had decided not to promote him to lieutenant general. His cavalry division has been reorganized and expanded to corps strength, but he is to retain his old rank of major general. What is more, his two new division commanders, Wade Hampton and Fitzhugh Lee, have been made major generals. Infighting and feuding among his staff and among men who did not receive promotions in the reorganization further disrupt the harmony of his camp. Finally, one of his sisters has died, and Flora, eight months pregnant, has been taken ill at Lynchburg.[35]

September 13. Everything has changed. About 7:30 this morning, General Alfred Pleasonton's cavalry crossed the Rappahannock and Hazel rivers in such force and at so many points that Stuart's men stood no chance. Behind the cavalry came the infantry and artillery of General Gouverneur K. Warren's II Corps, and the whole has converged on Brandy. The cavalry alone numbers 10,000 men—nine full brigades— to Stuart's six brigades. Apparently, Meade had learned that Lee's army had been thinned by the movement of James Longstreet's men to Tennessee and the scattering of Ewell's and Hill's men elsewhere. With Lee's army too depleted to rush to Stuart's assistance, Meade sees Culpeper as easy pickings.[36]

Stuart's scattered pickets and divided camps may have been saved by the swift action of his artillery, which moved from the Court House to Brandy to help intercept the main Federal column, led by John Buford. But by noon the artillery has already begun to withdraw. There are too many Yankees. The gunners enjoy small victories along the way. George Neese has turned his battery on a cluster of blue riders atop a knoll perhaps a half-mile away. His guns roar; one rider tumbles to the ground, and the others scatter. One Federal officer proclaims the precision of the Confederate guns "extraordinary." Yet fall back the Rebels do, ever closer to the Court House, where the fighting becomes tenacious. Federal sharpshooters have moved to within 150 yards of the Confederate batteries. Bullets whizz and zip between the gunners. Most of the lead whisks "harmlessly and unceremoniously" past them, but one of Neese's men falls with a painfully wounded ankle. Neese returns the favor by pouring canister into the threatening blue tide. These Yankees fight well, he thinks to himself; they mean business. The Yanks know they outnumber the Rebels, and this knowledge has imbued them with an "intoxicating inspiration," a boldness that usually produces victories on the battlefield. It is early afternoon by now, and the Federals have pushed the gray troops back to the outskirts of the Court House.[37]

Fortunately for the gray-clad gunners, Federal artillerists consistently overshoot their marks. Unfortunately for Court House residents, many Yankee shells crash through buildings along the northern and eastern portions of town. This being a Sunday, worship services had already started before the battle-lines reached town. When the shells began to fall, Reverend Barnett Grimsley dismissed his Baptist congregation, mounted his horse, and raced for his home in Rappahannock County. People of all denominations have flocked to the Episcopal rectory, the home of John Cole. It has one of the largest and deepest cellars in town, and people have learned to take sanctuary there when the Court House is subjected to bombardment. Confederate gunners return the favor by pummeling a Federal battery positioned by the Wallach house. The Wallach women have fled to their cellar, all the while cursing the Rebels in ladylike fashion.[38]

Finally, blue horsemen, some firing pistols, others wielding sabers, crash through Confederate batteries on the extreme right flank. General George A. Custer, youngest general in the Union army, leads this wild charge. Old Curly, as his Michigan troops call him, is a sight to behold, outfitted in a gold-trimmed hussar jacket, tight black velvet trousers, and gilt spurs; but Custer is undeniably brave. While leading the assault, his horse is shot from under him, and he suffers a nasty-looking leg wound. Custer's men plow ahead, but they are paying for their victory. Where they penetrate enemy lines, the Rebels fight fiercely, with "blazing pistols, flashing sabers, and excited men contending and wildly struggling like maddened demons in a furious melee for the mastery of the situation."[39]

By now fighting has reached the streets of town, but it is all over for the artillerists. When Vermont, Michigan, and New York regiments, all led by a remounted Custer, bore down upon them at such close quarters, the Confederate gunners were helpless. "Nothing but Rebel wind and first-class pluck for racing" has saved most of the men from being captured. They did get some help from the 5th and 6th Virginia cavalry, which swooped into the fray while the gunners withdrew to the safety of Rapidan and Robinson rivers; but superior numbers have told once more, and the Confederate riders are withdrawing beyond Mt. Pony. Confederate resistance everywhere is collapsing as heavy rainclouds move in from the west.[40]

A few civilians have been casualties of the day's fighting. The wife of the Reverend Richard Stone was wounded by a shell fragment at the Court House. One of the Curtis families—confusion reigns as to which one—suffered casualties when an artillery shell crashed into their house. Many more people suffer emotionally and psychologically as a Federal army settles down to occupy Culpeper for the second time in the war. As the smoke of battle clears, people carefully exit cellars all over the Court House. Haunted and haunting faces peer from windows as long columns of Federal cavalry ride into town. One old lady, dressed in mourning, has spent all day at her parlor window, gazing out into Main Street and muttering over and over again, "Oh, you sons of bitches!"[41]

The bluecoats have varying opinions of the Court House and surrounding countryside, though they are generally less than enthusiastic. A private in the 2nd Pennsylvania Cavalry believes Culpeper is not nearly so desolate as some portions of Virginia he has seen. He is impressed by the "nice looking" Court House with its "handsome" residences, although he notices that most of the houses are vacant. Other Federals are less generous in their appraisal. Impressions of the Court House range from "tumble-down 'Virginian,'" to "a nasty hole" and "a dirty-looking place." Most of the buildings, offers a New Yorker, appear "old and dingy," and he snickers at the location of the courthouse and jail on one of the main streets, a location that would not be "in the best of taste" in a northern town. More fairly, Colonel Joseph W. Keifer observes of the Court House, "It is built after the manner of almost all inland Southern towns—Occasional very fine dwellings, interspersed with rude negro quarters throughout." Nearly everyone comments on how deserted the town looks. There are plenty of soldiers, but few citizens. The white citizens who remain are the very young and the very old. The remaining blacks—a mere "sprinkling" at best—display the only happy faces.[42]

Meade does not care what Culpeper looks like so long as he can hold it. He pressed his attacks on the night of September 13 and hoped to resume fighting on the 14th, but he has come to see the impossibility of a direct assault across the Rapidan. He is fairly sure that he outnumbers Lee, but he sees no advantage in crossing the river and pushing back the Rebels any further unless he can push them all the way to Richmond, and he knows his force is inadequate to that task.[43]

Late September. Meade is even less certain of what to do. He is fairly confident that Lee will not attack him, although the occasional sortie has been launched across the Rapidan, and artillery bombards Federal pickets regularly. But light skirmishing has dwindled into sporadic firing, and while Meade outnumbers Lee 90,000 to 50,000, he seems content to spend the winter in Culpeper. The county swarms with his soldiers. Wagons carrying supplies and equipment to widespread encampments line country roads. With the Rappahannock bridge now rebuilt and the telegraph fully operational, Meade holds a strong position. Yet Meade has yet to find a way to hit Lee without suffering heavy casualties and risking his supply and communications lines. He remains uncertain of Lee's strength and the condition of the fords along the Rapidan.[44]

John Minor Botts (seated) and his daughters on the front porch of their house, Auburn, near Brandy Station. While taking up residence in Culpeper only after the start of the war, they became the county's most controversial unionists. (Courtesy Library of Congress)

This sketch by northern artist Alfred Waud depicts Federal artillery in action during the Saint Patrick's Day battle at Kelly's Ford. (Courtesy Library of Congress)

John Pelham, the young artillerist who became a favorite of Jeb Stuart and the ladies, was mortally wounded at Kelly's Ford on March 17, 1863. (Courtesy United States Military Academy Archives)

Below, Brandy Station as it appeared during the Federal winter encampment of 1863–64. (C. W. Bardeen, *A Little Fifer's War Diary*, 1910)

A northern artist's idealized impression of the cavalry battle at Brandy Station on June 9, 1863. (*Harper's Weekly*)

George G. Meade's staff in front of his headquarters at the William Douglas Wallace house, September 1863. (Courtesy Library of Congress)

This view of the battle at Rappahannock Station on November 7, 1863, by Edwin Forbes depicts the advance of the 44th New York Infantry. (*Leslie's Illustrated Newspaper*)

Another sketch of the Rappahannock Station fight, also by Forbes, captures the primitive nature of much of the fighting on that night. George G. Meade's victory forced Robert E. Lee to abandon Culpeper and permitted a prolonged Federal occupation. (Courtesy Library of Congress)

A view of Kelly's Ford during Federal occupation. The foreground shows the remains of Confederate breastworks once manned to repel the invader. (C. W. Bardeen, *A Little Fifer's War Diary*, 1910)

Meade's supply depot at Brandy Station, early 1864. (Courtesy United States Military Academy Archives)

Brandy Station headquarters and staff of the U.S. Sanitary Commission in early 1864. (Courtesy Massachusetts Commandery, Military Order of the Loyal Legion and the U.S. Army Military History Institute)

A sutler's store at Brandy Station in February 1864. (Courtesy Massachusetts Commandery, Military Order of the Loyal Legion and the U.S. Army Military History Institute)

These two "contra-band" (ex-slaves) worked as servants for Union officers in Culpeper in the autumn of 1863. Notice the tin cans strewn in the fore-ground, signs of Fed-eral abundance. (Courtesy Library of Congress)

The winter of 1863–64 became a season of repose for many officers, including these members of John Sedgwick's staff. (Courtesy United States Military Academy Archives)

The Army of the Potomac crosses the Rapidan River at Germanna Ford in May 1864 headed for the Wilderness. (Courtesy Massachusetts Commandery, Military Order of the Loyal Legion and the U.S. Army Military History Institute)

Daniel A. Grimsley of the 6th Virginia Cavalry in a postwar photograph. He was one of many Culpeper volunteers to fight through the entire war. (John N. Opie, *A Rebel Cavalryman with Lee, Stuart, and Jackson*, 1899)

The mood in the Federal camp fluctuates daily, as it does in any camp. Many of Meade's men, infantry especially, grow impatient with his cautious method of making war. They appreciate the formidable nature of the Confederate line, but they are tired of waiting for something to happen. A few men, accustomed to the Army of the Potomac advancing only to give way, believe that Lee *will* attack, and Meade will retreat, just like McClellan, Pope, Burnside, Hooker, and all the rest. Others think the army is "certain" to fight, and that Meade would not dare miss an opportunity to "strike at that wily old Gen" who has caused the army "so much trouble." Generally, though, high spirits predominate over sullen grousing. "Our camp is alive with pleasant scenes, and it is impossible to delineate our life at present with dark outlines," reports a Massachusetts soldier. Regimental bands serenade officers on most evenings. The program for one concert at Meade's headquarters included "Hell on the Rappahannock" in addition to selections from *Il Trovatore* and *Lucia di Lammermoor*. The men are animated because they were paid during the last week of September, some regiments receiving as much as six months' back pay. On the other hand, they complain about high prices charged by sutlers (a "lot of extortioners" insists one man) who demand 50 to 60 cents for a pound of butter, 40 cents for a pound of cheese, 50 cents for a pound of raisins, and 25 cents for three apples.[45]

Luckily, the soldiers do not depend on their meager pay to eat, for Culpeper's farmers are enjoying a bountiful harvest, and it is all there for the taking. "Seldom are soldiers permitted to live in a country of which it may be said as emphatically as of this," reports one man, "that it 'flows with milk and honey.'" Local crops, sheep, cattle, and poultry have become "the basis" of army rations. "The country abounds with sorghum, apple-butter, milk, honey, sweet potatoes, peaches, apples, etc.," reveals a New York cavalryman. Forage for horses is similarly "abundant." Unfortunately, Culpeper farmers are not always compensated for this apparent bounty, which remains but a fraction of past harvests. Union cavalrymen, in particular, with the ability to range far and wide over the county, take advantage of their distance from the camps to confiscate whatever they fancy. "You can have no idea how much better off this army is now than it was when you came to see me last Fall," a sergeant tells his father. "We fare better in all respects. . . . The boys are in better spirits, and much healthier." He claims that the men are no longer forced to live off the countryside as they were early in the war, but then he admits, "When we do any such thing, it is only because we see something which looks good, and so we take it as a luxury & not because we actually need it."[46]

Most of Meade's men coolly rationalize the ravaging of Culpeper's countryside. "We are so far into the heart of secessia now," the chaplain of a New York regiment informs his wife, "that we dont try to restrain the men much but let them forage to their hearts content." The chaplain is saddened by the way men have defaced a church near his camp, a church which, "like the lovely country about [it,] . . . may be said to be 'beautiful in ruins.'" Seats have been ripped from the building by "the ruthless hand of the soldiery," and the walls bear scribbled names of hundreds of men. Yet even this sacrilege the chaplain excuses as a product of both northern and southern soldiers. Churches and houses are considered fair game if their owners have abandoned them. "Abandoned property is an incentive to pillage," explains one man, "deserted dwellings are prompters to vandalism, . . . and the demon of destruction, roused by a spirit of resentment, prompts the best of men to deeds of rapine and plunder." Such reasoning will be cold comfort to some Culpeper families, who will find their residences mere shells should they ever return home.[47]

Culpeper's civilians try to limit the extent of the damage by selling what they can to the army. Women do most of the trading. They are the ones most in need of money and most vulnerable to threats of theft, especially if they have been left on a farm, perhaps with children, while their husbands fight for Lee. Milk, garden vegetables, and butter are the products most often sold, but they will part with anything they can spare. Sometimes they barter rather than sell for cash. One woman has been doing that in the camp of the 151st New York Regiment. "She would not take money," marvels one soldier in explaining the arrangement, "though some of the men offered her two dollars for what she had." The men have plenty of sugar, which they trade to the woman for butter. Both sides benefit. The men save close to two dollars over what they would have paid in cash for the butter; the woman acquires a commodity she can obtain nowhere else.[48]

But many men, whatever the luxuries they enjoy, find camp life tedious. "This camp is the dullest I have ever been in," complains a Pennsylvania cavalryman. "There is nothing to see or be seen." The men are restricted to camp when not on picket duty, and their only activity comes from drills and inspections, two detestable ingredients of army life that the men find totally unnecessary at this season of the year. By comparison, picket duty offers the only "real fun" to be found. The appeal of picket duty has grown recently after a tense period in which men fired at anything that moved. Most men have resumed the old relaxed style of guarding their lines. "Some of the Rebel pickets came over to our lines to-day and played 'Seven Up' with some of our men," an Ohio soldier, posted on the Rapidan at Raccoon Ford, confesses to his diary. On quiet evenings, Federal pickets can enjoy the music of Confederate bands playing for dress parades and serenading officers. Likewise, they can hear Rebel voices lifted in song at evening prayer meetings.[49]

Camp life has its sobering side, too, for another round of executions and punishments are being meted out for desertion and cowardice. Courts-martial convene virtually every day, and though some cases are sad ones, discipline and justice must be served. Most deserters continue to be bounty-jumpers, a group for which army veterans show little sympathy. Even Meade has issued an order forbidding conscripts and substitutes to serve on picket duty, fearing, evidently, that their proximity to Confederate lines will make it too easy for them to desert. Instead, they will be kept busy drilling in camp (at least four hours per day) and learning military duties. The veterans approve. "If those fellows are trusted on picket," offers one man, "the army will soon be in h—l." Men suspected of cowardice have a rough time, too. Three conscripted Quakers from New York have received severe physical punishments for refusing to bear arms.[50]

Veterans of the Army of the Potomac have also started to grumble about the fruits of the first Federal conscription. The dregs of society, these conscripts are, and even worse are the substitutes who have "volunteered" to serve in exchange for the government's bounty. They are "men in form," spits one veteran, but they possess "few of the traits that govern men." Many appear to have been thieves, gamblers, or thugs in civilian life, foul in language and cowards to boot. Their bounties collected, many desert at the first opportunity. Colonel Dawes proclaims them "a sorry looking set." "What a contrast between such hounds and the enthusiastic and eager volunteers of 1861," laments the colonel. "Our men thoroughly despise these cattle and certainly the honor of the old army will not be safe in such hands." For those misfits caught attempting to desert, the price can be high. The army has witnessed a series of public executions lately, performed with much pomp and display in order to impress the men with the gravity of the offense.[51]

The approach of autumn has brought a change in the weather that people alternately praise and curse. On the bright side, cooler weather has brought about the death of the flies and mosquitoes. The relentless heat has disappeared, and most days may be described as "fair." On the other hand, genuine cold spells set in quickly. A Pennsylvania soldier, who knows something about cold weather, has been shivering beneath three blankets on recent nights, and he has donned his overcoat on some days. Autumn also signals the onset of the rainy season. Tents flood on some nights; high winds batter canvas shelters; campfires hiss and die. When the rains cease, the mud, thick "Virginia mud," clings to men's boots, making it difficult to walk and impossible to stay clean. The contrast between the soldier's present life and his life as a civilian is revealing. On cold nights at home, these men went to bed to keep warm, and huddled snugly under quilts and comforters. As soldiers, they get *out* of bed to stay warm. Their heavy uniforms and coats conserve heat far more efficiently than their blankets, and a "brisk 'double quick'" upon rising "brings warmth to the skin and an appetite to the stomach." Only Meade is oblivious to the weather. Confident that he has the upper hand over Lee, his world is perfect. "We are having lovely weather at present," he informs he wife; "our camps are beautifully situated at the foot of the Blue Ridge, with the mountains in view, with pure air and plenty of good water; the best country in Virginia we have yet been in."[52]

As in the Confederate camp across the river, prayer meetings are proliferating this autumn in the Army of the Potomac. One chaplain is delighted with the new enthusiasm of his flock. At 7 P.M. on a recent evening, when the drummer sounded "Church Call," "every officer and nearly every man in the Regiment" drifted into the natural sanctuary he had carved out of the forest near camp. "I never preached to a congregation that gave me such breathless attention," he marveled, "and I think I never had *so good a time.*" Some men use the revival spirit to lecture their comrades on specific sins, especially intemperance. "There is need of reformation in the army with regard to this *great subject,*" insists a New Yorker. At a recent regimental ceremony, he complains, "scores" of officers and men had been drunk. "The Army tends more to demoralize than ennoble the soldier," he insists. He calculates that nineteen of every twenty men in the army drink, and that nine out of every ten curse. In his company alone, six out of seven men who professed a religious affiliation upon leaving home now play cards, and one of those men is a preacher.[53]

Some men pursue more lonely, even painful, assignments during their off-duty hours. Henry L. Abbott is a captain in the 20th Massachusetts Infantry, known as the "Harvard Regiment" because so many of its officers and men have attended the Cambridge college. One of Abbott's brothers, a captain in the 2nd Massachusetts, was slain—"murdered," says the family—in the fearful slaughter of Gordon's brigade at Cedar Mountain. Henry had been shaken terribly by the news. Now, little more than a year later, he finds himself encamped nearly upon the very field of his brother's death. Many men have visited this by-now-famous battle ground during the past year. Some have come from curiosity; others seek souvenirs. Few have visited with so heartfelt a mission as Abbott. Guided by a survivor of the battle, Abbott found the lonely spot where the 2nd Massachusetts lost so many good men. "Of course Wood [the guide] could not show me the spot where Ned lay," Abbott informs his mother. "But only the line of the brigade. I fancied a great many places." The memory of the place continues to haunt him. Nearly a week later, Abbott has written to his father, "When I was on the field where the 2nd fought, it seemed as if I could see Ned alive, looking as he did on the becan-club regatta."[54]

Meanwhile, the army enjoys a strained relationship with Culpeper's civilian population. All the unionists, of course, are glad to have the army here. If only, they pray, Meade's presence means a permanent Federal encampment. Meade has established his headquarters at the Wallach house. Wallach's winsome daughter, 23-year-old Nannie, directs household affairs with a decided "eye to business." Most of the soldiers are smitten with Nannie, who "carries herself superbly, serene and undisturbed." Her victims include Meade, who, if determined to resist Lee's advances, seems powerless against Miss Wallach. In return for giving up several rooms to Meade's staff for administrative purposes, she has received guards to watch over the barn, fences, and other properties on the family's nearly three hundred acres. Her remaining half-dozen servants, now freewomen—and about half the number of slaves the Wallachs kept before the war—have worked their wiles on the cooks and servants of Meade's staff. Thus have they "secured the complete stocking of their larder for weeks to come from the abundance of Uncle Sam's commissary." And, of course, in the evening, Miss Wallach opens the parlor to Meade's staff. The company sings war and college songs to the accompaniment of Nannie's skillful piano playing. "She is very fascinating," sighs a young New Yorker, "perfectly at ease, and brilliant as a dewdrop on a summer morn."[55]

Other families receive officers and a few enlisted men into their homes. Most of them appear to be unionists, but who can say how many are simply being cautious? Meade has received personal visits from John Botts, Jack Pendleton, and John Cole. Pendleton has persuaded Meade that he is a good Union man, which does not say much for the Yankee general's power of perception. The soldiers do not seem to care about the political inclinations or motives of the families they visit. It is enough for them to taste of whatever "social sweets" may be afforded them.[56]

Culpeper's most noted unionist, John Minor Botts, is also among the biggest entertainers in the county. Anyone passing through the neighborhood of Brandy can spot Botts's impressive house, Auburn. Botts also has three "charming" daughters to serve as hostesses, though few would think them as lovely or clever as Nannie Wallach. Botts generally uses these social occasions to rail against his treatment by the U.S. government. His ego offends some officers, who refuse his invitations, however inviting the thought of a home-cooked meal or the refinements of a parlor.[57]

Most families are less enthusiastic about this second Federal occupation of Culpeper. At least one civilian, a Miss Stringfellow, has been wounded as a result of skirmishing along the Rapidan. Less threatening but no less painful are the material losses that alternately sadden and anger people. "There is much grief among the old families here at seeing the landmarks of their childhood and days of the prosperity swept away," observes a Wisconsin soldier while watching a crew of men level acres of cedar trees and orange hedges for the sake of constructing their beds, "and their manifestation of sorrow is sometimes quite affecting." On the other hand, he, like so many others, reasons, "Sorry as it makes us feel, we have to stand it and take the trees." More slaves have been claimed as contraband by the army, including groups of blacks who had been spirited to safety in Madison and Rappahannock counties.[58]

And insult is occasionally added to injury. When one citizen approached General William H. French, encamped near the Court House, to request a safe guard for his cornfield, French replied that the man must first swear allegiance to the United States. The citizen retorted that he would be damned before he did any such thing. French replied that *he*, then, would be damned before supplying safe guards for Rebels. The citizen, sensing a determined opponent, protested that he would starve if his corn went unprotected, but French held firm, and the fellow went off muttering to himself. That night he did more than mutter; because he had not received the guard he had requested, foraging soldiers razed his entire field of corn.[59]

The people remain largely powerless. Their best hope of dislodging the Federals is to harass their supply lines through guerrilla raids and bushwhacking. Yet the best opportunities for doing this lie across the Rappahannock, in Fauquier County. Meade holds Culpeper firmly in his grasp.[60]

CHAPTER ELEVEN

EQUINOX

$\mathcal{T}$he autumnal equinox passed quietly on September 22, but Lee is not ready to go into hibernation for the winter. Having spent September digging rifle pits and fortifying his position below the Rapidan, he will not be content until Meade has been pushed beyond the Rappahannock. Lee set his army in motion yesterday, October 8, but cautiously. With most of Meade's infantry occupying the ridge north of the Court House, and a large cavalry contingent picketing the river on his right flank, the Federals could either defend or attack with equal effect.[1]

October 9. Last evening and early this morning Lee crossed two corps and Stuart's cavalry below the Robinson River. He intends to swing around and strike Meade's right flank by way of Madison Court House. His movements are based on information about the placement and strength of Meade's army received from civilians in Culpeper. The Federals have grown suspicious of some local people. They have arrested an as yet unidentified woman who has been selling milk and vegetables to Union soldiers. They accuse her of being a spy. This evening, Meade also arrested three prominent gentlemen—Henry Shackleford, C. P. Stallard, and Colonel Freeman—and sent them to Washington. It is doubtful that the Federals actually think them spies, and no charges have been made against them; but they will be held to exchange for unionist civilians arrested by the Confederates.[2]

October 11. Meade has received the worst of two days of fighting, and he is hopping mad. Here is what happened. When Stuart's men crossed the Robinson River and drove Federal cavalry under Judson Kilpatrick back toward James City, the two sides took up positions in the hills on either side of the town. Meade, realizing he was in danger of being enveloped, ordered John Buford's cavalry division across the Rapidan at Germanna Ford. Fitzhugh Lee quickly pushed back Buford, and early this morning, Stuart found that Kilpatrick had skedaddled during the night. With a praiseworthy combination of cunning and audacity, the outnumbered Stuart pursued and caught up with the Federals about three miles west of the Court House.[3]

Kilpatrick, desperately trying to shield Meade's retreating army, was still not out of the soup. As Fitz Lee steadily pushed back Buford's cavalry, first to Stevensburg and then on toward Brandy, Kilpatrick awoke to the new danger of being outflanked by the combined forces of Stuart and Lee. He retreated further east toward the heights of Fleetwood. Both sides recognized the necessity of seizing the high ground, and gray and blue units collided in running fights all through the late morning and early afternoon in a race for the prize. Fitzpatrick won, and breathed a further sigh of relief when he saw Buford's hard-pressed men, riding north to join him, make a tenacious stand against Lee around Brandy Station. "Like a tiger that is pursued too dangerously near its lair and at last turns in desperation on its pursuer and offers deadly combat," marveled one of Lee's artillerists, "so the Yanks that we chased all day at last turned and attacked us with . . . determined vigor and dashing intrepidity."[4]

George Custer's Michigan brigade typified Federal heroics. When General Thomas Rosser's Confederate brigade threatened Buford's command early in the fight, Custer led the 1st and 5th Michigan Cavalry in a charge against the gray wall. "Boys of Michigan," called out the 23-year-old general, "there are some people between us and home; I'm going home, who else goes?" The regiments responded with three hearty hurrahs; the band struck up "Yankee Doodle Dandy"; and the line leapt forward. After advancing a short distance, Custer—"the daring, terrible demon that he is in battle"—shouted out "Charge!" and the attack was on. The Wolverines had not advanced far when they encountered a wide ditch, which they had to detour around. They took a hammering from Rosser's men by doing so; Custer had two horses shot from under him. Before long, however, they had reformed their lines on Rosser's side of the ditch and easily claimed the field.[5]

Most of Meade's infantry and supply wagons had safely crossed the Rappahannock by this time, but Kilpatrick and Buford remained in a tight spot. They might have been pummeled convincingly were it not for the erratic behavior of Fitzhugh Lee. "I wish you could see him and hear his voice during a fight," boasts a member of the 3rd Virginia Cavalry of Lee. He is always in the thickest of the fight and above all the noise and confusion his full rich voice can be heard cheering on his men." Sadly, Lee has also become fond of drink—excessively fond think some observers—to the point where he hardly knows, on occasion, what commands he is giving. Whether or not influenced by drink, Lee miscalculated twice in rapid succession this afternoon. First, just as his regiments showed promise of pushing past Buford and seizing Fleetwood ahead of Kilpatrick, he called a momentary halt to their advance. Reacting to the rising volume of cheers and clashing sabers in the fight between Stuart and Kilpatrick, Lee mistook the clamor for indications of a Federal victory, perhaps accompanied by the arrival of reinforcements. So as not to rush into a trap, he retarded his advance just enough to ensure Federal success in gaining Fleetwood. Likewise, as Lee surveyed the converging columns of Kilpatrick and Stuart, Fitz mistook friend for foe. He ordered his artillery to open fire, and the the well-directed shells forced several Confederate regiments to halt or turn back. Confederate momentum had been lost, and Buford's men, by well-ordered degrees, fell back to help Kilpatrick secure Fleetwood.[6]

By midafternoon, Stuart believed he had no choice but to attack the reunited Federal cavalry, even though their artillery held the high ground and they enjoyed strong positions in the woods around Brandy. He had tried all day to out maneuver the Yanks. Now he would depend on the dash and courage of his horsemen to launch attacks from two directions. "For a little while the fight was severe," reports one Rebel, "and the crash of small arms crept out over the evening air with a similar fierceness and frightful roar of an infantry battle, and the deadly music was well interspersed with a deep hoarse growl of booming cannon on all sides." Like last June's struggle over this same terrain, horsemen today fought both mounted and dismounted, depending on circumstances. Perhaps the most courageous Confederate exercises of the day came when the 5th, 6th, and 15th Virginia Cavalry made no fewer than five saber charges against Federal positions. "On the great field were riderless horses and dying men," records a cavalryman; "clouds of dust from solid shot and bursting shell occasionally obscured the sky; broken caissons and upturned ambulances obstructed the way, while long lines of cavalry were pressing forward in the charge, with their drawn sabers, glistening in the bright sunlight." Culpeper has seen it all before.[7]

This evening, as the sun reluctantly slides below the Blue Ridge, both sides, gasping for breath and thankful for a reason to recess, have paused. Stuart and Lee pull back to Brandy; Buford and Kilpatrick withdraw toward the Rappahannock. The Federals have accomplished their mission. The infantry is safe and what supplies could not be moved have been destroyed. Little remains for the Rebels save the debris of the battlefield and the hastily evacuated Federal camps. The bluecoats even took time to destroy the track and railroad buildings at Brandy and Rappahannock stations, and the Rappahannock bridge. Once more, the Federals have fought Robert Lee's cavalry to a draw, a far cry from results during the first two years of the war. The Confederates have gone into camp around Brandy. A number of Little Fork Rangers have been wounded in the day's fighting.[8]

Robert E. Lee arrived on Traveller at the Court House in early afternoon. It was his first attempt to ride horseback in two days, since a flare-up of rheumatism forced him to travel in a wagon. But he felt better this morning, and his spirits were considerably raised by the warm welcome given him by the people of Culpeper. Only one resident wished to complain. She rushed forward to inform Lee that some of her neighbors had been overly friendly to the Yankees, and that some young ladies had even attended entertainments at General John Sedgwick's headquarters.

She pointed out some of the offenders in the crowd that now flocked to Lee. The young ladies so identified froze in terror, for Lee's gaze seemed severe. How relieved they were when his voice betrayed bemusement. "I know General Sedgwick very well," he offered, as the crowd waited breathless for his judgment. "It is just like him to be so kindly and considerate, and to have his band there to entertain them. So, young ladies, if the music is good, go and hear it as often as you can, and enjoy yourselves. You will find that General John Sedgwick will have none but agreeable gentlemen about him."[9]

Late in the afternoon, Lee retired to establish a camp near Griffinsburg, where he received frequent reports from Stuart on the course of the fighting. Learning that the Union cavalry had fallen back behind the Rappahannock, Lee breathed easier, but he has decided now to press the attack tomorrow. He will pursue the same plan he used to secure Culpeper from Pope last year: He will slip a portion of his army around the Union right flank, cut off its retreat, and intercept Meade on the Orange & Alexandria near Manassas.[10]

Dusk, October 12. Things have gone better than expected for Lee. His men broke camp early and, with Stuart's cavalry leading the way, crossed the Rappahannock between Jeffersonton and Waterloo. Meanwhile, Meade, ignorant of Lee's movements but having regained some confidence following his escape from Culpeper, sent Buford's cavalry division and II, V, and VI Corps back across the river. The cavalry tangled with a token force of Rebel horsemen near the Court House before rejoining the infantry at Brandy. All the while, the corps of Ewell and Powell Hill have penetrated deeper into Fauquier County. The Federals have spent most of the day burying dead comrades and removing wounded men who have lain here since yesterday's fighting. They are angered to find the dead stripped of clothing and equipment.[11]

Having missed the day's fight, Federal foot soldiers are not in a good mood. They crossed the river fully expecting a great battle and an even greater victory. They believe Meade pulled out far too soon yesterday, and they wanted to settle up with the Rebs today. The broad blue lines moving across Culpeper's rolling plains, the sun shining brightly for the first time in several days, "aroused an assurance of strength," asserts a Pennsylvanian, "and was such an incentive to valor and determination that the actual combat was earnestly looked for with no doubtful convictions of its results." Now, as the autumn twilight fades, so too do hopes of a "splendid pageant" and an anticipated "rout and ruin of the foe."[12]

Midnight. Meade, finally comprehending something of Lee's daring move, has ordered his army back across the Rappahannock. He must concentrate his force and prepare to attack. Or to defend? He is still uncertain. He even denies he is retreating from Culpeper for the second time in as many days. He calls it "a withdrawal of the army—to get into a proper position to offer battle." His men have just eaten a cold meal and settled down to catch a few hours' sleep when shrill bugle calls tell them to roll out and line up. Denied their anticipated glory, the infantrymen grumble about the hardships of another long march with no results. "We moved through level fields, blackberry bushes predominating, which stripped our clothes, tore out our flimsy shoes, and soon penetrating the stockings made our feet sore and bloody," reports a Massachusetts soldier of yesterday's march. "The men became lame and chafed, and when we camped . . . all were much worn and wearied." Now they must retrace their steps. A few soldiers try to make light of it. "Get up, you lazy lubber you," calls one broad-chested fellow in a deep voice; "do you want to sleep all the time?" The absurdity of his question produces tired laughter, and his comrades are in good spirits by the time they wind their way back toward the river.[13]

October 20. Lee has spent the past week pursuing the Army of the Potomac, as Meade, like Pope, has fallen back to Manassas. Lee gave chase, but A. P. Hill is no Jackson, and so, despite his head start, was unable to cut off the Federal retreat. To top that, Hill then bungled an excellent opportunity to crush Meade's III Corps at Bristoe Station, three miles south of Manassas Junction. For the only time in the war, Lee seems to have been disappointed in Hill, and Hill knows he has sinned. Hearing the hard tone in his commander's voice when Lee, after surveying the battlefield at Bristoe, ordered the dead buried, Hill

tried to placate him by accepting responsibility for the losses. "Yes,"
Lee is reported to have agreed, "it is your fault; you committed a great
blunder yesterday." He need not have said anything. Lee can wither a
man with his gaze. Perhaps his recurring rheumatism has made Lee
testy; perhaps he is frustrated over another missed opportunity to crip-
ple Meade. He cannot seem to finish off Meade as easily as he did
Pope, Burnside, and Hooker.[14]

For the moment, the campaign is over. Hill's corps has returned to
Culpeper; Lee has established headquarters near Rappahannock Station. The dreary mood has been made even more melancholy by several days of unceasing rain. Yet, given the season and the condition of
his army, Lee should be satisfied. His army has destroyed nearly twenty
miles of railroad from Bristoe to the Rappahannock. He tells both his
wife and James Seddon that he withdrew from Bristoe because he saw
no chance to force Meade to battle, and to have contested the region
any further would have fatigued his troops unnecessarily. "I think the
sublimest sight of the war," maintains the commander, "was the cheerfulness and alacrity exhibited by this army in the pursuit of the enemy
under all the trials and privations to which it was exposed." He reasons, "If they had been properly provided with clothes, I would certainly have endeavored to have thrown them north of the Potomac.
But thousands were barefooted, thousands with fragments of shoes, &
all without overcoats, blankets or warm clothing. I could not bear to
expose them to certain suffering, on an uncertain issue." Winter is approaching. Better to spend it resting in Culpeper.[15]

But if Lee's army has destroyed the O&A, Meade's men have desolated the countryside to which it returns. The weight of war is beginning to tell. The occupation of Pope and Meade and countless raids in
between have produced a dismal scene. Cavalrymen, artillerists, and
teamsters will find little forage here for horses and mules. In fact, the
scant supply of horses has reached a critical point for Lee and Stuart.
Men in several cavalry regiments will be sent home to secure fresh
mounts. Meanwhile, the men have settled in a region that stirs concern
about the condition of their own communities. "We cannot tell what
kind of buildings stood between the great number of blackened chim-

neys on every side through Fauquier & Culpeper," laments one soldier, "but in addition to these there is the framework of many a handsome residence stripped of all that could be useful to these fiends in building hovels, & the walls, where they remain, covered with obscenity. How much longer will the just retribution for these things tarry?"[16]

Lee's camps stretch from Rappahannock Station back to Brandy and southward to Stevensburg. Most of his 50,000 men assume they will spend the winter here, and so have started to build huts, complete with chimneys, to protect themselves from the already chilly weather. "I think it very likely that we stay in this section for some time," a North Carolinian informs his father in expressing general wisdom, "for the Yankees will hardly attempt a forward movement." A Georgian seconds his opinion: "One thing is certain we have crippled Meades army so bad I think he will not fight any more this winter." They take their example from Lee, who, after some little trouble finding a place to stay, has allowed his servant to make a hut for him, complete with chimney, in a nice pine thicket.[17]

Naturally, some soldiers complain. Mail is slow to arrive, and current newspapers are impossible to obtain. Clothing is threadbare or lacking entirely. The weather is fickle—rain one day, sun the next, clouds the day after that—but generally cold. Food is plentiful but plain, mostly bacon, beef, and bread. Of all complaints, this last may be heard most often. "Eating is the chief annoyance," insists a man in the 27th Virginia Infantry, for in this they know the Federals have the advantage over them. "The whole country around here is bright with tin cans used by the Yanks for vegetables, condensed milk, lobster, oysters, fruit & everything else," he grumbles, "while bottles in vast quantities attest the prevalence of 'spirits' and their devotion thereto. I go to bed & console myself with the reflection that this 'cruel war' will one day be over." And not a few men are dissatisfied with their half-victory over Meade.[18]

Most men, however, are perfectly content with the prospects of wintering in Culpeper. Perhaps Lee will relent in his attitude toward furloughs and allow them to visit their families. All who have invested time and energy in their winter quarters revel in the cozy comfort of their abodes. "No one who has not camped out can fully appreciate the luxury good warm fires are to the soldier," ruminates one man in his diary.

"We pitch our tents build our chimneys make our beds off the ground & consider ourselves luxuriously appointed." Wounded men have a chance to mend their bodies. All have an opportunity to bathe and to wash their vermin-infested clothes. After a few days in camp, new clothing for many troops arrives from several sources. Some of it originates in Richmond, but one South Carolina brigade has also received 800 pairs of shoes from a relief society at home. Generally, it is a time to relax and to think of the terrors of the battlefield as a distant threat.[19]

Camp life is not taxing. Picket duty is required, but little drill is demanded. Men spend most of their time "policing" the camps and preparing for winter. Green Samuels, a lieutenant in the 10th Virginia Infantry, describes the odd term "policing" in a letter to his wife Kathleen in Woodstock, Virginia. The men gather and burn all leaves, deadwood, and rubbish on their campgrounds. Then they cut tree stumps level with the ground, dig ditches for drainage, fill in any holes, and level the ground. His wife would be "surprised at the appearance of a well-regulated camp," he assures her; "it is a little town," though far cleaner than the civilian variety. "If it were not for you and our little baby," Samuels declares, "I would be almost tempted to remain a soldier all my life, the soldier's life in camp is the easiest and most careless thing imaginable."[20]

"Great hilarity prevails" in most camps. At least some humor can be seen in nearly every circumstance of army life. One morning a few days ago, Jubal Early exclaimed in a voice heard through half his camp, "Lord Jesus Christ, God Almighty!" When an aide rushed to see what disaster had befallen the general, he discovered that Early had only worked a button off his shirt. A South Carolinian who has been known to complain about the army's limited diet admits that if "grumbling fills in the courses" than "laughing at misfortune and tough beef & biscuit generally makes up the dessert." A few nights past, a picket on the upper Rappahannock caused some merriment. Seeing a portion of Rosser's brigade approaching from the other side of the river, he mistook them for Yankees. He raised an alarm and "created great confusion with the citizens" before his mistake was realized.[21]

Men also savor civilian company once again, particularly female company. Elijah Johnson, on picket duty with the 15th Virginia Cavalry between Jeffersonton and Waterloo, thinks this the best place he has ever served. Local residents, among them the Burks family, gladly supply him and his mates with far better eating fare than they receive in camp, "& as for pretty young ladies" to visit, he swears, "I never saw them more plentiful in any vicinity." He has become acquainted with "several nice girls," and is especially fond of Mittie and Roberta Weyman. Officers are frequently invited to stay in Culpeper homes, and generals and their staffs have the pick of the litter. Jedediah Hotchkiss, Ewell's topographer, recently spent a day seeking a suitable headquarters with his boss. They dismissed a Mrs. Taylor's house as being too "much injured and the furniture destroyed by the Yankees." They finally settled on Berry Hill, a "roomy old house," quite comfortable, although there, too, the Yankees have left piles of broken furniture. In the evenings, his map-making set aside, Hotchkiss visits neighboring families known to him from previous encampments, especially the Misses Wise, at Brandy.[22]

There are somber moments, to be sure. Powell Hill, still smarting and feeling blue from Lee's censure, has startled his old neighbors with a rare display of ill manners. Proud of their local hero, a contingent of Culpeper militia offered themselves to Hill as a personal bodyguard. Hill has told them bluntly that he does not require an escort, and that the 60 militiamen can better serve their country by enlisting in a volunteer regiment. The opportunity for a permanent camp also means courts-martial and punishments, measures that put a damper on any camp. A few men, most deserters, have been executed. These occasions are not intended to be pretty sights, but some executions are particularly unnerving. "At the stake I read the burial service," reported the Methodist chaplain of the 28th North Carolina. "They were tied to the stakes, the word was given, and one of them was killed, but the other had to be shot a second time. A most revolting spectacle." The parents of one poor fellow watched their son shot to death by a firing squad, and then carried his body home in a wagon to be buried. Lee fully endorses the executions and protests the tendency of the War Department to show leniency, particularly toward deserters. An army can only be maintained through discipline, warns Lee, and the sight of a fellow-soldier being executed for a breach of discipline is the best possible warning not to follow his example.[23]

Lee has a good deal more on his mind, too. He is uncertain of Meade's purpose. He had hoped the Yankee might sit out the winter in Manassas, but Meade quickly rebuilt the O&A as far as Warrenton, and his pickets appeared on the northern side of the Rappahannock within days of Lee's return to Culpeper. Lee has responded by transforming old Federal entrenchments above the river into a defensive line of rifle pits and two redoubts. The redoubts sit west of the railroad; they protect a pontoon bridge which, with the railroad bridge still unrepaired, provides the only means of crossing the icy water. General Early worries that the limited field of fire renders these defenses "very inadequate." Lee regards them as "slight, but . . . adequate." Most of the nongenerals are impressed by the entrenchments. "It is an utter impossibility for the Enemy to break our lines by a front attack," decides a Georgian.[24]

But Lee is also distracted by personal worries. His second son, Rooney, captured near Richmond while recuperating from his Brandy Station wound, is a Yankee prisoner. The approaching winter will revive the discomfort of his own rheumatism. In asking Mary to send him two jackets and two pairs of flannel drawers, he confesses, "I have suffered so from cold already, I hope I shall get used to it. But I have felt very differently since my attack last spring, from which I have never recovered." Yet military and personal cares fade away on those occasions when Lee is reminded of his army's purpose. In late October, he spoke to a South Carolina woman, in camp to present her husband with a new suit of clothes. "Said she was willing to give up everything she had in the world to attain our independence," Lee told Mary, "and the only complaint she made of the conduct of our enemies was their arming our servants against them."[25]

Lee frequently expresses concern about southern civilians, especially in this part of Virginia, which he believes has been ravaged by war. He is especially concerned about the destitute families of soldiers, and so has asked Governor Letcher to supply meat and flour to such families at the Court House and at Fredericksburg. "I find that there is great suffering among the people in this region for want of the necessaries of life," he explains to Letcher. "The farms and gardens have been robbed, stock and hogs killed, and these outrages committed, I am sorry to say, by our own army to some extent, as well as by the Federals." The condition of some people is pitiable. Before Lee's arrival, they had even taken to scavenging abandoned Federal campsites in search of food for themselves and abandoned equipment that could be sold to the Confederates.[26]

Other men besides Lee take time to reflect. Religious services are again held with some regularity, and several chaplains, anticipating a winter home in Culpeper, have constructed chapels. The men seem eager to attend not only divine services but Bible classes and prayer meetings, and Culpeper's civilian ministers still attract large audiences from the camps. Contemplation inevitably turns toward the Confederate cause, and many men, while discouraged that the war goes on, reassert their determination to whip the enemy. As he considers the scarred countryside, "without a fence or a planted field of any kind," a South Carolinian detects an iron will in Culpeper's people that should inspire the rest of the Confederacy. "They are intensely hostile to the Yankees," he informs his wife, "and there is certainly no submission in them." Other men draw strength from their families. Most soldiers need an occasional reminder of their duty, acknowledges one officer, and "there is no reminder so good as a letter from home which recalls in all their force the pure and high principles which should actuate every one of us in the war."[27]

November 7. The contemplation and complacency ended abruptly today. It is nearly evening, and all Hell has broken loose in the past few hours. You could see trouble coming late this morning. Pickets at Rappahannock Station and Kelly's Ford reported the advance of sizable Federal forces at 10:30 A.M. The Federal V and VI Corps under John Sedgwick, a total of 30,000 men, seemed bound for Rappahannock Station; I, II, and III Corps under William H. French, accompanied by Meade, moved toward Kellysville. By 1 P.M., Sedgwick had formed in line of battle less than two miles from the river. By 3:30 P.M., the Federals had driven in the remaining Confederate pickets, moved to within a mile of the redoubts, and unlimbered their guns. Two brigades of infantry—fewer than two thousand men plus four cannon—now stand between them and Culpeper.[28]

Downstream at Kelly's Ford, the danger was even greater, and collapse swift. French's men opened up on the south bank with three batteries of artillery at about 12:30 P.M. By 1:30 P.M., having battered two North Carolina regiments, they were in Culpeper. The Federals suffered 42 casualties as they forded the frigid Rappahannock and panted up the opposite bank, but the Rebel defenses crumbled rapidly. "As we rushed toward the entrenchments in double time and scrambled over its four-foot high walls," reports a Federal officer, "its defenders surrendered their guns without further resistance." It was over by 2 P.M.[29]

Some 350 Rebels gave up, and another 50 were killed or wounded. Hardy Bodman, 2nd North Carolina, lies bleeding from a bullet that struck him above his left ear and ploughed three inches under his scalp. Sergeant John G. Newsom, 30th North Carolina, is stunned by a bullet that grazed his scalp. Less lucky is another private in the 2nd North Carolina. He was struck by a musket ball in the pelvis, and his wound will be difficult to treat. He will likely die. Meanwhile, French's pioneers rapidly built two pontoon bridges, and all three corps are now in Culpeper.[30]

At Rappahannock Station, Sedgwick has unleashed a similar but far larger assault. First, artillery pounded the Confederate redoubts and connecting rifle pits. Skirmishers advanced, and four full regiments—men from Wisconsin, Maine, and Pennsylvania—have battled to within 250 yards of a redoubt on the Rebel right flank, defended by three Louisiana regiments. The Louisianians are good shots. Down goes William Attig, 49th Pennsylvania; a bullet has struck him in the left side of his forehead. Down goes John P. Patterson of the same regiment, from a bullet that fractures his skull. The VI Corps has advanced simultaneously against the Confederate left, again to within 250 yards of its stubborn North Carolina and Louisiana defenders. A horrendous artillery and rifle exchange has been maintained since then. Lee, Early, and Ewell have all arrived to inspect the scene. Early, whose troops hold the redoubts, crossed over to inspect the lines. He returns worried about the ability of his men to hold out, and he has brought up the rest of his division to fortify the southern bank, where eight artillery pieces are already positioned. Lee, who believes the action is only a reconnaissance in force, seems unwilling to commit more troops. It is growing dark; Lee may be right.[31]

5:30 P.M. Two blue columns advance at the double quick through the growing darkness. General David A. Russell, a New Yorker who graduated near the bottom of his West Point class in 1845, has ordered the 6th Maine and 5th Wisconsin to storm the redoubts. A night attack! Insanity, think Russell's men, but on they charge. They tumble over stumps and plow through thick underbrush. They slog across a ditch thick with mud. They strain on the grade of a steep slope, but they encounter no abatis. The Confederate defenders are stunned, but they battle back as Federals flood over their parapets yelling and screaming like so many Rebels. This is war at its most primitive. Combatants fire few rifles. An unlucky target is Lieutenant Horace G. Jacobs, 6th Maine, who falls when a bullet strikes him from behind in the left shoulder and exits below his clavicle. A Louisiana corporal is struck in the same shoulder, but the bullet has lodged in his body. Most blue and butternut warriors grapple with each other, thrust with bayonets, and swing once-fired muskets like Stone-Age clubs. The Rebels throw back the first line; they throw back the second line; but a third line of Pennsylvanians is too much for them. The Louisiana Tigers break and make a desperate lunge for the bridge to their rear.[32]

Lee, standing above the scene but opposite an intervening valley, does not appreciate the gravity of these events. He saw some flashes of musket fire in the initial assault, but high winds moving away from him muffle the sounds of battle. He still believes it is a skirmish. He is tired. He is cold. He will go to bed and reevaluate the situation at first light. He leaves Early to deal with it.

Minutes later, and Early has learned of the collapse of the redoubts. Not only that, but a second assault, led by another New Yorker, Colonel Emory Upton, West Point class of 1861, has been launched against rifle pits and entrenchments on the Confederate left flank. The left collapses, overwhelmed by superior numbers and taken by surprise. Early can do nothing to save the situation. He cannot send in more troops for fear of creating a bottleneck at the bridge; he cannot use his artillery for fear of killing his own men. He is mortified "to hear the final struggle of these devoted men and to be made painfully aware of their capture, without the possibility of being able to go to their relief."[33]

9 P.M. Sedgwick controls the north bank and has bagged 1,600 Confederate prisoners. His own losses amount to about four hundred. Informed of the situation, Lee has ordered Early to pull back beyond Brandy Station and await the inevitable attack. By now a few lucky Confederates have made their way to the south shore. Some men raced across the bridge. More desperate sorts leaped into the icy water and swam to safety. The North Carolinians who escaped Kelly's Ford have also been recalled so that Lee can concentrate his forces. Jubal Early orders the bridge burned to slow Federal pursuit, but Meade, as usual, seems disinclined to move too quickly. He already has a victory. Only chaplains and surgeons will work tonight.[34]

A hard snow fell yesterday, the day after the Rappahannock fiasco. Lee waited most of the day for Meade to attack, but the blow went undelivered. Seizing the opportunity, Lee ordered his army south of the Rapidan, out of Culpeper. Meade follows, but slowly. It has been a long, hard 48 hours. Lee's men have had no sleep and little to eat, certainly no hot meals. Many Confederate camps, including equipment, personal effects, cooking utensils, and stores, were simply abandoned. More than that, after chasing Meade all the way to Manassas only a month earlier, Lee's army chafes at this "disgraceful retreat." "Last night was almost as disagreeable and comfortless as the night we left Gettysburg and the night we crossed the Potomac," judges the chaplain of a North Carolina regiment. "The fences for miles along the line of march were all ablaze and such straggling I have never witnessed. Thousands were gathered around the fires. If the Yankee Cavalry [had] followed us closely, they would have captured many of them."[35]

Men are reluctant to say it, but Lee blundered badly at Rappahannock Station by underestimating his opponent. Only after the bridgehead force had been "completely annihilated," believe some, did Lee "wake from his reverie" to spare the rest of his army a similar fate. A surviving Louisiana Tiger has told folks at home, "You and everyone else will wonder why those brave men were not reenforced in time to save them from destruction, nobody knows but Genl. Lee, who I hope will account satisfactorily for it." Colonel Alexander "Sandie" Pendleton, a staff officer, has summed it up best. Today, November 10, as the last of Lee's men crosses at Rapidan Station, he observes, "I don't think Meade will come on. I earnestly hope General Lee will soon attack him, and let us retrieve our lost reputation. It is absolutely sickening, and I feel personally disgraced by the issue of the late campaign, as does every one in the command. Oh, how each day is proving the inestimable value of General Jackson to us!"[36]

Federal reaction is jubilant, though with a touch of disappointment. As Meade rides past a division of V Corps, the men greet "Old Foureyes" with "rousing, approving and appreciative cheers." A Federal surgeon calls it a "brilliant" victory, with so many Rebel dead that "the *ditches were full of them*." "It was some satisfaction, even though it came through death and blood," he assured his wife, "to thus pay back a little of the drubbing which we so unceremoniously had to receive upon previous fields." Even Abe Lincoln, so often disappointed in the commanders of this army, has telegraphed to say "Well done." Meade looks pleased. He has been so often criticized for being too slow and methodical that he savors the cheers of his men as a parched man craves drink. The victory will, he trusts, convince the "intelligent public" that his retreat to Centreville was intended "not to avoid battle, and that Lee . . . is really the one who has avoided battle." A few other men, however, whisper that Meade should have been more aggressive on November 8. "I do feel most decidedly that he has been over-cautious," insists a staff officer. "Our men were not used up, . . . but on the contrary were very fresh, and full of ardour."[37]

Few common soldiers complain. It is their turn to settle into winter camp at Culpeper. What is more, Lee's men have thoughtfully left a good many huts and quarters ready for immediate occupation. "This would be a splendid place to stop all winter," concludes a Pennsylvanian, "plenty of food and water." Many men set about improving the Rebel handiwork by patching chimneys and bringing in fresh pine boughs, or "Virginia feathers," for bedding. Unfortunately, there are not enough Rebel quarters to go around, so quite a few men must build winter homes from scratch, which has played havoc with local forests and fences. A few men assigned to the Court House take up residence in vacant houses in town. One cavalry captain establishes his company headquarters in the office of the Virginia House.[38]

Then, too, the Federal generals sometimes select campsites where none have been. Unaccountably, they too often select low, marshy places, "saturated with water," a practice that has produced a good many complaints from enlisted men and doctors. "Last night it rained in torrents," complained a surgeon encamped on Mountain Run, "and in five minutes the bottom of my tent held one or two inches of water." No wonder the Confederates had not stopped here. The surgeon also appreciates the wisdom of Rebel construction. Looking for ways to improve ventilation and heating in his hospitals, he will forsake stoves for fireplaces of sticks and clay, modeled, he says, after some he saw in a Confederate camp.[39]

Generals, naturally, take the nicest quarters. Sedgwick selects the Welford house, which, having been used as a Confederate hospital, had first to be cleared of amputated limbs. Emory Upton invited himself and his staff to stay as Mrs. Major's guests at Presqu' Isle while his brigade takes possession of the woods. General Alexander Hays commandeered the old Fitzhugh house at Carrico Mills, just north of Stevensburg. "I am as comfortable as if at home," claims the general, "with a good fire, and fancy furniture and a comfortable bed." What is more, rejoices Hays, the family, consisting of an old man and two old ladies, are the "most sensible people" he has met in Virginia, for they "do not talk 'secesh,' although they are full of it."[40]

As a relief from the arduous campaign, men and officers alike have gone on a binge of socializing, card playing, drinking, and amusing themselves. The peak period came on November 14 to 16, when Meade was in Washington to confer with Lincoln and Stanton on future operations. In his absence, good-natured "Uncle John" Sedgwick commanded the army and set the tone. Sedgwick immediately arranged a punch party for the officers of his corps. Upton's staff gave a dinner party at Presqu' Isle and enjoyed enough wine "to float the pontoons of the 50th Engineers." Nearly everyone, including the more serious-minded Meade, has called on John Botts at some time during the past few weeks. Botts, in turn, complains to everyone about how both armies have misused him. Many of the army's "lady-killing gentry" have flirted with one of Botts's three daughters, but she has reportedly surrendered the "citadel of her affections" to a sergeant from Massachusetts who, somewhat ironically, commands the "safeguards" at her father's house.[41]

Despite the sergeant's good fortune, most enlisted men must devise their own entertainments. Some soldiers enjoy innocent pastimes, such as baseball. Others seek livelier times in gambling and drinking. Cards, shell games, raffles, the men will bet on anything. Alcohol is officially forbidden to enlisted men, but many officers—too often poor examples for their men—turn a blind eye. So if a man can find a supplier, he can usually wet his whistle without fear of punishment, unless he becomes disorderly. Some officers even sign commissary orders that allow enlisted men to buy whiskey. French and Sedgwick, following reviews of their corps by a group of visiting British officers, held fine receptions, and any review, observes one officer, is generally "expected in this army to be a prelude to a big drunk."[42]

November 25. Despite much revelry, camp life in the Army of the Potomac has settled down into dull routine. The telegraph is fully operational, and an elaborate system of signal stations is being erected by Captain Lemuel B. Norton, chief signal officer. Most importantly, the Orange & Alexandria, its tracks replaced and the Rappahannock bridge restored, has been operating since November 19. Meade has constructed a railroad siding and depot at Brandy Station, which is more convenient to his camps than is the Court House station. He has created a second depot for livestock about a third of the way from Brandy to the Rappahannock.[43]

Men react variously to the inactivity. Most seem content to sit tight for the winter, especially as the weather has turned ugly in mid- and late November—much rain, very cold, and mud everywhere. No one can move in this mud. It would be easier to wage a winter campaign in New England snow, decides a soldier from Worcester, Massachusetts.

"War does not suit me," contends a member of the 37th Massachusetts Volunteers. "I dislike the work—fighting is not agreeable to my nature." He is proud to have played his role and done what he could "to sustain the old flag," but he admits, "I think I would not enlist again, unless the case was very urgent." Other men, mostly senior officers who will not be trudging in the mud and rain or charging across a battlefield, want action, and gossip about Meade's indecisiveness.[44]

December 3. Meade has finally moved, but no one is rejoicing. Feeling pressure from President Lincoln and the North's journalistic 'strategists'" to keep after Lee, Meade set the army in motion on November 26, Thanksgiving Day, across the Rapidan. From that time until its return last night and today, the Army of the Potomac has not known a happy moment. Foul weather, lack of food and sleep, and a running contest with Lee that culminated along Mine Run, in Orange County, have produced no gains. Meade lost 1,653 of 85,000 men; Lee lost 745 of 48,500. Many men feel personal anguish. A captain in the 17th Maine has lost one of his lieutenants. "I have felt his sudden death more than any other we have ever had," the captain confides to his diary. "Living together in the same tent so long, it seemed like losing a part of myself." "The battle did not occur, but great suffering and toil was undergone by our army," summarizes a Wisconsin volunteer. "I can hardly tell you how tired, sleepy and worn out we all are to-night."[45]

> A march in the ranks hard-prest, and the road unknown,
> A route through a heavy wood with muffled steps in the darkness,
> Our army foil'd with loss severe, and the sullen remnant retreating.

Meade returns "snappish and cross." He believes he will soon be relieved as commander of the army. Some officers and northern newspapers think that is a good idea, and speculation runs wild over who will succeed him. Meade may well have been justified in not storming Lee's position at Mine Run; undoubtedly many Federal lives would have been lost. But the affair smacks too much of nearly three years of Union disappointment in Virginia. The press reports that the army is "demoralized," "full of copperheads," and "fit only for observation work." Many people, it seems, consider Meade a second-rate mind with a first-rate string of luck. Some of his officers, like John Gibbon and Winfield Scott Hancock, support him, but others would like to see John Sedgwick, Joe Hooker, George Thomas, or Alfred Pleasonton placed in charge. Meade thinks it will be Hooker or Thomas. The army has been unsettled for several days now by all the rumors, not to mention fears that Lee is about to launch an attack at any moment.[46]

Whatever Meade's future, the army will remain here until spring. One sign of the camp's permanent status is measured by the number of visitors that flock to Culpeper. Officers' wives come to visit or to remain for at least part of the winter. Enlisted men, unable to have their wives present, enjoy the sight of "a *real live lady.*" "It does seem so good to catch a view of the ladies occasionally," admits one man. "It is a variety that softens the harsh, coarse, everyday life in the army, so full of everything hostile to society, and evils that blunt the finer sensibilities and feelings." An even more welcome sight for enlisted men is the many sutlers who have set up shop. Although official rations have improved significantly, the men now enjoy delicacies—canned peaches, sardines, and oysters—provided by these traveling merchants. Meade also entertains a succession of official guests, including foreign dignitaries, all eager to visit Rebel territory and see the army that pushed Lee out of Pennsylvania.[47]

As Christmas approaches, the weather is already quite cold, with strong winds, lots of rain, occasional snow, and "universal mud." Most of the men have finished building their winter quarters, but they frequently suffer from exposure when on duty. "The cold spell still holds on," complains one officer; "it is really severe, equal I think to anything we had during the whole of last winter." "Oh, how cold and miserable the poor devils looked," reports another officer of his pickets, "crouching around fires no larger than a tin pan. . . . The ground was frozen too hard for them to pitch their little bits of canvas." Even Jack Pendleton, inveterate Rebel that he is, has taken pity on a forlorn bunch of pickets posted in the vicinity of Redwood. He informed the officer in charge of the best roads by which to march his troops to assigned positions. Consequently, the men, in position before dark and able to gather wood for fires, enjoyed hot cups of coffee that night. In fact, Pendleton is a little concerned lest his neighbors learn of his action and misinterpret it. Some men whose camps are near the Court House have been ordered to occupy empty residences in town as protection against the cold.[48]

When off duty and sitting snug by their fireplaces, the men have plenty of time to debate the effect of the new conscription and reenlistment laws on their chances of getting Christmas furloughs. The army is eager to have these veteran soldiers reenlist. If Lee will stay below the Rapidan, and Meade's army can be resupplied and reoutfitted, the spring campaign could decide the war. Consequently, national, state, and even local governments have offered large bounties to men who reenlist. The Federal government will give $402 to soldiers who stay in the army for three years or the duration of the war. Most men also hope to receive a 30-day furlough along with the money, but the army can postpone the furlough to meet manpower needs. Add to this state, county, and city bonuses, and the financial inducement is rich indeed. Now there is also talk of a 30-day furlough for entire regiments if three-fourths of their numbers reenlist. Most men think such numbers are impossible. Infantrymen—the bulk of any army—even if willing to reenlist, want to transfer to the cavalry or artillery, even to the navy. They are tired of "transporting Government supplies in a knapsack."[49]

Some men, unwilling to await the results of their regiment's reenlistment drive, try other ways to get home. A soldier in the 16th Maine, recently engaged to his sweetheart back home, justified his application for leave by citing Deuteronomy 20:7, to wit: "And what man is there that hath betrothed a wife, and hath not taken her? Let him go and return unto his house, lest he die in battle, and another man take her." To his own delighted surprise, his application has been approved.[50]

Unfortunately, other men, desperate to escape the cold and hardships of camp life, have tried to desert or to leave camp without authorization. Brigade and division courts–martial are being held at nearly every camp, generally in unoccupied buildings. No tents, thank you, not in this sort of weather. One brigade uses an old store at Kellysville. A Massachusetts soldier assigned to a guard detail there finds the assignment "soft" and his circumstances "comfortable," but it is also inconvenient. His duties require only that he keep uninvited guests out of the courtroom, but in return, he and the other guards must keep in "Washington style—boots blacked and brass bright."[51]

One must pity some of the men on trial, for they are genuinely confused by the proceedings. They understand little about military justice, and only now do they appreciate the possibility of severe punishment for leaving camp. A Maine soldier who "skedaddled" from a work detail admits to his court that "he thought there would not be anything done about it." Nearly all such cases involve conscripts or new recruits, and not a few cases involve whiskey, which continues to flow abundantly in camp. The courts sometimes show leniency. A Pennsylvania private charged with desertion has been found guilty only of being AWOL (absent 12 days), and forced to forfeit only $5 in pay. The court was swayed by the man's "evident lack of mental capacity, almost idiocy." Boards looked less kindly on a 15-year-old recruit who "did not think there was any harm" in going to Washington to visit a friend, and on a German immigrant who went to Philadelphia to find a substitute.[52]

And not all cases involve desertion or naive conscripts, for the inactivity, a frequent problem in winter camps, has produced an alarming increase in drunkenness and general lawlessness. "This army is so demoralized by substitutes and conscripts that it seems to me it is in a critical condition," reported a Federal surgeon yesterday. "We have drunken rows and disturbances in the camps about us almost every night." The result has been a steady docket of courts-martial for crimes and misdeeds that range from petty theft to assault. The most sensational crime of late, about which the camps are still buzzing, was the murder of a Yankee captain by a disappointed suitor of the captain's fiancee.[53] More typically, of 57 cases tried in Culpeper since August for crimes and infractions committed in Culpeper, 15 have been for desertion, 5 for being AWOL, 10 for robbery or theft, 6 for insubordination, 4 for disobedience, 6 for conduct unbecoming an officer, 2 for assault, and 1 each for cowardice, marauding, and cruelty to an animal. And these cases do not include a whole slew of men tried for cowardice, straggling, being AWOL, or misconduct before the enemy during the Mine Run campaign.[54]

Then, too, there is the occasional odd case. The oddest in recent weeks has been that of Private George A. Francis of the 4th Regiment, U.S. Artillery. While awaiting trial for desertion, Francis suffered such anxiety that he began to masturbate compulsively. For two months he was so "entirely beyond control" that he required a 24 hour guard. The court hearing his case at Brandy Station on the day before Christmas certified a medical discharge for insanity and committed Francis to an institution.[55]

Not a few men pay the ultimate price for their crimes, and the sight of brigades and divisions forming hollow squares to witness executions is all too frequent. President Lincoln seems to commute most of the death sentences, but the Army of the Potomac, much like the Army of Northern Virginia a few months ago, finds it necessary to set an example that will deter others from misbehavior, especially desertion. Some men understand the necessity of such harsh measures, but the effect of the executions is usually more depressing than inspirational. "Such terrible scenes can only blunt men's finer sensibilities and burden them the more," decides one man; "and Heaven knows that the influences of a soldier's life are hardening enough already."[56]

Thankfully, the soldiers perpetrate most of their crimes against each other rather than against the people of Culpeper. There are, however, alarming exceptions. The most outrageous recent act occurred in September when approximately eight soldiers assaulted two black women near the home of Mrs. Brown, on Cedar Run. The men had been drinking, and whether they intended to rape the women is uncertain. Their trial is pending.[57]

While they are not always so violent, it is disheartening to see soldiers treat Culpeper's civilians as a subject people, with no respect for their privacy or property. Someone on a recent "rainy stormy night" killed an ox belonging to Mrs. Jamieson. The culprit has yet to be found. Cavalrymen are the worst offenders, for they are free to roam (officially and unofficially) through the countryside. The First Cavalry Division seems to be the worst of the lot. A number of civilians have complained about "depredations" committed by the men of this division, many of whom have entered and searched private homes under false pretenses. The division's First Brigade has been further accused of "brutal treatment of women and children." Orders have been issued to rein in those men who seem "determined to bring disgrace upon the command by such conduct as in civil life would subject them to punishment as criminals."[58]

Many soldiers dismantle Culpeper without scruple. A Massachusetts soldier reports that a foraging party of some two hundred men completely sacked the stone mansion of William Major. "Bureaus were pillaged or tipped over," he admits; "furniture smashed or stolen; crockery broken to pieces; mirrors stolen or broken; and a splendid piano . . . was smashed too." Senseless as is this destruction, the man justifies it to his own satisfaction. "It looked sad to destroy so much property," he tells his wife, "but this is the result of war. . . . It sickened me to look on. I did nothing in the way of sacking the house. . . . But I was busy tearing down negro huts to get the lumber. That was not destroying property needlessly; it was only getting stuff to make officers comfortable." One of those officers, also from Massachusetts, takes a similar view. To strip houses of their furnishings and lumber is "rather rough," he acknowledges, "but such is war, and war is what people wanted, especially the women, so I have not much pity for them. The owners had deserted this house or it would not have been molested."[59]

One of the hardest hit is Jack Pendleton. Despite his kindness to Federal pickets, Pendleton is not spared the vengeance of the occupying forces. Some soldiers dislike Pendleton. An Indiana soldier calls him "egotistical & vain." "The only good thing in my opinion he ever did for the world," the Hoosier expands, "was to build his excellent house for our Hd Qs." Pendleton complains to old political friends in the North that his estate has been "utterly and wholly destroyed. . . . The army, by night and by day, has destroyed every particle of my stock, except a few milch cows and one poor yoke of oxen. They have robbed me of all grain of two years growth. . . . They have burned every panel of fence. . . ; they have broken open, searched and robbed my house."[60]

General Patrick, Meade's formidable provost marshal, who is known as the "Deacon," has done his best to curb destruction. He is appalled by the "general relaxation of discipline, the disposition to plunder, burn & commit all sorts of depredations & vandalism" by the army, just as he was in the summer of 1862. Patrick, however, is pleased to see that

Meade, unlike Pope, has passed stringent orders against the destruction of private property. "The General is determined," says Patrick of Meade, "to make examples of all offenders." When a group of soldiers tried to confiscate Archibald Shaw's grindstone—very likely the only one still in civilian hands—a provost guard intervened to insist that the men secure written authorization for their action. They obtained an order, although the legal nicety has done little to ease Shaw's anxiety over his loss. Even though a unionist, and perfectly happy to let the army use the stone on his place, he dislikes having it carted away. "Well," Shaw told the men who took it, "don't destroy my grindstone, boys; bring it back when you are done with it." They assured him, chuckling to themselves, that they would return it.[61]

Culpeper's dwindling civilian population witnesses such trials and the establishment of the Union camps in stunned disbelief. It is bad enough that much of their surviving property is taken and their timber cut down for Yankee shelter, but they are cast into despair when forced to watch neighborhood churches, fences, outbuildings, slave quarters, and the unoccupied houses of absent neighbors torn down for their lumber. The number of people remaining to bear these insults is difficult to judge. One Federal soldier estimates that no more than eighty people now inhabit the county. The Court House, in particular, is a dismal place. The courthouse building and slave pen have been transformed into prisons for Confederates.[62]

Even without the thefts and wanton destruction, Culpeper by this time presents a sad picture. "The Palatinate, during the war of Louis XIV, could scarcely have looked so desolate as this country," admits a member of Meade's staff. "The houses that have not been actually burnt usually look almost worse than those that have: so dreary are they with their windows without sashes, and their open doors, and their walls half stripped of boards." Hundreds of acres of once flourishing forests have been replaced by stumps; once-cultivated fields support only weeds and wild berries. The scars of abandoned army camps pockmark the landscape with "the burnt spots, where fires were, the trenches cut round the tents, and the poles, and old bones and tin pots that invariably lie about." The scars of past battles add to the melancholy scene: fragments of shells, remains of caissons and wagons, animal bones, "and here and there, you come on a little ridge of earth, marked by a bit of board, on which is scrawled the name of a soldier, who lies where he fell, in this desert region."[63]

The young ladies of Culpeper have been slower to accept the visits and advances of Federal troops than they were when Lee's men occupied the county. Some women are downright defiant. When General Kilpatrick attempted to fly a Union flag from a window of the H. Triplet house, near Stevensburg, Eliza Triplet resisted the desecration almost to the point of getting herself imprisoned. Yet this "rebel she adder" so impressed the officers occupying the house with her spunk that they relented in the face of her "unreserved" expressions of devotion to the Confederate cause. At the Court House, another soldier reports, "The ladies keep themselves . . . in scornful seclusion. It would hurt their pride even to have a Yankee soldier look at them"[64]

Here and there one catches glimpses of kindness and hears words of sympathy. Not all Federal soldiers or Rebel citizens feel unmitigated hatred. Susan Coons has established a nice barter arrangement with a Pennsylvania soldier, Captain Charles Noble. She sends the captain and his company mutton and turkeys; he returns coffee, sugar, and cheese. When Mrs. Coons prepared a Christmas feast for the captain's men, he expressed his hopes to her that "ere many months have rolled around, this carnage shall have ceased and peace spread her broad wings over the whole land." Yet the Coons family, like so many others in Culpeper, have had little to remind them that this is a "festive season." Martha Coons has concluded, "The gloomy clouds of war which overshadow our land entirely obscure all mirth from our hearts."[65]

PART IV

Winter

CHAPTER TWELVE

A YANKEE VILLAGE

he weather here is about as reliable as usual, which is to say not
very. Winter began cold and windy with a little snow. Now, near
the end of February, it is again cold and windy, but in between there
have been many pleasant, even balmy days. Rain, too—lots of rain. So
begins 1864 in Culpeper. Both soldiers and civilians have accepted the
army's residence here until at least April; soldiers do not like to fight
in winter. The Federal camps are impressive. Meade has positioned
four of his five corps in a horseshoe configuration, with the open end
braced against the Rappahannock. The circumference of the horseshoe wraps around the county precincts, excluding very few civilians
from military supervision, and some of the finest remaining houses
serve as headquarters for various corps, division, and brigade commanders. Meade has set the army's headquarters on a knoll east of Fleetwood and just north of his main supply depot at Brandy Station.[1]

Additional space is required for the officers' wives, daughters, and
sisters who have descended upon Culpeper in defiance of the poor
weather. Someone estimates that 2,500 women have reported thus far.
"When they all arrive," one lieutenant speculates, "the women will be
the controlling power of these H.Q. & what measures they will adopt
for the prosecution of this war is very hard to conjecture." Provost

317

Marshal Patrick is annoyed by the invasion and thinks it "very unwise" to have so many women here. But since most of them are permitted only a visit of 20 days, the log jam may soon break up. Other men look on in amazement at the "perfect shoals of womankind" that have washed over the army. "I do believe that officers will next be trying to bring grand pianos," concludes one fellow.[2]

Accommodations and living conditions, even the "sea of mud" around Brandy Station, are nothing like what the ladies expected to find. Some soldiers discourage their wives from coming. "This is a country now from which civilisation has taken flight," writes Peter Welsh, color sergeant of the 28th Massachusetts, to Mrs. Welsh, "nothing left but the barren field and wild forrest." Even if his darling could find her way to his camp across miles of "mud and slush knee deep," he, as a noncommissioned officer, has only a tent, shared with three other men, for an abode. More impressive quarters are available to generals' wives. Many now reside in homes at the Court House. Others live at their husbands' headquarters, as does George Custer's new bride Libbie at Jack Barbour's home, Clover Hill. The Barbours, by now nearly destitute, continue to live downstairs while the Custers live upstairs. Custer's staff are tented in the yard, and, like staff officers across Culpeper, know the feeling of being displaced by female guests. "Crinoline has crowded me out of the house," complains one fellow, "& I am now in my tent shivering with cold." When they can gain entrance nowhere else, the women, too, live under canvas in "a sort of Bedouin life."[3]

Naturally, so many women must be entertained, a task the army undertakes with verve. Weather permitting, the women enjoy exploring this small corner of "Rebeldom." Women may be seen everywhere riding on horseback or traveling in carriages, converted ambulances, and "all kinds of vehicles." They view famous battle sites, especially Cedar Mountain, visit the hospitals, and inspect the homes of Culpeper residents known to their husbands. People touring the countryside are shocked by its desolate condition. "The whole country," complains one officer, "besides the mud, is now ornamented with stumps, dead horses and mules, deserted camps, and thousands upon thousands of crows." The explanation for so many crows—"nigger crows" one Irishman calls them—is grisly. They feast on the entrails of slaughtered animals and the carcasses of dead horses and mules. They blacken "acres of ground" near the camps.[4]

Some outings become comical in the extreme, and with just a touch of dissipation, as officers and ladies make merry. One staff officer, assigned to join a riding party of 13 women and 30 officers, arrived at General Andrew Humphrey's headquarters to find the rest of the group already drinking Champagne. The ladies had donned mock military garb for the occasion. One woman trimmed her jacket in "dragoon style" with orange tape. Another pinned the badge of III Corps to her hat. Still another stitched a major's insignia on her sleeve "in tarnished lace." The party spent the day riding from one headquarters tent to another, with each step accompanied by liquid refreshment, generally alcoholic. "Talk about cavalry raids to break down horses!" declares the initially tardy officer in dismay. "If you want to do that, put a parcel of women on them and set them going across the country."[5]

A round of balls, dinner parties, inspections, and reviews that began in mid-January has reached a peak in February. Some occasions inspire more glitter than others, but the finest affairs could have been staged in New York or Philadelphia. Ladies and gentlemen, often including prominent guests from Washington, dress "in the height of civil or military fashion." Officers deck themselves out in full dress, complete with colorful sashes, glistening sabers, and sparkling spurs. Regimental and brigade bands provide music. So many people attend these functions—hundreds of them by some counts—that special pavilions, with canvas roofs and plank floors, must be constructed to accommodate the dancing. The largest ball was given on George Washington's birthday. Vice President Hannibal Hamlin and several senators came down for that affair, described by one participant as "a scene of beauty, gallantry and chivalry." A novel affair occurred the following night when the ladies of the 6th New York Artillery sponsored a ball for their men, this being a leap year. Unlike entertainments at earlier Federal encampments, these recent occasions have been almost entirely northern affairs, with very few Culpeper women escorted to them. The most notable exceptions are the daughters of John Botts, and, indeed, Botts himself still entertains selected Federal officers in his home.[6]

It is all quite amazing, really, the way this Rebel community has been transformed into a combination northern military bastion and extended soiree. The positions of Confederate celebrities and southern admirers have been usurped by the invaders. A few months ago, Rebel ladies and gentlemen flocked to see Jeb Stuart's cavalry on review and in mock battle. Now northern women and their escorts—the "youth, beauty, & chivalry" of Yankeedom—applaud Union inspections and staged combats. Not long past, the sight of a blue uniform aroused passions. People feared the Yankees, and their presence angered the population; all were confident that gallant Confederate lads would quickly expel the intruders. But dullness has replaced passion. Fatalism reigns where optimism was assumed. Citizens sing humbly and sometimes bitterly a Confederate hymn that has been popular since the earliest days of the war:

> *God be our shield,*
> *At home or afield,*
> *Stretch thine arm over us,*
> *Strengthen and save.*

> *What tho' they're three to one,*
> *Forward each sire and son,*
> *Strike till the war is won,*
> *Strike to the grave!*[7]

Yet not all civilian invaders come only as mindless merrymakers, which is a source of some relief both to Culpeper's permanent residents and to Union soldiers. The United States Christian Commission and the United States Sanitary Commission have assigned representatives to Culpeper, and by late February, their presence is of some consequence. The Sanitary Commission is a civilian agency founded early in the war to care for sick and wounded soldiers. It employs hundreds of agents in army camps to provide medical care, warm meals, clothing, and shelter to soldiers in need. It has assigned 21 men, including agents, inspectors, messengers, teamsters, and three black laborers, to Culpeper. From its headquarters at Brandy Station (they also maintain a storehouse at the Court House), agents visit hospitals in all the corps encampments to determine the needs of sick and convalescent men. Warm underclothing, they have discovered, is the single greatest need, although agents also think that the blankets and quilts they have issued relieve much suffering and possibly save lives.[8]

Besides organized benevolent aid, a number of individuals have come to work in the army hospitals. A former mayor of Philadelphia and his wife are nursing Pennsylvania troops. "Mr Fay is one of the most distinguished and benevolent gentlemen I ever met," asserts one general. "He has left all the comforts of home, and resigned the office of Mayor, to come out here to the front to spend his time and money for the good of the soldiers." Walt Whitman, a prominent—and somewhat scandalous—northern poet, has been working as a nurse in Washington and Virginia hospitals. A witness to much suffering and death, Whitman has been moved by this war:

> Long there and then in vigil I stood, dimly around me the battle-field
>   spreading
> Vigil wondrous and vigil sweet there in fragrant silent night,
> Vigil for comrade swiftly slain, vigil I never forget, how as day brighten'd,
> I rose from the chill ground and folded my soldier well in his blanket,
> And buried him where he fell.[9]

But Whitman has been impressed by the healthy situation of Meade's army in Culpeper. He approves of the operation of the division hospitals, mostly in I, II, and III Corps. Happily, they hold few men, the most seriously ill patients having been sent to Washington. Most of the remaining cases are of diarrhea—"the great disease of the army"—although, unfortunately, the affliction is becoming "more & more prevalent, & chronic." The field hospitals he finds typical: a collection of tents with earthen floors, heated by hot rails in trenches that run the length of each tent.[10]

Not everyone would agree with Whitman's estimation of the hospitals. It is true that most accommodations are as clean and comfortable as conditions permit, but some facilities suffer for one reason or another. The hospital near the Barbour house is situated in what one man describes as "a nigger hovel," and a "disgustingly filthy" one at that. The nurses and attendants, he insists, are "unfeeling," and he suspects that they live high off the hog at the "Hotel Barbour" on supplies—particularly food—intended for their patients. "I have heard much about the treatment our men receive in Rebel prisons," he complains, "but it can not be much worse than this so-called hospital." Still all evidence suggests that this is an exceptional case.[11]

Cornelia Hancock, a New Jersey Quaker, is one of several women who have come south to nurse the army. She, like Whitman, is pleased with the hospital to which she has been assigned—Third Division, II Corps—although she laments the absence of a heat stove in the hospital tent. The men eat well: oysters, meat, and bread for breakfast; soup, turkey broth, corn, and lima beans for dinner; and oysters, farina, and bread and butter for supper. Besides the hospital tents, the compound includes tents for hospital personnel and for dining and cooking. Both she and the division surgeon, Dr. F. A. Dudley, reside in log houses. Corduroy walkways (made of logs laid crosswise) provide convenient avenues between the 14 structures. Dr. Dudley, though he spends too much time lounging in his tent and reading newspapers, is a first-rate surgeon, and he accords Miss Hancock far better treatment than she received at the hospitals in Washington. Here, on the front lines, everything she asks for is provided, and she actually eats free of charge, a real advantage compared to the $4 per week that she had to pay for meals in Washington. Dudley's only disappointing quality, according to Miss Hancock, is his lack of abolitionist enthusiasm. He attends all free black people who come to him for medical treatment, but he clearly dislikes them. He also keeps a black lad as a servant. Miss Hancock disapproves of Dudley's habit of making the poor boy "act the monkey and dance" for his amusement. Yet he is polite to Miss Hancock, and given the prejudice of many surgeons toward women, "that is enough."[12]

It is interesting to observe and listen to Miss Hancock, for she fills her free time in much the same way as the soldiers and expresses many of the same opinions. She spends many hours writing letters home, mostly to her mother, sister, and niece; and she is blue when they fail to respond promptly. She tells her family that they know far more about what is happening in the war than does she. "War is humbug," she declares. "It is just put out to see how much suffering the private can bear I guess." Miss Hancock also detests officers, and she knows scarcely one general who does not drink to excess. Everyone curses, too. "I do not think they attach any importance to it," she decides, "Just from habit." An alarming thought, she concedes, and warns her niece not to be surprised if *she* should return home with a more colorful vocabulary. She complains about rats who gnaw at her clothes, yet she has become almost immune to the sight of death. One of her favorite "resorts" is the "dead house," where corpses are stored, embalmed, and placed in coffins. There she observes the features of the "fine looking men" who have died and takes comfort in thinking that they will be "buried very decently." Following one operation to amputate a man's leg, she watched the doctors cut the dead limb into three additional pieces "for the sake of practice." She concludes: "One can get used to anything."[13]

But the longer the army remains encamped, the greater becomes Miss Hancock's boredom and the more unbearable she finds the tedium of military life. "I get so tired of the wan faces," she confesses, "and 'please to give me a lemon,' the pots, kettles and pans." She longs, like the men, for a furlough to visit home. Many men are almost "demented to go home," she decides, and she fears it will not take long for her to achieve that state as well. Sundays are the worst. With so few duties to perform, hours crawl by. She spent one Sunday evening nursing a stray dog and keeping score for two doctors while they played cards. When a "religious fit" suddenly struck the two men, they and Miss Hancock spent the remainder of the evening discussing the Bible. On the other hand, weekdays can be nearly as tedious. "There is nothing of importance happening here," she decided on a recent Wednesday, "The drums beat, the bugle sounds, the winds blow, the men groan—that is all."[14]

While the Sanitary Commission and volunteers like Whitman and Miss Hancock tend to the bodies of men, the Christian Commission assumes responsibility for their souls. Organized in New York in late 1861 by the Young Men's Christian Association, the Commission sometimes cares for the sick and wounded, but its principal goal is to promote moral behavior and religious devotion. Agents distribute Bibles, tracts, newspapers, and hymnals among the men. They converse with soldiers and persuade them to seek religious guidance from their chaplains. The Commission has also established headquarters at Brandy Station, where, like the Sanitary Commission, it is within range of all the corps encampments. Its present goal is to construct as many chapels in as many regiments as possible. If the men will construct the walls and floors, promise Commission agents, they will provide canvas roofs. From the look of things, the agents have struck a deal, for dozens of white-topped chapels may be seen across Culpeper. Not content with the bare necessities, some regiments have decorated the entrances with garlanded archways, and they embellish the interiors with fireplaces, chandeliers (made from tin cans), and lovingly crafted pulpits.[15]

And in point of fact, many soldiers lend an ear to the Christian Commission's preachings. The fledgling Federal revival of last autumn has carried over into the New Year as more men turn to God, or at least wonder about the fate of their souls. The army's chaplains and religiously inclined soldiers rejoice at this massive and seemingly sincere religious fervor. One hears reports of well-attended Scripture readings, prayer meetings, and worship services in all the camps, with men speaking to God in cautious tones. One colonel takes pride in the use made of his regiment's chapel. "Our little church is full every night," he assures his wife. "We have a grate deal of interest in religion in the regiment. Several have come out and taken a decided stand for Christ. . . . I do think that we are in the era of a greate revival among us."[16]

There are no chapels on the picket lines, which can extend for several miles in advance of the Union camps. This is a pity, for that is where the men most need cheering up. Picket duty is the most unpleasant chore they face in winter. It is tedious, lonely, and uncomfortable. And not entirely free of "anxiety and hard work," for despite the apparent peace and lack of activity in Lee's camps, one cannot trust the Rebels too far. On sunny, warm, windless, dry days the task is not bad, but such days have been rare. The presence of the enemy is almost a secondary concern in foul weather, when the men direct their main energy toward maintaining fires. In the coldest weather, a picket post daily burns a cord and a half of wood, a supply that can be acquired only by further stripping fences and buildings and denuding stands of timber. Some generals, Winfield Scott Hancock for one, forbid fires at night; this causes much grumbling and sickness.[17]

The standard stint of picket duty is three days, with each picket force divided into thirds: one group on post, another in reserve, and the third allowed to sleep. If a brigade is assigned permanently to picket, as has often happened this winter, it is rotated out of camp by thirds, so that each man spends six days in camp to every three on duty. Each post is manned by from four to six men, at least one of them a noncommissioned officer; but only one man at a time is required to stand watch, generally for two to three hours. "I go on at three o'clock this afternoon," a New Englander on duty at Mitchell's Station informs his wife by way of explanation, "and stay till six o'clock. Then I shall cook and eat my supper, and *go to bed* on a few boughs spread on the ground, and sleep till three o'clock tomorrow morning, when I go on post again to stay till six o'clock, then breakfast."[18]

There is less fraternization than last fall, even though Yank and Rebel lines along the Rapidan are close, very close, within speaking distance. But no one wants to start trouble, and Federal orders generally are not to fire on the Rebels. So the principal foes remain the weather and boredom. One man combats both by reflecting on the war and expressing his thoughts in rhyme. On a recent evening, inspired by the crisp air and comforting winter moon, he wrote the following:

> *On guard tonight; 'tis a lonely beat,*
> *And, with heavy heart and weary feet,*
> *Amid the gloom and the dark I dread,*
> *For I'm watching o'er the unburied dead.*
>
> *How sad the thought that another day*
> *Will bring again the battle fray;*
> *And ere the close of the morrow's light*
> *I, too, may sleep like these tonight.*[19]

Saturday, February 6. The battle fray echoes once again along the Rapidan, a reverberation of events far to the east. Apparently General

Benjamin F. Butler decided a couple of days ago to attempt a movement against Richmond from his position at Bermuda Hundred. For some reason, he thought a simultaneous move by Meade against Lee's lines would propel Confederate forces out of Richmond to Orange County. Halleck ordered Sedgwick—who again commands the army while Meade is in Washington—to cooperate. Sedgwick thinks it is a damn-fool idea, but he ordered a "demonstration" yesterday that has taken a nasty turn this morning.[20]

This morning, with Kilpatrick's cavalry providing reconnaissance on the flank and I Corps creating a diversion at Raccoon Ford, Sedgwick sent the infantry of Warren's II Corps bursting across Morton's Ford. A formidable position awaits them south of the Rapidan. First of all, the river bends toward Culpeper at this point, so that in crossing, the Federals will have their flanks exposed to Rebel rifles along a one-mile stretch. Next, the Rapidan's south bank rises gradually toward a high ridge, wooded and strongly entrenched about a mile from the river. Finally, the water, waist deep in most places, is damned cold as the bluecoats wade across. They must make their way slowly, too, for the safest portion of the narrow ford accommodates only four men abreast. The chill is offset somewhat by Rebel bullets that whizz past the men's ears as they clamber up the south bank.[21]

Mid-afternoon Despite the obstacles, these Federals—three infantry brigades of the Third Division and an artillery brigade—seem to be carrying the day. Indeed, Lee's pickets are falling back, and a few dozen of his men have been captured. Not bad for a "demonstration." As the Federals come to within a thousand yards of the main Rebel entrenchments, some ten pieces of artillery open up on them. The action intensifies. The Third Brigade, led by General Joshua T. Owen, has borne the brunt of the fighting as the Rebels, by now some 4,000 strong, extend their lines to encircle Owen's men. Reserves from the First and Second Brigades have moved up to bolster the blue line as fighting sweeps across largely open ground. The only substantial protection for the Yankees lies in some intervening ravines.[22]

Early evening—7 P.M. The Rebels launched a counterattack shortly before dark—about 4:30—but the Federals seem to have repulsed it.

The most intense fighting, some of it hand to hand, swirled around the Jeremiah Morton house, which sits astride the ridge. One Yankee regiment of immigrant recruits, the 39th New York—better known as the Garibaldi Guards—nearly caused disaster when a hail of Confederate fire forced them to break ranks. A "beastly set" of Dutch, Italian, and French troops is one assessment of the 39th, "the rag tag & bobtail of all creation," declares a Massachusetts officer. The situation was saved by the 14th Connecticut, which rapidly filled the gap left by the 39th. The 14th, which has suffered heavy casualties, was reinforced, in turn, by two more New York units.[23]

Both sides have lost heavily in this rare night fight. The Federals have been particularly handicapped, according to some reports, by the incoherent and occasionally reckless commands of General Alexander Hays, who totters unevenly and apparently drunkenly in his saddle. A young fifer in Company I, 111th, New York Volunteers, thinks it "a grand sight" to watch the armies battling at night. The firing looks "like litening bugs," he gasps, and it is "grand" to watch the shells bursting high in the air. The sky is illuminated further by flames that leap high into the night from the pitiful collection of buildings downriver at Raccoon Ford. About 300 men of I Corps have crept down to the "village" and torched it. Meanwhile, on the real battleground, the Federals have apparently lost over 200 dead and wounded, and surgeons have already made their way across the river to tend to the latter. Survivors are amazingly cheerful, despite cold temperatures and a light rain that has fallen intermittently during the entire day. Here and there, as the fighting fades, bands of men start fires to warm themselves and brew coffee.[24]

Sunday evening, February 7. Most of the Federals had recrossed the Rapidan by midnight last night. An orderly retreat began at about 7 P.M., with the rear guard following at about 10 P.M. Comrades carried wounded warriors across the river by means of wobbly footbridges constructed during the fight. Some men are in bad shape. A sergeant of the 19th Maine, shot in the head by a musket ball, probably will not live. Corporal Henry Clow, 108th New York, is in agony from a bullet that passed through his colon and exited near his spine. Private E. Holloway,

1st Delaware, must be operated on immediately to extract a ball that seems to be lodged near his bladder. A Connecticut private has had his left elbow smashed by a bullet; amputation is probably in order.[25]

Soldiers not wounded in the fight suffered from the bitter weather, and today are coughing and shivering from exposure. Yet, once again, they seem unruffled by either the cold or their losses. "We had a rough time, on the whole," reports a New York volunteer. "It was cold and rainy; besides we had no opportunity to dry our clothes from the time we forded the river until two o'clock the next morning—yet the men were in good spirits all the time." Walt Whitman is actually cheered by the men's appearance: "I talk'd with some of the men; as usual I found them full of gayety, endurance, and many fine little outshows, the signs of the most excellent good manliness of the world." The cavalry expeditions on the flanks have returned, too. It is well the men do not know of Butler's utter failure to advance against Richmond.[26]

The remainder of February has seen the Army of the Potomac settle into a predictable routine with one day much like another, "varied only by storm and sunshine." Men work when they must and amuse themselves as best they can. It is like any other winter encampment, only bigger. The men are better housed than last winter. Most of them have good huts and fireplaces. "I have been to a great many of the camps," reports Walt Whitman, "& I must say I am astonished how good the houses are almost every where—I have not seen one regiment nor any part of one, in the poor uncomfortable little shelter tents that I saw so common last winter." Viewed from a distance—say, from the signal tower on Mt. Pony—the village-like setting of the camps, with men cooking, washing, chopping wood, playing games, or lounging about, could be mistaken for a scene from a New York stage play; it looks like a Yankee village.[27]

Amusements, ways to pass the time, weigh heaviest on the men. Even though they are nearly drilled to death and invest much time in policing their camps, standing picket, and keeping corduroy roads in repair, the word most often used to describe camp life is "dull." Non-commissioned officers, kept busy writing reports and filling in forms, find their job "very laborious." "I would honestly prefer soldiering at the same price [pay] & stand the fatigue and exposure in Battle," insists a quartermaster sergeant, "than do what is to be done in my Capacity." Officers cannot concoct enough legitimate duties to keep their men busy all the time, and Lord knows how long they will be stuck here. One New Englander takes the long view of the uncertain nature of this soldiering business. "I think the experience must be good for us all," he concludes, "and learn us to take things as they come without fretting about the future."[28]

Meanwhile, they seem to be under constant scrutiny by a parade of visiting politicians—"gentlemen in silk hats and patent leathers"—who want to know why the army is sitting still. Oh! how the soldiers resent these creatures. Veterans returning to camp from furloughs are particularly resentful of civilian men—the "stay-at-home cowards"—who seem to "loathe and hate" the very soldiers that allow them to sleep peacefully in bed. A curious attitude to say the least, made all the harder to understand by the returning soldier's awareness that the war is far from over. "Going home seems like a fairy dream," confesses one man, which makes his return to a tent home and half-cooked rations all the more difficult to bear. "I am in a low spirited mood just now," he confesses.[29]

Elsewhere regiments continue to pair off in games of baseball; they stage sack races or greased-pig contests; and regiments, brigades, even entire corps pit their best horses against one another in spirited races. Cockfights provide another diversion, as well as an opportunity to wager. Many camps offer first-rate theatrical productions. One regiment recently staged a minstrel show, but many Federals take equal delight in the oddities of genuine local "nigs." Particularly fascinating to them are black prayer meetings, all enthusiasm and song, described by one soldier as "very interesting and laughable."[30]

A new diversion has been provided by the photographists and newspaper illustrators that now swamp the army. They are everywhere, and appear to be photographing and sketching everyone and everything. Well, almost everything, for they tend to record a sanitized version of army life for the public and for posterity. They seldom show men gambling, or being executed, or engaged in fistfights, or suffering from wounds. No images of war such as Walt Whitman is fashioning in verse, thank you; none of the "clotted rags and blood," "crush'd head," "amputated hand," "perforated shoulder," "frame all wasted," "yellow-blue countenance," or "gnawing and putrid gangrene." Rather, they portray comfortable living quarters; dress parades; Sanitary and Christian commission workers; tidy hospitals; costume balls; and vigorous, manly recreations like races, ballgames, and wrestling. A few photographists and illustrators had accompanied Pope's army, but their numbers pale beside the legions that have recently invaded Culpeper.[31]

Generals and enlisted men alike parade to the photographic galleries, where they may have their likenesses made for $1.50 each. General Alexander Webb has had six likenesses taken of his headquarters cabin at Stevensburg, one of them adorned by his wife and daughters, who are visiting here. To see a likeness of themselves is a curiosity for most soldiers, as is the experience of having one made. "I . . . tore up two machines before they got one that would stand the pressure," jokes a New Yorker in sending a photograph to his mother. "There was a little boy helping the artist," he continues, "he said that a rat or mouse would never stay in the house where that picture was." Keep it in the cupboard or cellar, the soldier instructs his mother, and it will spare her the expense of keeping a cat in "these hard times."[32]

Intellectual pursuits remain popular. Some divisions even invite civilian lecturers from the North to visit the camps and expound on issues of the day. A midwestern soldier is pleased to see a "crowded house" for the opening session of a lyceum in his regiment, and looks forward to the next lecture, which will address the issue of whether "civil liberty is more the result of individual culture than of physical suffering." Some regiments use their Christian Commission chapels for these and other high purposes, such as teaching illiterate men to read and write and for temperance meetings, Masonic gatherings, and concerts. One Pennsylvania colonel, seeking to combine instruction with recreation, has requested use of a Commission chapel as a lecture hall for the "instruction of Officers, in tactics, and sword and bayonet exercise etc. And also for meetings and lectures in science, literature and art."[33]

The sturdy log cabins of the 39th Massachusetts Infantry, encamped at Mitchell's Ford, are situated amid a "veritable Eldorado of firewood and drinking water." Ah, but food for thought is ever the New Englander's creed. The regiment has established a school in its Christian Commission chapel and ordered all men who cannot read or write to attend school daily. The ungrateful rabble so assigned produced "ugly mutterings" at first and exuded anything but a "teachable spirit," but they have been slowly won over as they noted with some amazement their swift progress in the mysteries of learning. Some men have progressed to the point where they can write letters to their families. The regiment's colonel has added further inducement by promising a gold pen and case to the man who gains the "greatest proficiency in reading."[34]

Not all learned discussion takes place in school or on a lecture platform. A debate over reenlistments that began last fall continues in tents and around campfires all across Culpeper. In early January, 6,000 men went home on furloughs as "veteran volunteers" after reenlisting. Since then, men who reenlisted upon the promise of being allowed to spend some time at home have been told that the army cannot release so many at one time. Soldiers now fear that they will never receive furloughs, at least not before the spring campaign. Other men had enlisted because of promised bounties, but these seem to have dried up, or to have been reduced in size and numbers. "For my own part," writes a Massachusetts soldier, "I should like the furlough well enough, but I don't want to be compelled to serve three years more. So far as the bounty is concerned, I can make money fully as fast at the wages now being paid, by working at my trade, and not be in danger of getting my head blown off."[35]

Now, understand, this reluctance to reenlist does not suggest a diminished patriotism in these good men. Edwin Wentworth, a private in the 37th Massachusetts Volunteers who fancies keeping his head on his shoulders, does not regret enlisting, but he believes it is time for another crop of able-bodied men to do their duty. "It angers me," he admits, "when I think of the cowardly hounds who were so ready, *before the war*, to whip the South and free the slaves, *with a war of their tongues*," who now "shrink" from this opportunity to "fight for their idol *Nigger*." One hears a lot of talk like that, for many Union soldiers are more haters of southern whites than they are friends of the southern blacks. Even men who pledge themselves to "equal rights to all men," and who believe "Freedom will certainly triumph in the end," are convinced that after three years of active duty, they have served their country long enough.[36]

Men are somewhat heartened by the steady flow of Rebel deserters coming into the Federal lines. The Johnnies desert by the dozens on cold, icy nights, with few clothes on their backs, no shoes on their feet, and a rumbling in their bellies. Jeb Stuart's cavalrymen complain that their horses are starving. "There is scarcely a night but some of them [Lee's men] desert & come into our lines," reports the colonel of the 12th New Jersey. "They appear to be almost in a starving condition & are tired of the war." Some Rebel deserters claim that Lee has established five lines of pickets between his camps and the Rapidan, intended not to buffer a Federal attack but to keep his own men from deserting. Maybe that is how the rumor began that two Mississippi regiments recently tried to *fight* their way through the Confederate lines and across the Rapidan.[37]

When school is out, the supply of lecturers runs dry, and men tire of debating the purpose of the war or the chances of victory, evening "hops"—cotillion parties—provide merriment and diversion. The lack of female dancing partners posed a problem at first, but the Federal army has solved that minor hurdle by searching nearby homes—both abandoned and occupied—for feminine apparel, to be donned by enough "ladies" in each company to correct the sexual imbalance. Add to the confiscated bonnets and petticoats an imaginative use of shelter tents and barrel hoops, and the "gentler sex" is counterfeited in abundance. Men reluctant to confiscate Rebel female garb write home for such finery. For those officers who might insist on a justification for such frivolity, an answer is quick in coming. The hops help to "educate the feet," or, failing that excuse, they provide instruction in tactics, as the dances allow men to "wheel in the waltz, change base in the quadrille, deploy in the lancers, charge in the polka, and execute flank movements in the Virginia reel."[38]

The "psychological effects of skirts" can have a curious effect on men, even to the point of arousing the "impulse of protection." Not many nights ago, the Excelsior Brigade invaded a hop being held by the 1st Massachusetts Regiment. As their hall was invaded, the New England

men instinctively leaped to protect their "female" partners. "Jim Mc-
Crae happened to be walking on my arm," recounts Charles Bardeen,
"and I put myself in front of him as inevitably as if he had been a girl 15
years old." The need lasted but an instant, for McCrae, a big, red-haired,
freckled-face Irishman, is always "spoiling for a row." When his mates
laid into the invaders in defense of their hall and their "women," Jim
"swished his skirts out of the way, pulled up [his] sleeves . . . , and sailed
into that Excelsior crowd with both fists."[39]

But it is just such hops and parties that require officers to keep a
short rein on their men. It is a familiar situation. Officers try to keep
their charges busy, but the excess of free time and lack of military action produce restiveness. Soldiers long for any opportunity to cut
loose, relieve the boredom, and take their minds off the impending
campaign—and home. The latter continues to be the larger danger.
"The thought of comfortable firesides comes up and makes men home-
sick," admits one soldier, "and this preys directly on their spirits."[40]

Some men respond to discipline, know-it-all officers, and sweaty
work details with outbreaks of drunkenness and insubordination,
which continue to plague the army. A private in a New York regiment
refused to cut a tree stump in his camp near Stevensburg. "I will be
damned if I will cut that stump for you or anyone else," he told his
sergeant. Another private in another New York regiment took exception to a surgeon's criticism of his tent during a recent inspection.
"Suck my ass," shot back the private, and when told that he would be
reported for a dirty tent he grabbed the doctor's hair and walloped him
on the side of the head. A Massachusetts private aroused his whole
company on a recent night when he staggered through camp singing
obscene songs and shouting profanities. When his sergeant tried to
quiet him, he called him a "cock-sucking son of a bitch."[41]

Many such harsh words are inspired by Demon Rum, and it is not
just the enlisted men who engage in rowdy behavior. Charges were recently preferred against the lieutenant colonel of the 121st New York
for "drunkeness, gambling and obscene behavior before the Regiment." Nearly all of the officers and many privates testified against
him, but he got off with a fairly light punishment—a severe reprimand

and threatened dismissal from the service. That was hardly sufficient in the eyes of some men. "He is, I am sorry to say," reported one officer of the colonel, "anything but a temperate, virtuous man. Wine and women are his Gods, and to indulge his appetite in the matter, he has taken to the card table to supply an empty purse."[42]

Some men are so intoxicated that they can recall nothing of their misdeeds. A private in the 13th Massachusetts, accused of striking another soldier with a stick, swears he was so "crazy drunk" he has no recollection of the attack. A New Yorker who went roaring through his company street, escaped the guard detail that arrested him, struck the sergeant of the guard when apprehended, and called the brigade adjutant a "son of a bitch" and another officer "a whore's bastard" claims, "I would not have done what I did but for the liquor. I was never drunk before." Another New Yorker entered a similar plea, but his captain, inquiring as to why the man had missed a Sunday morning inspection, elicited a response that has hurt the man's case. "By Jesus Christ," he snarled at the captain, "I was drunk then, I am drunk now, and I am going to get drunk as long as I have Green Backs in my pockets, and you or no other God-damned son of a bitch can prevent me." Less colorfully, a private in a Pennsylvania regiment declares, after having been drunk and disorderly in camp near the Court House and having threatened to kill a lieutenant, that he has "not the slightest knowledge of what occurred."[43]

Whatever the excuses, such behavior cannot be tolerated in this particular winter camp. The Army of the Potomac has never before wintered below the Rappahannock, in enemy territory. Then, too, there is the reenlistment controversy, and the possibility that the army will be severely undermanned should large numbers of men be furloughed. The presence of so many women in camp carries a certain obligation, too. However, most important is the changed character of the army. It is an army with more conscripts, bounty jumpers, and "outlaws" than in the past. The new elements are "turbulent and noisy," constantly engaged in gambling, skulduggery, and fistfights of "terrible brutality." Because such men require strict supervision, the entire army must suffer. Meade is determined to punish wrongdoers. Some soldiers believe these "mercenaries" have changed the character of the volunteer army of 1861-63. The "friendly feeling of cordial comradeship" between enlisted men and officers has vanished, think some observers.[44]

Yet the army knows when to rally, and men momentarily set aside their differences and prejudices in late February and early March when Meade sent men marching and galloping in all directions. It all started in the idle brain of General Judson Kilpatrick. Old "Kil-cavalry" (known as such for his habit of pushing man and beast to their limits) had been bored by the lack of activity in camp. On one occasion, he created his own excitement by riding a horse into his headquarters at Rose Hill, cantering down the hall, and exiting by the rear door. He then rode back in, retracing his route to exit at the front. Kilpatrick considers such exercises great sport. So while sitting around his campfire near Stevensburg, he concocted a raid on Richmond to free Union prisoners, burn the city, and capture Jeff Davis. Meade did not think much of the plan, and his cavalry chief, Pleasonton, said it was "not feasible." But Lincoln, after some hesitation, warmed to the scheme, and, well, Lincoln is boss. He saw it as a good way to spread word of his amnesty proclamation, announced last December, for all Rebels who will lay down their arms. Lincoln had also been alarmed by reports of suffering among Federal prisoners in Richmond.[45]

So Kilpatrick, "a frothy braggart, without brains," in the opinion of one staff officer, led 4,000 men across Ely Ford on February 28. As a diversion for Kilpatrick's force, Meade sent XI Corps and part of III Corps on a demonstration southwestward toward Madison Court House. He also dispatched George Custer and 1,500 cavalrymen toward Charlottesville to tear up the Gordonsville and Lynchburg Railroad.[46]

The diversions succeeded in a limited way, but Kilpatrick's raid was a bust. Custer had a helluva good time. His men destroyed a railroad bridge over the Rivanna River, burned three gristmills filled with grain and flour, captured over 50 men and 500 horses, and brought away over 1,000 slaves. As if that were not enough action, his command had the excitement of a hair-breadth escape. Having nearly been led into a trap by a Rebel guide, Custer's men fled to the protection of Sedgwick's infantry. Sedgwick's men, meanwhile, had sat around for two days, sleepless in rain and mud, before returning with Custer to Culpeper. None of this served to brighten the men's spirits when they learned that bold Kilpatrick had abandoned his mission at the very gates of Richmond. The Confederates had read rumors of an intended raid in northern newspapers, and although the Rebels knew not when or even if such a daring scheme would be launched, they were prepared to confront Kilpatrick's column. Kilpatrick fled, but over three hundred of his men have been captured. Tragically, his second in command, Colonel Ulric Dahlgren, 21-year-old son of a Yankee admiral, was killed.[47]

"The great raid was a great failure," Sedgwick has concluded. "It does not seem to have been made with any judgment." Still, Kilpatrick may not have been entirely to blame. After all, how did the Rebels learn of the raid? The element of surprise was entirely lacking, and at least one staff officer knows why. "A secret expedition with us is got up like a picnic, with everybody blabbing and yelping," he says disgustedly. "One is driven to think that not even the prospect of immediate execution will stop Americans from streaming on in their loose talking, devil-may-care ways." Now, a new wrinkle has developed that enrages the South. It is alleged that papers betraying a plan to burn parts of Richmond and kill President Davis and other government officials were found on Colonel Dahlgren's body. Whether for these reasons or because of the scheme's failure, an Indiana cavalryman reports, "The boys are ashamed of Kilpatrick and his raid."[48]

Meade's mood has not been improved by another round of demands for his resignation. Even while Kilpatrick's men retreated, Meade was bound for Washington to appear before the Committee on the Conduct of the War. General Daniel E. Sickles—he of the infamous Barton Key affair—and Abner Doubleday—whom some people credit with having invented baseball—have accused Meade of favoring retreat after the second day of fighting at Gettysburg. Furthermore, General Albion P. Howe has accused Meade and John Sedgwick of botching the Mine Run campaign. Meade had to answer questions relating to both sets of charges. At the same time, some of his fellow officers were demanding that Joe Hooker again lead the army. But much of that talk seems to have subsided now. It is mid-March, and Meade's friends—John Gibbon, Winfield Hancock, and others—have rallied behind him. Even more important, he seems to retain the confidence of Secretary of War Stanton.[48]

The people of Culpeper have not been so lucky, and now, as a third year of war draws to a close, their spirits have never been lower. People have fared according to the character of the Yankees they have encountered. As usual, it is the uncertainty of events that most depresses people. How long will the Yankees remain? Will the next patrol to pass our farm be kindly disposed or hostile? Will soldiers marching through the Court House steal what they want or respect private property? Merchants and farmers have met Federals of both stripes. The amounts of store goods, firewood, grain, and livestock confiscated are incalculable, and even though citizens are supposed to receive receipts for property so taken, no one trusts the bluecoats.[50]

The army officially sympathizes with the worst suffering citizens. Not only do officers insist that soldiers respect civilians and their property, but rations are issued to people on the verge of starvation. The same is true in neighboring Fauquier County, where a portion of Meade's army is encamped around Warrenton. Of course, by now the countryside has been pretty well stripped of subsistence, and some men derive perverse pleasure from hearing Rebels beg for food and clothing and admitting that the Confederacy is doomed. They chuckle at the adamant protests of less supine residents, too. Both Jack Pendleton and John Botts have complained to the army about not being properly compensated for confiscated or damaged property. Pendleton has even been to Washington to complain to President Lincoln. The president must have given him some satisfaction, because he has been "very independent" since his return, apparently thinking that "Abe will support him in any thing he may say or do." Botts claims to be a unionist, but, as one Federal officer observes, "his ardor cools when he fancies his pocket is to be touched."[51]

Most soldiers, considering the utter desolation of the countryside, cannot help but sympathize with these people, what remains of them, that is. One Union surgeon has even grown fond of Culpeper, and sees great potential here. "After the war, when evil passions are lulled to rest," he tells his wife, "this country will be a desirable one to live in. Northern men and Northern money and energy will develope its resources, and an unprecedented reign of prosperity will follow. On some accounts, I should like to live here." For the moment, however, the population is small and scattered. Few male residents remain, save the "lame, blind, and supernumerated." Old John Kelly still resides at Kellysville, waited on by a few old slaves who are more scared of leaving than of remaining with him. But even the once-ferocious Kelly is feeling his years—and the loss of his right arm. Two years ago, outraged by the conduct of one of his slaves, Kelly struck her so viciously that he cut his hand on her teeth. Blood poisoning necessitated an amputation. "Just retribution," comment some people. A few blacks remain, too, though it is hard for the Yanks to distinguish between former slaves and those who have never known bondage. Not that it matters much any more, and besides, the Federals have no use for blacks who cannot make themselves useful in camp.[52]

Some white men who have fled the county still contemplate a return. Until then, they try to maintain their homesteads from afar. James F. Brown, currently refuging in Charlottesville, served 16 months in the 4th Virginia Cavalry. He has sold grain and meat to the Confederate army at fair prices, and when at home, between Federal occupations, he has "never turned a soldier or refugee" away from his door. As a former soldier, a former justice of the peace, and a large landowner, he does not return for fear of being arrested by the Federals. So he stays in communication with his family, still residing in Culpeper, and bides his time. His dependents include his wife and ten children (the eldest being 17), several relations, and the family of an army comrade captured at Gettysburg that is "entirely dependent" on him for support. He even retains some of his slaves, which once numbered 19.[53]

Some of Culpeper's remaining Rebel women seem happy for the company of the soldiery, as long as the men behave themselves. The best behaved men, as in past Federal occupations, receive invitations into family parlors and are invited to supper. Neither side pretends to sympathize with the other's "cause," but bonds of human sympathy are sometimes formed. "We got a couple of girls to sing a song," reports one soldier to his sweetheart of an evening in one Culpeper home. "They sang the 'Home Spun Dress'—a very beautiful *Southern* song— in a quite commendable manner. One of the girls agreed to write the song off for me so I can send it north." The song also reminded the Union soldier of Confederate women's past loyalty:

> *The Southern land's a glorious land,*
> *And has a glorious cause,*
> *Three cheers, three cheers for Southern Rights,*
> *And for the Southern Boys!*
>
> *We've sent our sweethearts to the war,*
> *But dear girls, never mind,*
> *Your soldier-boy will ne'er forget,*
> *The girl he left behind.*[54]

Most residents, on the other hand, refuse to compromise their prin- ciples or associate with Yankees. When two Union officers called on Mrs. William Major near Cedar Mountain, she turned them away "gracefully," even while refusing their offerings of sugar and coffee. Re- turning disappointedly to camp, the same two men passed a farm where a young woman—"a handsome figure in her shortened skirts, her head bare, cheeks red, and eyes flashing"—valiantly beat at a grass fire that threatened the fences and buildings of her homestead. The officers volunteered their assistance, but the young woman, even with her house in danger, refused them "with the utmost scorn." The men finally gained entrance to a third abode, inhabited by a woman, her children, and her aged father. The woman's husband was in the army. The family was poor and too timid to resist the officer's well-intended effort to be cordial. "The faces of the old man and the woman were sad and fearful, and sharp with hope long deferred," observed one Yankee. "The children showed a half-frightened curiosity. It was a stiff recep- tion they gave us, and we had no right to expect anything different. I felt that our intrusion was unwelcome, almost an insult."[55]

Other people appear to receive the Yankees in a generous spirit, but then exploit their advantage. Consequently, Meade's provost marshal,

General Patrick, is in an uproar about spies. He is suspicious of many people, although the only person he has actually interrogated is Mrs. Payne, who still tries to operate the Virginia House. Patrick may close the establishment, as the Confederates nearly did some three years ago. In 1861, Mrs. Payne had been selling spirits to Confederate soldiers. This time she is collecting information. "We have captured her letters & a box," Patrick reports in his diary, apparently unwilling as yet to prefer charges against Mrs. Payne. "She is a hard case," he admits, "& yet our Officers *will* go there & tell her & her daughters every thing."[56]

The Federals are not a little annoyed, too, by scouting parties from Lee's army, many of them led by soldiers from Culpeper or adjoining counties. The Federals consider them guerrillas and bushwhackers who harass the Yanks on all sides. Above the Rappahannock, in Fauquier County, John Mosby's men make a nuisance of themselves at every opportunity. Cavalry pickets north of the Court House are pestered by Hill's guerrillas, who closely watch Federal movements along the Hazel River. The band is small but mobile and dangerous. "I do not think it safe to patrol to Hazel River with less than 20 to 30 men," the lieutenant of one picket force advises his brigade commander, "and shall not send a patrol unless you direct." Generals also recognize the danger. Earlier this month, Wesley Merritt acknowledged that only sizable reconnaissance forces can feel safe from "attack and capture by guerrillas" in this region.[57]

The assumed advantage of using home-grown boys to scout in Culpeper is that, knowing the terrain and inhabitants, they have the best opportunity to escape detection. Alas, it does not always work that way. Last January, four Little Fork Rangers—Isaac Lake, Hill Jeffries, Art McCormick, and Silas Newsome—were spending the night at Martha Rixey's house while on a scout. They assumed they would be safe there, but someone in the neighborhood informed the Federals of their presence. Well after midnight, the four lads were awakened by the shouts of some two hundred Union cavalrymen who had surrounded the house and were demanding their surrender. The spunky Rangers, all veterans of at least two years' service, wanted to fight their way out. The widow Rixey, however, fearful of reprisals, begged them to give up. They bowed to her wishes. Within days, they found themselves in the Old Capitol Prison.[58]

One other point about the Rixey incident: Major W. R. Parnell, commanding the Federal detachment, was incensed that the Rixey house, like most houses in the area, had a safeguard assigned to it. As his men surrounded the Rixey home, he heard the guard, a Private Williams of Company C, 5th New Jersey Volunteers, tell them that they had "no right to take those men prisoners." The implication is that Private Williams *knew* the Rebels were sleeping in the house (how could he not?), but that his sympathy for Mrs. Rixey (or perhaps a bribe) had convinced him to turn a blind eye. Thus Parnell's anger. "Such men are dangerous when outside of our lines," the major complained of Williams, and he has demanded a court-martial for the private.[59]

In other ways, too, these raids do not always turn out as planned. A few weeks ago, early in March, another party of Little Fork Rangers slipped into Culpeper intending to ambush a Federal wagon train near Jeffersonton. The train was more heavily guarded than they expected, so after firing a volley into the column, the Rangers beat a hasty retreat. However, one of their number, Adolphus Lloyd, was wounded and captured. Lloyd, just 18 years old, is the eldest of James and Ann Lloyd's five children, and the whole family are sick of the war. Tired, wounded, and captured, Adolphus decided to take the oath. That was bad enough in Confederate eyes, but then Lloyd, evidently to satisfy an old family grudge, turned in an elderly neighbor, Truman Harris, as a Rebel sympathizer. Mr. Harris has been hauled away to Point Lookout, Maryland, and Lloyd, in order to save his skin, has disappeared from the neighborhood.[60]

Serving on "detached service" near his home has led George H. Coons to think about getting out of the war, but he prefers a nobler exit than Lloyd's. Coons has served nearly two years with the Little Fork Rangers, but as he is nearly 40 years of age, his rheumatism, asthma, and weak lungs make active service extremely wearing. Having a chance to visit his wife and daughter this winter, he has seen the damage done to his farm by contending armies. Meade's army, in particular, did several thousand dollars' worth of damage last fall, as well as encouraging three of Coons's slaves to run away. This winter, he finds his family freezing and nearly starving. He has been able to purchase a few barrels of corn at $60 per barrel, but he finds "no sympathy" among neighbors who, while trying to keep their own heads above water, charge "*extortion* prices" for life's necessities. Coons is so troubled that he has asked Governor William Smith to appoint him to the vacant post of county commissioner of revenue in Culpeper's southern district. He would take office when the Yankees leave (which he expects to happen this spring) and hold it until an election could be held.[61]

March 25. Another general has arrived in Culpeper, but he is not just any other general. Ulysses S. Grant—Unconditional Surrender Grant—hero of Fort Donelson, Pittsburg Landing, Vicksburg, and Chattanooga, writes dispatches to Secretary of War Stanton and General Halleck at a table in his temporary headquarters, a plain brick home near the Court House depot. Grant is the new commanding general of the Union armies. By rights, he should be in Washington City, sitting at the desk occupied by Henry Halleck; but Grant is no desk general; he must be in the field. Yet he is not here to usurp Meade's authority or steal his thunder. Indeed, he has publicly expressed his confidence in the hero of Gettysburg. Meade has earned the right to lead his men. Grant wants only to travel with the army and whisper advice in Meade's ear.[62]

Grant is below average height, but he has a firm, square jaw, a "spare, strong build," and a type of "rough dignity." He is not unattractive, with light-brown hair, a short, full beard, clear blue eyes, and a high forehead, and his manner suggests calm determination. He first visited the army a fortnight ago, around March 10, when he was greeted with "true Virginia hospitality, i.e., mud by the square mile, and rain by the flood." This time, two days before his arrival, a monster snowstorm hit Culpeper, with high winds and frigid temperatures. The storm dumped six to eight inches of snow on the army. That gave the boys a high old time, with snowball fights breaking out in virtually every camp. Whole brigades sometimes paired off against each other in "brisk skirmishing." The snow has mostly melted now, and today, March 25, rain falls.[63]

Grant pays no mind; he is thinking about Lee. Grant is a lieutenant general now, the first United States soldier to hold that rank since George Washington. There is irony for you: George Washington, a Virginian, and now Grant, determined to whip Robert E. Lee, related by marriage to Washington, and to conquer Virginia. But to succeed, he must prepare this army for the spring campaign. "I have not been out of the house today," he tells his wife, Julia Dent Grant, in a break from official correspondence, "and from appearances should not be able to go for several days. At present however I shall find enough to do indoors." He pauses to consider this new army, the first eastern army he has accompanied in the field. He has confidence in these men. "From indications," he concludes to Julia. "I would judge the best of feelings animate all the troops here toward the changes that have been made."[64]

Ah, yes, the changes. There have been significant ones in the past few days. Life is always more or less uncertain, and life in an army at war has no guarantees at all. Grant's arrival, of course, is a major change for the army, and officers and men alike have been scrutinizing and discussing the merits of their new commander. "The feeling about Grant is peculiar," observes one officer, "a little jealousy, a little dislike, a little envy, a little want of confidence." His arrival by train at 2 P.M. on Thursday produced no noticeable enthusiasm in the ranks. Indeed, it went largely unnoticed. He did not look much like a warrior as he stepped onto the platform in plain dress, his eyes half closed. "I should have taken him for a clerk at headquarters rather than a general," asserts one man. A few officers and men glanced up from their work, but quickly returned to duty. A cockfight or a set-to between a pair of freedmen would have drawn a bigger crowd.[65]

Those men who react negatively to Grant do so for one of two reasons. A few soldiers fear they see another Pope in Grant, another western general come east to tell them how to fight. When men hear of Grant's reported remark that the Army of the Potomac "has got to *fight* this summer," they cannot conceal "a contemptuous smile." Grant did not see this army perform at Antietam, at Fredericksburg, at Chancellorsville, or at Gettysburg. Even in defeat they have won glory, and no army on either side of this contest has fought more stubbornly. And eastern soldiers believe they have been fighting foes superior to those faced by Grant in the West. Grant "had better look out or he may lose his Military reputation," believes a New England soldier, "for he has got a different style of Rebels and a different General to fight" out here. Lee, it seems clear, is no John Pemberton or Braxton Bragg.[66]

Part of this reaction stems from loyalty to Meade. The tall, stooped, round-shouldered general has few rabid supporters, but Meade possesses better-than-average intelligence, and he has beaten Lee already. Many men wonder why a known quantity should be replaced by an unknown. They are especially concerned by the new "duality of command" installed by Grant. Who commands the army, Meade or Grant? How can both command? "Old Spectacles," one of Meade's nicknames, "is nothing but an upper-adjutant now," some fear.[67]

On the other hand, men appreciate that their new commanding general has taken the field with them, rather than hiding behind a desk. Here he may judge the military situation first hand and identify the army's needs. Grant exudes "not only the will but the power to call for unlimited and unqualified resources" to subdue the Rebels. Even men who insist that Grant prove himself by *earning* their approval wish him well. A New Englander, perhaps displaying a touch of regional prejudice toward Grant, reports, "I have no idea that Grant is a genius. In fact, I am very sure that he is not. But still if he has only as much shrewdness & character as he is supposed to have, with the immense resources which he can command, I feel that it is pretty safe." Having the two generals—Meade and Grant—working together, each with his own strengths (Meade for his cleverness and tactical skill; Grant for his force and decisiveness) may be "the next thing to having a man of real genius" lead the army.[68]

The second great change, a complete reorganization of the Army of the Potomac, was announced on March 24. The move is not at all popular with much of the army. Some men attribute the change to Meade, who in fact initiated it last February; but Grant thoroughly approves of the reorganization and intends to see it through. The plan calls for consolidation of many units—from regiments to corps—to form a leaner army, with the addition of thousands of new recruits and conscripts. Two corps—I and III—have been broken up and merged into the three remaining corps, II, V, and VI, to be led, respectively, by Winfield Hancock, Gouverneur Warren, and John Sedgwick. Each surviving corps will be consolidated into two divisions. Additionally,

General Ambrose Burnside and IX Corps will join the army from Tennessee. The prevailing fear is that adulteration will injure the pride, spirit, and effectiveness of the army. Meade and Grant seem to be "breaking up families" and questioning the effectiveness of many brave men and renowned units.[69]

Officers and men make the best of the situation. "It was a heavy blow to veterans of the old 3rd Corps," concedes one man, "to sink their identity in another body [II Corps] but . . . there are no troops in the Army of the Potomac who wouldn't feel proud to fight under Hancock." Officers who have lost their commands, like General Alexander Hays, are less sanguine. "The enemies of our country have . . . assailed it in vain," he tells his wife rather grandly, "and now it dissolves by the action of our own friends." Some junior officers have held "indignation" meetings to protest this consolidation movement. Such rebels will likely be dismissed from service. Yet some men grieve sincerely at the loss of popular leaders. "General [John C.] Caldwell is our friend," laments a young officer upon the departure of his division commander. "He has been a father to us youngsters and ever ready to help in smoothing the pathway of official duty." On the other hand, people recognize that not a few incompetent officers have been justly removed from command. When William Blaisdell, colonel of the First Brigade, Second Division, II Corps, lost his command, a fellow officer cursed the colonel and his staff as an "uncouthed, wicked, meddlesome, and abominable pack. . . . They were disliked and detested by all, and we are glad that they are broken up and laid aside."[70]

Grant believes the consolidation will help end the war, and end it soon. He is ordering all available troops to the front, "all recruits, new organizations, and all the old troops it is possible to spare." He will need them, for he has concocted a bold scheme that will stretch the manpower and logistical efforts of the nation to an extent never imagined. He has called for the "co-operative action of all the Armies in the field" in as many as six simultaneous advances into the "interior" of Rebeldom. From Virginia, through Georgia, and into Louisiana and Arkansas, Grant wants to hit the Rebels and hit them hard. Virginia will receive the most attention, with campaigns in the Valley, against Richmond, and, most importantly, against Lee. He and Meade will personally go after Marse Robert. All he requires is enough men and Lee's cooperation, for Grant believes he must strike before Lee puts his own army in motion.[71]

April. Grant is working with Meade and his corps commanders to prepare the army for its sternest test of the war. That means more drill, inspections, target practices, and reviews than any veteran has ever seen. For despite Meade's efforts to maintain discipline and keep the men in a state of readiness, the cogs of his military machine can use some oil. It is so in any winter encampment. Lack of activity breeds lethargy, and the horrible weather—wind, rain, snow, and *mud*—that prevails has not helped. Then, too, Meade has had the distractions of appearing before Congress, hearing rumors of his replacement, the reorganization of the army, and the arrival of Grant. One feels sorry for this unassuming, goggle-eyed general whose ability so many people still question. Even his staff are unsure what to make of him. One moment he is cheerfully cracking jokes and telling stories; the next hour he is "going bang at someone, and nobody ever knows who is going to catch it next."[72]

No one can disguise the need for improvement. One brigade commander in early March expressed shock at the appearance and "inexcusable neglect" of his troops. Men appeared for inspection with "filthy arms, defective and abused equipment, clothing dirty and contrary to the prescribed uniform," some even attired in civilian dress. Colonel Joseph Keifer, 110th Ohio, expresses distress over the "unsoldierly and improper conduct" of some men in his command. "Any further indication of such conduct," he warns, "will make it necessary to again return to the old custom of keeping guards and a guardhouse." Even the commander of so elite a unit as Berdan's Sharpshooters complains that his men "are in a low state of discipline" and "poorly drilled."[73]

"A lively hum of preparation" is spreading through the army. One soldier insists that discipline is "more rigorous" than at any time in the war. "Every thing is done at the sound of the bugle," he declares. Infantry regiments practice complex maneuvers, such as forming columns against cavalry attacks and moving obliquely on the battlefield. They practice their marksmanship, too. Beginning in late March, every regiment in the army has taken target practice on Tuesdays, Thursdays, and Saturdays between 10 A.M. and noon, 10 rounds per man.[74]

And it is true that some of the displays of marksmanship are dismal. "After watching them fire at a target," observes one soldier of the practices, "one will not wonder that so few men are killed in a battle, for I have seen a great many of them fire at a target at the distance of only twenty rods, and not come within a rod of the mark." New York regiments are the worst, believes this New Englander, but accuracy in most of the army is poor. His regimental surgeon can attest to that. While riding today on the far side of a hill from a company practicing its marksmanship, he was hit in the wrist by a stray shot. The ball had spent itself before hitting him, so that he suffered nothing more than a severe bruise; but this instance is not an isolated case. It is as though the men had never before fired their rifles; and indeed that may sometimes be the case. "It is believed there are men in this army," reports Meade, "who have been in numerous actions without ever firing their guns, and it is known that muskets taken on the battlefield have been found nearly filled to the muzzle with cartridges." [75]

At least the cavalry will be ready; Grant has ensured that by summoning General Philip H. Sheridan to replace Alfred Pleasonton. Sheridan arrived at Brandy Station on April 5 and has not yet stopped to rest. He is pleased with the twelve thousand officers and men of his command. They are in good health and well equipped. Sheridan is troubled, however, that their horses are "thin and very much worn down" from picket duty. He is doing all he can to acquire new horses, and he has talked earnestly with Meade about the need to change the cavalry's mission. Rather than using it simply to shield infantry and guard wagons and railroads, "Little Phil" (just five feet five inches tall) wants to engage the Rebel cavalry "in a general combat." Meade does not seem inclined to alter his use of the cavalry, but he has promised to relieve it of excessive picket duty. So Sheridan has made his point, and, indeed, he "makes everywhere a favorable impression."[76]

CHAPTER THIRTEEN

AN UNSETTLED STATE

*I*n every direction, one sees signs of an army preparing to launch a campaign. The men are to pack all unnecessary articles of clothing and accoutrements for shipment to a central depot. Grant wants a lean, swift-moving army when he goes after Lee. Most civilians, with the exception of agents for the Sanitary Commission and Christian Commission, have been ordered to leave by April 16. The provost marshal has allowed the commission agents to stay a while longer because local ministers and army chaplains have requested it. A similar earlier order was to have cleared all women from the camps two weeks before Grant's arrival, but it was widely ignored. This time, an exodus of several thousand people has begun, with only a few nurses ignoring the decree. Cornelia Hancock intends to stay until "they stop bringing in 7 or eight sick per day."[1]

The men are sad to see these people leave. They will miss the Sanitary and Christian commissions and the hospitals. They present departing nurses with tokens of esteem. They are even sadder to see the sutlers go, despite complaints about exorbitant prices. "Since the expulsion of sutlers," laments one officer, "we have been obliged to confine ourselves to army rations." Not only that, but tobacco, which was a staple of the sutlers, has become exceedingly hard to obtain, and no other loss, claims some men, can so quickly demoralize an army. "[T]hey can go it without much to eat or drink," insists one man, "but Tobacco they must have."[2]

Some six hundred hospital patients are being evacuated along with the baggage and civilians. They are mostly sick or diseased, but the worst cases are men still recovering from wounds suffered at Morton's Ford in February. "How like Gettysburg it seemed to me," says Cornelia Hancock, who helped to load the men on trains bound for Washington. "I had all our worst cases put in a pile, took a whiskey bottle, and sat down and helped the poor souls to live while they were loaded." As the "groaning load" chugged out of Brandy Station, Hancock reflected, "[T]he idea of making a *business of maiming men* is not one worthy of a civilized nation." Not all men survive the journey. One lad groaned as he was borne on a stretcher all the way from the Washington depot to a hospital. He was dead by the time doctors came to examine him.[3]

This is not to say that Culpeper's three military hospitals have gone out of business. Daily sick calls bring new cases of measles, diarrhea, smallpox, pneumonia, rheumatism, and syphilis. Nor has the horror of the hospital wards diminished just because the wounded have been removed. "A wounded man is a sad sight," confesses Cornelia Hancock, "but saddest yet are the sights in our hospital now, cases of Chronic Diarrhea, men emaciated to a skeleton and blacker than a mulatto." In some ways, the sick are even more trouble to care for than the wounded, for they "have no appetite whatever" and are "full of notions." Many new recruits not quickly provided with shelter against the continuing rain, wind, and occasional snow enter the hospitals with severe colds, bronchitis, and pneumonia. "Nobody knows what soldiering is until they try it," reflects Hancock sardonically. "It will do in dry weather, but to have *water* dripping over you 23 hours out of 24 is not as pleasant as one might suppose." Or, as one soldier expresses it, "The danger of the battlefield is not so great as the danger of sickness, while getting acclimated."[4]

Healthy men cling to their amusements to the last minute. Baseball and snowball fights, lyceums and cotillions, theatricals and letter writing still hold sway. Horse races—or any excuse to bet—provide excitement, although not always as much as one recent contest in which the winning horse bolted into the crowd and knocked over several spectators. Itinerant performers occasionally cheer up the lads. A Wisconsin regiment recently applauded a "decided genius" who spoke and sang patriotic songs for two hours in their camp. "He was amusing, pathetic, patriotic, almost thrilling in his climaxes after the most approved style of oratory," claims one witness. "His utterances were encouraging to the soldiers . . . , wearied by the monotony of camp life." Some rowdiness persists, too, as exemplified by the men who have been tossing stones at passing trains along the O&A tracks in contests to hit the signal lights. Unfortunately, they occasionally hit the brakeman. Ah, well, it may only be high spirits.[5]

Civilians and soldiers maintain their uneasy truce, too, a calculated truce for many noncombatants. People have learned during the past three years that friendship with Federal officers improves their chances of saving their property from marauding soldiers and undue confiscation. And, of course, people usually respond to kindness with kindness. People follow the rule of thumb used across the Rappahannock in Fauquier County. "We are in the midst of them and are in their power," reasons a resident of Warrenton. "we only treat those kindly where kindness has been extended to us by them." A midwestern soldier has struck up an interesting friendship with old Mr. Mosee as they engage in a series of intensely competitive chess matches. Mosee tells the soldier that he "has beaten the Confederate army and is anxious to beat the Union army." His rival, Rufus Dawes of the 6th Wisconsin, concedes that Mosee, who lives isolated and alone except for his daughter "Puss," is a formidable opponent. "He spends his time studying calculus and chess for want of something else to do," observes Dawes.[6]

A few friendships have proved more scandalous. Martha Moore, who has boarded and housed several Union officers at her home in Stevensburg, became intimate with at least one Yankee, Captain S. N. Stanford of the 1st Ohio Cavalry. Some people describe Mrs. Moore as a woman of "ill character and repute." She admits to socializing—walking, riding, visiting— with Stanford and other officers, but she denies doing anything immoral. Nevertheless, Stanford admitted to having slept with her at his court-martial a fortnight ago, and the affair has turned out badly for him. The army has cashiered Stanford for neglecting his duty and engaging in conduct prejudicial to "good order and military discipline."[7]

Most enthusiastic in assisting the army, and genuinely so, are Culpeper's unionists. They dread the coming campaign, for they know that the army, most of it anyway, must depart. Until then, they make themselves useful and agreeable to the Federals, partly because they can profit by doing so, partly because it is their inclination. Jane Allen, a 62-year-old widow, is renting her house for $6 a month to a major and a lieutenant who work in the provost marshal's office. In addition, General Wesley Merritt's cavalry are camping in her fields. She frequently invites officers to dinner. She is also known for tenderly treating any soldier, officer or private, who reports sick to her, a common occurrence during this bitter winter. They come to her, she concedes, "like I was their mother." In return, her buildings and property are unscathed, and she is "treated as kind as could be."[8]

Robert and Sarah Thomas, in their early thirties, live on a 277-acre farm with five children near the Court House. Robert owned six slaves, but loyalty to the Union forbade him enlisting in the Confederate army, and poor health saved him from being conscripted. One slave, a mere girl named Pocahontas, remains with the family as a servant. The Thomases know "nearly all of the officers" of General David Birney's division, which uses their house as a picket post. Sarah feeds the division's officer of the day and its surgeon nearly all their meals. In return, Sarah receives passes through Federal lines to visit her father seven miles north of the Court House, and she is allowed to roam freely through Birney's camp and to purchase needed supplies from his quartermaster.[9]

Other people make a virtue of necessity. Martha Bailey, whose husband died in December 1862, now has five children to raise on her own. Since her husband's death, she lives with her brother, William Purks, but that has not spared her the need to try to support her family. A self-described uneducated woman who understood little about what started the war and cared little about which side might eventually win, Mrs. Bailey has now taken the oath along with her brother. This permits her to draw rations from the army, and it has earned her brother a safeguard for his farm. Now that she knows what the war is all about, Mrs. Bailey says, she stands by the Union. She also cooks and washes clothes for the soldiers.[10]

Of course, these unionists walk a fine line. On the one hand, they want the Federals to know they are loyal to Abe and the old flag. On the other hand, they know, as in the past, that another Confederate occupation is likely. Consequently, they cannot broadcast their feelings too widely. Several Union men live near Robert Thomas, yet only recently, after "many conversations" and much hemming and hawing, have they been able to reveal their true sympathies to one another. They have been "afraid to trust each other," admits Reuben Gains, for there is "danger in being an avowed Union man in this country." Jesse Burrows, who lives at the Court House, calls it a "delicate subject," to be talked of "only privately." Lewis Nelson, the merchant, refuses to support either side. He stays at home and does "not talk much." Neighbors seem "to fear each other," and no one dares "to talk about Unionism or the war either for or against it."[11]

The price of being suspected can be severe. Some people, like William Soutter early in the war, are threatened with physical harm. At the least, known unionists are ostracized. Jane Allen is still "stigmatized" for having her conscripted son released from the army. Old John Brown and John O'Neil do not try to disguise their loyalties, but they are "spoken against on account of it." Brown says to hell with them, but then he is an old fellow—in his sixties—and plain spoken. He openly visits the Federal camps and is on good terms with neighboring blacks, whom he keeps informed of Union military victories. He predicts a Yankee triumph and has consistently told local slaves that they are "as certain to be free as there . . . [is] a God in Heaven." Still, Brown's friends believe that if it were not for his age he would be in prison right now, or perhaps dead. Even Brown admits that if the Confederacy prevails he will be hounded out of the county. He knows that neighbors call him a "black republican" and other "hard names."[12]

Some unionists take advantage of Federal protection to escape Culpeper. Meade generously distributes passes to families and individuals seeking escape to a northern state or a Union-occupied portion of the South. One of the first to take advantage of this opportunity is

William Soutter. Soutter has been a pain in the Confederacy's neck since the war began. He has helped Federal prisoners in Culpeper to escape, and he twice avoided Confederate conscription because of his age and poor health. A neighbor once threatened to shoot him on sight. When conscripted a third time (the government never gives up), Soutter was forced into the army but deserted and was hiding in the woods near his home when the Army of the Potomac arrived. While he was in hiding, neighbors threatened to hang Soutter if they found him; even before he deserted, the county court refused to sell wheat to his family, an unheard-of rebuff. Given the opportunity to escape, he wasted no time in moving his family to Maryland.[13]

Other people remain enigmas where the question of loyalty is concerned, but that does not usually spare them persecution, sometimes from both sides. *Everyone* suspects Mary Payne of "disloyalty." Meade's provost marshal, General Patrick, has interrogated her and still keeps a wary eye on her activities. On the other hand, one of her formerly staunch Confederate daughters has been successfully courted by a major on John Pope's staff since the Federal occupation of 1862. Mr. Payne died in March 1863, having been partially paralyzed for a number of years. The trauma of the war hastened his end, and he could neither speak nor walk in his final weeks. Now his wife's hotel has been taken over completely by the Federals. Joseph Gorrell, the druggist, knows Mrs. Payne well, having boarded at the Virginia House before the war, but he is uncertain about her sentiments. He does think, however, that the hotel has become a "resort for Federal officers," whose presence Mrs. Payne welcomes. She has never welcomed Confederates in this way, a fact "remarked upon to some extent in the town." A few people also blame her for the arrest of Henry Shackleford and C. P. Stallard last year. The Shackleford family has publicly accused her of betrayal.[14]

Then there are the people who play along with the Federals in order to hang on to their property. It was the same during Pope's occupation. Isham Chewning, overseer for John Jameson, had some doubts about the wisdom of secession, but he supported the Confederacy until recently, when he took the oath. He denies to his neighbors that he has done so, probably out of embarrassment. He is now confused and not a little angry because even having sworn loyalty to the Union, his grain, hay, vegetables, cured meat, and livestock have not been spared by Yankee foraging parties. Delila Day has not taken the oath, but she presents a smiling face to any Yankee she meets. Because she is a woman, the Federals have not commented on her uncertain status. Indeed, she has been allowed to pass through the army's camps all winter taking in laundry without challenge.[15]

All that aside, the majority of people in Culpeper, like the people of Virginia generally, remain Rebels to the core, and they do what they can to thwart the Yankees. Trouble is, most of the remaining folk are women, children, and older men, which limits their range of activities. Some folk pilfer goods from Federal supply depots or act as spies. Martha Rixey is known in the Federal camps as a harmless woman who sells fresh-baked pies, but she keeps her ears open amongst the Yankees and passes on any information she gleans to Confederate scouts near her home. Local people also help disgruntled Union soldiers to desert, though this has proved to be a dangerous game. In late March, four Culpeper men, one of them a member of the 17th Virginia Infantry on "special duty" in the county, were arrested for enticing some New York soldiers to desert. The wife of one of the arrested men, Mrs. Hume, insists that her husband is a true Yankee, even an abolitionist. The officer who arrested him, however, has proof to the contrary, and retorts that Hume is a "*white washed* Yankee," and if an "abolitionist," then he intends to abolish the Federal army. Luckily, Hume was not one of the two men eventually tried by the Yanks. Of those two, one man, Robert Bowers of the 17th Virginia, has been sentenced to two years in prison.[16]

And so both sides, the massive Army of the Potomac and this puny Confederate enclave, temporarily occupy, quietly if uneasily, the same space. As the final days of April slip away, both sides increasingly recognize that this temporary marriage is drawing to a close. Both breathe easier at the prospect; both consider the inevitable separation with some apprehension. The soldiers want to escape the boredom of winter camp and end the war, but they do not want to die. The people of Culpeper wish to be rid of the army, but they wonder if worse times may not lie ahead and what damage this terrible force, once un-

leashed, may inflict on Lee's army and Confederate hopes. In such uncertain times, both sides continue to turn to religion. Local civilian
ministers call upon Jehovah to succor their Cause. "Oh Lord, help our
Southern Confederacy," a preacher beseeched recently at the Jeffersonton Baptist Church, "for it's in a mighty bad fix, I do assure you."[17]

The army's reaction is more complex. A member of the 3rd Indiana
Cavalry believes that three-fourths of the "intelligent men" in his regiment "would be pronounced *infidels* by an Orthodox Presbyterian." In
any case, he judges scornfully, the "majority are Universalists." Yet the
more immediate concern, whatever a man's denomination, is salva-
tion. The time "for action" draws near. Action means fighting, fighting
to the death for some, and who those unlucky ones might be, no one
can tell. As chapels are dismantled in preparation for the campaign—
oftentimes because departing Christian Commission agents retrieve
their canvas roofs—men hurry to the final sermons or to be baptized in
the waters of local rivers. Baptism may have been in the thoughts of
the preacher who expounded last week on Isaiah 55: "Lo, every one
that thirsteth, come ye to the waters." Unfortunately, the divine continued with the exhortation, "Come ye, buy, and eat; yea, come, buy
wine and milk without money and without price," which inspired
some jokesters to break out a barrel of beer and sell draughts to the departing congregation. The messages of the preachers are usually less
ambiguous, and surely no one could mistake the intent of the chaplain
who addressed the 2nd Rhode Island Infantry on "Our duty in the
coming campaign."[18]

Men secure in the destiny of their souls wonder just how ready this
army is to meet Lee. Most of them have fought that wily fox, sometimes successfully, more often not, but always with heavy losses. One
can see the Confederate camps quite clearly from Federal signal stations, especially on Stony Mountain. The Rebels have been "very busy
drilling & making great preparations to repel any attacks," observes
one soldier. "They appear very defiant & say come on yanks." As the
time to join battle draws closer, Grant has a new tactical worry: How
will he get across the Rapidan? Should he attempt to cross below Lee,
or above him? Men eye the Rebel earthworks and pray that Grant is

not fool enough to attack them directly. "I expect they will give us hell" in any case, considers a man who has already been wounded six times in the war.[19]

Is the army ready? Is it stronger and more efficient than four months ago? One hears mixed opinions around the campfires and at headquarters tents. Whether it is or not, many men want out. One New Englander hopes against hope that the campaign will be delayed two months longer, when he is due to be discharged. "I will be glad when this show is over," he confesses to a friend back home. "I have not got a ticket for the next one." A wave of excitement passed through the camps recently when Congress agreed to let soldiers with maritime experience transfer to the navy. Dozens of men, mostly New Englanders, have taken advantage of the offer, and although they will not be escaping the military, they will at least avoid the hardships and dangers of what is sure to be a rugged, deadly campaign. Desertion remains a problem for Grant, and many men who remain in the ranks no longer do so for patriotism, as they once did, but for money, "a very convenient article when there is a *family* to support," admits a Hoosier. Officers, too, seem uncertain about the changes wrought by Grant. A grim, almost fatalistic, mood prevails in some circles. "We are stripping for work, and we anticipate plenty of it—hot and heavy," thinks one of Sedgwick's staff. "You don't hear any big talk in the army now."[20]

The most optimistic men are the ones who feel rejuvenated by the thought that the war is now about slavery rather than disunion. The plight of the black population has been of particular concern in past weeks following news that captured black Federal soldiers at Plymouth, North Carolina, and Fort Pillow, Tennessee, have been murdered. But even patriotic men cannot help but recall the frustrations experienced by this army during the past two years. This is the furthest south they have penetrated, and their hold on Culpeper is so tenuous that they cannot truthfully claim to have conquered it. Some men are no more confident in their leaders than they were a year ago. Certainly Grant has yet to impress the majority. "I am of the opinion he will find that in confronting Lee he has more to contend with than he expects," judges one man. "I am afraid he is not adequate to the task he has undertaken."[21]

Grant may have private doubts, but he does not betray them. He has made several trips to and from Washington over the past few weeks. Such visits in the first half of April allowed him to see his wife Julia, but she has since gone to New York and plans to travel west to join her family in Missouri. There is less incentive for him to go north now, especially after his train narrowly escaped attack by Confederate guerrillas near Bristoe Station. It is just as well, he decides. Washington is tiresome, and while he is forever complaining about Virginia mud and Virginia weather, he seems to be content in Culpeper. Upon first arriving, he boarded at the Court House, where he could walk down to Gorrell's drug store to buy cigars and warm himself by the stove. He has since established more impressive headquarters at the Presley Rixey house. Now, at the end of April, he is getting testy, impatient to begin his work but knowing that it is useless, even dangerous, to move before the army is ready.[22]

The men, of course, have been speculating ever since Grant's arrival about when they would depart. It must be soon, for spring is close upon the land. "The country here is beginning to look as well as it can," one soldier proclaims. "The fruit trees where there are any left [are] all in blossom and the grass where it is permitted to grow at all is quite green." The change of seasons has set everyone to wondering what comes next. One soldier concedes, "What our campaign will be & how it will be has been thoroughly discussed by all & thoroughly understood by none."[23]

Few, however, question their ultimate target or the significance of their mission. A captain who deserted Lee's army and was captured by the Federals in Baltimore has given the War Department a detailed description of the deployment of the Rebels. Whether or not he can be trusted is, of course, open to question; but Grant, in any event, is ready to move his army of 120,000. The army will begin crossing the Rapidan at midnight tonight, May 3.[24]

May 4. The army is packed up and on the move. A "fearful Tornado" of dust and wind swept through the camps at dusk yesterday—an ill omen, said some—but the weather cleared today as camps were swiftly disassembled. "Where thousands of tents had covered the hills and plains . . . , now all was bare and desolate," marvels one soldier of the army's march into the predawn darkness. It was an arduous hike, conducted in "solemn procession" on a night that was black as vengeance. "There was none of the usual hilarity and enthusiasm that attend the breaking of camp," considers one man. All knew the grim business ahead, though some men, weary or in poor health, dreaded the march more than the battles to come. Even in the cool night air, many men discarded equipment and personal items along the roadside.[25]

Meade and his staff left headquarters before dawn and crossed the Rapidan at 8 A.M. Daylight lent confidence to the procession and inspired awe at the sight of this mighty war machine. On a hill near Stevensburg, Meade and his staff paused to survey the scene before plunging down toward the river. "As far as you could see in every direction," reports a staff officer, "corps, divisions, brigades, trains, batteries, and squadrons, were moving on in a waving sea of blue; headquarters and regimental flags were fluttering, the morning sun kissing them all, and shimmering gayly from gunbarrels." Grant mounted his horse Cincinnati and departed the Court House at about the time Meade approached Germanna Ford. By noon, he too had left Culpeper behind.[26]

May 5. Columns snaked toward and across the Rapidan all yesterday and last night. At least it had been a sunny day. Not until 2 P.M. today did the last of the troops and supply trains rumble into the Wilderness opposite Culpeper. They met remarkably little resistance as Lee pulled back before them, but no one pretends the quiet will long continue. "We are expecting a mighty hard time when the campaign opens," predicts a member of the 10th Massachusetts Volunteers. "I suppose we have a larger Army than ever before and so no doubt has Lee and the shock of battle will be terrible when the two Armies meet."[27]

All that remains of the mighty Army of the Potomac in Culpeper is a few soldiers who guard supplies the army could not carry away. The air hangs deathly still, and in the quiet, people slowly grasp the enormity of what has happened. They spoke before of devastation after Pope's withdrawal, but the Army of Virginia's sojourn was as nothing compared to the havoc wrought by Meade's minions. "The town has changed her features," asserts a man at the Court House, "sack cloth and ashes fill the place of wine and scarlet." Scores of houses, barns, sheds, structures of every conceivable type have been swept away. Hundreds of acres of forest have been leveled. Thousands of acres of farmland have been devastated. Thousands of head of livestock have been consumed or confiscated. All sense of security has been destroyed; the people feel violated. Perhaps the heaviest blow, the ultimate insult, fell when black troops from Burnside's corps, hitherto encamped around Warrenton, entered Culpeper to protect the tracks, warehouses, and rolling stock of the O&A. "We have hard times here," declares one citizen.[28]

But this is wartime, and quiet cannot prevail for long. Just hours after Grant's departure, Confederate cavalry have crossed the Rapidan and captured a number of guards at Federal supply depots. They have carried away the supplies, too, mostly tents and commissary stores. Their biggest prize is a quantity of salted beef, enough meat, rumor has it, to "supply the citizens of the area for two years." That may be, but the meat will doubtless go to Lee's army. The cavalrymen, who spent the winter on spare diets and in meager quarters, are amazed at the amounts of supplies the Federals have left behind. Even the remains of Federal quarters—luxurious by Confederate standards, and some still with blankets and equipment in them—seem the most "comfortably arranged" these men have seen in many a day.[29]

The Confederates send most of their prisoners below the Rapidan. Yesterday, however, May 8, upon encountering an undermanned detachment of black troops at Brandy Station, the Rebels reacted as they too often do in such instances. They despise the United States government for using black soldiers; they think it degrading to fight them. So rather than march the blacks down to the Rapidan and across Germanna Ford, they lined them up and shot them, just flat out murdered them. The bodies remain unburied. This sudden onslaught, with so many men suddenly captured, has made the Federals nervous. They stick close to their camps, fearful not only of Confederate patrols but of Rebel partisans. Culpeper, after all, is part of John Mosby's domain.[30]

In such an unsettled state, Culpeper's citizens strive mightily to resume normal lives. The county court reconvened on May 16 (not having met since last November 7) and called for elections to restore civil government. The people voted last week, but not everyone is happy with the results. Indeed, no little amount of discord has developed. Several of the men elected to office are viewed as shirkers, if not outright cowards, for never having served in the army. In fact, a few men who have been refugees outside of Culpeper for most of the war, and who have only just returned, now hold office. Men who have served in the army, or whose sons are serving, and who have endured every Yankee insult to Culpeper and its people, resent that. At least one man, Lewis Field, has protested the election results to Governor William Smith, though it is unlikely that the governor will intervene. The timing of this ill feeling is unfortunate, for news of a bloody fight at Spotsylvania has reached Culpeper. Early reports say that the 13th Virginia suffered many casualties.[31]

Mid-June. Conditions remain unsettled. One of the biggest threats to Culpeper security has been the many deserters—both Yank and Reb— that have been prowling through the countryside stealing whatever they find useful. "I know not what is to become of us," frets one old man, "unless something can be done to Rid us of such a vile pest." Even men belonging to organized Confederate units cannot always resist the temptation to raid a smokehouse or shed in hopes of finding a few sweet potatoes, turnips, or jars of apple butter. The raids stand in contrast to the urgent plight of many destitute people in the county. The court has ordered that nearly $1,000 earned from the sale of timber on poorhouse land be used to "aid in maintaining the poor." Regrettably, in an effort to pool all available finances, the court also ordered redemption of the county's Confederate bonds.[32]

And so it has gone through the summer. No universal catastrophes have befallen the population, but the people continue to bear small and individual ills and sorrows. Typhoid swept through the northern reaches of the county in July. It hit the Luttrell and Dulin families especially hard. The Dulins—now here is a case to make you doubt the beneficence of God. No more loyal Confederates reside in Culpeper. Ann Dulin, a widow, resided near Oak Shade with her three grown children, Mary, James, and Edwin, at the start of the war. James, a master carpenter, and Edwin, an apprentice, both joined the Little Fork Rangers. James, severely wounded in May 1862, is now disabled for life. Edwin, who, it is said, had a premonition of death before the battle of Spotsylvania, perished on that fateful field. Now Mary has been carried away by the fever.[33]

And there have been other battlefield losses, many others. News has slowly drifted in of seemingly constant fighting against Grant and Meade in the Wilderness, at Spotsylvania, Drewry's Bluff, Cold Harbor, until the Confederates have been forced back into Richmond. Culpeper has lost heavily, as men from all levels of society have been killed, wounded, and captured. Charles Crittenden (now a major) fell wounded at Spotsylvania, which some people are calling the bloodiest battle of the war. And for those infantrymen who insist they have never seen a dead cavalryman, the Little Fork Rangers have a bitter reply. They have lost seven men besides Edwin Dulin. Nearly as sad is the news that Jeb Stuart, a favorite in Culpeper, died in fighting at Yellow Tavern.[34]

Trade in Culpeper revives slowly. Some merchants, like G. F. Carter, have long since collected their wares and fled, in Carter's case to Lynchburg. Yet those who have weathered the Yankee storm, like Lewis Nelson, one of Culpeper's most solvent merchants, find eager customers both here and in surrounding counties. His most popular article of trade in recent months has been tobacco. Nelson cannot secure enough golden leaf to meet demand. He is currently seeking government permission—which seems necessary for every action nowadays—to transport 50 boxes of tobacco to the Court House from warehouses in Charlottesville and Lynchburg. The economy has been helped, also, by the way in which the O&A has speedily recovered. It now offers passenger and freight service from Culpeper to Orange Court House, Madison Court House, and Gordonsville.[35]

Nelson, to show he has something other than profits on his mind, has also interceded, along with Thomas O. Flint, on behalf of William Taylor. Taylor is a 27-year-old mulatto carpenter whom everyone likes, perhaps because white folk consider him to be "honest, polite, and industrious." He has lived quietly with his wife Kitty and their four children (the eldest being eight) in the Flatlands throughout the war, until recently, that is. Taylor has two things that few of the remaining white men in Culpeper possess: a team of horses and a strong back. When the Federals left, people at the Court House induced Taylor to take his team there and hire it and his aforementioned strong back to local folk whose horses and slaves had been taken by the enemy. He has been "constantly employed" since May. Now, three months later, he wishes to return to his family, so Nelson and Flint have used their influence with Governor Smith to obtain his release.[36]

Most of the rest of Culpeper's free blacks, like Taylor, have been as quiet and unobtrusive as they were before the war. They keep to their homes and converse among themselves—about the war, mostly, and with the very few white people they trust, mostly unionists. Their white neighbors do not bother them, but that does not mean they have been ignored, for the Federal army has preyed on them as much as on the whites. Most blacks have few possessions, but what they do own has been freely taken by Union soldiers. When black citizens dare protest, the Yankees laugh at them.[37]

Most blacks, however, remain as steadfast in their loyalty to the Union as do Culpeper's white unionists. During Federal occupations, they have washed and cooked for the Federals, served as guides, and provided useful information about their communities and neighbors. Some blacks fear that a Confederate victory will jeopardize their free-dom. Others, like George Mars, hope that a Union victory will free en-slaved members of their families. For Mars, that means his wife.[38]

Not a few black citizens have been on the move, although, unlike William Taylor, they have been leaving Culpeper, headed north. The biggest part of the exodus seems to have passed, for most of those want-ing to leave did so last fall, when Meade first arrived and offered free passage to Alexandria. A slew of people—mostly men—departed then, and they are now working for the United States government as team-sters or ostlers. Not all wanted to go, for the uncertainty of leaving their homes was at least as great as their misgivings about staying. Yet many saw little alternative. Randall Tate had just gathered and threshed four acres of wheat and was preparing to cut his two acres of corn when Gen-eral Hancock's men confiscated both crops. His prospects for a living gone, and fearful of similar treatment in the foreseeable future, Tate left for Alexandria. Even so, he is not bitter. He prefers serving the Union to his four months of impressed Confederate service after First Manassas.[39]

Willis Madden, the county's most prominent black citizen, has stayed put, but his son Slaughter has gone to Alexandria. Not that Willis has escaped the havoc of occupation. Meade's men took all of his horses and most of the rest of his livestock. They destroyed out-buildings and fences, and leveled three acres of woodland. Madden, in his 65th year, has been badly shaken by these events. All that he has worked for—his land, his livestock, his property—has been taken or destroyed. He has been financially ruined. It seems impossible that he will ever be able to regain what has been lost, or pay debts that he owes. He broods much these days and is depressed in spirit.[40]

Monday morning, September 19. The Yankees have returned. What this portends, no one can say. People only know that it is all too familiar. Bettie Browning wrote a letter to Daniel Grimsley two days ago prais-ing his father's Saturday sermon and wishing that Daniel had been here to enjoy it. "I think it would revive your spirits," she told her beau, who still serves in the field with his regiment. "It is indeed a dark time, but hope there will soon be a change." This is not the sort of change Bettie had in mind. She attended church again yesterday and prayed for the Confederate cause. Today, God, a whimsical if not per-verse God, has answered in his fashion.[41]

The Yankees, 325 men of the 13th and 16th New York Cavalry, ap-proached by a familiar route. They crossed the Rappahannock at Kelly's Ford well before dawn and headed for Rapidan Station. Their target seems to have been the O&A, Culpeper's link to Charlottesville and Lynchburg. At first light, Colonel Henry M. Lazelle attacked the small Confederate force guarding the railroad, no more than 70 men. Within an hour, the Yankees had dispersed all but a dozen Rebels, whom, along with some 200 horses, mules, and cattle, they promptly captured. They have proceeded to torch the railroad bridge, station house, telegraph of-fice, three railroad cars, several private dwellings, and a gristmill, which contains some 300 barrels of flour and large amounts of corn and wheat.[42]

Early morning, September 20. Lazelle's raiders grew too bold yesterday, paid for their boldness, and have scurried back across the Rappahannock. Having capped their destruction of Rapidan Station by pulling down the telegraph lines and tearing up an extensive section of track, the Federals, surprised by the light resistance they had encountered, pushed northeast toward the Court House. What they hoped to accomplish is uncertain, but they clearly did not expect to run smack into several hundred well-entrenched Confederates in the hills south of town, near Mt. Pony. Heavy skirmishing proved more than they bargained for, as nearly a third of Lazelle's command fled in panic. The remaining force followed in more orderly fashion by late afternoon, but Lazelle has abandoned his captured animals and over half of his prisoners. He also lost 27 men dead or missing and 11 wounded.[43]

November 1864. The country has suffered no serious threat since Lazelle's raid. The Yankees occasionally carry off citizens as hostages for a few days at a time, but this is intended more to harass than to harm. Culpeper these days is not as important to the strategic thinking of either North or South as it was for the past three and a half years. Culpeper is no longer the eye of the storm in Virginia. Ever since Grant crossed the Rapidan, the nation's attention has shifted elsewhere, toward Richmond and Petersburg, where Lee's army lies besieged, and toward the Shenandoah Valley, where Philip Sheridan threatens to destroy what remains of Virginia's once fruitful farmlands. On some days, Bettie Browning can hear the muffled sound of cannonading echo softly but "very distinctly here from some portions of the Valley."[44]

The passage of armies through the county has been replaced by rumors flying in every direction. The rumors are fed by the impossibility of getting reliable news that is less than several days old. Bettie Browning suffered for nearly a week from a false report that Daniel Grimsley had been captured. Of more importance to the ultimate fate of the Confederacy are reports of a Rebel defeat at Cedar Creek, the failure of a Confederate raid into Missouri, Lincoln's reelection as president of the northern states, and the departure of General William T. Sherman's army from Atlanta toward Savannah.[45]

But the reality of war forever hovers nearby, and nothing illustrates more forcefully the continued suffering of the men in uniform than the return of wounded and sick men from the army. Art McCormick, one of the Little Fork Rangers captured at Mrs. Rixey's place in January, has returned home on a 60-day furlough, released after seven months of captivity at Point Lookout. Rumors say he was badly mistreated in prison, and, while some people say he has "improved very much since he came home," Bettie Browning thinks he looks "dreadfully."[46]

McCormick is willing to return to service when he regains his strength, and Lord knows the army needs men, but fewer and fewer from Culpeper answer the call. Only romantically-inclined youths enlist now. In August, 16-year-old Woodford Wood joined the 4th Virginia Cavalry. He is a "dyed in the wool" Rebel who hates Yankees with a passion. Part of his hatred stems from the way in which Kilpatrick's cavalry plundered and pillaged his family's home near Jeffersonton some months ago. His father, Pollard Wood, opposed his going but, knowing the boy would likely run away to enlist anyway, reluctantly gave his consent. Bettie Browning's father, 44-year-old William L. Browning, was one of several men recently conscripted. He has obtained an exemption, but most who are summoned find themselves in uniform. The county had a narrow escape when conscription officers came for 41-year-old William C. Nalls. Nalls is one of the few millers left in Culpeper. When his neighbors learned that Nalls had been drafted, they petitioned for his release. His absence, insisted the petitioners, would produce "some suffering and much inconvenience." Happily, the army has shown its sympathy by assigning Nalls to the county as a miller.[47]

While the government calls on Culpeper for more men, Culpeper has appealed to the Confederate Congress for tax relief. The people have been patient with the Richmond government up until now. Some other parts of Virginia and the Confederacy seem to be crumbling inward. There have been bread riots in Richmond and angry protests nationwide over conscription, a tax-in-kind, requisitions for slaves, and the suspension of habeus corpus. Many poor folk and some portions of the middle classes resent the mounting human and material cost of a war that they believe increasingly is being waged for the benefit of slaveholders. Only a few in Culpeper voice these sentiments, usually the same people who spoke against secession. The county has been too busy hosting armies and maintaining life and limb to be affected by congressional actions.[48]

But now Culpeper has an issue of public concern and the leisure to seek redress. The people, through the county court, have asked exemption from 1863 and 1864 taxes. "Many of us are utterly unable to pay," reads the appeal. "Our people are a patriotic, law-loving, honest set of men, who really wish well to the Confederacy and are willing to suffer for it, but who feel . . . they must love their dependent ones, who cry for food, more than they are willing to suffer for their Mother Country." The petition lists the ravages of the Federal winter encampment, which has left "scarcely a panel of fence." By the time the army left, it was too late to plant crops even if people had the means to do so. Forty-two citizens from all walks of life have signed the petition. Merchant Lewis Nelson has boldly applied his signature, even though he is no longer the firm Rebel he once claimed to be. Most of the petitioners are once-comfortable farmers, but Hiram Amiss (a shoemaker) and Reverend Grimsley (Daniel's father) have also signed.[49]

As loyal Confederates feel the pinch of want, they become even less tolerant of unionists in their midst, but even some staunch Rebels, well-respected in the community, feel their allegiance weakening. They serve as living illustrations of Samuel Johnson's dictum that men may be sincere in their principles but lax in good practice. Thomas R. Rixey had initially opposed secession, but, like many other early unionists, came to favor separation after Fort Sumter. Still, he has never embraced the Confederacy enthusiastically. He neither applauds nor mourns Confederate victories. He only feels "oppressed, worn down," by the conflict, and he claims his health has suffered. Now Rixey, who was made a justice of the peace in recent elections, speculates privately that Culpeper might be "in a better condition under the rule of the northern people than of the southern people." Of course, he insists, he sympathizes with friends and neighbors serving in the army and with their families at home, but he can muster little enthusiasm for "the cause." When accused by neighbors of fluctuating loyalties, Rixey replies honestly, "A man cannot always say what his feelings were during three or four years. He may under-go many changes of feelings. It depends on his personal condition." Rixey's close friend Lewis Nelson concurs. He and Rixey speak confidentially about the condition of the country and their feelings about the war. As Nelson explains it, the county has been "overrun by both armies." Nothing remains to eat. He is "very anxious it [the war] should be terminated."[50]

Christmas Eve. December has been cold, so cold that when young William Nalle overheard a visitor to his father's house report fighting in Madison County a few days ago, he could not believe it. Too cold to fight, thought the lad. But the visitor had been right, and now General Alfred T. A. Torbert's cavalry is in Culpeper. On December 22, Torbert drove a brigade of Confederate cavalry out of Madison Court House. Today, young Nalle has met the Federals personally. He was riding on horseback to his grandmother's house, Fairview, about six miles north of the Court House on the Rixeyville Road. As he neared the house, he found it ablaze with light, with men carrying torches and causing a terrible "row." Yankees! and up to their usual tricks—cursing, breaking doors, smashing glassware. Nalle wheeled his horse and galloped away. Several Federals called after him, "Halt, you damned Rebel!" and fired their revolvers. But it was dark, and the boy made a small target.[51]

Just when he thought he was safe, four mounted figures dashed out behind him onto the road. They gave chase, but William rode the faster mount, and he knew the roads. He veered onto a side road and headed for John Payne's house nearby. When he reached it, he and one of the Payne boys rushed to warn neighbors of the invasion. No sooner had they started than they encountered yet another Federal patrol. The boys found a pine thicket, dismounted, and laid shivering in the snow for nearly three hours before returning to the Payne house.[52]

Christmas Day. The county is in an uproar. The main body of Torbert's raiding party has already passed through Culpeper en route to Gordonsville, but stragglers are looting neighborhoods as far north as Rixeyville and Jeffersonton. Some people believe they detect German accents—the hated Dutch! Local marksmen are already at work bushwhacking their uninvited guests, and some of Mosby's men, learning of the emergency, have made a swift appearance. Nalle and five other high-spirited lads, all equipped with revolvers, thought they would join the fun. They searched for bands small enough to harass safely, but the nearest they found was a wounded Federal, already the victim of a well-placed bullet, writhing in the road. Bored with their hunt, they dispersed. Nalle has returned to his grandmother's house, but is sickened by what he finds. What has not been stolen has been destroyed, including food, clothing, furniture. The Yankees, who seem ever to exalt the path of evil, have even raided the slave quarters, and forced one old servant to strip naked and dance in the snow.[53]

James W. Timberlake has retaliated with more success. When Federal stragglers visited Timberlake's farm near Rixeyville, the 50-year-old widower tried to accommodate them. He provided everything they demanded, including food for them and forage for their mounts, but the ruffians proceeded to rummage through the lower floor of his handsome brick house. The Yankees took what they wanted while Timberlake and several of his six children stood silent. Content with their booty, all but one soldier left. The remaining scoundrel, disappointed with his haul, went upstairs. Timberlake followed and watched as the man rifled a bedroom bureau. He continued to maintain a patient exterior as the soldier stuffed useful articles in his haversack and tossed unwanted items on the floor. But when the bluecoat scattered the clothes of Timberlake's deceased wife around the room, the farmer's emotions got the better of him. Grabbing a wrought-iron shovel from the fireplace, Timberlake swung mightily and felled the trespasser with a single blow to the head. Last night, after son Edward had turned the soldier's horse loose in a nearby wood, Timberlake and his 19-year-old daughter Senie buried the man in an unmarked and dishonored grave.[54]

December 31. There has never been a Christmas like it. Yesterday, while delivering some provisions from his parents' house to his grandmother's forlorn-looking residence, William Nalle encountered a Federal deserter on the road. His name was Barker, a sergeant in the 45th New York Cavalry. Nalle had a "long talk" with Barker, who claimed to have been drafted from his home in New York City. The Yankee said he was tired of war. He wandered away, whether toward home or back to his regiment, Nalle could not tell. Earlier today, Nalle found one wounded and three dead Yankees in the woods near his grandmother's house. The wounded man was carried to Sanford Payne's house. This evening, some of Mosby's men, hardened perhaps too much by the war, rode over to finish off the poor bastard. Nalle thinks it wrong. Even a Yankee, if wounded, he believes, deserves mercy. "I went over to look at the dead Yankees and see if they were buried," young Nalle writes to conclude the year.[55]

CHAPTER FOURTEEN

TO EVERY THING A SEASON

he first day of 1865 was cold, as befits this stark winter. It is now
mid-February, and the weather is still bitter. One snowfall barely
melts before another arrives. Snow and ice cling to rooftops and
fences. They chill the people of Culpeper, much as war news from east
and west chills Confederate hearts. This is not a season of hope. It is
very nearly a time of despair; it is a time of rumors and confusion and
apprehension. It is a time to keep silent.

As the preacher at the Jeffersonton Baptist Church wailed last
spring, the Confederacy is in a mighty bad fix. If there is good news to
be heard, none of it has reached Culpeper. Last month, unionist-con-
trolled constitutional conventions in Missouri and Tennessee adopted
laws to abolish slavery. The United States Congress has done the
same. John Bell Hood has resigned as commander of the Army of Tennessee, what is left of it anyway. Hood destroyed most of the army in
mad assaults against strong Union positions last November and December. Fort Fisher, North Carolina, fell to the Federals on January 15.
William T. Sherman, having ravaged Georgia last autumn, has moved
north from Savannah on a similar jaunt through South Carolina. No
doubt Charleston is his goal. Indeed, the most recent word is that Columbia is already in flames and Confederate authorities are evacuating

Charleston. On February 3, Federal and Confederate representatives met at Hampton Roads, Virginia, to discuss a possible armistice, but Lincoln, who personally attended the meeting, demanded nothing short of unconditional surrender. The Confederate delegation, led by Vice President Alexander Stephens, rejected this out of hand. Folks in Culpeper expected as much.[1]

Some members of the Confederate Congress then tried to negotiate an armistice, but that too failed. A North Carolina senator asked John Botts to assist in the effort, but Botts, objecting to any peace or armistice that would provide for an independent Confederacy, refused. "Calamitous and ruinous as this war has been," insists Botts, "I believe a separation from the North, with two peoples so immediately contiguous to each other, and with the bitterness of feeling that would be perpetrated under separate organizations, would prove to be even more ruinous and deplorable than the war itself has been, and *that* has left the Southern country little else than a general grave-yard or a desolate waste."[2]

Besides this more or less reliable news, the county is flooded by rumors. Most prevalent is a report that England and France are sending armaments to Richmond and that English troops are assembling in Canada for an invasion of the North. Most people recognize these reports for what they are, "sensationalist," and even a lad like William Nalle announces that such news is "hardly worth repeating." Other than the hope of foreign intervention, the most persistent rumor is that a 90-day armistice will soon be signed. People are desperate. They want to—they must—believe such rumors if they are to carry on.[3]

Men returning—or not returning—from the war keep the people of Culpeper constantly on edge. Even citizens who try to put the war out of mind daily encounter the shells of once-youthful men and hear their tales of imprisonment, lost battles, and missing comrades. Some men are eager to return to the fray, but most convalescing wounded and former prisoners have seen enough of war. James Hitt, just released from Point Lookout, says that while imprisoned he was "made to work hard at his trade [blacksmith] . . . every day to get something to wear and eat." James W. Stallard is also home safe from Point Lookout, as is Isaac Lake, one of the Little Fork Rangers captured at Mrs. Rixey's home a year ago; but other Culpeper men remain in enemy hands. At least six men have been at Point Lookout since last fall. They may soon be released, but for the moment, no one can predict their fate.[4]

The casualty list grows longer. Some men perish on battlefields; other succumb to fever and infection in hospitals. Many of those who have survived will suffer permanently from their wounds. They have lost eyes, had lungs punctured, survived amputations. Two members of the 13th Virginia, casualties of sorts, are spoken of only in whispers. William T. Bell has been absent without leave since October, and Mark A. Browning reportedly deserted his regiment last week. Both men supposedly "enlisted" in the army, but the truth is they were conscripted, and like the Yankee conscripts who tried every means possible to escape their army when encamped at Culpeper last winter, these southern lads wanted no part of the war. Bell, not yet 21, has been missing since shortly after his brother George, a year older, was captured at Winchester and sent to Point Lookout. The family, headed by 46-year-old Richard, are farmers of only modest means. As for Browning, well, he is approaching 40 years of age, and is in no condition to bear the strain of another campaign.[5]

John Tanner was wounded in the right arm almost three years ago while fighting with the 7th Virginia Infantry at Fraser's Farm. On the last day of December, Tanner shot and killed a 53-year-old carpenter named James F. Hackley, who rented a house and land from Judge Richard Field. No one is sure exactly what happened. The shooting occurred at the Field mill, where the old black miller Willis claims, "Hackley called Tanner some hard names." Tanner responded by drawing his pistol and shooting the carpenter through the heart. Hackley may have questioned why Tanner had not returned to the army. Tanner may have resented such implied criticism from someone who had never enlisted, never seen the elephant, and most certainly never been shot in the Confederate cause. Tanner likely believes that he has contributed enough to the fight for Southern independence, and that he has earned the right to stay home with his wife and two children. Still, it is tragic that neighbors should turn on each other in this way, and that Hackley leaves a widow and eight children.[6]

Some people are discouraged by reports from loved ones still in the thick of the fighting. Mary Corbin has been feeling blue lately. Her husband Lemuel, serving with Mosby, could not get home for Christmas or the New Year, and even though the raids of late 1864 left her house, Northcliff, untouched, she sees desolation all around her. Now she has received a letter from her husband that causes her more concern. He tries to be optimistic. He points out that Culpeper should be "truly thankful" for the good luck it has enjoyed thus far "in escaping the Yankees." Yet he cannot deny that hopes for independence seem to be slipping away. He concedes, "The way the Yankees carry on almost leads us to the conclusion that our cause must be unjust or the over Ruler of all things would not permit them to sow death and destruction broad cast over our once beautiful and happy country."[7]

To sow death and destruction: "To every thing there is a season," says Ecclesiastes 3. "A time to plant, and a time to pluck up that which is planted; . . . a time to rend, and a time to sew," that is, to mend. Yes, sowing and mending, think some people, is what must be done. If the Confederacy is, in fact, doomed, then gloomy faces will not save it. It has taken a superhuman effort, but some parts of Culpeper already look toward a possible end to the war.

March 1865. It helps to be young. Bettie Browning has been busy attending parties in Culpeper and Rappahannock counties. "I am sure I never heard of such enjoyment in my life as [there] has been this winter," she informs her beau, Daniel Grimsley, now a major. Bettie's friends—though not she, of course—have had gentleman callers in abundance, many of them discharged or recuperating veterans. Prewar flirtations have resumed, and some young men and ladies change partners in the game of romance. Some of the Little Fork Rangers are at home on furloughs. "They are seeing quite a gay time," Bettie assures Daniel. Jim Stallard is a particular favorite of the ladies, for he relates "many amusing anecdotes in regard to his capture and imprisonment." Bettie feels sad for these men. She knows that, whatever the Confederacy's prospects, they must soon return to war. It will not be easy for them. It is never easy to be home on furlough, to see the girls, eat home cooking, sleep in a bed, and then return to "the hardships of a soldier's life."[8]

Rumors continue to swirl, but people believe ever fewer of them. No one really thinks, as some reports have it, that Lee will invade Pennsylvania again this spring. Other rumors insist that the university at Charlottesville has been burned by Yankee raiders, and, closer to home, that Yankee patrols roam in the vicinity of Madison Court House and along the Hazel River. "Heard France had recognized our independence," scoffs William Nalle, "but I have heard it a hundred times before." Only the idle—and there are few such folk nowadays— have time for this prattle.[9]

Whether or not the Yankees return, whether or not France inter-venes, another spring approaches. Fields must be prepared and planted in March and April. Culpeper farmers, with whatever labor they can muster, with whatever tools they have preserved, must resume the eternal cycle: trimming orchards, planting potatoes, clearing and haul-ing brush, plowing, harrowing. Stray cattle must be retrieved; fences must be repaired.

April 5. Yet even as the hills and fields of Culpeper once again flaunt their luxurious green garments, restored to a beauty and freshness that not even war, sickness, and death can deny, the end seems near. News has reached Culpeper that Richmond has fallen. The outer defenses of Pe-tersburg fell three days ago, just hours after Robert E. Lee advised Presi-dent Davis that his government should evacuate the capital. Federal troops marched into Richmond the next day, and yesterday President Lincoln, like a conquering Caesar, inspected the city. Lee escaped with his army to Amelia Court House, where he hoped to resupply it. Having found no supplies there, Lee is considering alternative moves. His goal must be to link forces with Joe Johnston in North Carolina, but how he will get there and how he will obtain needed supplies are mysteries.[10]

April 14. Lee could not make it; he surrendered at Appomattox Court House, not very far east of here, on April 9. Word has been drifting into Culpeper for several days. Portions of Lee's paroled army have been passing through the Court House on their way home. Men who call Culpeper home return to tearful laughter. Families and friends embrace the scarred veterans. They rejoice that the war is over and that their men have survived even as they lament Confederate defeat and despair of the future. It is "a deuced finishing up blow to our cause," William Nalle has decided of the surrender. Continuing rumors of imminent French intervention, perhaps even of English recognition, produce bitter laughter now. Johnston's army is apparently still in the field, and several Confederate armies at last report hold out in the West, but the game is up in Virginia. The sad news of a few days ago that Powell Hill has been killed is swallowed up by this ultimate tragedy.[11]

More soldiers flood the county. Lieutenant John A. Holtzman of the Little Fork Rangers is among them. Holtzman shut down his school when the war started, borrowed a horse named John Brown from a cousin, and joined the Little Fork Rangers. Holtzman returned to the Court House a few days ago, still riding "old John Brown." When he returned the horse to his cousin, Holtzman "cried like a child." Men who live beyond Culpeper sometimes stop to visit friends they made during the war. A member of the Loudon County "Comanches" spent the night in the same house where his exhausted body recovered from the 1863 fight at Brandy Station. "How very different the circumstances of then and now," he muses. "Then we were going to Penn, now we are going to God knows where."[12]

There have been outbreaks of lawlessness. Cattle theft is high on the list. Perhaps anticipating more trouble, the court has ordered necessary repairs to the county jail, "so as to make it secure." Word of Lincoln's assassination underscores the impression that whirl is king, that all order is dissolving, that North and South border on chaos. Surprisingly, some people voice regret over the death of the Yankee president. "I am very sorry to hear of president Lincoln's death," William Nalle confides to his diary, "for though he was our enemy still from all I hear he must have been a most excellent, good hearted, kind man." To everything there is a season: A time of war, and a time of peace; a time to kill, and a time to heal.[13]

May 1911. Fifty years after Fort Sumter, Culpeper is preparing for a "home coming." Local newspapers promote it as a "week of reunion and friendship to bring back our old friends and acquaintances." The festivities, beginning on Monday, May 29, will include parades, baseball games, picnics, and ceremonies of all sorts. Not incidentally, the celebration will coincide with Confederate Memorial Day, on Saturday, June 3, and an appropriate program has been planned by the United Daughters of the Confederacy. But even this patriotic occasion will not be the highlight of the week. That honor goes, instead, to a ceremony to be held on Wednesday, May 31, when a monument honoring all Culpeper men who served in the Confederate army will be unveiled on the courthouse lawn. This will be the "banner day" that people have "looked forward to for so long."[14]

The poignancy and emotion of the event will doubtless overwhelm many people, for not a few see the coming ceremony as a symbolic end to the war. There have been several false starts in the past 45 years. In July 1881, more than three hundred veterans marched to Citizens' Cemetery to dedicate a 15-foot-tall granite shaft. The shaft crowned the remains of over 400 Confederate dead, disinterred and moved here from the old cemetery that once lay behind the Confederate hospital. People had talked about erecting such a monument for years. As early as 1868, citizens had been embarrassed by the casual appearance of the old burial ground, especially when compared to the well-manicured National Cemetery for Yankee dead established shortly after the war. "The people have done what they could to improve and embellish the cemetery in which sleep our 'boys in gray,'" noted one observer, "but it is in sad contrast with the Yankee cemetery . . . our poor boys sleep in their umble graves, unornamented save when our noble women bring their annual offering in flowers."[15]

In August 1902, the county witnessed two celebrations, one Federal, one Confederate. On August 8, survivors of the 28th New York Volunteers, Army of the Potomac, dedicated a 20-foot-tall granite monument in the National Cemetery. It joined several other Yankee monuments that already watched over the graves of nearly 1,400 Union soldiers. More widely attended, however, were the following day's festivities on the old Cedar Mountain battlefield. On this, the fortieth anniversary of the most famous event in wartime Culpeper, old men prowled the field in search of surviving landmarks, faded battle lines, and obscure graves:

Ashes of soldiers South or North,
As I muse retrospective murmuring a chant in thought,
The war resumes, again to my sense your shapes,
And again the advance of armies.
Noiseless as mists and vapors,
From their graves in the trenches ascending.[16]

Five thousand people reportedly attended the occasion. "Culpeper is in gala attire," a local newspaper boasted of the twin gatherings. "Red, white and blue bunting and the flags of the Union and of the Confederacy were everywhere, . . . the streets were filled with gray-bearded veterans, stalwart farmers and pretty girls."[17]

In May 1904, former lieutenant John Holtzman led 37 of the 116 men who had served under him in the Rangers to the Little Fork Church, at Oak Shade. There, near the spot where Culpeper's cavalrymen had received their company flag in 1861, eleven daughters of eleven veterans, including Esther Holtzman, unveiled a 15-foot-tall white marble memorial column. The column, firmly embedded in a granite base, was capped by a southern woman, also crafted from marble, bearing a saber and crowned with a laurel wreath. Former major Daniel Grimsley, by then a prominent judge, and former private Woodford Wood, the youngest man to serve in the company, and now a noted preacher in Baltimore, Maryland, delivered the principal addresses. An enthusiastic crowd of 3,000 people enjoyed a picnic dinner while a band played patriotic Confederate airs and the veterans posed for photographs around their monument.[18]

There have been other occasions for veterans to rendezvous since then. The Little Fork Rangers meet most years on the anniversary of their first muster, and they participated in a grand commemoration of the big Brandy Station fight in August 1906. Yet for those veterans still haunted by memories of bugle calls, crashing guns, splattered bodies, smoke, and chaos, none of these ceremonies and events has completely satisfied their need for recognition, either for themselves or for their cause. Now, in 1911, the rapidly dwindling number of men and women who have survived the war years will gather on the courthouse lawn one more time. Sadly, some faces will be missing.[19]

Daniel Grimsley died last year. He married Bettie Browning in 1866, and she and their six children survive him. Daniel studied law after the war, but practiced only a short time before being elected to the state senate. In 1880, after 10 years in the legislature, he was appointed judge of the Sixth Virginia Circuit Court, to replace the recently deceased Judge Henry Shackleford. Then came another term in the legislature, followed by a tenure of 24 years on the bench. In 1900, he published a brief history of the war in Culpeper.[20]

John Cole, the rector of St. Stephen's who did so much to maintain Culpeper's spiritual hopes during the war, spent his few remaining years—he died in 1868—raising money to rebuild local churches destroyed or damaged by repeated invasions. In early 1867, he estimated that it would take nearly $10,000 to repair just four churches. The chances of raising that much money seemed slim. "The truth is," Cole lamented to Jeremiah Morton during those grim days of Reconstruction, "the people are all absorbed in their own concerns & trying to keep out of the hands of the sheriff & get something with which to keep soul and body together."[21]

A few veterans have found their way to the Confederate Soldiers' Home in Richmond. First to enter, in 1894, was 70-year-old Simeon Hudson. However, Hudson soon recovered from the physical maladies that had forced him into the Home. Returning to Culpeper, he announced that he would rather live on his pension and be buried with relatives than to die alone in Richmond. William Smith Collins, who served as a private with the 6th Virginia Cavalry, is still at the Home. He suffers from kidney and bladder complaints as well as the disability of old age. Charles T. Crittenden, former captain of Company B, 13th Virginia Infantry and eventually a major in the regiment, entered the Home in 1902 suffering from war wounds. He passed away in 1907 and was buried at the foot of Cedar Mountain, not far from the battle line he and his men had defended so gallantly in August 1862. His mother Catherine passed on not long after the war; his sister Annie survives him.[22]

Many people regard William T. Ashby's exclusion from the Confederate Soldiers' Home as outrageous. Ashby, now in his early seventies, is absolutely destitute, unable to control his bladder, and dependent on his brother-in-law for care. Twice he has applied to the Home, first in 1908 and again this year, yet authorities have rejected both applications, probably because there is no record of his military service after April 1862. Ashby says he served through the war, and even government records show that he served for a year in the 7th Virginia Infantry. Some influential people have interceded on his behalf. Judge Grimsley endorsed his application, and the adjutant of A. P. Hill Camp No. 2, Culpeper's camp of the United Confederate Veterans, has very nearly insisted that Ashby be taken in; but it has all been for naught. Ashby's family will probably be forced to place him in the poorhouse.[22]

Some Culpeper notables are luckier than Ashby. John S. Pendleton died, like Dr. Cole, in 1868. His nephew and adopted son, George M. Williams, died earlier this year. Williams rejoined Gertrude in Culpeper after the war. They talked no more about moving to Arkansas, and gave no thought to leaving Redwood, which came into their possession when "Uncle Jack" Pendleton died. They survived Yankee Reconstruction, helped to restore Culpeper, and produced twelve children. Williams became a social and political force in the county as editor of the Culpeper *Exponent*. Gertrude survives her husband, as does Tina Suckers Hart, a former family slave, now 96 years old, who has stayed with the Williamses all these years.[24]

The Slaughter family still resides on the mountain that towers above their battlefield. Philip Slaughter departed this life in 1890. He became the historian of the Episcopal diocese of Virginia after the war, and wrote several pamphlets on the church and local history.[25]

John Minor Botts died at Auburn early in 1869, and many people remain unsure to this day of his wartime sympathies. He clearly opposed secession and courted the Federal army. His feuds with Jeb Stuart and other Confederate commanders served as sources of Confederate merriment during the war. Yet Botts, like a number of other residents, did not so much oppose the Confederacy as object to the political leaders of the Confederate government. To his dying day, Botts believed that southerners had been bullied and coerced into secession, and that once the Confederacy had been established, the nation's leaders shrank from personal military service to send, instead, the sons of farmers and mechanics to be slaughtered in the name of political principle. Botts was among the first to characterize the struggle as "the rich man's war and the poor man's fight."[26]

None of Culpeper's unionists suffered dire consequences for their wartime words and actions, although old Confederates sometimes viewed them with suspicion, even with contempt. Mary L. Payne, who has long since passed on, never escaped her reputation as a Union sympathizer. As a result, her hotel business suffered after the war. Her case was not helped when a daughter married a former Union officer, the same major who had flirted with her during the war, in 1868. Isaac C. Webster, a farmer and mechanic, had been an outspoken opponent of the rebellion, at one time announcing that he "wished an earthquake would come and swallow up the Confederacy." Many people have never forgotten that statement, and Webster and his wife have endured community hostility ever since. "They were so down on us," he remarked several years after the war, "that many of our former acquaintances will not notice or speak to us because we were guilty of loving the Union." Feelings even died hard within families. When James Shaw asked his brother Archibald to testify on his behalf before the Southern Claims Commission, Archibald replied to his brother's lawyer, "I told him James was as near to me as any of my brothers, but that I could not testify to his loyalty. He was in favor of secession."[27]

More often, with the Confederacy gone up the spout, people have let bygones be bygones. As early as the mid-1870s, when former unionists sought reimbursement through the Southern Claims Commission for property damaged or impressed by the Union army, some former Confederates testified on behalf of neighbors who they knew favored the Union cause. Anne Smoot, formerly Anne Crittenden, told the Commission that Ann C. Brandt had remained loyal to the United States, even though her son Logan had served and died in the Confederate cause. Similarly, Joseph B. Gorrell, who died in 1906, vouched for Mary L. Payne, and George Williams supported the claim of John C. Green. Some of these people even had to stretch the truth, or be careful to express their views in ways that would not injure their neighbor's case. They tried to dodge questions rather than lie. For example, Williams, who happened to be a cousin of Green's wife, replied, when asked by the Commission to comment on Green's political affiliations, "Well, I can hardly say that I can. He was at one time considered a whig, and at another time considered a democrat, and sometimes a little of one and then of the other." Williams spoke truer than he knew of many people in Culpeper.[28]

Perhaps the relatively small amount of tension to be observed between unionists and Confederates after the war may be explained by the fact that wartime unionism was, in fact, quite modest in Culpeper. The county as a whole certainly could not be regarded as disloyal to the Confederacy. Culpeper did lose its enthusiasm as the seasons of war progressed, but this may be attributed almost exclusively to war weariness. People grew tired of armies tramping through their fields, stealing their hogs, and destroying their fences. They grew tired of reading the names of neighbors and relatives who had been killed, wounded, or captured in a cause that seemed increasingly futile. When such things happened again and again, even people who had actively supported the Confederacy, like Thomas R. Rixey, began to take more neutral positions. Some people simply hedged their bets. John T. Hicks, who kept a hotel at the Court House during the war, played the game as successfully as anyone. John M. Wood, one of Culpeper's leading unionists, thought that Hicks was "about near neutral as a man could be." More to the point, however, Wood judged him a "not . . . very reliable man," a "tricky" man, who left a large "question of doubt about his sentiments."[29]

Culpeper Confederates remained bitter during the first couple of years after the war, particularly when the threat of forced Reconstruction darkened their lives. "The soreness consequent to the late war grows worse every day," reported a Freedmen's Bureau official in 1866, "and I believe the people as a mass are as disloyal as ever they were." A large part of the bitterness came from the visible reminders of war, which lingered long in Culpeper. Many neighbors, friends, and relations had given their lives for the Confederacy, and Yankee armies had scarred the landscape. "I think no county in the state suffered more than this county from the war," admitted the Freedmen's Bureau agent, "and it will require years to bring them back the state of prosperity they enjoyed before the war.[30]

In fact, the recovery progressed relatively swiftly, and, in any case, the people soon realized it was foolish to express undying love for Jeff Davis. Consequently, there appeared to be far more "unionists" after the war than during it, more people who for a variety of reasons wanted to appear as though they had disapproved of the Rebellion all along. As George Williams observed about a decade after the war, "I will say this, that I have heard of a great many loyal men since the war that I never heard spoken of before as such." Of the 125 claims from Culpeper considered by the Southern Claims Commission, 67 (54 percent) were rejected.[31]

Few can doubt, however, the sentiments of most black people about the war. Many members of the county's wartime black generation or their descendants have remained in Culpeper. In a total population of 13,472 in 1910, they numbered 5,262. As in all southern communities, racial accommodation and integration have not been easy since the war. Black citizens who prospered in the 1880s and 1890s have suffered in the era of Jim Crow. Yet, following a "race riot" at Rapidan Station in 1907, the nadir of race relations in the county, some harmony has been restored. Blacks operate more than two dozen businesses at the Court House. Henry Clay Lightfoot, a grocer, has even served on the town council. Blacks still live apart from whites and inhabit pretty much the same areas they did before the war, such as the Free State; but black ghettoes have also sprung up around the Court House and in rural areas like Bundytown and Maddenville.[32]

Other blacks, whether slave or free before the war, generally lie low, just as they have always done. George Mars and Ryburn Bundy farm small plots—six acres around Brandy Station for Mars—just as they did in 1860. William Yager, the lad who watched the Cedar Mountain fight from the roof of a shed, and who still recalls his encounter with a wounded Yankee soldier, resides in the county. He stayed with his "white family" for two or three years after the war, before going to work as a farmhand for $30 per month plus room and board on Dr. Strother's land in the Flats. William delights in pointing out that he and Dr. Strother had been boyhood playmates. Since then, he has hired out to several Culpeper families, including the Rixeys. He has been married twice, first to Lizzie Redman, who was free before the war, then, after Lizzie's death, to Ella Dickerson, who had been owned by the Ashby family. He fathered ten children, five with each wife.[33]

The county's leading antebellum black citizen, Willis Madden, fell on hard times after the war. Madden had his house in 1865, but precious little else. In 1871, he filed a claim for damages and goods confiscated by the Union army, but he collected only $879, about a third of his claim. The money allowed Madden to pay his debts and repair his house, but he possessed neither the energy nor the wherewithal to revive his once prosperous tavern and productive farmlands. He spent his remaining years tending a small garden and participating in church affairs. He died in 1879.[34]

As for other leading Confederate citizens, their fortunes varied after the war. Henry Shackleford served as a county and circuit court judge into the 1880s. Fayette Mauzy, long-time clerk of the court, served one term (1867–68) in the Virginia legislature. Robert E. Utterback, former captain of the Little Fork Rangers, became the county's first school superintendent in 1870, when Virginia established a public school system. He also practiced as a physician in the Rixeyville area until his death in 1881.[35]

Old John Kelly did not last long after the war, but he did mellow. The war wrecked his flourishing shops and sawmill, and his lands never revived once denied the unpaid attentions of slave labor. But Kelly "got religion," as they say. He joined and helped to rebuild Mt. Holly Church on the Fauquier side of the Rappahannock. His long-time neighbor and still bitter enemy George T. Wheatley only remarked, "Hell's for rent now." Kelly and Wheatley both died in 1877.[36]

Alfred Stofer, the indomitable editor of the *Observer*, revived his newspaper after the cessation of hostilities in order to oppose the "reconstruction" of Culpeper and Virginia by outsiders. He advocated, instead, the physical restoration and economic revitalization of the county by its own citizens. The *Observer* failed in the late 1870s, largely because of inroads made by the more conservative Culpeper *Times*. Stofer went on to help edit the Culpeper *Exponent*, established in 1881 by the Green family. Throughout his professional life, Stofer was known for his pungent, uncompromising editorials. Tragically, future generations may have been denied access to his work, for a fire earlier in this century destroyed a complete file of the *Observer*, from 1852 through 1877. Stofer died in 1909.[37]

The Field family lost more than it gained in the war. Three of Judge Richard H. Field's sons fell in Confederate service. A nephew, James G. Field, sacrificed a leg at Cedar Mountain; nonetheless he went on to practice law in Culpeper after the war until 1877, when he became Virginia's attorney general. James Field then roused himself from retirement to run for vice president on the Populist ticket in 1892. Culpeper gave him and presidential running mate James B. Weaver only 12 votes; they helped to elect, instead, Democratic nominee Grover Cleveland. On his lone campaign stop in Culpeper, Field attracted a "small and unsympathetic" audience of "Republicans and negroes," for most people in the county opposed the Populist Party's advocacy for small farmers and laborers. Still, when he died in 1902, Field was buried in Culpeper.[38]

May 31, 1911. As the streets swelled with visitors, Culpeper's surviving warriors assembled in the mayor's office at 9:30 A.M. this morning. They walked together, these last living remnants of Confederate courage, to the courthouse lawn. Surging around them, people who have been arriving in town since early morning moved toward the dedication site. The Culpeper Minute Men, accompanied by the militia company from Alexandria, marched toward the same spot, as did a dignified and quite serious-looking group of 250 Sunday-school children, all dressed in white with red sashes.

The ceremony began promptly at 10:30 with a prayer and the singing of "America." Then Henry Clay Burrows, formerly sergeant of Company E, 7th Virginia Infantry, now commander of A. P. Hill Camp No. 2, UCV, stepped forward. His complexion as fair as it was on the June day when he enlisted as a youth not yet 17, his hazel eyes just as clear, his six-foot frame only slightly stooped, Burrows described the fund-raising campaign that had led at long last to this momentous day. A prayer was offered, speeches were made. This time the granite memorial—a 12-foot-tall shaft—came from Vermont, and Powell Hill's grand-nieces, Frances Hill Horne and Mildred Hill, released the shroud from the monument. "Oohs" and "aahs" rose from the crowd, "a beautiful sight," whispered one person, an "inspiring moment," judged another tearfully. The band played "Dixie," and people cheered. The "faces of the old soldiers present brightened and their hearts must have warmed."[39]

Everyone is invited to attend a dinner now. People will mingle, and reminisce, and laugh, and slowly drift away. It is over.

NOTES

Chapter 1. A Place and a People

1. Eugene M. Scheel, *Culpeper: A Virginia County's History Through 1920* (Culpeper, 1982), pp. 1–38.

2. U.S. Bureau of the Census, *Seventh Census of the United States: 1850* (Washington, D.C., 1853), p. 259; *Population of the United States in 1860: Compiled from the Original Returns of the Eighth Census* (Washington, D.C., 1864), pp. 516–18; *Population Schedule of the Eighth Census, 1860, Culpeper County, Virginia*, National Archives Microcopy No. 653, Roll 1341. For comparison with a neighboring county, see T. Lloyd Benson, "The Plain Folk of Orange: Land, Work, and Society on the Eve of the Civil War," in Edward L. Ayers and John C. Willis, eds., *The Edge of the South: Life in Nineteenth-Century Virginia* (Charlottesville, 1991), pp. 60–61.

3. U.S. Bureau of the Census, *Agriculture of the United States in 1860; Compiled from the Original Returns of the Eighth Census* (Washington, D.C., 1864), pp. 154–62; *Eighth Census of the United States, 1860, Schedule 4: Productions of Agriculture During the Year Ending June 1, 1860, Virginia*, National Archives Microcopy No. T-1132, Reel 6; Avery O. Craven, *Soil Exhaustion as a Factor in the Agricultural History of Virginia and Maryland, 1606–1860* (Urbana, Ill., 1926), pp. 85–86, 96; Scheel, *Culpeper*, pp. 96–100; Charles W. Turner, "Virginia Agricultural Reform, 1815–1860," *Agricultural History*, XXVI (July 1952), pp. 80–89; Julius Rubin, "The Limits of Agricultural Progress in the Nineteenth-Century South," *Agricultural History*, XLVI (April 1975), pp. 362–64; G. Melvin Herndon, "Agricultural Reform in Antebellum Virginia: William Galt, Jr., A Case Study," *Agricultural History*, LII (July 1978), pp. 394–96, 406. On the general subject of Virginia's agricultural revival of the 1850s see William M. Mathew, *Edmund Ruffin and the Crisis of Slavery in the Old South: The Failure of Agricultural Reform* (Athens, Ga., 1988), pp. 94, 100–103, 109, 123; Mathew believes that Avery Craven exaggerates the extent of recovery. Also see Mathew, pp. 123–24, for the concept of agricultural diversification. The calculations of agricultural produc-

tion used here are based on the manuscript census. These numbers sometimes differ from the compilations published by the Bureau of the Census, but the general tendencies of production are the same in both sets of records.

4. Lewis Cecil Gray, *History of Agriculture in the Southern United States to 1860*, 2 vols. (Washington, D.C., 1932) II, pp. 792–800; John T. Schlebecker, *Whereby We Thrive: A History of American Farming, 1607–1972* (Ames, Iowa, 1975), pp. 100, 118, 120–23; Leo Rogin, *The Introduction of Farm Machinery in Its Relation to the Productivity of Labor in the Agriculture of the United States During the Nineteenth Century* (Berkeley, Calif., 1931), pp. 54–55, 59, 69–70, 77–78, 83–84, 155–59, 162; Scheel, *Culpeper*, pp. 105–106; *Eighth Census, Schedule 4*, Roll 234. According to the manuscript agricultural census, the average value of farm tools and machinery was nearly $230 per farm in Culpeper. That is a lot. Yet only a quarter of the farms actually possessed that much equipment.

5. Grady McWhiney, *Cracker Culture: The Celtic Tradition in the Old South* (University, Ala., 1987); John Otto, "The Great Plain Folk Migration," *Journal of Southern History*, LI (May 1985), pp. 183–200. Of course, planters sometimes had reason to emigrate, too, although there is not much evidence of this tendency for Culpeper. See generally James Oakes, *The Ruling Class: A History of American Slaveholders* (New York, 1982), pp. 69–95; Jane Turner Censer, "Southwestern Migration among North Carolina Planter Families: 'The Disposition to Emigrate,'" *Journal of Southern History*, LVII (August 1991), pp. 407–26.

6. Klaus Wust, *The Virginia Germans* (Charlottesville, 1969), pp. 20–25, 193; Arthur Dicken Thomas, Jr., and Angus McDonald Green, eds., *Early Churches of Culpeper County, Virginia: Colonial and Ante-Bellum Congregations* (Culpeper, 1987), pp. 1–4.

7. Mary Stevens Jones and Mildred Conway Jones, eds., *Historic Culpeper* (Culpeper, 1974), p. 132; Scheel, *Culpeper*, pp. 241, 344–45.

8. Jones and Jones, *Historic Culpeper*, pp. 132, 150; Scheel, *Culpeper*, pp. 345–46; Culpeper *Observer*, June 17, 1868.

9. Jones and Jones, *Historic Culpeper*, pp. 131–35; Scheel, *Culpeper*, pp. 336–58.

10. Scheel, *Culpeper*, pp. 337–38.

11. Scheel, *Culpeper*, pp. 77–84, 88–95; David R. Goldfield, *Urban Growth in the Age of Sectionalism in Virginia, 1847–1861* (Baton Rouge, La., 1977), pp. 221–25.

12. The numbers are tabulated from the 1860 manuscript census. See also Benson, "Plain Folk of Orange," pp. 63–64.

13. Lewis E. Atherton, *The Southern Country Store 1800–1860* (Baton Rouge, La., 1949), pp. 66–70, 171–76; Culpeper *Observer*, April 19, 1861, p. 3.

14. Scheel, *Culpeper*, pp. 100–101, 126–28; Arthur G. Peterson, "Flour and Grist Milling in Virginia: A Brief History," *Virginia Magazine of History and Biography*, XLIII (April 1935), pp. 98, 102–105; U.S. Bureau of the Census, *Manufactures of the United States in 1860; Compiled from the Original Returns of the Eighth Census* (Washington, D.C., 1865), 610, *Population Schedule of the Eighth Census*, pp. 827, 863, 904; Fletcher M. Green, "Gold Mining in Ante-Bellum Virginia," *Virginia Magazine of History and Biography*, VL (July 1937), pp. 227–35; *ibid.*, (October 1937), pp. 357–66. The statement that only seven mills produced goods in excess of $500 is based on the fact that only manufactories that produce in excess of that amount are listed in the census.

15. Charles W. Turner, "The Early Railroad Movement in Virginia," *Virginia Magazine of History and Biography*, LV (October 1947), pp. 350–53; Robert F. Hunter, "The Turnpike Movement in Virginia 1816–1860," *Virginia Magazine of History and Biography*, LXIX (July 1961), pp. 280, 285; Scheel, *Culpeper*, pp. 137–43.

16. Scheel, *Culpeper*, pp. 144–52; Jones and Jones, *Historic Culpeper*, p. 154; Donald S. Callaham, *The Rappahannock Canal* (Fredericksburg, 1972).

17. Charles W. Turner, "Virginia Railroad Development, 1845–1860," *Historian*, X (Autumn 1947), pp. 56–62, "The Early Railroad Movement in Virginia," pp. 353, 369–71; Joyce E. Wilkinson, "The Early Orange and Alexandria Railroad, 1849–1854," *Pioneer America*, I (July 1969), pp. 46–53.

18. Ticket Book No. 1, entry for July 20, 1860, Lemuel Armistead Corbin Papers, Virginia Historical Society; Charles W. Turner, "Railroad Service to Virginia Farmers, 1828–1860," *Agricultural History*, XXII (October 1948), pp. 239, 243–45; Atherton, *The Southern Country Store*, pp. 168–70; U.S. Bureau of the Census, *Seventh Census of the United States*, 259, *Population in 1860*, pp. 500, 518; Scheel, *Culpeper*, pp. 93–94, 153–57.

19. *Ibid.*; Rolla Milton Tryon, *Household Manufactures in the United States 1640–1860: A Study in Industrial History* (Chicago, 1917), pp. 308–309, 322–26, 370–75; John T. Schlotterbeck, "Plantation and Farm: Social and Economic Change in Orange and Green Counties, Virginia, 1716 to 1860" (Ph.D. diss., Johns Hopkins University, 1980), pp. 301, 310–17; Benson, "Plain Folk of Orange," p. 64. Schlotterbeck describes the change in neighboring Orange and Greene counties as the transition from a "social economy" toward a wider market economy. See also his essay "The 'Social Economy' of an Upper South Community: Orange and Greene Counties, Virginia, 1815–1860," in Orville Vernon Burton and Robert C. McMath, Jr., eds., *Class, Conflict, and Consensus: Antebellum Southern Community Studies* (Westport, Conn., 1982), pp. 1–28.

20. The calculations are based on the 6,653 slaves listed in the U.S. Bureau of the Census, *Population Schedule of the Eighth Census, 1860, Virginia [Slave Schedules], Culpeper County*, National Archives Microcopy No. 653, Roll 1389, rather than the 6,675 listed in the published census returns, *Population in 1860*, p. 511. See also Scheel, *Culpeper*, 159, and Michael Tadman, *Speculators and Slaves: Masters, Traders, and Slaves in the Old South* (Madison, Wis., 1989), p. 102.

21. Schlotterbeck, "Plantation and Farm," p. 174; Daniel E. Sutherland, *The Expansion of Everyday Life, 1860–1877* (New York, 1989), pp. 67–68; case of Alexander Jackson (No. 3008), Southern Claims Commission Case Files (1877–83), Records of General Auditor's Office, Records of Third Auditor's Office, Record Group 217, National Archives; *Population Schedule of the Eighth Census [Slave]*, 39; *Eighth Census, Schedule 4*, pp. 121–22. Jackson does not mention giving Day any portion of his earnings, and Loren Schweninger, *Black Property Owners in the South 1790–1915* (Urbana, Ill., 1990), p. 39, says this was generally the rule.

22. *Eighth Census, Schedule 4*, pp. 119–120; W. D. Gore, "Kelly's Ford," pp. 1–9, Works Progress Administration of Virginia, Historical Inventory for Culpeper County, Virginia, typescript in Culpeper County Courthouse.

23. U.S. Bureau of the Census, *Population in 1860*, pp. 516–18; Scheel, *Culpeper*, p. 161; Culpeper County Will Book U (1857–62), pp. 347–48, Culpeper County Courthouse.

24. Beverley B. Munford, *Virginia's Attitude Toward Slavery and Secession* (1909; Richmond, 1915), pp. 72–74; Catherine Thom Bartlett, ed., *"My Dear Brother": A Confederate Chronicle* (Richmond, 1952), pp. 24–25. Scheel, *Culpeper*, p. 162, also recounts the Thom story, but he mistakenly sets the episode in 1859.

25. Scheel, *Culpeper*, pp. 162–63; Munford, *Virginia's Attitude Toward Slavery and Secession*, pp. 121–22.

26. Scheel, *Culpeper*, p. 161; Thornton Stringfellow, "The Bible Argument: or, Slavery in

the Light of Divine Revelation," in E. N. Elliott, ed., *Cotton is King, and Pro-Slavery Arguments* (Augusta, Ga., 1860), pp. 462, 491.

27. Scheel, *Culpeper*, 163; Albert Ogden Porter, *County Government in Virginia: A Legislative History, 1607–1904* (New York, 1947), pp. 178–79; Harvey Wish, "The Slave Insurrection Panic of 1856," *Journal of Southern History*, V (May 1939), pp. 219–21; George M. Williams to Gertrude Long, December 23, 1856, [January 1, 1857], George M. Williams Family Papers, in possession of Janet LaValley, Culpeper, Virginia.

28. Charles L. Perdue, Jr. et al., eds., *Weevils in the Wheat: Interviews with Virginia Ex-Slaves* (1976; Bloomington, Ind., 1980), p. 294.

29. Scheel, *Culpeper*, p. 161; Philip J. Schwarz, *Twice Condemned: Slaves and the Criminal Laws of Virginia, 1705–1865* (Baton Rouge, La., 1988), pp. 291 n. 17, 301 n. 38; Culpeper County Court Minute Books, No. 24 (1858–64), pp. 52, 59–60, 109, 138–40, 158–59, Culpeper County Courthouse. Only five criminal cases involving slaves were brought before the county court between 1858 and 1861. This, of course, does not preclude the possibility of punishments by individual owners.

30. Scheel, *Culpeper*, p. 172.

31. E. M. Sanchez-Saavedra, " 'All Fine Fellows and Well-Armed': The Culpeper Minute Battalion 1775–1776," *Virginia Cavalcade*, XXIV (Summer 1974), pp. 4–11; George M. Williams to Gertrude Long, November 8, 21, and 24, 1859, Williams Family Papers.

32. George M. Williams to Gertrude S. Long, March 4 and May 18, 1860, Williams Family Papers.

33. Circuit Court Judgements, 1856–58, Drawer 3, Culpeper County Courthouse; Minute Book No. 24, pp. 147–48; Gore, "Kelly's Ford," 3, 7, 9, Historical Inventory for Culpeper. Virginia law also forbade the assembling of slaves for the purpose of teaching them to read and write, although individual slave-owners could teach their own slaves. See Janet Diutsman Cornelius, *"When I Can Read My Title Clear": Literacy, Slavery, and Religion in the Antebellum South* (Columbia, S.C., 1991), p. 33.

34. Scheel, *Culpeper*, pp. 164–65; Luther P. Jackson, *Free Negro Labor and Property Holding in Virginia, 1830–1860* (New York, 1942), pp. 60, 64–67, 70, 90–91; Raymond B. Pinchbeck, *The Virginia Negro Artisan and Tradesman* (Richmond, 1926), pp. 66–67; Goldfield, *Urban Growth in the Age of Sectionalism*, pp. 128–30; Ira Berlin, *Slaves Without Masters: The Free Negro in the Antebellum South* (New York, 1974), pp. 229–31, 348–67; Circuit Court Judgements, Drawer No. 3 (1856–58); Minute Book No. 24, pp. 148, 244, 296, 331, 336.

35. Scheel, *Culpeper*, pp. 165, 242; Berlin, *Slaves Without Masters*, pp. 251, 262–65; George M. Williams to Gertrude Long, January 25, March 17, July 12, 1860, Williams Family Papers. Runaway slaves seemed to favor such regions in other portions of Virginia, too. See Frederick Law Olmsted, *A Journey to the Seaboard Slave States*, 2 vols. (New York, 1856), I, pp. 111–13. For violence generally in antebellum southern society see McWhiney, *Cracker Culture*, pp. 146–70, and Elliott J. Gorn, " 'Gouge and Bite, Pull Hair and Scratch': The Social Significance of Fighting in the Southern Backcountry," *American Historical Review*, XC (February 1985), pp. 18–43. Bertram Wyatt-Brown, *Southern Honor: Ethics and Behavior in the Old South* (New York, 1982), pp. 352–61, 368–69, depreciates the significance of social class character in southern violence. Edward L. Ayers, *Vengeance and Justice: Crime and Punishment in the Nineteenth-Century American South* (New York, 1984), pp. 116–17, suggests why the people of the Flats were rarely prosecuted for being rowdy or drunk. Ervin L. Jordan, Jr., *Black Confederates and Afro-Yankees in Civil War Virginia* (Charlottesville, 1995), 130, documents one Culpeper interracial marriage in 1861.

36. These occupational and residential patterns were similar throughout the South. See Berlin, *Slaves Without Masters*, pp. 218–21, 235–38, 251; Schweninger, *Black Property Owners*, pp. 72, 124. For Bundy, see *Population Schedule of the Eighth Census*, pp. 833–34; Warner Bundy (No. 19,817), Southern Claims; Robertson Coons Account Book, 1846–61, in Coons Family Papers, Virginia Historical Society, Richmond.
37. *Population Schedule of the Eighth Census*, pp. 780, 782–83, 785, 787–88. For Virginia generally, see Jackson, *Free Negro Labor*, pp. 75–77. The Culpeper pattern conforms only partly to Schweninger's portrayal of the Upper South, *Black Property Owners*, pp. 84–87, 124. Most noticeably, free black women with property seem to be younger in Culpeper than elsewhere.
38. Jackson, *Free Negro Labor*, pp. 110–22; Berlin, *Slaves Without Masters*, pp. 279–80; 1860 Population Census, pp. 801, 894; cases of Randall G. Tate (No. 21,386) and Richard West (No. 20,596), Southern Claims. Contrary to the pattern described in the Upper South in Schweninger, *Black Property Owners*, pp. 73–74, the majority of Negro property owners in Culpeper were mulatto rather than black. The county's Negro population was evenly divided between blacks and mulattoes, but a vast majority of Court House Negroes (50 out of 66) were mulatto.
39. Scheel, *Culpeper*, pp. 163–65; Jones and Jones, *Historic Culpeper*, p. 134; T. O. Madden, Jr., *We Were Always Free: The Maddens of Culpeper County, Virginia: a 200-Year Family History* (New York, 1992), pp. 41–67.
40. Tax receipts for the 1850s and 1860s show that Madden owned only 87 acres, but he apparently rented or worked on shares an additional 194 acres. For tax rates and production figures for his farm see Madden Family Papers, Alderman Library, University of Virginia, Charlottesville; *Eighth Census, Schedule 4*, pp. 121–22; Willis Madden (No. 128), Southern Claims. For Epps, see Schweninger, *Black Property Owners*, pp. 121–23.
41. Scheel, *Culpeper*, pp. 164, 349; Madden, *We Were Always Free*, pp. 68–95.
42. Madden, *We Were Always Free*, pp. 86–90; Scheel, *Culpeper*, p. 349.
43. For the importance of community, neighborhood, and kinship in antebellum southern life see Robert C. Kenzer, *Kinship and Neighborhood in a Southern Community: Orange County, North Carolina, 1849–1881* (Knoxville, Tenn., 1987), pp. 6–51. For black communities see Schweninger, *Black Property Owners*, pp. 136–41, most of which applies to Culpeper.
44. George M. Williams to Gertrude S. Long, July 12, 17, 1860, Williams Papers.
45. *Ibid.*
46. *Ibid.*
47. George M. Williams to Gertrude S. Long, February 28, 1860, Williams Family Papers; Porter, *County Government in Virginia*, pp. 162–63. Circuit court judgments for 1859–64 were destroyed during the war, but a good idea of the types of suits being brought and the names of litigants may be ascertained from court minute books, execution books, law order books, and judgments from before and after the war. Indeed, the papers concerning many antebellum and wartime legal contests may be found among judgments passed after 1864 and into the 1870s, so long did some cases drag on in the courts. All of these records are housed in the Clerk's Office, Culpeper County Circuit Court. A convenient sampling of cases, though by no means a complete one, may be found in Dorothy Ford Wulfeck, comp., *Culpeper County, Virginia: Will Books B and C, Court Suits, Loose Papers, Inscriptions* (Naugatuck, Conn., 1965). See also Ayers, *Vengeance and Justice*, pp. 111–12.
48. County Court Minute Book No. 24, pp. 317–18, 334.
49. Scheel, *Culpeper*, pp. 136–37, 346; Gore, "Kelly's Ford," and Margaret Jeffries, "Wheatleyville," Historical Inventory for Culpeper.

50. Gore "Kelly's Ford," Historical Inventory for Culpeper.
51. Lyon Gardiner Tyler, *Encyclopedia of Virginia Biography*, 5 vols. (New York, 1915), II, p. 123; George M. Williams to Gertrude S. Long, May 5, 11, 1860, Williams Family Papers.
52. George M. Williams to Gertrude S. Long, July 10, September 10, 1860, Williams Family Papers.
53. John S. Pendleton to Dear Ellis, October 29, 1860, George M. Williams to Gertrude S. Long, September 10, 12, 1860, Williams Family Papers.
54. George M. Williams to Gertrude S. Long, May 22, September 10, 12, 1860, Williams Family Papers; Porter, *County Government in Virginia*, pp. 230–37; Scheel, *Culpeper*, pp. 104–105; Culpeper County Court Minute Book No. 24, inside flyleaf.
55. Scheel, *Culpeper*, pp. 365–66, 368–69. John S. Pendleton is erroneously labeled a Democrat (p. 365).
56. Scheel, *Culpeper*, pp. 363, 369.
57. George M. Williams to Gertrude Long, December 19, 1859, Williams Family Papers.

Chapter 2. A Promise of Glory and Greatness

1. E. B. Long, *The Civil War Day by Day: An Almanac, 1861–1865* (Garden City, N.Y., 1971), 60–61; William C. Davis, *"A Government of Our Own": The Making of the Confederacy* (New York, 1994), pp. 319–24.
2. Richmond *Enquirer*, January 1, 1861, p. 2.
3. Richmond *Enquirer*, January 1, 1861, p. 2; U.S. Bureau of the Census, *Population Schedule of the Eighth Census, 1860, Culpeper County, Virginia*, National Archives Microcopy No. 653, Roll 1341, pp. 781, 899, 911; *Population Schedule of the Eighth Census, 1860, Virginia [Slave Schedule], Culpeper County*, National Archives Microcopy No. 1389, Roll 1389, pp. 19–20, 23, 31, 41; *Eighth Census of the United States, 1860, Schedule 4: Productions of Agriculture During the Year Ending June 1, 1860, Virginia*, National Archives Microcopy No. T-1132, Roll 6, pp. 131–32, 135–36; Charles D. Walker, *Biographical Sketches of the Graduates and Élèves of the Virginia Military Institute Who Fell During the War Between the States* (Philadelphia, 1875), p. 425.
4. Lyon G. Tyler, *Encyclopedia of Virginia Biography*, 5 vols. (New York, 1915), V, p. 644; Richmond *Enquirer*, January 1, 1861, p. 2.
5. Richmond *Enquirer*, January 1, 1861, p. 2; *Population Schedule of the Eighth Census*, 788; *Population Schedule of the Eighth Census [Slave]*, p. 41; Daniel W. Crofts, *Reluctant Confederates: Upper South Unionists in the Secession Crisis* (Chapel Hill, 1989), p. 281.
6. Richmond *Enquirer*, January 1, 1861, p. 2; Culpeper *Observer*, January 11, 1861, p. 3; *Population Schedule of the Eighth Census*, 800; *Population Schedule of the Eighth Census [Slave]*, p. 5; Woodford B. Hackley, *The Little Fork Rangers: A Sketch of Company "D" Fourth Virginia Cavalry* (Richmond, 1927), p. 18.
7. Culpeper *Observer*, January 11, 1861, pp. 2–3.
8. Culpeper *Observer*, January 11, 1861, p. 3; *ibid.*, March 8, 1861, p. 3; Crofts, *Reluctant Confederates*, p. 138; Washington *Evening Star*, January 23, 1861, p. 2.
9. Crofts, *Reluctant Confederates*, pp. 267–68, 270–71; Frederic Bancroft, *The Life of William H. Seward*, 2 vols. (New York, 1900), II, p. 31; Richmond *Enquirer*, February 1, 1861, p. 2; Washington *Evening Star*, February 5, 1861, p. 2.
10. Case of Richard Wallach (No. 10,182), Southern Claims Commission Case Files, 1877–83. Records of the G.A.O., Records of the Third Auditor's Office. RG 217, National Archives; Culpeper *Observer*, January 11, 1861, p. 3; David R. Goldfield,

Urban Growth in the Age of Sectionalism: Virginia, 1847–1861 (Baton Rouge, La., 1977), pp. 251–56. For a similar shift in the North Carolina upcountry, see John C. Inscoe, *Mountain Masters, Slavery, and the Sectional Crisis in Western North Carolina* (Knoxville, Tenn., 1989), pp. 248–51.

11. Richmond *Enquirer*, February 1, 1861, p. 2; Crofts, *Reluctant Confederates*, p. 281.

12. William L. Loving to John S. Pendleton, October 16, 1860, George M. Williams to Gertrude S. Long, June 18, 20, 1860, Williams Family Papers, in possession of Janet LaValley, Culpeper, Virginia; Bancroft, *Life of William Seward*, II, pp. 534–36. For the general shift in Virginia toward unionism see Crofts, *Reluctant Confederates*, pp. 136–43.

13. Culpeper *Observer*, March 8, 1861, p. 2.

14. Long, *Civil War Day by Day*, pp. 42, 44; George H. Reese, ed., *Proceedings of the Virginia State Convention of 1861*, 4 vols. (Richmond, 1965), II, p. 246.

15. Reese, *Proceedings of the Virginia Convention*, II, pp. 605, 606, 671, 675, 680–81, 699.

16. Henry T. Shanks, *The Secession Movement in Virginia, 1847–1861* (Richmond, 1934), pp. 10, 206; Robert P. Sutton, *Revolution to Secession: Constitution Making in the Old Dominion* (Charlottesville, 1989), pp. 142–56; Goldfield, *Urban Growth in the Age of Sectionalism*, pp. 264–65; cases of John Brown (No. 15,556), William Heflin (No. 20,597), Sarah E. Thomas (No. 13,821), Southern Claims.

17. Cases of Mary L. Payne (No. 22,128), Susan P. W. Hall (No. 15,192), Simeon B. Shaw (No. 14,136), Southern Claims.

18. Culpeper *Observer*, April 19, 1861, p. 2. For continuing political divisions and the emergence of a "political culture" in the Confederacy, see George C. Rable, *The Confederate Republic: A Revolution Against Politics* (Chapel Hill, N.C., 1994).

19. Culpeper *Observer*, April 19, 1861, pp. 1, 2, 4; Little Fork Ranger Subscription Lists, in Coons Family Papers, Virginia Historical Society, Richmond. Hackley, *Little Fork Rangers*, p. 27, gives subscription lists similar to those in the Coons Papers, but his list for April 20 is longer.

20. Culpeper *Observer*, March 8, 1861, p. 2; Samuel P. Day, *Down South; or, An Englishman's Experience at the Seat of the American War*, 2 vols., (London, 1862), I, p. 314.

21. Mrs. Berkeley G. Calfee, *Confederate History of Culpeper County in the War Between the States* (Culpeper, 1948), pp. 1–2, 15–22; David F. Riggs, *13th Virginia Infantry* (Lynchburg, 1988), 84, 119; Hackley, *Little Fork Rangers*, p. 24; Lee A. Wallace, Jr., *A Guide to Virginia Military Organizations, 1862–1865* (Richmond, 1964), pp. 115, 121, 123, 268.

22. Reese, *Proceedings of the Virginia Convention*, IV, p. 90; Hackley, *Little Fork Rangers*, pp. 18–19, 25, 28, 31–32; Kenneth L. Stiles, *4th Virginia Cavalry* (Lynchburg, 1985), p. 128.

23. Hackley, *Little Fork Rangers*, pp. 26–28; *Population Schedule of the Eighth Census*, pp. 801, 841; *Population Schedule of the Eighth Census [Slave]*, pp. 5.

24. Hackley, *Little Fork Rangers*, pp. 27–28.

25. Culpeper *Observer*, April 19, 1961, p. 2; *Population Schedule for Eighth Census*, p. 777.

26. Cornelia Peake McDonald, *A Diary With Reminiscences of the War and Refugee Life in the Shenandoah Valley, 1860–1865* (Nashville, Tenn., 1934), p. 18; George M. Williams to Gertrude Williams, April 19 and 20, 1861, Williams Family Papers; Riggs, *13th Virginia Infantry*, pp. 1–3.

27. George M. Williams to Gertrude Williams, April 27, 1861, Williams Family Papers; Riggs, *13th Virginia Infantry*, p. 3.

28. Riggs, *13th Virginia*, p. 3; *Confederate Veteran*, I (April 1893), p. 103.

29. Richmond *Dispatch*, April 27, 1861, p. 1.

30. *War of the Rebellion: A Compilation of the Official Records of the Union and Confederate Armies,* 70 vols. in 128 books and index (Washington, D.C., 1880–1901, ser. 1, hereafter referred to as *War of the Rebellion,* and all references are to Series 1 unless otherwise noted) vol. 2, pp. 785, 786; Ezra J. Warner, *Generals in Gray: Lives of the Confederate Commanders* (Baton Rouge, La., 1959), pp. 56–57; Giles Buckner Cooke Diary, April 28, 29, 30, 1861, Virginia Historical Society, Richmond. Susan Leigh Blackford, *Letters from Lee's Army, or Memoir of Life In and Out of the Army in Virginia During the War Between the States* (New York, 1962), pp. 11–12; B. Rawlings to Philip St. George Cocke, April, 1861, Joseph B. Taylor to Philip St. George Cocke, May 4, 1861, James H. Buckley to Philip St. George Cocke, May 1861, Philip St. George Cocke Papers, Alderman Library, University of Virginia, Charlottesville.
31. *War of the Rebellion,* vol. 2, pp. 786–87, 804, 818.
32. *Ibid.,* pp. 798–99, 804–805.
33. *Ibid.,* pp. 806, 813, 817–19; Stiles, *4th Virginia Cavalry,* pp. 2–3; Cooke Diary, May 6–June 1, 1861.
34. *War of the Rebellion,* vol. 2, p. 824.
35. *War of the Rebellion,* vol. 2, pp. 836–37, 841–42, 845–47; Douglas Southall Freeman, *Lee's Lieutenants: A Study in Command,* 3 vols. (New York, 1942–44), I, pp. 90–91; Culpeper Baptist Church Minute Book, 1856–77, April 28, 1861, Virginia Baptist Historical Society, Richmond; Philip St. George Cocke to James L. Kemper, May 12 and 14, 1861, James L. Kemper Papers, Alderman Library, University of Virginia, Charlottesville.
36. John B. Cocke to Lucy Oliver Cocke, May 21, 1861, Cocke Papers; *War of the Rebellion,* vol. 2, pp. 841–42.
37. Lynchburg *Daily Virginian,* May 24, 1861, p. 3; Mildred T. Halsey to Joseph J. Halsey, June 5, 1861 and Samuel S. Halsey to Joseph J. Halsey, May 16, 1861, Morton-Halsey Papers, Alderman Library, University of Virginia, Charlottesville.
38. Mildred T. Halsey to Joseph J. Halsey, June 5, 1861; J. Morton Halsey to Joseph J. Halsey, June 5, 1861; both in Morton-Halsey Papers; S. Beckham to Philip St. George Cocke, May 31, 1861, Virginia Executive Papers, Virginia State Library and Archives, Richmond.
39. Mildred T. Halsey to Joseph J. Halsey, June 7, 1861, Morton-Halsey Papers; John Randolph to Millie [Payne], May 5, 1861, Randolph Family Papers, Alderman Library, University of Virginia, Charlottesville.
40. *Population Schedule of the Eighth Census,* p. 806; Michael P. Musick, *6th Virginia Cavalry* (Lynchburg, 1990), pp. 6, 120; Daniel A. Grimsley to Bettie Browning, April 18, 1861, Grimsley Family Papers, Virginia State Library and Archives, Richmond.
41. Daniel A. Grimsley to Bettie Browning, April 18, June 3, June 7, and June 14, 1861, Grimsley Family Papers.
42. Richmond *Daily Dispatch,* May 28, 1861, quoted in Hackley, *Little Fork Rangers,* p. 24; S. Beckham to Philip St. George Cocke, May 31, 1861, Virginia Executive Papers.
43. Jane A. Conway to Dear Sir, May 11, 1861, Grinnan Family Papers, Alderman Library, University of Virginia, Charlottesville; Margaret Jeffries, "Culpeper Military Institute," Works Progress Administration of Virginia, Historical Inventory for Culpeper County, Culpeper County Courthouse; Hackley, *Little Fork Rangers,* p. 24.
44. Lucretta Clore to John Letcher, June 15, 1861, Virginia Executive Papers.
45. Camp Henry Account Book, Culpeper Court House, 1861–62, pp. 1–7, Eleanor S. Brockenbrough Library, Museum of the Confederacy, Richmond; Alfred J. Stofer file,

Confederate Papers Relating to Citizens or Business Firms, War Department Collection of Confederate Records, RG 109, National Archives.

46. John W. Foushee, J. G. Miller and H. B. Miller files, Confederate Papers Relating to Citizens or Business Firms; *Population Schedule of the Eighth Census*, pp. 815–17, 851.

47. Camp Henry Account Book, pp. 7, 11–12.

48. Culpeper *Observer*, April 19, 1861, pp. 2–3.

49. Culpeper County Court Minutes Books, No. 24 (1858–1864), May 24, 1861, pp. 343–46, Culpeper County Courthouse.

50. *War of the Rebellions*, vol. 2, pp. 879–80; Lynchburg *Daily Virginian*, May 24, 1861, p. 3; Philip St. George Cocke to James L. Kemper, May 14, 1861, Kemper Papers; James L. Kemper to Philip St. George Cocke, May 25, 1861, Cocke Papers; Post Returns for Camp Henry, Culpeper Court House, May 21, June 9, 1861, War Department Collection of Confederate Records, entry 65, RG 109, National Archives.

51. Hackley, *Little Fork Rangers*, pp. 28–30.

52. James L. Kemper to Philip St. George Cocke, May 25, 1861, Cocke Papers; Post Returns for Camp Henry, June 9, 1861; Philip St. George Cocke to Lt. Col. Jordan, June 9, 1861, Cocke Papers.

53. Blackford, *Letters from Lee's Army*, p. 12; Post Returns for Camp Henry, May 21, 1861; *Population Schedule of the Eighth Census*, p. 896; David F. Riggs, *7th Virginia Cavalry* (Lynchburg, 1982), p. 75; John W. Murray to Ellen Murray, May 15, 1861, Murray Family Papers, Virginia State Library and Archives, Richmond; F. G. Skinner to Philip St. George Cocke, June 4, 1861, Virginia Executive Papers.

54. Thomas H. Covington to John C. Porter, May 27, 1861, Cocke Papers; Riggs, *7th Virginia Cavalry*, p. 61; Henry Shackleford to John Letcher, May 23, 1861, James G. Field to Richard H. Field, May 6, 1861, and Richard H. Field to Dear Sir, May 10, 1861, Virginia Executive Papers.

55. William A. Ross to F. H. Smith, May 5, 1861, William B. Ross to John Letcher, May 5, 1861, James Barbour to John Letcher, May 1, 1861, and John S. Pendleton to John Letcher, May 3, 1861, Virginia Executive Papers.

56. Cooke Diary, June 2, 1861.

57. Cooke Diary, June 2–June 10, 1861.

58. Sarah M. Bocock to James L. Kemper, July 2, 1861, Kemper Papers.

59. John W. Murray to Ellen Murray, May 15, 1861; Robert A. Hodge, comp., *A Death Roster of the Confederate Hospital at Culpeper, Virginia* (Fredericksburg, 1977), p. 3; Mrs. J. S. Pendleton to Philip St. George Cocke, June 10, 1861, Cocke Papers.

60. Lynchburg *Daily Virginian*, June 26, 1861, p. 1. For the role of Confederate women in the war generally see Drew Gilpin Faust, "Altars of Sacrifice: Confederate Women and the Narratives of War," *Journal of American History*, LXXVI (March 1990), pp. 1200–28; George C. Rable, *Civil Wars: Women and the Crisis of Southern Nationalism* (Urbana, Ill. 1989).

61. W. W. Payne to John Letcher, June 1, 1861, Virginia Executive Papers; *War of the Rebellion*, vol. 2, pp. 834, 850.

62. John B. Cocke to Lucy Oliver Cocke, May 21, 1861, Cocke Papers.

63. Eugene M. Scheel, *Culpeper: A Virginia County's History Through 1920* (Culpeper, 1982), p. 175; James Barbour to Dear Colonel, May 21, 1861, Virginia Executive Papers; cases of John Brown (No. 15,556) and Amiss, Southern Claims.

64. Cases of James B. Kirk (No. 636) and Archibald Shaw (No. 14,135), Southern Claims.

65. Cases of Ryburn Bundy (No. 19,818), Warner Bundy (No. 19,817), and Ira Field (No. 3003), Southern Claims; Culpeper County Court Minute Book No. 24, June 18, 1861, p. 356.

66. Cases of Ryburn Bundy, Warner Bundy, Ira Field, and Willis Madden (No. 128), Southern Claims.

67. Richmond *Daily Dispatch*, June 3, 1861, quoted in Hackley, *Little Fork Rangers*, p. 24.

68. *Population Schedule of the Eighth Census*, p. 884; *Population Schedule of the Eighth Census [Slave]*, p. 21; *Eighth Census, Schedule 4*, pp. 123–24; Catherine Crittenden to John Letcher, May 2, 1861, Virginia Executive Papers.

69. Riggs, *13th Virginia Infantry*, pp. 4, 99, 101, 113, 137, 144; Stiles, *4th Virginia Cavalry*, p. 133.

70. Riggs, *13th Virginia Infantry*, pp. 2–3; Mary Stevens Jones and Mildred Conway Jones, eds., *Historic Culpeper* (Culpeper, 1974), p. 17; James I. Robertson, Jr., *General A. P. Hill: The Story of a Confederate Warrior* (New York, 1987), pp. 5–8, 35–38.

71. McDonald, *A Diary With Reminiscences*, p. 18.

72. John B. Cocke to Uncle, June 20, 1861, Philip St. George Cocke "Last Will and Testament," May 30, 1861, Cocke Papers; *War of the Rebellion*, vol. 2, pp. 943–44; James I. Robertson, Jr., ed., *Proceedings of the Advisory Council of the State of Virginia, April 21–June 19, 1861* (Richmond, 1977), p. 133.

73. Hackley, *Little Fork Rangers*, pp. 33–35; Camp Henry Account Book, p. 23; Paul Glass and Louis C. Singer, eds., *Singing Soldiers: A History of the Civil War in Song* (New York, 1975), pp. 16–18. "The Bonnie Blue Flag" was one of the earliest songs of the Confederacy, sung as early as January 1861. Hackley's description of the departure of the Rangers says that the band played "The Homespun Dress." That song was not written until 1862, but it was sung to the tune of "The Bonnie Blue Flag."

74. Musick, *6th Virginia Cavalry*, p. 120; Daniel A. Grimsley to Bettie Browning, July 7, 1861, Grimsley Family Papers; Camp Henry Account Book, p. 24; Robert T. Bell, *11th Virginia Infantry* (Lynchburg, 1985), pp. 6–7; *Population Schedule of the Eighth Census*, p. 795; *Population Schedule of the Eighth Census [Slave]*, p. 1.

75. Day, *Down South*, I, pp. 313–14; William K. Scarborough, ed., *The Diary of Edmund Ruffin*, 2 vols. (Baton Rouge, La., 1972–76), II, p. 55; C. Vann Woodward, ed., *Mary Chesnut's Civil War* (New Haven, 1981), p. 95; Hospital Files: Report of Sick and Wounded, July 1861; Hodge, *Death Roster*, pp. 4, 52; Daniel A. Grimsley to Bettie Browning, July 7, 1861, Grimsley Family Papers; Cooke Diary [July, 14, 1861].

76. Wallace, *Virginia Military Organizations*, p. 268; John S. Barbour to John Letcher, July 18, 1861, Virginia Executive Papers.

77. Martha J. Cole to John Letcher, July 12, 1861, Virginia Executive Papers.

78. Samuel B. Halsey to Joseph J. Halsey, May 20, 1861, Morton-Halsey Papers.

Chapter 3. Glorious, Terrible War

1. Constance Cary Harrison, "Virginia Scenes in '61," in Robert Underwood Johnson and Clarence Clough Buel, eds., *Battles and Leaders of the Civil War*, 4 vols. (New York, 1887), I, p. 164.

2. David F. Riggs, *7th Virginia Infantry* (Lynchburg, 1982), pp. 3–4; Robert T. Bell, *11th Virginia Infantry* (Lynchburg, 1985), pp. 8–9; *War of the Rebellion: A Compilation of the Official Records of the Union and Confederate Armies*, 70 vols. in 128 books and index (Washington, D.C., 1880–1901, ser. 1 cited hereafter as *War of the Rebellion*, and, unless otherwise indicated, all references are to Series 1), vol. 2, pp. 464, pp. 572–73.

3. *War of the Rebellion*, vol. 2, pp. 572–73; Kenneth L. Stiles, *4th Virginia Cavalry* (Lynchburg, 1985), p. 5; Woodford B. Hackley, *The Little Fork Rangers: A Sketch of Company "D" Fourth Virginia Cavalry* (Richmond, 1927), pp. 32, 36–69.

4. Riggs, *7th Virginia Infantry*, pp. 3–4, 66, 69; U.S. Bureau of the Census, *Population Schedule of the Eighth Census, 1860, Culpeper County Virginia*, National Archives Microcopy No. 653, Roll 1341, pp. 776, 781.

5. David F. Riggs, *13th Virginia Infantry* (Lynchburg, 1988), pp. 4–6.

6. Riggs, *7th Virginia Cavalry*, p. 4.

7. Daniel A. Grimsley to Bettie Browning, July 24, 1861, Grimsley Family Papers, Virginia State Library and Archives, Richmond.

8. Mrs. Berkeley G. Calfee, *Confederate History of Culpeper County in the War Between the States* (Culpeper, 1948), p. 2; McHenry Howard, *Recollections of a Maryland Confederate Soldier and Staff Officer under Johnston, Jackson, and Lee* (Baltimore, 1914), p. 54; *Confederate Veteran*, 33 (October 1925), p. 396; Jesse W. Jordan to Sister, August 4, 1861, Jordan-Bell Family Letters, Virginia Historical Society, Richmond.

9. J. M. Broadus to J. A. Broadus, July 23, 1861, in Archibald T. Robertson, *Life and Letters of John Albert Broadus* (Philadelphia, 1901), p. 187; Calfee, *Confederate History of Culpeper*, pp. 2–3; *Population Schedule of the Eighth Census*, p. 786; U.S. Bureau of the Census, *Population Schedule of the Eighth Census of the U.S., 1860, Culpeper County, Virginia [Slave Schedules]*, National Archives Microcopy No. 653, Roll 1389, p. 41; Charleston *Courier*, September 16, 1861, p. 4; Washington *Evening Star*, August 12, 1861, p. 2.

10. Hospital Files: Virginia, Report for General Hospital at Culpeper Court House, July 1861, War Department Collection of Confederate Records, Box 19, RG 109, National Archives; Lynchburg *Daily Virginian*, June 26, 1861, p. 1.

11. Charleston *Courier*, August 16, 1861, p. 4.

12. Hospital Files, Report for General Hospital, July 1861, Discharges or Surgeon's Certificates and Deaths, Culpeper Court House, July 1861; Robert A. Hodge, comp., *A Death Roster of the Confederate Hospital at Culpeper, Virginia* (Fredericksburg, 1977), p. 74.

13. Hospital Files, Return of Medical Officers, August 1861; Riggs, *13th Virginia Infantry*, p. 117.

14. Giles Buckner Cooke Diary, July 7, [July 14], 1861, Virginia Historical Society, Richmond; John H. Bocock to James L. Kemper, July 27, 1861, James L. Kemper Papers, Alderman Library, University of Virginia, Charlottesville; T. C. Catchings to Millie Paine [sic], April 12, 1868, Randolph Family Papers, Alderman Library, University of Virginia; *Population Schedule of the Eighth Census*, pp. 796–97.

15. *Population Schedule for Eighth Census*, 890; Bunny [Herr] to Rachel Sisson, July 31, August 19, 1861, Sisson Family Papers, Alderman Library, University of Virginia Library, Charlottesville.

16. Cases of Matilda G. Hudson (No. 15,194), William A. Soutter (No. 17,756), Cases Disallowed by Commissioners of Southern Claims, Records of the U.S. House of Representatives, 1871–80, RG 233, National Archives.

17. George Graham Morris, "Confederate Lynchburg, 1861–1865" (M.A. thesis, Virginia Polytechnic Institute and State University, 1977), pp. 33–34; George Morris and Susan Foutz, *Lynchburg in the Civil War: The City—The People—The Battle* (Lynchburg, 1984), pp. 12–17; Washington *Evening Star*, August 17, 1861, p. 2; Jesse W. Jordan to Sister, August 4, 1861, Jordan-Bell Family Letters; Hodge, *Death Roster*, 11–106.

18. Mrs. Burton Harrison, *Recollections Grave and Gay* (New York, 1911), pp. 55–56; Arthur Dicken Thomas, Jr., and Angus McDonald Green, eds., *Early Churches of Culpeper County, Virginia: Colonial and Ante-Bellum Congregations* (Culpeper, 1987), p.

120; Monimia Cary to Clarence Cary, September 16, 1861, Burton Norvell Harrison Family Papers, Library of Congress.

19. Paul Glass and Louis C. Singer, eds., *Singing Soldiers: A History of the Civil War in Song* (New York, 1975), pp. 228–30. "Somebody's Darling" was sung in both North and South but was heard more frequently in the Confederacy. The song may be heard on the soundtrack of the film *Gone with the Wind*.

20. Monimia Cary to Clarence Cary, August 25, September 7, 1861 and Monimia Cary to Eliza Cary, September 11, 1861, Wilson Miles Cary Papers, Alderman Library, University of Virginia, Charlottesville; Harrison, *Recollections Grave and Gay*, 55–64; Harrison, "Virginia Scenes in '61," pp. 165–66. Another source says that the Wise daughters, a family with whom Monimia and Constance were staying, also participated in making the flags. See R. P. Rixey, *The Rixey Genealogy* (Lynchburg, 1933), pp. 218–19.

21. Monimia Cary to Mrs. A. F. Hopkins, September 10, 1861, Monimia Cary Papers; Monimia Cary to Clarence Cary, September 7, 1861, Wilson Cary Papers.

22. Hospital Records: Report of Sick and Wounded , September, October 1861; Hodge, *Death Roster*.

23. Culpeper County Court Minute Books, No. 24 (1858–1864), July 15, 1861, p. 358, Culpeper County Courthouse; Case of George T. Jennings (No. 13,069), Southern Claims (Disallowed); cases of Slaughter Madden (No. 13,673) and Lousia Vanlone (No. 965), Southern Claims Commission Case Files, 1877–83, Records of the General Accounting Office, Records of the Third Auditor's Office, RG 217, National Archives; *Population Schedule of Eighth Census*, p. 852; *Population Schedule of Eighth Census [Slave]*, p. 37; U.S. Bureau of the Census, *Eighth Census of the U.S., 1860, Schedule 4: Production of Agriculture During the Year Ending June 1, 1860, Virginia*, National Archives Microcopy No. T-1132, Roll 6, pp. 121–22.

24. Daniel A. Grimsley to Bettie Browning, July 24, August 3, 1861, Grimsley Family Papers.

25. *Population Schedule of the Eighth Census*, p. 844; Joseph W. Embrey to Sister, July 17, August 19, 1861, Joseph W. Embrey Letters, Alderman Library, University of Virginia, Charlottesville.

26. Joseph W. Embrey to Sister, August 19, 1861, Embrey Letters; Riggs, *13th Virginia Infantry*, p. 7.

27. Riggs, *13th Virginia Infantry*, pp. 7–8, 112; Joseph W. Embrey Diary, August 1861, Embrey Letters.

28. Case of James B. Kirk (No. 636), Southern Claims.

29. Case of William A. Soutter (No. 17,756), Southern Claims.

30. Hospital Reports: Report of Sick and Wounded, July, September, 1861; Bouldin, "Lynchburg, Virginia," p. 12. For the prevalence of venereal disease see Thomas P. Lowry, *The Story the Soldiers Wouldn't Tell: Sex in the Civil War* (Mechanicsburg, Pa., 1994), pp. 99–108.

31. Lynchburg *Daily Virginian*, September 23, 1861; *Population Schedule of the Eighth Census*, p. 814; County Court Minute Books, No. 24, October 21, 22, 1861, pp. 365–66; Clary Ann trial transcript dated October 21, 1861, James F. Brown to John Letcher, November 21, 1861, and Nancy Wayman to John Letcher, October 17, 1861, Virginia Executive Papers.

32. Thomas and Green, *Early Churches of Culpeper County*, pp. 54, 94, 291–92; Bettie Browning to Daniel A. Grimsley, November 18, 1861, Grimsley Family Papers; Donnie Johnston, *The Ghosts of Gourdvine Past: A History of the Gourdvine Baptist Church* (n.p., 1987), p. 25; Minutes of Baptist Church of Christ, Criglersville, Culpeper County,

entry of July 1861, Alderman Library, University of Virginia, Charlottesville; *Minutes of Shiloh Association, Seventieth Session, August 27, 1861* (Richmond, 1865), pp. 1–2.

33. Johnston, *Ghosts of Gourdvine Past*, p. 30; Thomas and Green, *Early Churches of Culpeper County*, pp. 194, 249; Pleasant Grove Baptist Church Minute Books, 1825–61, entry for August 17, 1861, Crooked Run Baptist Church Minute Books, 1846–49, entries for 1861, and Culpeper Baptist Church Minute Books, 1856–77, entry for September 9, 1861, all minute books at Virginia Baptist Historical Society, Richmond.

34. James LeGrand Wilson, *The Confederate Soldier*, ed. by James W. Silver (1902; Memphis, 1973), p. 111; Camp Henry Account Book, Culpeper Court House, 1861–62, pp. 27–28, Eleanor S. Brockenbrough Library, Museum of the Confederacy, Richmond.

35. Camp Henry Account Books, pp. 23–28, 30, 31; Charleston *Courier*, August 16, 1861, p. 4; A. S. Taylor to John Letcher, August 4, 1861, Virginia Executive Papers.

36. Camp Henry Account Book, pp. 32, 37–41, 47.

37. Camp Henry Account Book, pp. 43–48, 50, 53; files for J. G. and H. B. Miller, August–December 1861, Confederate Papers Relating to Citizens or Business Firms, War Department Collection of Confederate Records, RG 109, Microcopy M346, Reel 687, National Archives.

38. Culpeper County Circuit Court Execution Books, No. 13 (1857–90), November 1861, Culpeper County Courthouse; Susan Matthews to James L. Kemper, November 1, 1861, Kemper Papers; G. F. Carter Account Books, I, pp. 303, 349, 353, 355, 361, 375, Alderman Library, University of Virginia, Charlottesville.

39. Case of John C. Green (No 20,613), Southern Claims.

40. Bettie Browning to Daniel A. Grimsley, September 4, November 4, December 2, 1861, Grimsley Family Papers; Hackley, *Little Fork Rangers*, pp. 38–40; Stiles, *4th Virginia Cavalry*, pp. 8, 120, 134.

41. Riggs, *13th Virginia Infantry*, p. 113; Bettie Browning to Daniel A. Grimsley, November 18, 1861, Grimsley Family Papers; Bell, *11th Virginia Infantry*, pp. 16, 80; *Population Schedule of the Eighth Census*, p. 795.

42. Hodge, *Death Roster*, pp. 28, 42, 62; Riggs, *13th Virginia Infantry*, pp. 115, 125; *Population Schedule of Eighth Census*, pp. 776, 820, 906.

43. Hackley, *Little Fork Rangers*, p. 38; Stiles, *4th Virginia Cavalry*, pp. 133, 144; Lee A. Wallace, Jr., *A Guide to Virginia Military Organizations, 1862–1865* (Richmond, 1964), p. 123; Bettie Browning to Daniel A. Grimsley, November 18, November 4, 1861, Grimsley Family Papers.

44. Bettie Browning to Daniel A. Grimsley, September 4, 1861, Grimsley Family Papers.

45. Bettie Browning to Daniel A. Grimsley, November 4, November 18, 1861, December 2, Grimsley Family Papers; Culpeper County Marriage Registers, No. 2 (1850–80), 1861, Culpeper County Courthouse, Silas Bruce Marriage Register (1832–81), 1861, Virginia State Library and Archives, Richmond.

46. James S. Barbour to John Letcher, August 20, 1861, J. J. Halsey to Jackson Morton, September 1, 1861, and Charles E. Sinclair to John Letcher, October 28, 1861, Virginia Executive Papers; Perry J. Eggborn to James L. Kemper, July 30, 1861, Kemper Papers; *Population Schedule of the Eighth Census*, pp. 795–96; *Population Schedule of the Eighth Census [Slave]*, pp. 1–2; *Eighth Census, Schedule 4*, p. 107; Riggs, *7th Virginia Infantry*, p. 72.

47. Riggs, *7th Virginia Infantry*, pp. 3–4, 88; W. T. Patton to James L. Kemper, December 13, 1861, Kemper Papers. See also James W. Green to James L. Kemper, September 19, 1861, Kemper Papers.

48. *Population Schedule of the Eighth Census*, 809; *Population Schedule of the Eighth Census [Slave]*,

pp. 10–11; *Eighth Census, Schedule 4*, p. 109; James A. Beckham to James L. Kemper, August 19, 1861, Kemper Papers; Riggs, *7th Virginia Infantry*, p. 62.

49. James A. Beckham to James L. Kemper, August 19, 1861, Kemper Papers; John L. Brooke to John Letcher, August 26, 1861, Virginia Executive Papers.

50. Samuel S. Halsey to Joseph J. Halsey, November 19, 1861, Morton-Halsey Papers, Alderman Library, University of Virginia, Charlottesville.

Chapter 4. Invasion

1. *The War of the Rebellion, A Compilation of the Official Records of the Union and Confederate Armies*, 70 vols. in 128 books and index (Washington, D.C., 1880–1901, cited hereafter as *War of the Rebellion*, and all references are to Series 1 unless otherwise indicated), ser. 4, vol. 1, pp. 847–52.

2. Kenneth L. Stiles, *4th Virginia Cavalry* (Lynchburg, 1985), pp. 105, 115, 132; Bettie Browning to Daniel A. Grimsley, January 13, 28, 1862, Grimsley Family Papers, Virginia State Library and Archives, Richmond.

3. Culpeper *Observer*, February 21, 1862, p. 3; Bettie Browning to Daniel A. Grimsley, January 13, 1862, Grimsley Family Papers; Archibald T. Robertson, *Life and Letters of John Albert Broadus* (Philadelphia, 1901), p. 189.

4. Robertson, *Life and Letters of Broadus*, p. 189; Gertrude Williams to George M. Williams, March 8, 1862, George M. Williams Family Papers. For similarly high prices in neighboring Fauquier County see J. Michael Welton, ed., *"My Heart Is So Rebellious": The Caldwell Letters, 1861–1865* (Warrenton, Va., 1991), pp. 73–76.

5. Culpeper *Observer*, February 21, 1862, pp. 3–4; U.S. Bureau of the Census, *Population Schedule of the Eighth Census, 1860, Culpeper County, Virginia*, National Archives Microcopy No. 653, Roll 1341, p. 786.

6. *War of the Rebellion*, Series 4, vol. 1, pp. 923–25; Francis N. Boney, *John Letcher of Virginia: The Story of Virginia's Civil War Governor* (University, Ala., 1966), pp. 137, 139–41, 150–51, 156–57.

7. *War of the Rebellion*, Series 4, vol. 1, p. 944.

8. Culpeper *Observer*, February 21, 1862, p. 2.

9. Culpeper County Court Minute Books, No. 24 (1858–64), pp. 377–79, 381–82, Culpeper County Courthouse, Culpeper *Observer*, February 21, 1862, p. 3.

10. Charles Wager to John Letcher, February 27, 1862, Mrs. George Pennill to John Letcher, February 17, 1862, Mrs. M. E. Walker to John Letcher, February 25, 1862, Virginia Executive Papers, Virginia State Library and Archives, Richmond.

11. Culpeper *Observer*, February 21, 1862, p. 2; David F. Riggs, *13th Virginia Infantry* (Lynchburg, 1988), pp. 1–2, 84–85, 110; C. T. Crittenden to John Letcher, February 24, 1862, Virginia Executive Papers.

12. Riggs, *13th Virginia Infantry*, pp. 1–2, 84–85, 104, 119; David F. Riggs, *7th Virginia Infantry* (Lynchburg, 1982), p. 94; H. H. Hardesty, *Hardesty's Historical and Geographical Encyclopedia for Abelmarle, Orange, Greene, and Culpeper Counties* (New York, 1884), p. 441; Culpeper *Observer*, February 21, 1862, p. 3.

13. Michael P. Musick, *6th Virginia Cavalry* (Lynchburg, 1990), p. 8; Bettie Browning to Daniel A. Grimsley, March 4, 1862, Grimsley Family Papers.

14. *War of the Rebellion*, ser. 4, vol. 1, pp. 962–63, 966–69.

15. Joseph E. Johnston, *Narrative of Military Operations During the Civil War* (1874; Bloomington, Ind., 1959), pp. 83, 96–98, 102–103; *War of the Rebellion*, vol. 5, pp.

526–27, 1093, 1097–98; Craig L. Symonds, *Joseph E. Johnston: A Civil War Biography* (New York, 1992), pp. 140–43.

16. Jubal A. Early, *Narrative of the War Between the States* (1912; Wilmington, N.C., 1989), pp. 56–57; *War of the Rebellion*, vol. 5, pp. 526–27, 1061–62, 1096–98; Susan P. Lee, *Memoirs of William Nelson Pendleton* (Philadelphia, 1893), pp. 172–73; Johnston, *Narrative*, pp. 96–97, 106; Symonds, *Joseph E. Johnston*, pp. 145–46.

17. Carrie Spencer et al., comps., *A Civil War Marriage in Virginia: Reminiscences and Letters* (Boyce, Va., 1956), p. 131; John Rozier, ed., *The Granite Farm Letters: The Civil War Correspondence of Edgeworth and Sallie Bird* (Athens, Ga., 1988), pp. 72–74; Randolph A. McKim, *A Soldier's Recollections: Leaves from the Diary of a Young Confederate* (New York, 1910), p. 83.

18. Jeffrey N. Lash, *Destroyer of the Iron Horse: General Joseph E. Johnston and Confederate Rail Transport, 1861–1865* (Kent, Ohio, 1991), pp. 29–35; *War of the Rebellion*, vol. 5, pp. 1083, 1097–98; Angus J. Johnston, *Virginia Railroads in the Civil War* (Chapel Hill, N.C., 1961), pp. 40–41.

19. William N. Pendleton to Anzolette Pendleton, March 13, 1862, William Nelson Pendleton Papers, Southern Historical Collection, University of North Carolina at Chapel Hill; Lee, *Memoirs of William Pendleton*, p. 173; Robert T. Scott to Fanny Scott, March 18, 1862, Keith Family Papers, Virginia Historical Society, Richmond; Johnston, *Narrative*, p. 106; John B. Cary to Sally McHenry, March 24, 1862, Wilson Miles Cary Papers, Alderman Library, University of Virginia, Charlottesville.

20. Orders and Circulars Issued by the Army of the Potomac and the Army and Department of Northern Virginia, C.S.A., National Archives Microform M921, Special Orders 72, 75, and 77.

21. Lee, *Memoirs of Pendleton*, p. 174; Robert T. Scott to Fanny Scott, March 19, 1862, Keith Family Papers.

22. William N. Pendleton to Anzolette Pendleton, March 13, 1862, General Order of March 12, 1862, Pendleton Papers; Robert T. Scott to Fanny Scott, March 18, 1862, Keith Family Papers.

23. Symonds, *Joseph E. Johnston*, pp. 146–47; Johnston, *Narrative*, pp. 107–108; Woodford B. Hackley, *The Little Fork Rangers: A Sketch of Company "D" Fourth Virginia Cavalry* (Richmond, 1927), p. 41; Boney, *John Letcher*, pp. 159–60; *War of the Rebellion*, ser. 4, vol. 1, pp. 1009, 1011.

24. Aurelia Austin, ed., *Georgia Boys with "Stonewall" Jackson: James Thomas Thompson and the Walton Infantry* (Athens, Ga., 1967), pp. 28–29.

25. Boney, *John Letcher*, pp. 159–60; M. L. Gordon to John Letcher, March 14, 1862, Virginia Executive Papers; *War of the Rebellion*, ser. 4, vol. 1, pp. 1009, 1011–12, 1021–22; George M. Williams to Gertrude Williams, March 14, 1862, Williams Family Papers.

26. William N. Pendleton to Anzolette Pendleton, March 13, 1862, Pendleton Papers; James M. Farish to Tom Brown, March 23, 1862, Morton-Halsey Papers, Alderman Library, University of Virginia, Charlottesville.

27. George M. Williams to Gertrude Williams, March 10, 12, and 14, 1862, Williams Family Papers.

28. James M. Farish to Tom Brown, March 23, 1862, Morton-Halsey Papers; George M. Williams to Gertrude Williams, March 10, 1862; Camp Henry Account Book, pp. 60–61, Eleanor S. Brockenbrough Library, Museum of the Confederacy, Richmond.

29. John B. Cary to Sally McHenry, March 24, 1862, Wilson Cary Papers.

30. John B. Cary to Mrs. Wilson M. Cary, March 26, 1862, Wilson Cary Papers; *Population Schedule of the Eighth Census*, p. 899; Margaret Jeffries, "Annadale," Works Progress

Administration of Virginia, Historical Inventory for Culpeper County, Virginia, Culpeper County, Courthouse; McKim, *A Soldier's Recollections*, p. 82.

31. *War of the Rebellion*, vol. 12, pt. 1, pp. 412–17; John S. Mosby to Pauline Mosby, April 1, 1862, John Singleton Mosby Papers, Virginia Historical Society, Richmond; McKim, *A Soldier's Recollections*, 76.

32. *War of the Rebellion*, vol. 12, pt. 1, pp. 412–17; G. Campbell Brown to Mother, April 12, 1862, Polk-Brown-Ewell Papers, Southern Historical Collection, University of North Carolina at Chapel Hill; McKim, *A Soldier's Recollections*, pp. 76–79.

33. *Ibid.*; Welton, *My Heart Is So Rebellious*, p. 90.

34. U.S. Bureau of the Census, *Population Schedules of the Eighth Census, 1860, Virginia [Slave Schedules], Culpeper County*, National Archives Microcopy No. 653, Roll 1389, p. 28; *Eighth Census of the United States, 1860, Schedule 4: Productions of Agriculture During the Year Ending June 1, 1860, Virginia*, National Archives Microcopy, Roll 234, p. 117; Percy G. Hamlin, ed., *The Making of a Soldier: Letters of General R. S. Ewell* (Richmond, 1935), p. 110; G. Campbell Brown to Mother, April 12, 1862, Polk-Brown-Ewell Papers; John S. Mosby to Pauline Mosby, April 1, 1862, Mosby Papers.

35. McKim, *A Soldier's Recollections*, pp. 78–81.

36. *Ibid.*

37. McKim, *A Soldier's Recollections*, pp. vii, 79–81; John B. Cary to Mrs. Wilson M. Cary, March 26, 1862, Cary Papers.

38. Frank M. Myers, *The Comanches: A History of White's Battalion, Virginia Cavalry, Laurel Brigade, Hampton's Division, Army of Northern Virginia, C.S.A.* (Baltimore, 1871), p. 37; Paul M. Steiner, *Medical-Military Portraits of Union and Confederate Generals* (Philadelphia, 1968), pp. 287–88; Jack D. Welsh, *Medical Histories of Confederate Generals* (Kent, Ohio, 1995), 63–66. The best available biography of Ewell is Samuel J. Martin, *The Road to Glory: Confederate General Richard S. Ewell* (Indianapolis, 1991).

39. Hamlin, *The Making of a Soldier*, pp. 109–110; Richard S. Ewell to Joseph E. Johnston, April 8, 1862, Benjamin Stoddart and Richard Stoddart Ewell Papers, Perkins Library, Duke University, Durham, N.C.; Welton, *My Heart Is So Rebellious*, p. 97; *War of the Rebellion*, vol. 12, pt. 3, pp. 846–47. The date of "May" 23 given for the letter in Hamlin's book cannot be correct, as Ewell's division left Culpeper on April 19. Thus the correct date for this letter is probably April 13. For foreign-born troops generally see William L. Burton, *Melting Pot Soldiers: The Union's Ethnic Regiments* (Ames, Iowa, 1988).

40. Johnston, *Narrative*, pp. 109–110; *Confederate Veteran*, 6 (September 1898), p. 418.

41. *War of the Rebellion*, vol. 12, pt. 3, pp. 850–51; Hamlin, *Making of a Soldier*, p. 117.

42. G. Campbell Brown to Mother, April 12, 1862, Richard S. Ewell to Lizinka, April 13, 1862, Polk-Brown-Ewell Papers; Charles Short to Lemuel A. Corbin, April 23, 1862, Coons Family Papers, Virginia Historical Society, Richmond; McKim, *A Soldier's Recollections*, p. 73.

43. Special Orders and Circulars, Special Order 98, April 6, 1862; *War of the Rebellion*, ser. 1, vol. 12, pt. 3, pp. 851–53, 857–58, 868.

44. McKim, *A Soldier's Recollections*, pp. 77, 81–83; Emory M. Thomas, *Bold Dragoon: The Life of J. E. B. Stuart* (New York, 1986), 103; *War of the Rebellion*, vol. 12, pt. 3, p. 868.

45. Camp Henry Account Book, closed April 1862, p. 64; Mrs. Burton Harrison, *Recollections Grave and Gay* (New York, 1911), pp. 77–78; Charles Short to Mary Corbin, April 22, 1862, Charles Short to Lemuel A. Corbin, April 23, 1862, Coons Family Papers; *War of the Rebellion*, ser. 4, vol. 1, pp. 1095–1100.

46. Martha E. Coons to Mollie D. Corbin, April 22, 1862, Coons Family Papers; Minutes

of the Baptist Church of Christ, Criglersville, Culpeper County, April 1862, Alderman Library, University of Virginia, Charlottesville.

47. Charles Short to John Letcher, April 26, 1862, receipt of April 30, 1862 for Clary Ann, Virginia Executive Papers; Charles Short to Lemuel A. Corbin, April 23, 1862, Coons Family Papers.

48. McKim, *A Soldier's Recollections*, pp. 84–85; Martha E. Coons to Mary D. Corbin, April 22, 1862, Coons Family Papers.

49. *War of the Rebellion*, vol. 12, pt. 1, pp. 451–55, pt. 3, pp. 850–57; Torlief S. Holmes, *Horse Soldiers in Blue* (Gaithersburg, Md., 1985), pp. 28–29.

50. John Wiltshire, second affidavit in case of George Smith, Court of Claims, Congressional Jurisdiction Case File 7444, RG 123, National Archives; Daniel A. Grimsley, *Battles in Culpeper County, Virginia, 1861–1865* (Culpeper, 1900), pp. 4–5; Clark B. Hall, "Robert F. Beckham: The Man Who Commanded Stuart's Horse Artillery After Pelham Fell," *Blue & Gray*, IX (December 1991), pp. 34–35; *War of the Rebellion*, vol. 12, pt. 3, pp. 850–57.

51. Grimsley, *Battles in Culpeper*, p. 5; *Population Schedule of the Eighth Census*, pp. 775, 781, 785; Lemuel A. Corbin to Martha E. Coons, May 12, 1862, Coons Family Papers.

52. Bettie Browning to Daniel A. Grimsley, May 11, 1862, Grimsley Family Papers; Charles Short to Mary D. Corbin, May 24, 1862, Sarah T. Parr to Mary D. Corbin, June 10, 1862, Coons Family Papers; *Population Schedule of the Eighth Census*, p. 808; Grimsley, *Battles in Culpeper*, p. 5.

53. Mary A. B. Payne to Martha E. Coons, June 7 [1862], Coons Family Papers; Musick, *6th Virginia Cavalry*, p. 120; Bettie Browning to Daniel A. Grimsley, May 11, 18, 1862, Grimsley Family Papers.

54. Martha E. Coons to Mary D. Corbin, June 8, 19, 1862, Coons Family Papers.

55. Susan Coons to Mary D. Corbin, June 31, 1862, Sarah T. Parr to Mary D. Corbin, June 10, 1862, Coons Family Papers.

56. George M. Williams to Gertrude Williams, May 20, 1862, Williams Family Papers.

57. *Ibid.*, June 10, 11, 12, 17, 20, and 26, 1862.

58. *Ibid.*, June 5, 10, and 26, 1862.

59. *Ibid.*, June 10 and 26, 1862.

60. George M. Williams to Gertrude Williams, July 1, 1862, Williams Family Papers; Riggs, *13th Virginia Infantry*, pp. 15–19, 99–150; Musick, *6th Virginia Cavalry*, p. 120.

61. Paul Glass and Louis C. Singer, eds., *Singing Soldiers: A History of the Civil War in Song* (New York, 1975), pp. 267–69. "Weeping Sad and Lonely, or When This Cruel War is Over," was popular in both North and South with sheet music sales of over one million. It was so melancholy that some army officers forbid their men to sing it in camp.

62. Cecil D. Eby, Jr., ed., *A Virginia Yankee in the Civil War: The Diaries of David Hunter Strother* (Chapel Hill, N.C., 1961), pp. 64–66.

63. Welton, *My Heart Is So Rebellious*, pp. 141–42; *War of the Rebellion*, vol. 12, pt. 3, pp. 450–60, 465–69; Washington *Evening Star*, July 14, 1862, p. 1.

Chapter 5. Occupation

1. Jedediah Hotchkiss, *Make Me a Map of the Valley: The Civil War Journal of Stonewall Jackson's Topographer*, ed. by Archie P. McDonald (Dallas, 1973), pp. 59–63.

2. *The War of the Rebellion: A Compilation of the Official Records of the Union and Confed-*

erate Armies, 70 vols. in 128 books and index (Washington, D.C., 1880–1901, ser. 1, cited hereafter as *War of the Rebellion*, and all references are to Series 1 unless otherwise indicated), vol. 12, pt. 3, pp. 473–74.

3. Ezra J. Warner, *Generals in Blue: Lives of the Union Commanders* (Baton Rouge, La., 1964), pp. 376–77; Wallace J. Schutz and Walter N. Trenerry, *Abandoned by Lincoln: A Military Biography of General John Pope* (Urbana, Ill., 1990), pp. 76–89; [George A. Townsend], "Campaigning with General Pope," *Cornhill Magazine*, VI (December 1862), p. 758; Robert K. Krick, *Stonewall Jackson at Cedar Mountain* (Chapel Hill, 1990), pp. 3–5.

4. Schutz and Trenerry, *Abandoned by Lincoln*, pp. 91–103; Krick, *Stonewall Jackson at Cedar Mountain*, pp. 3–4.

5. New York *Tribune*, July 25, 1862, p. 1; *War of the Rebellion*, vol. 12, pt. 3, p. 915.

6. *War of the Rebellion*, vol. 12, pt. 3, pp. 472–82, 485–94.

7. *War of the Rebellion*, vol. 12, pt. 2, pp. 50–52.

8. *War of the Rebellion*, vol. 12, pt. 3, pp. 500–501; U.S. Senate, *Report of the Joint Committee on the Conduct of the War*, Senate Report No. 108, 37th Cong., 3rd sess. (Washington, D.C., 1863), part 3, 449–91. For a fuller discussion of these orders and circumstances under which they were issued see Daniel E. Sutherland, "Abraham Lincoln, John Pope, and the Origins of Total War," *Journal of Military History*, LVI (October 1992), pp. 567–86, and Christopher Mark Grimsley, "A Directed Severity: The Evolution of Federal Policy Toward Southern Civilians and Property, 1861–1865" (Ph.D. diss., Ohio State University, 1992), pp. 171–232.

9. *War of the Rebellion*, vol. 12, pt. 3, pp. 498–99, 514; Cecil D. Eby, Jr., ed., *A Virginia Yankee in the Civil War: The Diaries of David Hunter Strother* (Chapel Hill, 1961), pp. 69–70; Henry R. Pyne, *Ride to War: The History of the First New Jersey Cavalry*, ed. Earl Schenck Miers (New Brunswick, N.J., 1961), p. 46.

10. New York *Tribune*, July 19, 1862, p. 6, July 21, 1862, p. 4; New York *Herald*, July 20, 1862, p. 1; Mark to Darling Wife, August 7, 1862, Federal Soldiers Letters, Southern Historical Collection, University of North Carolina at Chapel Hill.

11. *Confederate Veteran*, XXV (August 1917), pp. 349–51; Clifford Dowdey and Louis H. Manarin, eds., *The Wartime Papers of R. E. Lee* (Rev. ed., New York, 1961), pp. 239–40, 949; Ella Lonn, *Foreigners in the Union Army* (Baton Rouge, La., 1951), 194; *War of the Rebellion*, vol. 11, pt. 2, p. 936; New York *Herald*, July 29, 1862, p. 5.

12. *War of the Rebellion*, ser. 2, vol. 4, pp. 329–30, 830–31, 836–37; Hudson Strode, *Jefferson Davis: Confederate President* (New York, 1959), pp. 290–91.

13. James Madison Stone, *Personal Recollections of the Civil War* (Boston, 1918), p. 57; New York *Herald*, July 28, 1862, p. 1; *Confederate Veteran*, IX (January 1901), p. 11; John Esten Cooke, *Stonewall Jackson* (1866; New York, 1894), pp. 251–54; Frederic Denison, *Sabre and Spurs: First Regiment Rhode Island Cavalry in the Civil War, 1861–1865* (Central Falls, R.I., 1876), pp. 114–15. The northerner quoted in Cooke was not so much concerned with the effect of this pillaging on the South as with the consequences for the North. He feared that "when the enlistments have expired we shall let loose a den of thieves upon the country."

14. Edward J. Stackpole, *From Cedar Mountain to Antietam* (Harrisburg, Pa., 1959), p. 25; New York *Herald*, July 28, 1862, p. 1; Washington *Evening Star*, August 1, 1862, p. 2; Regimental Order Book, First New Jersey Cavalry, Order No. 164, August 6, 1862, Records of Adjutant General's Office, RG 94, National Archives; Pyne, *Ride to War*, pp. 49–50.

15. Pyne, *Ride to War*, p. 50; Catherine Thom Bartlett, comp., *"My Dear Brother": A Confederate Chronicle* (Richmond, 1952), p. 67; "Philip Slaughter," manuscript in Jane C.

Slaughter Papers, Alderman Library, University of Virginia, Charlottesville; Richmond *Enquirer*, August 5, 1862, p. 2. Eby, *A Virginia Yankee*, p. 81, claims that Confederate soldiers destroyed the Slaughter house, but the family remembered it differently.

16. Percy G. Hamlin, ed., *Making of a Soldier: Letters of General R.S. Ewell* (Richmond, 1935), p. 113; Denison, *Sabre and Spurs*, p. 117.

17. Richmond *Enquirer*, August 5, 1862, pp. 1–2; Denison, *Sabre and Spurs*, p. 116; *Confederate Veteran*, IX (January 1901), p. 11.

18. New York *Herald*, August 7, 1862, p. 2; Cooke, *Stonewall Jackson*, pp. 251–54.

19. George M. Williams to Gertrude Williams, July 26 and 27 and August 5, 1862, George M. Williams Family Papers, in possession of Janet LaValley, Culpeper, Va.

20. Washington *Evening Star*, July 28, 1862, p. 2; Denison, *Sabre and Spurs*, p. 117; Richmond *Enquirer*, August 8, 1862, p. 4.

21. Richmond, *Enquirer*, August 5, 1862, p. 2; August 8, 1862, p. 4; claims of Willis Madden (No. 128), Ira Field (No. 3003), Alexander Jackson (No. 3008), Southern Claims Commission Case Files, 1877–83, Records of Government Accounting Office, Records of Third Auditor's Office, RG 217, National Archives; Myrta Lockett Avary, *A Virginia Girl in the Civil War* (New York, 1903), p. 49. On the issue of rape by soldiers see Thomas P. Lowry, *The Story the Soldiers Wouldn't Tell: Sex in the Civil War* (Mechanicsburg, Pa., 1994), pp. 123–31, and Reid Mitchell, *The Vacant Chair: The Northern Soldier Leaves Home* (New York, 1993), pp. 102–110. Lowry and Mitchell believe the principal victims of rape by northern soldiers were blacks.

22. New York *Herald*, August 7, 1862, p. 2; J. Michael Welton, ed., *"My Heart Is So Rebellious": The Caldwell Letters, 1861–1865* (Warrenton, Va., 1991), pp. 143–44; George M. Williams to Gertrude Williams, August 5, 1862, Williams Family Papers; Richmond *Dispatch*, August 23, 1862; Richmond *Enquirer*, August 5, 1862, p. 1. The young woman is variously described as Miss Slaughter and Miss Stringfellow. It was most likely Slaughter.

23. "Campaigning with Pope," p. 764; George Alfred Townsend, *Campaigns of a Non-Combatant* (New York, 1866), pp. 239–40, 242; Richmond *Dispatch*, August 23, 1862; Richmond *Enquirer*, August 5, 1862, p. 1. Townsend blames the famine conditions on the Confederate army, but he is the only person to suggest as much. But how honest are those who swear allegiance? See Harold M. Hyman, "Deceit in Dixie," *Civil War History*, III (March 1957), pp. 70–75.

24. Claims of William A. Soutter (No. 17,756), Archibald Shaw (No. 14,135), Simeon B. Shaw (No. 14,136), and Matilda G. Hudson (No. 15,194), Southern Claims.

25. Claims of Ryburn Bundy (No. 19,818), George Mars (No. 12,707), Southern Claims; *War of the Rebellion*, Ser. 4, vol. 1, p. 966.

26. William P. Lloyd Diary, July 21, 1862, Southern Historical Collection, University of North Carolina, Chapel Hill; Townsend, *Campaigns of a Non-Combatant*, p. 211; Mark to wife, August 7, 1862, Federal Soldiers' Letters.

27. Pyne, *Ride to War*, pp. 42–46; Denison, *Sabre and Spurs*, p. 115. See generally Hyman, "Deceit in Dixie," pp. 68–70.

28. *War of the Rebellion*, vol. 12, pt. 3, pp. 509, 513, 516–18, 521–22, 525–28, 530, 532, 539–40; Denison,*Sabre and Spurs*, pp. 116–17; Washington *Evening Star*, July 28, 1862, p. 2 and August 1, 1862, p. 2; Eby, *Virginia Yankee*, p. 70; Krick, *Stonewall Jackson at Cedar Mountain*, pp. 5–6.

29. Washington *Evening Star*, August 2, 1862, p. 3.

30. H. G. Ayer Diary, August 7, 10, 1862, Perkins Library, Duke University, Durham, N.C., Laura Virginia Hale, *Four Valiant Years in the Lower Shenandoah Valley, 1861–1865* (Strasburg, Va., 1968), p. 180; Mark to wife, August 7, 1862, Federal Sol-

diers' Letters. For female soldiers generally see Richard Hall, *Patriots in Disguise: Women Warriors of the Civil War* (New York, 1993).

31. Eby, *Virginia Yankee*, pp. 75–76; "Campaigning with Pope," pp. 764–65; Francis C. Kajencki, *Star on Many a Battlefield: Brevet Brigadier General Joseph Kargé in the American Civil War* (Rutherford, N.J., 1980), pp. 60–64; *War of the Rebellion*, vol. 12, pt. 2, pp. 88–89, 92–93, 129–30; *ibid.*, pt. 3, p. 547; Stackpole, *From Cedar Mountain to Antietam*, pp. 34–35.

32. Krick, *Stonewall Jackson at Cedar Mountain*, pp. 13–16; Joseph T. Durkin, ed., *Confederate Chaplain: A War Journal of Rev. James B. Sheeran* (Milwaukee, 1960), pp. 2–3.

33. Krick, *Stonewall Jackson at Cedar Mountain*, pp. 16–21, 25–38; Alexander Hunter, *Johnny Reb and Billy Yank* (New York, 1905), p. 239; James I. Robertson, Jr., *General A. P. Hill: The Story of a Confederate Warrior* (New York, 1987), pp. 100–102.

34. Krick, *Stonewall Jackson at Cedar Mountain*, pp. 31–32, 39–40; Hotchkiss, *Make Me a Map of the Valley*, pp. 65–66; Mary Anna Jackson, *Life and Letters of General Thomas J. Jackson* (New York, 1892), p. 324.

35. Richmond *Times-Dispatch*, August 27, 1911; J. William Jones, "Reminiscences of the Army of Northern Virginia, Paper No. 9, Cedar Run (Slaughter's Mountain)," *Southern Historical Society Papers*, X (January-February 1882), p. 84.

36. Townsend, *Campaigns of a Non-Combatant*, p. 243; Stackpole, *From Cedar Mountain to Antietam*, pp. 34–35; *War of the Rebellion*, vol. 12, pt. 3, pp. 547–61; Krick, *Stonewall Jackson at Cedar Mountain*, 43–50; George H. Gordon, *Brook Farm to Cedar Mountain in the War of the Great Rebellion* (Boston, 1883), p. 314.

37. "Campaigning with Pope," pp. 765–66.

38. Frederic Denison, *A Chaplain's Experiences in the Union Army* (Providence, R.I., 1893), pp. 18–19; Susan Leigh Blackford, comp., *Letters from Lee's Army, or Memoir of Life in and Out of the Army in Virginia During the War Between the States* (1947; New York, 1962), p. 104; Walter W. Lenoir Diary, January 10, 1863, Lenoir Family Papers, Southern Historical Collection, University of North Carolina at Chapel Hill.

39. "Campaigning with Pope," pp. 765–66; Townsend, *Campaigns of a Non-Combatant*, pp. 248–51; John S. Robson, *How a One-Legged Rebel Lives: Reminiscences of the Civil War* (Durham, N.C., 1898), pp. 94–96.

40. *Ibid.*

41. Descriptions of the battlefield may be found in Stackpole, *Cedar Mountain to Antietam*, pp. 58–60; Frederic Denison, *The Battle of Cedar Mountain: A Personal View* (Providence, R.I., 1881), pp. 11–13; Gordon, *Brook Farm to Cedar Mountain*, pp. 284–85. Krick, *Stonewall Jackson at Cedar Mountain*, offers the most comprehensive analysis of the battle. For brief but useful accounts see Time-Life Books, *Lee Takes Command: From Seven Days to Second Bull Run* (Alexandria, Va., 1984), pp. 101–109; J. Gay Seabourne, "The Battle of Cedar Mountain," *Civil War Times, Illustrated*, V (December 1966), pp. 28–41. Krick's book includes the best tactical maps of the battle.

42. Krick, *Stonewall Jackson at Cedar Mountain*, pp. 46–50; Frank M. Myers, *The Comanches: A History of White's Battalion, Virginia Cavalry, Laurel Brigade, Hampton's Division, Army of Northern Virginia, C.S.A.* (Baltimore, 1871), p. 88; U.S. Bureau of the Census, *Population Schedule of the Eighth Census, 1860, Culpeper County, Virginia*, National Archives Microcopy No. 653, Roll 1341, p. 888.

43. *War of the Rebellion*, vol. 12, pt. 2, pp. 227–29; Jubal A. Early, *Narrative of the War Between the States* (1912; New York, 1989), pp. 93–95; Krick, *Stonewall Jackson at Cedar Mountain*, pp. 75–76; David F. Riggs, *13th Virginia Infantry* (Lynchburg, 1988), pp. 20, 108, 110.

44. Jones, "Reminiscences," pp. 85; Walter W. Lenoir to brother, August 19, 1862, Lenoir Family Papers.

45. Samuel D. Buck, *With the Old Confederates: Actual Experiences of a Captain in the Line* (Baltimore, 1925), p. 44.

46. *War of the Rebellion*, vol. 12, pt. 2, pp. 228–29, 233–34; Early, *Narrative*, pp. 95–97; Krick, *Stonewall Jackson at Cedar Mountain*, pp. 86–87; Myers, *The Comanches*, pp. 89–90.

47. Krick, *Stonewall Jackson at Cedar Mountain*, pp. 95–99; McHenry Howard, *Recollections of a Maryland Confederate Soldier and Staff Officer under Johnston, Jackson, and Lee* (Baltimore, 1914), pp. 169–74. Not all of Winder's men mourned his passing. Some considered him an overly strict disciplinarian and claimed that he had been "spotted"–or targeted–for death in battle by his own men. See John O. Casler, *Four Years in the Stonewall Brigade* (1893; Dayton, Ohio, 1971), pp. 101–102, 104.

48. Denison, *Cedar Mountain*, pp. 19, 23.

49. Blackford, comp., *Letters from Lee's Army*, pp. 103, 110; William C. Oates, *The War Between the Union and the Confederacy* (New York, 1905), p. 129; J. P. Thompson, "Byrd Eastham Place–Cloverdale," Works Progress Administration of Virginia, Historical Inventory for Culpeper County, Virginia, Culpeper County Courthouse.

50. Townsend, *Campaigns of a Non-Combatant*, pp. 264–65; Margaret Jeffries, "Inskeep House," Works Progress Administration of Virginia; Mary Stevens Jones and Mildred Conway Jones, eds., *Historic Culpeper* (Culpeper, 1974), p. 109; David H. Strother, "Personal Recollections of the War, Part 8," *Harper's Magazine*, XXXV (August 1867), p. 292; Gordon, *Brook Farm to Cedar Mountain*, p. 285; Krick, *Stonewall Jackson at Cedar Mountain*, pp. 100–101, 411 n. 86. Some sources identify Curtis as George Curtis, but the only Curtis living near Inskeep is Abraham. Some sources also say a small boy (his son) accompanied him in flight, but no children resided in the Curtis household. There is also confusion in local lore between this incident and another one in September 1863 (see Chapter Ten).

51. William H. Tatum to Louisiana Tatum, October 9, 1862, William Henry Tatum Papers, Virginia Historical Society, Richmond; Charles L. Perdue, Jr. et al., eds., *Weevils in the Wheat: Interviews with Virginia Ex-Slaves* (Charlottesville, 1976), p. 335; U.S. Bureau of the Census, *Population Schedule of the Eighth Census, 1860, Virginia [Slave Schedule]*, Culpeper County, National Archives Microcopy No. 653, Roll 1389, p. 22; Jones and Jones, *Historic Culpeper*, p. 92; William Nalle, *Tales of Old Culpeper* (Culpeper, 1974), p. 31.

52. Townsend, *Campaigns of a Non-Combatant*, pp. 254–55; Washington *Evening Star*, August 11, 1862, p. 2; claim of Mary L. Payne (No. 22,128), Southern Claims; Eby, *Virginia Yankee*, p. 76.

53. Lloyd Diary, August 9, 1862.

54. Gordon, *Brook Farm*, p. 314; Strother, "Personal Recollections," p. 284; Stephen D. Engle, *Yankee Dutchman: The Life of Franz Sigel* (Fayetteville, Ark., 1993), pp. 131–34; *War of the Rebellion*, vol. 12, pt. 2, pp. 25–26. For the controversy over Banks's understanding of Pope's plan see Fred Harvey Harrington, *Fighting Politician: Major General N. P. Banks* (Philadelphia, 1948), pp. 81–83; Schutz and Trenerry, *Abandoned by Lincoln*, pp. 115–17; U.S. Senate, *Report of the Joint Committee on the Conduct of the War, Senate Report 142, 38th Cong., 2nd sess.* (Washington, D.C., 1865), Pt. 3, pp. 44–54.

55. "Letters of Davidson," p. 29; *War of the Rebellion*, vol. 12, pt. 2, pp. 226, 230–31, 234; Early, *Narrative*, pp. 98–99. A good biography of Pegram is Peter S. Carmichael, *Lee's Young Artillerist: William R. J. Pegram* (Charlottesville, 1995).

56. James Huffman, *Ups and Downs of a Confederate Soldier* (New York, 1940), pp. 58–59; Walter W. Lenoir to brother, August 19, 1862. Lenoir Diary, January 10, 1863, Lenoir Family Papers.

57. *War of the Rebellion*, vol. 12, pt. 2, pp. 226, 230–31, 234; Early, *Narrative*, pp. 98–99; Krick, *Stonewall Jackson at Cedar Mountain*, pp. 194–96; Buck, *With the Old Confeds*, p. 44.

58. *War of the Rebellion*, vol. 12, pt. 2, p. 234; Krick, *Stonewall Jackson at Cedar Mountain*, pp. 196–201; Early, *Narrative*, pp. 99–100; Buck, *With the Old Confeds*, pp. 44–45.

59. Krick, *Stonewall Jackson at Cedar Mountain*, pp. 202–218; Robert L. Dabney, *Life and Campaigns of Lieut. Gen. Thomas J. Jackson* (New York, 1866), pp. 500–501; G. F. R. Henderson, *Stonewall Jackson and the American Civil War* (1898; New York, 1949), pp. 409–11; Blackford, *Letters from Lee's Army*, pp. 104–105.

60. Robertson, *General A. P. Hill*, pp. 105–107; Eby, *Virginia Yankee*, p. 76; Strother, "Reminiscences," p. 284.

61. Walter W. Lenoir to brother, August 18, 1862, Lenoir Diary, January 10, 1863, Lenoir Family Papers.

62. Milo M. Quaife, ed., *From the Cannon's Mouth: The Civil War Letters of General Alpheus S. Williams* (Detroit, 1959), p. 100; *War of the Rebellion*, vol. 12, pt. 2, pp. 137, 146–47, 151–52; *Medical and Surgical History of the War of the Rebellion*, 2 vols. in 12 books (Washington, D.C., 1870–83), vol. 2, pt. 1, pp. 100, 117, and vol. 2, pt. 2, p. 85.

63. *War of the Rebellion*, vol. 12, pt. 2, pp. 151–52, 154; Julian W. Hinkley, *A Narrative of Service with the Third Wisconsin Infantry* (Madison, 1912), pp. 32–34; Russell Duncan, ed., *Blue-Eyed Child of Fortune: The Civil War Letters of Colonel Robert Gould Shaw* (Athens, Ga., 1992), pp. 229–30; Anthony J. Milano, "Letters from the Harvard Regiments. Part Two: The Second Massachusetts Regiment—From the Outbreak of War Through Cedar Mountain," *Civil War*, XIII (June 1988), p. 45.

64. *War of the Rebellion*, vol. 12, pt. 2, p. 161; Warner, *Generals in Blue*, p. 169; *Medical and Surgical History*, vol. 2, pt. 2, p. 830; Townsend, *Campaigns of a Non-Combatant*, p. 269; Hinkley, *Narrative of Service*, pp. 32–34; Quaife, *From the Cannon's Mouth*, p. 100. For more on Geary see Paul Beers, "General John W. Geary," *Civil War Times*, IX (June 1970), pp. 10–16; and William A. Blair, ed., *A Politician Goes to War: The Civil War Letters of John White Geary* (University Park, Pa., 1995).

65. Quaife, *From the Cannon's Mouth*, p. 101; Arthur A. Kent, ed., *Three Years With Company K: Sergt. Austin C. Stearns, Company K, 13th Mass. Infantry* (Rutherford, N.J., 1976), pp. 86–87.

66. Lenoir Diary, January 10, 1863; Susan W. Benson, ed., *Berry Benson's Civil War Book: Memoirs of a Confederate Scout and Sharpshooter* (Athens, Ga., 1992), p. 23.

67. Krick, *Stonewall Jackson at Cedar Mountain*, pp. 251–55, 283–86. The best biography of Early is Charles C. Osborne, *Jubal: The Life and Times of General Jubal A. Early, CSA, Defender of the Lost Cause* (Baton Rouge, La., 1994), although Gary W. Gallagher's forthcoming biography may be the definitive one.

68. Robson, *How a One-Legged Rebel Lives*, p. 94; Kent, *Three Years With Company K*, pp. 86–87; Townsend, *Campaigns of a Non-Combatant*, p. 258.

69. *War of the Rebellion*, vol. 12, pt. 2, pp. 234–35; Benson, *Civil War Book*, p. 23; Buck, *With the Old Confeds*, p. 45.

70. *War of the Rebellion*, vol. 141, pp. 231, 234–35; Early, *Narrative*, p. 100; Jones, "Reminiscences," p. 87; Buck, *With the Old Confeds*, p. 45; *Confederate Veteran*, X (January 1902), pp. 35–36; Krick, *Stonewall Jackson at Cedar Mountain*, pp. 252–55, 260–63; Stephen Z. Starr, *The Union Cavalry in the Civil War*, 3 vols. (Baton Rouge, La., 1979–85), III, pp. 294–95.

71. *War of the Rebellion*, vol. 12, pt. 2, p. 184; Jones, "Reminiscences," p. 87; Engle, *Yankee Dutchman*, p. 135; James I. Robertson, Jr., ed., " 'The Boy Artillerist': Letters of Colonel William Pegram, C.S.A.," *Virginia Magazine of History and Biography*, IIC

(April 1990), pp. 227–28; Krick, *Stonewall Jackson at Cedar Mountain*, pp. 304–306; Myers, *Comanches*, pp. 90–91.

72. Krick, *Stonewall Jackson at Cedar Mountain*, pp. 299–319; Robert Stiles, *Four Years Under Marse Robert* (New York, 1904), p. 189; Early, *Narrative*, pp. 100–101; *Confederate Veteran*, X (January 1902), p. 36.

73. Blackford, *Letters from Lee's Army*, pp. 108–109; Walter W. Lenoir to brother, August 19, 1862, Lenoir Family Papers.

74. Cornelius M. Buckley, trans., *A Frenchman, a Chaplain, a Rebel: The War Letters of Père Louis-Hippolyte Gache* (Chicago, 1981), pp. 103–31.

75. Jackson, *Life and Letters*, p. 326; George M. Neese, *Three Years in the Confederate Horse Artillery* (New York, 1911), pp. 87–88.

76. Eby, *Virginia Yankee*, p. 78; *Medical and Surgical History*, vol. 2, pt. 2, pp. 537–38; Townsend, *Campaigns of a Non-Combatant*, pp. 258–65.

77. Townsend, *Campaigns of a Non-Combatant*, p. 264.

Chapter 6. Liberation

1. Robert K. Krick, *Stonewall Jackson at Cedar Mountain* (Chapel Hill, 1990), pp. 326–32; Susan Leigh Blackford, comp., *Letters from Lee's Army, or Memoirs of Life In and Out of the Army in Virginia During the War Between the States* (1947; New York, 1962), pp. 108–109.

2. Jedediah Hotchkiss, *Make Me A Map of the Valley: The Civil War Journal of Stonewall Jackson's Topographer*, ed. Archie P. McDonald (Dallas, 1973), p. 67; Joseph T. Durkin, ed., *Confederate Chaplain: A War Journal of Rev. James B. Sheeran* (Milwaukee, 1960), p. 4.

3. [George A. Townsend], "Campaigning with General Pope, *Cornhill Magazine*, VI (December 1862), pp. 769–70; Cecil D. Eby, Jr., ed., *A Virginia Yankee in the Civil War: The Diaries of David Hunter Strother* (Chapel Hill, 1961), pp. 80–81; George A. Townsend, *Campaigns of a Non-Combatant* (New York, 1866), pp. 270–73; *New York Herald*, August 13, 1862, p. 8, August 15, 1862, p. 8.

4. R. M. Millan to Kate M. Grady, August 14, 1862, Catherine Jane (McGeachy) Buie Papers, Perkins Library, Duke University, Durham, N.C.; Townsend, *Campaigns of a Non-Combatant*, p. 273.

5. Krick, *Stonewall Jackson at Cedar Mountain*, p. 334; John N. Opie, *A Rebel Cavalryman with Lee, Stuart and Jackson* (Chicago, 1899), p. 40; Constant C. Hanks to sister, September 26, 1862, Constant C. Hanks Papers, Perkins Library, Duke University, Durham, N.C., Cornelius M. Buckley, trans., *A Frenchman, a Chaplain, a Rebel: The War Letters of Père Louis-Hippolyte Gache* (Chicago, 1981), p. 130; George F. Noyes, *The Bivouac and the Battlefield; or Campaign Sketches in Virginia and Maryland* (New York, 1863), p. 76.

6. Charles L. Perdue, Jr., et al., eds., *Weevils in the Wheat: Interviews with Virginia Ex-Slaves* (Charlottesville, 1976), p. 335.

7. Frank M. Myers, *The Comanches: A History of White's Battalion, Virginia Cavalry, Laurel Brigade, Hampton's Division, Army of Northern Virginia, C.S.A.* (Baltimore, 1871), p. 91; Krick, *Stonewall Jackson at Cedar Mountain*, pp. 338–39; James I. Robertson, Jr., *General A. P. Hill: The Story of a Confederate Warrior* (New York, 1987), p. 109.

8. Henry Kyd Douglas, *I Rode with Stonewall* (Chapel Hill, N.C., 1940), p. 128.

9. Blackford, *Letters from Lee's Army*, p. 109; Myers, *The Comanches*, pp. 94–95.

10. J. P. Thompson, "Byrd Eastham Place–Cloverdale," Works Progress Administration of Virginia, Historical Inventory for Culpeper County, Virginia, Culpeper County Court-

house; Frederic Denison, *The Battle of Cedar Mountain: A Personal View* (Providence, R.I., 1881), pp. 42–43; Blackford, *Letters from Lee's Army*, p. 110.

11. J. P. Thompson, "The Wiseman Place," "Hudson Place," and Margaret Jeffries, "Forest Grove," Works Progress Administration Historical Inventory; U.S. Bureau of the Census, *Population Schedule of the Eighth Census, 1860, Culpeper County, Virginia*, National Archives Microcopy No. 653, Roll 1341, p. 884.

12. Frederic Denison, *Sabre and Spurs: First Regiment Rhode Island Cavalry in the Civil War, 1861–1865* (Central Falls, R.I., 1876), pp. 127–28; *Medical and Surgical History of the War of the Rebellion*, 2 vols. in 12 books (Washington, D.C., 1870–83), Appendix to vol. 1, pt. 1, p. 121; case of Lucy Colvin (No. 21,015), Southern Claims Commission Case Files, 1877–83, Records of the G.A.O., Records of the Third Auditor's Office, RG 217, National Archives.

13. Mary S. Jones and Mildred Conway Jones, eds., *Historic Culpeper* (Culpeper, 1974), p. 93; William Nalle, *Tales of Old Culpeper*, (n.p., 1974), pp. 30–31; Eby, *A Virginia Yankee*, p. 79; David H. Strother, "Personal Recollections of the War, Part 8," *Harper's Magazine*, XXXV (August 1867), pp. 287–88; Mrs. Berkeley G. Calfee, *Confederate History of Culpeper County in the War Between the States* (Culpeper, 1948), p. 3; *Population Schedule of the Eighth Census*, p. 863.

14. *Medical and Surgical History*, vol. 2, pt. 2, p. 137; "Campaigning with General Pope," pp. 768–79; Townsend, *Campaigns of a Non-Combatant*, pp. 267, 270; claim of Mary L. Payne (No. 22,128), Southern Claims; Washington *Evening Star*, August 11 1862, p. 3.

15. Washington *Evening Star*, August 20, 1862, p. 2; Index to Virginia Hospitals, p. 18, Virginia Hospital Record Books, No. 640, pp. 35–41, 45–48, Field Records of Hospitals, RG 94, National Archives; *Medical and Surgical History*, Appendix to vol. 1, pt. 1, p. 111.

16. Townsend, *Campaigns of a Non-Combatant*, pp. 267–68.

17. *Ibid.*

18. David F. Riggs, *13th Virginia Infantry* (Lynchburg, 1988), pp. 88, 113, 121, 126; *Population Schedule of the Eighth Census*, pp. 778, 798, 842; U.S. Bureau of the Census, *Eighth Census of the United States, 1860, Schedule 4: Productions of Agriculture During the Year Ending June 1, 1860, Virginia*, National Archives Microcopy T-1132, Roll 6, pp. 119–120; U.S. Bureau of the Census, *Population Schedule of the Eighth Census, 1860, Virginia [Slave Schedule], Culpeper County*, National Archives Microcopy No. 653, Roll 1389, pp. 4, 34, 38; Raleigh T. Green, comp., *Genealogical and Historical Notes on Culpeper County, Virginia* (1900; Baltimore, 1958), p. 58.

19. Strother, "Personal Recollections," pp. 288–89; Douglas, *I Rode with Stonewall*, p. 127.

20. Strother, "Personal Recollections," p. 289; Hotchkiss, *Make Me a Map of the Valley*, pp. 67–68; Krick, *Stonewall Jackson at Cedar Mountain*, pp. 343–48; Rufus Mead Diaries, August 13, 1862, Rufus Mead Papers, Library of Congress; New York *Herald*, August 13, 1862, p. 8; Russell Duncan, ed., *Blue-Eyed Child of Fortune: The Civil War Letters of Colonel Robert Gould Shaw* (Athens, Ga., 1992), p. 231.

21. Krick, *Stonewall Jackson at Cedar Mountain*, p. 343; John S. Clark to Nathaniel P. Banks, August 11, 1862, Nathaniel Prentice Banks Papers, Library of Congress; Townsend, *Campaigns of a Non-Combatant*, pp. 273, 276.

22. Jedediah Hotchkiss to Sarah Ann Hotchkiss, August 16, 1862, Jedediah Hotchkiss Papers, Library of Congress, Sheeran, *Confederate Chaplain*, pp. 2, 4–5; David S. Sparks, ed., *Inside Lincoln's Army: The Diary of Marsena Rudolph Patrick, Provost Marshal General, Army of the Potomac* (New York, 1964), p. 122; Jubal Early, *Narrative of the War Between the States* (1912; Wilmington, N.C., 1989), p. 102; Hotchkiss, *Make Me a Map of the Valley*, pp. 67–68.

23. Townsend, *Campaigns of a Non-Combatant*, pp. 273–76; Blackford, comp., *Letters from Lee's Army*, pp. 110–11; Fitzgerald Ross, *Cities and Camps of the Confederate States*, ed. Richard B. Harwell (Urbana, Ill., 1958), p. 171; David E. Johnston, *The Story of a Confederate Boy in the Civil War* (Portland, Ore., 1914), p. 188.

24. Duncan, *Blue-Eyed Child of Fortune*, pp. 234–35; R. M. Millan to Kate M. Grady, August 14, 1862, Buie Papers.

25. James M. Binford to Carrie and Annie Gwathmey, August 13, 1862, Gwathmey Family Papers, Virginia Historical Society, Richmond; Alfred Kelly to Williamson Kelly, August 10, 1862, Williamson Kelly Papers, Perkins Library, Duke University, Durham, N.C.

26. Walter W. Lenoir Diary, January 10, 1863, Lenoir Family Papers, Southern Historical Collection, University of North Caroline at Chapel Hill.

27. Forrest P. Connor, ed., "Letters of Lieutenant Robert H. Miller to His Family, 1861–1862," *Virginia Magazine of History and Biography*, LXX (January 1962), pp. 88–90.

28. John Esten Cooke, *Stonewall Jackson* (1866; New York, 1894), pp. 266–67; Mary Anna Jackson, *Life and Letters of General Thomas J. Jackson* (New York, 1892), pp. 326–27; Percy G. Hamlin, ed., *The Making of a Soldier: Letters of General R. S. Ewell* (Richmond, 1935), p. 114.

29. Edward J. Stackpole, *From Cedar Mountain to Antietam* (Harrisburg, Pa., 1959), p. 75; Nathaniel P. Banks to wife, August 16, 1862, John S. Clark to Nathaniel P. Banks, August 12, 1862, Banks Papers; Strother, "Personal Recollections," 290; *War of the Rebellion*, vol. 12, pt. 3, p. 568.

30. John P. Hatch to father, August 13, 1862, John Porter Hatch Papers, Library of Congress; William P. Lloyd Diary, August 10, 1862, Southern Historical Collection, University of North Carolina at Chapel Hill; Krick, *Stonewall Jackson at Cedar Mountain*, p. 376; Sparks, *Inside Lincoln's Army*, p. 122; Samuel Gilpin Diary, August 12, 1862, E. N. Gilpin Papers, Library of Congress.

31. Krick, *Stonewall Jackson at Cedar Mountain*, pp. 351–56; Royall W. Figg, *"Where Men Only Dare to Go!"; or the Story of a Boy Company* (Richmond, 1885), p. 64.

32. *War of the Rebellion: A Compilation of the Official Records of the Union and Confederate Armies*, 70 vols. in 128 books and index (Washington, D.C., 1880–1901), ser. 1., vol. 12, pt. 3, pp. 564–65, 569, 571–72, 575–76 (cited hereafter as *War of the Rebellion*, and all references are to Series 1 unless otherwise indicated); Milo M. Quaife, ed., *From the Cannon's Mouth: The Civil War Letters of General Alpheus S. Williams* (Detroit, 1959), p. 105.

33. Percy H. Epler, *The Life of Clara Barton* (New York, 1946), pp. 34–35; Blanche Colton Williams, *Clara Barton: Daughter of Destiny* (Philadelphia, 1941), pp. 70–73; Stephen B. Oates, *A Woman of Valor: Clara Barton and the Civil War* (New York, 1994), pp. 58–63; Elizabeth Brown Pryor, *Clara Barton: Professional Angel* (Philadelphia, 1987), pp. 87–89.

34. Oates, *Woman of Valor*, pp. 61–64; Pryor, *Clara Barton*, pp. 89–91.

35. *War of the Rebellion*, vol. 12, pt. 3, pp. 571, 598; George E. Turner, *Victory Rode the Rails: The Strategic Place of the Railroads in the Civil War* (New York, 1953), pp. 192–98; Angus J. Johnston, III, *Virginia Railroads in the Civil War* (Chapel Hill, 1961), pp. 34–35; James A. Ward, *That Man Haupt: A Biography of Herman Haupt* (Baton Rouge, La., 1973), p. 124; Herman Haupt to wife, August 19, 1862, Lewis Muhlenberg Haupt Family Papers, Library of Congress; *Report of the Joint Committee on the Conduct of the War*, Senate Report No. 108, 37th Cong., 3rd sess. (Washington, D.C., 1863), pt. 2, p. 371.

36. Strother, "Personal Recollections," pp. 290–91; Krick, *Stonewall Jackson at Cedar Mountain*, 224; *War of the Rebellion*, vol. 12, pt. 3, p. 579; Sparks, *Inside Lincoln's Army*,

p. 122; Denison, *Sabre and Spurs*, p. 130; H. G. Ayer Diary, August 18, 1862, Perkins Library, Duke University, Durham, N.C.; George F. Noyes, *The Bivouac and the Battlefield; or Campaign Sketches in Virginia and Maryland* (New York, 1863), pp. 70–73.

37. Lloyd Diary, August 14, 1862; Strother, "Personal Recollections," p. 291; Eby, *Virginia Yankee*, pp. 81–82; Sparks, *Inside Lincoln's Army*, p. 123; "Philip Slaughter," in Jane C. Slaughter Papers, Alderman Library, University of Virginia, Charlottesville.

38. Noyes, *Bivouac and Battlefield*, pp. 62–63, 68.

39. John O. Beatty, *John Esten Cooke, Virginia* (1922; New York, 1949), p. 89; J. Michael Welton, ed., *"My Heart Is So Rebellious": The Caldwell Letters, 1861–1865* (Warrenton, Va., 1991), pp. 150–51.

40. Strother, "Personal Recollections," p. 291; Eby, *Virginia Yankee*, p. 81; Mary Jane Bouldin, "Lynchburg, Virginia: A City in War, 1861–1865" (M.A. thesis, East Carolina Univ., 1976), pp. 12–13; Mary Elizabeth Massey, *Refugee Life in the Confederacy* (Baton Rouge, La., 1964), pp. 5, 77; *Confederate Veteran*, XXXI (December 1923), p. 466.

41. Constant Hanks to sister, September 26, 1862, Hanks Papers; Strother, "Personal Recollections," p. 290.

42. Noyes, *Bivouac and Battlefield*, pp. 73–76.

43. *Ibid.*; Strother, "Personal Recollections," p. 291.

44. Jedediah Hotchkiss to Sarah Ann Hotchkiss, August 9, 1862, Hotchkiss Papers; Strother, "Personal Recollections," p. 289.

45. [William D. Wallach] to Henry W. Halleck, August 14, 1862, Consolidated Correspondence File, Box 222, RG 692, National Archives. One of the few recorded instances of an attempt at systematic inventory came in early August at two farms along the Rappahannock, one of them belonging to John Kelly. Why these two farms were selected is unclear, because both were owned by Rebels. See Ayer Diary, August 3, 1862, and inventories in back of diary.

46. U.S. Adjutant General, *General Orders Affecting the Volunteer Force, 1862* (Washington, D.C., 1863), pp. 102–103; *War of the Rebellion*, vol. 12, pt. 3, pp. 573, 577; *New York Herald*, August 17, 1862, p. 1; *Washington Evening Star*, August 18, 1862, p. 2.

47. *War of the Rebellion*, vol. 12, pt. 2, pp. 329–30, 551–52; *ibid.*, pt. 3, pp. 591, 598, 928–30; Emory M. Thomas, *Bold Dragoon: The Life of J. E. B. Stuart* (New York, 1986), pp. 142–44.

48. David H. Strother, "Personal Recollections of the War, Part 9," *Harper's Magazine*, XXXV (November 1867), p. 704; Sparks, *Inside Lincoln's Army*, p. 125; Noyes, *Bivouac and Battlefield*, pp. 80–82.

49. Julian W. Hinkley, *A Narrative of Service with the Third Wisconsin Infantry* (Madison, 1912), pp. 38–39; Sparks, *Inside Lincoln's Army*, p. 124; Gregory A. Coco, ed., *Through Blood and Fire: The Civil War Letters of Major Charles J. Mills, 1862–1865* (Gettysburg, 1982), pp. 7–9; *War of the Rebellion*, vol. 12, pt. 3, p. 603.

50. Darius Starr to mother, August 18, 1862, Darius Starr Papers, Perkins Library, Duke University, Durham, N.C.

51. Case of Anne C. Brandt (No. 21,180), Southern Claims; Denison, *Sabre and Spurs*, p. 131; Theodore B. Gates, *The "Ulster Guard" and the War of the Rebellion* (New York, 1879), p. 241; *Confederate Veteran*, VIII (September 1900), pp. 399–400. For black refugees generally see Ervin L. Jordan, Jr., *Black Confederates and Afro-Yankees in Civil War Virginia* (Charlottesville, 1995), pp. 69–90.

52. Noyes, *Bivouac and Battlefield*, pp. 82–84.

53. Eugene M. Scheel, *Culpeper: A Virginia County's History Through 1920* (Culpeper, 1982), p. 71; Calfee, *Confederate History of Culpeper*, pp. 4–5.

54. *New York Herald*, August 26, 1862, p. 1.

55. *War of the Rebellion*, vol. 12, pt. 3, pp. 940–41; Blackford, *Letters from Lee's Army*, pp. 112–14; G. F. R. Henderson, *Stonewall Jackson and the American Civil War* (1898; New York, 1949), pp. 423–27; Cooke, *Stonewall Jackson*, pp. 269–70; Abner C. Hopkins Diary, August 19, 1862, Virginia Historical Society, Richmond.

56. Thomas, *Bold Dragoon*, pp. 144–45; Henry B. McClellan, *Life and Campaigns of Major General J. E. B. Stuart* (Boston, 1885), p. 92; Woodford B. Hackley, *The Little Fork Rangers: A Sketch of Company "D" Fourth Virginia Cavalry* (Richmond, 1927), p. 44; *War of the Rebellion*, vol. 12, pt. 2, pp. 89–90, 726–27; *ibid.*, pt. 3, pp. 940–41; Douglas S. Freeman, *R. E. Lee: A Biography*, 4 vols. (New York, 1934), II, pp. 288–89; Samuel D. Buck, *With the Old Confeds: Actual Experiences of a Captain in the Line* (Baltimore, 1925), p. 48; Philip F. Brown, *Reminiscences of the War of 1861–1865* (Blue Ridge, Va., c. 1910), p. 18.

57. Richmond *Dispatch*, August 25, 1862, p. 1; Alexander D. Betts, *Experiences of a Confederate Chaplain, 1861–1864* (n.p., n.d.), p. 14; Daniel A. Grimsley, *Battles in Culpeper County, Virginia, 1861–1865* (Culpeper, 1900), p. 4; Helen Jeffries Klitch, ed., "Joseph Arthur Jeffries' Fauquier County, Virginia, 1840–1919," p. 16, typescript in author's possession; J. P. Thompson, "Hudson Place," Works Progress Administration of Virginia; Heros von Borcke, *Memoirs of the Confederate War for Independence*, 2 vols. (New York, 1866), I, pp. 110–11, Stuart Wright, trans., *Colonel Heros Von Borcke's Journal, 26 April-8 October 1862*, (Winston-Salem, N.C., 1981), p. 11.

58. Andrew J. Gillespie to Susan Gillespie, November 13, 1862, Randall Family Papers, Alderman Library, University of Virginia, Charlottesville, William H. Tatum to Louisiana Tatum, October 9, 1862, William Henry Tatum Papers, Virginia Historical Society, Richmond; Richmond *Dispatch*, August 25, 1862, p. 1; John B. Magruder to father, December 4, 1862, John Bowie Magruder Papers, Perkins Library, Duke University, Durham, N.C.

59. Brown, *Reminiscences*, pp. 18–19; Mills Lane, ed., *"Dear Mother: Don't Grieve About Me": Letters from Georgia Soldiers in the Civil War* (Savannah, 1977), p. 181; Figg, *Story of a Boy Company*, p. 64; Spencer G. Welch, *A Confederate Surgeon's Letters to His Wife* (New York, 1911), p. 20; P. Williams to William J. Hanks, August 23, 1862, Thomas Jonathan Jackson Papers, Perkins Library, Duke University, Durham, N.C.; Frank Moore, comp., *The Civil War in Song and Story, 1861–1865* (New York, 1889), p. 248.

60. None of the sources for the Mason incident agree exactly on the details. I have provided what seems to be the most likely scenario as drawn from William M. Owen, *In Camp and Battle with the Washington Artillery of New Orleans* (Boston, 1885), pp. 101–102; Gilbert M. Sorrel, *Recollections of a Confederate Staff Officer* (New York, 1905), p. 96; Brown, *Reminiscences*, p. 19; Culpeper *Exponent*, March 7, 1902, p. 3; John W. Stevens, *Reminiscences of the Civil War: A Soldier in Hood's Texas Brigade, Army of Northern Virginia* (Hillsboro, Tex., 1902), pp. 48–50; Francis W. Dawson, *Reminiscences of Confederate Service, 1861–1865*, ed. Bell I. Wiley (Baton Rouge, La., 1980), pp. 59–61; Blackford, *Letters from Lee's Army*, pp. 119–20; *Supplement to the Official Records of the Union and Confederate Armies*, 6 vols. (Wilmington, N.C., 1994), II, pp. 770–72.

Chapter 7. Lost in Admiration

1. *War of the Rebellion: A Compilation of the Official Records of the Union and Confederate Armies*, 70 vols. in 128 books and index (Washington, D.C., 1880–1901, ser. 1,

cited hereafter as *War of the Rebellion*, and all references are to Series I unless otherwise indicated), vol. 12, pt. 3, p. 552; Philip F. Brown, *Reminiscences of the War of
1861–1865* (Blue Ridge, Va, c. 1910), pp. 18–19.

2. John Esten Cooke, *Stonewall Jackson* (1866; New York, 1894), p. 270; Samuel D.
Buck, *With the Old Confeds: Actual Experiences of a Captain in the Line* (Baltimore,
1925), p. 48.

3. Heros von Borcke, *Memoirs of the Confederate War for Independence*, 2 vols. (1866;
New York, 1938), I, pp. 115–19; Henry B. McClellan, *Life and Campaigns of Major
General J. E. B. Stuart* (Boston, 1885), p. 93; Robert E. Lee to Mary Custis Lee, Au-
gust 25, 1862, Robert Edward Lee Papers, Virginia Historical Society, Richmond;
Richard W. Waldrop to father, August 24, 1862, Richard Woolfolk Waldrop Papers,
Southern. Historical Collection, University of North Carolina at Chapel Hill.

4. *War of the Rebellion*, vol. 12, pt. 2, pp. 552–53; Willard Glazier, *Three Years in the Fed-
eral Cavalry* (New York, 1874), p. 89; Borcke, *Memoirs*, I, pp. 119–20; Cecil D. Eby,
Jr., ed., *A Virginia Yankee in the Civil War: The Diaries of David Hunter Strother* (Chapel
Hill, 1961), p. 84.

5. John C. Ropes, *The Army Under Pope* (New York, 1889), pp. 36–37; George M.
Neese, *Three Years in the Confederate Horse Artillery* (New York, 1911), pp. 98–100;
James Longstreet, *From Manassas to Appomattox: Memoirs of the Civil War in America*,
ed. James I. Robertson, Jr. (Bloomington, Ind., 1960), p. 164; Thomas C. Elder to
Anna F. Elder, August 24, 1862, Thomas Claybrook Elder Papers, Virginia Historical
Society, Richmond.

6. George F. Noyes, *The Bivouac and the Battlefield; or Campaign Sketches in Virginia and
Maryland* (New York, 1863), pp. 88–98.

7. William M. Owen, *In Camp and Field with the Washington Artillery of New Orleans*
(Boston, 1885), pp. 102–109; Douglas W. Owsley et al., *The History and Archaeology
of St. James Episcopal Church, Brandy Station, Virginia* (n.p., 1992), pp. 10–11.

8. Susan Leigh Blackford, comp., *Letters from Jackson's Army, or Memoirs of Life In and
Out of the Army in Virginia During the War Between the States* (1947; New York, 1962),
pp. 116–20.

9. Blackford, *Letters from Lee's Army*, pp. 114–16; Daniel E. Sutherland, "Stars in Their
Courses," *America's Civil War*, IV (November 1991), pp. 41–45.

10. Jedediah Hotchkiss, *Make Me a Map of the Valley: The Civil War Journal of Stonewall
Jackson's Topographer*, ed. Archie P. McDonald (Dallas, 1973) p. 71; *War of the Rebel-
lion*, vol. 12, pt. 2, pp. 288–89, 294, 316–17, 605, 719–20, and pt. 3, p. 627; John W.
Stevens, *Reminiscences of the Civil War: A Soldier in Hood's Texas Brigade, Army of
Northern Virginia* (Hillsboro, Tex., 1902), pp. 51–52.

11. Emory M. Thomas, *Bold Dragoon: The Life of J. E. B. Stuart* (New York, 1986), pp.
145–52; John Hennessy, "Stuart's Revenge," *Civil War Times*, XXXIV (June 1995),
38–45. *War of the Rebellion*, vol. 12, pt. 2, pp. 730–34.

12. *War of the Rebellion*, vol. 121, pt. 2, pp. 705–708; Jubal A. Early, *Narrative of the War
Between the States* (1912; Wilmington, N.C., 1989), pp. 106–13; Buck, *With the Old
Confeds*, pp. 49–50.

13. Blackford, *Letters from Lee's Army*, pp. 123–24; Noyes, *Bivouac and Battlefield*, pp.
90–91; Alexander Hunter, *Johnny Reb and Billy Yank* (New York, 1905), p. 240;
Stevens, *Reminiscences of the Civil War*, pp. 51–52.

14. Stevens, *Reminiscences of the Civil War*, pp. 51–54.

15. Ropes, *The Army Under Pope*, pp. 37–40; Theodore B. Gates, *The "Ulster Guard" and
the War of the Rebellion* (New York, 1879), pp. 244–46.

16. U.S. Senate, *Report of the Joint Committee on the Conduct of the War, Senate Report No. 108, 37th Cong., 3rd sess.* 3 pts. (Washington, D.C., 1863), pt. 2, pp. 371–72; *War of the Rebellion*, vol. 12, pt. 3, pp. 602, 608–609; New York *Herald*, August 26, 1862, p. 1.

17. *War of the Rebellion*, vol. 12, pt. 2, pp. 553–54, 705–708, and pt. 3, pp. 631, 640–41, 647–48; Hotchkiss, *Make Me A Map of the Valley*, pp. 70–72; Early, *Narrative*, pp. 106–13; Buck, *With the Old Confeds*, pp. 49–50.

18. Angus J. Johnston, III, *Virginia Railroads in the Civil War* (Chapel Hill, 1961), pp. 81–82; *War of the Rebellion*, vol. 12, pt. 2, pp. 33–37, and pt. 3, pp. 603, 618, 624–25, 636–38, 648, 654, 662; Hotchkiss, *Make Me a Map of the Valley*, pp. 72–75; James M. McPherson, *Battle Cry of Freedom: The Civil War Era* (New York, 1988), pp. 526–28.

19. Mrs. Berkeley G. Calfee, *Confederate History of Culpeper County in the War Between the States* (Culpeper, 1948), p. 4; Catherine Thom Bartlett, ed., *"My Dear Brother": A Confederate Chronicle* (Richmond, 1952), pp. 66–67.

20. Index to Virginia Hospitals, pp. 18, 44, Field Hospitals, Records of Adjutant General's Office, RG 94, National Archives; Virginia Hospital Record Book No. 640, pp. 35–41, 45–80, Field Records of Hospitals, Records of Adjutant General's Office, RG 94, National Archives; T. H. Pearce, ed., *Diary of Captain Henry A. Chambers* (Wendell, N.C., 1983), p. 60; Report of Sick and Wounded at Culpeper Court House, September 11, 1862, Return of Medical Officers, September 1862, both in Hospital Files: Virginia, War Department Collection of Confederate Records, Box 19, RG 109, National Archives.

21. Ella Lonn, *Salt as a Factor in the Confederacy* (New York, 1933), pp. 13–17, 138–40; Francis N. Boney, *John Letcher of Virginia: The Story of Virginia's Civil War Governor* (University, Ala., 1966), pp. 150, 164–65, 168–69; Culpeper County Court Minute Books, No. 24 (1858–64), 387, 393, Culpeper County Courthouse; "Statement . . . of Bushels of salt contracted to the counties of Virginia," October, 1862, in Box 512, Virginia Executive Papers, Virginia State Library and Archives, Richmond.

22. George M. Williams to Gertrude Williams, September 16, 1862, Williams Family Papers, in possession of Janet LaValley, Culpeper. Emory M. Thomas, *The Confederate Nation: 1861–1865* (New York, 1979), 152–55, 234–35; George C. Rable, *The Confederate Republic: A Revolution Against Politics* (Chapel Hill, N.C., 1994), 344–47, 396–99; Richard N. Current et al., eds., *Encyclopedia of the Confederacy*, 4 vols. (New York, 1993), I, 344–47, 396–99.

23. *Ibid.*, September 12, 1862; U.S. Bureau of the Census, *Population Schedule of the Eighth Census, 1860, Culpeper County, Virginia*, National Archives Microcopy 653, Roll 1341, pp. 787, 869.

24. John N. Opie, *A Rebel Cavalryman with Lee, Stuart and Jackson* (Chicago, 1899), p. 67; George M. Williams to Gertrude Williams, September 12, 1862, Williams Family Papers.

25. Irvin L. Jordan, Jr., *Black Confederates and Afro-Yankees in Civil War Virginia* (Charlottesville, 1995), 177, 180, 254. Jordan says seventeen blacks were hanged as a result of the "conspiracy," but no evidence from within Culpeper verifies this.

26. William H. Tatum to Louisiana Tatum, October 9, 1862, Tatum Papers, Virginia Historical Society, Richmond; County Court Minute Book No. 24, p. 394.

27. William H. Tatum to Louisiana Tatum, October 9, 1862, Tatum Papers; *War of the Rebellion*, vol. 19, pt. 2, pp. 675, 685–87.

28. Andrew J. Gillespie to Susan Gillespie, November 13, 1862, Randall Family Papers, Alderman Library, University of Virginia, Charlottesville; T. C. Elder to wife, November 11, 16, 1862, Thomas Claybrook Elder Papers, Virginia Historical Society, Richmond.

29. Charles E. Cauthen, ed., *Family Letters of the Three Wade Hamptons, 1782–1901* (Columbia, S.C., 1953), p. 87; William H. Tatum to Louisiana Tatum, October 9, 1862,

Tatum Papers; William H. Runge, ed., *Four Years in the Confederate Artillery: The Diary of Private Henry Robinson Berkeley* (Chapel Hill, 1961), pp. 33–34; General Order No. 119, October 16, 1862, Orders and Circulars Issued by the Army of the Potomac and the Army and Department of Northern Virginia, C.S.A., 1861–1865, War Department Collection of Confederate Records, RG 109, National Archives; Richard Lewis, *Camp Life of a Confederate Boy of Bratton's Brigade, Longstreet's Corps, C.S.A.* (Charleston, S.C. 1883), pp. 34–35.

30. *War of the Rebellion*, vol. 21, 1016, 1018; Henry H. Campbell to Anna B. Campbell, November 7, 1862, Anna B. Campbell Papers, Perkins Library, Duke University, Durham, N.C.; Rufus Mead Diaries, August 12, 13, 1862, in Rufus Mead Papers, Library of Congress.

31. Stevens, *Reminiscences*, p. 84; Joseph C. Webb to Mrs. Robin N. Webb, November 5, 1862, Lenoir Family Papers, Southern Historical Collection, University of North Carolina at Chapel Hill.

32. David E. Johnston, *The Story of a Confederate Boy in the Civil War* (Portland, Ore., 1914), p. 165; David F. Riggs, *7th Virginia Infantry* (Lynchburg, 1982), pp. 17, 71, 81, 101.

33. Thomas, *Bold Dragoon*, pp. 188–89.

34. Andrew J. Gillespie to Susan Gillespie, November 15, 1862, Randall Papers; Henry M. Talley to Jane Talley, November 18, 1862, Henry M. Talley Papers, Virginia Historical Society, Richmond; Joseph C. Webb to Mrs. Robin Webb, November 5, 1862, Lenoir Family Papers.

35. General Order No. 125, November 7, 1862, Orders and Circulars; *War of the Rebellion*, vol. 19, pt. 2, p. 722.

36. T. C. Elder to wife, November 8, 1862, Thomas Claybrook Elder Papers, Virginia Historical Society, Richmond; Stevens, *Reminiscences*, p. 85; Johnston, *Confederate Boy*, pp. 166–67; Runge, *Four Years in the Confederate Artillery*, p. 34; Robert K. Krick, *9th Virginia Cavalry* (Lynchburg, 1982), p. 13; William H. Tatum to Louisiana Tatum, November 23, 1862, Tatum Papers.

37. Lewis, *Camp Life of a Confederate*, pp. 34–35; Johnston, *Confederate Boy*, p. 166; Henry M. Talley to Jane Talley, November 9, 1862, Talley Papers; Abner Crump Hopkins Diary, November 1, 1863, Virginia Historical Society, Richmond; *War of the Rebellion*, vol. 21, p. 1016; Special Order No. 243, November 15, 1862, Orders and Circulars.

38. [London] *Times*, December 27, 1862, p. 7; Robert E. Lee to Mary Custis Lee, November 13, 18, 1862, and to Mildred C. Lee, November 10, 1862, Lee Papers, Virginia Historical Society, Richmond; Robert E. Lee to Custis Lee, November 10, 1862, Robert Edward Lee Papers, Perkins Library, Duke University, Durham, N.C.

39. Henry A. Carrington to wife, November 1, 1862, Carrington Family Papers, Virginia Historical Society, Richmond; Joseph H. Singleton to Jefferson Davis, September 10, 1862, Phocian Rolfe and R. C. Bland to George W. Randolph, October 5, 1862, H. L. Zinn to Randolph, November 6, 1862, Charles Smith to Randolph, November 9, 1862, Samuel S. Clarke to Randolph, November 14, 1862, William M. Stone to Davis, November 18, 1862, Edward A. Truman to Randolph, November 19, 1862, all Letters Received by the Confederate Secretary of War, War Department Collection of Confederate Records, RG 109, National Archives.

40. Johnston, *Confederate Boy*, p. 166; Report of Sick and Wounded at Culpeper Court House, October 18, 1862, October 25, 1862, November 1, 1862; Mrs. Roger A. Pryor, *Reminiscences of Peace and War* (New York, 1905),p. 196; [London] *Times*, December 27, 1862, p. 7; William S. Hoole, *Lawley Covers the Confederacy* (Tuscaloosa, Ala., 1964), pp. 35–36; *Vizetelly Covers the Confederacy* (Tuscaloosa, Ala., 1957), p. 53.

41. Virginia Hospital Record Book No. 640, p. 70; Pryor, *Reminiscences*, pp. 195–97; Myrta Lockett Avary, *A Virginia Girl in the Civil War* (New York, 1903), pp. 51–52, 59–68.

42. Runge, *Four Years in the Confederate Artillery*, pp. 33–34; Joseph J. Halsey to Jeremiah Morton, December 5, 1862, Morton-Halsey Papers, Alderman Library, University of Virginia, Charlottesville; Record Book, General Hospital, Culpeper Court House, Virginia, 1862, War Department Collection of Confederate Records, Chapter VI, vol. 587, pp. 85–86, RG 109, National Archives; files for Lemuel Corbin, Mary S. Foushee, Thomas Hill, Elizabeth T. Major, Walter O'Bannon, John H. Rixey, John T. Stark, in Confederate Papers Relating to Citizens or Business Firms, War Department Collection of Confederate Records, RG 109, National Archives.

43. File of Philip C. Slaughter, Papers Relating to Citizens or Business Firms; Virginia Hospital Record Book No. 640, p. 80; *Population Schedule of the Eighth Census*, p. 867.

44. George M. Williams to Gertrude Williams, December 7, 1862, Williams Family Papers; Account Book No. 2, October–December, 1862, Lemuel Armistead Corbin Papers, Virginia Historical Society, Richmond; Joseph J. Halsey to Jeremiah Morton, December 5, 1862, Morton-Halsey Papers.

45. *War of the Rebellion*, vol. 19, pt. 2, pp. 701, 704, 716, 717; *ibid.*, vol. 21, pp. 1015, 1016; [London] *Times*, December 27, 1862, p. 7; Borcke, *Memoirs;* II, pp. 49–56, 60; John S. Mosby to Pauline Mosby, November 15, 1862, John Singleton Mosby Papers, Virginia Historical Society, Richmond.

46. John O. Collins to Catherine S. Collins, November 16, 1862; John Overton Collins Papers, Virginia Historical Society, Richmond; [London] *Times*, December 27, 1862, p. 7; *War of the Rebellion*, vol. 21, pp. 1020–21, 1026–28, 1035.

47. Boney, *John Letcher*, pp. 169–72; Lonn, *Salt in the Confederacy*, 141; County Court Minute Books, No. 24, p. 400; "Calculations & data for distribution of salt," November 11, 1862, Box 513, and James Barbour et al. to John Letcher, November 6, 1862, Fayette Mauzy to Letcher, December 16, 1862, John B. Stanard to John Letcher, November 21, 1862, Virginia Executive Papers; James H. Brewer, *The Confederate Negro: Virginia Craftsmen and Military Laborers, 1861–1865* (Durham, N.C., 1969), pp. 4, 6–8; [London] *Times*, December 27, 1862, p. 7.

48. Jane McVeigh to Jefferson Davis, November [c. 18] 1862, Letters Received by the Confederate Secretary of War, National Archives.

49. George M. Williams to Gertrude Williams, October 8, 24, November 11, 14, 18, 27, and December 11, 19, 1862, Williams Family Papers.

50. Joseph J. Halsey to Jeremiah Morton, December 5, 1862, Morton-Halsey Papers.

51. *War of the Rebellion*, vol. 21, p. 550.

Chapter 8. To Be a Confederate Soldier

1. For the weather see J. Michael Welton, ed., *"My Heart Is So Rebellious": The Caldwell Letters, 1861–1865* (Warrenton, Va., 1991), pp. 174, 178; Jedediah Hotchkiss, *Make Me a Map of the Valley: The Civil War Journal of Stonewall Jackson's Topographer*, ed. Archie P. McDonald (Dallas, 1973), pp. 105–17.

2. Charles E. Cauthen, ed., *Family Letters of the Three Wade Hamptons, 1782–1901* (Columbia, S.C., 1953), pp. 91–92. The harsh weather and hard campaigning was beginning to take its toll on Lee's cavalry by this stage of the war. See Charles W. Ramsdell, "General Robert E. Lee's Horse Supply, 1862–1865," *American Historical Review*, XXXV (July 1930), pp. 758–62.

3. Cauthen, *Hampton Letters*, pp. 91–92.

4. *War of the Rebellion: A Compilation of the Official Records of the Union and Confederate Armies*, 70 vols. in 128 books and index (Washington, D.C., 1880–1901, ser. 1, cited hereafter as *War of the Rebellion*, and all references are to Series 1 unless otherwise indicated), vol. 21, pp. 1097, 1100.

5. *War of the Rebellion*, vol. 21, pp. 1101, 1103; *ibid.*, vol. 25, pt. 2, pp. 623–24, 627; Clifford Dowdey and Louis H. Manarin, eds., *The Wartime Papers of R. E. Lee* (Boston, 1961), p. 401; Richard C. Price to Virginia E. Price, February 11, 1863, Richard Channinmg Price Papers, Virginia Historical Society, Richmond.

6. A good biographical sketch of Pelham is William W. Hassler, "John Pelham of the Horse Artillery," *Civil War Times*, III (August 1964), pp. 11–14. For fuller treatments see William W. Hassler, *Colonel John Pelham: Lee's Boy Artillerist* (Chapel Hill, N.C., 1960) and Charles G. Milham, *Gallant Pelham: American Extraordinary* (Washington, D.C., 1959). Also see Clark B. Hall, "Robert F. Beckham: The Man Who Commanded Stuart's Horse Artillery After Pelham Fell," *Blue & Gray*, IX (December 1991), p. 35.

7. Heros von Borcke, *Memoirs of the Confederate War for Independence*, 2 vols. (1866; New York, 1938), II, pp. 179–82; T.O. Madden, Jr., *We Were Always Free: The Maddens of Culpeper County, Virginia; A 200-Year Family History* (New York, 1992), pp. 103–106.

8. U.S. Bureau of the Census, *Population Schedule of the Eighth Census, 1860, Culpeper County, Virginia*, National Archives Microcopy No. 653, Roll 1341, p. 781; Borcke, *Memoirs*, II, 182–83; Milham, *Gallant Pelham*, pp. 221–22; Hassler, *John Pelham*, pp. 158–59.

9. Calfee, *Confederate History of Culpeper*, p. 5.

10. Eugene M. Scheel, *Culpeper: A Virginia County's History Through 1920* (Culpeper, 1982), p. 192.

11. Receipts for sale of slaves, January, 1863, March 26, 28, 1863, Coons Family Papers, Virginia Historical Society, Richmond.

12. Marriage Register, Culpeper County, February–May, 1863, Culpeper County Courthouse; Silas Bruce Marriage Register, April 19, 23, 1863, Virginia State Library and Archives, Richmond.

13. Paul Glass and Louis C. Singer, eds., *Singing Soldiers: A History of the Civil War in Song* (New York, 1975), pp. 286–87. "The Vacant Chair" was written around Thanksgiving 1861 by George F. Root, perhaps the North's most successful composer of wartime songs. This song, however, was universally popular.

14. Jeremiah Morton to Joseph J. Halsey, February 12, 1863, Mildred T. Halsey to Joseph J. Halsey, February 31, 1863, Morton-Halsey Papers, Alderman Library, University of Virginia, Charlottesville. For Vallandingham's career see Frank L. Klement, *The Limits of Dissent: Clement L. Vallandingham and the Civil War* (1970).

15. Crooked Run Baptist Church Minute Book, 1862, Virginia Baptist Historical Society, Richmond; Donnie Johnston, *The Ghosts of Gourdvine Past: A History of Gourdvine Baptist Church* (n.p., 1987), pp. 30, 34; Arthur D. Thomas, Jr., and Angus M. Green, eds., *Early Churches of Culpeper County, Virginia: Colonial and Ante-Bellum Congregations* (Culpeper, 1987), pp. 31, 78; George B. Taylor, *Virginia Baptist Ministers*, Third Series (Lynchburg, 1912), pp. 202–210.

16. Minutes of the Baptist Church of Christ, January 17, 1863, Alderman Library, University of Virginia, Charlottesville; Psalms 46: 1–5.

17. Crooked Run Baptist Church Minute Book, pp. 1846–69, entry of March 27, 1863, Virginia Baptist Historical Society, Richmond.

18. Minutes of Baptist Church of Christ, December 20, 1862, February 14, April 18, 1863.

19. Mary Stevens Jones and Mildred Conway Jones, eds., *Historic Culpeper* (Culpeper, 1974), pp. 21, 124–25; Thomas and Green, *Early Churches of Culpeper*, 154–56; George M. Williams to Gertrude S. Long, March 1, 1860, George M. Williams Family Papers, in possession of Janet LaValley, Culpeper; Jonathan Cole to Jeremiah Morton, March 25, 1863, Morton-Halsey Papers.

20. Richard H. Watkins to Mary P. Watkins, February 19, 1863, Richard Henry Watkins Papers, Virginia Historical Society, Richmond.

21. *Ibid.*

22. *Ibid.*, February 27, 1863.

23. *War of the Rebellion*, vol. 25, pt. 1, pp. 25–26; Henry H. B. McClellan, *The Life and Campaigns of Major General J. E. B. Stuart* (Boston, 1885), pp. 204–206; *Ibid.*

24. R.P. Rixey, *The Rixey Genealogy* (Lynchburg, 1933), pp. 213–14; Constance Cary to Wilson M. Cary, February 27, 1863, Wilson Miles Cary papers, Alderman Library, University of Virginia, Charlottesville.

25. *Ibid.*; Mrs. Burton Harrison, *Recollections Grave and Gay* (New York, 1911), pp. 98–104; Constance Cary to Clarence Cary, March 7, 1863, Burton Norvell Harrison Family Papers, Library of Congress.

26. Myrta Lockett Avary, *A Virginia Girl in the Civil War* (New York, 1903), pp. 116–19.

27. Harrison, *Recollections Grave and Gay*, p. 103.

28. James W. Biddle to Rosa Biddle, January 27, February 3, 1863, Samuel Simpson Biddle Papers, Perkins Library, Duke University, Durham, N.C.; Lucius C. Haney to sister, March 14, 1863, Jacob B. Click Papers, Perkins Library, Duke University, Durham, N.C.

29. James E. B. Stuart to Flora Stuart, March 13, March 15, 1863, James Ewell Brown Stuart Papers, Virginia Historical Society, Richmond; Douglas Southall Freeman, *Lee's Lieutenants: A Study in Command*, 3 vols. (New York, 1942–44), II, pp. 455–57; Hassler, *John Pelham*, p. 162; Milham, *Gallant Pelham*, p. 225; Scheel, *Culpeper*, p. 194.

30. Lawson Morrissett Diary, March 16, 1863, Eleanor S. Brockenbrough Library, Museum of the Confederacy, Richmond; Jennings C. Wise, *The Long Arm of Lee: History of the Artillery of the Army of Northern Virginia* (1915; New York, 1959), pp. 432–33. For a sketch of Averell see Robert B. Boehm, "The Unfortunate Averell," *Civil War Times*, V (August 1966), pp. 30–36.

31. Frederic Denison, *Sabre and Spurs: First Regiment Rhode Island Cavalry in the Civil War, 1861–1865* (Central Falls, R.I., 1876), pp. 208–10; McClellan, *Campaigns of Stuart*, pp. 207–208; Mary D. Robertson, ed., *Lucy Breckinridge of Grove Hill: The Journal of a Virginia Girl, 1862–1864* (Kent, Ohio, 1979), pp. 108–109.

32. *War of the Rebellion*, vol. 25, pt. 1, pp. 48, 57, 160–61. For two popular renditions of this and later action in the battle of Kelly's Ford see Wiley Sword, "Cavalry on Trial at Kelly's Ford," *Civil War Times*, XIII (April 1974), pp. 32–40, and Jerry Meyers, "Melee on Saint Patrick's Day," *America's Civil War*, IV (November 1991), pp. 30–37.

33. For this and the several following paragraphs see *War of the Rebellion*, vol. 25, pt. 1, pp. 48–50, 60–61; Freeman, *Lee's Lieutenants*, II, pp. 459–63; McClellan, *Campaigns of Stuart*, pp. 209–11; Stephen Z. Starr, *The Union Cavalry in the Civil War*, 3 vols. (Baton Rouge, La., 1979–8), I, pp. 343–50.

34. Wise, *The Long Arm of Lee*, pp. 433–34; McClellan, *Campaigns of Stuart*, pp. 211–16.

35. Freeman, *Lee's Lieutenant's*, II, p. 464–65; Hassler, *John Pelham*, pp. 164–66.

36. *War of the Rebellion*, vol. 25, pt. 1, pp. 50, 53; McClellan, *Campaigns of Stuart*, pp. 216–17; Sword, "Cavalry on Trial," pp. 33, 40.

37. McClellan, *Campaigns of Stuart*, p. 217; Freeman, *Lee's Lieutenants*, II, pp. 464–65;

Kenneth Stiles, *4th Virginia Cavalry* (Lynchburg, 1985), p. 105; Martha E. Coons to Frank A. Coons, March 25, 1863, Coons Family Papers, Virginia Historical Society, Richmond; Hassler, *John Pelham*, pp. 166–67; Thomas, *Bold Dragoon*, pp. 206–207; Borcke, *Memoirs*, II, pp. 188–90; *War of the Rebellion*, vol. 25, pt. 1, p. 60; Hall, "Robert F. Beckham," p. 35.

38. Lucius C. Haney to sister, March 21, 1863, Jacob B. Click Papers, Perkins Library, Duke University, Durham, N.C.; James E. B. Stuart to Flora Stuart, March 19, 1863, Stuart Papers.

39. Martha E. Coons to Frank A. Coons, March 25, 1863, Coons Family Papers; Lucius C. Haney to sister, March 21, 1863, Click Papers; Morrisett Diary, March 18–27, 1863; John J. Shoemaker, *Shoemaker's Battery, Stuart's Horse Artillery, Pelham's Battalion, Army of Northern Virginia* (Memphis, 1908), p. 29; *War of the Rebellion*, vol. 25, pt. 2, p. 683; John Bolling to Jesse Scott Armistead, April 8, 1863, John Bolling Letter, Virginia Historical Society, Richmond.

40. Richard H. Watkins to Mary Watkins, April 7, April 8, 1863, Watkins Papers, Virginia Historical Society, Richmond; Special Order, April 22, 1863, Fourth Virginia Cavalry Headquarters Book, Fourth Virginia Cavalry Papers, Museum of the Confederacy, Richmond.

41. David B. Ruggles, *Ruggle's Regiment: The 122nd New York Volunteers in the American Civil War* (Hanover, N.H., 1982), pp. 88–90.

42. Circular dated April 4, 1863, Fourth Cavalry Headquarters Book.

43. John Esten Cooke, *Outlines from the Outpost*, ed. Richard Harwell (Chicago, 1961), pp. 163–64; Jacob B. Click to Miss Evaline, March 23, 1863, Click Papers.

44. Richard H. Watkins to Mary Watkins, April 7, 1863, Watkins Papers.

45. William W. Blackford, *War Years with Jeb Stuart* (New York, 1945), p. 203; John Esten Cooke Diary, April 22, 1863, John Esten Cooke Papers, Perkins Library, Duke University, Durham, N.C.; Borcke, *Memoirs*, II, pp. 191–95.

46. Shoemaker, *Shoemaker's Battery*, pp. 29–31; Borcke, *Memoirs*, II, 195–200; *War of the Rebellion*, vol. 25, pt. 1, pp. 83–89; McClellan, *Campaigns of Stuart*, pp. 220–24; Richard C. Price to Virginia E. Price, April 24, 1863, Richard Channing Price Papers, Virginia Historical Society, Richmond; Sally Anne Armstrong Diary, April 16, 1863, Virginia Historical Society, Richmond; Helen Jeffries Klitch, ed., "Joseph Arthur Jeffries' Fauquier County, Virginia, 1840–1919," pp. 22–23, typescript in possession of author.

47. *Population Schedule of the Eighth Census*, p. 818; Mary S. Jones and Mildred C. Jones, eds., *Historic Culpeper* (Culpeper, 1974), p. 57; Armstrong Diary, April 3–5, 10, 16, 12–18, and 21, 1863.

48. *War of the Rebellion*, vol. 25, pt. 2, pp. 724–25, 736–37, 740–41; Ezra J. Warner, *Generals in Blue: Lives of the Union Commanders* (Baton Rouge, La., 1964), pp. 481–82. The Federals were also having trouble finding good horses at reasonable prices. They created a Cavalry Bureau in May. See John V. Barton, "The Procurement of Horses," *Civil War Times*, VI (December 1967), pp. 16–24.

49. Morrissett Diary, April 21, 25–27, 1863; Corson, *My Dear Jennie*, pp. 101–102; Armstrong Diary, April 26–28, 1863.

50. McClellan, *Campaigns of Stuart*, pp. 225–29; Borcke, *Memoirs*, II, pp. 202–208; Starr, *The Union Cavalry in the Civil War*, I, pp. 351–56; *War of the Rebellion*, vol. 25, pt. 1, pp. 1057–99.

51. Worthington Chauncey Ford, ed., *A Cycle of Adams Letters: 1861–1865*, 2 vols. (Boston, 1920), I, pp. 286–87.

52. Armstrong Diary, April 29–30, 1863; Ford, *Adams Letters*, I, pp. 286–89.

53. *War of the Rebellion*, vol. 25, pt. 1, 1072–80; Ford, *Adams Letters*, I, pp. 286–89; E. N. Gilpin Diary, April 30, 1863, Library of Congress.

54. Gilpin Diary, April 30, 1863; Denison, *Sabre and Spurs*, 221–22; Ford, *Adams Letters*, I, p. 288.

55. Ford, *Adams Letters*, I, p. 289.

56. *War of the Rebellion*, vol. 25, pt. 1, pp. 1072–80; Edward G. Longacre, *Mounted Raids of the Civil War* (South Brunswick, N.J., 1975), pp. 157–61.

Chapter 9. Perplexed, But Not in Despair

1. Sally Anne Armstrong Diary, May 3–5, 1863, Virginia Historical Society, Richmond.

2. Mary S. Jones and Mildred Conway Jones, eds., *Historic Culpeper* (Culpeper, 1974), p. 57; Armstrong Diary, May 6, 1863.

3. Helen Jeffries Klitch, ed., "Joseph Arthur Jeffries' Fauquier County, Virginia, 1840–1919," p. 25, typescript in possession of author.

4. Armstrong Diary, May 7–8, 1863.

5. Armstrong Diary, May 9, 10, 13, 15, and 17, 1863.

6. *War of the Rebellion: A Compilation of the Official Records of the Union and Confederate Armies in the War of the Rebellion*, 70 vols. in 128 books and index (Washington, D.C., 1880–1901, cited hereafter as *War of the Rebellion*, and all references are to Series 1 unless indicated otherwise), vol. 25, pt. 2, pp. 792, 820, 834.

7. Emory M. Thomas, *Bold Dragoon: The Life of J. E. B. Stuart* (New York, 1986), pp. 139, 202–202, 216; Charles E. Cauthen, ed., *Family Letters of the Three Wade Hamptons, 1782–1901* (Columbia, S.C., 1953), p. 93.

8. Thomas, *Bold Dragoon*, p. 216; John J. Shoemaker, *Shoemaker's Battery, Stuart Horse Artillery, Pelham's Battalion, Army of Northern Virginia* (Memphis, 1908), p. 37; *War of the Rebellion*, vol. 25, pt. 2, pp. 782–83, 807.

9. Jones and Jones, *Historic Culpeper*, p. 36; Myrta Lockett Avary, *A Virginia Girl in the Civil War* (New York, 1903), pp. 229–33.

10. Avary, *Virginia Girl*, pp. 233–34.

11. U.S. Bureau of the Census, *Population Schedule of the Eighth Census, 1860, Culpeper County, Virginia*, National Archives Microcopy No. 653, Roll 1341, p. 820; *Population Schedule of the Eighth Census, 1860, Virginia [Slave Schedule], Culpeper County*, National Archives Microcopy No. 653, Roll 1389, p. 19; Avary, *Virginia Girl*, pp. 235–36. Bradford's wife is listed as Sarah in the census.

12. Culpeper County Circuit Court, Law Order Book No. 6 (1856–66), pp. 477–81, Culpeper County Courthouse, Culpeper County Court, Minute Book No. 24 (1858–64), pp. 402–409, Culpeper County Courthouse.

13. *War of the Rebellion*, vol. 25, pt. 2, pp. 810, 840.

14. Susan P. Lee, *Memoirs of William Nelson Pendleton* (Philadelphia, 1893), pp. 274–76.

15. Douglas S. Freeman, *Lee's Lieutenants: A Study in Command*, 3 vols. (New York, 1942–44), III, pp. 26–27; H. C. Kendrick to father and sister, May 28, 1863, H. C. Kendrick Letters, Southern Historical Collection, University of North Carolina at Chapel Hill; *War of the Rebellion*, vol. 27, pt. 3, pp. 858–59; F. P. Summers, ed., *Borderland Confederate* (Pittsburgh, 1962), pp. 70–71.

16. Watkins Kearns Diary, June 7, 1863, Virginia Historical Society, Richmond; Randolph H. McKim, *A Soldier's Recollections: Leaves from the Diary of a Young Confederate* (New York, 1910), pp. 141–42.

17. William G. Bean, *Stonewall's Man: Sandie Pendleton* (Chapel Hill, 1959), pp. 132–33; Lee, *Memoirs of Pendleton*, pp. 274–76; Jedediah Hotchkiss, *Make Me a Map of the Valley: The Civil War Journal of Stonewall Jackson's Topographer*, ed. Archie P. McDonald (Dallas, 1973), pp. 148–50; Harold B. Simpson, *Hood's Texas Brigade: Lee's Grenadier Guard* (Waco, Tex., 1970), pp. 244–45; John C. West, *A Texan in Search of a Fight, Being the Diary and Letters of a Private Soldier in Hood's Texas Brigade* (Waco, Tex., 1901), p. 72.

18. Clifford Dowdey and Louis H. Manarin, eds., *The Wartime Papers of R. E. Lee* (Boston, 1961), pp. 482–83; *War of the Rebellion*, vol. 25, pt. 2, pp. 787, 814, 848.

19. Dowdey and Manarin, *Wartime Papers of Lee*, pp. 502–503; *War of the Rebellion*, vol. 27, pt. 3, pp. 868–69.

20. Confederate States of America, Quartermaster Department, Record of Quartermaster Stores Issued to and Condemned in Units of Army of Northern Virginia, 1862–63, chap. V, vol. 204, May–June 1863, Records of Army of Northern Virginia, RG 109, National Archives; McKim, *A Soldier's Recollections*, pp. 142–43.

21. Confederate States of America, Papers Relating to Citizens or Business Firms, files on R. S. Rixey, March 12, June 1, 1863, Alfred Stofer, March 20, 25, April 6, 8, 1863, War Department Collection of Confederate Records, RG 109, National Archives.

22. Emily G. Ramey and John K. Gott, comps., *The Years of Anguish: Fauquier County, Virginia, 1861–1865* (Warrenton, Va., 1965), p. 96; McKim, *A Soldier's Recollections*, pp. 142–43; John R. Porter Diary, June 6–8, 1863, Perkins Library, Duke University, Durham, N.C.; Alexander D. Betts, *Experiences of a Confederate Chaplain, 1861–64* (n.p., n.d.), p. 37; Samual J. Watson, "Religion and Combat Motivation in the Confederate Armies," *Journal of Military History*, LVIII (January 1994), pp. 29–55.

23. For historical accounts of the review and associated events see Freeman, *Lee's Lieutenants*, III, pp. 1–3; Thomas, *Bold Dragoon*, pp. 216–19; and Fairfax Downey, *Clash of Cavalry: The Battle of Brandy Station, June 9, 1863* (New York, 1959), pp. 79–81. For a fictional account by a participant, see John Esten Cooke, *Mohun; or, The Last Days of Lee and His Paladins* (Boston, 1869), pp. 5–27.

24. Daniel A. Grimsley, *Battles in Culpeper County, Virginia, 1861–1865* (Culpeper, 1900), p. 8; Leiper Moore Robinson Civil War Experiences, pt. 1, pp. 1–3, Virginia Historical Society, Richmond; George M. Neese, *Three Years in the Confederate Horse Artillery* (New York, 1911), pp. 166–69; Heros von Borcke, *Memoirs of the Confederate War for Independence*, 2 vols. (New York, 1866), II, pp. 264–67; Avary, *Virginia Girl*, p. 241.

25. H. C. Kendrick to mother, June 6, 1863, H. C. Kendrick Letters, Southern Historical Collection, University of North Carolina at Chapel Hill; Thomas, *Bold Dragoon*, p. 218; Stephen Z. Starr, *The Union Cavalry in the Civil War*, 3 vols. (Baton Rouge, La., 1979–85), I, p. 375; and Freeman, *Lee's Lieutenants*, III, pp. 51–52.

26. Avary, *Virginia Girl*, pp. 238–40.

27. Lee, *Memoirs of Pendleton*, p. 277; Robert E. Lee to Mary C. Lee, June 9, 1863, DeButts-Ely Collection of Lee Family Papers, Library of Congress, also in Dowdey and Manarin, *Wartime Papers of Lee*, pp. 506–507; *War of the Rebellion*, vol. 27, pt. 3, pp. 872–73.

28. Armstrong Diary, May 24 and June 1 and 8, 1863.

29. Freeman, *Lee's Lieutenants*, III, pp. 5–8; Henry B. McClellan, *Life and Campaigns of Major General J. E. B. Stuart* (Boston, 1885), pp. 262–63.

30. Paul Glass and Louis C. Singer, eds., *Singing Soldiers: A History of the Civil War in Song* (New York, 1975), pp. 152–53. "Tenting on the Old Camp Ground" was written by Walter Kittredge, a popular concert balladeer who had been deferred from military service. This song became one of the most popular of the war in the camps of both armies.

31. McClellan, *Campaigns of Stuart*, p. 264; *War, of the Rebellion*, vol. 27, pt. 1, pp. 902–903; Starr, *Union Cavalry*, I, pp. 371–73, 375–78. For sketches of Buford see Russell F. Weigley, "John Buford," *Civil War Times* V (June 1966), pp. 14–23, and Michael Phipps and John S. Peterson, *"The Devil's to Pay": Gen. John Buford, USA* (Gettysburg, 1994). The battle of Brandy Station has been the subject of several articles in recent years, partly in response to threats to the battlefield by industrial developers. The standard but far from adequate study for many years was Downey, *Clash of Cavalry*. It has been superseded in large part by Starr, *Union Cavalry*, I, pp. 372–95; Gary W. Gallagher, "Brandy Station: The Civil War's Bloodiest Arena of Mounted Combat," *Blue & Gray*, VIII (October 1990), pp. 8–22, 44–53; Clark B. Hall, "The Battle of Brandy Station," *Civil War Times*, XXIX (May–June 1990), pp. 32–42, 45, and "Buford at Brandy Station," *Civil War*, VIII (July–August 1990), pp. 12–17, 66–67; Marshall D. Krolick, "The Battle of Brandy Station," *Civil War Quarterly*, VII (December 1986), pp. 52–65. When completed, Clark B. Hall's book on the subject will likely be the definitive study.
32. McClellan, *Campaigns of Stuart*, p. 264; Luther W. Hopkins, *From Bull Run to Appomattox: A Boy's View* (Baltimore, 1908), pp. 89–91; *War of the Rebellion*, vol. 27, pt. 2, pp. 754–55.
33. *Ibid.*; for a sketch of Jones see [Editors], "'Grumble' Jones," *Civil War Times*, VIII (June 1968), pp. 35–41.
34. *Ibid*; John N. Opie, *A Rebel Cavalryman with Lee, Stuart and Jackson* (Chicago, 1899), pp. 147–49.
35. Shoemaker, *Shoemaker's Battery*, p. 38; McClellan, *Campaigns of Stuart*, 264–66; *War of the Rebellion*, vol. 27, pt. 2, pp. 754–55, 757, 772; Neese, *Three Years in Confederate Artillery*, p. 171.
36. Freeman, *Lee's Lieutenants*, III, pp. 5, 8; Douglas W. Owsley et al., *The History and Archaeology of St. James Episcopal Church, Brandy Station, Virginia* (n.p., 1992), pp. 14–15.
37. *War of the Rebellion*, vol. 27, pt. 1, pp. 949–50; Clark B. Hall to author, July 3, 1994.
38. *Ibid.*
39. Gallagher, "Brandy Station," pp. 15–17; Clark B. Hall, "Robert F. Beckham: The Man Who Commanded Stuart's Horse Artillery After Pelham Fell," *Blue & Gray*, IX (December 1991), pp. 34–37. While the record is inconsistent, Hall believes Stuart arrived at St. James's at about 9 A.M. Clark B. Hall to author, July 3, 1994.
40. Hall, "The Battle of Brandy Station," pp. 36–37; Neese, *Three Years in Confederate Artillery*, pp. 172–73; McClellan, *Campaigns of Stuart*, pp. 267–68; Gallagher, "Brandy Station," p. 18.
41. McClellan, *Campaigns of Stuart*, pp. 266–67; Gallagher, "Brandy Station," pp. 18–19.
42. Gallagher, "Brandy Station," pp. 19–20.
43. Freeman, *Lee's Lieutenants*, III, pp. 8–9; *War of the Rebellion*, vol. 27, pt. 2, p. 749; Frank M. Myers, *The Comanches: A History of White's Battalion, Virginia Cavalry, Laurel Brigade, Hampton's Division, Army of Northern Virginia, C.S.A.* (Baltimore, 1871), pp. 182–83; Hall to author, July 3 1994.
44. Freeman, *Lee's Lieutenants*, III, p. 9; *War of the Rebellion*, vol. 27, pt. 2, pp. 733–35; McClellan, *Campaigns of Stuart*, pp. 269–71.
45. Hall, "Battle of Brandy Station," pp. 35, 38–39; Gallagher, "Brandy Station," pp. 20–22, 44; Opie, *A Rebel Cavalryman*, pp. 152–54; George Baylor, *Bull Run to Bull Run; or, Four Years in the Army of Northern Virginia* (Richmond, 1900), pp. 143–44; McClellan, *Campaigns of Stuart*, pp. 271–72; Myers, *The Comanches*, pp. 183–84. For a sketch of Percy

Wyndham see Edward A. Longacre, "Sir Percy Wyndham," *Civil War Times*, VII (December 1968), pp. 12–19.

46. Neese, *Three Years in Confederate Artillery*, p. 177; Opie, *Rebel Cavalryman*, pp. 154–56; Borcke, *Memoirs*, II, pp. 273–76; Henry R. Pyne, *Ride to War: The History of the First New Jersey Cavalry*, ed. Earl Schenck Miers (New Brunswick, N.J., 1961), pp. 118–24; Hall, "Battle of Brandy Station," pp. 39–42; Gallagher, "Brandy Station," pp. 44–50; G. W. Beale, *A Lieutenant of Cavalry in Lee's Army* (Boston, 1918), p. 94.

47. *Ibid*; Justis Scheibert, *Seven Months in the Rebel States During the North American War, 1863*, trans. Joseph C. Hayes, ed. William Stanley Hoole (Tuscaloosa, 1958), pp. 90–91; Starr, *Union Cavalry*, I, pp. 385–86; Clark B. Hall to author, July 3, 1994.

48. McClellan, *Campaigns of Stuart*, pp. 277–79; *War of the Rebellion*, vol. 27, pt. 2, pp. 772–73; Neese, *Three Years in Confederate Artillery*, pp. 176–78; Gallagher, "Brandy Station," pp. 46–47.

49. Hall, "Battle of Brandy Station," pp. 40–42; Gallagher, "Brandy Station," pp. 47–51.

50. Hotchkiss, *Make Me a Map of the Valley*, pp. 149–50; Douglas S. Freeman, *R. E. Lee: A Biography*, 4 vols. (New York, 1934), III, p. 31; *War of the Rebellion*, vol. 27, pt. 3, p. 876; *ibid.*, vol. 51, pt. 2, p. 722.

51. Robert E. Lee to Mary Custis Lee, June 9, 1863, DeButts-Ely Collection, also in Dowdey and Manarin, *Wartime Papers of Lee*, pp. 506–507.

52. Hotchkiss, *Make Me a Map of the Valley*, pp. 149–50; Freeman, *Lee's Lieutenants*, III, pp. 11–12; Starr, *Union Cavalry*, I, pp. 388–89.

53. James E. B. Stuart to Flora Stuart, June 12, 1863, James Ewell Brown Stuart Papers, Virginia Historical Society, Richmond. Confusion exists over the final casualty figures. The ones provided here are estimated from McClellan, *Campaigns of Stuart*, pp. 292–93; Gallagher, "Brandy Station," p. 51; and Starr, *Union Cavalry*, I, pp. 389–90.

54. Mrs. Berkeley G. Calfee, *Confederate History of Culpeper County in the War Between the States* (Culpeper, 1948), p. 7.

55. Calfee, *Confederate History*, p. 7; Avary, *Virginia Girl*, pp. 244–52.

56. Kenneth L. Stiles, *4th Virginia Cavalry* (Lynchburg, 1985), pp. 28–29; William A. Hill to Anna Lee Major, June 6, 1863, Hill Family Papers, Virginia Historical Society, Richmond; John H. Williams to Cora Pritchartt, June 10, 12, 16, 1863, Williams Family Papers, Virginia Historical Society.

57. William W. Blackford, *War Years with Jeb Stuart* (New York, 1945), p. 217; John R. Porter Diary, June 9, 1863, Perkins Library, Duke University, Durham, N.C.

58. Glass and Singer, *Singing Soldiers*, p. 153.

59. Summers, *Borderland Confederate*, p. 72.

60. Robert E. Lee to George W. C. Lee, June 13, 1863, Robert Edward Lee Papers, Perkins Library, Duke University, Durham, N.C.; Robert E. Lee to Mary Custis Lee, June 14, 1863, Virginia Historical Society, Richmond; *War of the Rebellion*, vol. 27, pt. 3, p. 881.

61. Susan Leigh Blackford, comp., *Letters from Lee's Army, or Memoir of Life In and Out of the Army in Virginia During the War Between the States* (1947; New York, 1962), pp. 174–75; Gallagher, "Brandy Station," p. 51; William O. Harvie to Mrs. Lewis E. Harvie, June 14, 1863, Harvie Family Papers, Virginia Historical Society, Richmond.

62. *Richmond Examiner*, June 12, 1863, p. 2; Freeman, *Lee's Lieutenants*, III, pp. 18–19.

63. James E. B. Stuart to Flora Stuart, June 12, 1863, Stuart Papers; *War of the Rebellion*, vol. 27, pt. 2, pp. 679–85, 719–20. The Charleston *Mercury* of June 17 said Stuart had been "disgracefully surprised," and that his "head had been turned by the ladies and newspapers." Quoted in Torlief S. Holmes, *Horse Soldiers in Blue* (Gaithersburg, Md., 1985), p. 86. See also Thomas, *Bold Dragoon*, pp. 226–31.

64. Starr, *Union Cavalry*, I, pp. 391–95; Worthington C. Ford, ed., *A Cycle of Adams Letters: 1861–1865*, 2 vols. (Boston, 1920), II, p. 32; Joseph P. Hazelton, *Scouts, Spies, and Heroes of the Great Civil War* (Cleveland, 1892), p. 248; McClellan, *Campaigns of Stuart*, pp. 294–95; Gallagher, "Brandy Station," pp. 51–53; Charles W. Ramsdell, "General Robert E. Lee's Horses Supply, 1862–1865," *American Historical Review*, XXXV (July 1930), pp. 762–64; Opie, *Rebel Cavalryman*, pp. 158–59.

65. *War of the Rebellion*, vol. 27, pt. 2, pp. 313–14; *ibid.*, pt. 3, p. 886; Robert E. Lee to George W. C. Lee, June 13, 1863, Lee Papers, Perkins Library, Duke University; Summers, *Borderland Confederate*, p. 72; Neese, *Three Years in Confederate Artillery*, pp. 179–80; Hotchkiss, *Make Me a Map of the Valley*, pp. 150–52; George K. Harlow to parents, June 10, 1863, Harlow Family Papers, Virginia Historical Society, Richmond.

66. Henry T. Owen to Harriet A. Owen, June 13, 1863, Henry Thweatt Owen Papers, Virginia Historical Society, Richmond; H. C. Kendrick to mother, June 6, 1863, H. C. Kendrick Letters, Southern Historical Collection, University of North Carolina at Chapel Hill.

67. Woodford B. Hackley, *The Little Fork Rangers: A Sketch of Company "D" Fourth Virginia Cavalry* (Richmond, 1927), pp. 47, 85–86; H. C. Kendrick to mother, June 6, 1863, Kendrick Letters; Robert E. Lee to George W. C. Lee, June 13, 1863, Lee Papers, Duke University; William R. Aylett to Alice Aylett, June 9, 13, 1863, Aylett Family Papers, Virginia Historical Society, Richmond, Henry T. Owen to Harriet A. Owen, June 13, 1863, Owen Papers.

68. William H. Tatum to John C. C. Tatum, June 7, 1863, Tatum Papers; William O. Harvie to Lewis E. Harvie, June 14, 1863, Harvie Family Papers; Robert E. Lee to Mary C. Lee, June 14, 1863, Lee Papers, Virginia Historical Society; Blackford, *Letters from Lee's Army*, p. 176. Lee's letter refers to five Cole children, but the population census for 1860 (p. 783) lists only three children in the Cole household.

69. James H. Williams to Cora Pritchartt, June 13, 1863, Williams Family Papers; W. H. Tatum to Rosabelle Tatum, June 15, 1863, Tatum Papers; William N. Berkeley to wife, June 15, 1863, Berkeley Family Papers, Alderman Library, University of Virginia, Charlottesville; Summers, *Borderland Confederate*, pp. 72–73.

70. West, *A Texan in Search of a Fight*, pp. 74–75; Simpson, *Hood's Texas Brigade*, pp. 247–48.

71. *War of the Rebellion*, vol. 27, pt. 2, p. 315; James I. Robertson, Jr., *General A. P. Hill: The Story of a Confederate Warrior* (New York, 1987), pp. 200–201.

72. Neese, *Three Years in Confederate Artillery*, p. 180; Draughton Stith Haynes, *The Field Diary of a Confederate Soldier* (Darien, Ga., 1963), pp. 28–29; Francis Milton Kennedy Diary, June 16–18, 1863, Southern Historical Collection, University of North Caroline at Chapel Hill; James N. Bradshaw to wife, Samuel Simpson Biddle Letters, Perkins Library, Duke University, Durham, N.C.; Porter Diary, June 16, 1863.

73. Avary, *Virginia Girl*, pp. 252–55.

74. Avary, *Virginia Girl*, pp. 258–59.

75. Hassler, *General to His Lady*, pp. 248–49.

Chapter 10. Return of the Yankees

1. Robert K. Krick, *Parker's Virginia Battery, C.S.A.* (Berryville, Va., 1975), p. 179; Susan Leigh Blackford, Comp., *Letters from Lee's Army, or Memoir of Life In and Out of the Army in Virginia During the War Between the States* (1947; New York, 1962), p. 197; John O. Collins to Catherine S. Collins, July 27, 1863, John Overton Collins Papers, Virginia Historical Society, Richmond; Edward P. Alexander to wife, July 25, 1863, Edward P. Alexan-

der Papers, Southern Historical Collection, University of North Carolina at Chapel Hill; Lawson Morrissett Diary, July 24–25, 1863, Eleanor S. Brockenbrough Library, Museum of the Confederacy, Richmond; Everard H. Smith, "Chambersburg: Anatomy of a Confederate Reprisal," *American Historical Review*, LXXXXVI (April 1991), pp. 441–48; Mills Lane, ed., *"Dear Mother: Don't grieve about me." Letters from Georgia Soldiers in the Civil War* (Savannah, 1977), p. 258.

2. Charles D. Walker, *Biographical Sketches of the Graduates and Élèves of the Virginia Military Institute Who Fell During the War Between the States* (Philadelphia, 1875), pp. 425–27; David F. Riggs, *7th Virginia Infantry*, 2nd ed. (Lynchburg, 1982), pp. 65, 66, 79, 83, 85, 87, 88, 93; Robert T. Bell, *11th Virginia Infantry* (Lynchburg, 1985), p. 69; David F. Riggs, *13th Virginia Infantry* (Lynchburg, 1988), pp. 100, 101, 115; William Daniel Ross to sister, June 11, 1863, Ross Family Correspondence, Virginia State Library and Archives, Richmond.

3. Sally Anne Armstrong Diary, July 22, 24, 1863, Virginia Historical Society, Richmond; Francis Milton Kennedy Diary, July 24, 1863, Southern Historical Collection, University of North Carolina at Chapel Hill.

4. Luther W. Hopkins, *From Bull Run to Appomattox: A Boy's View* (Baltimore, 1908), p. 115.

5. Gary W. Gallagher, ed., *Fighting for the Confederacy: The Personal Recollections of General Edward Porter Alexander* (Chapel Hill, 1989), p. 274.

6. *Ibid.*, pp. 274–75.

7. Krick, *Parker's Battery*, p. 180; George Washington Hall Diary, July 26, 1863, Library of Congress; James M. Simpson to Addie Simpson, July 26, 1863, Allen and Simpson Family Papers, Southern Historical Collection, University of North Carolina at Chapel Hill.

8. Susan P. Lee, *Memoirs of William Nelson Pendleton* (Philadelphia, 1893), pp. 298–99; Blackford, *Letters from Lee's Army*, p. 197.

9. Robert A. Stiles to mother, July 29 [1863], Robert Augustus Stiles Papers, Virginia Historical Society, Richmond.

10. Fairfax Downey, *Clash of Cavalry: The Battle of Brandy Station, June 9, 1863* (New York, 1959); Emory M. Thomas, *Bold Dragoon: The Life of J. E. B. Stuart* (New York, 1986), pp. 254–56; James E. B. Stuart to Flora Stuart, July 25, 1863, James Ewell Brown Stuart Papers, Virginia Historical Society, Richmond. For a review of the Stuart controversy see Mark Nesbitt, *Saber and Scapegoat: J. E. B. Stuart and the Gettysburg Controversy* (Mechanicsburg, Pa., 1994).

11. Clifford Dowdey and Louis H. Manarin, eds., *The Wartime Papers of R. E. Lee* (Boston, 1961), pp. 551, 560, 564–65.

12. John S. Lewis, Jr. to mother, July 31, 1863, Harry Lewis Papers, Southern Historical Collection, University of North Carolina at Chapel Hill; Ray Mathias, *In the Land of the Living: Wartime Letters by Confederates from the Chattahoochee Valley of Alabama and Georgia* (Troy, Ala., 1981), p. 57; Thomas C. Elder to wife, July 30, 1863, Thomas Claybrook Elder Papers, Virginia Historical Society, Richmond; Morrissett Diary, July 26–30, 1863; John Rozier, ed., *The Granite Farm Letters: The Civil War Correspondence of Edgeworth & Sallie Bird* (Athens, Ga., 1988), pp. 126–31; James H. Williams to Cora Pritchartt, July 31, 1863, Williams Family Papers, Virginia Historical Society, Richmond; Jedediah Hotchkiss, *Make Me a Map of the Valley: The Civil War Journal of Stonewall Jackson's Topographer*, ed. Archie P. McDonald (Dallas, 1973), pp. 163–64; Richard T. Couture, ed., *Charlie's Letters: The Correspondence of Charles E. DeNoon* (n.p., 1982), pp. 177–78; Hall Diary, July 27–29, 1863; Blackford, *Letters from Lee's Army*, pp. 197–98; John O. Collins to Catherine S. Collins, July 31, 1863, Collins Papers.

13. Krick, *Parker's Battery*, pp. 180–81; Harold B. Simpson, *Hood's Texas Brigade: Lee's Grenadier Guard* (Waco, Tex., 1970), pp. 292–93; Thomas C. Elder to Anna F. Elder, July 30, 1863, Elder Papers; Hall Diary, July 30, 1863; *War of the Rebellion: A Compilation of the Records of the Union and Confederate Armies*, 70 vols. in 128 books and index (Washington, D.C., 1880–1901, ser. 1, cited hereafter as *War of the Rebellion*, and all references are to Series 1 unless otherwise indicated) vol. 29, pt. 2, pp. 649–50; William Hamilton to Roy Hamilton, August 25, 1863, William Hamilton Papers, Library of Congress; Washington *Evening Star*, August 15, 1863, p. 1; August 19, 1863, p. 1.

14. *War of the Rebellion*, vol. 27, pt. 3, p. 1049; Dowdey and Manarin, *Wartime Papers of Lee*, pp. 566–67; Stephen C. Smith to brother, August 2, 1863, Stephen Calhoun Smith Papers, Perkins Library, Duke University, Durham, N.C.; George G. Young to brother, August 2, 1863, George G. Young Letters, Alderman Library, University of Virginia, Charlottesville; *War of the Rebellion*, vol. 29, pt. 1, p. 9; Ulysses R. Brooks, *Stories of the Confederacy* (Columbia, S.C., 1912), pp. 189–91; George M. Neese, *Three Years in the Confederate Horse Artillery* (New York, 1911), pp. 203–204; Hotchkiss, *Make Me a Map of the Valley*, p. 164.

15. *War of the Rebellion*, vol. 29, pt. 2, 624, vol. 27, pt. 3, pp. 1049, 1075; Jubal A. Early, *Narrative of the War Between the States* (1912; Wilmington, N.C., 1989), p. 285.

16. Milo M. Quaife, ed., *From the Cannon's Mouth: The Civil War Letters of General Alpheus S. Williams* (Detroit, 1959), pp. 248–49; Rufus B. Dawes, *Service with the Sixth Wisconsin Volunteers* (Marietta, Ohio, 1890), pp. 195, 197–200; William Hamilton to Boyd Hamilton, August 11, 1863, Hamilton Papers; Hall Diary, August 3–4, 1863; *War of the Rebellion*, vol. 29, pt. 1, pp. 21–22; Neese, *Three Years in Confederate Artillery*, pp. 204–205; Hotchkiss, *Make Me a Map of the Valley*, 164.

17. William Clark Corson, *My Dear Jennie*, ed. Blake W. Corson (Richmond, 1982), p. 104; Armstrong Diary, July 29, 31, August 3, 5, 1863.

18. Daniel A. Grimsley, *Battles in Culpeper County, Virginia, 1861–1865* (Culpeper, 1900), pp. 14–15; *War of the Rebellion*, vol. 29, pt. 1, pp. 67–70, 80–81; Dawes, *Service with the Sixth Wisconsin*, pp. 197–98; Allen Nevins, ed., *A Diary of Battle: The Personal Journals of Colonel Charles S. Wainwright, 1861–1865* (New York, 1962), p. 276; Hopkins, *From Bull Run to Appomattox*, pp. 115–16.

19. Cases of Peter Sheldon (NN 209) and Wilbur W. Smith (NN 407), U.S. War Department, Court-Martial Cases, 1809–94, Judge Advocate General Records, RG 153, National Archives.

20. Worthington C. Ford, ed., *A Cycle of Adams Letters: 1861–1865* (Boston, 1920), II, pp. 68–69, 72; Neese, *Three Years in Confederate Artillery*, p. 202.

21. Dawes, *Service with the Sixth Wisconsin*, pp. 199–200; Henry N. Blake, *Three Years in the Army of the Potomac* (Boston, 1865), p. 237; Nevins, *Diary of Battle*, pp. 273–74; Ervin L. Jordan, Jr., *Black Confederates and Afro-Yankees in Civil War Virginia* (Charlottesville, 1995), 187–88; Constant C. Hanks to Florilla Hanks, August 5, September 13, 1863, Constant C. Hanks Papers, Perkins Library, Duke University, Durham, N.C.

22. Armstrong Diary, August 16–17, 1863.

23. Quaife, *From the Cannon's Mouth*, pp. 248–51.

24. Ford, *Cycle of Adams Letters*, II, pp. 71–72; Dawes, *Service with the Sixth Wisconsin*, p. 199.

25. Nevins, *Diary of Battle*, p. 271; James I. Robertson, Jr., ed., "An Indiana Soldier in Love and War: The Civil War Letters of John V. Hadley," *Indiana Magazine of History*, LIX (September 1963), pp. 248–49; William Hamilton to Boyd Hamilton, August 11, 21, 1863, Hamilton Papers.

26. John O. Collins to Catherine S. Collins, August 20, 1863, Collins Papers; Neese, *Three Years in Confederate Artillery*, pp. 205–206; Robert E. Lee, Jr., to Mary Custis Lee, August 21, 1863, Robert Edward Lee Papers, Virginia Historical Society, Richmond; James H. Williams to Cora Pritchartt, August 15, 1863, Williams Family Papers, Virginia Historical Society; Luther W. Hopkins, *From Bull Run to Appomattox: A Boy's View* (Baltimore, 1908), p. 116. For examples of fraternization among pickets on the Rappahannock see Alexander Hunter, *Johnny Reb and Billy Yank* (New York, 1905), pp. 429–31.

27. John O. Collins to Catherine S. Collins, August 17, 1863, Collins Papers; James E. B. Stuart to Flora Stuart, August 28, 1863, Stuart Papers.

28. Robert A. Stiles to mother, July 29, 1863, Stiles Papers; John C. West, *A Texan in Search of a Fight, Being the Diary and Letters of a Private Soldier in Hood's Texas Brigade* (Waco, Tex., 1901), p. 98; J. William Jones, *Christ in Camp, or Religion in the Confederate Army* (Atlanta, 1887), pp. 318–19; Kennedy Diary, September 21, 1863; Robert E. Lee, Jr., to Mary Custis Lee, August 21, 1863, Lee Papers, Virginia Historical Society; Alexander C. Haskell to mother, September 14, 1863, Alexander C. Haskell Papers, Southern Historical Collection, University of North Carolina at Chapel Hill. George G. Young to brother, August 22, 1863, Young Letters.

29. George G. Young to brother, August 22, 1863, Young Letters; John O. Collins to Catherine, August 20, 22, 1863, Collins Papers; John J. Shoemaker, *Shoemaker's Battery: Stuart's Horse Artillery, Pelham's Battalion, Army of Northern Virginia* (Memphis, 1908), pp. 51–52. Generally, see Drew Gilpin Faust, "Christian Soldiers: The Meaning of Revivalism in the Confederate Army," *Journal of Southern History*, LIII (February 1987), 63–90; Samual J. Watson, "Religion and Combat Motivation in the Confederate Armies," *Journal of Military History*, LVIII (January 1994), 29–55.

30. Ford, *Cycle of Adams Letters*, II, pp. 73–74. One example of a court-martial for marauding near Kelly's Ford is the case of Leonard Felter (NN 407), Court-Martial Cases.

31. *Ibid.*, II, pp. 74–75.

32. Armstrong Diary, August 7, pp. 11–12, 15–17, 22, 30, September 1, 1863.

33. Culpeper Law Order Books, County Circuit Court, Book No. 6 (1856–66), pp. 481, 487–88, Culpeper County Courthouse; Richard H. Field to John Letcher, August 6, 1863, Virginia Executive Papers, Virginia State Library and Archives, Richmond; James W. Stallard to Richard Luttrell, September 4, 1863, Luttrell Family Papers, Perkins Library, Duke University, Durham, N.C.; D. D. Pendleton to mother, September 1, 1863, William Nelson Pendleton Papers, Southern Historical Collections, University of North Carolina at Chapel Hill; John N. Opie, *A Rebel Cavalryman with Lee, Stuart and Jackson* (Chicago, 1899), p. 182; Confederate Papers Relating to Citizens or Business Firms, names of people cited, War Department Collection of Confederate Records, RG 109, Microcopy No. 346, National Archives.

34. Opie, *A Rebel Cavalryman*, p. 182; Lynchburg *Daily Virginian*, September 16, 1863, p. 2; Hotchkiss, *Make Me a Map of the Valley*, p. 175.

35. James E. B. Stuart to Flora Stuart, September 4, 17, 1863, Stuart Papers; Neese, *Three Years in Confederate Artillery*, p. 207; James H. Williams to Cora Pritchartt, September 9, 1863, Williams Family Papers; Hotchkiss, *Make Me a Map of the Valley*, p. 175; Thomas, *Bold Dragoon*, pp. 259–63. The result of this unrest plus the defeat of his cavalry in an action on the Rappahannock on September 13–14 led Stuart to speculate on life after the war in his September 17 letter to Flora, as though he were trying to escape present realities.

36. Louis P. Morrison to Rebecca Morrison, September 1, 1863, Louis Philip Morrison Papers, Southern Historical Collection, University of North Carolina at Chapel Hill; William D. Henderson, *The Road to Bristoe Station: Campaigning With Lee and Meade, August 1–October 20, 1863* (Lynchburg, 1987), pp. 30–36; McClellan, *Campaigns of Stuart*, pp. 372–73; G. W. Beale, *A Lieutenant of Cavalry in Lee's Army* (Boston, 1918), pp. 124–25; Grimsley, *Battles in Culpeper County*, pp. 15–16; *War of the Rebellion*, vol. 29, pt. 1, p. 9, and pt. 2, pp. 175, 179–80.

37. Neese, *Three Years in Confederate Artillery*, pp. 208–11; George R. Agassiz, ed., *Meade's Headquarters: Letters of Colonel Theodore Lyman from the Wilderness to Appomattox* (Boston, 1922), p. 16; Grimsley, *Battles in Culpeper County*, pp. 15–17.

38. Mrs. Berkeley G. Calfee, *Confederate History of Culpeper County in the War Between the States* (Culpeper, 1948), pp. 7–8; Grimsley, *Battles in Culpeper*, pp. 15–16; Washington *Evening Star*, September 18, 1863, p. 2.

39. Gregory J. W. Urwin, *Custer Victorious: The Civil War Battles of General George Armstrong Custer* (Rutherford, N.J., 1983), pp. 96–98; Willard Glazier, *Three Years in the Federal Cavalry* (New York, 1874), pp. 320–22; Neese, *Three Years in Confederate Artillery*, pp. 211–12.

40. Beale, *Lieutenant of Cavalry*, pp. 125–26; Grimsley, *Battles in Culpeper*, pp. 17–18; *War of the Rebellion*, vol. 29, pt. 1, pp. 111–12, 118–29; Frederic Denison, *Sabre and Spurs: First Regiment Rhode Island Cavalry in the Civil War, 1861–1865* (Central Falls, R.I., 1876), pp. 286–87.

41. Grimsley, *Battles in Culpeper*, pp. 16–17; Washington *Evening Star*, September 18, 1863, p. 2; Silas Wesson Diary, September 13, 1863, U.S. Army Military History Institute, Carlisle Barracks, Pa.; Thomas Francis Galwey, *The Valiant Hours*, ed. Wilbur S. Nye (Harrisburg, Pa., 1961), p. 143; Charles D. Page, *History of the Fourteenth Regiment, Connecticut Volunteer Infantry* (Meriden, Conn., 1906), p. 182. There is confusion in local lore between the Curtis episode and one occurring during the battle of Cedar Mountain.

42. William Hamilton to mother, September 21, 1863, Hamilton Papers; Robert G. Carter, *Four Brothers in Blue; or, Sunshine and Shadows of the War of the Rebellion* (Austin, 1978), pp. 351–52; Frank P. Deane, ed., *My Dear Wife: The Civil War Letters of David Brett, Union Cannoneer* (Little Rock, 1964), p. 82; Joseph W. Keifer to wife, September 27, 1863, Joseph Warren Keifer Papers, Library of Congress; John L. Smith, *History of the Corn Exchange Regiment, 118th Pennsylvania Volunteers* (Philadelphia, 1888), 307–308; Lemuel T. Foote to wife, September 24, 1863, Lemuel Thomas Foote Papers, Library of Congress.

43. Henderson, *Road to Bristoe Station*, pp. 38–47; George G. Meade, *Life and Letters of George Gordon Meade*, 2 vols. (New York, 1913), II, p. 148; *War of the Rebellion*, vol. 29, pt. 2, pp. 179–80.

44. Terry L. Jones, ed., *The Civil War Memoirs of Captain William J. Seymour: Reminiscences of a Louisiana Tiger* (Baton Rouge, La., 1991), pp. 84–85; *War of the Rebellion*, vol. 29, pt. 2, pp. 186, 188, 191–92, 195–96, 200–202, 206–208, 215–16, 244; Lemuel T. Foote to wife, September 24, 1863, Foote Papers. For fighting outside of Culpeper during the remainder of September and early October see Henderson, *Road to Bristoe Station*, pp. 53–71.

45. Lawrence F. Kohl, ed., *Irish Green and Union Blue: Civil War Letters of Peter Welsh, Color Sergeant, 28th Regiment Massachusetts Volunteers* (New York, 1987), p. 126; Glazier, *Three Years in the Federal Cavalry*, pp. 322–29; Henry L. Campbell to parents, September 20, 1863, Anna P. Campbell Papers, Perkins Library, Duke University,

Durham, N.C.; Gilpin Diary, September 27, 1863; Lemuel T. Foote to wife, September 24, 26, October 7, 1863, Foote Papers; Josiah Marshall Favill, *Diary of a Young Officer, serving with the armies of the United States during the War of the Rebellion* (Chicago, 1909), p. 261; Carter, *Four Brothers in Blue*, pp. 353; Frank Rauscher, *Music on the March, 1862–1865, with the Army Life of the Potomac* (Philadelphia, 1892), pp. 118–21; Deane, *My Dear Wife*, pp. 79, 82.

46. Darius Starr Diary, September 21, 1863, Darius Starr Papers, Perkins Library, Duke University, Durham, N.C.; Alonzo Pickard to Rosie Flagg, September 27, 1863, Alonzo C. Pickard Papers, Library of Congress; Glazier, *Three Years in the Federal Cavalry*, pp. 324, 328–29; Darius Starr to father, September 23, 1863, Starr Papers.

47. Lemuel T. Foote to wife, September 20, 26, 1863, Foote Papers; Smith, *Corn Exchange Regiment*, pp. 308–309.

48. Lemuel T. Foote to wife, October 7, 1863, Foote Papers.

49. William Hamilton to mother, September 21, 1863, Hamilton Papers; Dawes, *Service with the Sixth Wisconsin*, pp. 209–10; Rudolf Aschmann, *Memoirs of a Swiss Officer in the American Civil War*, ed. Heinz K. Meier (Bern, Switzerland, 1972), p. 127; Bigelow, *Civil War Diary*, pp. 228–29; Ruth L. Silliker, ed., *The Rebel Yell & the Yankee Hurrah. The Civil War Journal of a Maine Volunteer: Private John W. Haley, 17th Maine Regiment* (Camden, Maine, 1985), p. 120; Thomas Francis Galwey Diaries, September 28, 1863, Library of Congress; Galwey, *The Valiant Hours*, pp. 146–47; *Southern Historical Society Papers*, X (August–September 1882), pp. 422–23; Charles E. Davis, Jr., *Three Years in the Army: The Story of the Thirteenth Massachusetts Volunteers* (Boston, 1894), pp. 270–71; Alfred S. Roe, *The Thirty-Ninth Regiment Massachusetts Volunteers, 1862–65* (Worcester, Mass., 1914), pp. 107–107.

50. Favill, *Diary of a Young Officer*, p. 263; J. B. Frankenberg to Dear Friend, September 29, 1863, Federal Soldier Letters, Southern Historical Collection, University of North Carolina at Chapel Hill; Darius Starr to mother, September 20, 1863, Starr Papers; Galwey, *Valiant Hours*, pp. 143–45; James I. Robertson, Jr., *Tenting Tonight: The Soldier's Life*, vol. 10 in Time-Life Books, *The Civil War* (28 vols., Alexandria, Va., 1983-87), pp. 154–55; Roe, *Thirty-Ninth Massachusetts Regiment*, pp. 108–109; Ezra D. Simons, *A Regimental History: One-Hundred-and-Twenty-Fifth New York State Volunteers* (New York, 1888), pp. 152–53; Charles D. Page, *History of the Fourteenth Regiment, Connecticut Volunteer Infantry* (Meriden, Conn., 1906), p. 185; Smith, *Corn Exchange Regiment*, p. 308; Davis, *Three Years in the Army*, p. 270; Edward N. Wright, *Conscientious Objectors in the Civil War* (1931; reprinted New York, 1961), pp. 165–66.

51. Arthur A. Kent, ed., *Three Years With Company K: Sergt. Austin C. Stearns, Company K, 13th Mass. Infantry (Deceased)* (Rutherford, N.J., 1976), pp. 214–17; Nevins, *Diary of Battle*, pp. 270–71; Dawes, *Service with the Sixth Wisconsin*, p. 202; Rufus Mead to Dear Folks, August 29, 1863, Rufus Mead Papers, Library of Congress; Charles F. McKenna, ed., *Under the Maltese Cross: Campaigns 155th Pennsylvania Regiment* (Pittsburgh, Pa., 1910), pp. 208–209; Blake, *Three Years in the Army of the Potomac*, pp. 238–40; Theodore Gerrish, *Army Life: A Private's Reminiscences of the Civil War* (Portland, Maine, 1882), pp. 123–28.

52. Darius Starr Diary, September 19–October 8, 1863, Starr Papers; William Hamilton to mother, September 21, 1863, William Hamilton Papers; Carter, *Four Brothers in Blue*, pp. 353–54; Lemuel T. Foote to wife, September 24, October 20, 1863, Foote Papers; Meade, *Life and Letters*, II, p. 151.

53. Lemuel T. Foote to wife, September 28, 1863, Foote Papers; Kohl, *Irish Green and Union Blue*, p. 128; Alonzo Pickard to Rosie Flagg, September 20 and 27, 1863, Pickard Papers.
54. Robert Garth Scott, ed., *Fallen Leaves: The Civil War Letters of Major Henry Livermore Abbott* (Kent, Ohio, 1991), pp. 3, 11, 217–18, 220.
55. Robertson, *Personal Recollections of the War*, p. 69; Favill, *Diary of a Young Officer*, pp. 259–60.
56. Meade, *Life and Letters*, II, p. 150; Smith, *Corn Exchange Regiment*, p. 309; Gilpin Diary, September 30, 1863; Dawes, *Service with the Sixth Wisconsin Volunteers*, pp. 205–207; Silliker, *The Rebel Yell and the Yankee Hurrah*, p. 120.
57. Lemuel T. Foote to wife, September 20, 1863, Foote Papers; Robertson, *Personal Recollections*, pp. 71–73; Sparks, *Inside Lincoln's Army*, pp. 289, 291.
58. Dawes, *Service with the Sixth Wisconsin Volunteers*, p. 205; Denison, *Sabre and Spurs*, p. 290.
59. Lemuel T. Foote to wife, September 20, 1863, Foote Papers.
60. Joseph W. Keifer to Eliza Keifer, September 26, 1863, Keifer Papers; Lynchburg *Daily Virginian*, September 25, 1863, p. 2; Denison, *Sabre and Spurs*, p. 291.

Chapter 11. Equinox

1. *War of the Rebellion: The Official Records of the Union and Confederate Armies*, 70 vols in 128 books (Washington, D.C., 1888–1901, ser. 1, hereafter cited as *War of the Rebellion* and all references are to Series 1 unless otherwise indicated) vol. 29, pt. 2, pp. 757–58; Thomas Francis Galwey, *The Valiant Hours*, ed. Wilbur S. Nye (Harrisburg, Pa., 1961), p. 148.
2. George M. Neese, *Three Years in the Confederate Horse Artillery* (New York, 1911), p. 216; Jubal Early, *Narrative of the War Between the States*, (1912; Wilmington, N.C., 1989), p. 303; *War of the Rebellion*, vol. 29, pt. 1, p. 410; Lemuel T. Foote to wife, October 7, 1863, Lemuel Thomas Foote Papers, Library of Congress; David S. Sparks, ed., *Inside Lincoln's Army: The Diary of Marsena Rudolph Patrick, Provost Marshal General, Army of the Potomac* (New York, 1964), pp. 294–95; Bessie H. Shackleford to John Letcher, October 1863, Virginia Executive Papers, Virginia State Library and Archives, Richmond.
3. Josiah M. Favill, *Diary of a Young Officer, serving with the armies of the United States during the War of the Rebellion* (Chicago, 1909), p. 263; Frank Rauscher, *Music on the March, 1862–1865, With the Army of the Potomac* (Philadelphia, 1892), pp. 123–24; *War of the Rebellion* vol. 29, pt. 1, pp. 9–10, 230, 347–48, 410, 439–42, and pt. 2, pp. 757–58; G. W. Beale, *A Lieutenant of Cavalry in Lee's Army* (Boston, 1918), pp. 128–29; Henry B. McClellan, *The Life and Campaigns of Major General J. E. B. Stuart* (Boston, 1885), pp. 376–80. For a summary of actions on October 8–22, see William D. Henderson, *The Road to Bristoe Station: Campaigning With Lee and Meade, August 1–October 20, 1863* (Lynchburg, 1987), pp. 72–105.
4. Rufus B. Dawes, *Service with the Sixth Wisconsin Volunteers* (Marietta, Ohio, 1890), pp. 211–12; Margery Greenleaf, ed., *Letters to Eliza from a Union Soldier, 1862–1865* (Chicago, 1970), pp. 44–45; Alfred S. Roe, *The Thirty-Ninth Massachusetts Volunteers, 1862–65* (Worcester, Mass., 1914), pp. 110–13; *War of the Rebellion*, vol. 29, pt. 1, pp. 348, 442–43; William Clark Corson, *My Dear Jennie*, ed. Blake W. Corson (Richmond, 1982), pp. 111–12; Stephen Z. Starr, *The Union Cavalry in the Civil War*, 3 vols. (Baton Rouge, La., 1979–85), II, pp. 24–25; Beale, *Lieutenant of Cavalry*, pp. 128–30; Neese, *Three Years in Confederate Artillery*, pp. 217–19.

5. Starr, *Union Cavalry*, II, pp. 25–27; Gregory J. W. Urwin, *Custer Victorious: The Civil War Battles of General George Armstrong Custer* (Rutherford, N.J., 1983), pp. 102–104; Willard Glazier, *Three Years in the Federal Cavalry* (New York, 1874), pp. 335–36.

6. Richard H. Watkins to wife, October 21, 1863, Richard Henry Watkins Papers, Virginia Historical Society, Richmond; McClellan, *Campaigns of Stuart*, pp. 380–81; *War of the Rebellion*, vol. 29, pt. 1, p. 443; Neese, *Three Years in Confederate Artillery*, pp. 217–19.

7. McClellan, *Campaigns of Stuart*, pp. 381–83, *War of the Rebellion*, vol. 29, pt. 1, pp. 443–44; Neese, *Three Years in Confederate Artillery*, pp. 219–20; Glazier, *Three Years in Federal Cavalry*, pp. 337–38.

8. Lemuel T. Foote to wife, October 7, 1863, Foote Papers; James M. Greiner et al., eds., *A Surgeon's Civil War: The Letters and Diary of Daniel M. Holt, M.D.* (Kent, Ohio, 1994), p. 147; Woodford B. Hackley, *The Little Fork Rangers: A Sketch of Company "D" Fourth Virginia Cavalry* (Richmond, 1927), pp. 48–49.

9. Douglas S. Freeman, *R. E. Lee: A Biography*, 4 vols. (New York, 1934), III, pp. 171–73; Armistead L. Long, *Memoirs of Robert E. Lee: His Military and Personal History* (New York, 1887), p. 306.

10. Freeman, *R. E. Lee*, III, pp. 173–76.

11. *War of the Rebellion*, vol. 29, pt. 1, pp. 349, 444–45; and pt. 2, p. 293; Sparks, *Inside Lincoln's Army*, p. 298; Roe, *The Thirty-Ninth Regiment Massachusetts Volunteers*, p. 114.

12. John L. Smith, *History of the Corn Exchange Regiment, 118th Pennsylvania Volunteers* (Philadelphia, 1888), p. 320.

13. *War of the Rebellion*, vol. 29, pt. 1, pp. 293–94, 349; George G. Meade, *Life and Letters of George Gordon Meade*, 2 vols. (New York, 1913), II, p. 154; Robert G. Carter, *Four Brothers in Blue; or, Sunshine and Shadows of the War of the Rebellion* (Austin, Tex., 1978), pp. 354–55; Rauscher, *Music on the March*, pp. 124–25; Smith, *Corn Exchange Regiment*, p. 321; Henderson, *Road to Bristoe Station*, pp. 120–36.

14. Henderson, *Road to Bristoe Station*, pp. 137–205; James I. Robertson, Jr., *General A. P. Hill: The Story of a Confederate Warrior* (New York, 1987), pp. 234–40; Susan P. Lee, *Memoirs of William Nelson Pendleton* (Philadelphia, 1893), pp. 303–304; A. Kelly to brother, October 24, 1863, Williamson Kelly Papers, Perkins Library, Duke University, Durham, N.C.; William Y. Mordecai to mother, October 20, 1863, William Young Mordecai Papers, Perkins Library, Duke University; Spencer G. Welch, *A Confederate Surgeon's Letters to His Wife* (New York, 1911), p. 81; Terry L. Jones, ed., *The Civil War Memoirs of Captain William J. Seymour: Reminiscences of a Louisiana Tiger* (Baton Rouge, La., 1991), pp. 88–89.

15. James I. Robertson, Jr., ed., *The Civil War Letters of General Robert McAllister* (Rutherford, N.J., 1965), p. 347; Jones, *Civil War Memoirs of Seymour*, p. 89; *War of the Rebellion*, vol. 29, pt. 1, p. 408; Clifford Dowdey and Louis H. Manarin, eds., *The Wartime Papers of R. E. Lee* (Boston, 1961), p. 611.

16. *War of the Rebellion*, vol. 29, pt. 1, p. 452; Corson, *My Dear Jennie*, p. 113; Charles W. Ramsdell, "General Robert E. Lee's Horse Supply, 1862–1865," *American Historical Review*, XXXV (July 1930), pp. 764–65; Lee, *Memoirs of Pendleton*, pp. 304–305; William Y. Mordecai to mother, October 20, 1863, Mordecai Papers.

17. H. M. Wagstaff, ed., *The James A. Graham Papers, 1861–84* (Chapel Hill, 1928), pp. 158–59; C. Torrence to R. Lenoir, October 22, 1863, Lenoir Family Papers, Southern Historical Collection, University of North Carolina at Chapel Hill, Dowdey and Manarin, *Wartime Papers of Lee*, p. 615; Robert E. Lee to daughter, October 31, 1863, De-Butts-Ely Collection of Lee Family Papers, Library of Congress.

18. A. Kelly to brother, October 24, 1863, Williamson Kelly Papers; Edmund Cody Burnett, ed., "Letters of a Confederate Surgeon: Dr. Abner Embry McGarity, 1862–65, Pt. II," *Georgia Historical Quarterly*, XXIX (September 1945), p. 177; Carrie E. Spencer et al., comps., *A Civil War Marriage in Virginia: Reminiscences and Letters* (Boyce, Va., 1956), p. 197; Wagstaff, *Graham Papers*, pp. 159, 163–64; Tabulation of Supplies, October 20–31, 1863, Thomas Jonathan Jackson Papers, Perkins Library, Duke University, Durham, N.C.; Thomas C. Elder to wife, November 3, 1863, Thomas Claybrook Elder Papers, Virginia Historical Society, Richmond; Watkins Kearns Diary, October 22–30, 1863, Virginia Historical Society; Alexander C. Haskell to father, October 22, 1863, Alexander C. Haskell Papers, Southern Historical Collection, University of North Carolina at Chapel Hill.

19. Francis Milton Kennedy Diary, October 23, pp. 27–28, 1863, Southern Historical Collection, University of North Carolina at Chapel Hill; Kearns Diary, October 24 and 29, 1863; Wagstaff, *Graham Papers*, p. 162; Burnett, "Letters of a Confederate Surgeon," p. 176; Richard H. Watson to wife, October 25, 1863, Richard Henry Watkins Papers, Virginia Historical Society, Richmond; Alexander C. Haskell to father, October 27, 1863, Haskell Papers.

20. Spencer et al., *Civil War Marriage in Virginia*, p. 200.

21. Richard H. Watkins to wife, October 25, 1863, Watkins Papers; Peter W. Hairston to Fanny Hairston, October 30, 1863, Peter W. Hairston Papers, Southern Historical Collection, University of North Carolina at Chapel Hill; Alexander C. Haskell to father, October 27, 1863, Haskell Papers; Elijah S. Johnson Diary, November 3, 1863, Virginia Historical Society, Richmond.

22. Johnson Diary, October 31, 1863, November 3, 1863; Jedediah Hotchkiss, *Make Me a Map of the Valley: The Civil War Journal of Stonewall Jackson's Topographer*, ed. Archie P. McDonald (Dallas, 1973), pp. 179–80; Jedediah Hotchkiss to wife, October 22, 1863, Jedediah Hotchkiss Papers, Library of Congress.

23. Robertson, *General A. P. Hill*, p. 24; Kennedy Diary, November 4–5, 1863; A. Tedford Barclay to sister, October 26 and 27, 1863, A. Tedford Barclay Letters, Virginia State Library and Archives, Richmond; Charles W. Turner, ed., *Ted Barclay, Liberty Hall Volunteers: Letters from the Stonewall Brigade* (Berryville, Va., 1992), p. 111; *War of the Rebellion*, vol. 29, pt. 2, pp. 806–807.

24. Dowdey and Manarin, *Wartime Papers of Lee*, pp. 615–16; *War of the Rebellion*, vol. 29, pt. 1, pp. 610–11, 619; Burnett, "Letters of a Confederate Surgeon," p. 180.

25. Dowdey and Manarin, *Wartime Papers of Lee*, pp. 615–16; Robert E. Lee, Jr., *Recollections and Letters of General Robert E. Lee* (New York, 1904), pp. 112–13.

26. *War of the Rebellion*, vol. 29, pt. 2, pp. 823–24; George G. Young to sister, November 3, 1863, George G. Young Letters, Alderman Library, University of Virginia, Charlottesville.

27. Alexander D. Betts, *Experiences of a Confederate Chaplain, 1861–64* (n.p., n.d.), pp. 48–49; Thomas L. Norwood to Walter Lenoir, October 31, 1863, Lenoir Family Papers, Southern Historical Collection, University of North Carolina at Chapel Hill; Welch, *A Confederate Surgeon's Letters to his Wife*, pp. 81–82; Thomas R. Faucette to George Faucette, October 29, 1863, Faucette Family Papers, Mullins Library, University of Arkansas, Fayetteville; Alexander C. Haskell to mother, October 21, 1863, Haskell Papers.

28. Barry Popchock, "Daring Night Assault," *America's Civil War*, IV (March 1992), pp. 32–33; Jones, *Civil War Memoirs of Seymour*, p. 91. Confederate and Federal reports of operations on November 7–8, 1863 are in *War of the Rebellion*, vol. 29, pt. 1, pp. 553–637.

29. *War of the Rebellion*, vol. 29, pt. 1, pp. 555–56, 568, 612, 632; Popchock, "Daring Night Assault," 36; Rudolf Aschmann, *Memoirs of a Swiss Officer in the American Civil War*, ed. Heinz K. Meier (Bern, Switzerland, 1972), pp. 128–30.

30. *Ibid.; Medical and Surgical History of the War of the Rebellion*, 2 vols. in 12 books (Washington, D.C., 1870–83), vol. 2, pt. 1, pp. 99, 116; vol. 2, pt. 2, p. 220.

31. Popchock, "Daring Night Assault," pp. 32–35; *Medical and Surgical History*, vol. 2, pt. 1, pp. 124, 229; Jones, *Civil War Memoir of Seymour*, pp. 91–92; *War of the Rebellion*, vol. 29, pt. 1, pp. 612–13; Early, *Narrative*, pp. 309–11.

32. Popchock, "Daring Night Assault," pp. 35–36; Charles Sterling Underhill, ed., *"Your Soldier Boy Samuel": Civil War Letters of Lieut. Samuel Edmund Nichols* (Buffalo, N.Y., 1929), pp. 86–87; Mason W. Tyler, *Recollections of the Civil War*, ed. William S. Tyler (New York, 1912), pp. 122–23; *Medical and Surgical History*, vol. 2, pt. 2, pp. 512, 533; Allan Nevins, ed., *A Diary of Battle: The Personal Journals of Colonel Charles S. Wainwright, 1861–1865* (New York, 1962), pp. 298–99; Jones, *Civil War Memoirs of Seymour*, p. 93; Richard E. Winslow, III, *General John Sedgwick: The Story of a Union Corps Commander* (Novato, Ca., 1982), pp. 122–23.

33. Terry L. Jones, *Lee's Tigers: The Louisiana Infantry in the Army of Northern Virginia* (Baton Rouge, La., 1987), pp. 182–85; Popchock, "Daring Night Assault," pp. 36–37; *War of the Rebellion*, vol. 29, pt. 1, pp. 613, 621–24; Early, *Narrative*, pp. 311–14.

34. Winslow, *General John Sedgwick*, p. 123; Freeman, *R. E. Lee*, III, pp. 192–93; *War of the Rebellion*, vol. 29, pt. 1, pp. 613–16; Samuel D. Buck, *With the Old Confeds: Actual Experiences of a Captain in the Line* (Baltimore, 1925), pp. 93–98.

35. Early, *Narrative*, pp. 316–17; Spencer, *Civil War Marriage in Virginia*, p. 201; William H. Runge, ed., *Four Years in the Confederate Artillery: The Diary of Private Henry Robinson Berkeley* (Chapel Hill, 1961), p. 61; Kennedy Diary, November 8–9, 1863; Neese, *Three Years in Confederate Artillery*, pp. 235–36.

36. Richard H. Watkins to wife, November 11, 1863, Watkins Papers; Jones, *Lee's Tigers*, p. 186; Douglas S. Freeman, *Lee's Lieutenants: A Study in Command*, 3 vols. (New York, 1942–44), III, pp. 167–69; R. Lockwood Tower, ed., *Lee's Adjutant: The Wartime Letters of Colonel Walter Herron Taylor, 1862–1865* (Columbia, S.C., 1995), p. 82; Lee, *Memoirs of Pendleton*, p. 305.

37. Smith *Corn Exchange Regiment*, p. 347; Agassiz, *Meade's Headquarters*, pp. 45–46; Greiner et al., *A Surgeon's Civil War*, pp. 156, 157; *War of the Rebellion*, vol. 29, pt. 2, p. 443; Meade, *Life and Letters*, II, pp. 155–56; Nevins, *Diary of Battle*, p. 300.

38. Furst Diary, November 9, 1863; Robertson, *Civil War Letters of McAllister*, pp. 356–57; Agassiz, *Meade's Headquarters*, p. 47; Charles W. Bardeen, *A Little Fifer's War Diary* (Syracuse, N.Y., 1910), p. 273; Joseph W. Keifer, *Slavery and Four Years of War: A Political History of Slavery in the United States, Together with a Narrative of the Campaigns and Battles of the Civil War in which the Author Took Part, 1861–1865*, 2 vols. (New York, 1900), II, pp. 187–88; Lemuel T. Foote to wife, November 19, 1863, Foote Papers.

39. John G. Perry, *Letters from a Surgeon of the Civil War* (Boston, 1906), pp. 123–27.

40. Winslow, *General John Sedgwick*, p. 124; F. W. Morse, *Personal Experiences in the War of the Great Rebellion* (Albany, N.Y., 1866), pp. 65–66; George T. Fleming, ed., *Life and Letters of Alexander Hays, Brevet Colonel United States Army* (Pittsburgh, 1919), p. 516.

41. Winslow, *General John Sedgwick*, pp. 124–25, Morse, *Personal Experiences*, pp. 66–67; Agassiz, *Meade's Headquarters*, pp. 46–47; Robert Hunt Rhodes, ed., *All for the Union: A History of the 2nd Rhode Island Volunteer Infantry in the War of the Great Rebellion* (Lincoln, R.I., 1985), p. 133; Robertson, *Civil War Letters of McAllister*, pp.

357–59; Joseph W. Keifer to Eliza S. Keifer, November 15, 1863, Joseph Warren Keifer Papers, Library of Congress; Silliker, *Rebel Yell and Yankee Hurrah*, pp. 128, 133.

42. Tyler, *Recollections of the Civil War*, pp. 124–25; Rauscher, *Music on the March*, p. 139; Furst Diary, November 19, 1863; Bardeen, *Little Fifer*, pp. 273–74; Lemuel T. Foote to wife, November 19, 1863, Foote Papers; Agassiz, *Meade's Headquarters*, pp. 48–50; Robertson, *Civil War Letters of McAllister*, p. 360; Perry, *Letters from a Surgeon*, pp. 127–28; Furst Diary, November 20, 1863; Joseph H. Keifer to Eliza S. Keifer, November 16, 1863, Keifer Papers.

43. Clark B. Hall, "Season of Change: The Winter Encampment of the Army of the Potomac December 1, 1863–May 4, 1864," *Blue & Gray*, VIII (April 1991), pp. 14–15, 16–18.

44. Darius Starr to mother, November 16, 1863, Darius Starr Papers, Perkins Library, Duke University, Durham, N.C.; E. O. Wentworth to wife, November 29, 1863, Edwin Oberlin Wentworth Papers, Library of Congress; Sparks, *Inside Lincoln's Army*, p. 310.

45. Winslow, *General John Sedgwick*, pp. 125–26; Augustus Buell, *"The Cannoneer": Recollections of Service in the Army of the Potomac* (Washington, D.C., 1890), p. 137; Greiner et al., *A Surgeon's Civil War*, pp. 159–63; Philip N. Racine, ed., *"Unspoiled Heart": The Journal of Charles Mattocks of the 17th Maine* (Knoxville, Tenn., 1994), pp. 84–89; Dawes, *Service with Sixth Wisconsin*, p. 225. For the Mine Run campaign see *War of the Rebellion*, vol. 29, pt. 1, pp. 663–908; Jay Luvaas and Wilbur S. Nye, "The Campaign That History Forgot," *Civil War Times*, VIII (November 1969), pp. 11–42; Martin Graham and George Skoch, *Mine Run: A Campaign of Lost Opportunities* (Lynchburg, 1987).

46. Sparks, *Inside Lincoln's Army*, pp. 319–21; Meade, *Life and Letters*, II, pp. 156–61; Perry, *Letters from a Surgeon*, p. 148; Nevins, *Diary of Battle*, pp. 308–309; Furst Diary, December 4, 1863; Robertson, *Personal Recollections*, p. 79.

47. Ezra D. Simons, *A Regimental History: One Hundred and Twenty-Fifth New York State Volunteers* (New York, 1888), pp. 188–89; Joseph W. Keifer to wife, December 19, 1863, Keifer Papers; Bardeen, *Little Fifer*, p. 289; Wilbur Fisk, *Anti-Rebel: The Civil War Letters of Wilbur Fisk* (Croton-on-Hudson, N.Y., 1983), p. 173; Sparks, *Inside Lincoln's Army*, p. 321; Meade, *Life and Letters*, II, pp. 161–63.

48. James I. Robertson, Jr., ed., "An Indiana Soldier in Love and War: The Civil War Letters of John V. Hadley," *Indiana Magazine of History*, LIX (September 1963), p. 264; Fisk, *Anti-Rebel*, pp. 174–75, 181; Galwey, *Valiant Hours*, p. 184; David W. Blight, ed., *When This Cruel War is Over: The Civil War Letters of Charles Harvey Brewster* (Amherst, Mass., 1992), pp. 269, 273; Alonzo Pickard to Rozella Flagg, December 13, 27, 1863, Alonzo C. Pickard Papers, Library of Congress, Greenleaf, *Letters to Eliza*, pp. 58–59, 63–64; Charles E. Davis, Jr., *Three Years in the Army: The Story of the Thirteenth Massachusetts Volunteers* (Boston, 1894), p. 298; Nevins, *Diary of Battle*, pp. 307–311; Dawes, *Service in Sixth Wisconsin*, pp. 229–30, 234.

49. Starr Diary, December 24, 1863; Nevins, *Diary of Battle*, p. 309; Lawrence F. Kohl, ed., *Irish Green and Union Blue: Civil War Letters of Peter Welsh, Color Sergeant, 28th Regiment Massachusetts Volunteers* (New York, 1987), pp. 137–39; Dawes, *Service with Sixth Wisconsin*, pp. 231–35; Carter, *Four Brothers in Blue*, pp. 376–77.

50. Harold A. Small, ed., *The Road to Richmond: The Civil War Memoirs of Maj. Abner S. Small of the 16th Maine Vols.* (Berkeley, Ca., 1957), pp. 120–21. For a similar but less success effort see Thomas Chamberlin, *History of the One Hundred and Fiftieth Regiment, Pennsylvania Volunteers, Second Regiment, Bucktail Brigade* (Philadelphia, 1895), p. 167.

51. Greenleaf, *Letters to Eliza*, pp. 58–60. For a brief firsthand account of courts-martial procedures see General Du Chanal, "How Soldiers Were Tried," *Civil War Times*, VII (February 1969), pp. 10–13.

52. Racine, *Unspoiled Heart*, p. 90; cases of Edward Neffrey (LL 1377), James McCabe (NN 371), and Herman Barber (MM 916), U.S. War Department, Courts-Martial Cases, 1809–1894, Judge Advocate General Records, RG 153, National Archives.

53. Perry, *Letters from a Surgeon*, pp. 99–100; Robert Garth Scott, ed., *Fallen Leaves: The Civil War Letters of Major Henry Livermore Abbott* (Kent, Ohio, 1991), pp. 223–25; Favill, *Diary of a Young Officer*, p. 263.

54. Survey of courts-martial records; Perry, *Letters from a Surgeon*, pp. 99–100; Scott, *Fallen Leaves*, pp. 223–25; Henry N. Blake, *Three Years in Army of the Potomac* (Boston, 1865), pp. 267–68.

55. Case of George A. Francis (MM 1270), Courts-Martial Cases.

56. Buell, *The Cannoneer*, p. 139; James I. Robertson, Jr., "Military Executions," *Civil War Times*, V (May 1966), pp. 34–39; Darius Starr to father, December 4, 1863, Starr Papers; Fisk, *Anti-Rebel*, pp. 179–80. In April 1864, Meade refused to commute a death sentence for rape even though Lincoln seemed inclined to do so. See William Corby, *Memoirs of Chaplain Life: Three Years with the Irish Brigade in the Army of the Potomac*, ed. Lawrence F. Kohl (New York, 1992), pp. 220–28.

57. Case of Samuel H. Clark (LL 1377), Courts-Martial Cases.

58. Case of W. H. Green (LL751), Court-Martial Cases; Third Indiana Cavalry, Circular of November 12, 1863, General Order 10, December 4, 1863, Regimental Order Books.

59. E. O. Wentworth to wife, December 16, 1863, Wentworth Papers; Blight, *When This Cruel War is Over*, p. 271; Mrs. Berkeley G. Calfee, *Confederate History of Culpeper County in the War Between the States* (Culpeper, 1948), pp. 9–10.

60. Robertson, "Civil War Letters of Headley," p. 264; Calfee, *Confederate History of Culpeper*, pp. 9–10.

61. Hall, "Season of Change," p. 50; Sparks, *Patrick Diary*, pp. 321–22; Fisk, *Anti-Rebel*, pp. 176–77.

62. James H. Kidd, *Personal Recollections of a Cavalryman with Custer's Michigan Cavalry in the Civil War* (Ionia, Mich,, 1908), p. 230; Chamberlin, *History of the One Hundred and Fiftieth Regiment, Pennsylvania Volunteers*, p. 168; Calfee, *Confederate History of Culpeper*, pp. 10–11; Blake, *Three Years in the Army of the Potomac*, p. 268.

63. Agassiz, *Meade's Headquarters*, p. 48.

64. Ulysses R. Brooks, *Stories of the Confederacy* (Columbia, S.C., 1912), pp. 210–11; Lemuel T. Foote to wife, November 19, 1863, Foote Papers.

65. Kidd, *Personal Recollections*, pp. 231–32; Robert S. Robertson, *Personal Recollections of the War: A Record of Service with the Ninety-Third New York Volunteer Infantry* (Milwaukee, 1895), pp. 148–49; Silliker, *Rebel Yell and Yankee Hurrah*, p. 134; Charles Noble to Susan E. Coons, December 15, 17, and 24, 1863, and Martha E. Coons to George Dallas Coons, November 11, 1864, Coons Family Papers, Virginia Historical Society, Richmond.

Chapter 12. A Yankee Village

1. Charles W. Bardeen, *A Little Fifer's War Diary* (Syracuse, N.Y., 1910), pp. 290–94; Andrew A. Humphreys, *The Virginia Campaigns of '64 and '65: The Army of the Potomac and the Army of the James* (New York, 1894), pp. 1–2; Clark B. Hall, "Season of Change: The Winter Encampment of the Army of the Potomac December 1, 1863–May 4, 1864," *Blue & Gray*, VIII (April 1991), pp. 12–18.

2. Henry N. Blake, *Three Years in the Army of the Potomac* (Boston, 1865), p. 271; F. W. Morse, *Personal Experiences in the War of the Great Rebellion, from December, 1862, to July 1865* (Albany, N.Y., 1866), pp. 71–72; James I. Robertson, Jr., ed., "An Indiana Soldier in Love and War: The Civil War Letters of John V. Hadley," *Indiana Magazine of History*, LIX (September 1863), p. 267; David S. Sparks, ed., *Inside Lincoln's Army: The Diary of Marsena Rudolph Patrick, Provost Marshal General, Army of the Potomac* (New York, 1964), p. 327; George R. Agassiz, ed., *Meade's Headquarters 1863–1865: Letters of Colonel Theodore Lyman from the Wilderness to Appomattox* (Boston, 1922), pp. 64, 74.

3. Lawrence F. Kohl, ed., *Irish Green and Union Blue: Civil War Letters of Peter Welsh, Color Sergeant, 28th Regiment Massachusetts Volunteers* (New York, 1987), p. 143; Shirley A. Leckie, *Elizabeth Bacon Custer and the Making of a Myth* (Norman, Okla., 1993), p. 40; Arlene Reynolds, ed., *The Civil War Memories of Elizabeth Bacon Custer* (Austin, Tex., 1994), pp. 44–45; Robertson, "Civil War Letters of Hadley," p. 268; Agassiz, *Meade's Headquarters*, pp. 64, 74.

4. Charles B. Miller to Mary B. Miller, February 21, 1864, Federal Soldiers' Letters, Southern Historical Collection, University of North Carolina at Chapel Hill; Louis P. Morrison to wife, February 9, 1864, Louis Philip Morrison Papers, Southern Historical Collection, University of North Carolina at Chapel Hill; George T. Fleming, ed., *Life and Letters of Alexander Hays, Brevet Colonel, United States Army* (Pittsburgh, Pa., 1919), pp. 536–37; Agassiz, *Meade's Headquarters*, p. 65; Warren Lee Goss, *Recollections of a Private: A Story of the Army of the Potomac* (New York, 1890), Constant Hanks to Rose Hanks, February 6, 1864, Constant C. Hanks Papers, Perkins Library, Duke University, Durham, N.C.; Blake, *Three Years in the Army of the Potomac*, p. 272.

5. Robertson, "Civil War Letters of Hadley," pp. 270–71; Agassiz, *Meade's Headquarters*, pp. 65–66.

6. Alonzo Pickard to Rozella Flagg, February 21, 1864, Alonzo C. Pickard Papers, Library of Congress; Louis P. Morrison to wife, February 25, 1864, Morrison Papers; Joseph W. Keifer to Eliza S. Keifer, January 14, January 16, 1864, Joseph Warren Keifer Papers, Library of Congress; Morse, *Personal Recollections*, pp. 72–73; Charles P. Miller to Mary B. Miller, February 22, 1864, Federal Soldiers' Letters; Robert S. Robertson, *Personal Recollections of the War: A Record of Service with the Ninety-Third New York Volunteer Infantry* (Milwaukee, 1895), p. 83; James I. Robertson, Jr., ed., *The Civil War Letters of General Robert McAllister* (New Brunswick, N.J., 1965), pp. 383–86.

7. Robertson, "Civil War Letters of Hadley," p. 267, Paul Glass and Louis C. Singer, eds., *Singing Soldiers: A History of the Civil War in Song* (New York, 1975), pp. 30–31.

8. Charles J. Stille, *History of the United States Sanitary Commission* (New York, 1868), pp. 390–91; United States Sanitary Commission, *Bulletin*, I (New York, 1866), pp. 138–40, 207, 258, 276.

9. Robertson, *Civil War Letters of McAllister*, p. 390; verses from "Vigil Strange I Kept on the Field One Night."

10. Edwin H. Miller, ed., *The Correspondence of Walt Whitman*, 6 vols. (New York, 1961–77), I, pp. 195–99.

11. Ruth Silliker, ed., *The Rebel Yell and Yankee Hurrah: The Civil War Journal of a Maine Volunteer: Private John W. Haley, 17th Maine Regiment* (Camden, Maine, 1985), pp. 135–36.

12. Henrietta S. Jacquette, ed., *South After Gettysburg: Letters of Cornelia Hancock, 1863–1868* (New York, 1956), pp. 52–58, 61, 70.

13. *Ibid.*, pp. 58–69.

14. *Ibid.*, pp. 58–66.

15. Lemuel Moss, *Annals of the United States Christian Commission* (Philadelphia, 1868), pp. 411–16; Wilbur Fisk, *Anti-Rebel: The Civil War Letters of Wilbur Fisk* (Croton-on-Hudson, N.Y., 1983), pp. 200–201; Robert H. Rhodes, ed., *All for the Union: A History of the 2nd Rhode Island Volunteer Infantry in the War of the Great Rebellion* (Lincoln, R.I., 1985), p. 139.

16. Edwin O. Wentworth to wife, March 13, 1864, Edwin Oberlin Wentworth Papers, Library of Congress; Rhodes, *All for the Union*, p. 139; Blake, *Three Years in the Army of the Potomac*, p. 271; Robertson, *Civil War Letters of McAllister*, pp. 381, 383, 385. For a less kind view of army chaplains see Goss, *Recollections of a Private*, pp. 255–56.

17. Alonzo C. Pickard to Kate, March 21, 1864, Pickard Papers; Mason W. Tyler, *Recollections of the Civil War*, ed. William S. Tyler (New York, 1912), p. 133; Edwin O. Wentworth to wife, January 11, 1864, Wentworth Papers; John G. Perry, *Letters from a Surgeon of the Civil War*, (Boston, 1906), pp. 155–56.

18. Arthur A. Kent, ed., *Three Years With Company K: Sergt. Austin C. Stearns, Company K, 13th Mass. Infantry (Deceased)* (Rutherford, N.J., 1976), pp. 249–52; Edwin O. Wentworth to wife, January 11, 1864, Wentworth Papers.

19. Hall, "Season of Change," p. 16; Pliny A. Jewett to Stephen Jewett, March 27, 1864, Jewett Family Papers, Virginia Historical Society, Richmond; Edwin O. Wentworth to wife, January 11, 1864, Wentworth Papers.

20. Agassiz, *Meade's Headquarters*, p. 68; *War of the Rebellion: A Compilation of the Official Records of the Union and Confederate Armies*, 70 vols. in 128 books and index (Washington, D.C., 1880–1901, ser. 1, cited hereafter as *War of the Rebellion*, and all references are to Series 1 unless otherwise indicated), vol. 33, pp. 114, 138.

21. Thomas F. Galwey, *The Valiant Hours*, ed. Wilbur S. Nye (Harrisburg, Pa., 1961), pp. 187–89; Agassiz, *Meade's Headquarters*, pp. 69–70. The most complete account of the Morton's Ford fight is Bruce A. Trinque, "Rebels Across the River," *America's Civil War*, VII (September 1994), pp. 38–45, 88; but a good sketch from the Confederate perspective as prelude to the Wilderness campaign is Gordon C. Rhea, *The Battle of the Wilderness, May 5–6, 1864* (Baton Rouge, La., 1994), pp. 1–7.

22. *War of the Rebellion*, vol. 33, pp. 119–20, 132–33; Charles D. Page, *History of the Fourteenth Regiment, Connecticut Volunteer Infantry* (Meriden, Conn., 1906), pp. 218, 222.

23. *War of the Rebellion*, vol. 33, 115, 133; Page, *History of the Fourteenth Pennsylvania*, pp. 219–23; Robert Garth Scott, ed., *Fallen Leaves: The Civil War Letters of Major Henry Livermore Abbott* (Kent, Ohio, 1991), p. 237; Trinque, "Rebels Across the River," pp. 44–45.

24. Page, *History of the Fourteenth Pennsylvania*, pp. 219, 221–23; Harry F. Shinn, ed., "A Fifer's Diary," pp. 14–15, typescript in possession of author; *War of the Rebellion*, vol. 33, pp. 114–15; Trinque, "Rebels Across the River," pp. 42–43; Galwey, *The Valiant Hours*, pp. 189–90; Agassiz, *Meade's Headquarters*, p. 71. For a different appraisal of Hays's conduct see Fleming, *Life and Letters of Alexander Hays* pp. 541–42.

25. *War of the Rebellion*, vol. 33, pp. 115–16, 122, 133–34; *Medical and Surgical History of the War of the Rebellion*, 2 vols. in 12 books (Washington, D.C., 1870–83), vol. 2, pt. 1, p. 181; vol. 2, pt. 2, pp. 87, 304, 861.

26. Sanitary Commission, *Bulletin*, 278; Ezra D. Simons, *A Regimental History: One Hundred and Twenty-Fifth New York State Volunteers* (New York, 1888), p. 190; Walt Whitman, *Speciman Days*, in *Complete Prose Works* (Philadelphia, 1892), 49; *War of the Rebellion*, vol. 33, pp. 139–41.

27. Perry, *Letters from a Surgeon*, p. 158; Miller, *Correspondence of Whitman*, I, p. 197.

28. Louis P. Morrison to Rebecca Morrison, February 25, 1864, Morrison Papers; David

W. Blight, ed., *When This Cruel War Is Over: The Civil War Letters of Charles Harvey Brewster* (Amherst, Mass., 1992), p. 268.

29. Josiah M. Favill, *Diary of a Young Officer, serving with the armies of the United States during the War of the Rebellion* (Chicago, 1909), pp. 278–80; Robertson, *Personal Recollections*, p. 85; Blight, *When This Cruel War Is Over*, p. 267; Fisk, *Anti-Rebel*, pp. 187–88.

30. Charles E. Davis, *Three Years in the Army of the Potomac: The Story of the Thirteenth Massachusetts Volunteers* (Boston, 1894), pp. 308–309, 313; Favill, *Diary of a Young Officer*, p. 282; Richard E. Winslow, *General John Sedgwick: The Story of a Union Corps Commander* (Novato, Ca., 1982), p. 139; Samuel J. B. V. Gilpin Diary, January 23, 1864, E.N. Gilpin Papers, Library of Congress; Robertson, "Civil War Letters of Hadley," p. 269; Robert G. Carter, *Four Brothers in Blue; or, Sunshine and Shadows of the War of the Rebellion* (Austin, Tex., 1978), p. 381.

31. W. Fletcher Thompson, Jr., *The Image of War: The Pictorial Reporting of the American Civil War* (New York, 1960), pp. 132–37; Edwin Forbes, *Thirty Years After: An Artist's Story of the Great War* (1890; Baton Rouge, La., 1993); Frederic E. Ray, *"Our Special Artist": Alfred R. Waud's Civil War* (1974; Mechanicsburg, Pa., 1994); William L. Elder, Jr., *Culpeper: A Pictorial History* (Virginia Beach, Va., 1976). Whitman's phrases are taken from his poem "The Wound-Dresser."

32. Hall, "Season of Change," p. 48; Carter, *Four Brothers in Blue*, p. 380; Alexander S. Webb to father, March 15, 1864, Papers of Alexander Stewart Webb, Sterling Library, Yale University, New Haven, Conn.; William A. Frassantio, *Grant and Lee: The Virginia Campaigns, 1864–1865* (New York, 1983), pp. 28–29; Constant C. Hanks to mother, March 22, 1864, Constant C. Hanks Papers, Perkins Library, Duke University, Durham, N.C.

33. Robertson, *Personal Recollections*, pp. 83–84; Carter, *Four Brothers in Blue*, p. 380; Gilpin Diary, February 10, 12, 1864; Favill, *Diary of a Young Officer*, pp. 281–82; James Gwyn to W. E. Boardman, February 21, 1864, U.S. Christian Commission Letters, Communications Received at Central Office, Philadelphia, RG 94, National Archives; Alfred S. Roe, *Thirty-Ninth Massachusetts Volunteers, 1862–65* (Worcester, Mass., 1914), pp. 144–48; Philip N. Racine, ed., *"Unspoiled Heart": The Journal of Charles Mattocks of the 17th Maine* (Knoxville, Tenn., 1994), pp. 107, 115, 123; Robertson, *Civil War Letters of McAllister*, p. 389; Fisk, *Anti-Rebel*, pp. 202–203.

34. Roe, *Thirty-Ninth Massachusetts*, pp. 148–49.

35. *War of the Rebellion*, vol. 33, p. 357; Kohl, *Irish Green and Union Blue*, p. 155; Carter, *Four Brothers in Blue*, p. 382; Blight, *When This Cruel War Is Over*, pp. 273–74; Fisk, *Anti-Rebel*, pp. 186–87; Davis, *Three Years in the Army*, pp. 302–303; Edwin O. Wentworth to wife, January 17, 1864, Wentworth Papers.

36. Edwin O. Wentworth to wife, January 17, 1864, Wentworth Papers; Constant C. Hanks to mother, January 4, February 6, 1864, Hanks Papers. For the motivations of Union soldiers, especially with a view toward emancipation, see Earl J. Hess, *Liberty, Virtue, and Progress: Northerners and Their War for the Union* (New York, 1988), pp. 81–102; and James M. McPherson, *What They Fought For, 1861–1865* (Baton Rouge, La., 1994), pp. 56–69.

37. Joseph W. Keifer to Eliza Keifer, February 23, 1864, Keifer Papers; Davis, *Three Years in the Army of the Potomac*, pp. 301–302; Edward G. Longacre, *To Gettysburg and Beyond: The Twelfth New Jersey Volunteer Infantry* (Hightstown, N.J., 1988), p. 169; Robertson, *Civil War Letters of McAllister*, p. 384; Blight, *When This Cruel War Is Over*, pp. 275, 277.

38. Gilpin Diary, February 13, 1864; Blake, *Three Years in the Army of the Potomac*, p. 271; Robertson, *Personal Recollections*, p. 84. For the complex attitudes of northern soldiers

toward female roles see Reid Mitchell, *The Vacant Chair: The Northern Soldier Leaves Home* (New York, 1993), pp. 71–87.

39. Bardeen, *Little Fifer*, p. 295.

40. Regimental Letter Book of Thirty-seventh Massachusetts, circular of February 17, 1864, Regimental Letter and Order Book of the Seventeenth Maine, order of January 20, 1864, both in U.S. War Department, Regimental Record Books, Records of Adjutant General's Office, RG 94, National Archives.

41. Racine, *Unspoiled Heart*, p. 108; cases of William Graham (LL 1625), Jackson Coe (NN 1625), and J.M. Phillips (NN 1562), U.S. War Department, Court-Martial Cases, 1809–94, Judge Advocate General Records, RG 153, National Archives.

42. Racine, *Unspoiled Heart*, pp. 120–21, 127; James M. Greiner, et al., eds., *A Surgeon's Civil War: The Letters and Diary of Daniel M. Holt, M.D.* (Kent, Ohio, 1994), p. 169.

43. Cases of John Wilson (LL 1763), Stephen Mack (LL 1506), Charles Williams (LL 1814), and Jesse Loraine (NN 1273), Court-Martial Cases.

44. Davis, *Three Years in the Army of the Potomac*, p. 302; William Corby, *Memoirs of Chaplain Life: Three Years with the Irish Brigade in the Army of the Potomac*, ed. Lawrence F. Kohl (New York, 1992), p. 226; Frank Wilkeson, *Recollections of a Private Soldier in the Army of the Potomac* (New York, 1887), pp. 30–31.

45. Margaret Jeffries, "Rose Hill," p. 2, Works Progress Administration of Virginia, Historical Inventory for Culpeper County, Virginia, Culpeper County Courthouse; Edward G. Longacre, *Mounted Raids of the Civil War* (South Brunswick, N.J., 1975), pp. 227–38; V.C. Jones, "The Kilpatrick-Dahlgren Raid: Boldly Planned . . . Timidly Executed," *Civil War Times*, IV (April 1965), pp. 12–21; *War of the Rebellion*, vol. 33, pp. 169–71; George G. Meade, *Life and Letters of George Gordon Meade*, 2 vols. (New York, 1913), II, pp. 168–69, 170.

46. The fullest account of the raid is V.C. Jones, *Eight Hours Before Richmond* (New York, 1957).

47. *War of the Rebellion*, vol. 33, pp. 163, 170–71; Harold R. Woodward, Jr., *For Home and Honor: The Story of Madison County, Virginia, during the War Between the States, 1861–1865* (Madison, Va., 1990), pp. 83–85; Tyler, *Recollections of the Civil War*, pp. 135–37.

48. Winslow, *General John Sedgwick*, pp. 140–41; Agassiz, *Meade's Headquarters*, pp. 76–78; Gilpin Diary, March 18, 1864.

49. Winslow, *General John Sedgwick*, p. 141; Meade, *Life and Letters*, II, pp. 169–80.

50. J. Michael Welton, ed., *"My Heart Is So Rebellious": The Caldwell Letters, 1861–1865* (Warrenton, Va., 1991), pp. 204–205.

51. *War of the Rebellion*, vol. 33, 365; Percy G. Hamlin, ed., *The Making of a Soldier: Letters of General R. S. Ewell* (Richmond, 1935), p. 122; Longacre, *Gettysburg and Beyond*, p. 169; Frank Rauscher, *Music on the March, 1862–1865, With the Army of the Potomac* (Philadelphia, 1892), p. 144; Rudolf Aschmann, *Memoirs of a Swiss Officer in the American Civil War*, ed. Heinz K. Meier (Bern, Switzerland, 1972), p. 137; Robertson, "Civil War Letters of Hadley," p. 273; Racine, *Unspoiled Heart*, p. 98.

52. Greiner et al., *A Surgeon's Civil War*, p. 171; James W. Latta Diary, February 5, 1864, Library of Congress; Joseph W. Keifer to Eliza Keifer, January 9, 1864, Keifer Papers; Isaac Plumb Record, April 5, 1864, Civil War Miscellaneous Collection, U.S. Army Military History Institute, Carlisle Barracks, Pa.

53. Kenneth L. Stiles, *4th Virginia Cavalry*, 2nd ed. (Lynchburg, 1985), p. 101; U.S. Bureau of the Census, *Population Schedule of the Eighth Census, 1860, Culpeper County, Virginia*, National Archives Microcopy No. 653, Roll 1341, pp. 836–37; *Population*

Schedule of the Eighth Census, 1860, Virginia [Slave Schedules], Culpeper County, National Archives Microcopy No. 653, Roll 1389, pp. 30–31; James F. Brown to William Smith, March 2, 1864, Virginia Executive Papers, Virginia State Library and Archives, Richmond.

54. Joseph W. Keifer to Eliza Keifer, January 9, 1864, Keifer Papers; James H. Kidd, *Personal Recollections of a Cavalryman with Custer's Michigan Cavalry in the Civil War* (Ionia, Mich., 1908), pp. 229–32; New York [?] *Republican*, April 15, 1864; Alonzo Pickard to [unknown], February 21, 1864, Pickard Papers; Glass and Singer, *Singing Soldiers: A History of the Civil War in Song*, pp. 248–50. "The Southern Girl, or The Homespun Dress," was written in 1862 by Carrie Belle Sinclair, of Augusta, Georgia. Popular throughout the South, it was intended to show the loyalty of southern women to the Cause and to their men.

55. Harold A. Small, ed., *The Road to Richmond: The Civil War Memoirs of Maj. Abner S. Small of the 16th Maine Vols.* (Berkeley, Ca., 1957), pp. 127–28. For Federal views of Rebel women see Mitchell, *The Vacant Chair*, pp. 89–113.

56. Sparks, *Inside Lincoln's Army*, pp. 332, 343–44.

57. *War of the Rebellion*, vol. 33, pp. 361, 367, 570, 651, 697; William L. Royall, *Some Reminiscences* (New York, 1909), pp. 53–57; John Esten Cooke, *Wearing of the Gray*, ed. Philip Van Doren Stern (Bloomington, Ind., 1959), pp. 472–82; George Quintus Peyton Diary, Alderman Library, University of Virginia, Richmond; p. 22; Susan W. Benson, ed., *Berry Benson's Civil War Book: Memoirs of a Confederate Scout and Sharpshooter* (Athens, Ga., 1992), pp. 57–58.

58. *War of the Rebellion*, vol. 33, pp. 367–68; Woodford B. Hackley, *The Little Fork Rangers: A Sketch of Company "D" Fourth Virginia Cavalry* (Richmond, 1927), p. 64; Stiles, *4th Virginia Cavalry*, pp. 119, 121, 124, 128. Other examples of 4th Virginia Cavalry men being captured are in *War of the Rebellion*, vol. 33, pp. 364, 427.

59. *War of the Rebellion*, vol. 33, pp. 367–68.

60. Hackley, *Little Fork Rangers*, p. 67; Stiles, *4th Virginia Cavalry*, p. 122; *Population Schedule of the Eighth Census*, p. 830.

61. Stiles, *4th Virginia Cavalry*, p. 105; *Population Schedule of the Eighth Census*, p. 909; *Population Schedule of the Eighth Census [Slave]*, p. 33; G. H. Coons to William Smith, January 11, 1864, Virginia Executive Papers.

62. Horace Porter, *Campaigning with Grant* (New York, 1897), p. 24; John Y. Simon, ed., *The Papers of Ulysses S. Grant*, 20 vols. (Carbondale, Ill., 1967–95), X, p. 220; Meade, *Life and Letters*, II, pp. 182–83.

63. Goss, *Recollections of a Private*, pp. 258–59; Agassiz, *Meade's Headquarters*, pp. 80, 81; Carter, *Four Brothers in Blue*, pp. 383, 385; Bardeen, *Little Fifer*, p. 295; Gilpin Diary, March 23, 1864; Shinn, "A Fifer's Diary," p. 29.

64. Simon, *Papers of Grant*, X, pp. 218–25.

65. Wilkeson, *Recollections of a Private Soldier*, pp. 37–38; Worthington C. Ford, ed., *A Cycle of Adams Letters: 1861–1865*, 2 vols. (Boston, 1920), II, p. 128; Rufus B. Dawes, *Service with the Sixth Wisconsin Volunteers* (Marietta, Ohio, 1890), pp. 152–53; E. W. Locke, *Three Years in Camp and Hospital* (Boston, 1872), p. 279; Goss, *Recollections of a Private*, pp. 258–59.

66. Charles S. Underhill, ed., *"Your Soldier Boy Samuel": Civil War Letters of Lieut. Samuel Edmund Nichols* (Buffalo, N.Y., 1929), p. 101; Dawes, *Service with the Sixth Wisconsin*, pp. 239–40; Blight, *When This Cruel War Is Over*, p. 280.

67. Locke, *Three Years in Camp and Field*, pp. 276–78; Wilkeson, *Recollections of a Private*, p. 38; Goss, *Recollections of a Private*, p. 259.

68. Rauscher, *Music on the March*, pp. 152–53; Dawes, *Service with the Sixth Wisconsin*, pp. 239–40; Underhill, *Your Soldier Boy Samuel*, p. 101; Ford, *Cycle of Adams Letters*, II, p. 128; Scott, *Fallen Leaves*, pp. 242–44.

69. *War of the Rebellion*, vol. 33, pp. 722–23; Allen Nevins, ed., *Diary of Battle: The Personal Journals of Colonel Charles S. Wainright, 1861–1865* (New York, 1962), pp. 329–330, 335; Meade, *Life and Letters*, II, pp. 166–82; David M. Jordan, *Winfield Scott Hancock: A Soldier's Life* (Bloomington, Ind., 1988), p. 107; Joseph W. Keifer to Eliza S. Keifer, March 24, 1864, Keifer Papers; Goss, *Recollections of a Private*, p. 259; Wilkeson, *Recollections of a Private*, p. 38; Roe, *The Thirty-Ninth Massachusetts Volunteers*, p. 154.

70. Carter, *Four Brothers in Blue*, p. 385; Jordan, *Winfield Scott Hancock*, p. 108; Fleming, *Life and Letters of Hays*, pp. 562–63; case of James R. Bigelow (NN 1543), Court-Martial Cases; Favill, *Diary of a Young Officer*, p. 283; Robertson, *Civil War Letters of McAllister*, pp. 400–403. The most complete look at reorganization and the resulting bitterness is Frederick B. Arner, *The Mutiny at Brandy Station, The Last Battle of the Hooker Brigade: A Controversial Army Reorganization, Courts Martial, and the Bloody Days That Followed* (Kensington, Md., 1993).

71. Simon, *Papers of Grant*, X, pp. 240, 245–46, 251.

72. Agassiz, *Meade's Headquarters*, p. 73.

73. Regimental Letter and Order Book, 17th Maine, circular of March 9, 1864, Regimental Letter and Order Book, 110th Ohio, General Order No. 3, April 8, 1864, Regimental Record Books; Racine, *Unspoiled Heart*, pp. 110–11.

74. Dawes, *Service with the Sixth Wisconsin*, pp. 241–43; Gilpin Diary, March 23 and 26, and April 23, 1864; Davis, *Three Years in the Army*, p. 317; Luther C. Furst Diary, April 18, 1864, Harrisburg Civil War Round Table Collection, U.S. Army Military Institute, Carlisle Barracks, Pa.; Rhodes, *All for the Union*, p. 142; Joseph W. Keifer to Eliza S. Keifer, April 6, 1864, Keifer Papers; Letter Book, 37th Massachusetts Infantry, circulars of March 22, 1864, April 19, 1864, Regimental Record Books.

75. Darius Starr to Daniel Starr, April 21, 1864, Darius Starr Papers, Perkins Library, Duke University, Durham, N.C.; *War of the Rebellion*, vol. 33, pp. 907–908.

76. Meade, *Life and Letters*, II, p. 185; Stephen Z. Starr, *The Union Cavalry in the Civil War*, 3 vols. (Baton Rouge, La., 1979–85), II, pp. 72–82; Philip H. Sheridan, *Personal Memoirs of Philip H. Sheridan*, 2 vols. (New York, 1888), I, pp. 348–56; Roy Morris, Jr., *Sheridan: The Life and Times of General Phil Sheridan* (New York, 1992), pp. 154–58; Agassiz, *Meade's Headquarters*, p. 82.

Chapter 13. An Unsettled State

1. *War of the Rebellion: A Compilation of the Official Records of the Union and Confederate Armies*, 70 vols. in 128 books and index (Washington, D.C., 1880–1901, ser 1, cited hereafter as *War of the Rebellion*, and all references are to Series 1 unless otherwise indicated) vol. 33, pp. 816–17, 921–22; Wilbur Fisk, *Anti-Rebel: The Civil War Letters of Wilbur Fisk* (Croton-on-Hudson, N.Y., 1983), p. 205; Edwin O. Wentworth to wife, April 17, 1864, Edwin Oberlin Wentworth Papers, Library of Congress; Allen Nevins, ed., *Diary of Battle: The Personal Journals of Colonel Charles S. Wainwright, 1861–1865* (New York, 1962), p. 342; E. W. Locke, *Three Years in Camp and Hospital* (Boston, 1872), pp. 280–81; David S. Sparks, ed., *Inside Lincoln's Army: The Diary of Marsena Rudolph Patrick, Provost Marshal General, Army of the Potomac* (New York, 1964), p. 355; Army Chaplains' Representation, n.d., U. S. Christian Commission Letters, RG 94, National

Archives; F. W. Morse, *Personal Experiences in the War of the Great Rebellion* (Albany, N.Y., 1866), p. 75; Henrietta S. Jacquette, ed., *South After Appomattox: Letters of Cornelia Hancock, 1863–1868* (New York, 1956), pp. 86–87.

2. Fisk, *Anti-Rebel*, pp. 211–14; James I. Robertson, Jr., ed., *The Civil War Letters of General Robert McAllister* (New Brunswick, N.J., 1965), pp. 405–406; Joseph W. Keifer to Eliza S. Keifer, April 24, 1864, Joseph Warren Keifer Papers, Library of Congress; David W. Blight, ed., *When This Cruel War is Over: The Civil War Letters of Charles Harvey Brewster* (Amherst, Mass., 1992), p. 284.

3. Nevins, *Diary of Battle*, p. 340; Jacquette, *South After Gettysburg*, p. 73–74; Edwin H. Miller, ed., *The Correspondence of Walt Whitman*, 6 vols. (New York, 1961–77), I, pp. 204–205.

4. Register of Sick and Wounded at Hospital of 2nd Division, 1st Army Corps, Army of the Potomac, Army Corps Register 10, RG 94, National Archives; Jacquette, *South After Gettysburg*, pp. 74, 82–83, 85; E. O. Wentworth to wife, March 28, 1864, Wentworth Papers.

5. Blight, *When This Cruel War is Over*, pp. 281, 284, 286, 288; Samuel Gilpin Diary, March 27, April 3, 1864, E. N. Gilpin Papers, Louis P. Morrison to Rebecca Morrison, March 27, 1864, Louis Philip Morrison Papers, Southern Historical Collection, University of North Carolina at Chapel Hill; Luther C. Furst Diary, April 23, 1864, Harrisburg Civil War Round Table Collection, U.S. Army Military History Institute, Carlisle Barracks, Pa.; Rufus B. Dawes, *Service with the Sixth Wisconsin Volunteers* (Marietta, Ohio, 1890), 243; *War of the Rebellion*, vol. 33, p. 899.

6. Blight, *When This Cruel War Is Over*, pp. 281–82; Eugene M. Scheel, *Culpeper: A Virginia County's History Through 1920* (Culpeper, 1982), p. 212; George T. Fleming, ed., *Life and Letters of Alexander Hays, Brevet Colonel United States Army* (Pittsburgh, Pa., 1919), pp. 567–68; J. Michael Welton, ed., *"My Heart Is So Rebellious": The Caldwell Letters, 1861–1865* (Warrenton, Va., 1991), p. 221; Dawes, *Service with the Sixth Wisconsin*, pp. 241, 247–48.

7. Case of S. N. Stanford (NN 1549), U.S. War Department, Court-Martial Cases, 1809–94, Judge Advocate General Records, RG 153, National Archives.

8. Case of Jane L. Allen (No. 3264), Southern Claims Commission Case Files, 1877–83, Records of the G.A.O., Records of the Third Auditor's Office, RG 217, National Archives.

9. Case of Sarah E. Thomas (No. 13,821), Southern Claims.

10. Case of Martha Bailey (No. 18,467), Southern Claims.

11. Cases of Thomas, Mary L. Payne (No. 22,128), Southern Claims; case of George T. Jennings (No. 13,069), Claims Disallowed by Commissioners of Claims (Southern Claims Commission), Records of the U.S. House of Representatives, 1871–1880, RG 233, National Archives.

12. Cases of Allen and John Brown (No. 15,556), Southern Claims.

13. Case of William A. Soutter (No. 17,756), Southern Claims.

14. Case of Mary L. Payne (No. 22,128), Southern Claims.

15. U.S. Bureau of the Census, *Population Schedule of the Eighth Census, 1860, Culpeper County, Virginia*, National Archives Microcopy No. 653, Roll 653, 857; cases of Isham B. Chewning (No. 10,507) and Delila Day (No. 2858), Southern Claims Disallowed.

16. *War of the Rebellion*, vol. 33, p. 390; Scheel, *Culpeper*, p. 212; James I. Robertson, Jr., ed., "An Indiana Soldier in Love and War: The Civil War Letters of John V. Hadley," *Indiana Magazine of History*, LIX (September 1963), pp. 280–81; cases of W.T. Bowen (NN 1492) and R. Bowers (MM 1456), Court-Martial Cases. For an example of how

even seemingly intense anti-Confederate activity could be exaggerated see, Kenneth W. Noe, "Red String Scare: Civil War Southwest Virginia and the Heroes of America," *North Carolina Historical Review*, LXIX (July 1992), pp. 301–22.

17. Margaret Jeffries, "Jeffersonton Baptist Church," p. 4, Works Progress Administration of Virginia, Historical Inventory for Culpeper County, Virginia, Culpeper County Courthouse.

18. Gilpin Diary, April 4, 17, 1864; E. O. Wentworth to Dear Union, April 17, 1864, Wentworth Papers; Robertson, *Civil War Letters of McAllister*, p. 405; Arthur A. Kent, ed., *Three Years With Company K: Sergt. Austin C. Stearns, Company K, 13th Mass. Infantry* (Rutherford, N.J., 1976), p. 256; Robert Hunt Rhodes, ed., *All for the Union: A History of the 2nd Rhode Island Volunteer Infantry in the War of the Rebellion* (Lincoln, R.I., 1985), pp. 142–43.

19. L. P. Morrison to wife, March 27, 1864, Morrison Papers; *War of the Rebellion*, vol. 33, pp. 856–57, 922–24, 983, 993; John Y. Simon, ed., *The Papers of Ulysses S. Grant*, 20 vols. (Carbondale, Ill., 1967–1995, X, p. 274; Uncle Ned to Friend David, April 27, 1864, Unidentified Manuscript Collection, Library of Congress. For Lee's preparations see Gordon C. Rhea, *The Battle of the Wilderness, May 5–6, 1864* (Baton Rouge, La., 1994), pp. 18–29.

20. Uncle Ned to Friend David, April 27, 1864, Unidentified Manuscript Collection; L. P. Morrison to wife, April 18, 1864, Morrison Papers; Charles E. Davis, Jr., *Three Years in the Army: The Story of the Thirteenth Massachusetts Volunteers* (Boston, 1894), pp. 315–17; Robertson, "Civil War Letters of Hadley," pp. 280–81; Blight, *When This Cruel War Is Over*, p. 281; Richard E. Winslow, III, *General John Sedgwick: The Story of a Union Corps Commander* (Novato, Ca., 1982), pp. 148–49.

21. Fisk, *Anti-Rebel*, pp. 206–207; Constant C. Hanks to Florilla Hanks, December 13, 1863, April 1, 1864, Constant C. Hanks Papers, Perkins Library, Duke University, Durham, N.C.; Blight, *When This Cruel War Is Over*, p. 288; Lawrence Kohl, ed., *Irish Green and Union Blue: Civil War Letters of Peter Welsh, Color Sergeant, 28th Regiment Massachusetts Volunteers* (New York, 1987), p. 150; Henry N. Blake, *Three Years in the Army of the Potomac* (Boston, 1865), pp. 274–75; L. P. Morrison to wife, March 22, 1864, Morrison Papers. Clark B. Hall, in "Season of Change: The Winter Encampment of the Army of the Potomac December 1, 1863–May 5, 1864," *Blue & Gray* VIII (April 1991), believes the Army of the Potomac was materially and psychologically transformed during its stay in Culpeper, but this may have been more apparent in retrospect than at that time.

22. Simon, *Papers of Grant*, X, pp. 297, 315–16, 337, 377; Darius Starr to Daniel Starr, April 21, 1864, Starr Papers; Scheel, *Culpeper*, p. 212; Hall, "Season of Change," p. 60; Winslow, *General John Sedgwick*, p. 149; Alexander S. Webb to wife, April 29, 1864, Papers of Alexander Stewart Webb, Sterling Library, Yale University, New Haven, Conn. For Grant's campaign plan see Rhea, *Battle of the Wilderness*, pp. 49–58.

23. Blight, *When This Cruel War Is Over*, p. 289; Robertson, "Civil War Letters of Hadley," p. 284.

24. Augustus Buell, *"The Cannoneer": Recollections of Service in the Army of the Potomac* (Washington, D.C., 1890), 143; *War of the Rebellion*, vol. 33, pp. 853, 1022–23; Simon, *Papers of Grant*, X, p. 388; Andrew A. Humphreys, *The Virginia Campaigns of '64 and '65: The Army of the Potomac and the Army of the James* (New York, 1894), pp. 18–19; Rhea, *Battle of the Wilderness*, p. 33.

25. Charles W. Bardeen, *A Little Fifer's War Diary* (Syracuse, N.Y., 1910), p. 299; Robert S. Robertson, *Personal Recollections of the War: A Record of Service with the Ninety-Third*

New York Volunteer Infantry and First Brigade, First Division, Army of the Potomac (Milwaukee, 1895), p. 87; Ruth Silliker, ed., *The Rebel Yell & Yankee Hurrah: The Civil War Journal of a Maine Volunteer: Private John W. Haley, 17th Maine Regiment* (Camden, Maine, 1985), pp. 141–42.

26. Agassiz, *Meade's Headquarters*, pp. 85–87; Rhea, *Battle of the Wilderness*, pp. 67–68.

27. Robertson, *Personal Recollections*, pp. 88–89; Silliker, *Rebel Yell & Yankee Hurrah*, p. 142; Harold A. Small, ed., *The Road to Richmond: The Civil War Memoirs of Maj. Abner S. Small of the 16th Maine Vols.* (1939; Berkeley, 1957), pp. 130–31; Humphreys, *Virginia Campaign of '64 and '65*, p. 20; Blight, *When This Cruel War Is Over*, p. 290.

28. Newspaper clipping, n.d., George W. Bagby Scrapbooks, IV, George William Bagby Papers, Virginia Historical Society, Richmond; Robert E. Lee, Jr., comp., *Recollections and Letters of General Robert E. Lee* (New York, 1904), p. 104; William Marvel, *Burnside* (Chapel Hill, 1991), pp. 347–48; Nevins, *Diary of Battle*, p. 345; Lewis Y. Field to William Smith, May 30, 1864, Virginia Executive Papers, Virginia State Library and Archives, Richmond.

29. Charles W. Davidson, ed., "Major Charles A. Davidson: Letters of a Virginia Soldier," *Civil War History*, XXII (March 1976), p. 36; B. C. Willis, "Reminiscences of the Last Year of the War," April 7, 1864, Virginia State Library and Archives, Richmond.

30. Willis, "Reminiscences," May 8, 1864; Scheel, *Culpeper*, p. 213.

31. Culpeper County Court Minute Books, No. 24 (1858–64), May 16, 1864, Culpeper County Courthouse; Election Polls, Culpeper County, May 1864, Culpeper County Courthouse; Joseph J. Halsey to Mildred T. Halsey, May 21, 1864, Morton-Halsey Papers, Alderman Library, University of Virginia, Charlottesville; Lewis Y. Field to William Smith, May 30, 1864, Virginia Executive Papers; David F. Riggs, *13th Virginia Infantry* (Lynchburg, 1988), p. 89.

32. Lewis Y. Field to William Smith, May 30, 1864, Virginia Executive Papers; *Confederate Veteran*, XXXVII (February 1929), p. 63; Culpeper County Court, Minute Book No. 24, June 20–21, 1864.

33. John W. Munson, *Reminiscences of a Mosby Guerrilla* (New York, 1906), pp. 126–27; Bettie Browning to Daniel A. Grimsley, July 19, July 30, 1864, Grimsley Family Papers, Virginia State Library and Archives, Richmond; *Population Schedule of Eighth Census*, p. 810; Kenneth L. Stiles, *4th Virginia Cavalry*, 2nd ed. (Lynchburg, 1985), p. 108; Woodford B. Hackley, *The Little Fork Rangers: A Sketch of Company "D" Fourth Virginia Cavalry* (Richmond, 1927), pp. 65–66.

34. Robert T. Bell, *11th Virginia Infantry* (Lynchburg, 1985), p. 73; David F. Riggs, *7th Virginia Infantry*, 2nd ed. (Lynchburg, 1982), p. 62; Riggs, *13th Virginia Infantry*, pp. 104, 110, 121, 146; Stiles, *4th Virginia Cavalry*, pp. 96, 108, 117–18, 120, 125, 129, 134–35, 143.

35. G. F. Carter Account Books, II, pp. 444–61, Alderman Library, University of Virginia, Charlottesville; Welton, *My Heart Is So Rebellious*, pp. 231–32, 234–35, 236–37; Lewis P. Nelson to William Smith, August 12, 1864, August 15, 1864, Virginia Executive Papers; Orange & Alexandria Passenger and Freight Rates, September 1864, Board of Public Works Papers, Virginia State Library and Archives, Richmond.

36. *Population Schedule of the Eighth Census.* p. 851; Lewis P. Nelson and Thomas O. Flint to William Smith, August 19, 1864, Virginia Executive Papers.

37. Cases of Ryburn Bundy (No. 19,818) and George Mars (No. 12,707), Southern Claims; Ervin L. Jordan, Jr., *Black Confederates and Afro-Yankees in Civil War Virginia* (Charlottesville, 1995), 201–15.

38. Cases of Malcolm West (No. 20,609) and George Mars, Southern Claims.

39. Cases of Randall G. Tate (No. 21,386), Slaughter Madden (No. 13,673), Richard West (No. 20,596), and Malcolm West, Southern Claims.

40. Cases of Slaughter Madden and Willis Madden (No. 128), Southern Claims; T. O. Madden, Jr., *We Were Always Free: The Maddens of Culpeper County, Virginia; A 200-Year Family History* (New York, 1992), pp. 108–110.

41. Minute Books, County Court, No. 25 (1864–69), August 15, 1864; Bettie Browning to Daniel A. Grimsley, September 17, 1864, Grimsley Family Papers; *War of the Rebellion*, vol. 43, pt. 2, p. 120.

42. *War of the Rebellion*, vol. 43, pt. 2, pp. 120, 123, 133; William Nalle Diary, October 17, 1864, Virginia Historical Society, Richmond.

43. *War of the Rebellion*, vol. 43, pt. 2, pp. 133–34, 873, 877–78; Jubal A. Early, *Narrative of the War Between the States* (1912; Wilmington, N.C., 1989), pp. 407, 433; Creed Thomas Davis Diary, September 19, 1864, Virginia Historical Society, Richmond.

44. Nalle Diary, October 17, 1864; Scheel, *Culpeper*, pp. 213–14; Bettie Browning to Daniel A. Grimsley, October 26, 1864, Grimsley Family Papers.

45. Bettie Browning to Daniel A. Grimsley, October 26, 1864, Grimsley Family Papers; Stiles, *4th Virginia Cavalry*, p. 136.

46. Bettie Browning to Daniel A. Grimsley, October 26, 1864, Grimsley Family Papers.

47. Hackley, *Little Fork Rangers*, pp. 65, 68–69; *Population Schedule of the Eighth Census*, pp. 800, 825; James F. Hart to William Smith, August 27, 1864, Virginia Executive Papers; Riggs, *13th Virginia Infantry*, p. 130.

48. Emory M. Thomas, *The Confederate Nation: 1861–1865* (New York, 1979), pp. 202–5, 232–35, 260–61; Richard N. Current et al., eds., *Encyclopedia of the Confederacy*, 4 vols. (New York, 1993), I, 331–36, 344–45.

49. Culpeper Petition of November 1864, Memorials and Petitions to Congress, Legislative and Executive Papers, Petition No. 368, War Department Collection of Confederate Records, RG 109, National Archives.

50. Case of Louisa Vanlone (No. 965), Southern Claims; cases of John T. Hicks (No. 1006) and Edward W. Brown (No. 20,598), John R. Rixey (No. 20,612), Southern Claims Disallowed.

51. Nalle Diary, December 1864; *War of the Rebellion*, vol. 43, pt. 2, p. 829; Harold R. Woodward, Jr., *For Home and Honor: The Story of Madison County, Virginia, during the War Between the States, 1861–1865* (Madison, Va., 1990), p. 87; William Nalle, *Notes on the Nalle Family of Culpeper County, Virginia* (Culpeper, 1970), pp. 69–70.

52. Nalle, *Notes on Nalle Family*, pp. 69–70.

53. Hackley, *Little Fork Rangers*, p. 76; Nalle, *Notes on Nalle Family*, pp. 70–71.

54. *Population Schedule of the Eighth Census*, p. 806; Mary S. Jones and Mildred C. Jones, eds., *Historic Culpeper* (Culpeper, 1974), p. 62; Daniel A. Grimsley, *Battles in Culpeper County, Virginia, 1861–1865* (Culpeper, 1900), pp. 24–25.

55. Nalle Diary, December 24–31, 1864.

Chapter 14. To Every Thing a Season

1. E. B. Long, *The Civil War Day by Day: An Almanac, 1861–1865* (Garden City, N.Y., 1971), pp. 621–22, 639–40; William Nalle Diary, February 6, 1865, Virginia Historical Society, Richmond.

2. John Minor Botts, *The Great Rebellion: Its Secret History, Rise, Progress, and Disastrous Failure* (New York, 1866), pp. 320–21.

3. Nalle Diary, February 6–7, 1865.
4. Nalle Diary, February 21, 1865; William Major to John S. Mosby, February 8, 1864, John Singleton Mosby Papers, Virginia Historical Society, Richmond; David F. Riggs, *13th Virginia Infantry* (Lynchburg, 1988), pp. 100, 101, 139, 149; Kenneth L. Stiles, *4th Virginia Cavalry*, 2nd ed. (Lynchburg, 1985), pp. 96, 121, 123, 136, 145.
5. Stiles, *4th Virginia Cavalry*, pp. 98, 123, 136, 145; Riggs, *13th Virginia Infantry*, pp. 101, 104, 110, 124, 134, 146; *Population Schedule of the Eighth Census, 1860, Culpeper County, Virginia*, National Archives Microcopy No. 653, Roll 1341, pp. 798, 846.
6. David F. Riggs, *7th Virginia Infantry*, 2nd ed. (Lynchburg, 1982), p. 95; *Population Schedule of the Eighth Census*, pp. 811, 834; Nalle Diary, January 1, 1865. Nalle refers to Jeff Hackley, but James is the only adult male of that surname living near Field.
7. Lemuel A. Corbin to Mary Corbin, January 1, [1865], Coons Family Papers, Virginia Historical Society, Richmond.
8. Bettie Browning to Daniel A. Grimsley, February 18, March 5, 1865, Grimsley Family Papers, Virginia State Library and Archives, Richmond.
9. Bettie Browning to Daniel A. Grimsley, March 5, 1865, Grimsley Family Papers; Nalle Diary, March 7–April 7, 1865.
10. Nalle Diary, April 5, 1865; Long, *Civil War Day by Day*, pp. 663–67.
11. Nalle Diary, April 6–14, 1865; Woodford B. Hackley, *The Little Fork Rangers: A Sketch of Company "D" Fourth Virginia Cavalry* (Richmond, 1927), p. 92; James I. Robertson, Jr., *General A. P. Hill: The Story of a Confederate Warrior* (New York, 1987), pp. 317–18.
12. Hackley, *Little Fork Rangers*, p. 92; Eugene M. Scheel, *Culpeper: A Virginia County's History Through 1920* (Culpeper, 1982), p. 214.
13. Nalle Diary, April 14 and 21, 1865; Culpeper County Court Minute Books, No. 25 (1864–69), April 17, 1865, Culpeper County Courthouse.
14. Culpeper *Exponent*, May 26, 1911, p. 1; *ibid.*, June 2, 1911, p. 1.
15. Scheel, *Culpeper*, p. 288; Robert A. Hodge, comp., *A Death Roster of the Confederate Hospital at Culpeper, Virginia* (Fredericksburg, 1977), pp. 4–6; Culpeper *Exponent*, July 22, 1881, p. 3; *Confederate Veteran*, XI (1903), pp. 69–70.
16. "Ashes of Soldiers," a postwar poem by Walt Whitman.
17. Daniel A. Grimsley, *Battles in Culpeper County, Virginia, 1861–1865* (Culpeper, 1900), p. 49; Scheel, *Culpeper*, pp. 313–14.
18. Scheel, *Culpeper*, p. 314; Culpeper *Exponent*, May 27, 1904, p. 2; *ibid.*, June 10, 1904, p. 2; Hackley, *Little Fork Rangers*, pp. 104–106.
19. Scheel, *Culpeper*, p. 315; Culpeper *Exponent*, August 10, 1906, pt. 1, p. 5 and pt. 2, p. 2.
20. Michael P. Musick, *6th Virginia Cavalry* (Lynchburg, 1990), p. 120; Clement A. Evans, ed., *Confederate Military History: Virginia*, rev. ed., 13 vols. (Wilmington, N.C., 1987), IV, pp. 910–11; *Hardesty's Historical and Geographical Encyclopedia* (New York, 1884), p. 437; Culpeper *Exponent*, February 11, 1910, p. 1.
21. Raleigh T. Green, comp., *Genealogical and Historical Notes on Culpeper County, Virginia*, 2 pts. (1900; Baltimore, 1958), pt. 1, pp. 27–30; John Cole to Jeremiah Morton, February 7, 1867, Morton-Halsey Papers, Alderman Library, University of Virginia, Charlottesville.
22. Applications for admission, R. E. Lee Camp Confederate Soldiers' Home Records, Virginia State Library and Archives, Richmond. Culpeper *Exponent*, February 15, 1907, p. 8.
23. Riggs, *7th Virginia Infantry*, p. 61; application for admission, Soldiers' Home Records.
24. Redwood scrapbook and "Family Recollections," both in George M. Williams Family Papers, in possession of Janet LaValley, Culpeper; Scheel, *Culpeper*, p. 226; Culpeper *Exponent*, January 5, 1911, p. 3. Gertrude died in 1928.

25. Lyon G. Tyler, *Encyclopedia of Virginia Biography*, 5 vols. (New York, 1915), II, pp. 230–31; Family Sketches," in Jane C. Slaughter Papers, Alderman Library, University of Virginia, Charlottesville; Jane Chapman Slaughter, "Reverend Philip Slaughter: A Sketch," *William and Mary Quarterly*, 2nd ser., XVI (July 1936), pp. 435–56.

26. Tyler, *Encyclopedia of Virginia Biography*, II, pp. 100–101; Botts, *The Great Rebellion*, ix–x, p. 323.

27. Cases of Mary L. Payne (No. 22,128), Isaac C. Webster (No. 21,822), and Simeon B. Shaw (No. 14,136) Southern Claims Commission Case Files, 1877–83, Records of the G.A.O., Records of the Third Auditor's Office, RG 217, National Archives.

28. Cases of Anne C. Brandt (No. 21,180), Mary L. Payne, John C. Green (No. 20,613), Southern Claims.

29. Case of John T. Hicks (No. 1006), Claims Disallowed by Commissioners of Claims (Southern Claims Commission), Records of the U.S. House of Representatives, 1871–1880, RG 233, National Archives.

30. W. S. Chase to T. F. P. Crandon, February 28, 1866, and W. S. Chase to W. R. Morse, June 30, 1866, U.S. War Department, *Records of the Assistant Commissioner for the State of Virginia, Bureau of Refugees, Freedmen, and Abandoned Lands, 1865–1869*, Microcopy 1048, Roll 44, RG 105, National Archives.

31. Case of Richard Wallach (No. 10,182), Southern Claims; J. B. Holloway and Walter H. French, comps., *Consolidated Index of Claims Reported by the Commissioners of Claims to the House of Representatives from 1871 to 1880* (Washington, D.C., 1892).

32. Scheel, *Culpeper*, pp. 215–26; W. A. McNulty to O. Brown, August 31, October 31, 1866, *Freedmen's Bureau Records*; Ervin L. Jordan, Jr., *Black Confederates and Afro-Yankees in Civil War Virginia* (Charlottesville, 1995), 197.

33. Cases of George Mars (No. 12,707) and Ryburn Bundy (No. 19,818), Southern Claims; Charles L. Perdue et al., eds., *Weevils in the Wheat: Interviews with Virginia Ex-Slaves* (Charlottesville, 1976), 333–42.

34. T. O. Madden, Jr., *We Were Always Free: The Maddens of Culpeper County, Virginia; a 200-Year Family History* (New York, 1992), pp. 111–23.

35. Scheel, *Culpeper*, 216, 268–70, 354; Stiles, *4th Virginia Cavalry*, p. 140.

36. Scheel, *Culpeper*, p. 347; M. D. Gore, "Kelly's Ford," pp. 9–10, Works Progress Administration of Virginia, Historical Inventory for Culpeper County, Virginia, Culpeper County Courthouse.

37. Scheel, *Culpeper*, pp. 217, 232, 245, 288, 322.

38. Green, *Genealogical and Historical Notes*, pt. 1, pp. 57–58; John H. Moore, "James Gaven Field: Virginia's Populist Spokesman," *Virginia Cavalcade*, IX (Spring 1960), pp. 35–41; Scheel, *Culpeper*, pp. 312, 369.

39. Culpeper *Exponent*, May 26, 1911, pp. 1 and 5; *ibid.*, June 2, 1911, p. 1; Riggs, *7th Virginia Infantry*, p. 66.

BIBLIOGRAPHY

KEY TO ABBREVIATIONS

BHS   Virginia Baptist Historical Society, Richmond, Va.
CB   U.S. Army Military History Institute, Carlisle Barracks, Pa.
CCH   Culpeper County Court House, Culpeper, Va.
CL   Culpeper Town and County Library, Culpeper, Va.
DU   Perkins Library, Duke University, Durham, N.C.
LC   Library of Congress, Washington, D.C.
LSU   Department of Archives and History, Louisiana State University, Baton Rouge, La.
MC   Museum of the Confederacy, Richmond, Va.
NA   National Archives, Washington, D.C.
SHC   Southern Historical Collection, University of North Carolina at Chapel Hill, Chapel Hill, N.C.
UA   Mullins Library, University of Arkansas, Fayetteville, Ark.
UV   Alderman Library, University of Virginia, Charlottesville, Va.
VHS   Virginia Historical Society Library,, Richmond, Va.
VL   Virginia State Library and Archives, Richmond, Va.
WM   Swem Library, College of William and Mary, Williamsburg, Va.
YU   Sterling Library, Yale University, New Haven, Ct.

MANUSCRIPTS

Allen and Simpson Family Papers, SHC
Edward P. Alexander Papers, SHC
Sally Anne Armstrong Diary, VHS
H. G. Ayer Diary, DU
Aylett Family Papers, VHS
George William Bagby Papers, VHS

Nathaniel Prentice Banks Papers, LC
Baptist Church of Christ Papers, UV
James Barbour Family Papers, UV
A. Tedford Barclay Papers, VL
Barnes Family Papers, WM
Albert A. Batchelor Papers, LSU
Berkeley Family Papers, UV
Bethel Baptist Church Minute Book, 1850–68, BHS
Samuel Simpson Biddle Letters, DU
John Bolling Letter, VHS
Bowles Family Papers, UV
Silas Bruce Marriage Register, 1831–81, VL
Catherine Jane (McGeachy) Buie Papers, DU
Isabella N. Burnet Papers, UV
Camp Henry Account Book, Culpeper Court House, 1861–62, MC
Anna B. Campbell Papers, DU
Campbell Family Papers, WM
Carrington Family Papers, VHS
G. F. Carter Account Books, UV
Monimia Fairfax Cary Papers, DU
Wilson Miles Cary Papers, UV
Cedar Run Baptist Church Minute Book, 1830–79, BHS
Civil War Miscellaneous Collection, CB
John F. H. Claiborne Papers, LC
Jacob B. Click Papers, DU
Philip St. George Cocke Papers, UV
John Overton Collins Papers, VHS
Confederate States Army, Department of Henrico Papers, VHS
Confederate States of America, Papers Relating to Citizens or Business Firms, War Department Collection of Confederate Records, Record Group 109, NA
Confederate States of America, Memorials and Petitions to Congress, Legislative and Executive Papers, Petition No. 368, War Department Collection of Confederate Records, Record Group 109, NA
Confederate States of America, Record of Quartermaster Stores Issued to and Condemned in Units of Army of Northern Virginia, 1861–63, Chapter V, Vols. 198, 204, Records of Army of Northern Virginia, Record Group 109, NA
Confederate States of America, Treasury Department List of Collectors and Assessors, 1861–65, Chapter X, Vol. 190, War Department Collection of Confederate Records, Record Group 109, NA
Confederate States of America, War Tax Returns, Virginia, District 38 (Culpeper County), War Department Collection of Confederate Records, Record Group 109, NA
Confederate States War Department, Letters Received by the Confederate Secretary of War, 1861–65, Record Group 109, NA
Catlett Fitzhugh Conway Autobiography, VHS
Cook-Luttrell Family Papers, WM
Giles Buckner Cooke Diary, VHS
John Esten Cooke Papers, DU
Cooke Family Papers, VL
Coons Family Papers, VHS

Lemuel Armistead Corbin Papers, VHS
William Clark Corson Papers, VHS
Crooked Run Baptist Church Minute Book, 1856–69, BHS
Culpeper Baptist Church Minute Book, 1856–77, BHS
Culpeper County Birth Records, 1864–96, CCH
Culpeper County Chancery Court, Order Book No. 5, 1859–70, CCH
Culpeper County Chancery Court, Rule Docket, 1857–93, CCH
Culpeper County Circuit Court, Judgements, Drawers 3–5, 1856–67, CCH
Culpeper County Circuit Court, Execution Book No. 13, 1857–90, CCH
Culpeper County Circuit Court, Law Order Book No. 6, 1856–66, CCH
Culpeper County Circuit Court, Rule Book, 1837–93, CCH
Culpeper County Court, Fiduciary Record, 1850–90, CCH
Culpeper County Court, Minute Books Nos. 24 & 25, 1858–69, CCH
Culpeper County Death Register, 1864–98, CCH
Culpeper County Deed Book No. 14, 1858–64, CCH
Culpeper County Election Polls, May 1864, CCH
Culpeper County Land Taxes, 1859–70, VL
Culpeper County Marriage Register, 1850–80, CCH
Culpeper County Personal Property Taxes, 1857–70, VL
Culpeper County Will Books U–V, 1857–68, CCH
Creed Thomas Davis Diary, VHS
DeButts-Ely Collection of Lee Family Papers, LC
Thomas Claybrook Elder Papers, VHS
Joseph W. Embrey Letters, UV
Benjamin Stoddert and Richard Stoddert Ewell Papers, DU
Richard Stoddert Ewell Letter Book, DU
Faucette Family Papers, UA
Federal Soldiers' Letters, SHC
Lemuel Thomas Foote Papers, LC
Fourth Virginia Cavalry Papers, MC
Frazer Family Papers, UV
Luther C. Furst Diary, CB
Thomas Francis Galwey Diaries, LC
E. N. Gilpin Papers, LC
Gourdvine Baptist Church Books, BHS
Green Family Manuscripts, UV
William Green Papers, VHS
Grimsley Family Papers, VL
Grinnan Family Papers, UV
Gwathmey Family Papers, VHS
Franklin S. Hall Papers, UV
George Washington Hall Diary, LC
Peter C. Hamilton Papers, SHC
William Hamilton Papers, LC
Constant C. Hanks Papers, DU
Harlow Family Papers, VHS
Harrisburg Civil War Round Table Collection, CB
Burton Norvell Harrison Family Papers, LC
Harvie Family Papers, VHS

Alexander C. Haskell Papers, SHC
John Porter Hatch Papers, LC
Lewis Muhlenberg Haupt Family Papers, LC
Hebron Lutheran Church Papers, UV
H. C. Hendrick Letters, SHC
Hero Family Papers, LSU
Hill Family Papers, VHS
James Montgomery Holloway Papers, VHS
Abner Crump Hopkins Diary, VHS
Marcus S. Hopkins Diary, UV
Jedediah Hotchkiss Papers, LC
Hunter-Garnett Family Papers, UV
John Daniel Imboden Papers, UV
Thomas Jonathan Jackson Papers, DU
Jewett Family Papers, VHS
Elijah S. Johnson Diary, VHS
Jordan-Bell Family Letters, VHS
Watkins Kearns Diary, VHS
Joseph Warren Keifer Papers, LC
Keith Family Papers, VHS
Williamson Kelly Papers, DU
James L. Kemper Papers, UV
Francis Milton Kennedy Diary, SHC
Helen Jeffries Klitch, ed., "Joseph Arthur Jeffries' Fauquier County, Virginia, 1840–1919,"
    typescript in possession of author.
George Bolling Lee Papers, VHS
Robert Edward Lee Papers, DU
Robert Edward Lee Papers, VHS
R. E. Lee Camp Confederate Soldiers' Home Records, VL
Lenoir Family Papers, SHC
Harry Lewis Papers, SHC
Philip Lightfoot Papers, WM
William P. Lloyd Diary, SHC
John James Hervey Love Papers, LC
Luttrell Family Papers, DU
Jacob Lyons Diary, SHC
Charles D. McCoy Papers, UV
Craig Woodrow McDonald Account Book, VHS
Madden Family Papers, UV
John Bowie Magruder Papers, DU
Rufus Mead Papers, LC
Methodist Episcopal Church, South, Papers, UV
William Young Mordecai Papers, VHS
Louis Philip Morrison Papers, SHC
Lawson Morrissett Diary, MC
Morton-Halsey Papers, UV
John Singleton Mosby Papers, LC
John Singleton Mosby Papers, VHS
Munford-Ellis Family Papers, DU

Murray Family Papers, VL

Thomas B. Nalle Papers, DU

William Nalle Diary, VHS

New Salem Baptist Church Minute Books, 1834–72, BHS

Nelle Virginia Norman, "History of the Culpeper County Normans," manuscript in CL

Henry Thweatt Owen Papers, VHS

Payne Family Papers, VHS

Pegram-Johnson-McIntosh Family Papers, VHS

Dudley Digges Pendleton Papers, DU

William Nelson Pendleton Papers, SHC

Edward Thomas Perkins Family Papers, LC

George Quintas Peyton Diary, UV

John William Peyton Diaries, UV

Alonzo C. Pickard Papers, LC

Adam H. Pickel Letters, DU

Pleasant Grove Baptist Church Minute Book, 1825–61, BHS

Polk-Brown-Ewell Papers, SHC

John R. Porter Diary, DU

Powell Family Papers, WM

Richard Channing Price Papers, VHS

Randall Family Papers, UV

Randolph Family Papers, UV

A. J. Rhoades Letter, UV

Leiper Moore Robinson Civil War Experiences, 1863–65, VHS

Ross Family Correspondence, VL

Thomas Rosser Papers, UV

Richard Rouzie Papers, WM

Daniel Sayler Papers, DU

Joseph D. Shields Papers, LSU

Shipp Family Papers, VHS

M. Shuler Collection, LC

Sisson Family Papers, UV

Daniel French Slaughter Papers, DU

Jane C. Slaughter Papers, UV

Mrs. M. S. Slaughter Papers, UV

Cornelius Smith Papers, WM

Edward B. Smith Ledger, WM

Stephen Calhoun Smith Papers, DU

Darius Starr Papers, DU

Stevensburg Baptist Church Minute Book, 1833–1927, BHS

Robert Augustus Stiles Papers, VHS

James Ewell Brown Stuart Papers, VHS

George B. Sydnor Letter, VHS

Henry M. Talley Papers, VHS

William Henry Tatum Papers, VHS

Thom Family Papers, VHS

Unidentified Manuscripts Collection, LC

United States Christian Commission Letters, Communications Received at Central Office, Philadelphia, Record Group 94, NA

United States House of Representatives, Claims Disallowed by Commissioners of Claims (Southern Claims Commission), Records of House of Representatives, 1871–80, Record Group 233, NA

United States House of Representatives, Southern Claims Commission Case Files, 1877–83, Records of General Accounting Office, Records of Third Auditor's Office, Boxes 344–46, Record Group 217, NA

United States War Department, Consolidated Correspondence File, 1794–1915, Office of Quartermaster General, Boxes 101, 222, 1096–97, Record Group 92, NA

United States War Department, Court-Martial Cases, 1809–94, Judge Advocate General Records, Record Group 153, NA

United States War Department, Hospital Files: Virginia, Collection of Confederate Records, Box 19, Record Group 109, NA

United States War Department, Index to Virginia Hospitals, Field Records of Hospitals, Records of Adjutant General's Office, Record Group 94, NA

United States War Department, Indexes to Hospitals Army Corps I–VI, Records of Adjutant General's Office, Box 22, Record Group 94, NA

United States War Department, Post Returns for Camp Henry, Culpeper Court House, Virginia, Collection of Confederate Records, Record Group 109, NA

United States War Department, Proceeding of U.S. Army Courts-Martial and Military Commissions of Union Soldiers Executed by U.S. Authorities, 1861–66, Judge Advocate General Records, Record Group 153, NA

United States War Department, Record Book, General Hospital, Culpeper Court House, Virginia, 1862, Collection of Confederate Records, Chapter VI, Vol. 587, Medical Department, Record Group 109, NA

United States War Department, Records of the Assistant Commissioner for the State of Virginia, Records of the Bureau of Refugees, Freedmen, and Abandoned Lands, Record Group 105, NA

United States War Department, Regimental Record Books, Records of Adjutant General's Office, Record Group 94, NA

United States War Department, Register and Prescription Book of Artillery Brigade, 3rd Army Corps, and Artillery Brigade, 2nd Army Corps, Army Corps Register 121, Record Group 94, NA

United States War Department, Registers of Records of Proceedings of U.S. Army Courts-Martial, 1809–90, Records of Judge Advocate General, Record Group 153, NA

United States War Department, Register of Sick and Wounded at Hospital of 2nd Division, 1st Army Corps, Army of the Potomac, Army Corps Register 10, Record Group 94, NA

United States War Department, Register of Sick and Wounded of Artillery Brigade, 3rd Army Corps, Army of the Potomac, Army Corps Register 120, Record Group 94, NA

United States War Department, Virginia Hospital Record Book No. 640, Field Records of Hospitals, Records of Judge Advocate General, Record Group 94, NA

Virginia Board of Public Works, Orange and Alexandria Railroad Correspondence, 1860–65, VL

Virginia Executive Papers, VL

Virginia Overseers of the Poor, Annual Reports, Public Auditor's Records, VL

Richard Woolfolk Waldrop Papers, SHC

Richard Henry Watkins Papers, VHS

Robert W. Watts Letters, UV

Alexander Stewart Webb Papers, YU

Edwin Oberlin Wentworth Papers, LC
Silas Wesson Diary, CB
Williams Family Papers, VHS
George M. Williams Family Papers, Janet LaValley Collection
B. C. Willis Reminiscences, VL
Works Progress Administration of Virginia, Historical Inventory for Culpeper County, Virginia, CCH
Yancey Family Papers, WM
George G. Young Letters, UV

NEWSPAPERS AND CONTEMPORARY PERIODICALS

Culpeper *Exponent*
Culpeper *Observer*
DeBow's Review
Hunt's Merchant Magazine and Commercial Review
Lynchburg *Daily Virginian*
New York *Times*
Religious Herald
Richmond *Dispatch*
Richmond *Times-Dispatch*
Washington *Evening Star*

PUBLISHED RECORDS AND REPORTS

Culpeper Virginia Monument Commission, *Report of the Culpeper Virginia Monument Commission of Pennsylvania* (Harrisburg, Pa., 1914).
Moss, Lemuel. *Annals of the United States Christian Commission.* Philadelphia, 1868.
Reese, George H., ed. *Proceedings of the Virginia State Convention of 1861.* 4 vols. Richmond, 1965.
Robertson, James I., Jr., ed. *Proceedings of the Advisory Council of the State of Virginia, April 21–June 19, 1861.* Richmond, 1977.
Shiloh Association, *Minutes.* Richmond, 1860–65.
Supplement to the Official Records of the Union and Confederate Armies. 6 vols. Wilmington, N.C., 1994.
United States Bureau of the Census. *Agriculture of the United States in 1860, Compiled from the Eighth Census.* Washington, D.C., 1864.
United States Bureau of the Census. *Manufactures of the United States in 1860, Compiled from the Eighth Census.* Washington, D.C., 1865.
United States Bureau of the Census. *Population of the United States in 1860, Compiled from the Eighth Census.* Washington, D.C., 1864.
United States Bureau of the Census. *Population Schedule of the Eighth Census, 1860, Culpeper County, Virginia.* National Archives Microcopy No. 653, Roll 1341.
United States Bureau of the Census. *Population Schedule of the Eighth Census, 1860, Virginia [Slave Schedule], Culpeper County.* National Archives Microcopy No. 653, Roll 1389.
United States Bureau of the Census, *Seventh Census of the United States: 1850.* Washington, D.C., 1853.
United States Bureau of the Census. *Statistics of the United States (including Mortality, Prop-*

erty, etc.) in 1860, Compiled from the Eighth Census. Washington, D.C., 1866.

United States Sanitary Commision, Bulletin. New York, 1866.

United States Senate. Report of the Joint Committee on the Conduct of the War, Senate Report No. 108, 37th Cong., 3rd sess.. 3 pts. Washington, D.C., 1863.

United States Senate. Report of the Joint Committee on the Conduct of the War, Senate Report No. 142, 38th Cong., 2nd sess.. 3 pts. Washington, D.C., 1865.

United States Senate. Supplemental Report of the Joint Committee on the Conduct of the War to Senate Report No. 142, 38th Cong., 2nd sess.. 2 vols. Washington, D.C., 1866.

United States War Department, Medical and Surgical History of the War of the Rebellion. 2 vols. in 12 books. Washington, D.C., 1870–83.

United States War Department, Records of the Assistant Commissioner for the State of Virginia, Bureau of Refugees, Freedmen, and Abandoned Lands, 1865–1869. National Archives Microcopy No. 1048.

United States War Department, War of the Rebellion: A Compilation of the Official Records of the Union and Confederate Armies. 70 vols. in 128 books and index. Washington, D.C., 1880–1901.

Wulfeck, Dorothy Ford, compiler. Culpeper County, Virginia: Will Books B and C, Court Suits, Loose Papers, Inscriptions. Naugatuck, Ct., 1965.

PUBLISHED CORRESPONDENCE, DIARIES, AND MEMOIRS

Agassiz, George R., ed. Meade's Headquarters 1863–65: Letters of Colonel Theodore Lyman from the Wilderness to Appomattox. Boston, 1922.

Allen, Gay Wilson, et al., eds. Collected Writings of Walt Whitman. 6 vols. New York, 1961–77.

Aschmann, Rudolf. Memoirs of a Swiss Officer in the American Civil War. Ed. Heinz K. Meier. Bern, Switzerland, 1972.

Avary, Myrta Lockett. A Virginia Girl in the Civil War. New York, 1903.

Averell, William Woods. Ten Years in the Saddle: The Memoir of William Woods Averell. Ed. by Edward Eckert and Nicholas J. Amoto. San Rafael, Ca., 1978.

Bardeen, Charles W. A Little Fifer's War Diary. Syracuse, N.Y., 1910.

Bartlett, Catherine Thom, ed. and comp. "My Dear Brother": A Confederate Chronicle. Richmond, 1952.

Baxter, Nancy Niblack, ed. Hoosier Farm Boy in Lincoln's Army: The Civil War Letters of Pvt. John R. McClure. n.p., 1971.

Baylor, George. Bull Run to Bull Run; or, Four Years in the Army of Northern Virginia. Richmond, 1900.

Beale, G. W. A Lieutenant of Cavalry in Lee's Army. Boston, 1918.

Benson, Susan W., ed. Berry Benson's Civil War Book: Memoirs of a Confederate Scout and Sharpshooter. Athens, Ga., 1992.

Betts, Alexander D. Experiences of a Confederate Chaplain, 1861–1864. n.d., n.p.

Blackford, Susan Leigh, comp. Letters from Lee's Army, or Memoir of Life In and Out of the Army in Virginia During the War Between the States. Ed. by Charles Minor Blackford, III. New York, 1962.

Blackford, William W. War Years with Jeb Stuart. New York, 1945.

Blair, William A. ed. A Politician Goes to War: The Civil War Letters of John White Geary. University Park, Pa., 1995.

Blake, Henry N. Three Years in the Army of the Potomac. Boston, 1865.

Blight, David W., ed. *When This Cruel War Is Over: The Civil War Letters of Charles Harvey Brewster*. Amherst, Mass., 1992.

Booth, George Wilson. *Personal Reminiscences of a Maryland Soldier: 1861–1865*. Baltimore, 1898.

Borcke, Heros von. *Memoirs of the Confederate War for Independence*, 2 vols. New York, 1866.

Botts, John Minor. *The Great Rebellion: Its Secret History, Rise, Progress, and Disastrous Failure*. New York, 1866.

Brown, Philip F. *Reminiscences of the War of 1861–1865*. Blue Ridge, Va., 1910.

Buck, Samuel D. *With the Old Confeds: Actual Experiences of a Captain in the Line*. Baltimore, 1925.

Buckley, Cornelius M., trans. *A Frenchman, a Chaplain, a Rebel: The War Letters of Père Louis-Hippolyte Gache*. Chicago, 1981.

Buell, Augustus. *"The Cannoneer": Recollections of Service in the Army of the Potomac*. Washington, D.C., 1890.

Burnett, Edmund Cody, ed. "Letters of a Confederate Surgeon: Dr. Abner Embry McGarity, 1862–1865. Part II." *Georgia Historical Quarterly*, XXIX (September 1945), 159–90.

"Campaigning with General Pope," *Cornhill Magazine*, VI (December 1862), 758–70.

Carter, Joseph C. *Magnolia Journey: A Union Veteran Revisits the Former Confederate States*. University, Ala., 1974.

Carter, Robert G. *Four Brothers in Blue; or, Sunshine and Shadows of the War of the Rebellion*. Austin, 1978.

Casler, John O. *Four Years in the Stonewall Brigade*, Rev. ed. Dayton, Ohio, 1971.

Cauthen, Charles E., ed. *Family Letters of the Three Wade Hamptons, 1782–1901*. Columbia, S.C., 1953.

Chambers, Henry A. *Diary of Captain Henry A. Chambers*. Ed. by T. H. Pearce. Wendell, N.C., 1983.

Coco, Gregory A., ed. *Through Blood and Fire: The Civil War Letters of Major Charles J. Mills, 1862–1865*. Gettysburg, Pa., 1982.

Coe, Hamlin A. *Mine Eyes Have Seen the Glory: Combat Diaries of Union Sergeant Hamlin Alexander Coe*. Ed. by David Coe. Rutherford, N.J., 1975.

Confederate Veteran. 40 vols. Nashville, Tenn., 1893–1932.

Connor, Forrest P., ed. "Letters of Lieutenant Robert H. Miller to His Family, 1861–1862." *Virginia Magazine of History and Biography*, LXX (January 1962), 62–91.

Cooke, John Esten. *Outlines from the Outpost*. Ed. by Richard Harwell. Chicago, 1961.

Cooke, John Esten. *Wearing of the Gray: Being Personal Portraits, Scenes and Adventures of the War*. Ed. by Philip Van Doren Stern. Bloomington, Ind., 1959.

Corby, William. *Memoirs of Chaplain Life: Three Years with the Irish Brigade in the Army of the Potomac*. Ed. by Lawrence F. Kohl. New York, 1992.

Corson, William Clark. *My Dear Jennie*. Ed. by Blake W. Corson. Richmond, 1982.

Couture, Richard T., ed. *Charlie's Letters: The Correspondence of Charles E. DeNoon*. n.p., 1982.

Dame, William M. *From the Rapidan to Richmond and the Spotsylvania Campaign: A Sketch and Personal Narrative of the Scenes a Soldier Saw*. Baltimore, 1920.

Davis, Charles E., Jr. *Three Years in the Army: The Story of the Thirteenth Massachusetts Volunteers*. Boston, 1894.

Dawes, Rufus B. *Service with the Sixth Wisconsin Volunteers*. Marietta, Ohio, 1890.

Day, Samuel P. *Down South; or, An Englishman's Experience at the Seat of the American War*. 2 vols. London, 1862.

Deane, Frank P., ed. *My Dear Wife: The Civil War Letters of David Brett, 9th Massachusetts Battery, Union Cannoneer.* Little Rock, Ark., 1964.

Denison, Frederic. *The Battle of Cedar Mountain: A Personal View.* Providence, R.I., 1881.

Denison, Frederic. *A Chaplain's Experiences in the Union Army.* Providence, R.I., 1893.

Douglas, Henry Kyd. *I Rode With Stonewall.* Chapel Hill, N.C., 1940.

Dowdey, Clifford and Louis H. Manarin, eds., *The Wartime Papers of R. E. Lee.* Boston, 1961.

Duncan, Russell, ed., *Blue-Eyed Child of Fortune: The Civil War Letters of Colonel Robert Gould Shaw.* Athens, Ga., 1992.

Durkin, Joseph T., ed. *Confederate Chaplain: A War Journal of Rev. James B. Sheeran, 14th Louisiana, C.S.A..* Milwaukee, 1960.

Early, Jubal A. *Narrative of the War Between the States.* New edition. Wilmington, N.C., 1989.

Eby, Cecil D., Jr., ed. *A Virginia Yankee in the Civil War: The Diaries of David Hunter Strother.* Chapel Hill, N.C., 1961.

Everson, Guy R. and Edward H. Simpson, Jr., eds. *Far, Far from Home: The Wartime Letters of Dick and Tally Simpson, Third South Carolina Volunteers.* New York, 1994.

Favill, Josiah M. *Diary of a Young Officer, serving with the armies of the United States during the War of the Rebellion.* Chicago, 1909.

Figg, Royall W. *"Where Men Only Dare to Go!"; or the Story of a Boy Company.* Richmond, 1885.

Fisk, Wilbur. *Anti-Rebel: The Civil War Letters of Wilbur Fisk.* Croton-on-Hudson, N.Y., 1983.

Fleet, Betsy and John D. P. Fuller, eds., *Green Mount: A Virginia Plantation Family during the Civil War: Being the Journal of Benjamin Robert Fleet and Letters of of his Family.* Charlottesville, Va., 1962.

Fleming, George T., ed. *Life and Letters of Alexander Hays, Brevet Colonel United States Army.* Pittsburgh, 1919.

Forbes, Edwin. *Thirty Years After: An Artist's Story of the Great War.* Baton Rouge, La., 1993.

Ford, Worthington C., ed. *A Cycle of Adams Letters: 1861–1865.* 2 vols. Boston, 1920.

Fowle, George. *Letters to Eliza, from a Union Soldier, 1862–1865.* Ed. by Margery Greenleaf. Chicago, 1970.

Gallagher, Gary W., ed. *Fighting for the Confederacy: The Personal Recollections of General Edward Porter Alexander.* Chapel Hill, N.C., 1989.

Galwey, Thomas F. *The Valiant Hours.* Ed. by W. S. Nye. Harrisburg, Pa., 1961.

Gerrish, Theodore. *Army Life: A Private's Reminiscences of the Civil War.* Portland, Me., 1882.

Glazier, Willard. *Three Years in the Federal Cavalry.* New York, 1874..

Gordon, George H. *Brook Farm to Cedar Mountain in the War of the Great Rebellion.* Boston, 1883.

Goss, Warren Lee. *Recollections of a Private: A Story of the Army of the Potomac.* New York, 1890.

Greiner, James M. et al., eds. *A Surgeon's Civil War: The Letters and Diary of Daniel M. Holt, M.D..* Kent, Ohio, 1994.

Hamlin, Percy G., ed., *The Making of a Soldier: Letters of General R. S. Ewell.* Richmond, 1935.

Harrison, Mrs. Burton [Constance]. *Recollections Grave and Gay.* New York, 1911.

Hassler, William W., ed. *The General to His Lady: The Civil War Letters of William Dorsey Pender to Fanny Pender.* Chapel Hill, N.C., 1965.

Haupt, Herman. *Reminiscences of General Herman Haupt*. Milwaukee, 1901.

Haynes, Draughton S. *The Field Diary of a Confederate Soldier*. Darien, Ga., 1963.

Henderson, G. F. R. *Stonewall Jackson and the American Civil War*. New York, 1949.

Hopkins, Luther W. *From Bull Run to Appomattox: A Boy's View*. Baltimore, 1908.

Hotchkiss, Jedediah. *Make Me a Map of the Valley: The Civil War Journal of Stonewall Jackson's Topographer*. Ed. by Archie P. McDonald. Dallas, 1973.

Howard, McHenry. *Recollections of a Maryland Confederate Soldier and Staff Officer under Johnston, Jackson and Lee*. Baltimore, 1914.

Huffman, James. *Ups and Downs of a Confederate Soldier*. New York, 1940.

Hunter, Alexander. *Johnny Reb and Billy Yank*. New York, 1905.

Jackson, Mary Anna. *Life and Letters General Thomas J. Jackson*. New York, 1892.

Jaquette, Henrietta S., ed. *South After Gettysburg: Letters of Cornelia Hancock, 1863–1868*. New York, 1956.

Johnston, David E. *The Story of a Confederate Boy in the Civil War*. Portland, Ore., 1914.

Jones, J. William. *Christ in Camp, or Religion in the Confederate Army*. Atlanta, 1887.

Jones, Terry L., ed. *The Civil War Memoirs of Captain William J. Seymour: Reminiscences of a Louisiana Tiger*. Baton Rouge, La., 1991.

Keifer, Joseph Warren. *Slavery and Four Years of War: A Political History of Slavery in the United States, Together with a Narrative of the Campaigns and Battles of the Civil War in which the Author Took Part*. 2 vols. New York, 1900.

Kent, Arthur A., ed. *Three Years With Company K: Sergt. Austin C. Stearns, Company K, 13th Mass. Infantry*. Rutherford, N.J., 1976.

Kidd, James H. *Personal Recollections of a Cavalryman with Custer's Michigan Cavalry in the Civil War*. Ionia, Mich., 1908.

Kieffer, Harry M. *The Recollections of a Drummer-Boy*. Boston, 1883.

Kohl, Lawrence F., ed. *Irish Green and Union Blue: Civil War Letters of Peter Welsh, Color Sergeant, 28th Regiment, Massachusetts Volunteers*. New York, 1987.

LaBree, Ben, ed. *Camp Fires of the Confederacy*. Louisville, Ky., 1898.

Lane, Mills, ed. *"Dear Mother: Don't grieve about me. If I get killed, I'll only be dead." Letters from Georgia Soldiers in the Civil War*. Savannah, Ga., 1977.

Lee, Robert E., Jr., comp. *Recollections and Letters of General Robert E. Lee*. New York, 1904.

Lee, Susan P., ed. *Memoirs of William Nelson Pendleton*. Philadelphia, 1893.

Lewis, Richard. *Camp Life of a Confederate Boy of Bratton's Brigade, Longstreet's Corps, C.S.A.*. Charleston, S.C., 1883.

Locke, E. W. *Three Years in Camp and Hospital*. Boston, 1872.

Long, Armistead L. *Memoirs of Robert E. Lee: His Military and Personal History*. New York, 1887.

Longstreet, James. *From Manassas to Appomattox: Memoirs of the Civil War in America*. New York, 1992.

McClellan, Henry B. *The Life and Campaigns of Major General J. E. B. Stuart*. Boston, 1885.

McDonald, Cornelia Peake. *A Diary With Reminiscences of the War and Refugee Life in the Shenandoah Valley, 1860–1865*. Nashville, 1934.

McKay, Mrs. C. E. *Stories of Hospital and Camp*. Philadelphia, 1876.

McKim, Randolph H. *A Soldier's Recollections: Leaves from the Diary of a Young Confederate*. New York, 1910.

Mathias, Ray, ed. *In the Land of the Living: Wartime Letters by Confederates from the Chatta-hoochee Valley of Alabama and Georgia*. Troy, Ala., 1981.

Meade, George G. *Life and Letters of George Gordon Meade*. 2 vols. New York, 1913.

Melville, Malcolm L., comp. *Spilman Papers*. Forestville, Ca., 1965.

Merington, Marguerite, ed. *The Custer Story: The Life and Intimate Letters of General George A. Custer and His Wife Elizabeth.* New York, 1950.

Milano, Anthony J., ed. "Letters from the Harvard Regiments. Part Two: The Second Massachusetts Regiment—From the Outbreak of War Through Cedar Mountain." *Civil War,* XII (June 1988), 29–45.

Miller, Edwin H., ed. *The Correspondence of Walt Whitman.* 6 vols. New York, 1961–77.

Moore, Frank, ed. *The Rebellion Record: A Diary of American Events with Documents, Narratives, Illustrative Incidents, Poetry, etc.* 11 vols. and Suppl. New York, 1861–68.

Morgan, William H. *Personal Reminiscences of the War of 1861–65.* Lynchburg, Va., 1911.

Morse, F. W. *Personal Experiences in the War of the Great Rebellion, from December, 1862, to July, 1865.* Albany, N.Y., 1866.

Mosby, John S. *The Letters of John S. Mosby.* Richmond, 1986.

Munson, John W. *Reminiscences of a Mosby Guerrilla.* New York, 1906.

Nalle, William. *Tales of Old Culpeper.* Culpeper, Va., 1974.

Neese, George M. *Three Years in the Confederate Horse Artillery.* New York, 1911.

Nevins, Allan, ed. *A Diary of Battle: The Personal Journals of Colonel Charles S. Wainwright, 1861–1865.* New York, 1962.

Norton, Oliver W. *Army Letters: 1861–1865.* Chicago, 1903.

Noyes, George F. *The Bivouac and the Battlefield; or Campaign Sketches in Virginia and Maryland.* New York, 1863.

Oates, William C. *The War Between the Union and the Confederacy.* New York, 1905.

Opie, John N. *A Rebel Cavalryman with Lee, Stuart and Jackson.* Chicago, 1899.

Owen, William M. *In Camp and Battle with the Washington Artillery of New Orleans.* Boston, 1885.

Paxton, John R. *Sword and Gown.* Ed. by Calvin Dill Wilson. New York, 1926.

Perdue, Charles L., Jr., et al., eds. *Weevils in the Wheat: Interviews with Virginia Ex-Slaves.* Charlottesville, 1976.

Perry, John G. *Letters from a Surgeon of the Civil War.* Boston, 1906.

Porter, Horace. *Campaigning with Grant.* New York, 1897.

Pryor, Mrs. Roger A. [Sarah A.] *Reminiscences of Peace and War.* New York, 1904.

Quaife, Milo M., ed. *From the Cannon's Mouth: The Civil War Letters of General Alpheus S. Williams.* Detroit, 1959.

Racine, Philip N., ed. *"Unspoiled Heart": The Journal of Charles Mattocks of the 17th Maine.* Knoxville, Tenn., 1994.

Ramey, Emily G. and John K. Gott, comps. *The Years of Anguish: Fauquier County, Virginia, 1861–1865.* Warrenton, Va., 1965.

Rauscher, Frank. *Music on the March, 1862–1865, With the Army of the Potomac.* Philadelphia, 1892.

Ray, Jean S., comp. *The Diary of a Dead Man: Letters and Diary of Private Ira S. Pettit.* n.p., 1969.

Reid-Green, Marcia, ed. *Letters Home: Henry Matrau of the Iron Brigade.* Lincoln, Neb., 1993.

Reynolds, Arlene, ed. *The Civil War Memories of Elizabeth Bacon Custer.* Austin, Tex., 1994.

Rhodes, Robert Hunt, ed. *All for the Union: A History of the 2nd Rhode Island Volunteer Infantry in the War of the Great Rebellion as told by the Diary and Letters of Elisha Hunt Rhodes.* Lincoln, R.I., 1985.

Robertson, Archibald T. *Life and Letters of John Albert Broadus.* Philadelphia, 1901.

Robertson, James I., Jr., ed. "An Indiana Soldier in Love and War: The Civil War Letters of John V. Hadley." *Indiana Magazine of History*, LIX (September 1963), 189–288.

Robertson, James, I., Jr., ed. *The Civil War Letters of General Robert McAllister*. New Brunswick, N.J., 1965.

Robertson, Robert S. *Personal Recollections of the War: A Record of Service with the Ninety-Third New York Volunteer Infantry and First Brigade, First Division, Army of the Potomac.* Milwaukee, 1895.

Robson, John S. *How a One-Legged Rebel Lives: Reminiscences of the Civil War*. Durham, N.C., 1898.

Royall, William L. *Some Reminiscences*. New York, 1909.

Rozier, John, ed. *The Granite Farm Letters: The Civil War Correspondence of Edgeworth & Sallie Bird*. Athens, Ga., 1988.

Runge, William H., ed. *Four Years in the Confederate Artillery: The Diary of Private Henry Robinson Berkeley*. Chapel Hill, N.C., 1961.

Russell, Charles W., ed. *The Memoirs of Colonel John S. Mosby*. Boston, 1917.

Scarborough, William K., ed. *The Diary of Edmund Ruffin*. 2 vols. Baton Rouge, La., 1972–76.

Scheibert, Justus. *Seven Months in the Rebel States During the North American War, 1863.* Trans. by Joseph C. Hayes. Ed. by William Stanley Hoole. Tuscaloosa, Ala., 1958.

Scott, Robert Garth, ed. *Fallen Leaves: The Civil War Letters of Major Henry Livermore Abbott*. Kent, Ohio, 1991.

Sears, Stephen W., ed. *The Civil War Papers of George B. McClellan: Selected Correspondence, 1860–1865*. New York, 1989.

Sheridan, Philip H. *Personal Memoirs of Philip H. Sheridan*. 2 vols. New York, 1888.

Silliker, Ruth, L. ed. *The Rebel Yell and the Yankee Hurrah. The Civil War Journal of a Maine Volunteer: Private John W. Haley, 17th Maine Regiment*. Camden, Me., 1985.

Simon, John Y., ed. *The Papers of Ulysses S. Grant*. 20 vols. Carbondale, Ill., 1967–95.

Slaughter, Philip. *Views from Cedar Mountain, Present, Retrospective and Prospective.* Culpeper, Va., 1884.

Small, Harold A., ed. *The Road to Richmond: The Civil War Memoirs of Maj. Abner S. Small of the 16th Maine Vols*. Berkeley, Ca., 1957.

Sorrel, Gilbert Moxley. *Recollections of a Confederate Staff Officer*. New York, 1905.

Southern Historical Society Papers. 52 vols. Richmond, 1876–1959.

Sparks, David S., ed. *Inside Lincoln's Army: The Diary of Marsena Rudolph Patrick, Provost Marshal General, Army of the Potomac*. New York, 1964.

Spencer, Carrie E., et al., comps. *A Civil War Marriage in Virginia: Reminiscences and Letters.* Boyce, Va., 1956.

Stevens, John W. *Reminiscences of the Civil War: A Soldier in Hood's Texas Brigade, Army of Northern Virginia*. Hillsboro, Tex., 1902.

Stiles, Robert. *Four Years Under Marse Robert*. New York, 1904.

Stone, James M. *Personal Recollections of the Civil War*. Boston, 1918.

Stringfellow, Frank. *War Reminiscences: Life of a Confederate Scout Inside the Enemy's Lines.* n.p., 1892.

Strother, David H. "Personal Recollections of the War." *Harper's Magazine*, XXXV (August 1867), 273–95, (November 1867), 704–28.

Tower, R. Lockwood, ed. *Lee's Adjutant: The Wartime Letters of Colonel Walter Herron Taylor, 1862–1865*. Columbia, S.C., 1995.

Townsend, George A. *Campaigns of a Non-Combatant*. New York, 1866.

Turner, Charles W., ed. "Major Charles A. Davidson: Letters of a Virginia Soldier." *Civil War History*, XXII (March 1976), 16–40.

Turner, Charles W., ed. *Ted Barclay, Liberty Hall Volunteers: Letters from the Stonewall Brigade*. Berryville, Va., 1992.

Tyler, Mason W. *Recollections of the Civil War*. Ed. by William S. Tyler. New York, 1912.

Underhill, Charles S., ed. *"Your Soldier Boy Samuel": Civil War Letters of Lieut. Samuel Edmund Nichols*. Buffalo, N.Y., 1929.

Wagstaff, H. M., ed. *The James A. Graham Papers, 1861–1864*. Chapel Hill, N.C., 1928.

Welch, Spencer G. *A Confederate Surgeon's Letters to His Wife*. New York, 1911.

Welton, J. Michael, ed. *"My Heart Is So Rebellious": The Caldwell Letters, 1861–1865*. Warrenton, Va., 1991.

West, John C. *A Texan in Search of a Fight, Being the Diary and Letters of a Private Soldier in Hood's Texas Brigade*. Waco, Tex., 1901.

Whitman, Walt. *Complete Prose Works*. Philadelphia, 1892.

Wilkeson, Frank. *Recollections of a Private Soldier in the Army of the Potomac*. New York, 1887.

Wilson, LeGrand. *The Confederate Soldier*. New Edition. Ed. James W. Silver. Memphis, 1973.

Wilson, William L. *A Borderland Confederate*. Ed. by F. P. Summers. Pittsburgh, 1962.

Worsham, John H. *One of Jackson's Foot Cavalry: His Experience and What He Saw During the War 1861–1865*. New York, 1912.

Wright, Stuart, trans. *Colonel Heros von Borcke's Journal, 26 April–8 October 1862*. Winston-Salem, N.C., 1981.

UNIT HISTORIES

Beale, R. L. T. *History of the Ninth Virginia Cavalry in the War Between the States*. Richmond, 1899.

Bell, Robert T. *11th Virginia Infantry*. Lynchburg, Va., 1985.

Bennett, A. J. *The Story of the First Massachusetts Light Battery, Attached to the Sixth Army Corps*. Boston, 1886.

Chamberlin, Thomas. *History of the One Hundred and Fiftieth Regiment, Pennsylvania Volunteers, Second Regiment, Bucktail Brigade*. Philadelphia, 1895.

Denison, Frederic. *Sabre and Spurs: First Regiment, Rhode Island Cavalry in the Civil War, 1861–1865*. Central Falls, R.I., 1876.

Gates, Theodore B. *The "Ulster Guard" and the War of the Rebellion*. New York, 1879.

Hackley, Woodford B. *The Little Fork Rangers: A Sketch of Company "D," Fourth Virginia Cavalry*. Richmond, 1927.

Hinkley, Julian W. *A Narrative of Service with the Third Wisconsin Infantry*. Madison, Wis., 1912.

History Committee. *History of the Nineteenth Regiment Massachusetts Volunteer Infantry 1861–1865*. Salem, Mass., 1906.

Holmes, Torlief S. *Horse Soldiers in Blue*. [First Maine Cavalry]. Gaithersburg, Md., 1985.

Irby, Richard. *Historical Sketch of the Nottoway Grays*. Richmond, 1878.

Krick, Robert K. *9th Virginia Cavalry*, 2nd Ed. Lynchburg, Va., 1982.

Krick, Robert K. *Parker's Virginia Battery, C.S.A..* Berryville, Va., 1975.

Longacre, Edward C. *To Gettysburg and Beyond: The Twelfth New Jersey Volunteer Infantry, II Corps, Army of the Potomac, 1862–1865*. Hightstown, N.J., 1988.

McKenna, Charles F., ed. *Under the Maltese Cross: Campaigns 155th Pennsylvania Regiment, Narrated by the Rank and File*. Pittsburgh, Pa., 1910.

Musick, Michael P. *6th Virginia Cavalry.* Lynchburg, 1990.

Myers, Frank M. *The Comanches: A History of White's Battalion, Virginia Cavalry, Laurel Brigade, Hampton's Division, Army of Northern Virginia, C.S.A.*. Baltimore, 1871.

Nichols, G. W. *A Soldier's Story of His Regiment (61st Georgia): And Incidentally the Lawton-Gordon-Evans Brigade, Army of Northern Virginia.* Kennesaw, Ga., 1961.

Page, Charles D. *History of the Fourteenth Regiment Connecticut Volunteer Infantry.* Meriden, Ct., 1906.

Powell, William H. *The Fifth Army Corps (Army of the Potomac): A Record of Operations During the Civil War.* New York, 1896.

Pullen, John J. *The Twentieth Maine: A Volunteer Regiment in the Civil War.* Philadelphia, 1957.

Pyne, Henry R. *History of the First New Jersey Cavalry.* Trenton, N.J., 1871.

Roe, Alfred S. *The Thirty-Ninth Massachusetts Volunteers, 1862 65.* Worcester, Mass., 1914.

Riggs, David F. *7th Virginia Cavalry.* 2nd ed. Lynchburg, Va., 1982.

Riggs, David F. *13th Virginia Infantry.* Lynchburg, Va., 1988.

Shoemaker, John J. *Shoemaker's Battery, Stuart's Horse Artillery, Pelham's Battalion, Army of Northern Virginia.* Memphis, 1908.

Simons, Ezra D. *A Regimental History: One Hundred and Twenty-Fifth New York State Volunteers.* New York, 1888.

Simpson, Harold B. *Hood's Texas Brigade: Lee's Grenadier Guard.* Waco, Tex., 1970.

Smith, John L. *History of the Corn Exchange Regiment, 118th Pennsylvania Volunteers.* Philadelphia, 1888.

Stiles, Kenneth L. *4th Virginia Cavalry.* 2nd Edition. Lynchburg, 1985.

Swinfen, David B. *Ruggles' Regiment: The 122nd New York Volunteers in the American Civil War.* Hanover, N.H., 1982.

Wilkinson, Warren. *Mother, May You Never See the Sights I have Seen: The Fifty-Seventh Massachusetts Veteran Volunteers in the Army of the Potomac 1864–65.* New York, 1990.

ADDITIONAL CONTEMPORARY SOURCES

Conn, Granville P. *History of the New Hampshire Surgeons in the War of the Rebellion.* Concord, N.H., 1906.

Dabney, Robert L. *Life and Campaigns of Lieut. Gen. Thomas J. Jackson.* New York, 1866.

DuChanal, General François de. "How Soldiers Were Tried." *Civil War Times,* VII (February 1969), 10–15.

Elliott, E. N., ed. *Cotton is King, and Pro-Slavery Arguments.* Augusta, Ga., 1860.

Grimsley, Daniel A. *Battles in Culpeper County, Virginia, 1861–1865.* Culpeper, Va., 1900.

Hazelton, Joseph P. *Scouts, Spies, and Heroes of the Great Civil War.* Cleveland, Ohio, 1892.

Hilles, Lewis B. *Chickens Come Home to Roost.* New York, 1899.

Humphreys, Andrew A. *The Virginia Campaigns of '64 and '65: The Army of the Potomac and the Army of the James.* New York, 1894.

Kautz, August V. *The Company Clerk: Showing How and When to Make Out All Returns, Reports, Rolls, and Other Papers.* Philadelphia, 1865.

Moore, Frank, ed. *The Civil War in Song and Story, 1860–1865.* New York, 1889.

Plum, William R. *The Military Telegraph During the Civil War in the United States.* 2 vols. Chicago, 1882.

Rasmussen, Wayne D., ed. *Agriculture in the United States: A Documentary History.* 4 vols. New York, 1975.

Ropes, John C. *The Army Under Pope.* New York, 1889.

Slaughter, Philip. *The Culpeper Minute Men: Presentation of Flag, September 6th, 1887.* Culpeper, Va., 1887.

Stille, Charles J. *History of the United States Sanitary Commission.* New York, 1868.

Wharton, Henry M. *White Blood: A Story of the South.* New York, 1906.

SECONDARY SOURCES

Alotta, Robert I. *Civil War Justice: Union Army Executions under Lincoln.* Shippensburg, Pa., 1989.

Arner, Frederick B. *The Mutiny at Brandy Station, the Last Battle of the Hooker Brigade: A Controversial Army Reorganization, Courts Martial, and the Bloody Days That Followed.* Kensington, Md., 1993.

Atherton, Lewis E. *The Southern Country Store 1800–1860.* Baton Rouge, La., 1949.

Ayers, Edward L. *Vengeance and Justice: Crime and Punishment in the Nineteenth-Century American South.* New York, 1984.

Bean, William G. *Stonewall Jackson's Man: Sandie Pendleton.* Chapel Hill, N.C., 1959.

Beatty, John O. *John Esten Cooke, Virginian.* New York, 1949.

Benson, T. Loyd. "The Plain Folk of Orange: Land, Work, and Society on the Eve of the Civil War," 56–78 in Edward L. Ayers and John C. Willis, eds. *The Edge of the South: Life in Nineteenth-Century Virginia.* Charlottesville, 1991.

Berlin, Ira. *Slaves Without Masters: The Free Negro in the Antebellum South.* New York, 1974.

Black, Robert C., III. *The Railroads of the Confederacy.* Chapel Hill, N.C., 1952.

Boney, Francis N. *John Letcher of Virginia: The Story of Virginia's Civil War Governor.* University, Ala., 1966.

Bouldin, Mary Jane. "Lynchburg, Virginia: A City in War 1861–1865." M.A. Thesis, East Carolina University, 1976.

Boyle, Andrew J., comp. *The Church in the Little Fork: A History of Historic Little Fork Church.* Orange, Va., 1983.

Brewer, James H. *The Confederate Negro: Virginia Craftsmen and Military Laborers, 1861–1865.* Durham, N.C., 1969.

Brooks, Stewart. *Civil War Medicine.* Springfield, Ill., 1966.

Brown, R. Shepard. *Stringfellow of the Fourth.* New York, 1960.

Burton, William L. *Melting Pot Soldiers: The Union's Ethnic Regiments.* Ames, Iowa, 1988.

Calfee, Mrs. Berkeley G. *Confederate History of Culpeper County in the War Between the States.* Culpeper, Va., 1948.

Calfee, Mrs. Berkeley G., and Mrs. Mary G. Coleman. *Historical Sketch of St. Stephen's Episcopal Church, Culpeper, Virginia.* n.p., 1959.

Carlile, Peggy Jo. "Thornton Stringfellow, Proslavery Author." M.A. Thesis, Western Illinois University, 1976.

Carmichael, Peter S. *Lee's Young Artillerist: William R.J. Pegram.* Charlottesville, 1995.

The Civil War. 28 vols. Alexandria, Va., 1983–87.

Cornelius, Janet D. *"When I Can Read My Title Clear": Literacy, Slavery, and Religion in the Antebellum South.* Columbia, S.C., 1991.

Craven, Avery O. *Soil Exhaustion as a Factor in the Agricultural History of Virginia and Maryland, 1606–1860.* Urbana, Ill., 1926.

Crofts, Daniel W. *Reluctant Confederates: Upper South Unionists in the Secession Crisis.* Chapel Hill, N.C., 1989.

Cunningham, H. H. *Doctors in Gray: The Confederate Medical Service.* Baton Rouge, La., 1958.

Current, Richard N. et al., eds. *Encyclopedia of the Confederacy.* 4 vols. New York, 1993.

Daniel, W. Harrison. "Chaplains in the Army of Northern Virginia: A List Compiled in

1864 and 1865 by Robert L. Dabney." *Virginia Magazine of History and Biography*, LXXI (July 1963), pp. 327–40.

Daniel, W. Harrison. "The Christian Association: A Religious Society in the Army of Northern Virginia." *Virginia Magazine of History and Biography*, LXIX (January 1961), pp. 93–100.

Daniel, W. Harrison. "Virginia Baptists, 1861–1865." *Virginia Magazine of History and Biography*, LXXII (January 1964), pp. 94–114.

Davis, Burke. *They Called Him Stonewall: A Life of Lt. General T. J. Jackson, C.S.A.*. New York, 1954.

Davis, George K. and Gary M. Pequet. "Interest Rates in the Civil War South." *Journal of Economic History*, L (March 1990), pp. 133–48.

Davis, William C. *"A Government of Our Own": The Making of the Confederacy*. New York, 1994.

Dorman, John F. *The Farish Family of Virginia and Its Forebears*. Richmond, 1967.

Dorman, John F. *The Robertson Family of Culpeper County, Virginia*. Richmond, 1964.

Downey, Fairfax. *Clash of Cavalry: The Battle of Brandy Station, June 9, 1863*. New York, 1959.

Eaton, Clement. "Slave-Hiring in the Upper South: A Step toward Freedom." *Mississippi Valley Historical Review*, XLVI (March 1960), pp. 663–78.

Elder, William L., Jr. *Culpeper: A Pictorial History*. Virginia Beach, Va., 1976.

Engle, Stephen D. *Yankee Dutchman: The Life of Franz Sigel*. Fayetteville, Ark., 1993.

Epler, Percy H. *The Life of Clara Barton*. New York, 1946.

Faust, Drew Gilpin. "Altars of Sacrifice: Confederate Women and the Narratives of War." *Journal of American History*, LXXVI (March 1990), pp. 1220–28.

Faust, Drew Gilpin. "Evangelicalism and the Meaning of the Proslavery Argument: The Reverend Thornton Stringfellow of Virginia." *Virginia Magazine of History and Biography*, LXXXV (January 1977), pp. 3–17.

Faust, Drew Gilpin. "Christian Soldiers: The Meaning of Revivalism in the Confederate Army." *Journal of Southern History*, LIII (February 1987), pp. 63–90.

Frassantio, William A. *Grant and Lee: The Virginia Campaigns, 1864–1865*. New York, 1983.

Freeman, Douglas S. *Lee's Lieutenants: A Study in Command*. 3 vols. New York, 1942–44.

Freeman, Douglas S. *R. E. Lee: A Biography*. 4 vols. New York, 1934–35.

Gallagher, Gary W. "Brandy Station: The Civil War's Bloodiest Arena of Mounted Combat." *Blue & Gray*, VIII (October 1990), pp. 8–22, 44–53.

Garnett, William E. and Emma Garnett McCoy. *The Garnetts of Albemarle County, Virginia*. n.p., 1963.

Gilliam, Sarah K. *Virginia's People: A Study of the Growth and Distribution of the Population of Virginia from 1607 to 1943*. Richmond, 1944.

Glass, Paul and Louis C. Singer, eds. *Singing Soldiers: A History of the Civil War in Song*. New York, 1975.

Goldfield, David R. *Urban Growth in the Age of Sectionalism: Virginia, 1847–1861*. Baton Rouge, La., 1977.

Gorn, Elliott J. " 'Gouge and Bite, Pull Hair and Scratch': The Social Significance of Fighting in the Southern Backcountry." *American Historical Review*, XC (February 1985), pp. 18–43.

Graham, Martin and George Skoch. *Mine Run: A Campaign of Lost Opportunities*. Lynchburg, Va., 1987.

Green, Fletcher M. "Gold Mining in Ante-Bellum Virginia." *Virginia Magazine of History and Biography*, XLV (July 1937), pp. 227–35, and XLV (October 1937), 357–66.

Green, Raleigh T., comp. *Genealogical and Historical Notes on Culpeper County, Virginia.* Culpeper. Va., 1900.

Grimsley, Christopher Mark. "A Directed Severity: The Evolution of Federal Policy Toward Southern Civilians and Property, 1861–1865." Ph.D. dissertation, Ohio State University, 1992.

Hall, Clark B. "The Battle of Brandy Station." *Civil War Times,* XXIX (May–June 1990), pp. 32–42, 45.

Hall, Clark B. "Buford at Brandy Station." *Civil War,* VIII (July–August 1990), pp. 12–17, 66–67.

Hall, Clark B. "Robert F. Beckham: The Man Who Commanded Stuart's Horse Artillery After Pelham Fell." *Blue & Gray,* IX (December 1991), pp. 34–37.

Hall, Clark B. "Season of Change: The Winter Encampment of the Army of the Potomac, December 1, 1863–May 4, 1864." *Blue & Gray,* VIII (April 1991), pp. 8–22, 48–62.

Hall, Richard. *Patriots in Disguise: Women Warriors of the Civil War.* New York, 1993.

Hanson, Raus McDill. *Virginia Place Names: Derivations, Historical Uses.* Verona, Va., 1969.

Hardesty's Historical and Geographical Encyclopedia. New York, 1884.

Harrington, Fred H. *Fighting Politician: Major General N. P. Banks.* Philadelphia, 1948.

Harris, William C. "The Southern Unionist Critique of the Civil War." *Civil War History,* XXXI (March 1985), 39–56.

Hassler, William W. *Colonel John Pelham: Lee's Boy Artillerist.* Chapel Hill, 1960.

Henderson, William D. *The Road to Bristoe Station: Campaigning With Lee and Meade, August 1–October 20, 1863.* Lynchburg, Va., 1987.

Hess, Earl J. *Liberty, Virtue, and Progress: Northerners and Their War for the Union.* New York, 1988.

Hilliard, Sam B. *Hog Meat and Hoecake: Food Supply in the Old South, 1840–1860.* Carbondale, Ill., 1972.

Hodge, Robert A., comp. *A Death Roster of the Confederate Hospital at Culpeper, Virginia.* Fredericksburg, 1977.

Hodge, Robert A., comp. *Some Pre-1871 Vital Statistics on Colored Persons of Culpeper County, Virginia.* Fredericksburg, Va., 1978.

Holloway, J. B., and Walter H. French, comps. *Consolidated Index of Claims Reported by the Commissioner of Claims to the House of Representatives from 1871 to 1880.* Washington, D.C., 1892.

Hoole, William S. *Lawley Covers the Confederacy.* Tuscaloosa, Ala., 1964.

Hoole, William S. *Vizetelly Covers the Confederacy.* Tuscaloosa, Ala., 1957.

Hunter, Robert F. "The Turnpike Movement in Virginia 1816–1860." *Virginia Magazine of History and Biography,* LXIX (July 1961), 278–89.

Hyman, Harold M. "Deceit in Dixie." *Civil War History,* III (March 1957), pp. 65–82.

Inscoe, John C. *Mountain Masters, Slavery, and the Sectional Crisis in Western North Carolina.* Knoxville, Tenn. 1989.

Jackson, Luther P. *Free Negro Labor and Property Holding in Virginia, 1830–1860.* New York, 1942.

Johnston, Angus J., III. *Virginia Railroads in the Civil War.* Chapel Hill, N.C., 1961.

Johnston, Donnie. *The Ghosts of Gourdvine Past: A History of Gourdvine Baptist Church.* n.p., 1987.

Jones, Mary S., ed. *An 18th Century Perspective: Culpeper County.* Culpeper, Va., 1976.

Jones, Mary S., and Mildred C. Jones., eds. *Historic Culpeper.* Culpeper, Va., 1974.

Jones, Terry L. *Lee's Tigers: The Louisiana Infantry in the Army of Northern Virginia.* Baton Rouge, La., 1987.

Jordan, Ervin L., Jr. *Black Confederates and Afro-Yankees in Civil War Virginia*. Charlottesville, 1995.

Jordan, David M. *Winfield Scott Hancock: A Soldier's Life*. Bloomington, Ind., 1988.

Kajencki, Francis C. *Star on Many a Battlefield: Brevet Brigadier General Joseph Kargé in the American Civil War*. Rutherford, N.J., 1980.

Kaser, David. *Books and Libraries in Camp and Battle: The Civil War Experience*. Westport, Ct., 1984.

Keneally, Thomas. *Confederates*. New York, 1979.

Kenzer, Robert C. *Kinship and Neighborhood in a Southern Community: Orange County, North Carolina, 1849–1881*. Knoxville, Tenn., 1987.

Klingberg, Frank W. *The Southern Claims Commission*. Berkeley, Ca., 1955.

Krick, Robert K. *Lee's Colonels: A Biographical Register of the Field Officers of the Army of Northern Virginia*, rev. ed. Dayton, Ohio, 1992.

Krick, Robert K. *Stonewall Jackson at Cedar Mountain*. Chapel Hill, N.C., 1990.

Krolick, Marshall D. "The Battle of Brandy Station." *Civil War Quarterly*, VII (December 1986), 52–65.

Lash, Jeffrey N. *Destroyer of the Iron Horse: General Joseph E. Johnston and Confederate Rail Transport, 1861–1865*. Kent, Ohio, 1991.

Lebergott, Stanley. *Manpower in Economic Growth: The American Record Since 1800*. New York, 1964.

Leckie, Shirley A. *Elizabeth Bacon Custer and the Making of a Myth*. Norman, Okla., 1993.

Little, Lewis P. *Imprisoned Preachers and Religious Liberty in Virginia*. Lynchburg, Va., 1938.

Long, Charles M. *Virginia County Names: Two Hundred and Seventy Years of Virginia History*. New York, 1908.

Longacre, Edward C. "The Battle of Brandy Station: 'A Shock That Made the Earth Tremble.'" *Virgnia Cavalcade*, XXV (Winter 1976), pp. 136–43.

Longacre, Edward C. *Mounted Raids of the Civil War*. South Brunswick, N.J., 1975.

Lord, Francis A. *Lincoln's Railroad Man: Herman Haupt*. Rutherford, N.J., 1969.

Lowry, Thomas P. *The Story the Soldiers Wouldn't Tell: Sex in the Civil War*. Mechanicsburg, Pa., 1994.

Luvaas, Jay and Wilbur S. Nye. "The Campaign That History Forgot." *Civil War Times*, VIII (November 1969), pp. 11–42.

Madden, T.O., Jr. *We Were Always Free: The Maddens of Culpeper County, Virginia; A 200-Year Family History*. New York, 1992.

Martin, Edgar W. *The Standard of Living in 1860: American Consumption Levels on the Eve of the Civil War*. Chicago, 1942.

Martin, Samuel J. *The Road to Glory: Confederate General Richard S. Ewell*. Indianapolis, 1991.

Massey, Mary Elizabeth. *Refugee Life in the Confederacy*. Baton Rouge, La., 1964.

Mathew, William M. *Edmund Ruffin and the Crisis of Slavery in the Old South: The Failure of Agricultural Reform*. Athens, Ga., 1988.

McPherson, James M. *What They Fought For, 1861–1865*. Baton Rouge, La., 1994.

McWhiney, Grady. *Cracker Culture: Celtic Ways in the Old South*. Tuscaloosa, Ala., 1988.

Meyers, Jerry. "Melee on Saint Patrick's Day." *America's Civil War*, IV (November 1991), pp. 30–37.

Milham, Charles G. *Gallant Pelham*. Washington, D.C., 1959.

Mitchell, Reid. *The Vacant Chair: The Northern Soldier Leaves Home*. New York, 1993.

Monaghan, Jay. "Civil War Slang and Humor." *Civil War History*, III (June 1957), pp. 125–33.

Moore, John H. "James Gaven Field: Virginia's Populist Spokesman." *Virginia Cavalcade*, IX (Spring 1960), 35–41.

Morris, George G. "Confederate Lynchburg, 1861–1865." M.A. thesis, Virginia Polytechnic Institute and State University, 1977.

Morris, George G., and Susan Foutz. *Lynchburg in the Civil War: The City—The People—The Battle*. Lynchburg, Va., 1984.

Morris, Roy, Jr. *Sheridan: The Life and Times of General Phil Sheridan*. New York, 1992.

Naisawald, L. Van Loan. *Grape and Canister: The Story of the Field Artillery of the Army of the Potomac, 1861–65*. New York, 1960.

Nalle, William. *Notes on the Nalle Family of Culpeper County, Virginia*. Culpeper, Va., 1970

Nesbitt, Mark. *Saber and Scapegoat: J. E. B. Stuart and the Gettysburg Controversy*. Mechanicsburg, Pa., 1994.

Noe, Kenneth W. "Red String Scare: Civil War Southwest Virginia and the Heroes of America." *North Carolina Historical Review*, LXIX (July 1992), pp. 301–22.

Oates, Stephen B. *A Woman of Valor: Clara Barton and the Civil War*. New York, 1994.

Osborne, Charles C. *Jubal: The Life and Times of General Jubal A. Early, CSA, Defender of the Lost Cause*. Baton Rouge, La., 1994.

Owsley, Douglas W., et al. *The History and Archaeology of St. James Episcopal Church, Brandy Station, Virginia*. n.p., 1992.

Payne, Brooke. *The Paynes of Virginia*, 2nd Ed. Harrisonburg, Va., 1977.

Peavey, James D., ed. *Confederate Scout: Virginia's Frank Stringfellow*. Onancock, Va., 1956.

Peterson, Arthur G. "Flour and Grist Milling in Virginia: A Brief History," *Virginia Magazine of History and Biography*, XXXXIII (April 1935), pp. 97–108.

Pinchbeck, Raymond B. *The Virginia Negro Artisan and Tradesman*. Richmond, 1926.

Popchock, Barry. "Daring Night Assault." *America's Civil War*, IV (March 1992), pp. 30–37.

Porter, Albert O. *County Government in Virginia: A Legislative History, 1607–1904*. New York, 1947.

Pressly, Thomas J. and William H. Schofield, eds. *Farm Real Estate Values in the United States by Counties, 1850–1959*. Seattle, 1965.

Pryor, Elizabeth B. *Clara Barton: Professional Angel*. Philadelphia, 1987.

Rable, George C. *Civil Wars: Women and the Crisis of Southern Nationalism*. Urbana, Ill. 1989.

Rable, George C. *The Confederate Republic: A Revolution Against Politics*. Chapel Hill, N.C., 1994.

Radley, Kenneth. *Rebel Watchdog: The Confederate States Army Provost Guard*. Baton Rouge, La., 1989.

Ramsdell, Charles W. "General Robert E. Lee's Horse Supply, 1862–1865." *American Historical Review*, XXXV (July 1930), pp. 758–77.

Ray, Frederic E. *"Our Special Artist": Alfred R. Waud's Civil War*. Mechanicsburg, Pa., 1994.

Rhea, Gordon C. *The Battle of the Wilderness, May 5–6, 1864*. Baton Rouge, La., 1994.

Rixey, R. P. *The Rixey Genealogy*. Lynchburg, Va., 1933.

Robertson, James I., Jr. *General A. P. Hill: The Story of a Confederate Warrior*. New York, 1987.

Robertson, James I., Jr. "Military Executions." *Civil War Times*, V (May 1966), 34–39.

Robinson, William M., Jr. *Justice in Grey: A History of the Judicial System of the Confederate States of America*. Cambridge, Mass., 1941.

Rogin, Leo. *The Introduction of Farm Machinery in Its Relation to the Productivity of Labor in the Agriculture of the United States During the Nineteenth Century*. Berkeley, Ca., 1931.

Romero, Sidney J. *Religion in the Rebel Ranks*. Lanham, Md., 1983.

Royster, Charles. *The Destructive War: William Tecumseh Sherman, Stonewall Jackson, and the Americans.* New York, 1991.

Ruffner, Kevin C. "Civil War Desertion from a Black Belt Regiment: An Examination of the 44th Virginia Infantry," pp. 79–108 in Edward L. Ayers and John C. Willis, eds., *The Edge of the South: Life in Nineteenth-Century Virginia.* Charlottesville, 1991.

Ryland, Garnett. *The Baptists of Virginia, 1699–1926.* Richmond, 1955.

Sanchez-Saavedra, E. M. " 'All Fine Fellows and Well-Armed': The Culpeper Minute Men Battalion 1775–1776." *Virginia Cavalcade,* XXIV (Summer 1974), 4–11.

Savitt, Todd L. *Medicine and Slavery: The Diseases and Health Care of Blacks in Antebellum Virginia.* Urbana, Ill., 1978.

Schlebecker, John T. *Whereby We Thrive: A History of American Farming, 1607–1972.* Ames, Iowa, 1975.

Schlotterbeck, John T. "The 'Social Economy' of an Upper South Community: Orange and Greene Counties, Virginia, 1815–1860," pp. 3–28 in Orville Burton and Robert C. McMath, Jr., eds., *Class, Conflict, and Consensus: Antebellum Southern Community Studies.* Westport, Ct., 1982.

Schutz, Wallace J. and Walter N. Trenerry. *Abandoned by Lincoln: A Military Biography of General John Pope.* Urbana, Ill., 1990.

Schwarz, Philip J. *Twice Condemned: Slaves and the Criminal Laws of Virginia, 1705–1865.* Baton Rouge, La., 1988.

Schweninger, Loren. *Black Property Owners in the South, 1790–1915.* Urbana, Ill., 1990.

Scott, Robert Garth. *Into the Wilderness with the Army of the Potomac.* Bloomington, Ind., 1985.

Shanks, Henry T. *The Secession Movement in Virginia, 1847–1861.* Richmond, 1934.

Shattuck, Gardiner H. *A Shield and Hiding Place: The Religious Life of the Civil War Armies.* Macon, Ga., 1987.

Slaughter, Jane C. "Reverend Philp Slaughter." *William and Mary Quarterly,* 2nd Series, XVI (July 1936), pp. 435–56.

Stackpole, Edward J. *From Cedar Mountain to Antietam.* Harrisburg, Pa., 1959.

Starr, Stephen Z. *The Union Cavalry in the Civil War.* 3 vols. Baton Rouge, La., 1979–85.

Sutherland, Daniel E. "Abraham Lincoln, John Pope, and the Origins of Total War." *Journal of Military History,* LVI (October 1992), 567–86.

Sutherland, Daniel E. *The Confederate Carpetbaggers.* Baton Rouge, La., 1988

Sutherland, Daniel E. *The Expansion of Everyday Life, 1860–1876.* New York, 1989.

Sutherland, Daniel E. "Getting the 'Real War' into the Books." *Virginia Magazine of History and Biography,* LXXXXVIII (April 1990), pp. 193–220.

Sutherland, Daniel E. "Introduction to War: The Civilians of Culpeper County, Virginia." *Civil War History,* XXXVII (June 1991), 120–37.

Sutherland, Daniel E. "Stars in Their Courses." *America's Civil War,* IV (November 1991), pp. 41–45.

Sutton, Robert P. *Revolution to Secession: Constitution Making in the Old Dominion.* Charlottesville, 1989.

Sword, Wiley. "Cavalry on Trial at Kelly's Ford." *Civil War Times,* XIII (April 1974), pp. 32–40.

Symonds, Craig L. *Joseph E. Johnston: A Civil War Biography.* New York, 1992.

Tadman, Michael. *Speculators and Slaves: Masters, Traders, and Slaves in the Old South.* Madison, Wis., 1989.

Taylor, George B. *Virginia Baptist Ministers.* Third series. Lynchburg, Va., 1912.

Taylor, George B. *Virginia Baptist Ministers.* Fifth series. Lynchburg, Va., 1915.

Thomas, Arthur D., Jr., and Angus McDonald Green, eds. *Early Churches of Culpeper County, Virginia: Colonial and Ante-Bellum Congregations*. Culpeper, Va., 1987.

Thomas, Benjamin P., and Harold M. Hyman. *Stanton: The Life and Times of Lincoln's Secretary of War*. New York, 1962.

Thomas, Emory M. *Bold Dragoon: The Life of J.E.B. Stuart*. New, York 1986.

Thomas, Emory M. *The Confederate Nation: 1861–1865*. New York, 1979.

Thomas, Emory M. *The Confederate State of Richmond: A Biography of the Capital*. Austin, Tex., 1971.

Thompson, W. Fletcher, Jr. *The Image of War: The Pictorial Reporting of the American Civil War*. New York, 1960.

Trinque, Bruce A. "Rebels Across the River." *America's Civil War*, VII (September 1994), pp. 38–45, 88.

Tryon, Rolla M. *Household Manufactures in the United States 1640–1860: A Study in Industrial History*. Chicago, 1917.

Turner, Charles W. "The Early Railroad Movement in Virginia." *Virginia Magazine of History and Biography*, LV (October 1947), 350–71.

Turner, Charles W. "Railroad Service to Virginia Farmers, 1828–1860." *Agricultural History*, XXII (October 1948), pp. 239–48.

Turner, Charles W. "Virginia Agricultural Reform, 1815–1860." *Agricultural History*, XXVI (July 1952), pp. 80–89.

Turner, Charles W. "Virginia Railroad Development, 1845–1860." *Historian*, X (Autumn 1947), pp. 43–62.

Turner, George E. *Victory Rode the Rails: The Strategic Place of the Railroads in the Civil War*. New York, 1953.

Tyler, Lyon G. *Encyclopedia of Virginia Biography*. 5 vols. New York, 1915.

Urwin, Gregory J. W. *Custer Victorious: The Civil War Battles of General George Armstrong Custer*. Rutherford, N.J., 1983.

Walker, Charles D. *Biographical Sketches of the Graduates and Élèves of the Virginia Military Institute Who Fell During the War Between the States*. Philadelphia, 1875.

Walsh, Margaret. "The Value of Mid-Nineteenth Century Manufacturing Returns: The Printed Census and the Manuscript Census Compilations Compared." *Historical Methods Newsletter*, IV (March 1971), pp. 43–51.

Ward, James A. *That Man Haupt: A Biography of Herman Haupt*. Baton Rouge, La., 1973.

Watson, Samual J. "Religion and Combat Motivation in the Confederate Armies." *Journal of Military History*, LVIII (January 1994), 29–55.

Welsh, Jack D. *Medical Histories of Confederate Generals*. Kent, Ohio, 1995.

Wert, Jeffry D. *Mosby's Rangers*. New York, 1990.

Wiley, Bell I. "Soldier Newspapers of the Civil War." *Civil War Times*, XVI (July 1977), pp. 20–29.

Wilkinson, Joyce E. "The Early Orange and Alexandria Railroad 1849–1854." *Pioneer America*, I (July 1969), pp. 46–53.

Winslow, Richard E., III. *General John Sedgwick: The Story of a Union Corps Commander*. Novato, Calif., 1982.

Wise, Jennings C. *The Long Arm of Lee: History of the Artillery of the Army of Northern Virginia*. New York, 1959.

Wish, Harvey. "The Slave Insurrection Panic of 1856." *Journal of Southern History*, V (May 1939), 206–22.

Woodward, Harold R., Jr. *For Home and Honor: The Story of Madison County, Virginia, dur-*

ing the War Between the States, 1861–1865. Madison, Va., 1990.

Wright, Edward N. *Conscientious Objectors in the Civil War*. New York, 1961.

Wust, Klaus. *The Virginia Germans*. Charlottesville, 1969.

Yates, Robert S., comp. *A History of James Somerville of Culpeper County, Virginia, His Ancestors and Descendants from 1700 to 1987*. Decorah, Iowa, 1988.

Zornow, William F. "Aid for the Indigent Families of Soldiers in Virginia, 1861–1865." *Virginia Magazine of History and Biography*, LXVI (October 1958), pp. 454–58.

ACKNOWLEDGMENTS

*M*ore than a few acknowledgments are in order. First I express thanks to the many librarians and archivists who unearthed, copied, and supplied materials for me. The University of Arkansas libraries, including Special Collections and a fine Inter-Library Loan department, provided the most immediate service. On the road, I encountered unfailing courtesy and enthusiasm from the staffs of the Culpeper Town and County Library; the Clerk's Office of the Culpeper Circuit Court; the Virginia Historical Society and Virginia State Library and Archives, both in Richmond; the Manuscript Department of the Swem Library, College of William and Mary, Williamsburg; the Manuscript Department, Alderman Library, University of Virginia, Charlottesville; Library of Congress and National Archives, Washington, D.C.; Southern Historical Collection, University of North Carolina at Chapel Hill; the Manuscript Department of the Perkins Library at Duke University; and the Manuscript Department at the Louisiana State University Library, Baton Rouge. I extend particular thanks for favors done me by Guy R. Swanson at the Eleanor S. Brockenbrough Library, Museum of the Confederacy, Richmond; Michael P. Musick and Michael Meier in the Military Division of the National Archives; and Darlene F. Slater at the Virginia Baptist Historical Society, Richmond.

Of the several individuals who supplied documents or information concerning their families, my greatest debt goes to Janet LaValley of Culpeper, who invited me into her home, Redwood, and allowed me to transcribe family correspondence in rooms where Robert E. Lee, Jeb Stuart, John Pelham, and many other lords of the 1860s once visited. Running a close second is T. O. Madden, Jr., of Elkwood, Virginia, who graciously spent several hours with me discussing his family's history and the history of Madden's tavern. I also acknowledge my gratitude to Angus McDonald Green and Anna Marie Stringfellow, both of Culpeper; Lea Thom Aspinwall Cadwalader of Blue Bell, Pennsylvania; and William E. Norman of Gaithersburg, Maryland. Russell Guinn of Culpeper also supplied useful information.

Among professional colleagues, Richard Sommers confirmed for me the value of the Culpeper story, and Richard E. Beringer steered me away from an early, ill-advised approach to the topic. Fred A. Bailey and Carl H. Moneyhon forced me to analyze Culpeper's social class structure more carefully. James M. McPherson shared his ideas about the nature of total war and read with critical eye a manuscript, subsequently published, on John Pope. William Hanchett constructively challenged my interpretation of Abraham Lincoln's role in the evolution of total war. R. B. "Randy" Rosenburg pointed me toward the papers of the R. E. Lee Confederate Soldiers' Home. Robert K. Krick supplied valuable leads.

I am extremely grateful to those people who either volunteered or allowed themselves to be drafted to read portions of the manuscript. Willard B. Gatewood, Jr., Herman M. Hattaway, and Gary W. Gallagher all allowed me to impose upon their time. Clark B. Hall not only read my chapter on Brandy Station, but also at various times invited me into his home, generously supplied me with copies of his own research materials, and shared with me his vast knowledge of the war in Culpeper. Grady McWhiney read the entire manuscript, and no words can repay him for his quarter century of patient and steadfast friendship. Norah M. Vincent, my editor at The Free Press, saw the merit of the original manuscript, and worked closely with me to polish and refine it. Loretta Denner, my production editor, and Camilla Hewitt, my copy editor, were also most helpful and patient.

Non-historian Charles Whitman gave me a crash course in book-keeping and taught me how to read nineteenth-century ledgers, and Jerry W. "Jake" Looney tutored me in law and taught me the differences between county, circuit, and chancery courts. Three former graduate assistants deserve praise. Terri Castelow helped with court-martial records; Lori Bogle tracked down newspaper references; and Michael Strickland surveyed the medical records of the war. Randy W. Hackenburg at Carlisle Barracks, Mary Ison at the Library of Congress, Nick Natanson at the National Archives, and Charlyn E. Richardson at the United States Military Academy helped me locate most of the book's photographs Gary M. Shepard of the University of Arkansas provided quality prints from other sources, and Lloyd Fink and Bart Cohen, also of the University of Arkansas, made the maps. I am also grateful to Fulbright College of the University of Arkansas for a research grant that permitted completion of a vital stage of my research.

Above all, thanks to Anne for . . . well, everything.

INDEX

Abbott, Henry L., 285
Abbott, Ned, 285
Adams, Charles F., Jr., 275
Afton, 234, 254
Agriculture, 5
Alabama troops, 266, 268
  Infantry, 67, 141; 4th Regt., 64
Alcinda (slave), 271
Alcocke, Abner, 112, 113
Alcocke, Thomas A., 112
Alexandria, Va., 10, 41, 158, 175, 188,
  363–64
Allen, Jane, 352, 353
Allen, R.O., 244–45
Amiss, Hiram, 35, 53, 367
Amissville, Va., 42, 191, 198
Andrews, Richard S., 138
Annadale, 99–100
Apperson, Richard, 56
Armstrong, John S., 275
Armstrong, Sally, 224–25, 226, 227,
  231–32, 242, 264–65, 269, 271, 275,
  274–75
Army of the Potomac, 226, 281, 283–84,
  294, 306, 307, 311, 328, 334, 343,
  359
  First Cavalry Division of, 311–12
  reorganization of, 344–46
Army of Virginia, 114, 117, 129, 187

Ashby, John, 50
Ashby, William T., 379–80
Asher, Ann, 19
Asher, Nancy, 19
Attig, William, 301
Auburn, 239, 286, 380
Auger, Christopher, 140
Averell, William W., 217–18, 220, 227–29

Bailey, Martha, 352–53
Ball's Bluff, Va., 82
Baltimore, Md., 68, 215–16
Banks, Nathaniel P., 114, 130–31,
  139–41, 145, 165
Baptists, 21, 25
Barbour, Edwin, 51
Barbour, James, 32, 33, 34–35
Barbour, John S., Jr., 11, 59, 94–95, 252,
  318
Bardeen, Charles, 332–33
Barker, Sergeant, 369
Barnett's Ford (on Rapidan), 130–31
Barnett's Ford (on Rappahannock), 174
Barton, Clara, 167–68
Battle
  aftermath of, 149–54, 254–55
  nature of, 146–47
  preparation for, 133–34,
Bayard, George D., 131–32, 136, 162, 177

Beauregard, Pierre G.T., 62, 69, 88, 105
Beckham, Mr., 46
Beckham, Abner, 81, 112
Beckham, Beverly, 108, 112
Beckham, James A., 81, 108
Beckham, James T., 112
Beckham, Robert F., 207, 221, 240, 244, 245, 246, 252
Bell, George, 373
Bell, John, 27, 30
Bell, John W., 40, 56
Bell, Richard, 373
Bell, William T., 373
Bel Pre, 69, 215, 254
Berdan's Sharpshooters, 346
Berry Hill, 123, 250, 298
Beverly's Ford, 108, 243, 252
Birney, David, 352
Blackburn's Ford, battle of, 61–62
Blackford, Charles Minor, 256, 260
Blacks, free, 17–21, 54–55, 125–26, 362–64, 391 n.37, n. 38
  in Confederate service, 69–70, 127–28, 198
  Federal attitudes toward, 271, 357
  in Federal service, 271, 363–64
  postwar condition, 383–84
Blaisdell, William, 345
Bocock, John, 51, 66
Bocock, Sarah, 52
Bodman, Hardy, 301
Bonham, Milledge L., 48
"Bonnie Blue Flag," 58, 140, 217, 396 n.73
Borcke, Heros von, 207–209, 217, 221, 239
Botts, John Minor, 227, 239, 241, 265, 276, 286, 306, 319, 337, 372, 380–81
Bounty jumpers, 283–84, 334–35
Bowen, William, 101
Bowers, Robert, 355
Bowman, George, 55–56
Boyle, Cornelius, 95–96, 99
Bradford, Sally [Sarah], 234–35, 261
Bradford, Samuel, 234–35, 261
Bragg, Braxton, 191
Brandt, Ann C., 381
Brandy Rifles, 105
Brandy Station, Va., 8, 11, 37, 64, 91, 108, 193, 213, 220, 227, 268, 273, 277–78, 290–92, 303, 306, 360
  battle of, 242–53, 378
  cavalry reviews at, 238–42, 253
Breckinridge, James, 218
Bristoe campaign, 293–95

Bristoe Station, Va., 188, 294–95
Brooke, Daniel, 54
Brooke, John L., 82
Brown, C.B., 244
Brown, Captain, 274
Brown, J.B., 139
Brown, James F., 338
Brown, John, 53, 353
Brown, Mrs., 311
Brown, Polly, 15
Brown, Sarah, 139
Brown, Simeon A., 218
Brown, Thornton, 264
Browning, Bettie, 45, 58, 59, 63, 70–71, 74, 77–78, 79, 93, 110, 112, 364, 365, 366, 374, 379
Browning, Mark A., 373
Browning, William H., 45, 190
Browning, William L., 366
Browning, Willis, 190
Buford, John, 227, 243, 246–49, 277–78, 290–92, 293
Bundy, Ryburn, 127, 383
Bundy, Warner, 18, 54
Burks family, 298
Burnside, Ambrose, 344–45
Burrows, Henry Clay, 62, 264, 385
Burrows, Jesse, 352
Bushwhackers, 128, 129, 287, 340. *See also* Guerrillas
Butler, Benjamin F., 325–26, 328

Caldwell, John C., 345
Camp Henry, 43, 47, 48–49, 52, 64, 75, 106
Camp Lee, 190
Camp Pelham, 224
Camp Qui Vive, 207
Canady, John D., 264
Canals, in Culpeper, 10
Carrico Mills, 305
Carter, G.F., 77, 362
Carter, John W., 252
Cary, Clarence, 68
Cary, Constance, 68–69, 215, 216
Cary, Hetty, 68–69
Cary, Jenny, 68–69, 103–104
Cary, Monimia, 68–69
Casualties, 58–59, 62, 64–65, 67, 69, 70, 78, 101, 112, 115, 183, 214–15, 220–21, 253, 268, 301, 303, 307, 327–28, 361–62, 365, 373
Catchings, T.C., 66

Catlett's Station, Va., 95, 185–86
Cedar Creek, battle of, 365
Cedar Mountain, 134, 175, 193–94, 228,
    260, 285, 318
  battle of, 133–49, 276–77, 377
Cedar Run, 149, 162
Celts, 6, 7, 21, 39
Centreville, Va., 80, 93, 95
Chancellorsville, battle of, 229
Charlottesville, Va., 10, 114, 170, 362
Cheat Mountain, 82
Chewning, Isham, 354–55
Chinquapin Neck, 19–20, 226
Churches
  destruction of, 183, 282, 379
  role of, 64, 74–75, 107, 159, 211–13, 356
Civilians
  caring for sick and wounded, 52, 64,
    65–69, 158–59
  entertaining soldiers, 99–100, 102–103,
    197, 209, 268, 285–86, 297–98, 314,
    338–40, 351–52
  profit from war, 47–48, 75–77, 197–98,
    238, 276, 282–83
  reactions to battle, 138–40, 154, 279
  reactions to war, 43–47, 60, 63–64,
    66–67, 71–72, 79–80, 88–89, 97–99,
    104–105, 106–107, 109–11, 188–89,
    211, 224–25, 231–32, 264–65, 269,
    299, 375–76
  targets of war, 108–109, 119–26, 131,
    169–70, 176–77, 178–79, 270–71,
    274–75, 279, 281–82, 287, 295–96,
    299–300, 311–14, 368–69
  wavering morale, 73–75, 90–91, 105,
    224–25, 320, 327, 374
Clark's Mountain, 177
Clary Ann (slave), 73–74, 107
Class conflict, 21–22
Clore, Curran, 46–47
Clore, Lucretta, 46–47
Clover Hill, 252, 318
Cloverdale, 138, 156
Clow, Henry, 327
Cocke, John, 43
Cocke, Philip St. George, 41–43, 47,
    48–49, 49–50, 57
Colbert, Eveline, 73–74
Colbert, William, 73–74
Cold Harbor, battle of, 362
Cole, Frances, 260
Cole, John, 126, 212–13, 260, 278, 286,
    379, 425 n.68

Cole, Martha J., 59
Cole, William H., 38
Collins, William Smith, 379
Collman, Lucy, 19
Colvin, Gabriel, 62
Colvin, John N., 127
Colvin, Lucy, 157
Colvin, William D., 136
Colvin, William F., 76
Community, sense of, 212, 22–23, 27, 54–55
Confederate soldiers
  camp life, 96, 296–97
  clothing and equipment, 41, 49, 195,
    267–68, 295–97
  conditions of service, 40, 42–43, 49,
    71–72, 94, 97, 102, 106, 186–87,
    192–93, 194–97, 205–206, 213–14,
    216, 221–23, 237–38, 261, 263–64,
    295, 296–97
  discipline and punishments, 177, 195,
    222, 268, 298–99
  enlistment, 37–38, 42, 81–82, 89, 93
  morale of, 40, 53, 196–97, 223–24, 236,
    258–59, 263–64, 266–68, 300
  pleasures, 103, 196, 297–98
  reaction to battle, 63, 70–71, 148
  reaction to war, 51, 80–81
  religious nature, 238, 259–60, 266, 274,
    300
  sickness and wounds, 52, 58, 62–69,
    77–78, 149–50, 189, 197, 366, 373
  training, 39–40, 42, 49
  transfers, 50–51, 80, 196
Confederate commemorations, 376–78,
    385–86
Confederate Soldiers' Home (Richmond),
    379–80
Confiscation, by Federal soldiers, 122–23,
    123–24, 169–70, 172–73, 176,
    178–79
Connecticut troops, 328
  Infantry, 5th Regt., 144; 14th Regt.,
    327
Conscription, 55, 89–90, 97–98, 106,
    189–90, 309, 366
Conscripts, 283–84, 310, 334–35, 369
Conway, Jane, 46
Cooke, Giles B., 42, 51, 59, 66
Cooke, John Esten, 261–62
Coons, Dallas, 220
Coons, George H., 341–42
Coons, Martha, 106–107, 110
Coons, Robertson, 18

Coons, Susan, 110, 111, 314
Copperheads, 192, 211
Corbin, Mary, 110, 374
Corbin, Lemuel, 109, 197, 198, 2210, 374
Corinth, Miss., 191
Court days, 22–23
Courts-martial, 268, 270, 283, 298,
    309–11, 351–52
Crackers, 18, 22, 24. *See also* Plain folk;
    Whites, poor
Craftsmen, in Culpeper, 8–9, 11, 48
Crawford, Samuel M., 132–33, 140, 144,
    162
Crigler, William, 88
Criglersville, Va., 6
Criglersville Baptist Church, 211–12
Crittenden, Anne, 55, 138–39, 210, 379
Crittenden, Catherine, 55–56, 134,
    138–39, 156–57, 379
Crittenden, Charles T., 55, 91–92, 113,
    136, 362, 379
Crooked Run Baptist Church, 74, 132,
    211, 212
Culpeper Baptist Church, 43, 64, 74
Culpeper Circuit Court, 23, 235
Culpeper County
    physical description, 3–4, 126–27, 227,
        279–80, 295–96, 313- 14, 318–19,
        358, 359–60
    population, 5, 17, 313, 383
Culpeper County Court, 22–23, 48,
    69–70, 235, 360–61
Culpeper Court House, 8, 11, 30, 32, 33,
    39, 41, 42, 46, 47, 49, 64, 67, 75–76,
    95–96, 107, 108, 114–15, 126–27,
    140–41, 158- 60, 167, 174, 176–77,
    193, 227–28, 250, 252–53, 277–80,
    292- 93, 305, 313, 314, 358, 359–60,
    365, 376–77, 383, 385–86
    battle at, 277–79
Culpeper *Exponent*, 380, 384
Culpeper Methodist Church, 64, 68
Culpeper Military Institute, 46
Culpeper Minute Men, 16, 32, 37, 38–39,
    55, 56–57, 78, 79, 91–92, 105, 385
Culpeper *Observer*, 31, 34, 36, 39, 40–41,
    89, 90, 92, 384–85
Culpeper Riflemen, 37, 39, 70, 79, 92
Culpeper Road, 132–33, 134, 149
Culpeper Yellow Jackets, 46
Cunningham, Richard H., 49, 101–102, 108
Curtis, Abraham, 139, 407 n.50
Curtis family, 279, 407 n.50
Custer, Elizabeth B., 318

Custer, George A., 278–79, 290–91, 318,
    335–36

Dahlgren, Ulric, 336
Daniel, Samuel A., 139, 157
Daniel, Sarah, 157
Danville, Va., 170
Davis, Benjamin F. "Grimes," 243, 245
Davis, Jefferson, 62, 63–64, 94, 121–22,
    221, 256, 267, 335–36, 375
Dawes, Rufus B., 270–71, 272, 284, 351
Day, Delila, 354
Day, William, 12
Debtors, 23
Delaware troops
    Infantry: 1st Regt., 327–28
Denison, Frederic, 137
Desertion, 129–30, 161, 177, 194, 268,
    283–84, 298–99, 310, 311, 332, 355,
    357, 361, 373
Dickerson, Ella (slave), 384
Diley (slave), 212
Dixie Hotel, 159
Doggett, Charles, 179
Doubleday, Abner, 336
Douglas, Stephen, 26, 32
Drewry's Bluff, battle of, 362
Dudley, F.A., 322
Duffie, Alfred, 219, 250
Dulin, Ann, 361–62
Dulin, Edwin, 361–62
Dulin, James, 361–62
Dulin, Mary, 361–62
Duncan, T.J., 144
Dunn, James, 167
Dutch. *See* Germans

Early, Jubal A., 94, 136, 146–47, 148–49,
    161–62, 186, 187–88, 276–77, 297,
    301–302, 303
Economy, wartime, 47–48, 75–77, 88–89,
    197–98, 238, 276, 362
Eggborn, Jacob, 80
Eggborn, Perry J., 80
Eggborn, William, 80
Eggbornsville, Va., 15
Elections
    in Culpeper, 25–27, 360–61
    in North, 192, 211, 365
Ellis, Lewis, 15
Ely's Ford, 229, 335
Elzey, Arnold, 71, 104
Emancipation Proclamation, 191, 209–210
Embrey, Joseph W., 71–72

England. *See* Great Britain
Episcopalians, 25
Epps, William, 20
Ewell, Richard S., 94, 97, 100–101, 102,
    103–106, 119, 123–24, 131, 133,
    136, 156, 165, 235, 252–53, 258,
    301–302

Fairfax Court House, Va., 45, 93
Fairview, 368, 369
Falmouth, Va., 214
Fanny (slave), 210
Farmers, 5, 19, 193, 223, 238, 264,
    280–81, 337, 375
Farm machinery, 5–6
Farms and farming, 5–6, 19, 20, 387–88
    n.3, 388 n.4
Farish, Gabriel, 48
Farish, James, 56
Faulkner, David, 91
Fauquier County, Va., 14, 24, 101, 104,
    198–99, 269, 273, 276, 287, 295–96,
    337, 340, 351
Fay, Mr., 321
Federal soldiers
    camp life, 328–35
    conditions of service, 130, 280–81,
        283–84, 306–307, 308–309,
        324–25, 328–29, 346–47
    discipline and punishments, 270,
        283–84, 309–11, 333–35, 346
    entertainments, 283, 305–306, 319,
        329, 330–31, 350–51
    morale of, 117–18, 119, 120–21,
        168–70, 175, 272–73, 281–82,
        293–94, 333, 334–35, 357
    reenlistment debate, 309, 330–31
    religious nature, 284–85, 324, 356
    sickness and wounds, 65, 67, 130, 350
    training, 346–47
    treatment of blacks, 125–26, 271–72,
        311, 338, 369
    treatment of white civilians, 122–25,
        126–27, 128–29, 167–68, 270–72,
        274–76, 285–86, 311–14, 337,
        339–40, 369
Feuds, in Culpeper, 23–26, 381, 391 n.47
Field, Ira, 19, 54, 126
Field, James G., 50, 64, 160, 385
Field, Judy, 19
Field, Lewis, 361
Field, Richard H., 373, 385
Field, Richard Y., 78
Field, Ruben, 19

Fitzgerald, Captain, 122–23
Fitzhugh family, 305
Fitzhugh, Thomas, 19
Fitzhugh, Wash, 57
Flats, the, 18, 22, 97, 128, 169–70, 228,
    362–63
Fleetwood Hill, 242, 245, 248, 249,
    250–52, 255, 290–91
Flint, Edward, 62
Flint, Eliza, 64
Flint, Thomas O., 64, 362–63
Flint, William, 157
Flournoy, C.E., 243–44
Foraging, 102, 265, 281–82
Ford, C.E., 252
Forest Grove, 139, 157
Forno, Henry, 135
Fort Donelson, Tenn., 89
Fort Fisher, N.C., 371
Fort Hatteras, N.C., 82
Fort Pillow, Tenn., 357
Fort Pulaski, Ga., 105
Foushee, John, 47
Foushee, Mary, 197
Fowler, Jeff (slave), 215
France, 372, 374
Francis, George A., 311
Fraser's Farm, battle of, 373
Fraternization, 222, 238, 290, 273, 283, 325
Fredericksburg Plank Road, 250
Fredericksburg, Va., 10, 12, 20, 41, 95, 114,
    174, 199, 225–26, 233, 299–300
    battle of, 202, 205, 268
Freedmen's Bureau, 382
Freeman, Colonel, 289–90
Freeman, Harris, 23
Freeman, Ned, 109
Freeman, William H., 78
Freeman's Ford, 185, 227
Frémont, John C., 82
French, as soldiers, 327
French, William H., 287, 300–301, 306
Front Royal, Va., 114, 258
Furloughs, 194–95, 296, 309, 329, 331,
    374

Gaines, Argelon F., 78
Gaines, Mary F., 78
Gaines, Mildred, 78
Gains, Reuben, 353
Garcelon, Alonzo, 159
Garner, Andrew J., 50
Garnett, James, 132, 211
Geary, John W., 145

General Orders
  No. 5, 119, 173
  No. 11, 120
  No. 19, 173
  No. 54, 172
George, Cumberland, 43, 170
Georgia troops, 94, 97, 196, 206, 251, 259,
  263–64, 295, 299
  Infantry, 240; 12th Regt., 143; 14th
  Regt., 266
Germanna Ford, 226, 228–29, 290, 359
Germanna, Va., 6
Germans
  settlers, 6–7
  soldiers, 104, 170, 173, 310, 327, 368
Gettysburg, battle of, 263–64, 266–67, 336
Gibbon, John, 308, 336–37
Gibbs, Hannah (slave), 67
Gibson, D.W., 91
Gibson, Bruce, 243
Gilmor, Harry, 219–20
Glebe, The, 254
Glenmore, 254
Gordon, Churchill M., 70
Gordon, George H., 144
Gordon, John J., 210
Gordonsville and Lynchburg Railroad, 335
Gordonsville, Va., 10, 94, 102, 106, 114,
  119, 129, 174, 226, 362, 368
Gorrell, Joseph B., 89, 178, 354, 358, 381
Gorrell, Mary, 89
Gourdvine Baptist Church, 74, 211
Grant, Julia Dent, 343, 358
Grant, Ulysses S., 342–46, 356–57, 358–59
Gray, George, 33
Great Britain, 88–89, 372
Green, Daniel S., 52, 59, 64–65, 69, 93
Green, John C., 25, 381–82
Greene County, Va., 206–207
Gregg, David M., 243, 245–46, 249–50, 277
Grey, Daniel, 234, 254
Grey, Myrta, 234, 254, 261–62
Griffinsburg, Va., 7, 293
Grimsley, Barnett, 45, 96, 211, 278, 367
Grimsley, Daniel A., 45, 58, 59, 63, 70–71,
  110, 112, 249, 364, 365, 374, 378,
  379, 380
Guerrillas, 118–19, 119–20, 287, 340, 358

Hackley, James F., 373
Hall, Ann, 13
Hall, Susan, 35
Halleck, Henry W., 121, 166–67, 172–73,
  187, 326, 342

Halsey, Joseph, 44–45, 60, 83, 200–202
Halsey, Mildred, 44–45
Halsey, Samuel, 83
Hamlin, Hannibal, 319
Hampton Roads Conference, 372
Hampton, Wade,193, 205–206, 207,
  233–34, 245, 246, 277
Hancock, Cornelia, 322–23, 349, 350
Hancock, Winfield Scott, 308, 325,
  336–37, 344–45
Hardy, William B., 141
Harper's Ferry, Va., 15, 39, 41, 42, 56
Harris, James, 5
Harris, Truman, 341
Harrison, Burton N., 69
Hart's Mill, 185
Hartsuff, George L., 162
Hartwood Church, Va., 214–15, 220
Haskell, Joe, 265–66
Hatch, John B., 114–15, 119, 165–66
Haupt, Herman, 168, 188
Hawkins, John, 62, 88
Hawkins, Ned (slave), 176
Hays, Alexander, 305, 327, 345
Hazel River, 8, 184, 185, 224, 245, 246,
  263, 270, 277, 340, 375
Hazelwood Volunteers, 37, 50
Heflin, John, 15
Heflin, William, 35
Henry (slave), 15
Herndon, Thomas, 189
Herr, Mabel, 66–67
Herr, Mrs. William ("Bunny"), 66–67
Heth, Stockton, 37
Hicks, George, 19
Hicks, John T., 382
Hill, Ambrose Powell, 56, 71, 119, 131,
  133, 144, 148, 155, 191, 235–36,
  260–61, 294–95, 298, 376
Hill, Edward, 56
Hill, Henry, 206–207
Hill, Mildred, 385
Hill, Philip, 144
Hill, Thomas, 197, 276
Hill, William A., 78
Hill, William A. (of Madison County),
  254–55
Hill, William H., 264
Hinson's Mill, 188
Hitt, James, 372
Holcomb, Martin, 58–59
Holloway, E., 327–28
Holtzman, Esther, 378
Holtzman, John A., 376, 378

Home Guard, 41, 90
"Homespun Dress," 339, 441 n.54
Hood, John Bell, 260, 371
Hooker, Joseph, 225, 228, 243, 260, 308, 336
Hoop, C.B., 89
Horne, Frances Hill, 385
Horses, condition of, 205–206, 216, 225–26, 237, 295, 347
Hospitals, 52, 58–59, 64–65, 70–71, 149, 156–60, 189, 320–23, 349–50
Hotchkiss, Jedediah, 298
Howard, McHenry, 138
Howard, Oliver O., 100–101
Howe, Albion P., 336
Hoxton, William, 252
Hudson, Garnett, 9–10
Hudson, Matilda, 67, 127
Hudson, Robert, 134, 139, 171–72
Hume, Charles, 66–67
Hume, Mr., 355
Hume, Mrs., 355
Humphreys, Andrew, 319
Humphreys, Rufus, 158
Hurley, Sarah (slave), 12–13
Hussey, Obed, 6

Illinois troops
   Cavalry: 8th Regt., 244
Indiana troops, 312, 357
   Cavalry, 166, 336: 3rd Regt., 228, 244, 356
Inskeep, James, 139
Inskeep, John A., 39
Irish
   as settlers, 7
   as soldiers, 170
Italian soldiers, 327

Jackson, Alexander (slave), 12, 126
Jackson, Anna, 162
Jackson, Thomas J., 104, 105–106, 119, 121, 130–32, 143, 148–50, 153, 156, 161, 164–65, 166, 167, 177, 183–85, 199, 232
Jacobs, Horace G., 302
James City, Va., 290
James, Mr., 272
James (slave), 272
Jameson, James H., 58, 78
Jameson, John, 354
Jameson, Mary, 78
Jamieson, Mrs., 311
Jefferson Academy, 7
Jeffersonton Baptist Church, 356, 371

Jeffersonton, Va., 7, 38. 79, 182, 199, 216, 225, 242, 341, 366, 368
Jeffries, Hill, 340
Jennings, Fannie, 224, 232
Jennings, George T., 70
Johnson, Elijah, 297–98
Johnson, T.D., 62
Johnston, Albert Sidney, 105
Johnston, Joseph E., 62–63, 69, 93–95, 97, 102, 104, 106, 375–76
Jones, D.T., 76
Jones, S., 41, 42
Jones, William E. "Grumble," 244, 245, 246, 249
Jordan, Jesse, 67
Jordan, Margaret Brandon, 67
Journalists, 95, 133–34, 159–60, 178, 187, 197, 257, 267, 307

Karge, Joseph, 123
Keifer, Joseph W., 280, 346
Kelly, Dennis, 78
Kelly, Granville, 12, 272
Kelly, John P., 12–13, 17, 23–24, 124, 271–72, 338, 384, 412 n.45
Kelly's Ford, 177, 182, 207, 224, 226, 243, 245–46, 300–301, 364
   battle of, 217–20
Kellysville, Va., 12, 23–24, 124, 271–72, 300, 309–10
Kemper, Henry, 24
Kemper, James L., 43, 52, 61, 71, 80–81
Kilby, Andrew J., 264
Kilpatrick, Judson, 224, 251, 290–92, 314, 326, 335–36
   raid of, 335–36
Kirby, Sarah Ann, 38
Kirk, James B., 54, 72

Lake, Isaac, 340, 372
Latham, Emma, 57, 227
Latham, Fayette M., 24–25
Latham, Mary (slave), 12–13
Latimer, Joseph W., 137
Lawlessness, 73, 91, 376
Lazelle, Henry M., 364–65
Lee, Custis, 196
Lee, Fitzhugh, 207, 214–15, 217–20, 226, 246, 277, 290–91
Lee, Mary Custis, 196, 207, 253, 267, 295
Lee, Mildred, 196
Lee, Robert E., 41, 42, 43, 82, 104, 114, 121–22, 174, 177–79, 181–82, 187–88, 192, 194, 195–96, 198–99,

Lee, Robert E. (*cont.*)
  200, 206–207, 213, 221, 225–26,
  233–34, 235, 236–37, 241–42,
  252–53, 256, 258, 259–61, 267,
  268–69, 280–81, 289–95, 296,
  298–300, 301–302, 303–304,
  345–46, 356–57, 375
Lee, William H.F. "Rooney," 245, 248–49,
  252, 256, 299
Lenoir, Walter, 140–43, 162
Letcher Artillery, 37, 62
Letcher, John, 29, 42, 47, 59, 82, 87,
  89–90, 93, 97, 299–300
Lewis, Robert, 64
Lewis, Thomas, 109
Liberty Mills, Va., 131
Lightfoot, Charles E., 46
Lightfoot, Henry Clay, 383
Lincoln, Abraham, 26, 29, 31, 33–34, 87,
  113–14, 118, 199–20, 161–62,
  172–73, 304, 307, 311, 335, 365, 372,
  376
Little Fork, 6, 185
Little Fork Rangers, 37–38, 49, 56, 57–58,
  62, 77–78, 177, 216, 259, 292, 340,
  341, 362, 374, 376, 378
Lloyd, Adolphus, 341
Lloyd, Ann, 341
Lloyd, James, 341
Longstreet, James, 61, 94, 104, 177, 179,
  187–88, 199, 235, 236, 260, 277
Louisiana troops, 301–302
  Artillery: Washington Artillery, 183
  Cavalry: 15
  Louisiana Tigers: 302, 303–304
Luckett, Samuel, 158
Luray, Va., 121
Lutherans, 21
Luttrell family, 361
Lynchburg, Va., 10, 67, 114, 170, 189, 362

Madden, Elizabeth, 19
Madden, Jack, 20
Madden, Kitty, 20
Madden, Slaughter, 364
Madden, Willis, 19–21, 55, 126, 208, 365,
  384, 391 n.40
Madison County, Va., 39, 50, 131, 194,
  206–207, 254
Madison Court House, Va., 129, 199, 289,
  335, 362, 368, 395
Maine troops, 310
  Cavalry, 251; 1st Regt., 108–109

Infantry, 301; 6th Regt., 302; 16th
  Regt., 309; 17th Regt., 307
Major, Langdon C., 38, 276
Major, Mrs. William, 305, 339
Major, William, 134, 276, 312
Manassas, Va., 10, 41, 42, 44, 57, 58, 93,
  94–95, 187–88, 293
  1st battle of, 61–63, 70, 82
  2nd battle of, 191
Mann, J.T., 244
Manufacturing, in Culpeper, 8–10, 11, 12,
  388 n.14
Mars, George, 127–28, 363, 383
"Maryland," 69, 102–103
Mason, Charles, 179
Mason, James, 82
Mason, Mary, 189
Masonic Hall, 157
Massachusetts troops, 145–46, 175, 199,
  281, 294, 306, 309–10, 312, 327, 333
  Infantry, 1st Regt., 65, 332–33; 2nd
  Regt., 144–45, 249, 285; 10th Regt.,
  359; 13th Regt., 334; 20th Regt., 285;
  21st Regt., 122; 28th Regt., 318; 37th
  Regt. 306–307, 331; 39th Regt.,
  330–31
Matthews, Joseph O., 264
Mauzy, Fayette, 199–200, 384
McClellan, George B., 93, 95, 97, 111, 114,
  192
McClellan, Henry B., 249–50, 253, 258
McCormick, Art, 340, 366
McCormick, Cyrus, 6
McCrae, Jim, 332–33
McDowell, Irvin, 57, 59, 114, 130–31,
  145, 172
McGuire, Hunter, 156–57
McIntosh, Joe, 127
McPharlin, Thomas A., 159
McVeigh, Jane, 200
McVeigh, L.W., 89
Meade, George Gordon, 264, 272, 276,
  277, 280–81, 284, 286, 289- 90,
  293–96, 303–304, 305–308,
  312–12, 335, 336–37, 342, 343,
  345–46, 347, 359, 363
Merchants, in Culpeper, 8–9, 33, 36,
  47–48, 75, 76–77, 89, 99, 197, 337,
  362
Merritt, Wesley, 340, 352
Michigan troops, 270–71
  Cavalry, 278–79; 1st Regt., 290–91; 5th
  Regt., 290–91

Military service, avoiding, 55–56, 59, 69–70, 72–73, 90–92, 97- 98, 112
Militia, 52–53, 55, 58, 59, 75, 82, 89–90, 97
Miller, Henry, 47
Miller, J.G., 47
Mine Run campaign, 307, 310, 336
Mississippi troops, 268
    Infantry, 17th Regt, 58
Mitchell, Billy, 8
Mitchell's Ford, 330–31
Mitchell's Station, Va., 8, 11, 46
Monitor, 105
Moore, Martha, 351–52
Moore, Ned, 137–38
Morris, Robert, 248
Morrissett, Lawson, 217, 218
Morrisville, Va., 218
Morton, Jeremiah, 30–31, 211, 327, 379
Morton's Ford, fight at, 325–28
Mosby, John S., 100, 102, 199, 270, 340, 360, 368, 370, 374
Mosee, Mr., 352
Mosee, "Pus," 351
Mt. Holly Church, 384
Mt. Pony, 279, 365
Mt. Pony Baptist Church, 74
Munford, Thomas, 246

Nalle family, 157–58
Nalle, Thomas B., 157–58
Nallie, William, 139–40, 368–70, 372, 375–76
Nalls, William C., 366
Needham, Thomas, 65
Neese, George, 274, 278
Nelson, Kate, 80
Nelson, Lewis, 353, 362–63, 367, 368
New Bern, N.C., 105
New Madrid, Mo., 105
New Hampshire troops, 130
New Jersey troops
    Cavalry, 251; 1st Regt., 123, 130, 250, 251; 5th Regt., 341
    Infantry, 12th Regt., 332
New Salem Baptist Church, 74
Newby, James, 219
Newsom, John G., 301
Newsome, Silas, 340
New York troops, 171, 218, 270, 280, 282, 283, 285, 286, 328, 330, 33–34, 347, 355
    Artillery, 6th Regt., 319
    Cavalry, 251, 279; 8th Regt., 243, 244;

13th Regt., 364–65; 16th Regt., 364–65; 45th Regt., 369
    Infantry, 9th Regt., 130; 28th Regt., 122–23, 144, 377; 39th Regt., 327; 108th Regt., 327; 111th Regt., 327; 121st Regt., 333–34; 151st Regt., 282–83; Excelsior Brigade, 332–33
    Militia, 20th Regt., 271
Noble, Charles, 314
Norris, D.J., 62
North Carolina troops, 193–94, 194–95, 261, 268, 296, 298
    Infantry, 301, 303; 2nd Regt., 301; 30th Regt., 301; 37th Regt., 141–42
Northcliff, 106–107, 110–11, 374
Norton, Lemuel B., 306

Oak Shade, Va., 38, 49, 259, 378
Occupations, nonfarming, in Culpeper, 8–10, 18–19
Oden, Alexander, 264
Ohio troops, 283
    Cavalry, 1st Regt., 351
    Infantry, 82nd Regt., 189; 110th Regt., 346
Old Capitol Prison, 340
O'Neil, John, 353
Orange & Alexandria Railroad, 8, 10–11, 40–41, 94–95, 100, 114, 168, 185, 187, 249, 263, 295, 306, 351, 360, 362
Orange County, Va., 14, 31, 39, 68, 99, 104, 131–32, 166, 194, 217, 233, 236, 307
Orange Court House, Va., 106, 108, 269, 362
Owen, Joshua T., 326

Paducah, Ky., 82
Pannill, Mrs. George, 91
Parnell, W.R., 341
Parr, Sarah, 109–10, 111
Parr, Thomas, 48
Patrick, Marsena S., 166, 312–13, 317–18, 339–40, 354
Patterson, John P., 301
Patton, P.F., 30
Patton, Waller Tazewell, 16, 30, 39, 40, 80–81, 91, 264
Payne daughters, 128, 140, 340, 354
Payne, George S.M., 66
Payne, John, 368
Payne, Mary A.B., 110

Payne, Mary L., 35, 75, 340, 354, 381
Payne, Millie, 45, 66
Payne, Sanford, 370
Payne, William, 127, 158, 354
Peace Convention, 32, 34
Pegram, William J., 141, 148
Pelham, John, 207–209, 217–21
Pender, William Dorsey, 256–57, 262, 263
Pendleton, Alexander "Sandie," 304
Pendleton, Inez, 52
Pendleton, John S., 24–25, 33, 51, 98, 169,
    209, 265–66, 286, 308–309, 312,
    337, 380
Pendleton, William N., 95, 96, 241–42, 260
Peninsula (of Virginia), 82, 106, 111, 114
Pennsylvania troops, 218, 273, 284,
    293–94, 304, 310, 334
  Cavalry, 166, 283; 1st Regt., 128, 147;
    2nd Regt., 279–80; 6th Regt., 248,
    253
  Infantry, 301–302; 46th Regt., 144; 49th
    Regt., 301
Perry, Malinda (slave), 15
Perry, William H., 54
Perryville, Ky., 191
Petersburg, Va., 365, 375
Petty, Cornelia, 135
Photographers, 168–69, 329–30
Piedmont Academy, 36
Piedmont Hotel, 19, 159
Plain folk, 6. See also Crackers, Whites, poor
Pleasant Grove Baptist Church, 74–75
Pleasonton, Alfred, 243, 246, 252,
    253–54, 258, 277, 308, 335, 347
Plymouth, N.C., 357
Poague, William T., 137
Pocahontas (slave), 352
Point Lookout, Md., 341, 366, 372–73
Politics, in Culpeper, 25–27
Poor Institute, 64
Pope, John, 114, 117–22, 129, 130–31,
    132–33, 134–36, 140–41, 145–46,
    161, 165–66, 168–69, 172–74, 182,
    185–86, 187–88, 191
  orders of, 119–21, 122–23, 169,
    172–74; Confederate response,
    121–22, 172
Pope, John (of Culpeper), 137
Presqu' Isle, 305–306
Price, Thomas R., 207
Prices, wartime, 77, 88–89, 111, 193,
    197–98, 199, 224, 265, 281, 341–42
Prisoners, treatment of, 67, 360, 366, 372
Pryor, Roger A., 194

Pryor, Sarah, 197
Puller, John, 221
Purks, William, 72, 352

Railroads, 10–11. See also specific railroads
Raccoon Ford, Va., 66, 130, 177, 283, 326,
    327
Randolph, George W., 195, 239
Randolph, John, 45
Rapidan River, 7, 8, 66, 97, 106, 118–19,
    130–32, 133, 166–67, 174, 177, 207,
    222, 224, 226, 236, 269, 279, 280,
    303, 307, 325–26, 356–57, 358–59
Rapidan Station, 11, 99, 228, 304, 383
Rappahannock bridge, 100, 129, 252, 280,
    299
Rappahannock Canal, 10
Rappahannock County, Va., 14, 110, 194,
    374
Rappahannock River, 24, 49, 93, 97,
    100–101, 104, 105–106, 107, 114,
    117, 119, 166, 174, 175–76, 182, 184,
    186, 198, 205, 207, 214–15, 216, 218,
    222, 224, 225–26, 233, 236–37,
    242–43, 252, 258, 268–70, 272–73,
    277, 290–94, 299, 364–65
Rappahannock Station, 11, 49, 99, 101,
    108, 129, 174, 182, 199, 207, 224,
    249, 263, 292, 364–65
  battle of, 300–304
Redmon, Arthur, 19
Redmon, Betty, 19
Redmon, Lizzie, 383–84
Redmon, Martha, 19
Redwood, 111, 124–25, 200, 209, 217,
    219, 265, 308, 380
Refugees, 44, 98, 101, 109–110, 170–71,
    191, 199–200, 215, 338
  blacks as, 363–64
Remington, Va., 49
Rhode Island troops
  Cavalry, 114; 1st Regt., 122, 138, 157,
    218, 228
  Infantry, 2nd Regt., 356
Richardsville, Va., 10
Richmond, Va., 97, 98, 111–12, 114, 190,
    200–202, 237, 262, 325–26, 335–36,
    362, 365, 375
Richmond Examiner, 257
Rixey, Charles W., 88
Rixey family, 8, 197, 383
Rixey, John H., 197
Rixey, Margaret, 216
Rixey, Martha, 340–41

Rixey, Presley, 358
Rixey, Richard, 216
Rixey, Thomas R., 367–68, 382
Rixeyville, Va., 8, 216, 368, 369, 384
Roads, in Culpeper, 10, 97, 174
Roanoke Island, N.C., 89
Roberts, Benjamin S., 162
Robertson, Beverly, 88, 177, 246, 249–50
Robinson River, 130, 279, 289
Rose Hill, 224–25, 335
Ross, James P., 56, 79
Ross, William Daniel, 264
Rosser, Thomas, 221, 290–91
Rough and Ready Rifles, 37, 58
Rudasill, James, 9
Russell, David A., 302

Salt, 189–90, 199–200
Samuels, Green, 297
Samuels, Kathleen, 297
Scotch-Irish settlers, 6–7
Scott, Fanny, 95
Scott, Robert, 95. 96
Secession, 29, 53
    public reaction to, 29–34, 35–36,
        53–55
Seddon, James A., 207, 237, 242, 295
Sedgwick, John, 292–93, 300–301,
        305–306, 308, 326, 335–36, 344- 45
Settle, Joseph, 225
Settle, Judie, 225
Seward, William, 32, 33, 35, 172
Shackleford, Bessie, 208–209, 217,
        219–20, 224
Shackleford, Henry (Jr.), 30, 31, 50, 109,
        209, 289–90, 354, 379, 384
Shackleford, Henry (Sr.), 30
Shaw, Archibald, 54, 127, 313, 381
Shaw, James, 381
Shaw, Sarah, 35
Shaw, Simeon, 35
Sharpsburg, Md., 191
Sheads, George, 78
Sheads, Robert, 78
Shenandoah Valley, 56–57, 95, 104,
        105–106, 114, 276, 365
Sheridan, Philip H., 347, 365
Sherman, William T., 365, 371
Shiloh, Tenn., 105
Shirkers, 146, 150
Short, Charles, 106, 107, 109
Sickles, Daniel E., 336
Sigel, Franz, 121, 130–31, 140–41, 148, 175
Simms, Albert Gallatin, 176

Simpson, James M., 266
Sisson, Garland, 11
Slaughter, Ella, 126
Slaughter, Martha, 19–20
Slaughter, Martin, 19–20
Slaughter, Philip, 14, 57, 59, 65, 72, 123,
        169, 198, 276, 381
Slaveholders, 11–12, 13–14, 55, 99, 125,
        190, 191, 199–200, 209- 110, 276
Slavery, 11–13
    abolished, 371
    defense of, 14, 16
    protection of, 32–34
Slaves, 48, 111, 212, 269, 272, 338
    colonization of, 13–14
    in Confederate service, 199–200
    emancipated, 13, 124, 125–26, 175–76,
        209–210, 212, 271, 287
    in Federal service, 271, 287
    hired, 11–12, 20, 238
    punishment of, 15, 16–17, 73–74, 390
        n.29
    rebellious, 14–16, 73–74, 191,
        209–210
Slaymaker, H.C., 89
Slidell, John, 82
Smith, Eliza, 19
Smith, Ellen, 23
Smith, Frank, 19
Smith, Gustavus W., 94, 96
Smith, William, 342, 362
Smoot, Anne. *See* Crittenden, Anne
Smoot, James R., 210
"Somebody's Darling," 68, 398 n.19
Somerville Ford, 236
Somerville, Mr., 125–26
Somerville, Robert B., 264
Sorrel, Gilbert M., 179
South Carolina troops, 206, 250, 251, 274,
        297, 300
Southern Claims Commission, 381–82, 383
Southern Rights Association, 31
Soutter, William A., 72–73, 353–54
Sperryville, Va., 10, 130–31
Spies, 120, 129, 131, 174, 177, 179, 207,
        289–90, 339–40, 355
Spotsylvania, battle of, 361, 362
Spring Hill, 211
St. James's Episcopal Church, 183, 244,
        245, 246, 250, 253
St. Stephen's Episcopal Church, 64, 209,
        212–13
Stallard, C.P., 289–90, 354
Stallard, David, 109

Stallard, James W., 372, 374
Stanford, S.N., 351–52
Stanton, Edwin, 342
Stark, John, 80
Stark, John T., 9, 47
Starr, Darius, 175
Staunton, Va., 170
Steinwehr, Adolph von, 121
Stephens, Alexander, 372
Stevensburg, Va., 37, 183, 213, 245, 250, 274, 290, 333, 335, 359
Stevenson, George W., 248–49
Stofer, Alfred J., 31–32, 34, 36, 39, 47, 90, 238, 276, 384–85
Stofer, Ann, 39
Stone, Jack, 36
Stone, John A., 91
Stone, Mrs. Richard, 279
Stoneman, George, 226, 227
Stony Mountain, 356
Stowell, D. Porter, 108–109
Stringfellow, Ann, 67
Stringfellow, Benjamin F., 131
Stringfellow, Dr., 66–67
Stringfellow, Miss, 287
Stringfellow, Thornton, 14
Strother, David, 114, 120
Strother, Dr., 383
Strother, George, 48
Strother, John, 48, 92
Stuart, Flora, 194, 221, 257, 274, 277
Stuart, James E.B., 97, 100, 104, 106, 153, 162, 185–86, 187–88, 194, 198–99, 206, 209, 217, 218, 221, 223–24, 226, 233–35, 238–43, 245–46, 249–50, 251, 253–54, 255–57, 267, 269, 273-74, 277, 290–92, 362
Stuart, Mary (slave), 64
Sudley, Private, 252
Sulphur Springs Ford, 174
Sutlers, 281, 349–50
Swartz Woolen Mill, 38
Sweeney, Sam, 234

Taliaferro, Alexander G., 30, 99
Taliaferro, Margaret, 99–100
Taliaferro, May, 99–100
Taliaferro, Sarah, 99–100
Taliaferro, William B., 141, 142
Tanner, John, 373
Tate, Randall, 19, 363–64
Taxes, 366–67
Taylor, A.S., 75–76, 81
Taylor, James P., 155

Taylor, John, 37, 123
Taylor, Kitty, 362–63
Taylor, Mrs., 298
Taylor, William, 362–63
Tennessee troops, 268
"Tenting on the Old Camp Ground," 242–43, 255, 422 n.30
Terrett, George H., 48
Texas troops, 183, 193, 236
  Infantry, 186; 4th Regt., 260; 5th Regt., 260
Thom, J. Pembroke, 13–14
Thom, Lucy, 123
Thomas, Edward L., 141, 143
Thomas, George, 308
Thomas, Robert, 352, 353
Thomas, Sarah, 352
Thompson, Fannie, 213
Thompson, William, 56
Thompson, William M., 189
Thornhill, Frances, 12
Thoroughfare Gap, 95, 188
Timberlake, Edward, 369
Timberlake, James W., 369
Timberlake, Senie, 369
Torbert, Alfred T.A., 368
Total war, 119–21
Trimble, Isaac R., 104, 136, 185
Triplet, Eliza, 314
Triplet, H., 314
Turner, John, 110

Unionists, 33, 34, 35–36, 72–73, 112, 127–28, 158–59, 172–73, 175–76, 190, 285–86, 352–54, 363, 367–68, 381–83
United Confederate Veterans, 380, 385
United Daughters of the Confederacy, 377
U.S. Christian Commission, 320, 323–34, 349–50
U.S. Sanitary Commission, 320–21, 349–50
U.S. troops
  Artillery, 4th Regt., 311
  Black, 360
  Cavalry, 6th Regt., 248
  Corps, I, 300, 321, 326, 327, 344–45; II, 277, 293, 300, 321, 322, 326, 344–45; III, 294, 300, 321, 335, 344–45; V, 293, 300, 304, 344–45; VI, 293, 300, 344–45; IX, 344–45, 360; XI, 226, 335; XII, 226
  Sharpshooters, 2nd Regt., 175
Upton, Emory, 302–303, 305–306

Utterback, Robert E., 49, 57–58, 62, 92, 384
Utz, Burr, 62

"The Vacant Chair," 210–11, 418 n.13
Val Verde, 157–58, 168, 171
Vallandingham, Clement, 211
Van Dorn, Earl, 69, 191
Veighney, Adeline, 198
Vermont troops, 279
Vicksburg, Miss., 267
Virginia, 105
Virginia General Assembly, 31, 32, 89–90
Virginia House Hotel, 75–76, 140, 158,
    159–60, 217, 224, 305, 340, 354, 381
Virginia Military Institute, 16, 50, 81
Virginia secession convention, 31–32,
    34–35, 43
Virginia troops, 196, 216
    Artillery, 191; Chew's Battery, 274;
        Culpeper Battery, 207;
    Richmond Howitzers, 178; Rockbridge
        Artillery, 137
    Cavalry, 206, 273–74; 1st Regt., 101,
        218; 2nd Regt., 108, 218, 219; 3rd
        Regt., 213, 215, 218–19, 222, 291; 4th
        Regt., 77–78, 79, 88, 92, 101, 217,
        219, 220, 222, 292, 366; 5th Regt.,
        218, 221, 279; 6th Regt., 44–45, 243,
        245, 279, 292, 379; 7th Regt., 244,
        245; 9th Regt., 226; 10th Regt., 199,
        248, 274; 11th Regt., 246; 12th Regt.,
        246, 250, 255; 13th Regt., 226; 15th
        Regt., 214, 292, 297–98; 35 Batt., 246,
        250; Loudon
    Comanches, 376; Powhatan, 42, 50;
        Rappahannock, 45
    Infantry, 259; 7th Regt., 51–52, 61–62,
        71, 80–81, 92, 194, 264, 373, 380; 8th
        Regt., 95; 10th Regt., 104, 297; 11th
        Regt., 58, 61–62, 78, 264; 13th Regt.,
        39, 62–63, 71, 92, 104, 113, 136–37,
        141, 142–43, 146–47, 186, 196, 264,
        361, 373, 379; 14th Regt., 195, 264;
        17th Regt., 355; 18th Regt., 52,
        258–59; 19th Regt., 57; 21st Regt.,
        101, 162–63, 182, 258; 27th Regt.,
        296; 31st Regt., 142–43; 55th Regt.,
        200
    Militia, 52–53; 5th Regt., 59

Wager, Mrs. Charles, 254
Wager, Charles W., 52–53, 59
Walker, James A., 136–37, 142–43,
    147–49

Walker, Mrs. M.E., 91
Wallach family, 278
Wallach, Margaret, 98
Wallach, Nannie, 286
Wallach, Richard, 33
Wallach, William Douglas, 33, 112, 114,
    120, 172–73, 278, 286
Walsh, Michael, 144
Warren, Gouverneur K., 277, 326, 344–45
Warrenton, Va., 73, 94, 101, 114, 185, 188,
    198–99, 299, 337, 351, 360
Washington, D.C., 158, 161, 350
Washington *Evening Star*, 33, 171
Watkins, Mary, 213–14
Watkins, Richard, 213–14, 223
Waterloo bridge, 185
Waterloo, Va., 10, 188, 224–25
Weather, 94, 102, 105–106, 107, 117, 131,
    133, 153, 160, 174, 186, 195, 205,
    207, 214, 216, 221, 225, 261, 269,
    273, 284, 306–307, 308–309, 317,
    342, 346, 371
Webb, Alexander, 330
Webster, Isaac C., 381
"Weeping, Sad and Lonely," 113, 403 n.61
Welford, Robert, 48
Welford's Ford, 245
Wells, George, 47
Welsh, Peter, 318
Wentworth, Edwin, 331
West, Richard, 19
Weyman, Mittie, 298
Weyman, Roberta, 298
Wharton, John, 8
Wharton, John J., 46
Wheatley, Garland T., 23–24, 218
Wheatley, George T., 23–24, 384
Wheatleyville, Va., 24
White, James L., 189
White (slave), 13
Whites, poor, 18, 122, 124, 128–29,
    169–70, 361, 366–67. See also Crack-
    ers; Plain folk
Whitman, Walt, 321, 328
Wickham, William C., 222
Wilderness, battle of, 362
Williams, Alpheus S., 140, 144, 145, 165,
    271–72
Williams, George, 254–55
Williams, George M., 16, 25–27, 39, 40,
    51, 89, 98, 111–12, 124- 25, 191, 198,
    200, 380, 381–82, 383
Williams, Gertrude, 39, 89, 98, 111–12,
    124–25, 200, 209, 380

Williams, James, 254
Williams, Private, 341
Willis, 373
Wilson, Bill, 255–56
Wiltshire, John, 102, 108
Winchester, Va., 56–57, 62–63, 189, 258
Winder, Charles S., 131–32, 133, 137–38, 407 n.47
Wisconsin troops, 270–71, 287, 307, 351
    Infantry, 301; 3rd Regt., 144–45, 248–49; 5th Regt., 302; 6th Regt., 351
Wise family, 69, 215, 254, 398 n.20
Wise, Annie, 215, 298
Wise, Fannie, 215, 298

Wise, Mary, 254
Women
    in camp, 308, 317–19
    as soldiers, 130
    wartime roles, 52
Wood, Jacque, 190
Wood, John M., 382
Wood, Lewis L., 31
Wood, Pollard, 79, 366
Wood, Woodford, 366, 378
Wyndham, Percy, 250–51

Yager, William (slave), 155, 383–84
Yancey, Robert, 210
Yew Ridge, 248, 253

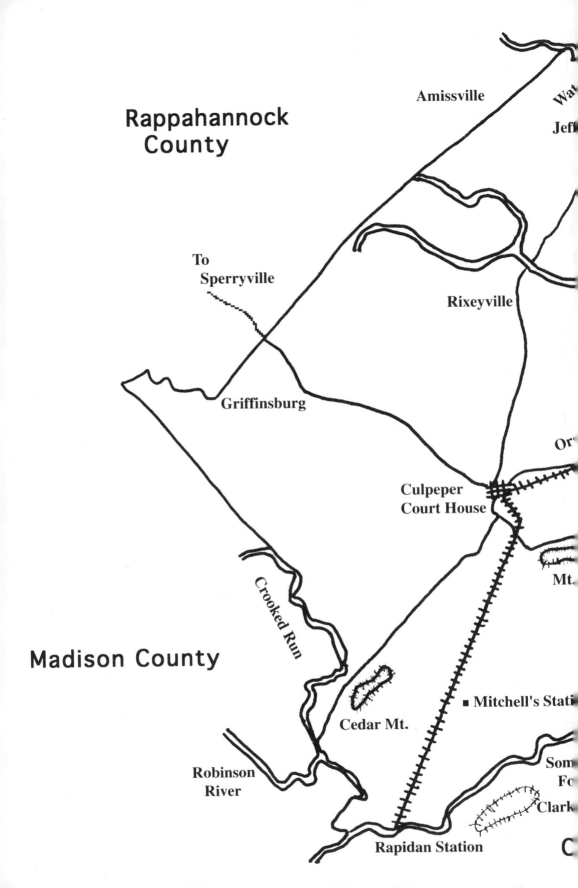